SECOND EDITION

INTEGRATED MARKETING COMMUNICATIONS

STRATEGIC PLANNING PERSPECTIVES

KEITH J. TUCKWELL

ST. LAWRENCE COLLEGE

PEARSON

Prentice
Hall

Toronto

Library and Archives Canada Cataloguing in Publication

Tuckwell, Keith J. (Keith John), 1950–

    Integrated marketing communications: strategic planning perspectives / Keith J. Tuckwell. — 2nd ed.

Includes index.
ISBN-13: 978-0-13-219912-4
ISBN-10: 0-13-219912-2

1. Communication in marketing—Textbooks. 2. Sales promotion—Textbooks. 3. Advertising—Textbooks.
I. Title.

HF5415.123.T82 2007   658.8'02   C2006-906397-4

ISBN-13: 978-0-13-219912-4
ISBN-10: 0-13-219912-2

Editor-in-Chief: Gary Bennett
Acquisitions Editor: Don Thompson
Marketing Manager: Eileen Lasswell
Developmental Editor: Lisa Cicinelli
Production Editor: Cheryl Jackson
Copy Editor: Leanne Rancourt
Proofreader: Claudia Forgas
Production Coordinator: Sharlene Ross/Andrea Falkenberg
Compositor: Phyllis Seto
Photo and Permissions Researcher: Lisa Brant
Art Director: Julia Hall
Cover and Interior Design: Anthony Leung
Cover Image: Jupiterimages Unlimited

4 5 6   12 11 10 09

Printed and bound in the United States.

To Esther…and our children, Marnie, Graham, and Gordon

Brief Contents

Preface   xvii

Part One   UNDERSTANDING INTEGRATED
MARKETING COMMUNICATIONS   1

Chapter 1   Integrated Marketing Communications: An Overview   2

Chapter 2   Strategic Planning Principles   35

Chapter 3   Branding Strategy   68

Part Two   PLANNING FOR INTEGRATED MEDIA   99

Chapter 4   Advertising Planning: Creative   100

Chapter 5   Advertising Planning: Traditional Media   133

Chapter 6   Planning for Direct Response Communication   166

Chapter 7   Planning for Online and Interactive Communications   190

Part Three   PLANNING FOR INTEGRATED MARKETING   219

Chapter 8   Sales Promotion   220

Chapter 9   Public Relations   252

Chapter 10   Event Marketing and Sponsorships   279

Chapter 11   Personal Selling   311

Part Four   MEASURING PLAN PERFORMANCE   337

Chapter 12   Evaluating Marketing Communications Programs   338

Appendix 1   Media Buying Principles and
Media Information Resources   367

Appendix 2   Integrated Marketing Communications Plan: Mr. Sub   392

Glossary   419

Index   428

Contents

Preface   xvii

Part 1   **UNDERSTANDING INTEGRATED MARKETING COMMUNICATIONS**   1

1 Integrated Marketing Communications: An Overview   2

Learning Objectives   2

THE INTEGRATED MARKETING COMMUNICATIONS MIX   3
Advertising   4
Direct Response Communications   6
Interactive Communications   6
Sales Promotion   6
Personal Selling   8
Public Relations   8
Event Marketing and Sponsorships   8

FACTORS ENCOURAGING INTEGRATED MARKETING COMMUNICATIONS   9
Media Consumption Trends   9
Customer Relationship Management   10

IMC HIGHLIGHT   EVEN THE EXPERTS CAN'T KEEP UP   10
Expanding Role of Database Management Techniques   11
Digital Communications Technologies   11
The Demand for Efficiency and Accountability   12

CONSUMER BEHAVIOUR ESSENTIALS   12
Needs and Motives   13
Personality and Self-Concept   15
Attitudes and Perceptions   15
Reference Groups   17
Family Influences   17

IDENTIFYING AND SELECTING CONSUMER TARGET MARKETS   19
Demographic Segmentation   19
Psychographic Segmentation   23

IMC HIGHLIGHT   TAKE ME SERIOUSLY   23
Geographic Segmentation   24
Direct (Customized) Segmentation   26

IMC HIGHLIGHT   MILLENNIALS: A VERY DIFFERENT TARGET   28

BUSINESS MARKETS AND BUYER BEHAVIOUR   29
Integration and Partnering Influences B2B Communications Strategies   29

Summary   31
Key Terms   32

Review Questions 32
Discussion and Application Questions 33
Endnotes 33

2 Strategic Planning Principles 35

Learning Objectives 35

FACTORS INFLUENCING STRATEGIC PLANNING 36
Economic Influences 36
Competitor Influence 37
Social and Demographic Influences 38
Technology Influence 38
Legal and Regulatory Influence 40
Strategic Planning Process 41

THE CORPORATE PLAN 42

MARKETING PLANNING 45
Market Background 47

IMC HIGHLIGHT   WEST 49: POPULAR DESTINATION FOR TEENS 47

Marketing Plan 50

MARKETING COMMUNICATIONS PLANNING 56

IMC HIGHLIGHT   TIM HORTONS: NOBODY DOES IT BETTER! 58

Marketing Communications Objectives 59
Marketing Communications Strategies 59
Measuring and Evaluating Marketing Communications 64

Summary 65
Key Terms 66
Review Questions 66
Discussion and Application Questions 66
Endnotes 67

3 Branding Strategy 68

Learning Objectives 68

DEFINING THE BRAND 69

IMC HIGHLIGHT   MAZDA'S DNA 71

THE BENEFITS OF BRANDING 73
Brand Loyalty 74
Brand Equity 75

BUILDING THE BRAND 76
Establishing Core Values and Brand Positioning 76

BRAND POSITIONING CONCEPTS 78
Product Differentiation 81
Brand Leadership Positioning 82

Head-on Positioning (Comparative Positioning) 83
Innovation Positioning 83
Price (Value) Positioning 83
Channel Positioning 85
Lifestyle (Image) Positioning 85
Planning and Implementing Marketing and Marketing
    Communications Programs 85

PACKAGING AND BRAND BUILDING 88

IMC HIGHLIGHT   FAME AND FORTUNE DO NOT COME BY CHANCE 88

Protecting the Product 89
Marketing the Product 90
Providing Convenience 92

BRANDING BY DESIGN 93

IMC HIGHLIGHT   BRAND BY DESIGN: THE CHRYSLER 300 SEDAN
    IS A WINNER 94

Summary 96
Key Terms 97
Review Questions 97
Discussion and Application Questions 98
Endnotes 98

Part 2   PLANNING FOR INTEGRATED MEDIA 99

4 Advertising Planning: Creative *100*

Learning Objectives 100
COMMUNICATIONS ESSENTIALS 101
Marketing Communications Planning Process 104
Advertising Planning—Creative 105
POSITIONING STRATEGY STATEMENT 112
Creative Objectives 114
Creative Strategy 115
Appeal Techniques 117

IMC HIGHLIGHT   ECHO TARGETS 30-SOMETHING WOMEN 119

IMC HIGHLIGHT   LIGHTS, CAMERA, ACTION 125

Creative Execution 126

Summary 129
Key Terms 130
Review Questions 130
Discussion and Application Questions 131
Endnotes 132

5 Advertising Planning: Traditional Media   *133*

Learning Objectives   133

MEDIA PLANNING   134
Market Profile   134
Competitor Media Strategy   134
Target Market Profile   135
Media Objectives   136
Media Budget   136

THE MEDIA PLAN   136
Media Objectives   136
Media Strategy   138

IMC HIGHLIGHT   BMW MINI'S LIFESTYLE MEDIA PLAN   141

Media Execution   146

ASSESSING MEDIA ALTERNATIVES   148
Television   149

IMC HIGHLIGHT   IS TV LOSING ITS LUSTER?   152

Radio   153
Newspapers   154
Magazines   156
Out-of-Home Advertising   157

Summary   162
Key Terms   163
Review Questions   164
Discussion and Application Questions   164
Endnotes   165

6 Planning for Direct Response Communications   *166*

Learning Objectives   166

DIRECT RESPONSE COMMUNICATIONS AND DIRECT MARKETING   167

THE ROOTS OF DIRECT RESPONSE COMMUNICATIONS: DATABASE
MANAGEMENT   169
Internal Data Sources   170
Collecting Data   171
Accessing Data   171

IMC HIGHLIGHT   SHOPPERS OPTIMUM STRATEGY BENEFITS CLARITIN   172

External Sources   173
Online Databases   173

THE TOOLS OF DIRECT RESPONSE COMMUNICATIONS   175
Direct Mail   175
Direct Response Television   178
Direct Response Print Media   179

IMC HIGHLIGHT   INFOMERCIALS ARE CATCHING ON   180

Telemarketing   181
Catalogues   183

Summary   186
Key Terms   187
Discussion and Application Questions   188
Review Questions   188
Endnotes   189

7 Planning for Online and Interactive Communications   *190*

Learning Objectives   190
INTERNET PENETRATION AND ADOPTION   191
ONLINE AND INTERACTIVE MARKETING COMMUNICATIONS   192
The Internet and Online Marketing Communications   194
IMC HIGHLIGHT   INTEGRATED CAMPAIGN DELIVERS RESULTS AT CANADIAN TIRE   194

ONLINE AND INTERACTIVE COMMUNICATIONS PLANNING   196
ONLINE AND INTERACTIVE COMMUNICATIONS OBJECTIVES   197
Creating Awareness   198
Branding and Image Building   198
Offering Incentives   199
Generating Leads   199
Providing Customer Service   199
Conducting Transactions   201
ONLINE AND INTERACTIVE COMMUNICATIONS STRATEGIES   202
Search Advertising   202
Banner Advertising   203
Pop-up and Pop-under Ads   205
Rich Media   205
Sponsorships   205
IMC HIGHLIGHT   GENERAL MOTORS GOES ONLINE   207

Email Advertising   208
Company Websites   209
Webcasting (Webisodes)   211
MOBILE MEDIA   212
Text Messaging   212
Online and Commercially Purchased Video Games
(Advergaming)   214
IMC HIGHLIGHT   GAMES REACH THE MALE TARGET   215

Summary   215
Key Terms   216
Review Questions   217
Discussion and Application Questions   217
Endnotes   218

Part 3   PLANNING FOR INTEGRATED MARKETING   *219*

8 Sales Promotion   *220*

Learning Objectives   **220**

SALES PROMOTION   221

SALES PROMOTION PLANNING   222
Market Profile   222
Competitor Activity Profile   223
Target Market Profile   223
Sales Promotion Objectives   223
Budget   224

THE SALES PROMOTION PLAN   224
Sales Promotion Objectives   225

SALES PROMOTION STRATEGY   226
Logistics and Fulfillment   229
Measurement and Evaluation   229
Consumer Promotion Execution   231

IMC HIGHLIGHT   BUZZ MARKETING PAYS OFF FOR CADBURY   236

Trade Promotion Execution   243

IMC HIGHLIGHT   CANADIAN TIRE SCORES BIG   243

ADDITIONAL CONSIDERATIONS FOR SALES PROMOTION PLANNING   247
Frequency of Promotions   248
Brand Image and Promotions   248
Building Brand Equity   248

Summary   249
Key Terms   249
Review Questions   250
Discussion and Application Questions   250
Endnotes   251

9 Public Relations   *252*

Learning Objectives   **252**

DEFINING PUBLIC RELATIONS   253

THE ROLE OF PUBLIC RELATIONS   254
Corporate Communications   254
Reputation Management   254
Product Publicity   257
Product Placement, Branded Content, and Product Seeding   258

IMC HIGHLIGHT   BUZZ PAYS!   259

Community Relations and Public Affairs   260
Fundraising   261

PUBLIC RELATIONS PLANNING   261
Public Relations Objectives   263

Public Relations Strategy 264
Public Relations Execution 266
Timeline and Budget 271
Measurement and Evaluation 273

PUBLIC RELATIONS AS A COMMUNICATIONS MEDIUM 274
Advantages of Public Relations 274

IMC HIGHLIGHT PR BRINGS RESULTS FOR LEE AND LABATT 274

Disadvantages of Public Relations 275

Summary 276
Key Terms 277
Review Questions 277
Discussion and Application Questions 277
Endnotes 278

10 Event Marketing and Sponsorships *279*

Learning Objectives 279
AN INTRODUCTION TO EVENT MARKETING 280
Sports Marketing Sponsorship 281
Entertainment Sponsorships 286
Culture and the Arts Sponsorships 288
Cause Marketing Sponsorships 289

IMC HIGHLIGHT L'ORÉAL SPONSORS *CANADIAN IDOL*: BECAUSE IT'S WORTH IT 289

Experiential Marketing: Product Promotional Tours and Tour
Sponsorships 291

CONSIDERATIONS FOR PARTICIPATING IN EVENT MARKETING 291

MEASURING THE BENEFITS OF EVENT MARKETING AND SPONSORSHIP 292

PLANNING THE EVENT 293
Event Concept Development 294

IMC HIGHLIGHT HOOKING UP WITH THE RIGHT EVENT 294

Designing the Event 296
Setting Objectives 297
Planning Tools 298

MARKETING THE EVENT 298
Product Strategy: Defining the Event 298
Pricing Strategy 300
Marketing Communications Strategy 301

EVENT MARKETING EXECUTION 301
Site Selection and Staging 302
Staffing 305
Operations and Logistics 305
Safety and Security 307

Summary 307
Key Terms 308
Review Questions 309

Discussion and Application Questions 309
Endnotes 310

11 Personal Selling *311*

Learning Objectives 311

PERSONAL SELLING AND INTEGRATED MARKETING COMMUNICATIONS 312
Retail Selling 312
Business-to-Business Selling 314
Direct Selling 314

THE EVOLUTION OF SELLING 315
Partnership Selling 318

PERSONAL SELLING: THE HUMAN COMMUNICATIONS ELEMENT 318
Personal Characteristics 318

IMC HIGHLIGHT GREAT SALESPEOPLE TAKE CARE OF BUSINESS 321
Preparation and the Importance of Knowledge 322

ROLES AND RESPONSIBILITIES OF SALESPEOPLE 325
Gathering Market Intelligence 325
Problem Solving 325
Locating and Maintaining Customers 325
Follow-up Service 325

PERSONAL SELLING STRATEGIES 325
Prospecting 326
Pre-approach 327
Approach 327
Sales Presentation 327
Handling Objections 328
Closing 329
Follow-up 330

SELLING IN A CHANGING BUSINESS ENVIRONMENT 330
Selling Is a Team Effort 330
Companies Sell Relationships, Not Products 331
Technology Is Changing Selling 332

IMC HIGHLIGHT SOME SUCCEED WHILE MANY FAIL. WHY? 332

Summary 333
Key Terms 334
Review Questions 334
Discussion and Application Questions 335
Endnotes 335

Part 4 MEASURING PLAN PERFORMANCE 337

12 Evaluating Marketing Communications Programs 338

Learning Objectives 338

THE ROLE AND SCOPE OF MARKETING RESEARCH 339

RESEARCH TECHNIQUES FOR MARKETING COMMUNICATIONS 340
Primary Research 340

IMC HIGHLIGHT SCOTT PAPER AND P&G DIG DEEP FOR CLUES 344

IMC HIGHLIGHT E.D. SMITH: PASSIONATE ABOUT JAM 348

MEASURING AND EVALUATING ADVERTISING MESSAGES 351
Client Evaluation 351
External Research Techniques and Procedures 352

MEASURING AND EVALUATING SALES PROMOTIONS 355

IMC HIGHLIGHT BRANDING OREGON 356

MEASURING AND EVALUATING DIRECT RESPONSE AND INTERNET
COMMUNICATIONS 357

MEASURING AND EVALUATING PUBLIC RELATIONS COMMUNICATIONS 359

MEASURING AND EVALUATING EVENT MARKETING AND SPONSORSHIPS 360

MEASURING THE INTEGRATED MARKETING COMMUNICATIONS EFFORT 361

Summary 362
Key Terms 363
Review Questions 364
Discussion and Application Questions 365
Endnotes 365

Appendix 1 Media Buying Principles and Media Information Resources 367

MEDIA BUYING PRINCIPLES 367
Newspaper Advertising 367
Magazine Advertising 373
Television Advertising 377
Radio Advertising 382
Out-of-Home Advertising 386
Direct Mail Advertising 389
Internet Advertising 391

MEDIA INFORMATION RESOURCES 395
Television Resources 395
Radio 397
Magazines 397
Newspapers 398
Out-of-Home Media 399
Internet Data Sources 399

RESEARCH DATA BY INDIVIDUAL MEDIA 400
Key Terms 401
Review Questions 401
Endnotes 403

Appendix 2 Integrated Marketing Communications Plan:
Mr. Sub 404

MARKET BACKGROUND 404
Market Analysis 404
External Influences on the Market 404
Consumer Data 405
Competitive Analysis 405
Brand Analysis (Mr. Sub) 406
SWOT Analysis 406
MARKETING COMMUNICATIONS PLAN 407
Target Market 407
Marketing Objectives 408
Marketing Communications Goal (Challenge) 408
Marketing Communications Objectives 408
Marketing Communications Strategy 408
Advertising Plan—Creative 409
Advertising Plan—Media 410
Sales Promotion Plan 412
Online and Interactive Plan 414
Event Marketing Plan 414

Glossary 419
Index 428

Preface

Teachers face many challenges in the classroom. Reviewers of this textbook and others which I have written identify three primary challenges: It is difficult to get students to read a textbook; multicultural classrooms present language problems; and it is difficult to cover course material in the time allotted. This textbook is designed to conquer these problems.

Before addressing the changes that were made to the second edition, I must say that the world of marketing communications is one that is changing rapidly. The impact of new technologies makes it very difficult for educators and practitioners to keep pace. Active practitioners, particularly in the media, are perplexed by the sudden emergence of new media alternatives such as cell phones, personal digital assistants, and MP3 players. Terms such as podcast, video on demand, blog, and webcast have entered the media arena and, as a result, practitioners are struggling to determine how new and old media must blend together to resolve clients' problems. Emerging technologies have placed everyone on a learning curve! Given the rapid pace of change, every effort has been made to ensure that the content is as up to date as it can be at the time of publication.

From a teaching perspective, textbook readability has always been an issue with me. Readability is a primary strength of *Integrated Marketing Communications: Strategic Planning Perspectives*. The book is written in a straightforward, easy-to-understand manner and is full of examples and illustrations that students will quickly identify with. If you accept the notion that being familiar with something makes it easier to understand and apply, then your students will be better equipped to develop a marketing communications plan once they have read this book. Its clear, concise, and informative nature solves the first two challenges (getting students to read and language problems) teachers face.

Most courses in marketing communications are one semester (14 to 15 weeks) in length with only 45 to 60 course hours available for teaching. You will find the format of this textbook ideal for such a course. The textbook includes 12 core chapters that cover all aspects of integrated marketing communications. A common planning model is presented in relevant chapters that bind the various components of marketing communications together. **Appendix 1** offers information about how to plan and buy media time and is an ideal supplement to all media-related chapters. **Appendix 2** presents an integrated marketing communications plan, something you will not find in any other textbook. Therefore, this book solves the third problem a teacher faces. You can cover all the material in the allotted time frame!

The goal of most IMC courses is to provide students with the vital information they need to create, implement, and evaluate an integrated marketing communications plan. To accomplish this goal, the student must appreciate what the various components of IMC are and how they may interact with one another to solve marketing problems. This textbook is designed to meet this goal! Core content of the book pays equal attention to the various components of the integrated marketing communications mix and stresses the need to include those components that are relevant into an integrated plan.

With regard to coverage of the various marketing communications components, you will find that each component gets equal treatment. There are individual chapters devoted to advertising (creative and media issues are treated separately), direct response communications, online and interactive communications, sales promotion, public relations, event marketing and sponsorships, and personal selling. The objective is to show students how the various components might interact with each other in order to create and implement a marketing communications plan that will resolve a business problem. Students will be able to apply the concept of integrated marketing communications!

The book is divided into four essential parts.

ORGANIZATION OF THE TEXT

Part 1: Understanding Integrated Marketing Communications

This section presents an overview of essential inputs that a manager would consider when developing a marketing communications plan. The content included in Chapter 1, Integrated Marketing Communications: An Overview, introduces the various components of the marketing communications mix and summarizes the essential concepts dealing with consumer behaviour, organizational behaviour, and target marketing. This material typically occupies four or five chapters in competing textbooks.

Chapter 2 shifts the focus to strategic planning. Relationships are drawn between plans and planning at various levels of an organization and how they are integrated. The structure and content of a marketing plan and a marketing communications plan are examined in order to show how plans work together to resolve marketing problems. Chapter 3 introduces the concept of branding and branding strategy. Discussion about branding is strategically located in the textbook to precede detailed coverage of the components of the marketing communications mix. Branding strategies and brand positioning strategies are often the foundation upon which marketing communications strategies are devised.

Part 2: Planning for Integrated Media

This section examines planning considerations for traditional media choices and new media choices. Chapter 4, Advertising Planning: Creative, introduces the communications process and the various planning concepts that are considered when briefing an agency about message requirements. The role of strategies and tactics—and the distinctions between them and creative objectives—is considered. Chapter 5, Advertising Planning: Traditional Media, presents the media planning process and stresses the importance of planning an effective yet efficient media plan. The various strategic decisions that apply to using traditional media alternatives are presented in detail.

Chapter 6 introduces the rapidly expanding field of direct-response communications. Since direct response relies on database management techniques, there is considerable emphasis on customer relationship management practices and the key role played by individualized marketing communications strategies in fostering solid customer relationships. Chapter 7 examines the emerging role of the Internet and other interactive media such as mobile communications devices and video games. Contemporary marketing communications plans merge new media with old media to generate better results.

Part 3: Planning for Integrated Marketing

Because organizations look for synergy, the objective is to integrate related marketing and marketing communications practices with the media strategies already presented in the book. Chapter 8 introduces the various sales promotion alternatives that are frequently employed in integrated marketing communications plans. The roles of consumer promotions and trade promotions are examined in detail. Chapter 9 examines the role of public relations in communications. The content focuses on the various techniques that are available, planning procedures, and measurement techniques.

Chapter 10 examines the emerging role of event marketing and sponsorships in contemporary marketing. It introduces the criteria for participating in event marketing and the steps and procedures for planning an event. Chapter 11 covers the role of personal selling in a variety of business settings. Personal selling adds a human component to the integrated marketing communications mix, and for this reason plays a very important role in establishing and building solid customer relationships.

Part 4: Measuring Plan Performance

This section examines the role of various research procedures for evaluating the effectiveness of marketing communications programs. Chapter 12 introduces some fundamental methodologies for collecting and analyzing primary research data and distinguishes between qualitative and quantitative data. The role and influence of collecting and interpreting information on the development of marketing communications strategies are considered.

UNIQUE FEATURES

- This text is presented in a **practical, friendly, student-oriented style** and provides a good balance between theory and practice. The emphasis on planning makes it an excellent resource for courses that involve developing marketing communications plans or for courses that want to introduce students to the various components of the marketing communications mix.

- This book is written from a **Canadian perspective**. Careful consideration was given to all of the input that was gathered from Canadian instructors during the review process. The book and much of its illustrative content will be very familiar to your students. Such familiarity will make it easier for students to apply the planning concepts that are presented.

- The **key topics that comprise a complete IMC course** are presented in 12 chapters. The amount and depth of content is ideally suited for courses of 14 or 15 weeks' duration. You, the instructor, will have time to cover all of the material.

- **Essential topics that are important for the development of integrated marketing communications strategies** are reviewed in only one chapter. Chapter 1 (Integrated Marketing Communications: An Overview) introduces the concept of integrated marketing communications, reviews various consumer behaviour and organizational behaviour concepts that are considered when an organization identifies targets, and develops communications strategies.

- The latest **issues and trends** affecting the marketing communications industry are presented in Chapter 1 and various other media chapters. The combination of new technology and changing consumer media habits is creating new challenges for industry practitioners. This information sets the stage for the **merging of old media with new media** in the quest to solve clients' problems.

- There is a unique emphasis on **marketing communications planning** throughout the book. Chapter 2 provides an overall model for organizing and structuring a marketing communications plan. Each of the individual chapters on the various components of the marketing communications mix includes a model for developing that component of the plan, while showing how it is integrated with other components to form an integrated marketing communications plan. The concept of integration is reinforced throughout the book.

- Many advertisers are moving away from the standard 30-second television commercial toward **new media alternatives** or to new television alternatives such as product placement, branded content, product seeding, buzz marketing, and experiential marketing. The impact of this trend and the presentation of these new opportunities are discussed in various chapters: Chapter 5 (Advertising Planning: Media), Chapter 6 (Planning for Direct Response Communications), Chapter 7 (Planning for Online and Interactive Communications), Chapter 8 (Sales Promotion), and Chapter 9 (Public Relations).

- **Chapter 7: Planning for Online and Interactive Communications** has been completely rewritten, a true reflection of the rapid pace of change in this area of communications. New topics such as search advertising, viral marketing, mobile communications and video games communications are now included.

- **Chapter 10: Event Marketing and Sponsorships** has been revised to incorporate better balance between event marketing and event planning. Event marketing as a means of communicating with customers continues to grow in importance. That role is reflected in new chapter content.

- Each chapter includes at least two **IMC Highlight vignettes**. These short inserts reflect important aspects of marketing communications planning or provide actual illustrations of how organizations apply marketing communications concepts. Among the featured organizations and brands are familiar names such as West 49, BMW Mini, Canadian Tire, Tim Hortons, Toyota, L'Oréal, Scott Paper, Labatt, Procter & Gamble, and Cadbury.

- The book includes countless **visual illustrations** that specifically demonstrate an important application of marketing communications. Most will be well-known names to your students and include companies and brands such as Scott Paper, Old Spice, Mazda, Wendy's, Harley-Davidson, Via, Diesel, Glad, Red Zone, Chrysler, McCain's, Oral-B, Gillette, L'Oréal, and many more. Many new illustrations, typically in the form of marketing communications messages, have been added to each chapter.

- **Three new cases** are available on the Website and in the Instructor's Manual. Each case is presented in the form of a "Communications Brief" in a manner much like a client would brief their communications agency. These cases are ideal for applying marketing communications concepts in either a case study format or a marketing communications plan format.

- **Appendix 1 Media Buying Principles and Media Information Resources** is a supplement that provides additional media details, and shows students some fundamental procedures for estimating costs and buying media time and space in a variety of media and other components or the marketing communications mix. Students can quickly refer to media-buying information in this specific section of the book. Review questions will challenge the students to understand and apply rate card information.

- **Appendix 2 Integrated Marketing Communications Plan: Mr. Sub** provides an example of a marketing communications plan so that students can quickly see the relationship between various planning principles such as objectives, strategies, and execution and between the various components of the marketing communications mix with respect to how each contributes to achieving objectives. The plan embraces traditional media advertising, online and interactive communications, sales promotions and event marketing. No other textbook offers an illustrative marketing communications plan.

PEDAGOGY

Learning Objectives. Each chapter starts with a list of learning objectives directly related to the key concepts contained in the chapter

Advertisements, Figures and Charts. Throughout each chapter, key concepts and applications are illustrated with strong visual material. Sample advertisements and other forms of marketing communications augment the Canadian perspective and demonstrate key aspects of marketing communications strategy and execution.

Key Terms. Key terms are highlighted in boldface in the text and in colour in page margins, where they are accompanied by definitions. Students also have quick access to key terms and definitions in the glossary at the end of the book.

Chapter Summaries. The summary at the end of each chapter reinforces major points and concepts.

Review Questions, Discussion and Application Questions. Both sets of questions allow students to review material and apply concepts learned in the chapter.

Appendix 1 Media Buying Principles and Media Information Resources. The essentials of buying media time and space in various media outlets are covered in this section. Review questions that will test the students understanding of and ability to apply rate card information are included.

Appendix 2 Integrated Marketing Communications Plan: Mr. Sub. This plan shows how various elements of marketing communications combine to form an integrated marketing communications plan. A variety of charts and figures are included to show how media and marketing communications budget allocations are presented in a plan.

Glossary. A glossary of all key terms and definitions appears at the end of the textbook.

SUPPLEMENTS

Instructor's Resource CD-ROM

This valuable tool is an all-in-one resource package that provides quick and easy access to the following supplements.

Instructor's Resource Manual

Prepared by the author, the Instructor's Resource Manual includes learning objectives, chapter highlights that can act as lecture outlines, additional illustrations of key concepts that can be built into lectures, and answers to review and discussion questions. A selection of Canadian case studies is included. Each case is presented in the form of a "communications brief" much like those used when clients are briefing their communications agencies. These cases are ideal for developing marketing communications strategies and plans. The manual also provides summary commentaries on each of the video segments in the video library that accompanies the textbook.

TestGen

A series of questions for each chapter has been prepared to test students on the material they have studied. The mix of questions will challenge the student's ability to understand concepts and apply concepts. The TestGen software enables instructors to view and edit questions, generate tests, and print the tests in a variety of formats. It also allows instructors to administer tests on a local area network, have tests graded electronically, and have their results prepared in electronic or printed reports.

PowerPoint® Slides

A complete set of slides that are specifically designed or culled from the textbook is available electronically. Full-colour versions of ads, photos, and figures from the textbook, found in the Image Library, can be inserted into your presentations.

Image Library

The Image Library contains various full-colour images from the textbook such as photos, ads, and figures. Instructors can integrate these images in their own presentations.

CBC/Pearson Education Canada Video Library

The videos that accompany the first edition of the textbook cover a broad range of marketing communications topics. Appropriate video segments have been secured from CBC shows such as *Venture*. These are available as separate supplements in both DVD and VHS formats, or you can link to the videos online at the Companion Website.

Companion Website (www.pearsoned.ca/tuckwell)

The Companion Website is a handy reference for students. The site includes practice questions, case studies, weblinks related to sites, CBC videos, and more. Visit the site for a learning experience.

ACKNOWLEDGMENTS

Many organizations and individuals have contributed to the development of this book. I would like to sincerely thank the following organizations for their cooperation and contribution:

3M Canada
ACLC Advertising
Apple Computers, Inc.
Ashton Green Limited
Audi of America
BBC News
BBM Canada
BMO Bank of Montreal
BMW Canada Inc.
Canada Post
Canadian Advertising Rates and Data
Canadian Curling Association
Canadian Geographic Magazine
Canadian National Sportsmen's Shows
CKCO-TV
The Clorox Company of Canada
Cottage Life
Crain Communications, Inc.
Dairy Farmers of Canada

Dell Canada
Diesel
Foote, Cone, and Belding
Frito-Lay, Inc.
General Motors of Canada
The Gillette Company
Glad Products Company
The *Globe and Mail*
Grocery Gateway, Inc.
Harley-Davidson Motor Company
Harry Rosen
Harvey's Restaurants
Interactive Advertising Bureau
john st. advertising
KAO Brands Canada
Kimberley-Clark Worldwide Inc.
Kraft Canada
Maple Leaf Foods, Inc.
The Martin Agency
Mazda Canada

McNeil Consumer Healthcare
Millward Brown Goldfarb
Mountain Equipment Co-op
Nottawasaga Resort
The Old Mill Inn & Spa
Open & Save
Parmalat
Pepsi-Cola Canada Ltd.
Procter & Gamble Canada
RBC Financial
Resolve Corporation
Rogers Publishing Limited
Rolex Canada Limited
Samsung Electronics Canada
Saturn Canada
Save.ca

Sears Canada, Inc.
Shell Canada Limited
Shoppers Drug Mart
Suzuki Canada
TaylorMade-adidas Golf
TDL Group Corp.
Ultima Foods
Unilever Canada, Inc.
UPS
VIA Rail Canada
Viceroy Homes
Visa Canada Association
Volvo Cars of Canada Corp.
Wendy's International, Inc.

For undertaking the task of reviewing this book at various stages of development, and for the time and energy they devoted to the review process, I would like to sincerely thank the following people:

Judith Nash, Southern Alberta Institute of Technology

Janice Shearer, Mohawk College of Applied Arts and Technology

Steve Finlay, Conestoga College

Dwight Dyson, Centennial College

Stephanie Koonar, Langara College

Maria F. Vincenten, Red River College

Marina Jaffey, Camosun College

From Pearson Education Canada I would like to thank Laura Forbes, Acquisitions Editor; Lisa Cicinelli, Associate Editor; Cheryl Jackson, Production Editor; Leanne Rancourt, Copy Editor; Karen Alliston, Proofreader; Lisa Brant, Photo and Permissions Researcher; Andrea Falkenberg, Production Coordinator; Anthony Leung, Designer; and Phyllis Seto, Compositor.

I would sincerely like to thank Michael Young, former vice-president and editorial director at Pearson Education Canada, for the guidance and wisdom he provided during the years we worked together. It was a pleasure working with you. Best wishes for continued success with Pearson Education in Australia.

As always I would also like to thank my family for their support and cooperation. Finding the time to write yet another book presents challenges for all of you. To Marnie, Graham, and Gord—thanks so much! As always, a very special thank you goes to my wife, Esther, for her patience, understanding, support, and guidance!

Keith J. Tuckwell
2007

A Great Way to Learn and Instruct Online

The Pearson Education Canada Companion Website is easy to navigate and is organized to correspond to the chapters in this textbook. Whether you are a student in the classroom or a distance learner you will discover helpful resources for in-depth study and research that empower you in your quest for greater knowledge and maximize your potential for success in the course.

[www.pearsoned.ca/tuckwell]

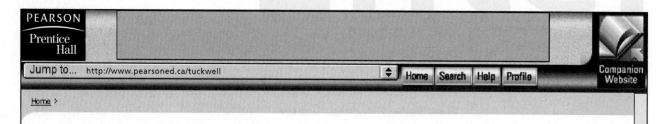

PEARSON
Prentice Hall

Jump to... | http://www.pearsoned.ca/tuckwell | Home | Search | Help | Profile

Companion Website

Home >

Integrated Marketing Communications: Strategic Planning Perspectives, Second Edition, by Keith J. Tuckwell

Student Resources

The modules in this section provide students with tools for learning course material. These modules include:

- Learning Objectives
- Destinations
- Quizzes
- Internet Exercises
- PowerPoint® Presentations
- Glossary
- CBC Videos

In the quiz modules students can send answers to the grader and receive instant feedback on their progress through the Results Reporter. Coaching comments and references to the textbook may be available to ensure that students take advantage of all available resources to enhance their learning experience.

Instructor Resources

A link to this book on the Pearson Education Canada online catalogue (www.pearsoned.ca) provides instructors with additional teaching tools. Downloadable PowerPoint Presentations and an Instructor's Manual are just some of the materials that may be available. The catalogue is password protected. To get a password, simply contact your Pearson Education Canada Representative or call Faculty Sales and Services at 1-800-850-5813.

Part 1

Understanding Integrated Marketing Communications

Part 1 focuses on several introductory issues that are associated with the development of integrated marketing communications programs. Chapter 1 introduces the components of the integrated marketing communications mix and the factors that encourage their use. The focus then shifts to a variety of essential consumer behaviour concepts and business-to-business buying characteristics that organizations consider when developing communications strategies.

Chapter 2 introduces the student to essential strategic planning principles while drawing relationships between planning at various levels of an organization. The structure and content of a marketing plan and marketing communications plan are presented in detail. The intent is to show how integrated planning provides solutions to marketing problems.

Chapter 3 concentrates on issues related to branding strategy. Essentially, marketing communications strategies are the primary vehicle for building the image of a brand or company. Since brand positioning is the focal point of most marketing communications strategies, the role that positioning strategy statements play in the development of communications campaigns is examined in detail. The role and influence of packaging and product design strategies and their effect on brand image are also examined.

1

INTEGRATED MARKETING COMMUNICATIONS: AN OVERVIEW

After studying this chapter you will be able to

1. appreciate the role of integrated marketing communications planning in business today

2. identify the components of the integrated marketing communications mix

3. identify the conditions that have led to the emergence of integrated marketing communications

4. explain how consumer behaviour concepts influence marketing communications strategies

5. assess the information needed to identify and select target markets

6. explain how unique characteristics of organizational buying behaviour influence marketing communications

Organizations today are searching for complete solutions to their communications needs. In the past, it was quite common for separate departments within an organization to prepare communications plans independently. If communications plans were prepared externally, various tasks would be assigned to distinct and separate organizations that were specialists in certain areas. Typically, an advertising agency would handle creative and media assignments, a company with expertise in sales promotion would develop consumer promotion programs, while a public relations firm would develop programs to build an organization's image. In such a system, each firm operated independently, not knowing what the others were doing. When communications plans were implemented, they often headed in different directions or delivered a different message about the company.

The environment that businesses operate in today continues to change at a very rapid pace. The influence of technology alone has forced business organizations to examine how they deliver messages to their target markets. Generally speaking, there has been a movement toward targeted media and away from mass media. As well, companies are experimenting with new communications concepts such as *branded content* and *product seeding* to create a "buzz" for new products. Peoples' media habits have changed. The average consumer relies less on newspapers and television and more on computers and telephones for receiving news and commercial messages. And the nature of competition has moved from being just competitive to being hypercompetitive. Companies are going to market with new products much more quickly than they used to.

Changes like these have influenced how an organization communicates with its customers. No longer do companies rely on disjointed strategies from a variety of sources, even though those sources are experts at what they do. The goal of communications now is to deliver the same message through a variety of media to have a synergistic impact on the target. Furthermore, the development of message strategy is now in the hands of fewer external suppliers. Many traditional advertising agencies have evolved into full-fledged marketing communications agencies and offer services in areas such as public relations, sales promotion, and direct response and online communications. The range of services and the level of specialization that agencies provide are much greater than before. In effect, these agencies are changing with their client's needs and are providing integrated marketing communications solutions.

THE INTEGRATED MARKETING COMMUNICATIONS MIX

Integrated marketing communications

The coordination of all marketing communications in a unified program that maximizes the impact on the intended target audience.

Integrated marketing communications involves the coordination of all forms of marketing communications in a unified program that maximizes the impact on consumers and other types of customers. It embraces many unique yet complementary forms of communication: media advertising (a focus on message strategies and media strategies in a traditional media environment); direct response communications (communications that encourage immediate action); digital communications that include online, mobile (cell phone), and CD-DVD communications; sales promotion (both consumer and trade promotions); public relations; event marketing and sponsorships; and personal selling (see Figure 1.1). Effective communications integration also considers the role of packaging and its impact on consumers at point-of-purchase and the role that all employees of an organization play in communicating a positive attitude about a company to its various publics. Any customer touch-point is part of integrated marketing communications.

How an organization plans and manages the various components of the mix is important. Rarely does an organization employ all components at one time, but rather selects and uses those components that are deemed appropriate for resolving the situation at hand. For the components used, the message delivered by each must be complementary. Integration of message strategy, regardless of the medium, is crucial to generating maximum impact on the target audience.

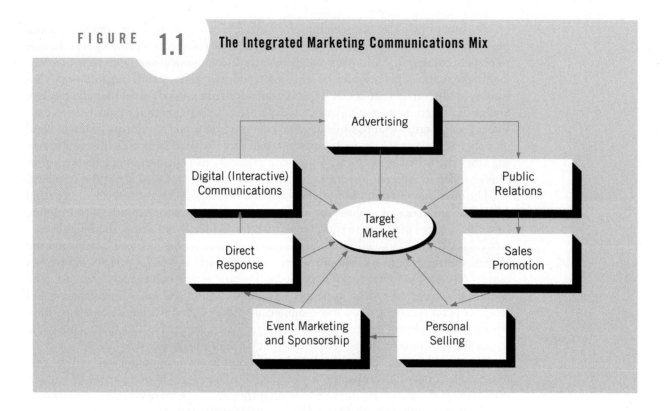

FIGURE 1.1 The Integrated Marketing Communications Mix

Clients look for a "total solutions" communications approach to resolve their business problems. There is a demand for comprehensively planned, seamless campaigns. However, since the communications industry is structured in a rather fragmented manner, with specialized agencies competing for a client's attention, a total solutions approach is not always feasible. The industry is restructuring itself, however, and as the concept of integrated marketing communications takes hold, the "total solutions" approach will be available.

Managing branded communications through today's ever-evolving matrix of potential consumer/customer touch-points is becoming increasingly complex. Both marketing organizations and their agencies need to stop for a moment and re-evaluate their long-term goals. Key issues remain the level and intensity of the planned service, organizational structures and execution processes, and the overall approach to compensation, performance, and accountability.[1]

Let's start the discussion about integrated marketing communications by clearly explaining the fundamental nature of each form of marketing communication.

Advertising

Advertising is a persuasive form of marketing communication designed to stimulate a positive response from a defined target market. In the context of the integrated marketing communications mix, good advertising (advertising that has an impact on the audience) will influence the behaviour of that audience—that is its primary function. Once a positive attitude toward a specific product or company is created in the customer's mind, that customer may be motivated to purchase the product or look favourably upon it.

Advertising can be either product oriented or promotion oriented. **Product advertising** provides information and helps build an image for the product, whether it's a brand or a company. In doing so, the features, attributes, and benefits of the product are presented in a persuasive manner. With reference to Figure 1.2, the ad for SpongeTowels stresses one key benefit to potential users: the product truly soaks up big spills (like a sponge!). That is a compelling argument for buying this product.

Advertising
A form of marketing communications designed to stimulate a positive response from a defined target market.

Product advertising
Advertising that provides information about a branded product to help build its image in the minds of customers.

FIGURE   **1.2**   **A Benefit-Oriented Advertisement for SpongeTowels**

Source: ® Registered trademarks and TM trademarks of Kruger Products. © 2005 Kruger Products.
Registered trademark of Kimberly-Clark Worldwide Inc. Used under licence.

General Motors Canada
www.gm.ca

Several large companies are among the leading product advertisers in Canada: General Motors, Procter & Gamble, Ford Motor Company, Sears Canada, and HBC (Hudson's Bay Company). These companies are also among the leaders in integrated marketing communications. General Motors, for example, communicates online through its company website, is active in direct response communications with prospective customers, uses sales promotions extensively to offer more attractive prices to customers, employs personal selling at the dealer level, and is constantly in the news thanks to the success of its public relations program.

Promotional advertising

Advertising that communicates a specific offer to encourage an immediate response from the target audience.

Promotional advertising is designed to accomplish a specific task—usually to communicate a specific offer to elicit some kind of immediate response from the customer. Including some kind of coupon or contest promotion with a print advertisement, for example, is a form of promotional advertising. In this case, the content of the ad presents the features and primary benefit to help build the image, and the coupon provides an incentive for customers to buy. Automobile manufacturers, for example, are well known for their rebate programs and low-cost financing programs, both of which are advertised heavily to attract customers. Packaged goods manufacturers use coupons and other incentives to encourage more immediate action by consumers. These form an integrated marketing communications strategy even though they involve only two components of the marketing communications mix.

Direct Response Communications

Direct response communications

The delivery of a message to a target audience of one; the message can be distributed by direct mail, direct response television, or telemarketing.

Direct response communications involves the delivery of a message to a target audience of one. As the term implies, "direct" means direct from the marketing company to a specific user or prospective user of a company's product. Direct mail is a common form of direct response communications. Other forms of direct response include direct response television (DRTV), telemarketing, and cell phone communications. This segment of the communications industry is growing at a much faster pace than traditional forms of advertising. Time-pressed consumers, for example, find the convenience of direct response appealing. They can learn of a product's benefit and actually buy it if they so desire, all in one stage.

Figure 1.3 includes the content of a direct mail package that was used as part of the launch strategy for Tylenol 8 Hour tablets. The mailing includes product information, sample tablets, and a $2.00 coupon on the first purchase of the product. The direct mail execution was a key element of the launch campaign since it was designed to encourage trial purchase. A television and print advertising campaign was implemented to generate awareness and interest for the brand, another example of successful integration.

Interactive Communications

Technology is changing so rapidly that there is little doubt that communications by way of electronic devices will be the future of marketing communications. Thus far, however, consumers have been reluctant to accept marketing communications distributed on the Internet; they do not see the Internet as a medium, like they would television or radio. While Internet users try to avoid commercial messages, advertisers are experimenting with more effective ways of delivering messages online. Consumers must realize that the online services they take for granted have to be paid for by someone. Advertising revenue is vital for the survival of Internet service providers.

The new emphasis that business organizations place on *customer relationship management (CRM)*, combined with their ability to manage internal databases, is forcing them to move toward direct and interactive communications. At present, organizations communicate through their own websites and through various forms of online advertising such as banner ads, pop-ups, and sponsorships. These and other new forms of communications will play an increasing role in the communications mix in the future.

Sales promotion

An activity that provides incentives to bring about immediate response from customers, distributors, and an organization's sales force.

Sales Promotion

Sales promotion involves special incentives to stimulate an immediate reaction from consumers and distributors. An organization's promotion expenditures tend to be divided between consumers and distributors. Strategies that include coupons, free samples, con-

FIGURE **1.3**

A Direct Mail Package Containing Product Information and Trial Purchase Incentives

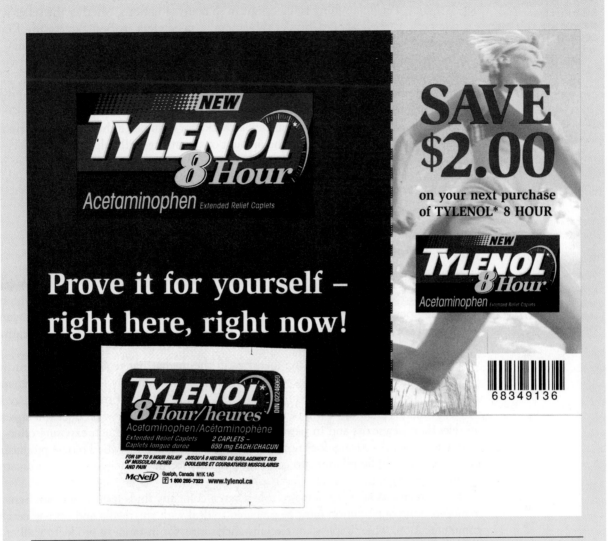

Source: Provided by McNeil Consumer Healthcare.

tests, and cash refunds are classified as consumer promotions. The direct mail campaign included in Figure 1.3 is a good example of how sales promotions are integrated with media advertising. Offering price discounts to distributors for purchasing goods in large quantities or for performing some kind of marketing or merchandising task on behalf of a marketing organization is classified as a trade promotion.

The marketing organization is constantly challenged on how to divide the sales promotion budget between consumers and trade customers. Regardless of how the budget is allocated, it is imperative that consumer promotion strategies be aligned effectively with consumer advertising programs (to pull the product through the channel of distribution) and that trade promotions be aligned effectively with personal selling programs (to push the product through the channel of distribution). In business, it is the integration of various marketing communications programs that pays off for the organization.

Personal Selling

Personal selling

Face-to-face communication involving the presentation of features and benefits of a product or service to a buyer; the objective is to make a sale.

As the term implies, **personal selling** involves the delivery of a personalized message from a seller to a buyer. That message presents the features, attributes, and benefits of a product or service. Personal selling is important in so many situations, whether the seller is a car salesperson in a DaimlerChrysler showroom, a store clerk in Best Buy, or the Kraft sales representative presenting a new product to a buyer at the head office of Loblaws.

Compelling advertising campaigns for new automobiles encourage consumers to visit dealer showrooms. That money can go to waste if a salesperson at a dealership is unprepared to handle customer inquiries effectively. And what about that new line of Post cereal that Kraft is trying to sell to Loblaws? If the buyer doesn't accept the offer put forth by the Kraft sales representative, Kraft faces a significant setback. For example, if the listing discounts or quantity discounts are not sufficient, no amount of advertising will help sell the product—it simply will not be available at Loblaws. The job of the sales representative is to secure distribution of the product in a timely manner. The availability of the product in stores must coincide with the scheduling of media advertising. If that is not the case, a lot of advertising money could be wasted.

Public Relations

Public relations

A form of communications designed to gain public understanding and acceptance.

Public relations communications are primarily directed toward gaining public understanding and acceptance. Public relations messages influence the attitudes and opinions of interest groups to an organization. Consequently, progressive-minded marketing organizations fully appreciate the role that public relations campaigns can play in generating positive attitudes toward products.

Public relations involve placing messages in the media that require no payment. In effect, they can generate "free" exposure. For example, a company issues a press release announcing a new product. The release includes all the virtues of the product, where it will be available, and how it will be advertised. Stories about the new product will appear on television newscasts and in newspaper and magazine articles. Such exposure offers a legitimacy that advertising does not have. To demonstrate, Hollywood movie producers rely heavily on public relations to generate publicity for new movie releases—it creates the necessary hype they desire!

Public relations also play a major role when a company finds itself in a crisis. Senior managers of an organization must be prepared to deal with the media and issue effective communications when unpleasant circumstances arise, for instance, a product recall or a matter of public safety involving the company.

Michelin
www.michelin.ca

Such was the case when Michelin found a flaw in its tires following qualifying runs at the 2005 US Grand Prix at Indianapolis Motor Speedway. After Michelin's requests for rule changes and track changes were denied, Michelin advised all of its teams not to compete. After the Michelin teams pulled out, only six cars were left to compete in the race! Michelin's intentions were good as they cited driver safety as paramount. However, their decision touched off a PR nightmare with racing fans.[2]

Event Marketing and Sponsorships

Event marketing

The process, planned by a sponsoring organization, of integrating a variety of communications elements with a single event theme.

Sponsorship

The act of financially supporting an event in return for certain advertising rights and privileges.

Event marketing and sponsorships are related yet different activities. **Event marketing** involves planning, organizing, and marketing an event, whether it is an event for a company or a brand of a company that integrates a variety of communications elements. **Sponsorship** simply means that a company provides money to an event to enjoy specified marketing privileges for being associated with the event. Molson, for example, is involved in event marketing through Champ Car Racing (the Molson Indy races that run in Toronto and Montreal each summer). Molson defrays the cost of holding such events by selling sponsorships to other companies. Those companies have advertising and signage privileges at the event and can use the event logo to help market their product to the public.

In the past decade, event marketing and sponsorships have become more prominent in the marketing communications mix. Although the benefits of event marketing are difficult to measure, an organization does know that it can reach its target market directly when it associates with the right event. Molson, for example, knows that beer drinkers often enjoy watching auto racing, hence its association with Champ Car Racing. In a strategic manner, Molson effectively combines its racing association with other elements of marketing communications. In the months leading up to the various Canadian races, Molson is active with media advertising, public relations, and sales promotions. All activities are designed to create awareness and interest—and sell tickets to the races.

In summary, contemporary organizations realize there are significant benefits to be achieved if all forms of marketing communications are integrated successfully. For certain, integration fosters a cooperative approach to communications planning, presents a unified message, and creates a higher level of impact on the target audience.

Molson
www.molson.com

FACTORS ENCOURAGING INTEGRATED MARKETING COMMUNICATIONS

Selecting the right combination of marketing communications alternatives to solve unique business problems is the key to success today. And that is a difficult challenge. In the past, strategies for the various forms of marketing communications (advertising, sales promotions, public relations, and so on) were implemented independently of each other. Each alternative was a silo. Contemporary thinking suggests a different approach, an approach in which each communications alternative is an equal partner; an approach where there is media neutrality; an approach in which creative solutions are recommended to solve business problems. This way of thinking is the foundation on which integrated marketing communications strategies are built.

Several key issues and trends will continue to affect marketing and marketing communications practice. Among these issues and trends are the following:

- consumers' media habits are changing in a manner that makes them more difficult to reach;
- the strategic focus on relationship marketing, commonly referred to as customer relationship management (CRM);
- the expanding role of database marketing;
- the sudden and dramatic impact of the Internet and other communications technologies; and
- the greater demand for efficiency and accountability in organizations.

Media Consumption Trends

There is definitely a trend moving toward newer, electronic forms of communication and away from traditional forms of communication. For example, the cost of network television advertising continues to rise each year while households viewing network prime-time TV are declining. How long will advertisers tolerate such an inequity?

Consumers are also multi-tasking with the media. One survey observes that 54 percent of television watchers are talking on a cell phone while watching TV, and 30 percent of radio listeners are using a cell phone at the same time.[3] Statistics such as these point advertisers in the direction of cell phones! Could the cell phone be the next big medium?

Procter & Gamble
www.pg.com

Procter & Gamble is one of North America's largest advertisers. The company is rethinking its communications strategy on a brand-by-brand basis. When all P&G brands are combined, P&G has reduced its television advertising budget by about 20 percent. While the company doesn't have a strategy that excludes television, it does have a strategy to be with consumers wherever they are, which embraces online and cell phone communications and product placement opportunities.[4]

For additional insight into how media consumption trends are influencing communications strategies, refer to the IMC Highlight **Even the Experts Can't Keep Up!**

Customer Relationship Management

Business today is all about relationships: the relationships that an organization has with its customers, distributors, and suppliers. A relationship may involve numerous compa-

---

IMC HIGHLIGHT

EVEN THE EXPERTS CAN'T KEEP UP!

The ability of the traditional mass media (television, radio, newspapers, magazines, and outdoor advertising) to reach consumers is dwindling, and for good reason. In the 1950s, the placement of one, 60-second TV commercial would reach 80 percent of North America's population. Today, to reach that many people would take more than 100 commercials!

The media landscape has changed, and how people use the media has also changed. Today, consumers are using technology to avoid watching commercials, and consumers, particularly young ones, are talking on their cell phones, surfing the web, and watching TV all at once. Therefore, marketers that cling to traditional media strategies are doomed for failure.

For certain, television advertising is not as dominant as it was. The proliferation of new technologies such as the Internet, digital TV, cell phones, personal digital assistants (PDAs), and iPods has resulted in a variety of new ways of reaching consumers. Now consumers can download TV shows, pass over regular radio for streamed music, and generally watch and listen when they want to. The media no longer control when and where people watch and listen.

It's been tough for the media experts employed by ad agencies to keep up with the changes. Traditional full-service agencies have given way to boutique-style agencies specializing in new media such as online communications, word of mouth, viral campaigns, product placement, and branded content. Any agency clinging to the old business model is stumbling while those that have learned to manipulate new technologies are profiting.

There was also a time when "message" issues dominated communications strategies, but now both clients and agencies believe that determining when and where a target

customer will notice their advertising is as important as the message itself. Not surprisingly, Procter & Gamble, the world's biggest advertiser, has shifted its communications thinking accordingly. P&G used to rely heavily on TV, but has moved from media planning (just thinking about TV) to communications planning. P&G carefully considers who the target is and where the target is going to be most receptive to a message.

Traditional media buyers must alter their approach in this new environment. The days of specialists on media such as television, magazines, and newspapers are so yesterday. Today, media strategists are expected to understand and make recommendations about all media channels. They must find ways of blending traditional media with new media to reach and influence the target market.

Clients are also changing. They are showing an adventurous side and are taking some risks with new media options. It was only five years ago that clients were being "educated" about online communications. In 2005, revenues generated from Internet advertising amounted to $520 million, a 43 percent increase over 2004. Chrysler now allocates 20 percent of its media budget to online communications. In the United States, advertisers like Cadbury Schweppes, Levi's, and Ralph Lauren are running carefully planned word-of-mouth campaigns.

There is little doubt that integrating the old with the new is essential for brand success. The challenge for clients and communications agencies is to stay on top of the changes that are occurring while making appropriate recommendations to resolve business problems.

Adapted from Laura Bogomolny, "Advolution: The ad industry's struggle to keep up," *Canadian Business*, February 13–26, 2006, pp. 61–64.

Intrawest
www.intrawest.com

nies working together to achieve common goals, or it may only involve one company trying to build a meaningful relationship with its consumers. **Customer relationship management** programs are concerned with establishing, maintaining, and enhancing long-term relationships; they involve collecting information about customers that can be used to develop and sustain those relationships. These programs call for marketing and marketing communications programs that are designed to approach customer groups (targets) collectively and each customer individually, when applicable.

To demonstrate CRM, let's examine the marketing communications used by Intrawest. Intrawest is North America's largest ski and golf destination operator. Instead of marketing each ski mountain or golf destination separately, Intrawest uses permission-based marketing and careful segmentation to turn winter skiers into summer golfers and mountain bikers.

By analyzing its own data about customers, Intrawest identified six different customer segments. One segment, called "valuable detached experts," are regular skiers that own Intrawest properties. They respond to clear and direct communications. In contrast, "family vacationers" like to comparison shop, look for bargains, and respond to images of social experiences and offers of ski and spa packages. At Intrawest, unique communications strategies that embrace direct mail and permission-based email are purposely designed to reach targets with unique needs.[5]

In today's very competitive business environment, equal consideration must be given to attracting new customers and to retaining existing customers. Typically, the more traditional means of communications are used to pursue new customers, and non-traditional media such as telemarketing, online communications (email), and loyalty programs are used to retain and enhance the customer relationship. Specific loyalty programs such as AIR MILES and Canadian Tire 'Money' keep customers coming back.

Expanding Role of Database Management Techniques

Database management systems involve the continuous collection of information about customers and have been developing and growing rapidly. Consequently, companies can contact consumers directly more easily than they were previously able to. Companies analyze the information to predict how likely the customer is to buy, and then develop a message precisely designed to meet that customer's unique needs. Technological advances allow a company to zero in on extremely small segments of the population, often referred to as niches. The ultimate goal is to aim directly at the smallest segment—the individual.

Database marketing has emerged as a major thrust to which more traditional forms of communications are added. Bell Canada, for example, is one of Canada's largest advertisers in the traditional mass media. Bell is also one of Canada's largest database and direct response marketing organizations. Bell keeps in close contact with its customers to serve them better and generate incremental business from them.

Bell Canada
www.bell.ca

Database marketing and customer relationship marketing are closely related. The database is the internal vehicle that facilitates implementation of customer relationship management programs. For additional information about database marketing and CRM, see the section on "Direct (Customized) Segmentation" later in this chapter.

Digital Communications Technologies

The Internet is now a vital means for communicating information about goods and services and conducting business transactions with customers. Companies are exploring new forms of advertising made available by the Internet, and in many cases are adding an online component to their traditional media advertising. The Internet is an exciting medium and is becoming a primary medium to reach customers on an individual basis.

Due to its relative newness, even the largest of advertisers have struggled in integrating Internet communications effectively. Many organizations jumped in very quickly, and as the old saying goes, learned from their mistakes. Online communications differ from traditional forms of communications. "It's a bit of direct response, it's a bit of broadcast, it's a bit of print, and it's a bit of technology," comments one observer.[6] The web is a challenging medium for advertisers, but a medium that seems to offer unlimited potential.

Text messaging refers to the transmission of short text-only messages on wireless devices such as cell phones and PDAs. As the penetration of cell phones continues to grow, more and more marketers will look at this medium more seriously. According to a Trendscan study, 52 percent of Canadian youths have their own cell phones. Sharp marketing communications managers wanting to reach this elusive target market are already using text messaging.[7] Cell phones are now capable of handling colour pictures, video, and hi-fi sound, so the flow of multimedia messages has contributed to the growth of the medium. Marketers have a personal link to consumers wherever they are!

The Demand for Efficiency and Accountability

Organizations now understand that scarce resources can be put to better use if the efforts of individual activities are coordinated. A coordinated effort encourages synergy, which in turn should have a stronger impact on the target audience. There is intense pressure on managers today to be more accountable for producing tangible results for their marketing communications investment. Therefore, communications strategies that are efficient are popular, as are strategies that can be measured easily in terms of return on investment. Senior management likes the idea of tangible results. Such a demand is fuelling interest in electronic communications because consumer responses to the communications can be tracked electronically and without cost. Similar measurements are not possible when traditional forms of communications are employed.

Toyota Canada was quick to recognize how integrated media and marketing strategies produce efficient communications. Many of its campaigns embrace both traditional forms of advertising as well as public relations, direct marketing, and online communications. Toyota management restructured the company so that all communications departments work together in one integrated group.

Toyota Canada
www.toyota.ca

According to Peter Renz, Toyota Canada's national manager of public relations and advertising, "We combined all departments in order to ensure that we were speaking with a consistent voice and were sending out a consistent message all the time. It's given us an opportunity to think more 'out of the box' in terms of ideas. With all disciplines working together there are tremendous efficiencies."[8]

CONSUMER BEHAVIOUR ESSENTIALS

A basic understanding of some important behavioural concepts is essential, because such knowledge is applied directly in the development of marketing communications strategies. Knowledge in the areas of needs and motives, personality and self-concept, attitudes and perceptions, reference groups, and families are considered when an organization plans its marketing communications strategies.

Consumer behaviour

The combined acts carried out by individuals choosing and using goods and services, including the decision-making processes that determine these acts.

Consumer behaviour is defined as the acts that individuals perform in obtaining and using goods and services, including the decision-making processes that precede and determine these acts.[9] In the context of marketing and marketing communications, it is imperative that organizations understand what influences consumers' behaviour. Consequently, organizations invest considerable sums of money on marketing research to understand consumers better. Information is power, as they say.

Needs and Motives

Need
The perception of the absence of something useful.

Motive
A condition that prompts an individual to take action to satisfy a need.

There is a direct link between needs and motives. Individuals have a **need** when they perceive the absence of something that is useful to them. A **motive** is a condition that prompts the individual to take action to satisfy the need. Consumers are motivated by friends and family members (word of mouth), or they can be influenced by what they see and read in the media, or by broadcast messages on radio and television. An appealing presentation of a product's features and benefits as they relate to a target's needs is often good enough to stimulate action—a purchase decision. For example, you might say to yourself, "I need (want) a fresh meat sandwich for lunch, so I'm going to a SUBWAY restaurant. "SUBWAY...Eat Fresh!" That's the power of advertising!

Maslow's *hierarchy of needs* and *theory of motivation* have had a significant impact on marketing and marketing communications strategies. Maslow classified needs from lower level to higher level. His theory is based on two assumptions:

1. When lower-level needs are satisfied, a person moves up to higher-level needs.
2. Satisfied needs do not motivate. Instead, behaviour is influenced by needs yet to be satisfied.

Maslow states that individuals move through five levels of needs, as shown in Figure 1.4. Numerous advertising examples can be cited to show how needs theory is applied. For example, safety needs are used to motivate people to buy life insurance and retirement plans. A tagline such as "Like a good neighbour, State Farm is there," captures the message of protection and security.

Beauty and personal care products are famous for appealing to social and esteem needs of women. A brand like Dove, for example (soap and skin care lotions), has almost always been aspirational: "I wish I could look like her...perhaps if I buy Dove I will!" But the modern-day Dove takes a widely different approach. Its latest ad campaign, titled "Campaign for Real Beauty," is quite progressive. It features real women. Outdoor and

Dove
www.dove.com

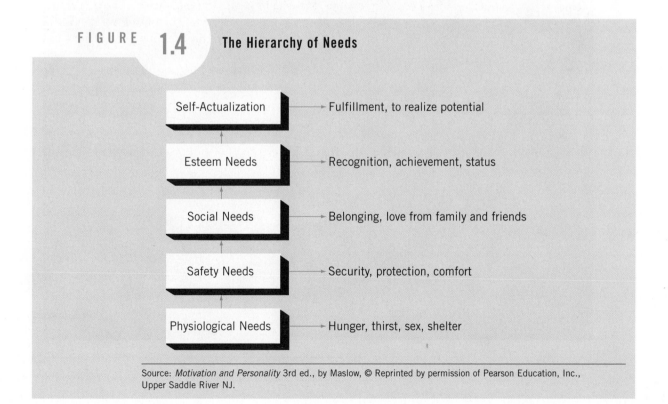

FIGURE **1.4** **The Hierarchy of Needs**

Self-Actualization → Fulfillment, to realize potential

Esteem Needs → Recognition, achievement, status

Social Needs → Belonging, love from family and friends

Safety Needs → Security, protection, comfort

Physiological Needs → Hunger, thirst, sex, shelter

Source: *Motivation and Personality* 3rd ed., by Maslow, © Reprinted by permission of Pearson Education, Inc., Upper Saddle River NJ.

print ads show women stripped down to their plain white undies—gleefully showing us their "real curves."

In terms of needs satisfaction, a female consumer might now say, "That chick in the ad sort of looks like me, and yet she's real and happy...perhaps if I buy Dove I'll stop hating myself."[10] Apparently, Dove has struck a real chord with modern-day women! "The brand has capitalized on a trend in society of self-acceptance and being comfortable in your own skin," says William Wackermann, publisher of *Glamour* magazine.[11]

The sporty-looking Porsche that appears in Figure 1.5 appeals to potential buyers at the esteem level. Porsche is the type of automobile one buys to demonstrate status or to reflect success, whether it be on a personal or professional level. In contrast, someone looking for functionality would pay significantly less for an automobile.

FIGURE **1.5** **The Porsche Appeals to Esteem Needs of Buyers**

Source: Courtesy of Dick Hemingway.

Personality and Self-Concept

Personality
A person's distinguishing psychological characteristics that lead to relatively consistent and enduring responses to the environment in which that person lives.

Personality refers to the individual's distinguishing psychological characteristics that lead to relatively consistent and enduring responses to the environment in which that person lives. Personality is influenced by self-perceptions, which in turn are influenced by family, reference groups, and culture. An understanding of that self-concept provides clues as to how to communicate with consumers. According to Maslow, we have certain needs that must be satisfied. The self-concept, however, goes a step further and focuses on our desires.

According to self-concept theory, the self has four components: real self, self-image, looking-glass self, and ideal self.[12]

1. **Real Self:** An objective evaluation of one's self. You as you really are.
2. **Self-Image:** How you see yourself. It may not be your real self, but a role you play with yourself.
3. **Looking-Glass Self:** How you think others see you. This can be quite different from how they actually see you.
4. **Ideal Self:** How you would like to be. It is what you aspire to.

Based on these descriptions, the real self and self-image are less significant. In contrast, the looking-glass self and ideal self seem dynamic—they focus more on desires, the way we would like to be perceived. Consequently, many communications campaigns revolve around the looking-glass self and the ideal self. Marketing communicators know that consumers buy on emotion, so they present messages for goods and services that make consumers feel and look better, for they know the next level of fulfillment is attractive.

To demonstrate, why is it that a man will spend $1500 or more on a suit at Harry Rosen when a less expensive suit could be purchased at Moores? The answer lies somewhere in the looking-glass self or the ideal self. The image created by high prices and effective communications attracts an upscale clientele to Harry Rosen stores. Harry Rosen has cultivated its image using a combination of media advertising, public relations, personalized service, and customer relationship management programs. Their job is to make the customers feel good about every purchase they make. Those customers are on the move and they want to make a statement about themselves.

How men react to the aging process provides another good illustration of the self-concept theory. Today's men are being influenced by body images presented in magazines like *Maxim* and *Men's Health*. It seems that physical imperfection can be a crippling disability! Brands such as Old Spice, Gillette, and L'Oréal have responded with a complete range of face scrubs, moisturizers, and cleansing products for men. Yes guys...it's all about image! See the illustration in Figure 1.6.

Attitudes and Perceptions

Attitude
An individual's feelings, favourable or unfavourable, toward an idea or object.

Attitudes are an individual's feelings, favourable or unfavourable, toward an idea or object. People form attitudes based on what they hear, read, and see about a product as well as from the opinions of others they have faith in. Friends, for example, certainly have a dramatic impact on the attitudes held by youth. Trendsetters and opinion leaders who embrace new products quickly also influence how consumer attitudes are shaped.

As a rule, organizations present their product in accordance to attitudes held strongly by their target audience. It makes little sense to go against the grain—many an organization has discovered it is very expensive to try to change an attitude.

A more liberal-minded society and a more vocal gay and lesbian community have altered how marketers view attitudes and perceptions. Only a few years ago it would be difficult for a brand to target the gay community. Marketers were almost afraid to

FIGURE **1.6**   Old Spice Helps Men Feel More Confident

Source: Courtesy of P&G Canada.

approach it for fear of doing something wrong or alienating their core consumers. So far, major efforts to target the gay and lesbian market have come from the tourism, automotive, alcohol, and financial sectors.[13] One television commercial for the Toyota Corolla shows a young woman jumping into the car and then kissing her female partner. Such a commercial reflects a very progressive attitude by Toyota. The company does not seem to worry that this ad campaign could alienate present customers—a true reflection of current times and changing attitudes!

Perception
The manner in which individuals receive and interpret messages.

Perception refers to the manner in which individuals receive and interpret messages. Given the prevailing model of human behaviour, it is safe to say that consumers accept messages that are in line with their needs, personality, self-concept, and attitudes, and ignore or reject messages that are not. Theory states that we are selective about the messages we receive and that there are three levels of selectivity:

1. **Selective Exposure:** Our eyes and minds notice only information that interests us.
2. **Selective Perception:** We screen out messages that conflict with our attitudes.
3. **Selective Retention:** We remember only what we want to remember.

To demonstrate how perception works, consider the situation Chrysler faces in the automobile market. The design and styling of an automobile usually leads to a "love it" or "hate it" attitude among consumers. Chrysler's PT Cruiser, for example, is perceived by some consumers to be too toy-like and they hate it, while others really like the retro look and love it. Consumers on the "hate it" side of the equation won't pay much attention to commercial messages about the vehicle.

In contrast, consumers will quickly tune in to messages for items they are contemplating purchasing. A pending purchase of a digital camera or a cell phone represents situations where consumers will be receptive to information—ads for these products suddenly become relevant and get noticed.

Reference Groups

Reference group (peer group)
A group of people who share common interests that influence the attitudes and behaviour of its members.

A **reference group**, or **peer group**, is a group of people with a common interest that influences the attitudes and behaviour of its members. Reference groups include schoolmates, sports teams, fraternities and sororities, and hobby clubs. There is considerable pressure on members to conform to the standards of the group—a desire to "fit in." Take, for example, the mild hazing that occurs among rookies of a college or university sports team, or the rituals associated with joining a fraternity.

In terms of marketing and marketing communications, it is common for brands to associate with a particular situation or lifestyle the target consumer could become interested in. There are risks with such associations, though. For example, if targeting youth, a brand like Mountain Dew tries to appeal to the extreme sports enthusiast and McDonald's uses a rap song to sell burgers. The target sees this practice for what it is: a disingenuous attempt to attract youth consumers without having a clue about their actual tastes.[14]

Apparently, reaching youth only works if the message is authentic. Therefore, if a brand "goes underground" (the place where most pop culture originates), it has a better chance of connecting with the target; it will be ahead of the curve in "buzzworthiness." Microsoft has carved itself a place in youth communities through a blogging site called theSpoke.net, an offline component targeting university clubs, and a loyalty program. TheSpoke.net gives students a place to converse about programming, digital music, movies, and anything else that strikes their fancy.[15] These activities keep Microsoft products at the top of the minds of a very important target.

Family Influences

Each member of a family has some influence on the behaviour of other family members and thus an influence on buying decisions. Perhaps the biggest influence on behaviour within families today relates to the *changing roles* and *responsibilities* of family members.

FIGURE **1.7**   **The Sporty Mazda 5 Appeals to a Young Contemporary Family**

NEVER LOSE YOUR COOL.

zoom-**ZOOM**

INTRODUCING THE ALL-NEW MAZDA**5**. THE FIRST TRUE MULTI-ACTIVITY VEHICLE. Just because you have a family now doesn't mean you have to give up your daily blast of zoom-zoom. Because the all-new Mazda5 is here. It's practical, yet sized for manoeuvrability. It's affordable, yet loaded with what you want. And, like the wildly successful Mazda3, it was created to remind you why you fell in love with the road in the first place. Mazda5 is a cleverly designed Multi-Activity Vehicle – meaning it combines six-passenger seating with versatile fold-flat cargo capability, along with the safety of available dual front side air bags and dual side air curtains for all three rows of seats. And when it comes to on-road performance, you can bet it's pure Mazda. So take the wheel of the new Mazda5 and get ready for some major grins...both from the child in the backseat, and the one that still lives in you.

2006 MAZDA5
FROM $19,995 MSRP*

GT model shown. *Starting MSRP available on the new 2006 Mazda5 GS. Freight and P.D.E. of $1,310 is not included. License, insurance, registration, taxes, and other charges extra. Dealer may sell for less. See your dealer for details.

Source: Courtesy of Mazda Canada.

Traditional attitudes, roles, and responsibilities are out—nothing is what it seems anymore.

Households are also different. There are same-sex households, lone-parent households, and dual-income (two-worker) households. In the dual-income household, much of the decision making is shared between partners. No longer can the maker of a household product assume the woman is the primary buyer, and a financial advisor cannot assume that the man makes all of the investment decisions. To do so would be foolish. Companies that are in tune with these types of changes are double targeting—they are devising marketing strategies that reach both genders effectively. Financial companies and automobile manufacturers recognize the role and influence of women in matters of financial planning and major buying decisions and are devising new campaigns that take advantage of such knowledge. See the illustration in Figure 1.7.

IDENTIFYING AND SELECTING CONSUMER TARGET MARKETS

Market segmentation

The division of a large market into smaller homogeneous markets based on common needs and characteristics.

Knowledge and understanding of consumer behaviour provide the foundation on which potential target markets are identified and pursued. In today's business environment, businesses devise their marketing and marketing communications strategies based on the concept of **market segmentation.** When a market is segmented, it is divided into smaller homogeneous markets or segments based on common needs or characteristics. Typically, it is a three-step process: identifying market segments by profiling the primary user, selecting the segments that offer the greatest profit potential, and positioning the product so it appeals to the target market. Volvo, the Swedish car company, develops and markets cars to a target market interested in safety. Through effective marketing communications, Volvo cars are positioned in the customer's mind as the safest cars to drive.

Micro-segmentation (micro-marketing)

The identification of very small yet profitable market segments.

Continual changes in technology are dramatically affecting how companies identify and pursue target markets. For example, with the capability to reach individual consumers directly with unique marketing strategies, segments (targets) are now potentially so small that new terms such as **micro-segmentation** and **micro-marketing** have emerged. Now a company can make sufficient profits in a very small segment through efficient production and marketing. At one time, for example, automobile makers needed to sell a volume of 250 000 cars for a new car to be a success. Today, the figure is as low as 50 000. Unique cars are being marketed to unique customer groups. The MINI, once a working-class car for the masses in Britain, is now targeted directly at twenty-something urban professionals in North America.

When a target market is identified, the result is a profile of the primary customer, and perhaps secondary customer, based on demographic, psychographic, and geographic variables.

Demographic Segmentation

Demographic segmentation

The identification of target markets based on characteristics such as age, income, education, occupation, marital status, and household formation.

With **demographic segmentation**, target markets are identified and pursued on the basis of variables such as age, gender, income, occupation, marital status, household formation, and cultural mix. For planning purposes, an organization must keep track of trends in each of these areas so it can adjust its strategies when necessary. Let's examine some essential demographic trends that will influence the direction of future marketing and marketing communications planning.

The Population Is Getting Older

Canada's population is growing older. Perhaps the most talked about groups in the past decade have been the baby boomers (those people born between 1946 and 1964), and the grey market (those people born prior to 1946). These groups are and will continue to be a major buying influence for decades to come.

Older age segments tend to be wealthier—they are free of financial obligations associated with children and mortgages—so they are seen as an attractive market to pursue. Luxury goods and premium brand marketers are enjoying much success due to this trend. The sales of BMW cars have risen 18 percent in the past five years, while mid-range domestic automobiles have grown by only 4 percent.[16] For a summary of the population and how it is aging, see Figure 1.8.

The baby boomer generation spawned another blip in the age curve known as the echo boom. The children of boomers, referred to as Generation X (born between 1965 and 1981), and Generation Y (born between 1982 and 2003) are causing headaches for marketers of goods and services that are aging with the population. Each generation has a different outlook and different values, so it is a challenge for marketers to retain older customers while trying to attract new, younger customers.

FIGURE **1.8** **Canada's Population and Growth Rates by Age Segments**
(All population figures in millions)

Age Segment	1991	2001	2011	% Growth 2001–2011
0–4	1.91	1.70	1.64	–3.1
5–12	3.04	3.23	2.77	–14.1
13–24	4.57	4.81	4.98	3.6
25–34	4.87	3.99	4.17	4.4
35–44	4.37	5.10	4.51	–11.5
45–64	5.37	7.29	9.47	29.9
65–69	1.07	1.13	1.49	31.3
70–79	1.44	1.82	1.99	8.9
80+	0.66	0.93	1.33	42.7
Total	**27.30**	**30.01**	**32.36**	**7.8**

Source: Adapted from the Statistics Canada publication "Profile of the Canadian population by age and sex: Canada ages, 2001 Census (Analysis series)," Catalogue 96F0030, July 2002.

Levi Strauss
www.levi.com

To illustrate the effect of age change, consider the condition of a company such as Levi Strauss. Boomers grew up with Levi's—in fact, they built the brand. But youth today see the brand as a relic from the past, and despite many good attempts to rekindle interest in the brand among youth, Levi's has failed. Eventually, Levi's will be out of business if they can't turn things around.

Urban Growth

The trend toward urbanization continues in Canada. The 2001 census shows 79.4 percent of Canadians live in an urban area with a population of 10 000 or more. As well, the population continues to concentrate in four broad urban regions: the extended Golden Horseshoe in southern Ontario, Montreal and its adjacent region, the Lower Mainland of British Columbia and southern Vancouver Island, and the Calgary–Edmonton corridor. In 2001, 51 percent of Canada's population lived in these regions, compared to 49 percent in 1996. It is not surprising, then, that successful marketing and advertising programs have an urban orientation and reflect contemporary households dealing with contemporary issues.

The nature of Canada's urban population has a direct effect on marketing and marketing communications planning. With the population so clustered, companies now devise plans that are regional in nature or dwell specifically on key urban areas. A brand may be available nationally in terms of geography, but the way it is positioned and the nature of the message could be very different from one area to another. Such a trend also helps explain the popularity of regional brands. In Atlantic Canada, for example, Alexander Keith's is a leading brand of beer. A national brand like Molson Canadian has to adapt its national strategy to suit the needs of Atlantic beer drinkers if it is to make any headway in that region.

Household Formations Are Different

Trends such as the postponement of marriage, the pursuit of careers by women, increases in divorce rates, and same-sex partnerships are producing new households in Canada. The mythical "Ozzie and Harriet" family with a working father, stay-at-home mother, and a couple of children, is long gone. Modern households are described as lone-parent families (either from divorce or absence of a partner), blended families (divorce and remarriage), and same-sex families (openness and acceptance of gay lifestyles).

Other changes are also occurring. Households are becoming smaller (in terms of the number of inhabitants) and one- or two-person households represent the fastest-growing segment in Canada. In fact, there are now as many one-person households as there are those with four or more people. The average household size decreased in the same period from 2.9 to 2.6 persons.[17]

No longer can marketing and marketing communications strategies be tailored to the traditional family. Products and services must be fashioned to fit all kinds of family situations, and again this calls for more micro-marketing strategies. Companies in the household and packaged-goods business, for example, have to offer a variety of sizes to meet the needs of such household variation. They must also be cognizant of who is making the buying decisions. To present a product improperly or in an old-fashioned way—that is, according to traditional roles and responsibilities—could be harmful to a brand's development.

Ethnic Diversity Continues

Canada's ethnic diversity continues to present new challenges for marketing organizations. Canadian culture is represented by many diverse subcultures (subgroups of a larger population). These subcultures have distinct lifestyles based on religious, racial, and geographic differences. The 2001 census revealed that visible minorities represent 5.7 million people in Canada, or about 18 percent of the population. The largest minority groups are Chinese (23 percent of the ethnic population), South Asian (21 percent), black (19 percent), and West Asian/Arab (13 percent). More recent immigrants (those arriving during the 1990s) have a tendency to migrate to large urban areas. Nearly 73 percent of immigrants who arrived in the 1990s live in three areas: Toronto, Vancouver, or Montreal. In Toronto alone, visible minorities now comprise 43 percent of the population.[18]

Frito Lay Canada is targeting Chinese and South Asian populations with a new line of Asian-inspired potato chips that include flavours like Wasabi, Spicy Curry, and Shrimp. The new line is being introduced in Vancouver and Toronto, markets where a majority of these ethnic populations reside. "The Asian-inspired chips will also appeal to Canadians who continue to seek new flavour experiences," says vice-president of brand marketing, Dale Hooper. The launch was supported with print ads in Chinese-language newspapers and 30-second spots on Chinese-language TV channels.[19] An example of the ad appears in Figure 1.9.

Gender Economics

Gender has always been a primary means of distinguishing product categories. Personal care products, magazines, and fashion goods are typically categorized to the gender of the buyer. As discussed earlier, more and more women are pursuing careers, so their changing roles and responsibilities in a household have influenced the buying decision process.

Women may, on average, earn less money than their male counterparts, but they make more than 80 percent of buying decisions in all homes. "Today's woman is the chief purchasing agent of the family and marketers must recognize that," says Michael Silverstein, principal at Boston Consulting Group.[20] Canadian Tire, a long-time popular spot for the neighbourhood handyman, is working hard to show its feminine side.

FIGURE **1.9** **Frito Lay Appeals Directly to the Chinese and South Asian Populations in a Manner They Understand**

Source: Reprinted by permission of FRITO-LAY, INC.

Redesigned stores now include complete model kitchens, wider aisles, brighter lighting, and more "touch-and-feel" displays—an unabashed attempt to attract female shopping dollars.[21] Ditto at Home Depot, where television commercials show families roasting marshmallows on their decks, a departure from its image as a haven for contractors. Home Depot also runs a "Do-it-Herself" series of home repair and decorating seminars.[22]

How organizations perceive gender roles has to be reflected in their marketing communications campaigns. The self-concept theory plays a key role in how females are portrayed in advertising—it is essential to communicate to a woman based on how she sees herself or wants to see herself. It should speak to her as an individual, one who defines her individuality today differently from how she will define it tomorrow. It understands that women are different from men. Aero chocolate bar experienced a 42 percent increase in sales, moving from number eight to number two in a very competitive market, when it targeted women specifically.

For more insight into the importance of reaching women, see the IMC Highlight **Take Me Seriously**.

Psychographic Segmentation

Psychographic segmentation
The identification of a target market according to lifestyle characteristics such as activities, interests, and opinions.

Psychographic segmentation examines individual lifestyles in terms of activities, interests, and opinions (commonly referred to as AIOs). Psychographics supplement demographics and serve a very useful purpose. An examination of lifestyle trends helps marketing organizations understand why two people who are demographically identical behave in different ways and purchase different types of goods and services. Included in lifestyle trends are people's media consumption habits (for example, which media do they refer to most often?)

Messages about products are delivered to targets in such a manner that they are associated with the targets' lifestyle. The personality of the product matches the personality

IMC HIGHLIGHT

TAKE ME SERIOUSLY

First, some facts about women:
- Women constitute 46.4 percent of Canada's labour force.
- Women make up 52.7 percent of professionals.
- Employed women and female entrepreneurs are the primary decision makers in households, influencing 95 percent of purchasing decisions.

Why are women so important to marketers? In addition to the above statistics, about 25 percent of women earn more money than their husbands or boyfriends. She is the chief purchasing agent for the family, is extremely brand-attuned, and does a lot of research before buying. She can't afford to buy everything and will decide where to trade up or down.

For example, it is widely accepted that women influence at least 80 percent of all car purchases. There are approximately 1.1 million cars sold annually in Canada, so that means women have a say in 800 000 car-buying decisions a year. Such data should make an automobile company take notice. And the smart companies do!

Volvo of Canada may pull away from its competitors with the launch of its first SUV, the XC90. It has been designed specifically for the needs and tastes of the primary family caregiver—the mother. Female focus groups

contributed input during the drawing-board stage and throughout the development of the XC90. The car is advertised on television programs and networks that attract the greatest number of female viewers.

Mazda is another company viewing women through a different lens. With reference to the ad that appears in Figure 1.7, the woman is shown as a mother, a wife, and a career woman. The television commercial for the same vehicle shows the husband with baby in tow, picking up his wife at the end of a long teaching day. Clearly, this is a situation of role change in a modern household.

Women are also the hottest target market among general merchandise retailers. Zellers recently launched several initiatives that target mothers directly. "She spends twice as much as others in our stores," said David Strickland, senior vice-president of marketing. Retailers that understand the multi-task nature of a mother's daily routine are trying to make the shopping experience less stressful, a little more relaxed, and a little more fun. If they can do so, shoppers will spend more money.

Adapted from "How a woman spends her money," *Business Week Online*, February 14, 2005, www.businessweek.com, Terry Poulton, "The 80% factor," *Strategy*, November 18, 2002, pp. M11–12, and Marina Strauss, "Merchants making moms their mark," *Globe and Mail*, March 25, 2002, p. B1.

of the target. Canada's beer industry uses psychographic information to devise one campaign after another for a variety of beer brands. The two leading national brands, Labatt Blue and Molson Canadian, continually present images and lifestyles that are attractive to male beer drinkers aged 19 to 29. Such campaigns tend to dwell on the concept that guys need to get together to do their thing—anything from enjoying the rugged outdoors, to frequenting bars, to watching sports on television.

Numerous research studies have been conducted in an effort to classify consumers into psychographic cells. A study conducted by Millward Brown Goldfarb of Toronto classifies Canadians into nine psychographic cells: protective providers, up and comers, *les petite vie*, mavericks, contented traditionalists, joiner activists, passive malcontents, disinterested outsiders, and tie-dyed greys. For insight into each of these cells, refer to Figure 1.10.

Millward Brown Goldfarb
www.goldfarbconsultants.com

Psychographic information shows how an interest in a particular product depends on one's lifestyle. For example, a trendy sports car such as the Mazda Miata or Pontiac Solstice will appeal to an up and comer (outgoing, ambitious, materialistic types), whereas a Ford Freestar minivan might appeal to a contented traditionalist (someone motivated by family, conservative values, and security). The nature of the message and the imagery presented in advertising will certainly be different for these automobiles. Refer to the illustration in Figure 1.11.

Psychographics allow a company to position its products better in the marketplace. Purchase decisions based on needs not yet satisfied, or based on a self-concept yet to be realized, furnish ammunition for compelling campaigns that focus on lifestyle associations. Such campaigns tap into the emotional side of the brain. For consumers who take the plunge and buy, the decision often has to be justified to others. Have you ever had to present rational arguments for an emotional purchase decision?

Geographic Segmentation

Geographic segmentation
The identification of a target market based on the regional, urban, or rural location of the customers.

Geographic segmentation refers to the division of a geographically expansive market into smaller geographic units. In Canada and the United States, for example, many companies manage their companies regionally with specific marketing plans for certain areas. A plan in Atlantic Canada would be different from a plan in Ontario. A plan for the Northeastern United States would be different from a plan for the South (Georgia, Florida, and Louisiana), and so on.

In Canada, Quebec presents the biggest challenge in terms of marketing and marketing communications. Many companies assume that translating a message from English to French is sufficient to attract the French-speaking population. Such a flawed premise only leads to alienation and rejection of the brand in question. The Brick suffered such a fate when it served up a French translation of a Calgary-based ad to Quebecers. It didn't work! Figure 1.12 highlights some important differences between English Canada and French Quebec.

Pepsi-Cola is the leading brand of soft drink in Quebec, a position it doesn't hold in any other region of Canada. Pepsi has used separate French and English campaigns for over 20 years. The French campaign featured the personality of Claude Meunier, a popular French comedian. The campaign worked because Quebecers are far more supportive of Quebec stars than English Canadians are of their counterparts. Two years ago Pepsi introduced a new advertising strategy. The popularity of the Meunier campaign gave Pepsi licence to go in another direction now that the brand was credible. The new theme is a celebration of Quebec culture. Pepsi's market share continues to grow in Quebec.[23]

Pepsi
www.pepsi.ca

Toyota Canada is another company that pays specific attention to Quebec. According to Chris Pappas, manager of vehicle marketing, "We try to make sure backdrops could be Montreal or Quebec City, as Quebecers are more sensitive to the appear-

FIGURE **1.10**   Lifestyle Segments in Canada

Millward Brown Goldfarb has identified nine different consumer segments in Canada. Each segment is motivated by a unique set of attitudes and beliefs.

Protective Providers

- Hardworking and value personal initiative and commitment to family
- Financially strained
- Unlikely to be involved in politics or social activist groups
- Price conscious and less brand loyal

Up and Comers

- Outgoing but like time alone for solitary pursuits
- Materialistic and seek instant gratification
- Enjoy the latest gadgets (anything new)
- Optimistic outlook and ambitions for wealth and power
- Traditional values and friendships are important

Les Petite Vie

- Uncomfortable with the pace of modern life
- Friends and family are very important; respect business leaders
- Favour government involvement in economic and social programs
- Open-minded on sexual matters
- Overwhelmingly French-speaking and Roman Catholic

Mavericks

- Individual's rights are important; dislike government intervention
- Confident and self-reliant
- More likely to engage in risky activities and adventures
- Tend to be leaders and enjoy challenges
- Seek wealth and power

Contented Traditionalists

- Well-adjusted, happy individuals
- Family more important than personal goals
- Loyal and trustworthy
- Active in community; religious focus; conservative values
- Brand loyal

Joiner Activists

- Value education and personal growth
- Liberal social attitudes
- Active in community
- Optimistic outlook and non-religious approach to life
- Concerned about health, environment, and cultural issues

Passive Malcontents

- Unhappy and dissatisfied with job, family, and social life
- Strong belief in law and order
- Live day-to-day; do not strive to get ahead
- Patriotic and trusting of government
- Not health conscious

Disinterested Outsiders

- Casual indifference to problems facing society
- Not very interested in anything beyond their daily lives
- Willing to bend the rules and lack respect for authority
- Dislike change
- Not health conscious and watch a lot of television

Tie-Dyed Greys

- Progressive attitudes about social issues
- Less materialistic and more independent than their peers
- Open-minded on moral issues
- Suspicious of big business ethics
- Environmentally conscious and slightly uncomfortable with technology

Source: Millward Brown Goldfarb, TrendZ 2003.

ance of their geographical landmarks. We think the awareness and perception of Toyota is better in the Quebec market because of it."[24]

Given the migration of the population to urban markets (discussed earlier in this chapter), it is possible to devise marketing and marketing communications strategies that are tailored specifically to regions or individual urban centres. Where possible, however,

FIGURE 1.11 **An Understanding of a Target's Psychographic Profile Leads to Lifestyle Imagery in Advertising**

Source: Courtesy of Mazda Canada.

many companies will develop universal strategies that are appropriate for all of North America, or even for the global marketplace. The phrase "thinking globally and acting locally" is a common theme among marketing organizations today. Either approach can work if the strategy is the right one. The key to success seems to be flexibility and a willingness to make changes when and where necessary.

Direct (customized) segmentation

The identification of a target audience at the level of the individual; marketing programs designed for and communicated to individual customers.

Direct (Customized) Segmentation

Direct or customized segmentation means that a company provides differentiated products and services, prices, and delivery strategies for each customer. By marketing online, companies are also capable of interacting with individual customers by personalizing messages, products, and services. The combination of operational customization—that is, the

FIGURE **1.12**   The Uniqueness of the French-Quebec Market

Many marketing executives must decide whether to develop unique marketing strategies for the Quebec market. Are the language and cultural differences significant enough to justify such an investment? Here are a few unique characteristics of the French-Quebec market that tend to justify unique marketing communications.

Lifestyle Habits (*joie de vivre*)

Quebecers like to indulge—cigarette smoking, lingerie, and hedonistic products usually index higher in Quebec. In Quebec there is greater permissiveness and there are fewer restraints on what is socially acceptable—homosexuality and extramarital affairs. Advertising that dares strikes a chord.

Consumer Habits: Heart over Head

Quebecers like to "do things right" while English Canadians "do the right thing." Appearance, image, and social relations are very important, such as dressing smartly and being more brand-image conscious. Advertising that appeals to emotions instead of rational benefits is usually quite effective.

Star Quality of Local Celebrities

The most popular television programs are produced in Quebec and French Quebecers are the stars. Leveraging Quebec talent will always be an asset in any advertising execution.

Adapted from Yves Léveillé, "What Quebec wants now," *Marketing*, June 20, 2005, p. 46.

Mass customization
The development, manufacture, and marketing of unique products to unique customers.

development and manufacture of unique products for unique customers—and marketing customization is often referred to as **mass customization**.

As discussed earlier in the chapter, contemporary organizations focus much of their efforts on customer relationship management (CRM). CRM enables a company to provide real-time service by developing an ongoing relationship with a valued customer by effectively using information the company has about that individual. CRM is designed to attract, cultivate, and maximize the return from each customer the company does business with. By effectively using information that is stored in a database, a company can increase the life of a customer relationship, enhance customer sales and profits, and convert low-profit customers into more profitable ones.

An organization may compile information about customers: past volumes, prices and profits generated, buying practices, frequency of purchase, and so on. This information is used in **database marketing** and can be combined with demographic, psychographic, media-related, and consumption information on customers to target them more effectively. Information is available from a variety of external sources, including Statistics Canada, Canada Post, and marketing intelligence companies such as Nielsen Media Research and Millward Brown Goldfarb.

Database marketing
The use and analysis of accumulated information on customer buying behaviour to develop more effective marketing strategies.

The electronic era has resulted in an information explosion that allows for the storage and transfer of great amounts of customer data in a short time. What has emerged is a concept called data mining. **Data mining** is the analysis of information to establish relationships among pieces of information so that more effective marketing strategies can be identified and implemented. Data mining techniques look for informational patterns and nuggets within the database.[25] The goal is to identify prospects most likely to buy, or buy in large volume, and to provide input on how best to communicate with the customer.

Data mining
The analysis of information to determine relationships among the data and enable more effective marketing strategies to be identified and implemented.

To demonstrate how new forms of segmentation are changing the ways companies do business, consider the following example. In the past, neighbourhoods were classified and described on the basis of the profile of the typical resident. It was believed that all households had similar characteristics—demographics, attitudes, and lifestyles. This was called

Geodemographic
segmentation (cluster
profiling)

The identification of target
markets according to
dwelling areas defined by
geographic and demographic
variables; based on the
assumption that like people
seek out residential neighbourhoods in which to cluster
with their lifestyle peers.

cluster profiling or **geodemographic segmentation**. Information was analyzed, clusters emerged, and they were given descriptions, such as "Mortgaged in Suburbia," "Canadian Establishment," or "Suburban Nesters." The descriptions alluded to the neighbourhood's profile.

Now it is possible to pinpoint individual houses by satellite and obtain the name of the owner through local property assessment rolls. The name is combined with data available from Statistics Canada and other sources described above. The marketing organization now has sufficient information to develop a customized offer that is sent to someone personally; neighbours may not receive the same offer. That's direct (customized) marketing!

Technology like this is changing the nature of marketing communications. There will be much greater use of direct response, online, and mobile communications between organizations and their customers in the future. Furthermore, organizations are collecting all kinds of valuable information about their customers through websites that can be added to a database. It seems that many visitors to a site willingly give up personal information to access the information they want at the website.

For more information about how segmentation and targeting concepts are applied in a marketing communications environment, see the IMC Highlight **Millennials: A Very Different Target**.

IMC HIGHLIGHT

MILLENNIALS: A VERY DIFFERENT TARGET

Based on their distinct demographic characteristics and lifestyle tendencies, a target group known as millennials represents a distinct segment of Canada's population. The eldest of millennials, those born between 1980 and 2000, are now in their early to mid-twenties. Marketers yearn to reach such an age group since they are just starting to from loyalties to brands.

By 2010, this group will outnumber both baby boomers and Gen-Xers among those 18 to 49 years old. The 18- to 49-year age bracket is a crucial target for all kinds of businesses, and a target that has traditionally been reached effectively by television and newspaper advertising.

Millennials are different from their predecessors. They have grown up with digital technology and use it instinctively. They are avid video gamers; they produce their own websites and blogs; they download music and television shows; and they use instant messaging to communicate with friends.

Also unlike their predecessors, millennials don't watch prime-time television. They download shows without commercials and watch whenever the mood strikes them. Millennials don't read newspapers, either. If they want information, they read it online or from a network of electronic contacts. These habits have a significant impact on advertisers. How does an advertiser reach a moving target?

From a psychographic perspective, this group is different because its social network revolves around technology, and according to some experts, the technology is forming a sort of group mentality (as opposed to individual thinking). Jack MacKenzie, senior vice-president with Frank N. Magid

Associates, a research consulting firm, calls this "the democratization of social interaction, a process that changes this generation's relationship with almost everything they come in contact with."

Essentially, networks of kids and young adults are incredibly loyal to each other. They are bound to certain ethics and values that, in some ways, prevent them from developing as individuals. They place considerable trust in non-traditional sources. They rely on their friends and their technology-based network for advice. These sources have much greater influence on their behaviours than traditional advertising.

Advertisers, mindful that young consumers have migrated away from traditional media outlets, are now experimenting with ads and short video messages for mobile phones, cell networks with dedicated game channels, and $1.99 TV programs to download to iPods and computers. They are also employing street-level marketing tactics (street teams to deliver the word about new products), participating more actively in events that reach younger targets, and designing their own blogs to communicate positive word of mouth about their products.

The moral of the story is quite simple: a marketer must truly understand how a target audience behaves and know what external factors influence the target the most. Keeping pace in a rapidly changing technology-based environment is extremely difficult and costly for marketers, but so essential if they want to communicate effectively.

Adapted from Tom Zeller Jr., "A generation serves notice: It's a moving target," *New York Times*, January 26, 2006, www.nytimes.com.

BUSINESS MARKETS AND BUYER BEHAVIOUR

The buying process of organizations is very different from consumer buying. In a nutshell, organizations exhibit more rational behaviour than consumers—consumers do a lot of buying based on emotion. The **business-to-business (B2B) market** is managed by individuals in an organization responsible for purchasing goods and services needed to produce a product or service or promote an idea. This market includes business and industry, governments, institutions, wholesalers and retailers, and professionals.

Business-to-business (B2B) market
A market of goods and services needed to produce a product or service, promote an idea, or operate a business.

The business market has several characteristics that distinguish it from consumer markets. Business markets have fewer buyers, and those buyers tend to be concentrated in industrial areas in and near large cities. The buying criteria are very practical, with decisions based on the best buy according to predetermined requirements, and there is usually a formal buying process for evaluating product and service alternatives. Business buying processes have changed dramatically because of advancing technology and the benefits derived from buying goods online.

Regardless of location or the numbers of buyers, the key issues that a business organization must address when marketing to other businesses are the criteria established by the buying organization. In most situations, those requirements are established in advance and companies can compete with each other by submitting bids. The buyer customarily chooses the bid with the lowest price, assuming the criteria have been met. So, what are those requirements?

- **Quality:** Buyers want consistent quality on every order. What they buy could have a direct impact on the quality of goods they in turn produce and market.
- **Service:** Buyers want reputable suppliers who provide prompt service and believe that the initial order is simply the start of a business relationship.
- **Continuity of Supply:** Buyers want suppliers that can provide goods over the long term. A steady source of supply ensures consistent production scheduling.
- **Price:** Buyers evaluate price in conjunction with the other criteria. The lowest price is not always accepted. Potential long-term savings could outweigh an initial low price.

To ensure that the right buying decision is made, organizations employ a formal or informal approach. A formal approach involves a **buying committee**. The committee is made up of key representatives from various functional areas of the company, such as finance, marketing, manufacturing, purchasing, and so on. A committee takes a very rational approach when evaluating alternatives, and participants need to know that costly decisions are shared decisions.

Buying committee
A formal buying structure in an organization that brings together expertise from the various functional areas to share in the buying decision process.

Buying centre
An informal purchasing process in which individuals in an organization perform particular roles but may not have direct responsibility for the actual decision.

A **buying centre** is an informal purchasing process with individuals in an organization involved in the purchasing process, but not necessarily having direct responsibility for the actual decision. These roles are summarized in Figure 1.13.

In terms of marketing or marketing communications, the seller must know who on the committee or within the buying centre has the most influence. It could be one person or several people. Once that is known, the best means of communicating can be determined. Based on the nature of business buying, it becomes clear that personal selling and direct forms of communications are vital components when trying to influence the decisions of business buyers.

Integration and Partnering Influences B2B Communications Strategies

Business markets have embraced customer relationship management in an attempt to establish efficient business systems. CRM promotes the seamless transfer of information

FIGURE **1.13**   **The Buying Centre**

Role	Description	Example
Users	Those in the organization who use the product directly.	If the product is a personal computer, any end-user in the organization.
Influencers	Those who define the product specifications.	An engineer.
Buyers	Those with the authority to buy.	A purchasing manager.
Deciders	Those with the power to finalize the purchase.	Where high-cost decisions are involved, the CEO may be the decider.
Gatekeepers	Those who control the flow of information to the members of the buying centre.	A purchasing manager may also fulfill the role of gatekeeper.

Eprocurement

An online, business-to-business marketplace through which participants can purchase goods and services from one another.

throughout the channels to ensure the efficient and continuous flow of goods. Forming partnerships with suppliers implies a long-term relationship. Therefore, to be part of a CRM system, the marketer must be more familiar than ever with the role the product plays in the customer's operations. Collecting information about the customer and operations is crucial.

The Internet has created buying opportunities through **eprocurement**. This is an Internet-based, business-to-business buying marketplace through which participants can purchase supplies and services from one another. It is an all-inclusive system that allows buyers to solicit multiple bids, issue purchase orders, and make payments. The combining of CRM practices with eprocurement systems fosters long-term relationships between buyers and sellers and presents a situation where participants are directly influenced by the decisions of other participants. This clearly is the future of business-to-business buying and marketing. Companies will either be part of the system or they will watch it unfold from the sidelines.

The strategies employed to reach business customers are also evolving. Yet, in spite of all the technological advances and the direct nature of the buying and selling process, customers must still be made aware of the product alternatives that are available. Creating awareness is always the first step. Therefore, the need for print advertising directed at business customers will continue, along with the need for strong personal sales contacts. The inclusion of sales promotion programs to assist salespeople is also important. Event marketing in the form of trade show participation will help keep marketing organizations on a buyer's radar screen, and direct marketing techniques such as direct mail and Internet-based communications will become more of a priority. A website containing essential product information is indispensable in B2B marketing situations. The same tools are employed in consumer marketing; they are just given different priority.

A recent survey published by the Center for Media Research provides interesting insights into business buying behaviour and the media that influence buyers. It suggests that simultaneous media usage presents a challenge for business-to-business marketers. Nearly half the respondents said traditional communications methods such as print, direct mail, and outdoor advertising are "not important" to them. In contrast, 44 percent

Center for Media Research
www.centerformediaresearch.
com

said the Internet was "somewhat important," 81 percent said word of mouth was "very important" or "important," and 88 percent said they "sought the advice of others" before making a decision.[26] This clearly indicates that products must live up to the promise made by any form of marketing communications.

Summary

The rapid pace of change in business today has forced organizations to re-examine and change the way they communicate with customers. More than ever before, organizations are demanding integrated marketing strategies to help resolve marketing problems and to take advantage of new opportunities.

The integrated marketing communications mix is composed of seven unique yet complementary components: advertising, direct response communications, interactive communications, sales promotion, personal selling, public relations, and event marketing and sponsorships. The organization evaluates marketing situations and employs the components of the mix that will effectively and efficiently reach its target market.

Several key issues and trends have led to the emergence of integrated marketing communications. Among the key issues are consumers' changing media habits, the strategic focus on customer relationship management (CRM), the expanding role of database marketing, the dramatic impact of the Internet, and greater demand by senior managers for efficiency and accountability for the resources that are invested in marketing communications.

In the process of developing marketing communications strategies, an organization must understand and apply various consumer behaviour concepts. Among these concepts are needs and motives, personality and self-concept, attitudes and perceptions, reference groups, and family. Research into these factors provides clues on how to reach customers with a more effective message.

Marketing communications programs consider the unique needs and desires of a specific target market. Target markets are identified on the basis of common characteristics that are classified according to demographic, psychographic, and geographic variables. Trends in each of these areas are analyzed and a consumer profile of a designated target market emerges. Organizations then determine which targets are worth pursuing. Contemporary technology now allows for direct communications with individual customers. These new techniques are part of CRM programs. CRM is a practice that is designed to attract, cultivate, and maximize the return from individual customers.

Business buying behaviour is different from consumer buying behaviour. While consumers tend to be swayed by emotion, business buyers maintain a rational approach when making buying decisions. Business buying is based on predetermined criteria according to quality, service, continuity of supply, and price. Decisions are made formally by a buying committee or informally by a buying centre. Technology and relationship marketing practices have taken hold in business-to-business (B2B) marketing. Companies must adapt to this way of doing business or perish. Tools such as personal selling, event marketing, direct response, and interactive communications will play a prominent role in the future.

Key Terms

advertising, 4	integrated marketing communications, 3
attitude, 15	market segmentation, 19
business-to-business (B2B) market, 29	mass customization, 27
buying centre, 29	micro-marketing, 19
buying committee, 29	micro-segmentation, 19
cluster profiling, 28	motive, 13
consumer behaviour, 12	need, 13
customer relationship management (CRM), 11	peer group, 17
data mining, 27	perception, 17
database management system, 11	personal selling, 8
database marketing, 27	personality, 15
demographic segmentation, 19	product advertising, 4
direct or customized segmentation, 26	promotional advertising, 6
direct response communications, 6	psychographic segmentation, 23
eprocurement, 30	public relations, 8
event marketing, 8	reference group, 17
geodemographic segmentation, 28	sales promotion, 6
geographic segmentation, 24	sponsorship, 8

Review Questions

1. Identify and briefly explain the components of the integrated marketing communications mix.
2. Briefly describe the key issues and trends that have led to the emergence of integrated marketing communications.
3. "An understanding of Maslow's hierarchy of needs and theory of motivation has a direct influence on advertising strategy." Explain.
4. According to the self-concept theory, the self has four components. Identify and briefly describe each component.
5. How important is assessing customer attitudes when developing an advertising campaign? Explain.
6. What role and influence do reference groups play when a consumer is deciding what products to buy?
7. What are the key elements of demographic segmentation, psychographic segmentation, and geographic segmentation?
8. Identify the basic trends in Canada that must be considered when identifying and selecting demographic targets.
9. What is meant by the term "direct or customized segmentation"?
10. What essential criteria do organizational buyers consider when making buying decisions?
11. What is the difference between a buying committee and a buying centre?

Discussion and Application Questions

1. How have integration and partnerships influenced marketing communications strategies in business-to-business markets? Explain.

2. "Relationship marketing practices will dramatically alter marketing communications strategies in the future." Is this statement true or false? Conduct some online secondary research and form an opinion on this statement.

3. "Due to the geographic and cultural diversity in Canada, regional marketing communications strategies should be commonplace; instead, organizations rely upon national strategies." What direction should companies be taking, and why? Consider both sides of the situation before making a decision.

4. From the following list of goods and services, identify what you think is the most important marketing communications tool for building and sustaining the brand. Provide some justification for your choices.
   a) Labatt Blue
   b) BMW automobiles
   c) Michelin tires
   d) RBC Financial Group

5. Cite some examples and provide actual illustrations of companies or brands that use the following consumer behaviour theories when developing communications strategies. Provide a description that relates the theory to the practice.
   a) hierarchy of needs and theory of motivation
   b) personality and self-concept
   c) reference groups
   d) family influences

6. Visit the Statistics Canada website and gather the most up-to-date statistics on Canadian household formations. Consider two or three prominent brands of Canadian household goods or retail organizations: do they reflect contemporary households? If not, what are the potential consequences?

7. The chapter discusses various methods (demographic segmentation, psychographic segmentation, and geographic segmentation) for identifying target markets. Provide some new examples of companies or brands that employ each of these methods when attempting to motivate their target customer to buy.

Endnotes

1 Kevin Astle, "Mending broken eggs," *Marketing*, July 14–21, 2003, p. 9.

2 Rich Thomaselli and Jean Halliday, "Formula One crashes spectacularly in U.S.," *Advertising Age*, June 29, 2005, **www.adage.com**.

3 "Crowned at last," *Economist*, April, 2005, p. 9.

4 Raymond Snoddy, "The man with the $6B plan," *Independent News*, June 28, 2005, **www.news.independent.co.uk**.

5 Eve Lazarus, "Intrawest digs deep," *Marketing*, May 31, 2004, p. 4.

6 Bernadette Johnson, "Advertisers revisiting the web: Study," *Strategy*, February 12, 2001, pp. 1, 14.

7 Karen Whitney-Vernon, "How to target teenage textualists," *Financial Post*, June 28, 2004, p. FP6.

8 Richard Rotman, "When worlds combine," *Marketing*, September 29, 2003, p. 8.

9 James F. Engel, David T. Kollatt, and Roger D. Blackwell, *Consumer Behavior*, 2nd ed. (New York: Holt Rinehart Winston, 1973), p. 5.

10 Seth Stevenson, "When tush comes to Dove," *Slate*, August 2, 2005, **www.slate.com**.

11 Rich Thomaselli, "Nike steers advertising toward reality anatomy," *Advertising Age*, August 15, 2005, **www.adage.com**.

12 John Douglas, George Field, and Lawrence Tarpay, *Human Behavior in Marketing* (Columbus, OH: Charles E. Merrill Publishing, 1987), p. 5.

13 Michelle Halpern, "They're here, they're queer, and they love to shop," *Marketing*, September 20, 2004, pp. 10, 11.

14 San Grewal, "Manufactured cool," *Toronto Star*, February 22, 2005, p. C4.

15 Lisa D'Innocenzo, "Two-faced marketing," *Strategy*, October 2004, pp. 25, 26.

16 Hollie Shaw, "Skip the Chevy—buy yourself a Beemer," *Financial Post*, July 10, 2003, pp. FP1, FP8.

17 Barbara Wickens, "How we live," *Maclean's*, November 4, 2002, p. 46.

18 "Proportion of foreign-born population, census metropolitan areas," Statistics Canada, **www.statcan.ca**.

19 "Frito-Lay Canada rolls out Asian flavour snacks," *Advertising Age*, March 20, 2006, p. 20.

20 Pallavi Gogoi, "I am woman, hear me shop," *Business Week*, February 2005, **www.businessweek.com**.

21 Kristen Goff, "A male bastion no more," *Whig-Standard*, August 20, 2005, p. 19.

22 Paul Brent, "Home Depot turns to women to lift market share," *Financial Post*, August 20, 2003, p. FP4.

23 Samson Okalow, "Vive la difference," *Strategy*, October 2004, pp. 31, 32.

24 Nancy Carr, "Does a distinct society need distinct creative?" *Strategy*, April 9, 2001, p. 13.

25 Ross Waring, "The promise and reality of data mining," *Strategy*, June 7, 1999, p. D9.

26 Media Post, **www.mediapost.com**, June 19, 2003.

STRATEGIC PLANNING PRINCIPLES

After studying this chapter you will be able to

1. identify essential external trends and conditions that influence organizational planning

2. describe the steps in the strategic planning process

3. identify the distinctions and relationships among the various types of plans

4. characterize the essential elements of a corporate plan

5. outline the structure and content of a marketing plan

6. outline the structure and content of a marketing communications plan

7. show how integrated marketing planning provides solutions to marketing problems

All business planning is an integrated process that involves planning at three levels of an organization: corporate planning (planning conducted by senior executives), marketing planning (planning conducted by brand and marketing managers), and marketing communications planning (plans designed by communications specialists based on guidelines provided by brand and marketing managers). When a planning system works properly, each level of planning is linked to the other levels. Corporate plans provide guidance and direction for marketing plans, and marketing plans provide direction for marketing communications plans.

How plans are struck varies considerably from company to company. There is no perfect model to follow. Some organizations produce very detailed plans, while others take a more action-oriented approach. The common factor among all companies should be integration, meaning integrating one plan with another and integrating all the pieces of a plan together so that a consistent strategic direction is followed when the plans are implemented. What this chapter presents is a potential model for preparing strategic plans. Students should recognize that it can be altered to fit the specific needs of an organization.

FACTORS INFLUENCING STRATEGIC PLANNING

Strategic planning (corporate strategy)
The process of determining objectives (setting goals) and identifying strategies (ways to achieve the goals) and tactics (specific action plans) to help achieve objectives.

Strategic planning, or the **corporate strategy**, is the process of determining objectives (setting goals) and identifying strategies (ways to achieve the goals) and tactics (specific action plans) to help achieve objectives. Based on this definition, a strategic plan includes three common variables:

- **Objectives:** Statements of what is to be accomplished in terms of sales, profit, market share, or other measures.
- **Strategies:** Statements that outline how the objectives will be achieved, such as the direction to be taken and the allocation of resources needed to proceed.
- **Tactics:** Action-oriented details, including precise details about the cost and timing of specific activities.

Strategic planning is a cyclical process in most organizations. It is an annual occurrence that calls for plans to be updated constantly based on the latest conditions that prevail in the marketplace. Therefore, the essential ingredient in any plan is a firm understanding of the external factors that will influence the potential direction a company will proceed in. Furthermore, in the business marketplace today, change is occurring so fast that it is absolutely essential that a company keep abreast of change. A company's strategic plan is influenced by changes in the economy, among consumers, technology, laws and regulations governing business practices, and competitor activities. Occurrences and trends in each of these areas have an impact on the nature and direction of corporate plans, marketing plans, and marketing communications plans. This section discusses briefly the nature and implications of these influences (see Figure 2.1).

Economic Influences

The general state of the economy has a direct impact on how aggressive or conservative a company is with its business plans. Should it be investing in marketing and marketing communications to expand its business, or should it conserve funds to protect profit margins? The general state of the economy is determined by growth rates in the gross domestic product, inflation rates, levels of employment, the value of the Canadian dollar in relation to foreign currencies, and income distribution among consumers. The relationship among these variables is dynamic. For example, and in very general terms, if the value of the gross domestic product has dropped for a few consecutive years, if levels of employment have been dropping, and if real income has been dropping marginally from

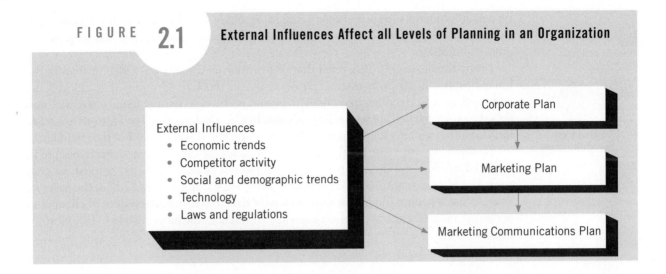

External Influences Affect all Levels of Planning in an Organization

External Influences
- Economic trends
- Competitor activity
- Social and demographic trends
- Technology
- Laws and regulations

Corporate Plan

Marketing Plan

Marketing Communications Plan

year to year, the economy could be in recession. If consumers aren't spending, marketing organizations might adopt a conservative approach and control investment in marketing and marketing communications. Conversely, if the marketplace is booming, levels of employment are high, and consumers are in spending mode, marketing organizations may adopt a more aggressive stance to their marketing and marketing communications efforts.

Based on all kinds of factors, a country's economy goes through cycles. Those cycles are recession, depression, recovery, and prosperity. In contrast to the scenario described above, an economy where gross domestic product is expanding, where real incomes are expanding, and employment is plentiful would indicate recovery or prosperity. Such an economy would call for aggressive investment in marketing and marketing communications to take advantage of the increases in consumer spending.

As North Americans witnessed in 2005, natural disasters such as Hurricane Katrina can have an immediate impact on the economy. Fuel prices rose significantly and many consumers changed their driving behaviour and car-buying behaviour. Automobile brands such as Toyota Corolla, Honda Civic, and Ford Focus were in greater demand, while full-size trucks and sport-utility vehicles were in less demand. It is difficult for manufacturers to react to such sudden changes in the marketplace.

Competitor Influence

Oligopoly
A market situation in which only a few brands control the market.

Monopolistic competition
A market in which there are many competitors, each offering a unique marketing mix; consumers can assess these choices prior to making a buying decision.

Direct competition
Competition from alternative products and services that satisfy the needs of a target market.

Indirect competition
Competition from substitute products that offer the same benefit as another type of product.

Assessing the activities of competitors is probably the most thoroughly analyzed aspect of marketing planning. Such analysis provides input into how one brand can differentiate itself from the others and perhaps stand out more in the eyes of consumers. Most Canadian markets are very competitive and described as being an **oligopoly** (a market with a few major brands) or as being **monopolistically competitive** (a market with all kinds of brands). In either case, the consumer has a choice of what brand to buy, and the effectiveness of the marketing and marketing communications strategies will influence the decision.

Competition comes in two forms: direct competition and indirect competition. **Direct competition** is competition from alternative products and services that satisfy the needs of a target market. **Indirect competition** is competition from substitute products that offer customers the same benefit. In today's hypercompetitive marketplace, the lines between direct and indirect competition are becoming blurred. McDonald's true competitors at one time were other hamburger restaurants such as Burger King and Wendy's. But now, based on expanding menus (due to competitive influences), McDonald's competes with KFC, Swiss Chalet, and Pizza Hut, and with even more upscale roadhouse-type establishments such as Kelsey's. Since McDonald's is in the restaurant business, it has to be conscious of what all other restaurants are doing so it can develop new strategies to grow its business.

Krispy Kreme quickly discovered that competition in Canada was different than in the United States. It was a marketing phenomenon in the United States that enjoyed the endorsements of celebrities like Nicole Kidman, and whose donuts found their way into episodes of *Sex and the City* and other programs. In Canada, however, Tim Hortons was ready for Krispy Kreme's arrival and taught its competitor a few lessons about fast food marketing.

Krispy Kreme
www.krispykreme.com

Nothing is going right for Krispy Kreme: its sales are falling, some franchisees are in financial trouble, and the company has been tainted by an accounting scandal. In contrast, Tim Hortons continues to flourish, growing to 2400 stores from 1700 in the past five years. What separates Tim Hortons from Krispy Kreme is its understanding of changes in consumer taste (see the section on consumer influences for more insight). Tim Hortons capitalized on the customer's desire for less-fattening food and adjusted its menu to include sandwiches in the late 1990s.[1]

Social and Demographic Influences

Chapter 1 presented in detail several demographic trends that must be considered when developing a strategic plan. Here is a quick recap of the key trends in Canada:

- The rate of population growth is slowing down and the population is getting older.
- The population is concentrated in urban markets.
- Households are getting smaller and the structure is changing (there are fewer traditional households and more non-traditional households).
- The population is becoming more ethnically diverse.
- Gender equality is altering decision-making processes.

In addition to these trends, the lifestyles of Canadians are changing. As a population, Canadians are generally more health conscious than ever before. They are concerned about social issues, such as education, health, and welfare, and the natural environment in which they live. People have awakened to how fragile nature is and they no longer take for granted natural resources such as water.

Issues such as obesity have also come to the foreground. A recent survey indicates that 65 percent of Canadians view the nutritional content of food as being "very important." SUBWAY restaurants, for example, enjoyed much success with spokesperson Jared, who lost a significant amount of weight while eating nothing but their "under 6 grams of fat" sandwiches. SUBWAY was very quick to react to the health-conscious trend that eventually went category wide.[2]

The consumer trend to cocooning resurfaced in the post–9/11 era in the form of "hiving." Hiving is about reaching out to others, not retreating. It's about friends and family and finding comfort in social relationships and connections. In this regard, the home has become the hub for a range of activities involving other people, most significantly entertaining and socializing. Products such as personal video recorders (PVRs), game consoles, personal digital assistants (PDAs), cell phones, MP3 players, satellite TV, LCD screens, and high-definition TV (HDTV), as well as kitchen gadgets like espresso machines, blenders, and grills have helped drive the trend toward hiving.[3] High-profile marketing communications programs have supported all brands in these product categories. See the illustration in Figure 2.2.

Technology Influence

New products are coming to market so fast that consumers simply cannot grasp them all. Can anyone possibly keep up with the changes occurring in the telecommunications

FIGURE **2.2** **An Ad Appealing to the "Home as an Entertainment and Social Centre" Trend**

Source: Courtesy of Samsung Electronics Canada.

industry? How many electronic gadgets do we need simply to stay in touch? The technological environment consists of the discoveries, inventions, and innovations that provide for marketing opportunities. New products, new packaging, and new forms of communications are the direct result of technological advancement.

Apple iPod
www.apple.com/ipod.html

In terms of product development, companies are harnessing the power of virtual reality, the combination of technologies that allows users to experience three-dimensional, computer-generated environments through light, sound, and touch. Virtual reality has helped firms to gather reactions to new car designs and other potential products.[4] How people communicate and conduct buying transactions is also affected by technology. The Internet has had an overwhelming impact on commerce and communications as websites and web-based communications seem imperative for reaching a tech-savvy public. Products like the iPod demonstrate why Apple Computer is a great company. With elegant hardware and friendly software, Apple's portable player made a profitable business out of digital music—a trick that eluded record labels and other companies, such as Sony, Microsoft, and Napster.[5]

Canadians have embraced automated teller machines (ATMs) and debit cards at an unprecedented rate, and 65 percent of customers already use banking eservices. In fact, new electronic person-to-person payment systems (called P2P) now allow the transfer of money instantly by email.[6]

It is forecast by many experts that the Internet will become a preferred channel for communicating with customers and for conducting transactions. A survey conducted by Statistics Canada revealed that the Internet is an ideal medium for reaching a desirable target market described as male and female between the ages of 15 and 44, college or university educated, household incomes of $40 000 plus, with an urban skew. In conjunction with customer relationship management (CRM) programs, the Internet offers direct and interactive contact with a desirable group of customers.

Legal and Regulatory Influence

Strategic plans are affected by new developments in the political and legal arenas. Most laws and regulations governing business practice are created by federal and provincial legislation. As well, many industries establish and abide by their own self-regulation policies and practices. In some cases, the self-regulation guidelines are more stringent. Industry Canada regulates Canadian businesses through the *Competition Act*. The act has three purposes: to maintain and encourage competition, to ensure small businesses have equal opportunity to participate in trade, and to provide consumers with product choice and competitive prices.

It cannot be assumed that all businesses follow the letter of the law. In terms of marketing communications, companies have to be careful about what they say to consumers. Exaggerated product claims to promote an important benefit that lack proper substantiation, claims that improperly quote sale prices to make a sale look better than it really is, and any other form of misleading advertising will cause problems for a company.

In 2005, Sears Canada was fined $487 000 for misrepresenting the sale price of tires. A year earlier, clothier Suzy Shier paid a $1 million penalty due to a legal issue dealing with misleading prices.[7] In the battle for razor market supremacy, Gillette made claims that the M3POWER razor "raises hair up and away from the skin." A federal court judge ruled the claim inaccurate and greatly exaggerated. The ruling forced Gillette to relabel millions of razors on store shelves at a cost of about $1.6 million—a lesson well learned![8]

Advertisers should follow the Canadian Code of Advertising Standards. The code contains regulations about gender portrayal, product claims, price claims, advertising involving product comparisons, and advertising to children. The code is administered by Advertising Standards Canada, a group representing advertisers and advertising agencies.

At present, the federal government and several provincial governments are revising consumer protection laws to reflect the explosive growth in ecommerce and the surge of complaints by people and small businesses doing business on the Internet. It seems that Canadian laws are well behind the changes in the marketplace.

Strategic Planning Process

Organizations that develop strategic plans have their own unique ways of doing so. A fairly common approach to planning is to start the process at the top or senior level of the organization and work downwards. In other words, the strategic plan, or corporate plan, devised by senior executives will influence the nature of the various brand marketing plans developed by middle managers, and the brand marketing plans will influence the nature of the marketing communications plan.

In the corporate plan developed by senior executives, most objectives are financial in nature and become the goals that must be shared by all of the company's divisions or products. Typically, the **corporate plan** is not an exhaustive document. Once the corporate plan has been struck, the various functional areas, including marketing, start their planning process. Refer to Figure 2.3 for a visual illustration.

A **marketing plan** is developed for each one of a company's products and sets out the objectives for all brands. The plan determines how the various elements of the marketing mix will be employed so that they have the desired impact on the target market. The target market is identified through some combination of demographic, psychographic, and geographic variables, and a positioning strategy statement guides the development of the plan.

Once the role of marketing communications has been determined, specific plans are then developed for the various components of the marketing communications mix. At this stage, the goal is to develop a synergistic communications plan that will improve the well-being of the product or service. As discussed in Chapter 1, advertising will achieve awareness and interest objectives and help build brand image over an extended period. Other variables, such as sales promotions, event marketing, public relations, and personal selling, perform more immediate tasks and are designed to achieve desire and action—a purchase. The integration of all components in a strategic plan will help achieve short-term and long-term objectives. The saying, "A chain is only as strong as its weakest link" appropriately describes the relationships among various components of the marketing communications mix and the relationship between marketing and marketing communications. As in war, a unified attack has a better chance of success!

Corporate plan

A strategic plan formulated at the executive level of an organization to guide the development of functional plans in the organization.

Marketing plan

A short-term, specific plan of action that combines strategy and tactics.

FIGURE **2.3** **Strategic Planning: Links among Various Organizational Plans**

The corporate plan provides guidance for the marketing plan and the marketing plan provides guidance for the marketing communications plan. All plans are based on the same background information and any analysis stemming from that information. Corporate plans are strategic in nature. Marketing plans and marketing communications plans are both strategic and tactical in nature.

THE CORPORATE PLAN

Mission statement

A statement of an organization's purpose and operating philosophy; provides guidance and direction for the operations of the company.

The mission statement is the guiding light for all forms of strategic planning. A **mission statement** is a statement of an organization's purpose and an indicator of the operating philosophy the organization follows. A good mission statement is customer and marketing oriented, considers the competition, and looks to the long term. In other words, once a company establishes its mission, it must provide adequate time and resources to carry through with it.[4] Figure 2.4 lists Mountain Equipment Co-op's purpose, vision. mission, and values—the components of their strategic plan.

FIGURE **2.4** **Key Components of Mountain Equipment Co-op's Strategic Plan**

Our Purpose

To support people in achieving the benefit of wilderness-oriented recreation.

Our **purpose** is what we resolve to do.

Our Vision

Mountain Equipment Co-op is an innovative, thriving co-operative that inspires excellence in products and services, passion for wilderness experiences, leadership for a just world, and action for a healthy planet.

Our **vision** is our picture of the future and outlines where we want to go.

Our Mission

Mountain Equipment Co-op provides quality products and services for self-propelled wilderness-oriented recreation, such as hiking and mountaineering, at the lowest reasonable price in an informative, respectful manner. We are a member-owned co-operative striving for social and environmental leadership.

Our **mission** tells us what business we are in, who we serve, and how. It represents the fundamental reason for MEC's existence.

Our Values

We conduct ourselves ethically and with integrity. We show respect for others in our words and actions. We act in the spirit of community and co-operation. We respect and protect our natural environment. We strive for personal growth, continual learning, and adventure.

Our **values** influence our conduct both collectively as an organization, and individually as employees, directors and members of our community. We strive to have our actions reflect these values, demonstrate personal accountability, and be publicly defensible.

Source: Courtesy of Mountain Equipment Co-op.

With the mission confirmed, executive attention turns to setting corporate objectives, determining strategic direction, and allocating resources. **Corporate objectives are statements of a company's overall goals. These objectives are usually financial in nature and are used to evaluate the effectiveness or ineffectiveness of a company's strategic plan and the people who manage the organization.** At the end of the year, actual financial results are compared to the objectives. The degree of success is there for all concerned to see. Corporate objectives can also be qualitative in nature, which are perhaps more difficult to measure immediately. Here are a few examples of corporate objectives, both quantitative and qualitative:

Corporate objective

A statement of a company's overall goal; used to evaluate the effectiveness or ineffectiveness of a company's strategic plan.

- To increase company sales revenue from $50 000 000 to $60 000 000 in 20XX.
- To increase category market share (share in a market for all company brands) from 25 percent to 30 percent in 20XX.
- To increase return on investment from 10 percent to 15 percent in 20XX.
- To exhibit constructive social responsibility by investing in research and development to discover environmentally friendly new products.

The last objective on the list above is qualitative in nature. At the end of the year, however, the organization will evaluate in some way its investment in social responsibility programs. The first three objectives on the list are quantitative in nature. Objective statements like these have direct impact on the development of marketing objectives and strategies. All company brands must contribute to achieving the company's goals. It is the total of sales revenues for various brands, for example, that constitutes overall company sales revenue. The market share of several company brands (for example, Maxwell House, Chase & Sanborn, Nabob, and General Foods International Coffees) make up Kraft Canada's total market share in coffee.

When an organization determines its corporate strategy, it considers several factors: marketing strength, degree of competition in current or new markets under consideration, financial resources, research and development capabilities, and management commitment to particular goals. It is common for a company to follow numerous strategic directions at the same time, largely due to the dynamic nature of the marketplace. To follow one direction and fail could have a negative long-term effect on the company.

A variety of strategic options are given due consideration. Among the options are a penetration strategy, an acquisition strategy, a new product development strategy, and a strategic alliance strategy. All these strategies imply a desire for growth. In some cases, a company may decide to get smaller. While that may seem odd, many companies find that too much expansion can have disastrous results on profits. Growing sales at the expense of profit doesn't make sense!

In such cases, a company may decide to consolidate operations by selling off various divisions or products. The goal is to return to the business it knows best. Molson did just that in the 1990s. The company's profits were declining sharply, so the decision was made to exit the retailing market (Beaver Lumber), the chemical market (Diversey Chemical), and the sports and entertainment market (Montreal Canadiens and the Molson Centre in Montreal). Molson returned to its roots—beer! In 2005, Molson merged with the Coors Brewing Company of the United States to form Molson Coors Brewing Company.

Molson Coors
www.molsoncoors.com

Penetration strategy

A plan of action for aggressive marketing of a company's existing products.

A penetration strategy involves aggressive marketing of a company's existing products. The goal is to build the business by taking customers from the competition or by expanding the entire market. Wendy's, for example, is constantly juggling its menu, altering its prices, and revamping restaurants to differentiate itself from other restaurants (see Figure 2.5). Coca-Cola invests considerable sums of money into Coca-Cola Classic, its core brand, to retain leadership in the soft drink category. It does so because Pepsi-Cola also invests considerable sums of money to take market share away from Coca-Cola Classic. It is a real marketing and marketing communications battle between the two brands!

Source: Courtesy of Wendy's International, Inc.

New product development strategy
A marketing strategy that calls for significant investment in research and development to develop innovative products.

New products, the result of a **new product development strategy**, offer another option for growth-minded companies. New products create new revenue streams at a much greater rate than simply trying to expand existing products. Apple Computer has enjoyed much success with new products recently. At Apple, sales have never been stronger, earnings have never been better, and Apple's popularity as a company has never been as pervasive. This is all thanks to savvy marketing and engineering, which has made the iPod more popular in a shorter period of time than Sony's famous Walkman.[9] Apple's latest new products include the iPod mini and the iPod nano.

Acquisition strategy
A plan of action for acquiring companies that represent attractive financial opportunities.

Rather than invest in something new, some companies prefer to buy their way into a market by following an **acquisition strategy.** Why did PepsiCo buy the Quaker Oats Company at a cost of $13.4 billion? To get its hands on Gatorade, the dominant brand in the growing sports drink beverage category.[10] With such a purchase, PepsiCo is more of a competitive threat to Coca-Cola; both companies are now in the beverage business, not just the soft drink business. In the athletic shoe market, Adidas-Salomon acquired Reebok International in a $3.8 billion deal that unites two shoe giants as well as their cast of celebrity endorsers. The acquisition will boost Adidas's share of the US shoe market to 20 percent and enhance its competitive position against Nike.[11]

Strategic alliance
The combination of separate companies' resources for the purpose of satisfying their shared customers; the companies have strengths in different areas.

Strategic alliances, when separate companies with complementary strengths join resources to satisfy their shared customers, are now very popular among companies searching for ways to reduce costs or improve operating efficiency. Couche-Tard, the owner of Mac's convenience stores, formed alliances with several food service providers in an attempt to stay ahead of competitors. Mac's has now added food service counters for SUBWAY, A&W, and Timothy's World Coffee. In some larger stores, all three partners are in one Mac's location. Alliances like this one benefit all partners. Timothy's, for example, could not expand at the same rate if it was doing things on its own. They see the partnership as a great opportunity.[12]

Senior executives also make decisions about the financial resources that are allocated to marketing and other functional divisions of the company. Prior to embarking on marketing plans for individual products, the vice-president of marketing usually knows how much money is available for marketing purposes. That person distributes the money among each of the company's brands. Competition among brand managers for such a scarce resource creates some very interesting marketing plans and presentations. Most companies have brands that are stars, and they are given budget priority. What's left is divided among the remaining brands.

MARKETING PLANNING

Marketing planning
The analysis, planning, implementing, and controlling of marketing initiatives to satisfy target market needs and achieve organizational objectives.

Contingency plan
The identification of alternative courses of action that can be used to modify an original plan if and when new circumstances arise.

With the details of the corporate plan determined, the marketing department starts the process of marketing planning. **Marketing planning** involves analyzing, planning, implementing, and controlling marketing initiatives to satisfy target market needs and achieve organizational objectives. In contrast to corporate plans, marketing plans are short term in nature (one year), specific in scope (they involve precise actions for one product), and combine both strategy and tactics (they are action oriented). The marketing plan should also include a **contingency plan** to provide alternative courses of action in the event that new circumstances arise.

The process involves four basic steps:

1. **Analyzing Market Opportunities:** The market conditions are evaluated to identify the best opportunities for the company, considering its expertise and resources.

2. **Developing Marketing Strategies:** A positioning strategy is designed in the context of satisfying target market needs and managing a product through its life cycle. During the life of a product, positioning strategies can change.

3. **Planning and Implementing Marketing Programs:** Basic decisions are made about how the marketing mix will be used. A budget is drawn up to allocate resources to the various activities recommended.

4. **Managing Marketing Programs:** Programs are put in place to evaluate and control the effectiveness of the marketing effort.

There is no perfect format for a marketing plan, although Figure 2.6 offers an illustration. Marketing plans vary considerably from one organization to another in length, detail, and content. This section will examine the content of a marketing plan, but readers must realize that the content of a plan is modified to suit the needs of each specific organization. Essentially, a marketing plan is divided into two major sections. The first section is a compilation of background information about the market, target market, competition, and product. The second section is the plan itself; it contains the objectives, strategies, and tactics for the product for the year ahead and provides specific details about how the budget is allocated and the timing of all activities.

FIGURE **2.6**   **The Marketing Planning and Control Process**

Once plans are developed and implemented, evaluation and control procedures are implemented during the plan period (e.g., quarterly reviews). At that stage there is an opportunity to revise marketing objectives and strategies according to current market conditions.

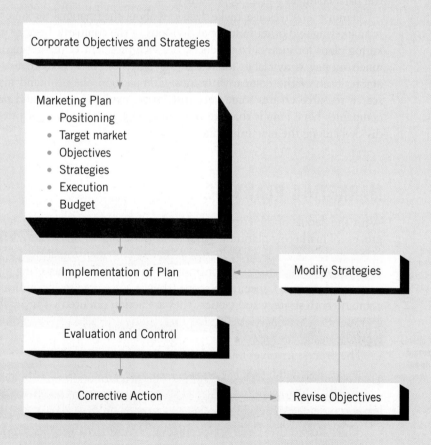

For additional insight into the importance of strategic planning, read the IMC Highlight **West 49: Popular Destination for Teens.**

Market Background

The direction a marketing plan takes is directly influenced by internal conditions (strengths and weaknesses) and external conditions (opportunities and threats). As indicated earlier, the first step in planning is analysis. In marketing terms, such an analysis is referred to as a **SWOT analysis**. The acronym SWOT stands for strengths, weaknesses, opportunities, and threats.

SWOT analysis
An analysis procedure that involves an assessment of an organization's strengths, weaknesses, opportunities, and threats; strengths and weaknesses are internal variables, whereas opportunities and threats are external variables.

Strengths and Weaknesses The internal capabilities and resources are reviewed to determine the relative condition of a brand and determine its capability to pursue new directions. The review considers a variety of controllable marketing factors and may extend to the areas of manufacturing, finance, human resources, and technology. Any limits on current strengths may justify developing new strengths.

IMC HIGHLIGHT

WEST 49: POPULAR DESTINATION FOR TEENS

Spotting a new trend—actually, spotting the trend before it becomes the trend—is one of the secrets to many companies' success. And that formula certainly applies to West 49. Chief executive officer Sam Baio was a self-proclaimed "passionate" skateboarder, but the question was whether he could take the popularity of a "fringe" sport and build a successful retail business around it. The answer was yes!

When Baio started out, the *X Games* were just hitting the television airwaves. At the same time, he realized that skating was becoming very popular with his son and nephews. Was that insight enough to start a business? To capitalize on the trend, he sought capital to open stores in suburban malls, places where teens congregated.

The bankers agreed with Baio's marketing instincts. Skateboarding would become a $12-billion industry worldwide. Over a 10-year period, skateboarders have grown in numbers by 61 percent and snowboarding has increased by 243 percent. With that kind of growth any business should excel!

The company lost money for the first three years, so some careful and precise marketing strategies were needed to help turn things around. In assessing the situation, Baio determined that West 49 was catering to too broad of a clientele; it was trying to do too much for too many age groups. He decided to zero in on the 12- to 18-year-old segment, and boom! business started to pick up. West 49 is now seen as a very cool place to hang out. The stores offer a complete range of products dedicated to boarding sports

along with clothing fashions that appeal to teenage extreme sports enthusiasts.

To effectively click with teenagers, Baio knew his marketing strategy would have to cultivate the lifestyle of the age group, not just offer them products. This marketing philosophy permeates the stores, particularly the multimedia stores that act as a gathering place for teens, complete with Nintendo games and live local bands on occasion.

Over the past year, West 49 has opened 10 new stores, bringing the total number of stores in the chain to 63. To grow further, Baio realizes West 49 must broaden its customer base beyond "boarding." Consequently, West 49 is eyeing companies that share complementary business strategies, reach similar customers, and have sound relationships with suppliers. West 49 recently acquired Off the Wall, a Vancouver-based 11-store chain that sells women's clothing. Off the Wall will help develop the female side of the business. West 49 also operates three stores in Canada for Australia's Billabong chain, a retailer that sells sporting goods and clothing to a youthful target.

Whatever the situation, Baio believes that the real challenge lies in spotting the trends and not jumping on fads. "Rollerblading was a fad," he says, "whereas skateboarding has been a long-term trend." Spotting trends and developing effective marketing strategies to take advantage of the trends equals success!

Adapted from Eric Vanden Bussche, "West 49 rides extreme sports craze," *Globe and Mail*, August 22, 2005, p. B3.

Opportunities and Threats The manager reviews relevant external data that may impact on the direction of the marketing plan. Such a review may include economic trends, social and demographic trends, legal and regulatory influences, competitive activity, technology influences, and social responsibility issues. Opportunities are prioritized, and threats are classified according to their seriousness and probability of occurrence. The absence of marketing action in either area could hinder the development of a brand.

A variety of information is collected and analyzed. The goals of a SWOT analysis are to capitalize on strengths while minimizing weaknesses and to take advantage of opportunities while fending off threats. Typically, a SWOT analysis should review the following information (refer to Figure 2.7 for an illustration of a marketing plan model).

FIGURE **2.7** **An Illustration of a Marketing Plan Model**

MARKETING BACKGROUND	MARKETING PLAN	
External Influences • Economic trends • Social and demographic trends • Technology trends • Regulatory trends	**Positioning Strategy** • Positioning strategy statement	Corporate Plan
Market Analysis • Market size and growth • Regional market size and growth • Market segment analysis • Seasonal analysis	**Target Market Profile** • Demographic • Psychographic • Geographic **Marketing Objectives** • Sales volume • Market share • Profit • Other	Marketing Plan • Marketing Background (SWOT Analysis) • Marketing Plan
Competitor Analysis • Market share trends • Marketing strategy assessment	**Marketing Strategies** • Product • Price • Marketing communications • Distribution	Marketing Communications Plan
Target Market Analysis • Consumer data • Consumer behaviour	**Marketing Execution (Tactics)** • Product • Price • Marketing communications • Distribution • New products • Marketing research • Service • Partnerships and alliances	
Product (Brand) Analysis • Sales volume trends • Market share trends • Distribution • Marketing communications • New product activity	**Budget and Financial Summary** • Budget allocations (by activity, by time of year) • Brand financial statement	
SWOT Analysis* • Strengths • Weaknesses • Opportunities • Threats	**Timeline or Calendar** • Activity schedule	

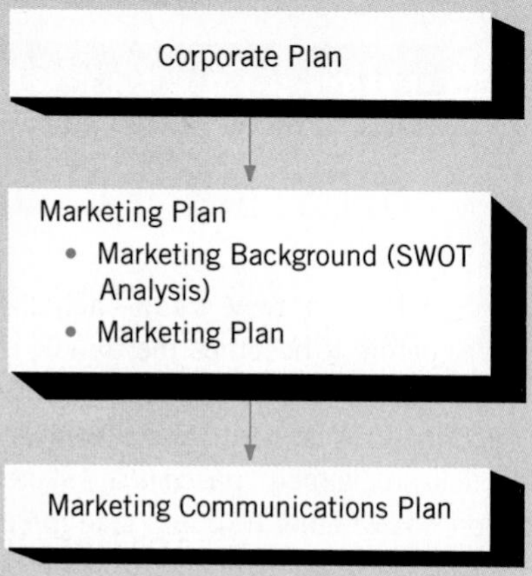

*Note: Including a SWOT analysis is optional. Some planners believe that the SWOT analysis occurs when the information is compiled in the preceding sections of the plan. Other planners believe that such information must be analyzed further to determine priorities. The latter is the intention of a SWOT analysis.

External Influences

- **Economic Trends:** The current and predicted states of the economy are considered. Is the economy growing (recovery or prosperity) or is it sputtering (recession)? Appropriate statistical information is evaluated in this section of the plan.
- **Social and Demographic Trends:** Basic trends in age, income, household formation, immigration, migration, and lifestyles are evaluated to identify potential target markets. For example, the aging of Canada's population will be a factor influencing positioning strategies in the future. There will be a new emphasis on older age groups.
- **Technology Trends:** Technological trends that affect buyer behaviour have to be determined. Technology quickens the speed with which new products come to market and the way companies deliver messages about products to customers.
- **Regulatory Trends:** A company should always stay abreast of changes to any laws and regulations affecting the marketing of its products. For example, new privacy laws have been introduced in Canada to protect consumers and regulate companies engaged in emarketing practices and ecommerce.

Once plans are developed and implemented, evaluation and control procedures are applied during the plan period (e.g., quarterly reviews). At that stage there is an opportunity to revise marketing objectives and strategies according to current market conditions.

Market Analysis

- **Market Size and Growth:** A review of trends over several years is considered for the purposes of making sales projections for the year ahead. Is the market growing or declining, and how fast?
- **Regional Markets:** Sales trends by region are analyzed to determine what areas need more or less attention in the year ahead. Some markets may be growing while others are not. A regional analysis helps determine priorities.
- **Market Segment Analysis:** There could be numerous product segments in a market. For example, in the hotel industry there are budget hotels, mid-priced hotels, and luxury hotels. Are all segments growing at the same rate, or are some segments doing better than others? Interpretive comments about the various segments should be included.
- **Seasonal Analysis:** Seasonal or cyclical trends over the course of a year are examined. For example, volume trends for beer and barbecue-related items would be much higher in the spring and summer seasons. The timing of proposed marketing activities needs to consider such trends.

Target Market Analysis

- **Consumer Data:** The profile of primary users (and secondary users, if necessary) is reviewed for any changes during the past few years. The aging population and lifestyle changes could be affecting the profile of product users.
- **Consumer Behaviour:** The degree of customer loyalty to the market and products within a market is assessed. To what degree are customers brand loyal? Do they switch brands, and how frequently do they do so? Knowledge of such behaviour has a direct influence on advertising and promotion strategies. Should the plan attract new customers, prevent existing customers from departing, or do both?

Product (Brand) Analysis

An assessment of a brand's past performance is included in this section of the plan. An attempt is made to link past marketing activities to the performance of the brand. Have previous strategies been successful, and will changes be needed in the year ahead?

- **Sales Volume Trends:** Historical volume trends are plotted to forecast sales for the year ahead.

- **Market Share Trends:** Market share is a clear indicator of brand performance. Market share trends are examined nationally, regionally, and by key markets to determine areas of strengths and weaknesses. Is the brand's market share growing faster or slower than competitors' shares? Where are the priorities for improving market share?

- **Distribution:** The availability of the product nationally and regionally is reviewed. Regional availability will affect how much marketing support a brand will receive. Should the new plan focus on areas where distribution is high or low?

- **Marketing Communications:** Current activities are assessed to determine if strategies need to be retained or changed. A review of expenditures by medium, sales promotions, and events and sponsorships is necessary to assess the impact of such spending on brand performance.

- **New Product Activity:** Sales performance of recently implemented initiatives is evaluated. For example, the performance of new product formats, sizes, flavours, and so on is scrutinized to determine the impact of those factors on sales and market share.

Competitor Analysis

In order to plan effectively, a manager should know competitors' products as well as his or her own product. A review of marketing mix activities for key competitors provides essential input on how to revise marketing strategies. A brand must react to the actions of another brand or suffer the consequences of lack of action.

- **Market Share Trends:** It is common to plot and review the market share trends of all brands from year to year. Such analysis provides insight into what brands are moving forward and what brands are moving backward.

- **Marketing Strategy Assessment:** An attempt is made to link known marketing strategies to competitor brand performance. What is the nature of the competition's advertising, sales promotions, events and sponsorships, and interactive programs? How much are the competitors investing in these areas? Have they launched any new products or implemented any new distribution, pricing, or communications strategies? What changes are anticipated in the year ahead?

Marketing Plan

The SWOT analysis leads directly into the development of the action plan. The plan section clarifies the positioning strategy of the company's brands, establishes objectives for the year, determines how the various elements of the marketing mix will be employed, and outlines the investment and timing of all activities that are recommended.

Positioning Strategy

Positioning
The selling concept that motivates purchase, or the image that marketers desire a brand to have in the minds of consumers.

Positioning strategy statement
A summary of the character and personality of a brand and the benefits it offers customers.

Positioning refers to the selling concept that motivates purchase, or the image that marketers desire a brand to have in the minds of customers. The **positioning strategy statement** has a direct impact on the nature of the message that must be communicated to consumers. For example, Harvey's positioning strategy statement might read as follows:

Harvey's serves a premium hamburger that appeals to hearty male appetites; a hamburger of the same size and quality a male adult would prepare on his home barbecue.

The positioning statement clearly identifies where the company wants the product to be in the market and helps provide direction to the message that will ultimately be communicated to customers. Furthermore, it serves as the standard for considering what strategies to use and not use. For example, if a marketing communications agency presents a new creative strategy for the brand, the client will evaluate it against the positioning strategy statement to see whether the new creative plan fits with the strategy.

In the case of Harvey's, the company identified an opportunity to grab hold of the adult premium burger and really run with it. From research, customers expected Harvey's to deliver barbecue-style hamburgers. The advertising agency developed the male-friendly slogan "Long live the grill" and a successful campaign that featured mouth-watering hamburgers and grilled chicken tailored specifically for hungry males.[13] See the illustration in Figure 2.8.

FIGURE **2.8** **Harvey's Positioning Strategy Appeals Directly to Adult Males**

Source: Courtesy of Dick Hemingway.

Target Market Profile

At this stage, the manager identifies or targets a group of customers that represents the greatest profit potential. As discussed earlier, a target market is defined in terms of similar needs and common characteristics based on the following:

- **Demographic Profile:** Characteristics such as age, gender, income, education, and ethnic background are considered. Depending on the nature of the product, some characteristics are more important than others. Some may not be important at all. For example, is the brand for males, females, or is it gender neutral? If the product is expensive, income will be an important factor.

- **Psychographic Profile:** The lifestyle profile includes three essential characteristics: the target's activities, interests, and opinions. Knowledge about customer behaviour provides clues on how to best reach the customer with a compelling message. As discussed in Chapter 1, many advertising campaigns are designed in such a way that a brand associates itself with a lifestyle or desired lifestyle of the target market (refer back to Millward Brown Goldfarb's nine lifestyle segments in Figure 1.10). Information about media consumption is also relevant to the customer profile. Knowledge about what media customers refer to most frequently affects how funds are allocated across different media and other forms of marketing communications. For example, if the target market spends a lot of time online and less time watching television than it used to, such knowledge could influence media strategy.

- **Geographic Profile:** The urban nature of Canada's population means geography has a significant influence on marketing strategy. Therefore, the profile considers the location of the target market in terms of region or key market. Geography is typically a key influence on how a budget is allocated across the country. Does a brand invest in regions of strength or regions that need shoring up?

Target market profile

A description of a customer group based on demographic, psychographic, and geographic variables.

To demonstrate **target market profiling**, consider the description of the primary customer for a Harley-Davidson motorcycle. Biker gangs do not keep Harley-Davidson in business! Their customer is described as

> Males, 40 to 55 years of age, earning $75 000 plus annually, living in major cities. They are "weekend warriors" who want to get away from the office. They are lawyers, doctors, or corporate executives looking for a way to alleviate stress. About 25 percent are new to biking and 45 percent have previously owned a Harley; 30 percent have come from a competing brand. Women account for 15 percent of purchasers.

Harley-Davidson
www.harley-davidson.com

This description aptly portrays a combination of demographic, psychographic, and geographic characteristics, at least the ones that are important to Harley-Davidson.[14] Figure 2.9 shows a sample of Harley-Davidson communications.

Marketing Objectives

Marketing objective

A statement that identifies what a product will accomplish in a one-year period, usually expressed in terms of sales, market share, and profit.

Marketing objectives are statements that identify what a product will accomplish in a one-year period. Similar to corporate objectives, they tend to focus on financial measures, such as sales and profits or other quantitative yardsticks. Objectives may also be qualitative in nature and include new product introductions, product line extensions, launching of new packaging, and so on. Here, the objective may be to simply get the new activity into the market at the planned time. Did we or did we not do it on time? Objectives do not always have to be measured in terms of dollars or market share.

To illustrate how marketing objectives are written, let's assume you are the brand manager for Crest toothpaste. You are developing objectives for 2007 based on your present market share of 28 percent. Crest is the challenger in the market following the brand leader, Colgate, which owns 40 percent market share. The toothpaste market is growing by 5 percent a year and is currently estimated to be worth $150 million.

FIGURE **2.9** Harley-Davidson Motorcycles Targets Middle-Aged Males by Placing Ads in Magazines that Segment Reads

Source: Courtesy of Harley-Davidson Motor Company.

You might set out the marketing objectives for Crest for the year ahead like this:

- To increase market share from 28 percent to 30 percent in 2007.
- To increase dollar sales from $42 000 000 in 2006 to $47 250 000 in 2007 (assumes a market growth of 5 percent and achievement of market share objective).

- To successfully introduce three new line extensions in 2007 to extend Crest's presence further in the oral care market.
- To improve distribution levels in Quebec from 75 percent to 85 percent (in stores carrying toothpaste) in 2007.

Objectives are written so they can be measured to facilitate evaluation at the end of the plan period. Were the objectives achieved or not? Was the plan too aggressive or not aggressive enough? It will depend on the dynamics of the marketplace over the next 12 months.

Marketing Strategies

Marketing strategy

A plan of action that shows how the various elements of the marketing mix will be used to satisfy a target market's needs.

Marketing strategies are the master plans for achieving the objectives. The importance of having a good strategy must be emphasized. There is a saying that "Good strategy with weak execution can produce reasonable results." Likewise, there is another saying: "Poor strategy with good execution produces terrible results." The reason these have become such common sayings is that they are true. The goal should be to have the right strategy and then simply to work on better execution as time goes on. Most professional hockey or football coaches would agree with this principle.

In the development of the marketing strategy, the role and contribution of each component of the marketing mix are identified. Priority may be given to certain components depending on the nature of the market. For example, the success of a brand of beer depends largely on the impact of advertising on the target market. The nature of the message and the amount of money invested in advertising are critical decision areas for achieving differentiation.

In the transportation market, the product environment (a combination of product and additional services) is an important consideration among travellers. VIA Rail, for example, stresses the benefit of staying connected with Wi-Fi service on select rail cars and calls their railway "a more human way to travel." See the illustration in Figure 2.10.

The budget allocated to the product will be identified in the strategy section of the plan. There are various methods for arriving at a budget. Some methods estimate sales first and then base the marketing or marketing communications budget on sales. Other methods develop the budget first, a method based on the premise that investing in marketing communications creates sales, so the budget is not the outcome of sales. Regardless of the method used, the budget must be carefully calculated and defended when the plan is presented to the marketing managers. Figure 2.11 shows further details about budget methodologies.

Marketing Execution (Tactics)

Tactics (execution)

Action-oriented details that outline how a strategic plan will be implemented.

The **tactics (execution)** outlined in the plan are program details drawn directly from the strategy section of the plan. Such details will identify what programs are to be implemented, how much they will cost, what the timing will be, and who will be responsible for implementation. The unique action plan provides specific details regarding how the various elements of the marketing mix will be used to achieve the marketing objectives. This section of the plan may also include a description of activities in areas such as marketing research, service programs, and potential partnerships and alliances.

Typically, only the key elements of various marketing communications plans (advertising, sales promotion, Internet communications, public relations, direct response, and so on) are included in the marketing plan. The assumption is that specific communications plans are based on the same marketing objectives and marketing strategies described in the marketing plan. Specific and lengthier information about marketing communications strategies and tactics is presented in their respective plans or a marketing communications plan.

FIGURE **2.10**   **VIA Rail's Differential Advantage Is a Promise of Staying Connected when Travelling**

Source: Courtesy of VIA Rail Canada.

Budget and Financial Summary

In order for a marketing plan to be improved, it is crucial to show the financial implications of the activities to be undertaken. Senior executives like to know how the company's money will be spent and how profitable the investment will be. Therefore, the budget section will itemize all activities and indicate the associated cost. Major areas such as media, consumer promotion, trade promotion, and marketing research are often subdivided into more specific activities.

FIGURE **2.11**   **Methods for Determining a Marketing Budget**

Method	Procedure
Percentage of Sales	A predetermined percentage of forecasted sales is allocated to marketing or marketing communications.
Fixed Sum/Unit	A predetermined dollar amount per unit sold is allocated to marketing or marketing communications.
Industry Average	The average amount (current or forecasted) spent on marketing or marketing communications by all brands in a market is allocated to marketing.
Advertising Share/Market Share	Invest at a level to retain share (ad share equals market share); invest at a level to build market share (ad share is greater than market share).
Task (Objective)	Define the task, determine the activities to achieve the task, and associate a cost to the activities.

In many companies, the brand managers and marketing managers are responsible for bottom-line profitability for their brands. If so, a financial statement for the brand is included. Such a statement should provide some financial history for the previous year, current year, and a forecast for the plan year. Senior executives are interested in seeing progress in marketing terms and financial terms. The financial statement will include such measures as sales, market share, cost of goods sold, gross profit, marketing expenses, and net profit before taxes.

Evaluation and Control

It is quite common for an organization to plan for semi-annual or quarterly reviews to assess its financial position. Marketing and marketing communications managers often fear such reviews because it is a time when budgets are frequently given the axe. Nonetheless, evaluation of activities is essential, because changes will likely be necessary while a plan is in midstream. **Marketing control** is the process of measuring and evaluating the results of marketing strategies and plans and then taking corrective action to ensure the marketing objectives are attained. Refer back to Figure 2.6 for a visual illustration of evaluation and control.

The evaluation process also provides an opportunity to change marketing strategies if necessary. If financial obligations are not being achieved, then new strategies must be explored. Furthermore, it is an opportunity to review key financials, such as sales, costs, and profits, and reforecast the figures for the balance of the year. If the original objectives are not achievable, they should be modified, as should the marketing activities and expenditures that support the product.

MARKETING COMMUNICATIONS PLANNING

Since plans have to be struck well in advance of their implementation date, the marketing communications plan is developed simultaneously with the marketing plan so that its key components can be integrated into the marketing plan. The various components of

Marketing control

The process of measuring and evaluating the results of marketing strategies and plans and of taking corrective action to ensure marketing objectives are achieved.

FIGURE **2.12**   **A Marketing Communications Plan Model**

MARKETING COMMUNICATIONS OBJECTIVES

- Identify what is to be accomplished

MARKETING COMMUNICATIONS STRATEGIES

- Identify the role/importance of mix components
- Budget available

CREATIVE PLAN

- Objectives (what to say)
- Strategies (how to say it)
- Execution (specific details)

MEDIA PLAN

- Objectives
- Strategies
- Criteria for reaching target
- Rationale for media selection
- Execution (cost, coverage, and timing details)

DIRECT RESPONSE PLAN

- Objectives
- Strategies
- Tactics
- Budget

DIGITAL (INTERACTIVE) PLAN

- Objectives
- Strategies
- Tactics
- Budget

SALES PROMOTION PLAN

- Objectives
- Strategies
- Tactics
- Budget

PUBLIC RELATIONS PLAN

- Objectives
- Strategies
- Tactics
- Budget

EVENTS AND SPONSORSHIP PLAN

- Objectives
- Strategies
- Tactics
- Budget

PERSONAL SELLING PLAN

- Objectives
- Strategies
- Tactics
- Budget

CALENDAR OF EVENTS

- Week
- Month

BUDGET SUMMARY

- Total and allocation by various plans

Note: These plans assume adequate input is provided from the background section of the marketing plan. See Figure 2.7 for details.

Corporate Plan

↓

Marketing Plan

↓

Marketing Communications Plan
- Advertising Plan
- Direct Response Plan
- Interactive Plan
- Sales Promotion Plan
- Public Relations Plan
- Event and Sponsorship Plan
- Personal Selling Plan

marketing communications rely on the same input (background information, target market profiles, and positioning strategy statements) as do other components of the marketing mix. A marketing communications plan model is included in Figure 2.12. To demonstrate how marketing plans and marketing communications plan are integrated, read the IMC Highlight **Tim Hortons: Nobody Does It Better!**.

TIM HORTONS: NOBODY DOES IT BETTER!

How did Tim Hortons become the largest quick-serve restaurant chain in Canada? A successful blend of marketing and marketing communications is the key to Tim's success. With more than 2400 restaurants and $3 billion in sales annually, Tim Hortons is operating on all of its marketing cylinders.

Good marketing planning and good execution of the plans have been an effective combination for the company. Many experts firmly believe that Tim Hortons's "made in Canada" appeal is its strongest attribute, even though it is now owned by Wendy's, an American company. It seems that Tim's homegrown experience and success strikes a chord with Canadians from coast to coast. Despite its ominous size and marketing clout, Tim Hortons retains a certain small-town flavour. The company even markets its roots in commercials that feature Canadian travellers in distant locations yearning for a cup of Tim's coffee.

The Timbits Minor Sports Program has been an effective community-based marketing program that supports local minor hockey and soccer leagues by providing free uniforms. Giving back to the community has certainly had very positive brand-building implications for the company.

Keeping abreast of food preferences is another key to Tim's success. Tim Hortons started to give McDonald's a run for its money in the early 1990s when it introduced items such as chili, soup, bagels, and fresh sandwiches. Regular customers could now visit the chain beyond the typical coffee-shop busy hours of early morning and mid-afternoon. Even though many new food items have been introduced, the fact that all items are offered with the same consistency at every location is a tribute to the operations side of the business.

Perhaps Tim's biggest marketing innovation was the drive-through. Tim's was one of the first restaurants to recognize that portability and convenience would encourage consumer snacking, and they mastered the drive-through concept better than anyone. A decade ago, only one in ten quick-serve meals served in Canada was bought at a drive-through. Today the number is one in five, largely due to Tim Hortons. At Tim Hortons specifically, drive-through sales account for 55 percent of revenue. Experts say it's all about convenience.

Marketing communications also play a key role. Tim Hortons's communications strategies embrace long-term brand-building campaigns (mainly through its well-known "True Stories" campaign) combined with short-term tactical campaigns that create awareness for new products. Whenever a new product is introduced, it is given the royal treatment in the media and through in-store advertising. The ads play up Tim's low-key, down-home image, from the office worker mistakenly called "Toffee" (an ad used to introduce a toffee-flavoured donut) to a man who rushes off to meet his lunch date—a bowl of steaming beef stew. It doesn't seem to matter who you are, you can see yourself in the values that are represented by Tim's style of advertising.

Etching its way further into Canada's culture, Tim Hortons is now the title sponsor of the Brier, the country's national men's curling championship. You can't get more Canadian than that! More smart marketing by a national icon.

Adapted from Hollie Shaw, "Staying fresh with smart marketing," *National Post*, March 1, 2006, p. FP3, and Rebecca Harris, "A cup of Canadiana," *Marketing*, December 13/20, 2004, pp. 25–26.

Marketing communications plan

A plan that identifies how the various elements of marketing communications will be integrated into a cohesive and coordinated plan.

A **marketing communications plan** is usually prepared by an outside organization. Depending on the nature of the plan, it could be an advertising agency, a public relations company or sales promotion company, or any combination thereof. At some point, all the agencies working on the same plan must compare notes to ensure that their strategies are synchronized. Each aspect of the marketing communications plan has its own objectives, strategies, and tactical plans. In fact, it is crucial that the role and contribution of each component—advertising, sales promotion, public relations, direct response, interactive communications, event marketing and sponsorships, and personal selling—be identified.

The role of the marketing communications components will vary depending on the nature of the product and the market. As well, some components are suited for achieving long-term objectives while others are suited for short-term objectives. The key to success is the integration of the various components to produce a unified approach to building the brand (or company).

Marketing Communications Objectives

In general terms, marketing communications objectives are very diverse and tend to involve

- building awareness and interest in the product,
- changing perceptions held by consumers about the product,
- differentiating the product from others by presenting unique features and benefits,
- attracting new target markets to the product,
- encouraging greater usage of the product,
- offering incentives to get people to buy the product,
- creating goodwill and fostering a positive public image (usually for a company),
- creating leads for follow-up at a later date, and
- motivating distributors to carry the product.

Crest
www.crest.com

To continue with the Crest toothpaste example in the "Marketing Objectives" section, Crest is a firmly established and well-known brand, so awareness objectives are not relevant. However, here are some examples of other marketing communications objectives Crest might identify:

- To achieve a brand preference score of 40 percent among primary buyers of toothpaste products.
- To achieve a trial purchase rate of 25 percent among competitive brand users by offering incentives that encourage brand switching.
- To alter consumers' perceptions about the brand's image so that potential users perceive Crest to be an innovative product and market leader.

These objectives imply that marketing communications will be an integrated effort including activities beyond advertising. For certain, sales promotions (both consumer and trade), public relations, and Internet communications will be employed. Advertising and sales promotions will satisfy the first two objectives, and public relations and Internet communications will satisfy the third objective. A brand such as Crest uses all components of the marketing communications mix to retain its position in the marketplace relative to Colgate (another leading brand). The ad for Crest that appears in Figure 2.13 creates awareness for a new line extension. Crest has incorporated Scope mouthwash (another Procter & Gamble brand) into the Crest formula to offer a dual benefit to consumers.

Marketing Communications Strategies

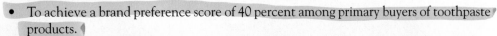

The marketing communications strategy provides a basic outline of how the various components of the mix will be used. As indicated by the Crest toothpaste example, all components may not be used, and those that are used are often ranked in terms of priority and what they are able to achieve.

This section of the strategy also identifies the budget allocated to marketing communications and how funds will be allocated to the various activities. What percentage of the budget will be allocated to advertising, to sales promotions, to event marketing, and so on?

Advertising Plan

Creative plan

A plan that outlines the nature of the message to be communicated to the target audience; involves the development of creative objectives, creative strategies, and creative execution.

The advertising plan is divided into two primary areas: creative (message) and media. The **creative plan** is concerned with what message will be communicated and how it will be communicated to the target market. The message usually stresses the most important attribute of the product—that which is most important to the customer. Where claims of

FIGURE **2.13**   **An Ad Creates Awareness for a New Line Extension**

Source: Courtesy of P&G Canada.

performance are made, proper substantiation is provided. That hints at the "how" aspect of creative planning. Agencies draw on such techniques as humour, sex, emotions, and even facts to tempt us to buy something. To illustrate, consider the ad for Diesel that appears in Figure 2.14. A sexual appeal technique certainly draws attention to the ad and the brand name. Diesel markets jeans, footwear, bags, and shades. Complete details about creative planning are presented in Chapter 4.

FIGURE **2.14** **A Sexual Appeal Technique Grabs the Reader's Attention Quickly**

Source: Courtesy of Diesel.

Media plan

A strategy that outlines the relevant details about how a client's budget will be spent; involves decisions about what media to use and how much money to invest in the media chosen to reach the target audience effectively and efficiently.

The **media plan** involves strategic decisions about what media to use and how much money to invest in the media that are chosen. The overall goal of any media plan is efficiency: the plan must effectively reach the target audience at the lowest possible cost. Since a company invests considerable sums in media advertising, wise decisions about usage are critical. Other media decisions involve timing, what markets to advertise in, how much money to allocate to regional markets and to key markets (cities), how long the campaign should last, and so on. Developing a media plan is complicated and best left to media specialists. More details about media planning for traditional mass media options are presented in Chapter 5.

Direct Response Plan

Direct response communications have a significant advantage over traditional mass media advertising: the direct results of the investment can be determined. The fact that direct response techniques can be accurately measured for success or failure makes it attractive to companies that stress accountability in their operations. It has taken considerable time for large companies to adopt direct response techniques. The negative image of direct mail advertising, for example, formerly made such a technique unattractive. Advancing technology, database marketing practices, and customer relationship management programs have fostered interest in marketing and communicating directly to individuals. Now all forms of direct response are popular. More details about direct response communications are included in Chapter 6.

Interactive Communications Plan

Earlier discussion about Internet communications stated that acceptance of advertising messages online was growing very slowly. Online consumers perceive Internet ads to be an intrusion, forgetting that the Internet is a medium much like television or newspapers. However, with each passing year, as consumers spend more time online, the commercial aspects of the Internet are becoming more acceptable. Certainly among youth, the Internet is becoming the medium of choice for personal communications. Widespread acceptance of commercial communications is just around the corner.

Among the communications alternatives available to companies wanting to advertise online are banner ads, sponsorships at websites where a target market congregates, and email correspondence. Other interactive options include CD-ROMs and instant text messaging through mobile telephones. Interactive communications strategies are discussed in more detail in Chapter 7.

Sales Promotion Plan

Sales promotions concentrate on reaching and influencing consumers, trade customers (distributors), and a company's sales force. Funds allocated to promotion strategies are traditionally divided between consumer promotions and trade promotions. Consumer promotions focus on objectives such as encouraging trial purchase, repeat purchase, or simply getting customers to buy a product in greater quantity. Refer to Figure 2.15 for an illustration of a promotion incentive designed to achieve trial and repeat purchases.

Trade promotions are designed to encourage merchandising and marketing support among distributors. Getting a product listed and on the store shelves of major supermarkets, for example, requires offering financial incentives to retailers such as Safeway, Sobeys, Loblaws, and others. In Canada, prominent retailers have significant clout with manufacturers, and as a result, considerable sums are spent on trade promotions each year. Sales promotion planning is discussed in detail in Chapter 8.

FIGURE 2.15 Manufacturers Offer Incentives to Encourage Trial and Repeat Purchases

Source: Courtesy of Parmalat.

Public Relations Plan

Public relations involve communicating with various groups beyond customers. For example, companies communicate with governments, prospective shareholders, the financial community, the media, and community groups. Typically, the goal of such communications is to enhance the company's public image. Public relations can be either corporate oriented or product oriented. At the corporate level, public relations are an important communications tool in times of crisis that show the public what the company is doing to resolve the crisis. PR can also be used to tell the public about the positive things a company is doing, for example, creating awareness of its environmental programs.

In a product sense, public relations play a role in generating interest in new products or spreading "news" about an existing product. Such communications are designed to secure media support for newsworthy information. The nature of public relations is such that written or broadcast news about a company or its products can be of more value. A third-party endorsement through public relations can have greater impact on consumers than advertising. Unlike advertising, public relations are an "unpaid" form of communications for the most part. For that reason alone, its usefulness must be exploited. The role and impact of public relations are presented in detail in Chapter 9.

Event Marketing and Sponsorships

Events and sponsorships now play a more prominent role in the marketing communications mix. Organizations are attracted to events because they present opportunities to reach a target market as a group in one location. The audience can be quite large, as in the case of a major-league sports event, or comparatively small, such as a local theatre production. Decisions about what events to support are important and careful planning is needed if the organization is to achieve maximum value from participation. A variety of communications elements must be built into the plan to show how the event will be supported. All of this information is documented in the communications plan. Event marketing and sponsorship planning are presented in Chapter 10.

Personal Selling Plan

Personal selling plays a key role in marketing, especially in business-to-business market situations. As indicated earlier, personal selling techniques create desire and action. The role of a sales representative is to present the benefits of products and show how they resolve a customer's problem. The sales representative is also responsible for presenting the marketing and merchandising support plans to distributors who resell the company's products. In this regard, there is a direct link to the media advertising, trade promotion, consumer promotion, and event marketing and sponsorship components of the marketing communications plan. Customers must be made aware of all activities that will potentially influence sales.

A sales manager directs the activities of the sales department and is responsible for setting sales objectives that are part of the marketing communications plan. The sales manager is also responsible for developing the sales strategies and tactics that will be employed by the sales representatives. Personal selling is discussed in more detail in Chapter 11.

Measuring and Evaluating Marketing Communications

The final step in the marketing and marketing communications planning process involves measurement and evaluation. It is essential that an organization monitor all programs to distinguish effective activities from ineffective activities. There's a famous expression about marketing planning and budgeting: "50 percent of my budget works and 50 percent doesn't work. But I don't know which is which." Yes, a lot of marketing decisions are made on instinct, but many more are based on hard and fast measurements.

In marketing communications, some activities are difficult to measure and very often too much burden is placed on communications. It is such a visible aspect of marketing that it is convenient for senior managers to be critical of it. Each element of marketing communications should be accountable for what it can accomplish. If it is advertising, awareness scores can be measured; if it's public relations, brand mentions in the press may be a means of measuring success; if it's event marketing, the number of new clients that come on stream may be a useful measure. Each component can be measured and evaluated in unique and different ways. This topic is discussed in detail in Chapter 12.

Summary

Strategic planning is an integrated process that involves developing plans at three different levels of an organization. The planning process is cyclical and is subject to constant change based on conditions in the marketplace. To stay on top of things, an organization monitors changes in the economy, competitive activity, consumer behaviour, technology, and laws and regulations.

A marketing communications plan (its direction and content) is influenced by a marketing plan and a corporate plan. When one plan is complete, it provides direction to the next plan. Planning usually starts with the corporate plan, a document prepared by senior executives. Corporate planning starts with the development of a mission statement followed by corporate objectives and strategies. When deciding upon a strategy, the organization evaluates its marketing strength, degree of competition, financial resources, research and development capabilities, and management expertise.

Marketing planning involves four steps: analyzing market opportunities, developing marketing strategies, planning and implementing marketing programs, and managing marketing programs. In performing these steps, target markets are identified, positioning strategies are developed, and marketing strategies and tactics for all components of the marketing mix and marketing communications mix are documented in a marketing plan.

The marketing communications plan identifies the various communications objectives for the year and the strategies that will be employed to achieve them. The plan is subdivided into specific areas, depending on which components of the mix will be employed. The advertising plan focuses on creative and media decisions. In the creative plan, objectives and strategies (what to say and how to say it) are identified. The media plan states the media objectives by identifying the target market, how often its members should be reached, and when they should be reached. The media strategies rationalize the use of media alternatives and provide detailed information about how the budget is allocated.

If the plan is an integrated plan, other components of the mix are included. Depending on the situation a brand or company faces, the plan could include sales promotion, public relations, events and sponsorships, direct response communications, interactive communications, and personal selling. Objectives, strategies, and tactics for each are included in the plan. The goal is to have a unified plan—all forms of marketing communications delivering a single message to a target market in a convincing manner.

Key Terms

acquisition strategy, 45

contingency plan, 45

corporate objective, 43

corporate plan, 41

corporate strategy, 36

creative plan, 59

direct competition, 37

indirect competition, 37

marketing communications plan, 58

marketing control, 56

marketing objective, 52

marketing plan, 41

marketing planning, 45

marketing strategy, 54

media plan, 62

mission statement, 42

monopolistic competition, 37

new product development strategy, 45

oligopoly, 37

penetration strategy, 43

positioning, 50

positioning strategy statement, 50

strategic alliance, 45

strategic planning, 36

SWOT analysis, 47

tactics (execution), 54

target market profile, 52

Review Questions

1. What are the external trends and conditions that should be considered when commencing a new planning cycle?

2. What are the key components of a corporate plan? What guidelines does the corporate plan provide to operational plans such as marketing and marketing communications?

3. What is a mission statement and what role does it play in planning?

4. Marketing planning involves four essential steps. Identify and briefly describe each step.

5. What role does a positioning strategy statement play in developing a marketing strategy?

6. "Marketing strategies are the master plans for achieving objectives." What does this statement mean?

7. What is the difference between marketing strategy and marketing execution?

8. What is meant by marketing control and how does it influence marketing planning?

9. What are the essential decision areas for a creative plan and a media plan?

10. What is the relationship between the various components of an integrated marketing communications plan?

Discussion and Application Questions

1. "Marketing communications objectives are diverse by nature, but a good campaign must have a specific focus." What does this mean?

2. Review the IMC Highlight **West 49: Popular Destination for Teens**. West 49 has been successful in appealing to teenagers in a niche segment of the sporting goods market. What strategies should West 49 be considering to expand its business further? Assess the present market situation and make some specific marketing recommendations.

3. Review the IMC Highlight **Tim Hortons: Nobody Does It Better!** Despite intense competition from other quick-serve restaurants, Tim Hortons continues to be a dominant leader in Canada. What are the key factors contributing to its success? If you were the marketing director at

Tim Hortons, what strategies would you be considering for the next few years? Are any changes in direction needed? Assess the situation and make some specific recommendations.

4. Evaluate the marketing situation for the following companies. What makes them unique and what is their differential advantage(s) compared to their primary competitors? Develop a positioning strategy statement for each company based on your assessment of the situation.

   a) Canadian Tire
   b) Best Buy
   c) Roots

5. Using a variety of online sources, conduct a market analysis for a branded product of your choosing. The market analysis should include the following information:

   a) market size and growth
   b) importance of regional markets
   c) market segment analysis (which segments are growing, declining, etc.)
   d) seasonal analysis

What conclusions can you draw from your analysis?

6. Compare and contrast the marketing communications strategies of two competing brands (a brand leader and a brand challenger). Do these brands use all elements of the marketing communications mix or do they selectively use only certain elements? What conclusions can you draw based on your analysis of each brand? Some brands to consider might be

   a) Coca-Cola and Pepsi-Cola
   b) Colgate toothpaste and Crest toothpaste
   c) Dove soap and Olay soap

7. Analyze the marketing communications strategies for an automobile (car or truck) of your choosing. Based on the images portrayed in any and all forms of marketing communications, describe in detail the target market that the automobile is pursuing. Provide a profile based on demographic, psychographic, and geographic characteristics.

Endnotes

1 Derek DeCloot, "How Krispy got creamed," *Globe and Mail*, December 22, 2004, **www.workopolis.com**.

2 Samson Okalow, "Fighting fat fright," *Strategy*, August 25, 2003, **www.strategymag.com**.

3 Serra Shular, "A new buzzword," *Marketing*, July 18/25, 2005, p. 20.

4 Philip Kotler, *A Framework for Marketing Management*, 2nd ed. (Upper Saddle River, NJ: Prentice-Hall, 2003), p. 104.

5 Bill Alpert, "Cell phones may bite off Apple," *Financial Post*, June 27, 2005, p. FP7.

6 Tyler Hamilton, "Cash is in the e-mail," *Toronto Star*, February 11, 2002, pp. E1, E2.

7 Marina Strauss and Simon Tuck, "Tribunal rules Sears broke law inflating tire savings," *Globe and Mail*, January 25, 2005, **www.globeandmail.com**.

8 Jack Neff, "Court rules against Gillette razor package claim," *Advertising Age*, June 23, 2005, **www.adage.com**.

9 M. Corey Goldman, "iPod's been sweet to Apple but could things go sour?" *Toronto Star*, June 13, 2005, p. D4.

10 Brad Foss, "Pepsi seals Quaker deal," *Globe and Mail*, December 5, 2000, p. B4.

11 Hoag Levins, "Adidas to acquire Reebok for $3.8 billion," *Advertising Age*, August 3, 2005, **www.adage.com**.

12 Sean Silcoff, "Couche-Tard to take on Hortons," *Financial Post*, August 11, 2004, pp. FP1, FP6.

13 Michelle Halpern, "Long live the underdog," *Marketing*, December 13/20, 2004, pp. 20, 21.

14 "Money hog," an advertorial appearing in the *National Post*, Driver's Edge Section, January 3, 2002, p. DO11.

BRANDING STRATEGY

After studying this chapter you will be able to

LEARNING OBJECTIVES

1. describe the concept of branding and the role it plays in marketing communications and other business-building programs

2. identify the various components of a brand

3. describe the benefits of branding for organizations and consumers

4. characterize the various stages of brand loyalty

5. describe the role and importance of brand positioning and its relationship to marketing communications plans

6. explain various brand positioning strategies commonly used in marketing communications

7. describe the role and influence of packaging and product design in the brand-building process

Think of marketing and marketing communications as a loop. The loop starts somewhere and ends somewhere, but exactly where? Well, it starts with the brand and ends with the brand. Marketing and marketing communications programs create awareness for the brand (the start of the loop). All kinds of messages are sent to consumers through a variety of touch-points such as packaging, personal selling, events, promotions, news articles, and advertising. Collectively, these messages heighten the interest and desire for the brand. While all this is happening, competing brands are doing the same thing. The goal for all brands is to get the consumer into the store to buy their brand. The consumer is now standing in front of a store shelf looking at all the different brands. Which one does he or she buy? The customer takes action and places one brand in the shopping cart. Which one? The loop just closed.

What this loop principle suggests is that every form of communication is going to have some kind of impact. The impact of the message and its ability to stimulate action are determined by what a brand has to offer (e.g., a compelling reason why someone should buy it) and the convincing way in which the message is delivered to potential customers. Essentially, the brand offering and the message communicated to consumers form the backbone of brand strategy and positioning strategy. This chapter provides insights into how brand strategy and positioning strategy are developed and show the influence of marketing communications in developing a relationship between the customer and the brand. Communications is the glue that holds or binds the customer to the brand.[1]

DEFINING THE BRAND

Just what is a brand? Ask the question and you will get hundreds of different answers. Every "expert" has a different take on what a brand is. The *Dictionary of Marketing Terms* defines a **brand** as an identifying mark, symbol, word(s), or combination of same, that separates one company's product from another company's product. Brand is a comprehensive term that includes all brand names and trademarks.[2]

In today's hypercompetitive marketing environment, branding is a hot button. Marketing executives are busy trying to find or build their brand essence, brand architecture, or brand DNA. Maybe it's a little overdone! That said, brands and branding have been around for centuries; only recently has the concept worked its way into everyday conversation.

Marketing communications in any form has an impact on how customers perceive a brand. It seems that a brand is more than just a tangible product. It can embrace intangible characteristics as well. Customer perceptions of brands are largely based on the brand name and what it stands for. It is an image they hold of a brand over an extended period and that image is based on what they have learned about the brand. For example, such brand names as Rolex or Jaguar suggest a certain quality or status. Nike sells shoes, but the brand represents a kind of rebellious spirit. Apple is a contemporary, user-friendly manufacturer of computers and portable music players, and Volvo is well known for making safe automobiles. These images are the result of good marketing and marketing communications programs. Perhaps Landor, a branding consulting firm, offers the best and simplest definition of a brand: a brand is "the sum of all characteristics, tangible and intangible, that make the offer unique."[3]

It is the various components of the brand working together that distinguish one product from another. The key components of a brand are as follows:

Brand Name   The **brand name** is the part of the brand that can be spoken. It may consist of a word, letter, or group of words and letters. Nike, Starbucks, Gatorade, WD-40, eBay, Tide, and Wal-Mart are all brand names. Brand names are usually presented with their own unique font style. The stylized treatment of the brand name serves the same function as a symbol and is referred to as a **wordmark**.

Brand
An identifying mark, symbol, word or words, or combination of mark and words that separates one product from another product; can also be defined as the sum of all tangible and intangible characteristics that make a unique offer to customers.

Brand name
That part of a brand that can be spoken.

Wordmark
The stylized treatment of the brand name; serves the same function as a symbol.

Brandmark or Logo The unique design, symbol, or other special representation of a brand name or company name is referred to as the **brandmark** or **logo**. Some interesting brandmarks include Apple Computer's famous apple with a bite taken out of it, Coca-Cola's unique bottle design and red cap, and Nike's famous swoosh (see Figure 3.1 for some famous brandmarks). A recent research study indicates that 97 percent of American citizens recognize Nike's swoosh logo. From a marketing perspective, you couldn't ask for anything more. However, so ubiquitous is the logo that it represents negative images to many consumers; for many it represents two social ills: the commercialization of sports and the globalization of capitalism.[4] That's not good for business!

FIGURE **3.1** **A Selection of Famous Logos**

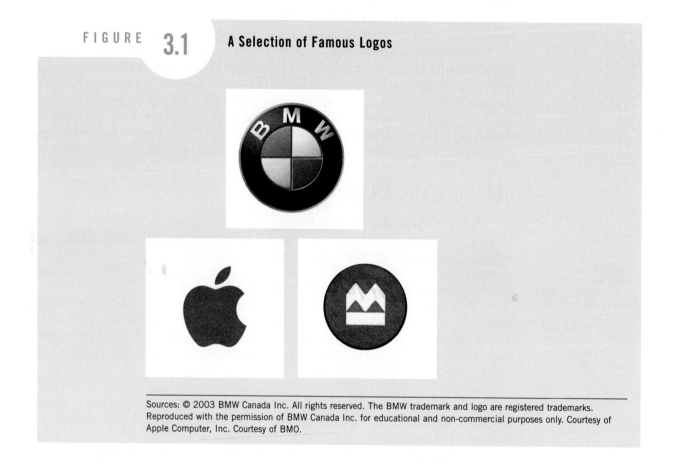

Trademark A **trademark** is that part of a brand that is granted legal protection so that only the owner can use it. The symbol ™ designates trademark claims. The ® symbol is used when the trademark has not only been claimed, but registered with the government trademarks office. Trademarks can include the brand names and symbols described above. "Coke"® and "Coca-Cola"® and the unique style in which these names are printed are registered trademarks of the Coca-Cola Company.

What to name a brand is a critical decision. Consequently, companies spend considerable amounts of time and money developing and testing brand names. When you think of it, virtually every marketing activity undertaken revolves around the brand name. It has to be distinctive and meaningful. It has to be the right name. What to name a product involves a creative decision and a strategic decision.

Brand names come in many different forms. They can be based on people (Calvin Klein and Tommy Hilfiger), places (Air France, Air Canada, and Monte Carlo), animals

(Mustang and Dove), inherent product meaning (Ticketmaster and Lean Cuisine), product attributes (Bounty paper towels and DieHard batteries), or they can be completely made up to simply sound scientific or attractive. For example, Sony has family names like Cyber-shot for its cameras, Wega for televisions, and Handycams for its camcorders.

Brands are more than just a tangible product. A company adds other dimensions that differentiate it in some way from other products designed to meet the same need. These differences may be rational and tangible, or they may be emotional or intangible entities related to what the brand represents. Through marketing communications, the "personality" of a brand evolves, and the combination of brand attributes (tangibles) and brand personality (intangibles) are what influence brand choices by consumers. The key for any brand is to be perceived as offering something unique. You could probably name at least 10 different brands of deodorant. Why does one person buy Gillette, another Mennen, another Right Guard, another Axe, and so on?

Brand management has played a key role in the growth and development of Mazda automobiles. The word "Mazda," however, was around long before the first Mazda vehicle went into production. It can be traced back to the ancient Orient, where Ahura Mazda was the god of wisdom and light. While the name dates back to the beginning of civilization, the corporate logo, the winged "M," symbolizes the way Mazda is stretching its wings as it moves into the future. It captures the spirit of the company and its aspirations.[5] See the illustration in Figure 3.2.

IMC HIGHLIGHT

MAZDA'S DNA

"Zoom-Zoom." It's a memorable slogan for a very effective advertising campaign. For the past six years, Mazda has been airing television commercials that are very different from anything it had done before. Gone is the previous message "The Practical Car, The Enjoyable Car. That's Mazda." The initial campaign that started in 1999 was based on the creative concept of "New Ideas that Stir Emotions." In 2002, that concept evolved into "Zoom-Zoom."

Let's trace the steps and see why Mazda altered its communications strategy. The "New Ideas that Stir Emotions" concept was to be a key aspect of Mazda's rebranding strategy. According to Mazda, the globalization of free markets, the emergence of "borderless" economies, and the subsequent intensification of competition mean the strength of a company's brand is more important than ever. In fact, the development of a strong, consistent brand that consumers identify with is a necessary condition for survival in the marketplace.

Brand management is now the centre of Mazda's business strategy. One of the company's overall goals is to develop a keen understanding of Mazda target customers and to delight them through concentrated efforts in the areas of product, service, and communication. Mazda has become a customer-driven company that wants to attract customers to its brand and foster the development of a

long-lasting, emotional connection with them.

The new communications campaign was part of a worldwide brand positioning strategy. Mazda describes its brand in terms of product attributes and personality. Like human DNA, the unique attributes of the product are distinctive design, exceptional functionality, and superbly responsive handling and performance. On the personality side, Mazda defines itself as stylish, insightful, and spirited. When these brand attributes and personality are combined, you have "New Ideas that Stir Emotions." Now an integral aspect of Mazda's corporate culture, this strategic direction provides a foundation for developing new products, services, and communications at every level of the company.

In 2002, the campaign evolved into "Zoom-Zoom." Zoom-Zoom aims to recreate the fun-to-drive feeling of Mazda vehicles. Zoom-Zoom is a phrase children use when they imitate the sound of a car engine. It expresses fascination with motion experienced by a child playing with a toy car or riding a bike. The Mazda brand conveys this feeling in its products, and Zoom-Zoom captures this feeling perfectly. Mazda offers driving experiences for customers who still have that childlike fascination with motion. This is the emotional connection that Mazda seeks with its customers. The Zoom-Zoom theme and the boy who appears in the commercials are easy to remember. It is a very likeable advertising campaign that has made an impact all over the world.

FIGURE **3.2** **The Winged "M" Symbolizes the Way Mazda Is Stretching Its Wings as It Moves into the Future**

Source: Courtesy of Mazda Canada.

"Zoom-Zoom," a phrase that has been popularized based on the success of an integrated marketing communications campaign, expresses Mazda's unique combination of brand attributes and brand personality. For more insight into Mazda's branding strategy, read the IMC Highlight **Mazda's DNA**.

Brands are more than physical products and services. Whenever and wherever a consumer is choosing between alternatives, brands play a role in the decision-making process. While brands provide customers with an assurance of quality, they also express a set of values that customers can identify with. The Coca-Cola brand is more than just a sweet-tasting soft drink; it carries a set of American values that strike a chord with consumers all over the world. Similarly, a brand like Virgin represents a youthful, rebellious attitude, much like that of Virgin's maverick founder, Richard Branson.[6]

Branding also applies to retail organizations. Canadian Tire, for example, is ranked among the best-managed brands in Canada—a testament to its consistent marketing practices over the years. While some retail brands such as the Bay and Zellers are fading, Canadian Tire has survived as a great brand despite the assault of formidable US-based competitors such a Home Depot and Wal-Mart. A number of factors have assisted Canadian Tire: it is an innovative company that experiments with new ways of offering value, and it consistently delivers what it promises. In short, the Canadian Tire brand stands for something in Canada.[7]

Canadian Tire
www.canadiantire.ca

THE BENEFITS OF BRANDING

Based on the discussion of branding in the preceding section it can be seen that consumers and organizations benefit from branding. Some of the benefits for consumers are as follows:

- Over time, the brand name suggests a certain level of quality. Consumers know what to expect; they trust and have confidence in the brand.
- There can be psychological rewards for possessing certain brands. For example, buying a brand new BMW automobile might suggest achievement to the owner. The automobile says something about the driver; it expresses his or her self-image.
- Brands distinguish competitive offerings, allowing consumers to make informed decisions. Such brand names as Cup-a-Soup (Lipton), Mr. Clean (Procter & Gamble), and Frosted Flakes (Kellogg) suggest clear messages or benefits about the product.

Over time, a relationship develops between a consumer and the brand; it's like a bond. Consumers offer their trust and loyalty in return for consistent product quality from the brand. A brand is a promise delivered. A brand protects its place in the consumer's mind by keeping its promise.[8]

The issue of trust is very important. A recent poll conducted by Ipsos Reid found that almost one-third of Canadians surveyed "strongly" believed it is more difficult to trust products and brands today than it was 20 years ago. Consumers today are more informed—they tend to ask more questions and have access to more information. The poll also revealed that Canadians have a set of trusted brands across many product categories: Robin Hood flour, Campbell's soup, Becel margarine, Kellogg's cereal, and Ford pickup trucks.[9] Brands like these become an integral part of people's lives.

Brands play a key role and offer numerous benefits to an organization as well. At the operational level, they help to plan production runs, maintain inventory counts, and facilitate order processing and delivery. In a marketing context, the key benefits are as follows:

Unique selling point (USP)

The primary benefit of a product or service that distinguishes it from its competitors.

- A good brand name communicates the point of difference, or **unique selling point (USP)**, and highlights the distinctive value added. A name such as Lean Cuisine, for example, addresses two benefits: "lean" communicates low calories and "cuisine" implies it tastes good. The brand name is meaningful and pleasant sounding.
- Branding allows for the creation and development of an image. For example, Nike suggests an independent spirit. Maytag stands for dependability. For these brands, extensive advertising campaigns have instilled such images in the customer's mind.

- Satisfied customers will make repeat purchases and hopefully remain loyal to the brand. Such loyalty stabilizes market share and provides for certain efficiencies in production and marketing. Reliable estimates of future sales facilitate internal brand planning.

A recent survey among automobile buyers shows the importance of branding and brand loyalty. Apparently, brand loyalty to a specific manufacturer's brand is at an all-time low, as almost two-thirds of respondents said they were likely to change nameplates with their next purchase. In assessing the decision to buy a domestic or imported brand, there was a stronger loyalty to imports.[10] That's bad news for General Motors and Ford.

In summary, branding decisions are important decisions. A brand name stands for much more than simply differentiating one brand from another. Decisions about brand name, benefits offered, package design, and the desired image form the foundation for marketing and marketing communications strategies.

Brand Loyalty

Brand loyalty

The degree of attachment to a particular brand expressed by a consumer. There are three stages of brand loyalty: brand recognition, brand preference, and brand insistence.

Brand loyalty is defined as the degree of consumer attachment to a particular brand. Loyalty is influenced by such factors as marketing communications (what is said about a brand), family or peer pressure, and friendship with a salesperson. For example, someone intending to buy a new car might return to the same dealer and person he or she has bought from before. Satisfaction based on experience with a product or an individual breeds loyalty.

Brand loyalty is measured in three distinct stages: brand recognition, brand preference, and brand insistence (see Figure 3.3).[11]

FIGURE **3.3** **The Stages of Brand Loyalty**

Brand Recognition
Consumer is aware of the name, benefit, and package.

Brand Preference
Brand is top-of-mind and considered a good alternative. Consumer will buy if available.

Brand Insistence
Consumer buys one brand only. If brand is not available, the purchase is postponed.

Brand recognition

Customer awareness of the brand name and package.

In the early stage of a brand's life, the marketing objective is to create **brand recognition**. It is imperative to communicate the brand name, the unique selling point, and what the product looks like (e.g., the package if it is a consumer good, or the look and style if it is a shopping good such as an automobile or appliance). A marketing communications campaign plays a key role here.

Brand preference

The situation where a brand is perceived as an acceptable alternative by a customer and will be purchased if it is available.

When a brand achieves the status of **brand preference**, it is on a short list of brand alternatives that the consumer will consider buying. Such a position is good because consumers only retain a select group of brand names in their minds for any product category. Furthermore, it is an indication that the message strategies and other marketing strategies are working; the customer knows something about the brand, has evaluated it in relation to his or her needs, and will purchase it if available when it is needed.

Brand insistence

A situation where the consumer searches the market for the specific brand.

At the **brand insistence** stage, a consumer will search the market extensively for a particular brand. No alternatives are acceptable, and if the brand is not available the consumer will likely postpone the purchase until it is. Such an enviable position shows the type of bond that can develop between a brand and a consumer.

Coca-Cola
www.coca-cola.com

As suggested earlier, consumers want consistent quality from their brands. The famous Coca-Cola marketing debacle of 1985 confirms how brand insistence works. Coca-Cola made the decision to replace Coca-Cola with a new formula. When the change was implemented, the backlash from customers was so swift and strong that the company had to bring back the original formula under the name Coca-Cola Classic. Some critics insist that Coca-Cola is a brand that has gone beyond brand insistence. So strong is the bond with consumers, the product cannot be changed—ever.

Since one of the tasks of marketing is to keep customers loyal, smart companies plan and implement loyalty programs. Retailers such as Canadian Tire, Costco, and Holt Renfrew have their own rewards programs, as do all major gasoline chains. More than 15.4 million people in Canada collect AIR MILES, a figure that represents more than 72 percent of Canadian households.[12] Loyalty-oriented marketing programs are presented in Chapter 8.

Brand insistent consumers often become advocates for the brand—they like the brand so much they will openly recommend it to others. As discussed in Chapter 1, a word-of-mouth network is a powerful communications tool that influences buying decisions. To illustrate, many users of Apple computers are advocates. They often belong to Mac user groups (MUGs) and frequently end up in "religious wars" with PC users. The same can be said of owners of Harley-Davidson motorcycles, commonly known as HOGs. To Harley owners, there is no other kind of motorcycle.

Brand Equity

Brand equity

The value (monetary or otherwise) of a brand to its owners; determined by the success of marketing activities; influenced by brand name awareness, degree of customer loyalty, perceived quality, etc.

Brand equity is a confusing term that has been historically defined in different ways for different purposes. For our purposes, **brand equity** is defined as the value of a brand in its holistic sense to its owners as a corporate asset.[13] The value of the asset reflects the brand's position and status in the marketplace and in the hearts and minds of the customers who purchase it regularly. In the Coca-Cola example cited earlier, the attitudes and feelings that consumers showed for Coca-Cola suggests it has extremely high brand equity. Brand equity is influenced by several variables: brand name awareness, the degree of loyalty expressed by customers, perceived quality, and the brand's association with a certain attribute. The quality and effectiveness of marketing and marketing communications play a key role in linking brands and consumers together. Coca-Cola is consistently ranked as the leading global brand in terms of value, at US$67.5 billion.[14] Seven of the world's top 10 brands are American (see Figure 3.4).

FIGURE **3.4**   **Brand Equity: The World's Top 10 Brands**

Rank	Brand	Value ($ billion)	Origin
1	Coca-Cola	67.0	USA
2	Microsoft	56.9	USA
3	IBM	56.2	USA
4	General Electric	48.9	USA
5	Intel	32.3	USA
6	Nokia	30.1	Finland
7	Toyota	27.9	Japan
8	Disney	27.8	USA
9	McDonald's	27.5	USA
10	Mercedes	21.8	Germany

Source: Interbrand (2006 data). Data published by BBC News, www.newsvote.bbc.uk.

Apple iPod
www.apple.com/ipod.html

To illustrate the concept of brand equity, consider Apple's iPod brand. iPod created the portable music player category. It offered innovative design and was launched just as digital music hit the mainstream (the right product at the right time). iPod achieved default status quickly, meaning that when consumers think about buying a music player they think first of iPod—the iPod is the Kleenex of music players.[15] A new brand name like iPod helps enhance the value of the corporate Apple brand name.

BUILDING THE BRAND

Brand manager

An individual assigned responsibility for the development and implementation of marketing programs for a specific product or group of products.

Building a brand (building brand equity) is the responsibility of the brand manager (or category manager or marketing manager, depending on a company's organizational structure). A **brand manager** is responsible for developing and implementing the marketing plans for the brands he or she is responsible for. The process of building a brand involves four essential steps (see Figure 3.5 for a visual illustration):

1. Identify and establish brand values and positioning strategy.
2. Plan and implement brand marketing programs.
3. Measure and interpret brand performance.
4. Grow and sustain brand equity (managing a brand through its life cycle).

Since the concept of brand equity has already been discussed, the remaining discussion in this chapter will focus on brand values and positioning, and the development of marketing programs.

Core values

The primary attributes and benefits a brand delivers to the customer.

Attribute

A descriptive feature of a product.

Benefit

The value a customer attaches to a brand attribute.

Establishing Core Values and Brand Positioning

What does a brand stand for? The answer to that question will relate to the core values of a brand. **Core values** are the primary attributes and benefits a brand delivers to the customer. An **attribute** is a descriptive feature; a **benefit** is the value consumers attach to a

FIGURE **3.5**   **The Brand-Building Process**

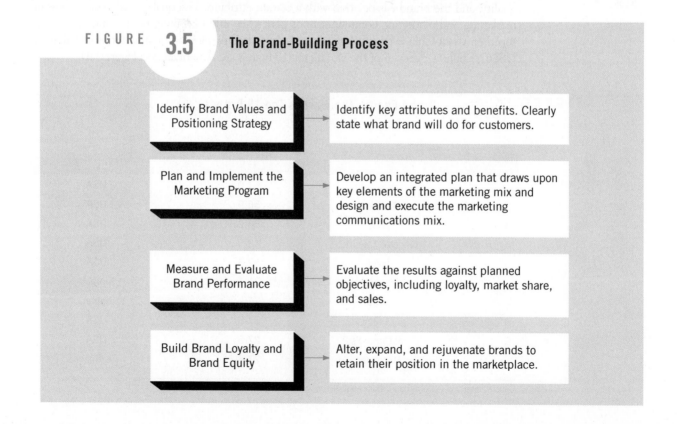

Identify Brand Values and Positioning Strategy	Identify key attributes and benefits. Clearly state what brand will do for customers.
Plan and Implement the Marketing Program	Develop an integrated plan that draws upon key elements of the marketing mix and design and execute the marketing communications mix.
Measure and Evaluate Brand Performance	Evaluate the results against planned objectives, including loyalty, market share, and sales.
Build Brand Loyalty and Brand Equity	Alter, expand, and rejuvenate brands to retain their position in the marketplace.

FIGURE **3.6**   **Brands Differentiate by Focusing on Unique Attributes**

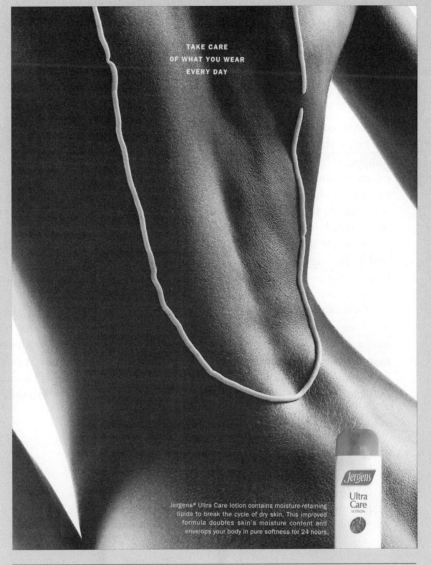

TAKE CARE
OF WHAT YOU WEAR
EVERY DAY

Jergens® Ultra Care lotion contains moisture-retaining
lipids to break the cycle of dry skin. This improved
formula doubles skin's moisture content and
envelops your body in pure softness for 24 hours.

Jergens
Ultra
Care
LOTION

Source: Courtesy of KAO Brands Canada.

brand attribute. Very often the core values can be expressed in a very short statement about the brand. Here are a few examples from various skin care products:

- Dove tells women to focus on internal beauty and the health of their skin; everyone should be happy with who they are (a self-esteem message). Dove emphasizes an attitude more than the product itself.

- Olay tells women to "love the skin you're in." Olay communicates how it adds moisture to protect the skin. Olay focuses on a key attribute.

- Jergens tells women to "take care of what you wear every day" (your skin). Product-specific attributes focus on moisture-retaining capabilities that leave the skin feeling soft.

The skin care category is large and very competitive. Every brand has a different means of communicating essentially the same message. They all offer the same proprietary benefit. Some brands focus on psychological benefits, while others focus on product-specific attributes. Each brand takes a different angle on how to communicate the key benefit. That's brand differentiation. With reference to the ad that appears in Figure 3.6 (previous page), Jergens Ultra Care Lotion communicates how the product helps retain moisture in a person's skin. The visual imagery, which is sensuous yet simple, aptly portrays the usefulness of the product.

BRAND POSITIONING CONCEPTS

Positioning
The selling concept that motivates purchase, or the image that marketers desire a brand to have in the minds of consumers.

As discussed in Chapter 2, **positioning** is the selling concept that motivates purchase, or the image that marketers desire a brand to have in the minds of customers. It is a strategy influenced by core brand values and the values offered by competing brands. Simply stated, each brand wants to differentiate itself from competitive offerings. Therefore, positioning involves designing and marketing a product to meet the needs of a target market and creating the appropriate appeals to make the product stand out from the competition in the minds of the target market.

A clearly defined positioning strategy statement provides guidance for all marketing and marketing communications strategies. The strategy statement provides a compelling reason why potential customers should buy the brand. Figure 3.7 illustrates the importance of positioning.

Typically, a brand sticks to a single-benefit positioning strategy, but for many brands and companies the competition is so intense that additional benefits become the focus of marketing communications. For example, Scope, a popular mouthwash, offers the primary benefit of fresher breath, and by introducing new flavours, it offers variety to users (see Figure 3.8 for an illustration). Some products offer multiple benefits and by doing so may have an edge on the competition. Crest toothpaste, for example offers a line that

FIGURE **3.7** **The Importance of Positioning**

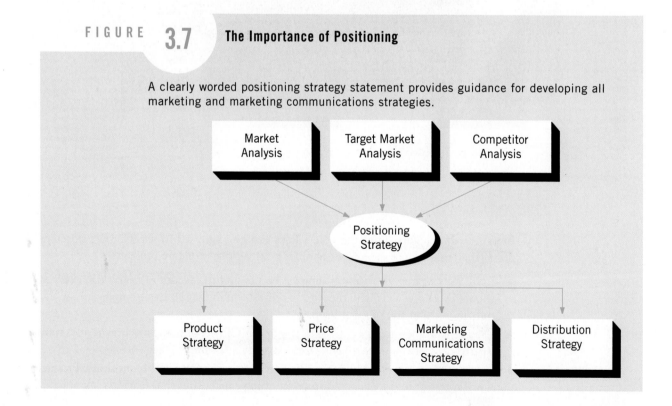

A clearly worded positioning strategy statement provides guidance for developing all marketing and marketing communications strategies.

Market Analysis · Target Market Analysis · Competitor Analysis → Positioning Strategy → Product Strategy · Price Strategy · Marketing Communications Strategy · Distribution Strategy

FIGURE **3.8**   **Advertising Communicates Scope's Primary Benefit and the Introduction of a New Flavour**

Source: Courtesy of P&G Canada.

combines two leading brands in toothpaste. Crest toothpaste now includes Scope mouthwash in its formula.

The positioning strategy statement should be clear, concise, and uncomplicated while addressing the target market's need and the primary benefit to be offered. Here is an actual positioning strategy statement for the Visa credit card:

> To reinforce our leadership position in the credit card market, and to establish it as the preferred provider for all future products.

Visa
www.visa.ca

One can start to see how such a statement is used as input for developing a communications strategy. All consumer-directed communications for Visa use the tagline "All you need" as a means of summarizing their primary benefit. When you look back at the positioning statement, the relationship between the positioning strategy and the communications strategy starts to crystallize. For an illustration of Visa advertising, see Figure 3.9.

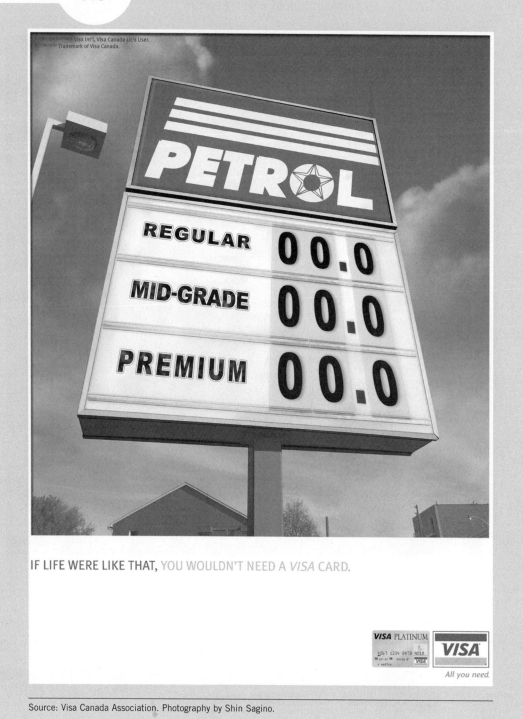

Source: Visa Canada Association. Photography by Shin Sagino.

There are all kinds of ways a product can be positioned in the minds of customers, but typically they relate back to some crucial element of the marketing mix such as product or product differentiation, price (low or high price), channel of distribution advantages, or the desired image a brand can create for itself through marketing communications. Let's discuss some of these positioning strategies.

Product Differentiation

Here's what the product is! Here's what the product does! That's product differentiation—nothing could be more straightforward. When a **product differentiation strategy**
is employed, the product will communicate meaningful and valued differences to distinguish itself from competitive offerings. Such differences focus specifically on what the
product may offer, and refer to the form of the product (size, shape, or physical structure),
performance quality (it lasts longer!), durability (ability to withstand stress), reliability
(it won't breakdown), or style (the look and appearance of the product or package). Glad
products, for example, consistently differentiate on the basis of how a unique seal keeps
things fresh. See the illustration in Figure 3.10.

FIGURE **3.10**   **A Unique Method of Sealing from Glad Keeps Products Fresh**

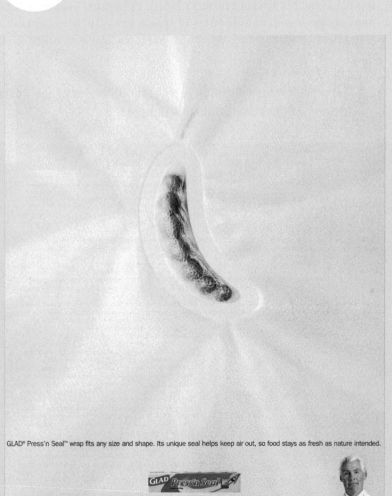

GLAD® Press'n Seal™ wrap fits any size and shape. Its unique seal helps keep air out, so food stays as fresh as nature intended.

Depend on it.™

Source: GLAD, the GLAD logo and PRESS'N SEAL are registered trademarks of the Glad
Products Company. Used with permission. © The Clorox Company. Reprinted with permission.

In the fast food restaurant category, Harvey's has taken a bold step to differentiate itself from other chains. While a perception exists that fast food is fattening, and competitors such as McDonald's and Wendy's are promoting healthier menus, Harvey's returned to its roots and promoted great-tasting grilled hamburgers served with the toppings that their customers want. Harvey's identifies itself with the guy who likes to barbecue beef.[16] Harvey's advertising slogan aptly portrays their positioning strategy: "Long live the grill." See the illustration in Figure 3.11.

Brand Leadership Positioning

Leadership positioning

A marketing strategy in which a product presents itself as a preferred choice among customers.

As the name suggests, **leadership positioning** is a strategy often employed by brand leaders. Good marketing and marketing strategies from the past have helped such a product achieve an enviable position in the marketplace and in the minds of customers. These brands have high brand equity. The message such a brand delivers is designed to reinforce its lofty position. Probably the classic example (pardon the pun) of leadership positioning is Coca-Cola Classic. In most North American markets, Coca-Cola Classic is the number-one brand, and in terms of brand equity, it is recognized as the most valuable brand name globally. In advertising, Coca-Cola Classic struts its stuff. The brand has used

FIGURE **3.11**   **Harvey's Differentiates from Other Fast Food Restaurants by Promoting Grilled Hamburgers**

Source: Harvey's Restaurants.

phrases such as "Coke is it," "Can't beat the real thing," "Always Coca-Cola," and "Real" to reinforce its position. The Visa example cited earlier serves as another illustration of leadership positioning. The slogan "All you need" aptly communicates Visa's position in the market.

Head-on Positioning (Comparative Positioning)

Head-on positioning A marketing strategy in which one product is presented as an equal or better alternative than a competing product.

Head-on positioning involves a comparison of one brand with another. Typically, the brand doing the advertising presents itself as being better than another brand. The message focuses on an attribute that is important to the target market. To dramatize the claim of superiority or whatever the claim may be, it is common to demonstrate how both brands perform. For example, we often see popular brands of household products use head-on positioning strategies. One brand of detergent compares its cleaning benefits to a competitor in a pre-laundry "dirty clothes" to post-laundry "clean clothes" experiment.

Perhaps the most famous illustration of this strategy is the "Pepsi Challenge." In television commercials, non-believers were challenged in a taste test. Once they experienced the taste of Pepsi-Cola, their conclusion was rather obvious. Another execution actually shows a Coca-Cola deliveryman enjoying the taste of an ice-cold Pepsi.

Pepsi World
www.pepsi.com

Innovation Positioning

Innovation positioning A marketing strategy that stresses newness (based on a commitment to research and development) as a means of differentiating a company or a brand from competing companies and brands.

An innovation is a product, service, or idea that is perceived by consumers as new. **Innovation positioning** is a marketing strategy that stresses that newness as a way to differentiate its brand from the competition. Adding oat bran to a breakfast cereal is considered a *continuous innovation* since it only constitutes a small change in the nature of the product. A *discontinuous innovation* is something that has an impact on society and the way we do things. The iPod, for example, altered the way we listen to music. A company that employs innovative strategy uses continuous innovation to stay one step ahead of the competition. Periodically, it will also discover and launch that breakthrough product that will separate it from competitors. Innovation is a mindset of the company!

3M is a company that invests heavily in research and development to constantly improve its products and bring new products to market. Its range of products is diverse, including anything from unique consumer products, such as Post-It Notes and Scotch tape, to highly technical electronic equipment used in hospitals and industry. From a branding perspective, the 3M brand stands for trust, leadership, and quality. To the customer, it is a guarantee of quality and reliability. 3M is proud of its innovations and promotes that message loud and clear to all of its publics. Phrases such as "Innovative and practical solutions" and "Leading through innovation" tie all its communications together into an integrated package.[17]

3M
www.3m.com

Price (Value) Positioning

Price positioning A marketing strategy based on the premise that consumers search for the best possible value given their economic circumstances.

A **price positioning** strategy is based on the premise that consumers search for the best possible value given their economic circumstances. Some consumers search for low prices, others are willing to pay more for something perceived as offering good value, and still others don't even look at price. Some people shop for high-end goods and services and expect to pay a lot for the products they buy.

Wal-Mart seems to have a lock on the low price positioning strategy in the North American retail marketplace. So firmly entrenched is its image in the minds of consumers, based on persistent messages that show prices being slashed on store signs, that consumers automatically think Wal-Mart offers the best value. Their slogan "We sell for less. Everyday." reinforces that message.

Harry Rosen
www.harryrosen.com

Another retailing example shows how high price positioning is also an effective strategy. In terms of men's fashion, Harry Rosen comes to mind. Harry Rosen has survived all kinds of economic and fashion trends over the years and has remained at the high end of the market. The Harry Rosen image has been carefully cultivated over time so that customers know exactly what to expect when they shop there—a quality suit that can cost anywhere from $1500 to $10 500.

Harry Rosen keeps its edge on the competition by carrying many exclusive products and by moving to customer relationship marketing and pitching wares directly to individual customers in mailings and through special events. According to retail consultant John Williams, Harry Rosen is "unique in North America and maybe the world. There's no other chain of high-quality menswear of any significance." Put a bit differently, Larry Rosen (president and son of the founder) states, "A man looks powerful, authoritative, confident and professional in a suit. To get the right suit that man knows where to shop—Harry Rosen."[18] See the illustration in Figure 3.12.

FIGURE **3.12**   **A High-Price, High-Quality Positioning Strategy Works for Harry Rosen**

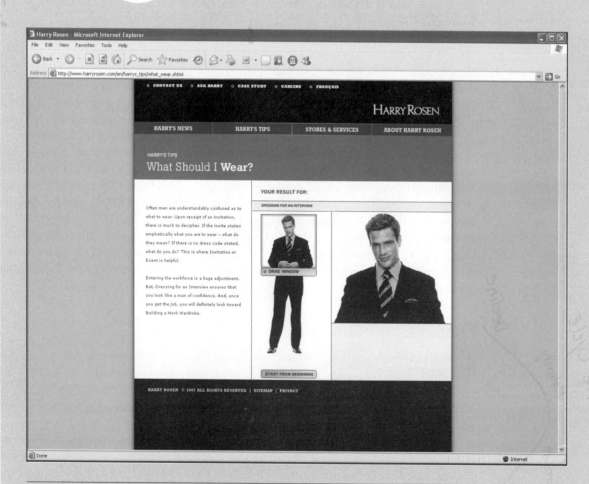

Source: Reprinted by permission of Harry Rosen.

Channel Positioning

Channel positioning
A marketing strategy based on an organization's position in its distribution channel and its market coverage.

Dell Canada
www.dell.ca

Some companies gain competitive advantage based on their **channel positioning** and their degree of market coverage. To demonstrate, consider the enviable position Dell Computer finds itself in. From nowhere, Dell conquered such corporations as IBM, Compaq, and Apple based solely on its methods of selling and delivering computers to customers. Dell was the first (an innovator) to sell computers directly to customers—by telephone initially, and then by the Internet with no retail outlets. The entire business was built on a non-conventional strategy for the industry.

Awareness of such a selling strategy was the responsibility of an extensive marketing communications program that embraced all of the mass media. Consumers were convinced that buying computers directly would save them money. Dell made the promise and then delivered the goods. The rest is history. Dell is now the leading personal computer company in North America.

In the soft drink business, consumers can purchase Coca-Cola and Pepsi-Cola in virtually any supermarket in North America. These brand leaders have significant leverage among distributors based largely on their brand equity. Being readily available certainly enhances the prospects of purchase. Distribution is an important factor, because it must be tied closely to the timing of marketing communications execution.

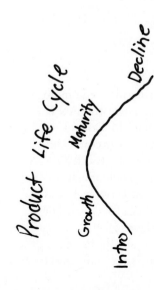

Lifestyle (Image) Positioning

Lifestyle (image) positioning
A marketing strategy based on intangible characteristics associated with a lifestyle instead of tangible characteristics.

Coors Light
www.coorslight.com

In very competitive markets where product attributes of so many brands are perceived to be equal by consumers, it is difficult to follow the positioning strategies outlined above. **Lifestyle** or **image positioning** involves moving away from the tangible characteristics of the product toward the intangible characteristics (things that aren't there, for example).

A lifestyle positioning strategy has moved the market share of Coors Light in Canada from 5.5 percent to 8.8 percent in a very short period of time. Coors Light (or the Silver Bullet) was showing its age; a favourite of older guys looking to lose their paunch. The brand was destined for "Dad's beer" status. A revitalized advertising campaign, however, showed the brand as younger. Television ads showed young guys drinking the brand and having fun in a variety of social situations with some very attractive women not far away. Coors Light's association with a younger target and lifestyle rejuvenated the brand.[19]

The use of psychographic information allows companies to develop campaigns based on the lifestyle or desired lifestyle of the target market. Generally speaking, lifestyle positioning involves using emotional appeal techniques such as love, fear, adventure, sex, and humour to influence the target. The image must be communicated through every media vehicle and brand contact, including logos and special events. The automobile industry effectively uses lifestyle imagery to sell cars. It is common to see the rugged outdoors associated with SUVs and young urban professionals driving a luxury car. Volvo accomplishes both of these situations in the ad that appears in Figure 3.13.

Planning and Implementing Marketing and Marketing Communications Programs

To build brand loyalty and brand equity requires effective marketing programs: activities that produce a strong and favourable association to a brand in a consumer's memory. It is an information transfer process that considers two essential factors. First, decisions must be made about how to employ various brand elements. These decisions involve brand names, trademarks, and characters. Second, appropriate marketing strategies must be developed to communicate the brand values and brand positioning strategy.

The most common brand elements are brand names, logos, symbols, characters, packaging, and slogans. The content of most advertising in any medium, from television to

FIGURE **3.13**   **Lifestyle Imagery Positions Competing Brands in the Customer's Mind**

Source: Courtesy of Volvo Cars of Canada Corp.

print to websites, usually includes these elements. Characters sometimes become more famous than the brand itself. Some very popular brand characters include the A&W Great Root Bear, the Pillsbury Doughboy, Tony the Tiger, and Ronald McDonald, to name only a few. Slogans are commonly used in advertising to summarize the core value of the brand. Phrases such as "Because I'm worth it" (L'Oréal), "Eat fresh" (SUBWAY restaurants), and "Impossible is nothing" (Adidas) have an impact on people. Such slogans state the main benefit of the product or brand, imply a distinction between it and other firms' products, and allow a brand to adopt a distinct personality of its own. For more insight into the role that advertising slogans perform, refer to Figure 3.14.

Based on the numerous examples already cited in this chapter, it should be abundantly clear that marketing communications is the "voice" of a brand's (or company's)

FIGURE **3.14**   **Some Famous Advertising Slogans**

Slogans are an effective means of drawing attention to a product. Typically, they make claims about a product or offer a significant benefit to the consumer. A good slogan reflects the positioning strategy of the brand and helps develop the personality of the brand. A good slogan is a memorable slogan.

Here are some famous slogans from the past:

From Canada

"At Speedy, you're a somebody"	Speedy Muffler
"Harvey's makes a hamburger a beautiful thing"	Harvey's
"Coffee Crisp makes a nice, light snack"	Nestlé Coffee Crisp
"It's mainly because of the meat"	Dominion Stores

From the United States

"You're in good hands"	Allstate Insurance
"Just do it"	Nike
"The king of beers"	Budweiser
"M'm, M'm good"	Campbell's Soup
"Kills bugs dead"	Raid
"The breakfast of champions"	Wheaties

positioning strategy. Regardless of the medium selected, that voice must deliver a message with clarity and continuity. If the communications strategies are executed effectively and with sufficient financial support, the desired message and image should be planted in the customer's mind.

To illustrate, consider the stark contrast with which Apple computers and accessories are presented to potential customers. Personal computers are technical in nature, and while competitors dwell on all kinds of technical jargon in their communications, Apple talks about why its computers are fun to use. Apple doesn't want to be seen as just another computer company. It wants to be perceived as a different kind of computer company. The same can be said of the communications that launched the iPod music player. The urban lifestyle and imagery that was attached to the brand caught on quickly with the primary target—young, urban males.

In terms of how the various elements of the marketing communications mix are employed, advertising should be viewed as an aerial attack on the audience it reaches. It is the most visible form of communications—a form of communications that creates awareness and interest in a brand. Advertising gets people talking about a brand. It creates hype. The other forms of marketing communications play more specific roles and should be viewed as the ground attack. Communications in the form of sales promotions, street-level and buzz marketing, and event marketing, for example, help create desire and action. They provide the stimulus that gets the wallet out of the pocket or purse. The Internet has become a useful vehicle for providing detailed information. Therefore, with all points of contact delivering the same message, a brand begins to build momentum—the brand-building process has begun.

For more insight into brand-building strategies, read the IMC Highlight **Fame and Fortune Do Not Come by Chance**.

Apple Computer
www.apple.com

FAME AND FORTUNE DO NOT COME BY CHANCE

Every day people are bombarded with brands pursuing their cash. Only a select few brands rise above the rest, their names instantly recognizable, desirable, and durable. They are the "superbrands." Some of the names in this category include Ferrari, Gucci, Nike, and Coca-Cola.

Brands like these teach marketers valuable lessons. Fame and, especially, fortune do not come by chance. Brand experts from the advertising, manufacturing, and retail communities point to a complex strategy of identity, creativity, quality, investment, and, above all, a magical relationship with the customer as the keys to success.

The first thing a brand needs is desirability. People have to really want to associate themselves with it. The emotional appeal might be the exclusivity of a Rolex watch or the sense of belonging that comes with owning a Harley-Davidson motorcycle. In a retailing environment, great brands go well beyond the concept of brand identity, with advertising, shop layouts, and products blending together into a personality.

Nike, one of the world's most readily identifiable brands, has a mission: "To bring inspiration and innovation to every athlete in the world." So successful is Nike that the "swoosh" logo has become a synonym for sporting success rather than just a shoe label.

Once a brand has captured the imagination of the public, its identity needs to be nurtured and protected, and targeted at specific customers frequently. Automobile brands such as BMW and Volkswagen have attracted car buyers with new versions of the famous MINI and the Beetle, very popular brands in their own right that sell because of their name and funky modern-looking designs.

But for all of the hefty investment in marketing, a brand's eventual success relies on the most fickle and least controllable element—the customer. "The strength of your brand comes from the customer. You have to respect and feed what the customer expects from you, maintain your identity and authenticity," says Franco Cologni, head of the watch division at Swiss luxury group Richemont.

Earning customer loyalty and proving a brand's real worth is going to be more important than ever before. Trademarks and brands, if they are authentic and truly connect the buyer to the brand, will be perceived as more of a "trustmark" than a trademark. Successful brands consistently prove their value and authenticity to consumers.

Adapted from Jane Barrett, "Careful nurturing drives superbrands," *Financial Post*, November 15, 2002, p. DO13.

PACKAGING AND BRAND BUILDING

The package is what consumers look for when they are contemplating a purchase. For new products especially, the look of the package must be instilled in the customer's mind. For that reason, it is very common for the package to play a key role in introductory marketing communications programs. Over time, consumers start associating specific colours with a brand, and they know exactly what they are looking for when trying to spot a brand on a cluttered store shelf. Coca-Cola, for example, is strongly associated with the colour red, while arch-rival Pepsi-Cola is strongly associated with blue.

In today's competitive environment, packaging is playing a more significant role in differentiating one brand from another. Over the life cycle of a product, it may change several times to spruce up the image of a brand. As well, a common package design across all product lines that make up a brand (e.g., various sizes, shapes, and formats) helps maintain brand identity. Old Spice deodorant, for example, is available in spray, powder, and roll-on formats in several different packages. From one container to the other, the design of the package has a common look and colour scheme (red). See Figure 3.15 for an illustration.

A revolution is occurring in packaged-goods marketing, as marketers see packages having a growing influence on purchase decisions amid ongoing media fragmentation. Changes in media and consumer lifestyles are now forcing a dramatic shift, making the package itself an increasingly important selling medium. Church & Dwight discovered

FIGURE **3.15**   Consistent Brand Identification across All Product Lines Is Important

Source: Paul Reynolds Photography.

this when it started marketing condoms directly to women. Two years of extensive research conceived Elexa, a line of "sexual well-being products" designed for females. The brand name Elexa Natural Feel Condoms is intended to overcome female perceptions that condoms are a barrier to intimacy. Since women tend to be uncomfortable looking for condoms in the condom aisle, Church & Dwight convinced retailers to display Elexa in the feminine care aisle, where it is shelved in cosmetic-inspired packaging that is very different from other condom packages. Advertising touts Elexa as a brand that revolutionizes the way women approach sex.[20].

The package is a very important touch-point with consumers. Familiarity with a package helps build trust between the consumer and the brand, so ultimately, the package is a factor that can influence consumer loyalty. A good package serves three functions: it protects the product, it markets the product, and it offers convenience to consumers.

Protecting the Product

How much protection a product needs depends on how often it changes hands in the distribution process. For example, how long does it sit in a warehouse, how will it be transported, what kind of handling will it experience, and how much protection from exposure to heat, cold, light, and moisture will it need? Milk, for example, is traditionally packaged

FIGURE **3.16**   **New Packaging Helps Alter the Image of Milk**

Source: Courtesy of Dick Hemingway.

in bags and cartons, but the recent introduction of plastic containers in single serving sizes (yes, milk is being positioned as a "refreshing" beverage) has increased the shelf life of milk. See Figure 3.16 for an illustration. Potato chips are packed in oversized bags to protect the chips while being transported or handled.

Marketing the Product

In its marketing role, the package does the same thing an advertisement in any medium would do. The design and colour scheme should be coordinated so that the overall look of the package creates a good impression. The package should be attractive and eye catching to grab the attention of consumers. It should contain useful information and tell consumers what the product's benefits are so they will have a reason to buy it. Red Zone body spray, body wash, and deodorant collectively promise a male he will smell great for long periods of time. That promise appears on the package and in advertisements that feature the package. See the illustration in Figure 3.17.

A change in package design often breathes new life into an existing brand. Making changes to colours, graphics, or configuration can dramatically alter a consumer's perception of the same product. To illustrate, consider the case of Nabisco Bits & Bites Snack Mix (marketed by Kraft Foods in Canada). The product was packaged in a

Kraft Canada
www.kraftcanada.com

FIGURE **3.17**   **A Combination of Packaging and Advertising Effectively Communicates the Benefit of Using Red Zone**

Source: Courtesy of P&G Canada.

cracker-style box, and sales had stagnated. Insight obtained through marketing research revealed that the package undermined the social image of a snack. Nabisco needed a package that would be as convenient as a potato chip bag. The solution was a standup foil pouch with a resealable opening. Over a four-year period, sales of Bits & Bites tripled and the resealable standup pouch package would become the standard for many other products in the snack food market.[21]

Packages can also be used to communicate information about promotional offers such as coupons, contests, and giveaways. Since promotions of this nature are temporary, a package "flash" is usually added to the front panel of the package to draw attention to the offer. Details of the offer would appear on the side, back, or inside the package (see Figure 3.18).

Source: Courtesy of Wanda Goodwin.

Beyond transferring essential information about a brand, marketers must be aware of legal and regulatory requirements associated with packaging. The universal product code (UPC) symbol (a series of black lines that identify each item of a product line) is mandatory on all packaged goods. Other mandatory information includes the volume or weight designation and the company name and address. On pre-packaged food products, nutritional information is now mandatory. Where appropriate and with substantiation from marketing research and approval from the appropriate government authority, a company can now make specific health claims about brands on the packages.

Providing Convenience

A package should be easy to carry, open, handle, and reseal (if appropriate). Liquid detergents, for example, should be easy to pour without spills (on some brands the plastic lid is the measuring device for dispensing the product). No-drip spouts on products such as mustard and ketchup also offer convenience. If a product is heavy or bulky, handles should be built into the package design. Other examples of convenience include resealable plastic lids on margarine containers, twist-off caps on beer, wine, and soft drinks, straws on fruit juice containers, and canned goods with moulded metal bottoms that allow for stacking on store shelves.

BRANDING BY DESIGN

Not all kinds of product are sold in a package. What attributes sell an appliance, an automobile, a computer, the services offered by a bank, and so on? For durable goods like cars and computers, the key influencer in the buying decision could be the design—the look and style of the product and the image it projects about itself. Consumers want products that fit in with their lifestyle or the decor of their home furnishings. For products like mutual funds, trusts, and other financial offerings—products that are truly intangible—consumers are primarily influenced by the brand image as perpetuated by effective marketing communications programs.

In the durable goods market, designers have traditionally followed one basic premise: form follows function. This is a good premise because consumers want durable goods to perform specific functions dependably and reliably. Shopping for a stove or a dishwasher involves comparing the interior and exterior features of various brands. Since all brands offered the same benefits, the decision was based largely on the brand name and the perceptions the consumer held about the brand name. At some point, manufacturers started offering kitchen appliances in a variety of colours; design elements became very important in the buying decision. Today, kitchen appliances are electronic in nature and have a very modern appearance.

The onslaught of new technologies has brought design standards to new heights. The goal for design is to make technology less hostile, less intrusive, and more friendly.[22] This new way of thinking is reflected in the design of many new automobiles. The PT Cruiser wasn't loved immediately by all. A kind of "love it" or "hate it" relationship formed among consumers. Of course, designers look for more love than hate when designing automobiles. The Chrysler 300 sedan has been another design success; its sleek lines and bold grille made it an instant hit with young and middle-aged men (see Figure 3.19). For specific insight into the importance of design, see the IMC Highlight **Brand by Design: The Chrysler 300 Sedan Is a Winner.**

FIGURE **3.19** **The Design Characteristics of the Chrysler 300 Appeals to Several Target Markets**

Source: Courtesy of Dick Hemingway.

BRAND BY DESIGN: THE CHRYSLER 300 SEDAN IS A WINNER

People have a fascination with automobiles unlike any other product. Let's face it, what gets a middle-aged man more excited than a car? (Don't answer that!) Needless to say, men, much more so than women, are drawn to an automobile based on its look and style.

The Chrysler 300 sedan, a design created by Ralph Gilles, a hot new Canadian designer, was launched in 2004. Gilles's mission when undertaking the project was to "bring the romance back to the auto industry." And he succeeded! The 300 model has been an overwhelming success for Chrysler. Gilles himself has benefited from the 300's success. He has appeared in a *GQ* magazine photo spread and graced the cover of *Black Enterprise*. Gilles gets "turned on" by taking the ordinary and making it extraordinary. While most cars take three years to get from design pad to production, Gilles's design team took six years working on the 300 model. Spending so much time on one project clearly suggests the importance of design in the branding equation.

The Chrysler 300 is commonly referred to as the "baby Bentley." Its aggressive and powerful stance, classic lines, and bold grille appealed immediately to the hip-hop crowd and middle-aged males. It's amazing how different people can react to an automobile design!

The grille itself suggests a big, hungry engine behind it. It's a car with lots of power for the highway, but with elegance fit for the city. The grille design plays a key role in communicating things about a car. Some observers refer to the grille as the mouth of the car, while others see it as the family crest of the brand. Its shape and detail could be part of a message of defiance and aggression, tradition and totem.

The fact that the Chrysler 300's innovative design was able to attract so many different kinds of buyers is a real bonus in a market that is highly fragmented. Not only is it generating significant sales, it is bringing in new customers to dealerships to look at other Chrysler models. Named *Motor Trend* magazine's Car of the Year in 2004, the 300 has literally revitalized a brand that had become very tired.

When Gilles approaches a design project his goal is to bring tension to the design, create trends rather than follow them, craft with confidence, and rely on timeless styling. He says, "A car can be an appliance or an escape. That's the underlying mission of a designer—to get the romance back."

Adapted from Mira Oberman, "Chrysler designer wants to romance the automobile," *National Post*, August 19, 2005, p. DO11, and Phil Patton, "Automakers put their best face forward," *National Post*, January 18, 2004, pp. FP1, FP6.

Chris Bangle, chief designer for BMW, takes an aesthetic viewpoint to the BMWs he designs. He considers consumer preferences that involve how people use cars and how they feel about them. He also considers opposing views of men and women. Women will say they need room for their purses in a car, and while men won't say they need room for a briefcase, they will demand that space just the same. As a designer, you try to accommodate both.

Oliver Boulay, head of design for Mitsubishi Motors, offers another perspective for pooling customer preferences into automobile designs: "Think of the customer as a family, with a forceful father, a stylish mother, a son influenced by technology, and a daughter influenced by fashion."[23]

Technology has also influenced the television industry. Sexy-looking, flat plasma screen televisions have replaced the black boxes of yesterday. The television remains the focal point of the family room, but in a very different manner. Mounted on a display stand or right on the wall, the new televisions offer a feeling of contemporary stylishness that is very attractive to consumers who now spend more money and time on home entertainment. See the illustration in Figure 3.20.

On the services side of things, consider the problem that the Bank of Montreal was facing. The bank had dropped significantly in ranking despite major expansion into wealth-management products. People were not aware that they could get anything from mutual funds to complex financial planning assistance from the bank. It embarked upon

BMO
www.bmo.com

FIGURE **3.20** **The Impact of Technology on Design Plays a Key Role in Building a Brand Image**

imagine a TV that fills the room with drama.

Imagine cinematic sound, DNIe™ picture enhancement and 3,000:1 dynamic contrast ratio. A television whose design and picture are equally arresting. With the Samsung 40" LCD TV, it's not that hard to imagine. To learn more, visit www.samsung.ca

SAMSUNG

Source: Courtesy of Samsung Electronics Canada.

a rebranding program that had to communicate the perception that what they were offering was above banking and better than banking.

FutureBrand, a company specializing in developing brand strategies, worked on the Bank of Montreal's branding program. "The critical element of any rebranding is to understand what the current narrative about the brand is, as well as the business strategy to date. Then you clarify what's going to change and distill it into a narrative explaining why the changes are a good thing."[24]

Distilling a complex rebranding into an instantly recognizable message is crucial. The result was a new persona for the bank, which is now known as BMO. The new BMO positioned all of the bank's product lines under one consistent brand. The new identity system introduced the name "BMO Financial Group," but linked it back to the Bank of Montreal. The bank's new identity appears in Figure 3.21. An extensive marketing communications program was implemented to communicate the new name to the Canadian public. All touch-points with consumers—from stationery to ATMs to websites to bank signage—carry the BMO name. Such a change represents a huge internal and external undertaking.

FIGURE **3.21** BMO Bank of Montreal Logo

Source: Courtesy of BMO.

Summary

Developing a sound brand strategy and positioning strategy is the first step in the brand-building process. Having the right strategy is important since consumers form their impressions about a brand based on what they hear and see about it. Therefore, marketing organizations use branding as a means of identifying products and building an image.

Branding offers several benefits for consumers. It suggests a consistent degree of quality, provides psychological rewards (e.g., a better self-image) for possessing certain brands, and it distinguishes competing brands from one another. Good brands are personal and they often become integral parts of people's lives. For manufacturers, the brand name communicates a point of difference, allows for the creation of an image, and helps build brand loyalty. Over time consumers come to trust what a brand stands for and express their satisfaction in varying degrees of brand loyalty. Loyalty is expressed in terms of brand recognition, brand preference, and brand insistence.

The brand-building process involves four essential steps: identifying brand values and positioning strategy, planning and implementing a brand marketing program, measuring and interpreting brand performance, and growing and sustaining brand equity. Brand values are the primary attributes (descriptive features) and benefits (the values consumers attach to a brand). Positioning refers to the image a marketer wants the brand to have in the customers' minds. A positioning strategy is based on an important element of the marketing mix. Some of the common positioning strategies include product differentiation, brand leadership, head-on (comparative), innovation, price and value, channel efficiency, and lifestyle.

When implementing a brand strategy, all elements of the marketing mix and the marketing communications mix come into play. The marketing communications mix is the voice of a brand's positioning strategy. A good strategy that is executed efficiently should instill the desired image about a brand in the customer's mind. In this regard, all elements of the communications mix work together to deliver a consistent message.

Packaging and product design play key roles in differentiating brands and help determine consumer perceptions. A good package design will protect the product, market the product, and provide consumers convenience in handling and using the product. Package designs should be unique and attractive to grab the attention of consumers as they pass by. Expensive durable goods rely on the design of the product to create images in the consumer's mind. The design must be functional yet attractive to the eye. Style and appearance are important influences on buying decisions for cars, appliances, computers, and other consumer electronic goods. Goods such as these are often an expression of one's self-image.

Key Terms

attribute, 76

benefit, 76

brand, 69

brand equity, 75

brand insistence, 74

brand loyalty, 74

brand manager, 76

brand name, 69

brand preference, 74

brand recognition, 74

brandmark, 70

channel positioning, 85

core values, 76

head-on positioning, 83

image positioning, 85

innovation positioning, 83

leadership positioning, 82

lifestyle positioning, 85

logo, 70

positioning, 78

price positioning, 83

product differentiation strategy, 81

trademark, 70

unique selling point (USP), 73

wordmark, 69

Review Questions

1. Identify and briefly explain the key components of a brand.

2. Identify two benefits of branding for consumers and two benefits of branding for organizations.

3. Identify and briefly explain the three stages of brand loyalty.

4. What is brand equity and how does a brand build it?

5. "A brand is a set of core values." What does this statement mean?

6. Define what positioning is and state the importance of having a clearly worded positioning strategy statement.

7. What is the difference between head-on positioning and brand leadership positioning? Provide an example of each not mentioned in the chapter.

8. If a brand is using a product differentiation positioning strategy, what will the advertising message focus on? Provide an example of this strategy not mentioned in the chapter.

9. If a brand is using a lifestyle positioning strategy, what will the advertising message focus on? Provide two examples of this strategy not mentioned in the chapter.

10. What essential roles does a package perform in the marketing of a brand? Briefly explain.

11. Explain the role and influence that the design of a product can have on prospective buyers.

Discussion and Application Questions

1. "A brand is more than the physical product." Explain.

2. "Selecting the name for a new product is a critical decision." What are the essential issues in naming a brand? Conduct some online secondary research to get to the bottom of this issue.

3. Select a lifestyle advertising campaign that you think is particularly effective. Write a brief report or make a brief presentation on why you think it is effective.

4. Explain the relationship between brand positioning and the development of an effective marketing communications strategy.

5. Evaluate the marketing situation for one of the following companies or brands. What makes this company (brand) unique and what is its differential advantage(s) compared to the primary competitors? Based on what you know of this company (brand) and what you see or hear in terms of marketing communications, develop a positioning strategy statement for the company (brand).

a) Apple
b) Wal-Mart
c) La Senza
d) Listerine
e) Gatorade

6. Using a company or brand of your choosing, examine the relationship between its name, logo, and advertising slogan (e.g., "GE brings good things to life"). Are these brand and communications elements permanently entwined or can any of the elements be changed to build the brand's image? What are the benefits and risks associated with any kind of change?

7. Assess the role that package design plays in building a brand's image. To justify your position, provide an example of a package design that you perceive to be good and a design that you perceive to be less than good. What is the relationship between the package design and other forms of marketing communications?

Endnotes

1 Jo Marney, "Bringing customers back for more," *Marketing*, September 10, 2001, p. 33.

2 *Dictionary of Marketing Terms*, Barron's Educational Series, Inc., 1994.

3 Lander, "A dictionary of branding terms," **www.landor.com/index.cfm?fuseaction= cBranding.getLexicon** (accessed November 2003).

4 Kevin Keller, *Strategic Brand Management* (Upper Saddle River, NY: Pearson Education, 2003), p. 106.

5 "A Proud History of Making Mazdas," *InterSections*, Welcome Edition, 2004, p. 4.

6 David Dunne and Julia Moulden, "Personal branding: Applying the lessons of successful brands to yourself," *Globe and Mail*, October 21, 2003, p. B9.

7 Timothy Woolstencroft, "The best hands-on brands," *Marketing*, June 13, 2005, p. 17.

8 Allan P. Adamson, "What's your brand's job?" *Advertising Age*, September 16, 2002, p. 18.

9 Marina Strauss, "Consumers less trusting of brands," *Globe and Mail*, February 13, 2003, p. B3.

10 "Buyers show little brand loyalty," *Globe and Mail*, June 9, 2005, p. G22.

11 Dale Beckman, David Kurtz, and Louis Boone, *Foundations of Marketing* (Toronto: Holt Rinehart and Winston, 1988), pp. 316–317.

12 "A thank you for the shopper," *National Post*, October 7, 2005, p. JV1.

13 Lander, "A dictionary of branding terms," **www.landor.com/index.cfm?fuseaction=Branding. getLexicon** (accessed November 2003).

14 "Coca-Cola still world's top brand," BBC News, July 22, 2005, **www.newsvote.bbc.uk.**

15 Mark Evans, "Apple's iPod is the Kleenex of MP3 players," *Financial Post*, July 15, 2005, p. FP7.

16 Dana Flavelle, "Harvey's busks lean trend with Big Harv," *Toronto Star*, September 18, 2003, p. C2.

17 3M Worldwide, **www.3M.com** (accessed November 2003).

18 Virginia Galt, "Return of the suit seen in 'dress to impress' times," *Globe and Mail*, September 6, 2002, p. B5.

19 Paul Brent, "Repositioning of brand pays off for Coors," *Financial Post*, August 16, 2004, p. FP4.

20 Lisa D'Innocenzo, "Design matters," *Strategy*, October 2005, p. 28.

21 Carey Toane, "Success is in the bag," *Marketing*, October 9, 2000, p. 25.

22 "Connecting with design," *Globe and Mail*, October 18, 2002, p. B13.

23 Paul Ferris, "All the right designs," *Marketing*, April 26, 2004, p. 4.

24 Terry Poulton," Communicating the new you," *Strategy*, October 7, 2002, p. 23.

Part 2

Planning for Integrated Media

Part 2 examines the steps, considerations, and procedures for developing message strategies and media strategies in the traditional media: television, radio, newspaper, magazines, various forms of out-of-home advertising, and direct response media. Message and media strategies for interactive media are also presented.

In Chapter 4, the basic elements of the communications process are introduced along with the various stages of creative (message) planning. Because creative plans are based on clearly defined objectives, strategies, and executions, the chapter draws clear distinctions among these three planning concepts. It finishes with a discussion of various creative appeal techniques and execution techniques that are employed by advertisers to present compelling messages to customers.

Chapter 5 describes the media planning side of advertising. Media planning involves identifying media objectives, creating media strategies, and executing those plans. The development of a sound media strategy is crucial, so considerable time is devoted to discussing primary issues that influence the strategy. Strategic decisions are largely influenced by the budget available and the strengths and weaknesses of each medium in the context of the problem the advertiser is attempting to resolve.

Chapter 6 examines the growing field of direct response communications. Direct response plans rely on database management techniques, and the chapter devotes considerable time to how organizations use information sources. Various direct response media options are introduced and the strengths and weaknesses of each option are examined.

In Chapter 7, the focus is on digital communications. The various strategies for delivering effective online messages are discussed and perspectives are offered regarding how to effectively integrate online messages with offline messages and related communications strategies. The emerging area of mobile communications is also examined in this chapter.

ADVERTISING PLANNING: CREATIVE

After studying this chapter you will be able to

1. identify the basic elements of the communications process

2. explain the various stages of creative planning

3. explain the role of a creative brief and describe the content of such a document

4. distinguish between creative objectives, creative strategies, and creative execution

5. describe the role of creative objective statements

6. appreciate the variety of appeal techniques for developing creative strategies

7. identify various execution techniques for best presenting creative strategies

From the previous chapter you have learned about the strategic planning process and seen how various elements of the marketing and marketing communications mix converge in a master plan of some kind. The role and nature of the individual plans—the plans for advertising, direct response, Internet, sales promotion, public relations, events and sponsorships, and personal selling—are the focus of the remainder of the book. Separate external organizations may be responsible for developing these plans. Therefore, in the planning and development stages there is much communication between a company and its external suppliers.

This chapter will focus specifically on one aspect of advertising: the development and implementation of the message. The initial section discusses some fundamental communications concepts that are common to all of the components of the marketing communications mix. It is followed by a discussion of the creative planning process. Creative planning relies upon essential input from the marketing plan and involves the development of a separate plan that outlines the creative objectives, creative strategies, and creative execution (tactics).

COMMUNICATIONS ESSENTIALS

The marketplace is dynamic and consumers are exposed to hundreds of messages each day from all kinds of sources. What do consumers recognize and recall at the end of the day? Can they say with certainty they saw a television commercial for Coca-Cola and recall that people looked like they were being poured from a bottle into a glass in the middle of a cobblestone square? Do they remember that Ford automobiles are "Built for life in Canada"? Do they recall the brand of cough syrup that says of itself, "It tastes awful but it works"? The answer is not likely. In very simple terms, there is so much commercial clutter out there that consumers remember very little. The challenge, therefore, is to develop a message in any form (broadcast or print) that will break through the clutter and leave a lasting impression on the audience. Easier said than done!

An understanding of the communications process and how consumers receive and interpret messages is essential. In Chapter 1, various consumer behaviour concepts were introduced—concepts such as needs and motives, attitudes and perceptions, reference groups and family influences. Knowledge and application of these concepts influence the nature and content of a commercial message and the degree to which it is accepted and retained by consumers.

Communication
The transmission, receipt, and processing of information between a sender and a receiver.

Encoding
The transformation of a message into a meaningful format, such as an advertisement, a mailing piece, or an article in a newspaper.

Transmission
The sending of a message through a medium such as television, radio, newspapers, magazines, outdoor advertising, Internet, and so on, or through personal selling.

Communication is defined as transmitting, receiving, and processing information. Communication occurs when the message that was sent reaches its destination in a form that is understood by the intended audience. Commercial communications do not have to be a complex science. Simply stated, an organization develops a message, selects the right media to deliver it, and, if all things are planned effectively, it will reach the consumers and have an impact on them. Developing the message is referred to as **encoding**; that is, the message is transformed into some attention-getting form, such as a print advertisement, a direct response mailing piece, an article about the product in a newspaper, and so on. The message is then **transmitted**, usually by the media (television, radio, newspapers, magazines, outdoor advertising, Internet, and so on) or through personal selling. Refer to Figure 4.1 for an illustration.

In the delivery of the message, however, certain complications arise along the way. For example,

- the message was not in line with customer attitudes,
- the message did not reach the intended target with the desired frequency,
- the message delivered by the competition was more convincing,
- the competition spent more on advertising and had higher share of mind, or
- new competitors entered the market and invested heavily in advertising.

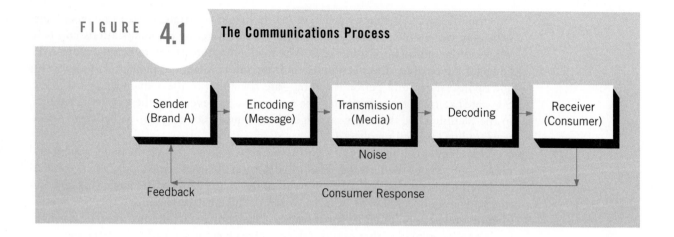

FIGURE **4.1**   **The Communications Process**

Sender (Brand A) → Encoding (Message) → Transmission (Media) → Decoding → Receiver (Consumer)

Noise

Feedback   Consumer Response

Noise

Any potential form of disruption in the transmission of a message that could distort the impact of the message; competitive advertising or the clutter of advertising messages in a medium are forms of noise.

Circumstances such as these are referred to as **noise** and dilute the impact of an advertiser's message. Whether or not a message breaks through the clutter is usually determined by the relationships between three separate factors: the quality of planning when developing message strategy, the execution of the plan being on target with the right timing and frequency, and the impact of competitive messages. The advertiser has control over the first two factors, but no control over the third.

Competing products are sending very similar messages to the same target market, creating noise. The objective, therefore, is to break through the noise. To do so, the message must be relevant to the consumer. For instance, the product's benefits must satisfy a need or suit the lifestyle of the target and be presented in such a manner that the brand becomes a preferred alternative.

Dove
www.dove.com

If the message does not break through (if it is perceived as dull, uses the wrong types of appeals, or is simply confusing to the target), then no action will occur. Lack of action indicates a need to revisit the creative strategy and execution and make changes where necessary. For example, many soap and skin care brands make similar claims and usually include good-looking females in their ads. Dove, in an effort to standout, launched a "real beauty" campaign that encouraged women to celebrate themselves as they are. It was a bold and compelling message that regular women of all ages and sizes identified with—it broke through the clutter. The love-your-beauty attitude expressed by Dove lead to the launch of several new Dove skin care products.[1]

A consumer passes through a series of stages on the way to taking action. Advertising can influence the consumer at each stage. One such model is referred to as ACCA— awareness, comprehension, conviction, and action. This model is part of a theory called DAGMAR, which stands for Defining Advertising Goals for Measured Advertising Response. An advertising goal is a specific communication task to be accomplished among a defined audience in a given period. The task should be measurable, with benchmarks in existence to assess achievements.

The effectiveness of an advertising campaign is usually linked back to this model. For example, an advertiser wants to know (in percentage terms) the level of awareness of its product among the target market, and whether or not it is perceived as being a preferred brand. Furthermore, the advertiser may want to know what percentage of the target market has tried the product (in the case of a new product campaign). Post-campaign marketing research studies measure the achievement of the objectives.

An advertisement (or campaign) that achieves good scores with respect to awareness, comprehension, and conviction is likely to succeed. The desired action in the form of someone buying the product will likely occur. To protect its investment in advertising, an organization may also conduct marketing research while the message strategy is in the development stage. The message is tested for likeability, persuasiveness, and likelihood of purchase. Research measures that exceed the norms of other products in the category would suggest the advertiser is on to something. The various marketing research techniques used to evaluate advertising effectiveness are discussed in Chapter 12. The following is a description of each behaviour stage:

- **Awareness:** In this stage, the customer learns something for the first time. In an advertising context, a message tries to plant the brand name and the primary benefit offered in the customer's mind. Awareness can be measured by aided and unaided recall tests.

- **Comprehension:** At this stage, the consumer is expressing interest. The message is perceived as relevant. The brand is evaluated on the basis of need satisfaction. It is in the consumer's cognitive realm, and becomes a candidate for potential purchase. A like or dislike for a brand can be measured using attitude scales.

- **Conviction:** At this stage, the consumer expresses stronger feelings toward the brand based on the perceived benefits it offers. The brand has moved higher in the consumer's frame of reference and become a preferred brand in his or her mind. In other words, a new attitude or a change in attitude about something has occurred. There may be sufficient motivation to take action and buy the product.

- **Action:** At this stage, the desired action occurs. The consumer buys the brand for the first time, visits the dealer showroom, or calls that 1-800 number!

This is the beginning of a customer relationship. An organization will invest a considerable amount of money in advertising and other forms of marketing communications to achieve one basic goal: to get the target customers to buy the product. The message delivered by marketing communications is nothing more than a promise—a promise that motivates someone to buy. The product must then live up to the expectations created by the marketing communications. As we say, no amount of advertising can make up for a lousy product.

Foote, Cone, and Belding
www.fcb.com

A second theory of communications revolves around the degree of involvement the consumer has with a product in the purchase decision-making process. The extent of involvement, described as either high involvement or low involvement, has implications for the development of marketing communications strategy. Referred to as the FCB Grid, the grid was developed by Richard Vaughn, a senior vice-president of Foote, Cone, and Belding Advertising (see Figure 4.2).[2]

FIGURE 4.2   **An Illustration of the FCB Grid**

HIGH INVOLVEMENT

Quadrant 1	**Quadrant 2**
High Importance (expensive)	High Importance (expensive)
Rational Decision	Emotional Decision
Example: Automobile or computer	**Example:** Designer Clothing
Quadrant 3	**Quadrant 4**
Low Importance (less expensive)	Low Importance (less expensive)
Rational Decision	Emotional Decision
Example: Detergent	**Example:** Soft drink, beer

LOW INVOLVEMENT

Source: Adapted from www.public.iastate.edu/~geske/FCB.html. Reproduced with permission.

Products that are included in Quadrant One are expensive and require a rational decision-making process during which alternatives are evaluated. Since the consumer will probably spend an extended period of time assessing alternatives, the message strategy should have an informative tone and style, and the media selected to deliver the message should be conducive to a long copy format (e.g., newspapers and magazines, websites, and CD-ROMs). Products in Quadrant Two are also high involvement, but consumers evaluate alternatives more on emotion. For example, designer clothing is bought to make the consumer feel good, feel sexy, or show status. Marketing communications must generate emotional responses and create an image that people will buy. The message will appeal to higher-level needs, the looking-glass self, and the ideal self. Television ads, glossy and visual magazine ads, and special inserts are effective media for such products.

Products that are included in Quadrant Three are low-involvement products that require rational decisions. Products such as household cleaning products, paper products, and other everyday items are in this category. Marketing communications should give the consumer a compelling reason to buy (e.g., it lasts longer, as in a battery, or it is fast acting, as in a headache remedy). Consumers are unlikely to read extensive copy for these types of products, so the message must be short. A catchy slogan might act as a reminder. When ScotTowels changed its name to SpongeTowels, the slogan stated "Our new name SUCKS! Literally!" It effectively communicated the number-one attribute consumers seek in a paper towel—absorbency.[3] Television, magazine ads with strong visuals, and point-of-purchase material are effective media choices for these kinds of products.

Products that are included in Quadrant Four are low-involvement products purchased on emotional decisions. The products are not expensive, but they make the consumer feel good. Examples of such products include snack foods, beer and alcohol, and soft drinks. There are not many rational reasons for buying these types of products, so it is common for messages to adopt a "feel good" strategy. For example, there is an abundance of lifestyle-oriented messages among popular Canadian beer brands. It is the image or lifestyle association that the consumer buys into. Television, outdoor advertising, and point-of-purchase play a role in delivering messages for these products.

Marketing Communications Planning Process

The various elements of the strategic planning process were presented in Chapter 3. This chapter concentrates on the advertising planning process, but will recognize the relationships between advertising and the other forms of communication. Once the relationships are established, the chapter will then focus on creative planning. Media planning concepts for traditional media alternatives are presented in Chapter 5.

All aspects of a marketing communications plan are based on the same set of information. The current situation a brand or company faces is analyzed, a problem or opportunity is identified, and a plan of action is developed and implemented. As part of the planning process, the role and contribution of the various elements in the marketing communications mix are identified and those that are most appropriate are included in the plan. Separate plans, designed to achieve specific objectives, are developed for each element of the mix. Once completed, the key elements of these plans are integrated into the master plan—the marketing plan (see Figure 4.3).

With reference to Chapter 3 again, marketing communications plans are devised to meet a variety of challenges and are usually documented as communications objectives in the marketing communications plan. As you will see in this chapter and subsequent chapters, certain elements of the marketing communications mix are better suited to achieving certain objectives. Marketing communications objectives can be diverse and tend to involve challenges, such as

- building awareness and interest for a product,
- encouraging trial purchase,

FIGURE **4.3**   **Creative Planning**

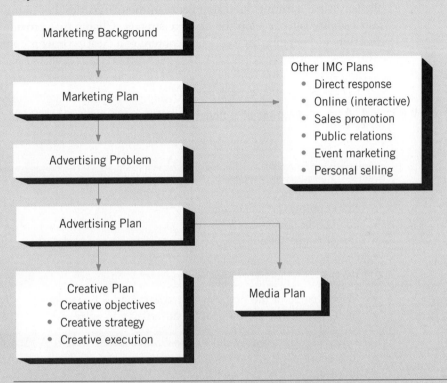

Creative and media solutions are planned together to form an advertising plan. Key recommendations from all IMC plans are integrated into the marketing plan.

Marketing Background

Marketing Plan

Advertising Problem

Advertising Plan

Creative Plan
• Creative objectives
• Creative strategy
• Creative execution

Media Plan

Other IMC Plans
• Direct response
• Online (interactive)
• Sales promotion
• Public relations
• Event marketing
• Personal selling

Note: The "Advertising Problem" is often stated as an "Overall Goal" of a campaign. All plans are based on the same marketing background information.

• attracting new target markets,
• encouraging brand preference,
• altering perceptions held by consumers,
• creating goodwill and fostering a positive public image, or
• motivating distributors to carry a product.

As indicated above, certain components of the marketing communications mix are more appropriate than others for achieving specific communications objectives. In this chapter you will see how advertising helps achieve some of these objectives.

Advertising Planning—Creative

Advertising

A form of marketing communications designed to stimulate a positive response from a defined target market.

Advertising is defined as a paid form of a non-personal message communicated through the various media by industry, business firms, not-for-profit organizations, and individuals. Advertising is persuasive and informational and is designed to influence the behaviour or thought patterns of the audience.[4] The advertising plan is usually developed by an advertising agency, an external partner that works closely with the client. The agency is responsible for developing and managing the client's advertising. Historically, agencies focused their energy on creative and media planning, but in today's environment they have expanded into other areas, such as direct response, marketing research, digital communications, and public relations.

Creative brief

A document developed by a client organization that contains vital information about the advertising task at hand; it is a useful tool for discussions between the client and its advertising agency.

The starting point for any new advertising project is the creative brief. A **creative brief** is a business document developed by the company that contains vital information about the advertising task at hand. The information is discussed with advertising agency personnel so that copywriters, art directors, and creative directors fully understand the nature of the assignment. The brief is a discussion document and the content can change based on the nature of discussion between the client and agency. In some cases, certain sections are actually left blank, awaiting discussion between the two parties. For example, the agency's key responsibility is to develop the creative strategy. Clients that provide too much strategic direction are "stepping on toes." The content of a creative brief is contained in Figure 4.4.

FIGURE 4.4 **Content of a Creative Brief**

Market Information (information from marketing plan)

- Market profile
- Brand profile
- Competitor profile
- Target market profile
- Budget

Problem and Overall Objective

- Identification of the problem that advertising will resolve
- Statement of the overall goal for advertising to achieve

Advertising Objectives (based on problem or goal)

- Awareness
- Interest
- Preference
- Action
- New image
- New targets

Positioning Strategy Statement

- A statement of brand benefits, brand personality, or desired image

Creative Objectives

- Key benefit statement
- Support claims statement

Creative Strategy

- Central theme ("big idea")
- Tone and style
- Appeal techniques

Creative Execution

- Tactical considerations
- Production decisions

Note: The nature and content of a creative brief varies from company to company. A working model is presented here to show the typical content of a creative brief. Some companies include a problem statement or an overall goal, while others include both. Advertising objectives usually concentrate on one or two issues so the campaign remains focused on the problem at hand.

Information that is provided by the client includes essential market background information, a statement that identifies the problem to be resolved or the overall goal to be achieved, and a list of communications objectives. The client also provides a positioning strategy statement to guide the development of the creative plan. The positioning strategy statement directly influences the creative objectives. For our discussions here, creative objectives deal with the content of the message to be delivered (e.g., what is the primary attribute and benefit to be communicated to the target market?). The remaining elements of the creative brief—the creative strategy and creative execution—are the responsibility of the agency. That's what they get paid to do!

Once the creative brief is finalized, the spotlight shines upon the copywriter and art director, a team charged with developing the creative concept or the "big idea," as it is often referred to, that will be the cornerstone of the campaign. At this point, the agency's creative team immerses itself in details about the brand, target market, and competition so that it can fully appreciate the current situation.

Let's examine the content of the creative brief in more detail. Since the market background information is drawn from the marketing plan, that section will not be discussed in this chapter. Simply refer back to Chapter 3 if you need more details. The market background section includes information about the market, brand, key competitors, a profile of the primary target market, and budget. Knowing a brand's market position and how consumers perceive it is important to developing message strategies. Knowing how competitors advertise their products is also important. The agency wants to ensure it recommends new and innovative ideas to its clients. An example of a creative brief is contained in Figure 4.5.

Problem Identification

Advertising plans are usually designed to resolve a particular problem or pursue an opportunity. For example, an established brand will review its marketing strategy each year and make changes in strategic direction when necessary. Factors such as the stage at which a brand finds itself in the product life cycle, the intensity of competition, and changing preferences among target consumers are evaluated in the review process. Changes in these areas have an impact on marketing communications strategies.

Problem statement

A brief statement that summarizes a particular problem to resolve or an opportunity to pursue and serves as the focus of a marketing strategy.

Overall goal

The objective of an advertising campaign.

Based on this creative brief model, the situation is encapsulated in a **problem statement**. Other models may require a statement that describes the **overall goal** of the campaign. Regardless of which option is used, advertising can only accomplish one thing at a time. A campaign must have a central focus. Simply stated, it's "Here's what we want to achieve!" To illustrate, consider the following examples:

- To create or increase brand awareness.
- To alter perceptions currently held by consumers about a brand.
- To present a completely new image for a brand.
- To launch a new product into the marketplace.
- To attract a new target market to a brand.
- To create awareness and trial purchase for a brand line extension.

Scott Paper
www.scottpaper.ca

These examples suggest focus. When ScotTowels was replaced by SpongeTowels (a new generation of paper towel), the advertising campaign needed focus. ScotTowels had a long history in Canada and had built up brand equity over the years. The campaign was designed to focus specifically on the name change to make consumers understand the change and to ensure they would have confidence in the new brand. A campaign that tries to resolve too many problems at one time would only confuse consumers who see and hear the message.

FIGURE **4.5**   **An Example of a Creative Brief**

This is an example of a creative brief for a public service campaign designed to increase awareness for the Centre for Addiction and Mental Health and its efforts to make the public more understanding of depression and what can be done for those who suffer from it.

BACKGROUND INFORMATION

- 3 million Canadians suffer from clinical depression.
- Only one third of sufferers seek help because they are afraid of being "labelled."
- 80 percent of suicides are by people suffering from a depressive illness.
- 40 percent of cases are diagnosed in people under the age of 20.
- Depression accounts for 30 percent of all disability claims in Canada.

PROBLEM

- The public knows little about depression. It is a silent disease with a prevailing stigma surrounding it. Many perceive it to be a simple coping deficiency that "weak" people have and that those people will, and can, snap out of it. Or they are just feeling "blue." Depression is a misunderstood illness.

OVERALL GOALS

- To create awareness about depression as a disease and to influence the public's attitudes about how to deal with people suffering from it.
- To make the public aware of the Centre for Addiction and Mental Health and the services it provides.

COMMUNICATIONS OBJECTIVES

- To remove the social stigma that surrounds depression and sell understanding of the disease.
- To encourage those who may have the disease to seek help.
- To raise awareness of the Centre for Addiction and Mental Health.

CREATIVE OBJECTIVES

- To communicate that depression is an illness and is the result of a chemical imbalance in the brain of sufferers, and that it can be controlled with modern medication and professional counselling.
- To communicate that people with depression can't help themselves. Those who have it or think they have it need to know they are not to blame, and that there is compassionate help available to deal with it.

CREATIVE STRATEGY

- Dramatically portray the real suffering situations (at work, at home, etc.) that people with depression go through each day by using compelling, human, and empathetic headlines and images.

CREATIVE EXECUTION

- Black and white ads of various sizes will be placed in the print media.
- Similar images will be depicted on Centre's website.
- Images will portray empathy and compassion.

Compiled with the assistance of David Sharpe, Vice-President and Creative Director, Remtulla Euro RSCG Advertising.

Advertising Objectives

Once the overall goal is determined, specific advertising objectives are identified. Wherever possible, advertising objectives should be quantitative in nature so that they can be measured for success or failure at a later date. Advertising objectives may be behavioural in nature or they may focus on issues related to the overall problem. For example, an objective may focus on creating a new image or on attracting a new target market.

Advertising objectives should only deal with issues that advertising (the creative plan and media plan) can resolve. For example, a new product campaign will focus on awareness objectives. The objective is to build awareness gradually by presenting a message that informs consumers about what the product is and what it will do for them. If the market is very competitive and several brands are strong, the advertising objectives will focus on building preference. The message will focus squarely on unique attributes that show how the advertised brand performs better than other brands.

To demonstrate how advertising objectives are written, consider the following examples:

- To achieve an awareness level of 60 percent for Brand X in the defined target market within 12 months of product launch.
- To achieve a trial purchase rate of 25 percent for Brand Y in the defined target market within 12 months of product launch.
- To reposition (or re-image) Brand Z in the customer's mind by presenting images that will attract a younger target market.

The first two examples are quantitative in nature and can be easily measured for achievement at the end of the plan period. If the objectives are achieved, it indicates that current advertising strategies are working. If they are not achieved, the client and agency can re-evaluate the situation and make appropriate changes. The third example is not quantitative in nature, but it can be measured. Assuming the current image of the brand is known, a marketing research study near the end of the plan period can be conducted to determine if the brand has caught on with younger customers.

Let's examine a few of these challenges in more detail and determine how they influence the direction of creative planning and the message strategy that is ultimately employed.

Creating or Increasing Brand Awareness

Creating awareness is always the first challenge for advertising. The higher the level of awareness, the stronger the likelihood consumers will buy the product. Achieving high levels of awareness depends on how memorable the message is and perhaps how frequently the message is delivered. The medium used to deliver the message will also influence awareness levels. The right plan will use the right medium, but the size of the budget often dictates media selection. Nonetheless, the use of a medium such as television may create higher levels of awareness than magazines or outdoor advertising, and so on. An example of an awareness-raising ad appears in Figure 4.6.

Encouraging Trial Purchase

Creating awareness and interest in a brand is one thing, but getting the wallets out is another. Sometimes incentives have to be offered to give consumers an extra nudge. If the timing of the incentive is right, positive action will be taken. Therefore, many advertisements are designed specifically to include special offers, anything from cents-off coupons to manufacturers' rebates to low-cost financing. These incentives serve a specific purpose. They help reduce the risk associated with purchasing something for the first time. For expensive goods such as cars and computers, where the risk is very high,

FIGURE   4.6   An Advertisement that Raises Awareness of a New Product

Source: Courtesy of Gillette.

incentives help encourage consumers to buy in a time frame that is desirable for the manufacturer.

Considering how the consumer's mind works, people want to know they are making the right decision. If the product lives up to the promise presented in the advertising, subsequent purchases will be made without incentives. Consumers today are looking for better value in the products and services they buy and, as a result, incentive-oriented advertising is now more prominent than in the past.

Attracting New Target Markets

In order to attract a new target market, say a younger age group than the audience the brand currently appeals to, a new message strategy is needed. The tone and style of adver-

Heineken
www.heineken.com

tising may have to change. To illustrate, consider some recent communications for Heineken beer in Canada. Heineken beer had two primary advertising objectives: to advance Heineken to the top of the super-premium segment (ahead of competing brands like Stella Artois) and to strengthen its connection with younger beer drinkers. Heineken was popular with older age groups, but the key to growth was to attract young drinkers.

To achieve these objectives Heineken adopted a fun and uninhibited-lifestyle approach in its television ads. The message encouraged people to be outgoing and spontaneous but did so in an intelligent way, very different from the senseless partying often associated with mainstream brands. Heineken summarized its message with the tagline "Meet you there," an expression that allows the beer drinker to participate in the communication, to figure it out on his own.[5] See the illustration in Figure 4.7.

Encouraging Preference

For an established brand in growth or mature markets, the objective is to stand out from competing brands. Therefore, the thrust of marketing activities is on product differentiation. Advertising messages focus on the attributes the brand offers. Where continuous improvement programs are in place, it is possible for a brand to become better with age, so there may be new things to communicate. Such was the case in the battle for frozen pizza supremacy between McCain Foods (Rising Crust Pizza) and Kraft Foods (Delissio Pizza). Both brands were being compared to delivery pizza, and Delissio was winning the battle.

To fight back, McCain improved its product, changed the brand name to Crescendo, and launched a new ad campaign that bypassed the traditional shopper aiming directly at teens, the influencers on purchase decisions. Preference among teens was the key to success. Using lines like "Nothing rises like a Crescendo," the commercials poke fun at teens so marvelled by watching the pizza crust rise as it bakes that they walk away from

FIGURE **4.7**   **Heineken, a Premium Beer, Is Targeting Younger Beer Drinkers**

Source: Courtesy of Dick Hemingway.

FIGURE **4.8** **New Ads by Crescendo Encourage Preference among the Teen Target Market**

Source: Courtesy of Dick Hemingway.

the oven sporting oven-window shaped tans on their faces.[6] The campaign helped move Crescendo into the leadership position in the category. See the illustration in Figure 4.8.

As this case indicates, unique attributes that are important to consumers play a key role in differentiating one brand from another and in creating preference for one brand over another. But changes such as these must be communicated to consumers. Having advertising messages focus on something new about the brand may be just enough to position the brand in a better light with consumers.

Altering Perceptions Held by Consumers

Building a brand sometimes requires consumers to adopt a different view of the brand. The quickest way to alter an image is to launch a completely new advertising campaign with an entirely different message. The style and personality of the message will be different to create a new image in the customer's mind.

Wal-Mart Canada
www.walmart.ca

Wal-Mart faced numerous perception problems when it entered Canada. Wal-Mart was that big, bad American bully that would invade Canada leaving Canadian retailers in its wake. "The biggest challenge was to find a way of connecting with Canadians," says Lou Puim, marketing director at Wal-Mart. To connect with Canadians, Wal-Mart developed a campaign that included real people, a strategy that was unheard of when the campaign first broke in 1994. Today, Wal-Mart's customer-testimonial approach seems natural and remains the backbone of its marketing communications program. "The real people strategy made Wal-Mart really Canadian." Wal-Mart has extended this strategy further by including ethnic Canadians in commercials and print ads where they talk about their experiences with Wal-Mart in their native language.[7]

POSITIONING STRATEGY STATEMENT

Positioning strategy has been discussed in the previous two chapters. Therefore, comments here will simply reinforce the necessity of having a clearly worded positioning strategy statement and how it is applied in developing an ad campaign. The positioning strategy statement identifies the key benefit a brand offers, states what the brand stands for, and is a reflection of a brand's personality. These are the essential inputs assessed by the creative team when it develops the message strategy. It can be the trigger that leads to discovery of the "big idea."

The Keg
www.kegsteakhouse.com

To illustrate how the positioning strategy influences creative planning, consider a recent repositioning effort by The Keg Steakhouse & Bar. The Keg began a renewal strategy and revamped its service, menu, décor, and logo. The Keg repositioned itself from being a bar with a steakhouse component to being a great steakhouse with a bar component. The Keg's positioning strategy statement might read as follows:

> A great steakhouse and bar where customers can relax with friends and enjoy good food in a comfortable and relaxing environment.

With the new positioning, The Keg has delivered consistent messages to consumers. A series of TV spots focus respectively on steaks, unpretentious service, and the bar component. One ad shows a single guy approaching the bar, who is suddenly surrounded by "friends" he doesn't know. The message is, "It's a comfortable relaxing place whether you're in a group or on your own." The Keg's target customer was 24 to 44 years old, white collar, high income, well educated, with a single male skew.[8] See Figure 4.9.

Crescendo Pizza was repositioned in the minds of consumers by focusing on a unique feature that wasn't being exploited by any other brand (see earlier discussion under "Encouraging Preference" in this chapter). Going into the development of the new campaign, Crescendo's positioning strategy statement might have read as follows:

> Crescendo is to be positioned as a hearty, great-tasting, rising-crust pizza that will uniquely appeal to the teen segment of the market.

In devising the new campaign, finding ways to communicate the impact of the rising crust would be the creative challenge.

FIGURE **4.9**   The Keg Repositioned Itself as a Great Steakhouse with a Bar Component to Reach a New Segment of the Market

Source: Courtesy of Dick Hemingway.

Creative Objectives

Creative objectives are statements that clearly indicate the information to be communicated to the target audience. What to say about a brand in general terms is usually included in the creative brief. While formats may vary, objective statements tend to involve a key benefit statement and a support claims statement, because the content of an ad or an ad campaign needs focus.

When determining what to say about a brand and how to say it, the copywriter and art director refer to the advertising objective for context. As discussed earlier in the chapter, the advertising objective may be *to achieve brand awareness, encourage trial purchase, attract a new target, encourage preference,* or *alter a perception.* Somehow, the objective and the primary reason for buying the brand must be related together so that a cohesive message is presented to the consumer.

- **Key Benefit Statement:** The **key benefit statement** expresses the basic selling idea, service, or benefit that the advertiser promises the consumer. This benefit should be the primary reason for buying a particular brand instead of competitive brands. The benefit can be something tangible, such as better performance, better quality, lower price, longer lasting, and so on, or it can be something intangible or psychological, such as the status and prestige that come with ownership. With reference to the Crescendo positioning strategy described above, the key benefit for Crescendo is the "rising crust." In previous campaigns this benefit was not exploited, but it would become the focal point of the new campaign to attract teenagers who are the primary consumers of the product.

- **Support Claims Statement:** A **support claims statement** describes the characteristics that will substantiate the promise. It provides proof of the promise based on criteria such as technical performance data, comparative product testing, and any other data generated from marketing research. Good support claims give customers a real reason why they should buy the product. In the case of Crescendo Pizza, Crescendo would make the claim that it was the "only rising-crust pizza" and that claim would be dramatized through visual imagery that shows the crust rising. Delissio, the primary competitor, makes the claim that Delissio is "better than take out." Both brands are making different claims in their respective advertising campaigns. Support claims statements are less important for brands touting intangible benefits. Lifestyle imagery, for example, relies on the image presented and the connection between the image and the consumer who sees it to substantiate the promise.

Pine-Sol
www.pinesol.com

To further demonstrate the application of and relationships between advertising objectives, key benefits, and support claims statements, consider the situation that Pine-Sol was facing. Pine-Sol ranks second in market share behind Mr. Clean and ahead of Lysol. Research showed Pine-Sol was thought to be old fashioned, too strong for everyday use, with an overpowering smell. It suffered from back-of-the-cupboard syndrome. The advertising objective was to alter these perceptions. The solution was found in consumer research. Younger women wanted strength, but not the strength Pine-Sol stood for. In exploratory research, the women talked about different types of clean: the clean for when friends dropped by and the clean for when the mother-in-law dropped by. Out of this came the idea for a new level of clean: the thorough clean. Therefore, the *key benefit statement* for Pine-Sol might read as follows:

> For mothers in search of a cleaner that will *thoroughly* clean their floors and counters, Pine-Sol works best (the promise).

The *support claims statement* might read like this:

> While other leading brands get your floors and counters clean, Pine-Sol cleans and disinfects more thoroughly. It even cleans the dirt you don't know about, such as accidents and spills that go undetected (the proof).

FIGURE **4.10**   **An Ad Focusing on a Key Benefit: "A Thorough Clean"**

"BAD AIM"

VIDEO: Open on a shot of an empty bathroom.
Now a little boy runs into the bathroom.
The little boy begins to pee in the toilet.
SFX: Tinkling in toilet.
SUPER: Pine-Sol cleans the dirt you know about.
VIDEO: Suddenly, his mom calls from downstairs. The boy turns to
respond to her call, and in doing so pees on the floor.
MOM: Max! We're going!
SFX: Tinkling on floor.
VIDEO: He turns back and casually finishes up.
SUPER: And the dirt you don't.
VIDEO: Cut to a mid-shot of Pine-Sol Original bottle.
SUPER: The thorough clean.

Source: PINE-SOL is a registered trademark of The Clorox Company. Used with permission.© The Clorox Company of Canada.

Pine-Sol's message was communicated in a unique manner. The ads charmingly dramatize real life and included situations mothers could readily identify with (see Figure 4.10). One commercial showed a small boy whose "aim" is off in the bathroom. Another showed a dog resting on the kitchen table instead of his basket. In research, women said "That's my life." In short, the ads make them think of Pine-Sol differently than before.[9]

An ad campaign by the Dairy Farmers of Canada for milk effectively communicated that milk strengthened bones and teeth, but also that there are so many other benefits milk offers that consumers are not aware of. Using the same visuals as previous campaigns, additional copy (in the form of support claims) was added to communicate the additional nutrients milk offers. The ad clearly and convincingly presents a solid case for including milk as part of a balanced diet. Milk fits nicely with the health and wellness trend that is so prominent among many consumers today. See the illustration in Figure 4.11.

Creative Strategy

With the decisions about what to say in advertising determined, the creative team turns its attention to creative strategy. This is where the advertising agency starts to earn its keep. What the team searches for is the "big idea," or the central concept or theme that an entire campaign can be built around. All kinds of discussion and experimentation take place. It is an exercise in brainstorming. The guiding light is the positioning strategy. When the ad

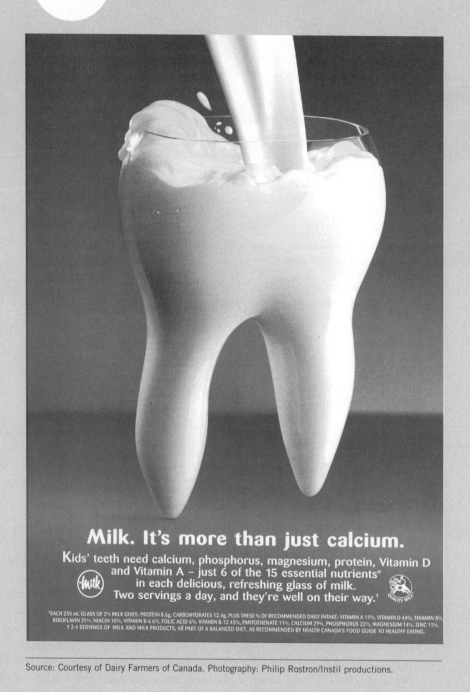

FIGURE **4.11**   **An Ad that Creates Awareness of the Additional Benefits Milk Offers**

Source: Courtesy of Dairy Farmers of Canada. Photography: Philip Rostron/Instil productions.

Creative strategy

A plan of action for how the message will be communicated to the target audience, covering the tone and style of message, the central theme, and the appeal techniques.

agency pitches its ideas to the client, the client evaluates the idea based on how it fits with the positioning strategy. Simply put: Is the big idea on strategy or off strategy?

The **creative strategy** is a statement of how the message will be communicated to the target audience. It deals with issues such as the theme, the tone and style of message that will be adopted, and the appeal techniques that will be employed. It is a statement about the personality a brand will project to consumers.

- **Central Theme:** The **central theme** or **"big idea"** is the glue that binds the various creative elements of the campaign together. As such, the theme must be transferable from one medium to another. For example, when someone sees an ad in print form (newspaper, magazine, or outdoor), it should conjure up images and meaning from something they have seen on television (a 30-second commercial). What the theme will be is truly the key decision the creative team makes. For the theme to see the light of day, it must be presented to the client in a very convincing manner. For a brand such as Maytag (appliances), the central theme is dependability. That is also the key benefit the brand offers. The idle Maytag repairman, a character strongly associated with the brand name, is the means by which dependability is communicated.

- **Tone and Style:** In an attempt to break through the clutter of competitive advertising, copywriters and art directors agonize over decisions about tone and style. Such a fundamental decision has direct impact on how a campaign evolves over time and how the brand's personality gets ingrained in the customer's mind. Single words often describe the tone and style that is recommended. For example, the message will be presented in a persuasive manner, an informative manner, a conservative manner, a friendly manner, a contemporary manner, a straightforward manner, an upbeat manner, and so on and so on. What approach will have the most impact on the target audience? Obviously, knowledge about the target audience that is gleaned from the demographic and psychographic profiles plays a key role in this decision.

Diet Pepsi
www.dietpepsi.com

A recent advertising campaign for Diet Pepsi aptly demonstrates how good decisions about theme, tone, and style have a positive impact on consumers. Diet Pepsi was losing ground to Diet Coke, and Diet Pepsi was being ruled by the image of regular Pepsi. Diet Pepsi's primary target market is young adults (the twenty-something crowd). They are making their first big, important decisions such as where to live, their career choice, and who to have relationships with. Marketing research revealed they didn't want to lose their spontaneity and spirit even though they were getting older. Therefore, the big idea had to consider the youthful feelings of a maturing audience. Too much youth and Diet Pepsi would wind up back in regular Pepsi territory. Too little, and the brand would be just plain dull.

The creative team recommended a "Forever Young" theme (see Figure 4.12). The tone and style of ads, particularly on television, were "kind of wacky." They portrayed characters on a temporary break from maturity, not a breakdown in their entire way of life, just a longing for some crazy moments of their past. In one ad a young man working in a men's shop spots a customer's underwear peeking out of his pants and gives him a wedgie. He then asked, "How's that fit?" The ad ends with the tagline "Taste the one that's forever young."[10] In the race for market share, Diet Pepsi and Diet Coke are now in a dead heat, proof that the right kind of advertising works.

For additional insight into how and where the "big idea" comes from, read the IMC Highlight **Echo Targets 30-Something Women**.

Appeal Techniques

How to make an advertisement appealing to the customer is another key decision. What techniques will be employed to bring the product benefit claims and theme to life? What can we do creatively to break through the perceptual barriers in the consumer's mind? There isn't a single, definitive formula for success, but there is a tendency to classify appeal techniques into certain areas. For example, when you see an ad, does it make you snicker? Does it draw a tear? Does it make you think? How consumers respond to an ad is usually related to the effectiveness of the appeal. The following is a discussion of some of the more common appeal techniques.

FIGURE **4.12** An Illustration of Diet Pepsi's Central Theme or "Big Idea"

Agency:	BBDO Canada	Title:	"Comb-Over"
Client:	Pepsi-Cola Canada Ltd.	Length:	30-second English Television
Product:	Diet Pepsi	Date:	01.02

We open on a balding man standing on a sidewalk somewhere. He is looking away, but turns towards camera as the camera approaches him
ANNOR VO: I see you're drinking Diet Pepsi. Is there anything else youthful you'd like to experience?

MAN: (thinking for a moment and then pointing at his bald head) Yeah...I'd like to have back all the hair I had in high school.

MUSIC: (The song "I Ran" from the Flock of Seagulls starts to play.)
Panning up we follow our hero walking towards camera - indeed he has his high school hair back - it's unfortunately the same 1980s Flock of Seagulls hairstyle he wore as teenager.

We see our hero in the middle of a serious business meeting.

His hair is casting an unusual shadow on the projection screen - disrupting the meeting.

Then we see our hero waiting for a serve.

His new hair is blocking 90% of his vision. His opponent winds up and serves. Just as our hero takes the ball in the head.

We match-dissolve back to our original scene – our hero looks back towards camera.

MAN: (thinking) Oh second thought, I'll stick to the Diet Pepsi.

FOREVER YOUNG

ANNOR VO: Taste the one that's forever young. Diet Pepsi.

Source: Pepsi-Cola Canada Ltd.

Positive Appeals

McDonald's Canada
www.mcdonalds.ca

Presenting the message in a positive manner is always a safe approach, but it is also a very common approach. If combined effectively with the right theme, positive appeals will work. However, if the creative execution lacks impact, it will wind up being just another ad. McDonald's is one of the country's biggest advertisers and dominates its market. The company is proud of its accomplishments so its ads reflect its position. The theme of McDonald's advertising does change from time to time, but the ads remain consistent in how they appeal to their target.

Typically, ads for McDonald's include music and positive interactions among family members and between family members and employees. The message is delivered in an

IMC HIGHLIGHT

ECHO TARGETS 30-SOMETHING WOMEN

Quebecers have always loved small cars, and Toyota has always been a leader there due to its quality, durability, and frugal gas consumption in smaller models. But, facing new competition, Toyota had to take action to protect its leadership position in the sub-compact segment.

Toyota Quebec and ad agency Bleu Blanc Rouge examined the Echo inside and out for untapped strengths. How could they make the little sub-compact desirable again? One amazing characteristic would ultimately do the trick. The Echo could be accessorized 36 different ways with a barrage of goodies available to customers. Among the goodies were sport wheels, sport suspension, and spoilers. The creative strategy was starting to take shape. What if tuning became an expression of one's personality? What if the Echo was unique rather than mass produced? Voila! An idea was born.

Echo would be positioned as unique; people would buy it as a reflection of their personality rather than buying a car they wanted to resemble. When assessing target market opportunities, the 30-something female offered the greatest potential. She has spent most of her adult life working and doing for others and is ready to pamper herself a bit. She is ready to assert her unique personality and be a little selfish in the process. *Égoïsme* (or selfishness in English) would be the key feature in developing the campaign. By shifting from *égoïste* to Echoïste, the creative team had an expression that would inspire the entire campaign.

Giving the idea more thought, the creative team concluded that they must express selfishness in a contemporary way. A light perspective would be needed, and it had to be a sexy expression of personality—nothing too heavy or complex. The end result was a series of commercials that portrayed the close relationship between the woman and her car. Maxim Roy, a French-speaking personality, was spokesperson, and in the ads she dressed in a manner that brought the association to life. A second series of ads showed the car with human tendencies—being playful and sexy.

Did it work? You bet! Echo sales shot up by 40 percent and plenty of new customers were inquiring about ways to personalize their car. The campaign created a buzz on the street, and Toyota was once again perceived as a fun brand.

Adapted from Bernard Lebourdais, "The Echoïste Zone," *Marketing*, April 11, 2005, p. 16.

upbeat manner. McDonald's latest campaign "I'm lovin' it" is global in scope and its success helps the company maintain its dominant leadership position in the quick-serve restaurant market. Taglines such as "I'm lovin' it" and "There's a little McDonald's in everyone" (from a previous campaign) aptly reflect a positive style of advertising. Admit it...the McDonald's tagline is a phrase you sing along to!

Negative Appeals

Unless you are Buckley's cough mixture, you don't say bad things about your product. "Tastes awful, but it works" is now a famous slogan coined by Buckley's. Following a philosophy of "do what your momma says and you will get better," Buckley's has experienced new popularity and a positive increase in market share based solely on its negative style of advertising.

For other products, though, negative appeals usually present a situation the consumer would like to avoid. Vim, a multi-purpose cleaner for kitchens and bathrooms, showed a dishevelled woman toiling away at cleaning a wall (see Figure 4.13). It appeared she was in prison because of the way she was dressed, and she was separated from her daughter by a glass wall. The daughter asks, "When are you going to get out?" A wider shot reveals the mother is in a tub behind a glass sliding door slowly cleaning the tile walls. Cleaning bathrooms is a task nobody enjoys. The message: use Vim and spend less time cleaning. This commercial won Best of Show at the 2005 Bessie Awards.

FIGURE **4.13**   **A Negative Appeal Technique Works Effectively to Show How Quickly Vim Works**

TITLE: Prison Visitor
PRODUCT: Vim–Unilever
ADVERTISER: Unilever Canada, Toronto
AGENCY: Zig, Toronto
CREATIVE DIRECTORS: Elspeth Lynn and Lorraine Tao
ART DIRECTOR: Stephen Leps
WRITER: Aaron Starkman
AGENCY PRODUCER: Janet Woods
PRODUCTION HOUSE: Reginald Pike
DIRECTOR: The Pelorian Brothers
EDITOR: Michelle Czukar, Panic & Bob Editing
SOUND DESIGN: Ted Rosnick,
Rosnick MacKinnon Webster
ACCOUNT EXECUTIVE: Christine Harron

"PRISON VISITOR"
VIDEO: We open on a woman in prison. She is being visited by her daughter. They are separated by a glass wall. The daughter puts her hand on the glass and the mother does, too. It's an emotional moment. DAUGHTER: When are you going to get out of here? MOTHER: In a while. (pause) I gotta get back. VIDEO: At this point, we cut to a wider shot and we discover that the mother is actually in a bathtub and the glass wall is the sliding shower door. The mother starts to clean with a generic spray. We can see it's not working. DAUGHTER: I love you, momma! MOTHER: I love you too, baby! VIDEO: The mom goes back to scrubbing. Fade to white. SUPER: Spend less time cleaning. VIDEO: Dissolve to Vim cream bottle. SUPER: Cleans the tough stuff. Easily.

Source: © Unilever Canada Inc.

Humorous Appeals

Kellogg Canada
www.kelloggs.ca

Taking a light-hearted approach to communicating benefits can work effectively. In fact, many critics believe that for advertising to be successful it must entertain the audience. If true, then an advertisement that causes the audience to break into a smile or giggle should break through the clutter. When Kellogg launched Raisin Crunch, a television commercial entitled "Fired" used humour to its advantage. In the commercial, a young man in an office is shown eating the cereal while his boss is trying to talk to him. The cereal is so loud and crunchy that the guy can't hear what his boss is saying. The boss is asking why the guy is still there, since he's been fired. Then the boss says, "I want you out!" The guy still can't hear a thing, so he gives his boss a feeble "thumbs up." The humour leaves little doubt about what the primary benefit of the product is.

Sport Chek, a sporting goods retailer, used humour effectively in a series of TV commercials about people buying sports gear. Apparently, equipment buyers want to look authentic and, through highly technical duds, possibly fool people (and ourselves) into illusions of athletic grandeur. One commercial features a guy coming off the ice who confuses a woman delivering the usual "good game" kudos when he starts behaving like he's being interviewed by a sportscaster. The woman seems slightly ticked off, but in a realistic, deadpan kind of way simply says, "I'll be in the car." The ad ends with the tagline, 'When you look like a pro, you feel like a pro."[11]

A major weakness of using humour is that it can wear out prematurely. After a few exposures, the audience may not find the message funny. Advertisers must also be wary of sarcastic humour that could insult cultural groups. Humour can backfire and bring on unwanted negative publicity. Furthermore, the use of humour allows for considerable creative latitude. The creative team must ensure that the humour does not get more attention than the product. To keep the message fresh, a pool of commercials is needed so that individual spots can be rotated in and out of a media schedule.

Sexual Appeals

Sex in advertising! It will spark some controversy, some good, some not so good. When sexual appeals are used in advertising, certain values and attitudes toward sex are being sold to consumers along with the products. Consider, for example, a recent commercial for Labatt Blue Light. The commercial, titled "Lip Gloss," was one of the most controversial ads shown in Canada in 2004. After the introductory shots of babes with beer, a woman says she likes her friend's lip gloss. The friend then shares the gloss through a passionate kiss as a group of men watch in awe. While gay and lesbian relationships may be okay with the 20-something crowd that Blue Light was targeting, there was considerable conservative backlash from many Canadians.

A recent award-winning campaign for Jergens effectively uses the female body in a sexy, smart, and simple way. The sensuous images and minimal copy portray the usefulness of the product. In a variety of executions, lines of lotion suggest clothing on an otherwise nude woman, which sparks consideration of that universal undergarment—your skin. Refer to Figure 4.14 for an illustration.

FIGURE **4.14**   **A Simple and Tasteful Use of a Sexual Appeal Technique**

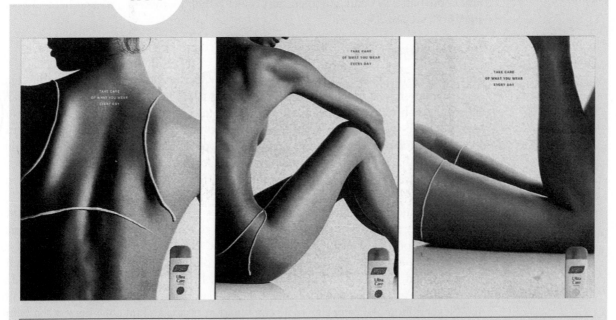

Source: Courtesy of KAO Brands Canada.

As demonstrated by these two examples, some sexual advertisements are subtle, while others are blatant. Doug Robinson, chair and creative director at Ammirati Puris, says, "It's simply a reflection of general trends in the entertainment world. People are using more provocative imagery and language. Whether you like it or not, videos and movies are opening doors."[12] Robinson's ad agency developed a controversial television ad for Carlsberg beer in which a woman alludes to her friend's prowess at giving oral pleasure. The ad raised a few eyebrows, to say the least!

Sex is a strong physiological need, just behind self-preservation, and sexual desire is an instinctive reaction, so why not use it in advertising? The only real issue is the way in which it is used. Clearly, explicit sex increases the risks for the advertiser, since it may alienate consumers at large. But, if core customers do not find it offensive, the advertiser may truly be on to something.

Emotional Appeals

Emotional appeals presented effectively will arouse the feelings of an audience. To demonstrate, consider the style of advertising used to promote social causes: anything from drinking and driving to spousal abuse to quitting smoking. In one TV ad that encourages people to stop smoking, a mature woman talks of the perils of second-hand smoke. Her husband, a smoker, is dead and she suffers from emphysema due to second-hand smoke. Such a message leaves the viewer with a disturbing feeling.

Tim Hortons
www.timhortons.com

Tapping into people's emotions also works in a positive setting. There is no disputing the popularity and dominance of Tim Hortons in Canada. With over 2500 restaurants and $2.9 billion in sales annually, it is Canada's largest restaurant chain. Part of Tim Hortons's success is attributed to effective and sometimes emotional advertising that resonates with consumers. Their "True Stories" series of commercials connects with Canadians everywhere by depicting the emotional bonding that actually exists between customers and the company.

A recent television spot tells the story of a retired couple travelling from British Columbia to Newfoundland, and two young men travelling form Newfoundland to BC. They go the distance only stopping at Tim Hortons along the way. The two parties unknowingly cross paths (actually wave at each other) at the entrance to a Tim's restaurant at the half-way point, and then carry on with their journey. Yes, it's another feel-good story from a Canadian icon.

Lifestyle Appeals

Advertisers using lifestyle appeal techniques try to associate their brand with the lifestyle or desired lifestyle of the audience they are trying to reach. Some of the appeals already discussed, such as sexual appeals and emotional appeals, are frequently included as elements of a lifestyle campaign. Other elements may include action, adventure, and excitement to stimulate desire. Lifestyle appeals are popular among advertisers owing to the greater availability of psychographic information about Canadian consumers. Many beer brands use lifestyle appeals to establish an image firmly in the minds of drinkers 19 to 29 years of age. If you are what you drink, then there is a brand of beer for you.

The automobile industry uses lifestyle messages heavily, particularly in the sport utility and luxury segments of the market. The need to experience adventure, for example, is effectively portrayed simply by placing a vehicle in an exciting situation. The need to experience recognition and status is portrayed by showing a young executive-type individual behind the wheel of a luxury automobile. Images like these speak much louder than words! Audi, for example, connects with executives on their way up the ladder with its "Never Follow" ad campaign. The combination of images and copy suggest the vehicle is for leaders, for people on the move, for people on their way up the ladder. See the illustration in Figure 4.15.

FIGURE **4.15**   **Audi Uses Lifestyle Appeals to Attract Potential Buyers**

Source: Courtesy of Audi of America.

Comparative Appeals

In comparative advertisements, the promise and proof are shown by comparing the attributes of a given product with those of competing products—attributes that are important to the target market. The comparison should focus on the primary reason for buying the product. Comparisons can be direct, such as when the other brand is mentioned and shown, or they can be indirect, with only a reference to another leading brand or brands. The Pepsi Challenge led to an all-out assault on Coca-Cola when Pepsi advertising made claims of taste preference for Pepsi-Cola by Coca-Cola drinkers. Now comparisons are more subtle, yet very convincing. One recent TV spot shows a Coca-Cola deliveryman hopping out of his truck while stopped at a rail crossing. He steals a few cases of Pepsi-Cola from the Pepsi driver's truck parked beside him. In the last scene the Coke driver is seen enjoying a Pepsi.

Comparative campaigns are usually undertaken by a "challenger" brand, a brand that ranks behind the category leader in terms of market share. Showing comparisons where the challenger performs better than the market leader is a convincing presentation. It will make consumers think more about the brand they currently use. Such a strategy presents several risks. For one thing, the brand leader could fight back. If so, the brand that made the comparison may need adequate financial resources to fight an advertising war. As well, any claims must not mislead the public. If they do, the market leader could instigate legal proceedings to get the offending brand to offer proof of its claims. Critics of comparative appeals firmly believe a brand should stand on its own merits. Why cloud the issue by bringing in competing brands?

Factual Appeals

Certain product categories lend themselves to a straightforward style of advertising. The ads simply state what the product will do and back it up with information that is easy for the customer to understand. Over-the-counter pharmaceuticals use this technique frequently. Brands in this category rely on technical information or scientific data to validate claims. Advil says it's for "today's kind of pain." Advil offers fast relief for the things that slow you down. Phrases such as "safe, reliable, and doctor recommended" verify the claim.

And what do the competitors say? Motrin ads say, "it's for people who don't fool around with pain." Unlike acetaminophen pain relievers, which alter perceptions of pain, Motrin works at the source of the pain (which makes it sound better!). Category leader Tylenol says, "doctors recommend Tylenol more than all other brands combined to reduce fever and temporarily relieve minor aches and pains." The third-party endorsement by doctors has a definite impact. These competitive examples aptly depict the intent of factual appeals.

Factual appeals are also appropriate for products that are expensive or complex, such as expensive LED televisions or space-age kitchen appliances. Yes, these types of products have to look good, but they must also be dependable. Consumers want some hard and fast facts! In these cases, there is usually a high degree of involvement by consumers in the decision-making process. Information (detailed information) provided by advertising is helpful.

For more insight into the nature of creative strategy, how creative concepts develop, and creative execution (the next section in this chapter), read the IMC Highlight **Lights, Camera, Action**.

LIGHTS, CAMERA, ACTION

Imagine you are watching a movie and a bank is being robbed—tense drama at its best is unfolding right before your eyes. The getaway vehicle is parked outside the front door. What kind of vehicle would it be? An inconspicuous van that will blend in with traffic? A souped-up car that will dart between vehicles while being pursued by police? How about a Kia Rio?

Just like a typical chase seen in movies like *Bullitt* or *The French Connection*, a Kia commercial entitled "Switcharoo" features a bright red Kia Rio sports coupe. The Kia Rio careens its way through city streets at outrageous speeds. It's thrilling, it's exciting, and it's advertising! To upgrade the image of the lowly Kia Rio, Canada's least expensive automobile, Kia went to great lengths to make the car look exciting.

The payoff comes at the end of the commercial. After the driver loses the cops he pulls up to another vehicle hidden under a canvas cover, left there so he and his buddies can complete their getaway. The driver pulls off the cover with a flourish to reveal...a bright red Kia Rio sedan! In the movies they always switch cars. In the commercial the guy

was so impressed with the coupe that in a moment of weakness he bought the sedan as well.

The commercial is odd, but it's funny and it gets the viewer's attention. And that's half the battle in the cluttered world of television advertising. In terms of creative objectives, Kia is attempting to reinforce the idea that Kia is a fun, quirky brand—a brand with a little personality. Dramatizing the personality in a high-speed chase is a strategy that no other car in its category has ever done before.

Consumers will look at all kinds of factual information about various cars before buying, but buying a car is not always a rational decision. The key is to make the buyer want the car, and that's often based on an emotional influence. A heart that wants a car will soon convince the brain that it's the right thing to buy. And that's what Kia is counting on. With 10 competitors in the same market segment, it's often the best commercial that captures the hearts and minds—and hopefully the wallets—of potential customers.

Adapted from Jerry Langton, "Shooting for the heart—and the wallet," *Globe and Mail*, September 22, 2005, p. B11.

Creative Execution

In the creative execution stage of creative planning, specific decisions are made regarding how to best present the message. If product comparisons are used, what kind of demonstration technique will be employed? Will sexual appeals be subtle or blatant? If lifestyle appeals are used, what kind of backdrops and settings will be needed? If music is called for, what kind of music will it be? If it is a print campaign, will the ads be copy dominated or image dominated? Will artwork or photography be the key visual element? How big will the ads be? There are a host of decisions to be made.

The agency creative team evaluates specific ideas that it thinks have the potential to convert its vision of an ad into reality. In doing so, the team must answer two basic questions:

1. What is the best or most convincing way to present the brand's benefits to motivate the consumer to take action?
2. Is there a specific technique that will effectively convince consumers that this is the right brand for them?

For example, if a decision is made to use a celebrity as a spokesperson, who will the celebrity be? Will it be a famous rock star, movie star, or sports personality? A lot of behind-the-scenes discussion goes on for decisions of this magnitude. The following are some of the more commonly used presentation tactics.

Product Demonstrations

For products that want to make claims regarding performance (e.g., dependability, reliability, speed), demonstrations work well. As mentioned above, the simplest appeal is to say or show the product and what it will do. In print advertising, "a picture says a thousand words." On television, showing the product in use is often the simplest and most direct way to make a claim. The intensity of competition among brands sometimes calls for more dramatic demonstrations. A technique referred to as **product as hero** (the product comes to the rescue when the consumer is facing a really tough situation) is often the answer. Categories such as household cleaning products and personal care products are famous for such a technique (see Figure 4.16).

If a product really wants to drive home an important claim, there's the **torture test**. This technique was made famous by Timex watches with its "It takes a licking and keeps on ticking" campaign. The exaggerated demonstrations for the watch certainly verified the primary claim of durability at a reasonable price.

Product as hero
A creative execution technique in which the advertised product is shown coming to the rescue (e.g., of a consumer in a difficult situation).

Torture test
A creative execution technique in which the product is subjected to extreme conditions to demonstrate its durability.

Testimonials

Advertisers that follow a traditional approach to advertising frequently use testimonials. In a testimonial, a typical user of the product presents the message. Real people in ads are often perceived to be more credible than models and celebrities who are paid handsomely to sell a certain brand. The Wal-Mart campaign that involved customers participating in TV commercials and the "True Stories" Tim Hortons campaign (both referred to earlier in the chapter) are good examples of the effectiveness of testimonials. In the case of Tim Hortons, everyday customers tell a story about why Tim Hortons plays such an important and enjoyable role in their lives. The commercials present kind of a "folksy" image that regular customers can identify with. When you think about it, after all, Tim Hortons is part of the daily grind of a lot of people.

The popularity of reality-based television has spawned *reality-based advertising*. Labatt Breweries adopted this technique in a campaign for Blue. The Blue campaign featured the slogan "Cheers. To Friends," and realistically depicted what guys do when they are hanging out together. One of the first ads in the campaign showed a montage of scenes that looked like they were shot by a hand-held video camera. The guys knock over an outhouse with a friend inside and show another guy being launched head first into a paper towel display in a supermarket. Another ad shows an unsuspecting guy opening a car door only to have thousands of golf balls spill out. His friends giggle from an apartment above the car. Anything goes![13] These kinds of commercials are produced for a

Labatt Blue
www.labattblue.com

FIGURE **4.16** | **An Ad that Clearly Communicates the Primary Benefits of the New Oral-B Toothbrush**

Source: Courtesy of P&G Canada.

fraction of the fees of regular commercials, which is a real bonus for advertisers—assuming they work.

Endorsements

Endorsement
A situation where a celebrity speaks highly of an advertised product.

Star power is the heart of a celebrity **endorsement** execution. Stars from stage, screen, music, and sports form the nucleus of celebrity endorsers. Among the biggest and most expensive celebrities are Tiger Woods (Nike, American Express, and Buick, among other brands and companies) and Britney Spears (Pepsi-Cola).

Ford of Canada and its dealer associations have built a campaign in Canada around retired hockey star Wayne Gretzky. The new campaign aims to provide a unified message from all Canadian Ford dealers by using a "Canadian icon" who appeals to all demographics. The campaign uses the theme and tagline "Built for life in Canada." Gretzky appears in television and print ads, dealer advertising, promotional materials, and on Ford's website.[14]

Hockey sensation Sidney Crosby will soon be seen as the lead spokesperson for a countless number of products. By all accounts, even from the Great One himself, Sidney Crosby is the next Wayne Gretzky. Even before playing a game in the NHL, Crosby had signed a five-year, $2.5-million deal with Reebok to promote their high-tech line of hockey gear. For Reebok, a new entrant into the hockey market (Reebok acquired CCM in 2004), a rising star like Sidney Crosby puts Reebok on a more level sheet of ice with competitors like Nike. Crosby has also signed a deal with Gatorade that is rumoured to be the highest-paid celebrity endorsement ever by the sports drink giant.[15]

Do celebrities work? That's a tough question to answer, but one asked frequently by clients. There isn't a definitive answer but let's look at a situation and try to pass judgment. Where would Nike be in the golf business without Tiger Woods? Nike has invested millions in Woods, and in return, he alone has put Nike on the golf map. Star power like that does attract advertisers, and an audience.

Reebok
www.rbk.com

Taglines and Slogans

Tagline
A short phrase that captures the essence of an advertised message.

Slogan
A short phrase that captures the essence of an entire advertising campaign; reflects the positioning strategy of the brand and is shown in all ads in all media.

Despite all of the time, energy, and money that go into developing an ad campaign, consumers only remember bits and pieces of the message. The most important thing for them to remember is the brand name and the primary benefit. To reinforce the primary benefit and the central theme of a campaign, and to reflect the positioning strategy of the brand, the creative team develops a **tagline** for individual ads, or a **slogan** that will appear in all forms of advertising. The slogan provides continuity within an advertising campaign. Several ads that appear in figures in this chapter include a slogan. Audi, for example, says "Never follow," and Diet Pepsi is "Forever young."

Of the things that consumers remember about a brand, the slogan is something they have a tendency to recall. The repetition of messages consumers receive over an extended period helps ingrain the slogan in the customer's mind. From time to time the slogan will change, especially when a brand or company wants to change its image. However, it is more common for the slogan to remain in place even if the creative strategy and creative execution are completely new.

Moores
www.mooresclothing.com

Moores (a menswear store) encountered this situation when its creative strategy shifted in the direction of humour. Previous ads were somewhat highbrow and had more of a Harry Rosen feel. Through research, Moores discovered some triggers for why men buy suits: weight gain, being out-of-date, and so on. In one commercial a man bends over only to hear a threatening rip in his pants; another commercial shows a man arriving at his wedding in a powder-blue tux, much to the dismay of his bride. Even though the style of advertising changed, the slogan remained constant: "Moores clothing for men. Well made. Well priced. Well dressed." Moores realized that the brand name and slogan are important variables that help build a brand's equity.

The best slogans are short, powerful summations that companies use alongside their logos to drive the brand message home to consumers. Some of the more popular and longstanding slogans appear in Figure 4.17.

FIGURE **4.17**   **Some Popular Brands and Slogans**

Visa	"All you need."
Volkswagen	"Drivers wanted."
Burger King	"Have it your way."
Avis	"We try harder."
Nike	"Just do it."
Allstate	"You're in good hands with Allstate."
M&Ms	"Melts in your mouth, not in your hand."
Timex	"Takes a licking and keeps on ticking."

A slogan is a key element of brand identification. Many of these slogans have stood the test of time. They are strongly associated with the brand name and appear in all forms of advertising.

Summary

The marketing communications process begins with a sender (the advertiser) developing a message to be sent by the media to the receiver (the consumer or business customer). The goal of marketing communications is to break through consumers' perceptual barriers while recognizing that competitors' messages are trying to do the same. When messages are developed, consideration is given to how consumers receive and interpret messages. The consumer's mind goes through a series of stages: awareness, comprehension, conviction, and action.

Creative planning is a sequential process that involves analyzing market and customer information, identifying problems and opportunities, setting goals and objectives, and developing creative strategies and tactics. The planning cycle starts with a creative brief, a document prepared by the client for discussion with the advertising agency. The brief includes relevant background information, and identifies problems, goals, and advertising objectives. The document acts as a guideline for the creative team when it is brainstorming for new ideas.

Once the advertising objectives are identified, the creative team begins work on creative objectives, strategies, and execution. Advertising objectives provide focus to the creative challenge (e.g., the objective is to create awareness, build preference, alter perceptions, encourage trial purchase, and so on). Creative objectives are statements that clearly identify the information to be communicated to the target market. They include a key benefit statement (a promise) and a support claims statement (proof of promise). Usually the client and agency collaborate when finalizing these statements.

Creative strategy is concerned with the tone, style, theme, and appeal techniques that are used to influence consumers to take action. Among the more commonly used strategies are positive and negative approaches, using humour, sexual, emotional, and lifestyle appeals, offering factual information, and comparisons with other products.

At the creative execution stage, specific decisions are made on how to implement the strategy. Some of the specific techniques that are commonly used include product demonstrations, testimonials from everyday users of the product, and celebrity endorsements. A good campaign will include a slogan. The slogan serves two essential roles. First, it communicates the essential idea the advertiser wants associated with the product, and second, it maintains continuity within an advertising campaign. In combination with the brand name, a good slogan helps build brand equity.

Key Terms

advertising,   105

"big idea",   117

central theme,   117

communication,   101

creative brief,   106

creative objective,   114

creative strategy,   116

encoding,   101

endorsement,   128

key benefit statement,   114

noise,   102

overall goal,   107

problem statement,   107

product as hero,   126

slogan,   128

support claims statement,   114

tagline,   128

torture test,   126

transmission,   101

Review Questions

1. Briefly explain the behavioural stages a consumer passes through prior to making the decision to buy a particular product.

2. What is a creative brief and what role does it play in the development of an advertising campaign?

3. In the context of creative planning, what is meant by the "big idea"?

4. Ad campaigns should have focus and aim toward an overall goal. Identify and briefly explain three specific goals a campaign may try to achieve.

5. How important is a positioning strategy statement and what role does it play in creative planning?

6. What is the difference between a key benefit statement and a support claims statement?

7. Briefly describe the various appeal techniques commonly used in advertising.

8. Briefly explain the following creative execution terms:
   a) product as hero and torture test
   b) testimonial and endorsement
   c) tagline and slogan

Discussion and Application Questions

1. Are humorous advertising campaigns effective? Conduct some online secondary research on humour in advertising and present a case for or against the use of humour.

2. "Lifestyle advertising strategies are ineffective because they communicate little about the product." Is this statement true or false? Conduct some online secondary research about lifestyle advertising and present a position on this issue.

3. "Good execution of a poor creative strategy will create positive results for the brand (company)." Is this statement true or false? Assemble some data that either support or refute this statement.

4. Clip an ad that catches your attention from a magazine in your household. After assessing the ad, try to determine the advertising objective, the creative objective (key benefit statement), and the creative strategy (appeal technique). Can you figure out what the advertiser intended when the ad was in the development stages?

5. Assess a series of advertisements for one brand (pick a popular brand that uses several different media). Based on everything you know about that brand and the marketing communications you are exposed to, write a positioning strategy statement that reflects the intentions of the brand. What message or image does the company want to instill in the customer's mind?

6. Select two brands that compete directly against one another. Assess the creative strategies and creative executions used by each brand. Since both brands are trying to reach and influence the same target market using advertising, which brand has more impact on consumers? Which style of advertising is more effective? Justify your position.

7. Find separate products or services that use the following creative appeal techniques:
   a) negative appeals
   b) humorous appeals
   c) comparative appeals
   d) emotional appeals
   e) lifestyle appeals

8. What is your assessment of each of the above strategies in terms of potential impact on the target market? Justify your position.

9. Assess a brand advertising campaign that features a celebrity spokesperson. Will that spokesperson have an influence on the intended target? What are the benefits and drawbacks of using a celebrity spokesperson?

Endnotes

1 Theresa Howard, "Ad campaigns tell women to celebrate who they are," *USA Today*, September 7, 2005, **www.usatoday.com**.

2 "Ad Education," Iowa State University, **www. public.iastate.edu/~geske/FCB.html**.

3 Stephen Blythe, "Two TV solitudes," *Marketing*, November 7, 2005, p. 19.

4 *Dictionary of Marketing Terms*, Barron's Educational Series, Inc., 1994, p. 13.

5 Michelle Halpern, "Fun with the suds," *Marketing*, August 29/September 5, 2005, p. 7.

6 Natalie Williams, "The McCain makeover," *Strategy*, January 2005, p. 15, and Keith McArthur, "Teens, moms targeted in oven-ready pizza war," *Globe and Mail*, February 21, 2005, **www. globeandmail.com**.

7 Annette Bourdeau, "Mr. Retail," *Strategy*, October 2005, pp. 16–17.

8 Rebecca Harris, "Consistency pays off," *Marketing*, September 6, 2004, p. 4.

9 "Packaged goods other," Cassie's insert in *Marketing*, November 18, 2002, p. 5.

10 Susan Heinrich, "Forever young: Pepsi campaign wins top Cassie," *Financial Post*, November 6, 2002, p. FP7.

11 Mary Maddever, "It's all in the gear," *Strategy*, September 2004, p. 21.

12 Wendy Cuthbert, "Racy ads pushing the boundaries," *Strategy*, September 25, 2000, p. 20.

13 Susan Heinrich, "Advertisers say it's time to get real," *Financial Post*, March 3, 2003, p. FP4.

14 "Gretzky driving Ford campaign," *Marketing*, November 25, 2002, p. 1.

15 Rich Thomaselli, "Searching for Michael Jordan," *Advertising Age*, September 5, 2005, p. 12.

ADVERTISING PLANNING: TRADITIONAL MEDIA

After studying this chapter you will be able to

1. describe the steps involved in media planning

2. distinguish among media objectives, media strategies, and media execution

3. describe the various factors that influence media strategy decisions

4. outline the characteristics, strengths, and weaknesses of mass media advertising alternatives

As mentioned in Chapter 4, the creative plan and media plan are developed at the same time and depend on the same information from the marketing plan. This chapter will focus specifically on the development and implementation of the media plan. Developing a media plan is a complex process. The primary goal of the agency media planners is to reach a target market efficiently. In doing so, they consider all kinds of strategic issues, along with conditions in the marketplace and what competitors are doing.

Efficiency in media planning can be loosely defined as gaining maximum exposure at minimum cost. In following this mantra, the agency planners must develop and execute a plan that achieves the client's objectives within certain financial constraints. As in the case of the creative plan, the media plan is part of a broader marketing communications plan and marketing plan. Therefore, the direction a media plan takes must fit in with and be coordinated (timed) with activities recommended in other marketing communications areas. Coordinating various communications activities creates synergy and maximizes the impact of the plan on competitors in the channel of distribution and on consumers.

Media planning is a complex task, and with consumer's media habits changing, mainly due to technology, it is more difficult than ever to reach people with advertising messages. In general terms, people are spending less time with traditional media and more time with digital media (online and mobile communications). Other forms of media entertainment include video on demand, satellite radio, digital video recorders, and video games.

It seems clear that consumers aren't going to be as receptive to the 30-second spot as they once were, and with the emergence of TiVo and digital video recorders (DVRs), many consumers zap right by the commercials that advertisers are paying top dollar to run. From a media planning perspective, new strategies have to be devised to reach an increasingly mobile and elusive consumer.

MEDIA PLANNING

Media planning involves developing a plan of action for communicating messages to the right people (the target market), at the right time, and with the right frequency. Both the client and the agency play a role in media planning (see Figure 5.1). The client's role focuses on providing necessary background information and then evaluating the recommendations that the agency makes. The agency assesses the information provided by the client and then prepares a strategic plan that will meet the client's objectives. Because there is a considerable amount of money involved, clients scrutinize media plans carefully.

Media brief
A document that contains essential information for developing a media plan; used to stimulate discussion between a client and agency.

Information provided by the client is contained in a **media brief** (much like the creative brief discussed in Chapter 4). The media brief is a document that contains essential information for developing the media plan and is used as a starting point in the discussion between a client and the agency. It includes some or all of the following information.

Market Profile

Any relevant information about the current state of affairs in the market is useful to media planners. Such information includes historical sales data for leading brands, market share trends of leading brands, and rates of growth in the market. Is the market growing, flat, or declining?

Competitor Media Strategy

In general terms, what media do major competitors use, and how much money do they invest in media advertising? What the competitors are doing has some influence on the strategic directions that will be recommended. For example, if key competitors dominate

FIGURE **5.1** **Media Planning Model**

Decisions made by the creative team about message strategy will influence media strategy (e.g., the choice of media). There should be good communications between the creative team and the media team.

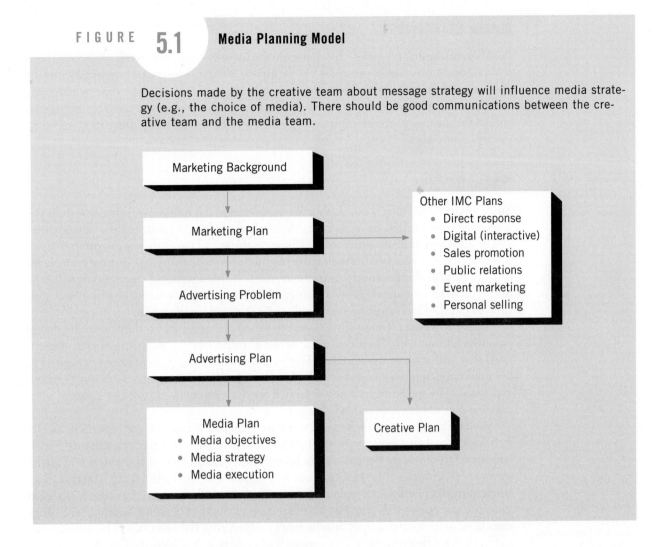

a particular medium, it may be prudent to select another medium to reach the same target. Whatever competitive information is available should be in the hands of the media planners.

Target Market Profile

Perhaps the most important ingredient for a media plan is a thorough understanding of the target market. As discussed earlier, targets are described on the basis of demographic, psychographic, and geographic variables. The target profile must be clearly defined and key variables must be expanded upon. For example, knowing the activities and interests of the target (psychographic considerations) enables a media planner to select the best times and best places to advertise.

Information about how the target interacts with the media (e.g., what media the target refers to most frequently) is also important as it helps the planner to allocate funds across the recommended media. As indicated above, media consumption habits are changing. One study in the United States revealed that 71 percent of consumers viewed word of mouth as the most influential factor in a car-buying decision. Television advertising ranked ninth on the list, yet television is the most prominent advertising medium used by automobile manufacturers. Direct mail advertising and other forms of direct response advertising were second and third on the list. This kind of information suggests that traditional advertisers will have to change their way of thinking—and quickly![1]

Media Objectives

Based on marketing priorities, the client usually identifies key objectives. Objectives tend to focus on target market priorities by identifying primary targets and secondary targets, the nature of the message and its influence on media selection, the best time to advertise, and the geographic market priorities. Depending on the problem at hand or the overall goal of the campaign, the client may also identify priorities for reach, frequency, and continuity of message.

Media Budget

Since media advertising is but one media expenditure, the funds available come from the marketing plan budget. In most cases, the client has already identified the amount that will be allocated to media advertising. Knowing the size of the budget is essential, because it provides the framework for the media planner's strategic thinking. Is there enough for television? Will this be strictly a print campaign? Is this a national campaign or will it be restricted to regional markets? Will this campaign rely on a few media or will it be a multimedia effort? The budget points the planners in a certain direction.

Once the media planners have been briefed on the assignment, they begin discussing potential alternatives. Their goal is to devise a media strategy and tactical plan (execution) that will achieve the stated objectives. Once the media plan has been presented to the client and approved, agency media buyers negotiate with the media to buy the time and space. The media buyer's task is to deliver the maximum impact (on a target audience) at a minimum cost (client's budget).

Media planning is quantitative by nature. Agency personnel are experts in media trends and have all kinds of statistical information available to figure out what media are best suited to the client's needs. Furthermore, the sophistication of computers and media software has enhanced the ability of media planners and media buyers to generate more efficient media plans. Once a plan has been implemented, the agency evaluates the plan in a post-buy analysis. A **post-buy analysis** is an evaluation of actual audience deliveries calculated after a specific spot or schedule of advertising has been run. The actual audience may be different from the estimated audience that was identified in the plan. The question to be answered is whether the plan delivered the audience it was supposed to.

Post-buy analysis
An evaluation of actual audience deliveries calculated after a specific spot or schedule of advertising has run.

THE MEDIA PLAN

The **media plan** is a document that outlines the relevant details about how a client's budget will be spent. Objectives are clearly identified, strategies are carefully rationalized, and execution details are precisely documented. The costs associated with every recommendation are put under the microscope when the agency presents the plan to the client. Because of the money involved, media plans often go through numerous revisions before being approved by the client. The structure and content of a media plan are the focus of this section of the chapter. Figure 5.2 summarizes the content of a media plan, although the content of a media plan varies from one agency to another. This model is strictly a guideline.

Media plan
A strategy that outlines the relevant details about how a client's budget will be spent; involves decisions about what media to use and how much money to invest in the media chosen to reach the target audience effectively and efficiently.

Media Objectives

Media objectives are clearly worded statements that outline what the plan is to accomplish. They provide guidance and direction for developing media strategies. If worded correctly, priorities will emerge. For example, there could be customer priorities, regional market priorities, and timing priorities. These priorities are based on historical information,

Media objective
A statement that outlines what a media plan is to accomplish (who, what, when, where, or how).

FIGURE **5.2**   **The Structure and Content of a Media Plan**

Media Budget

- Total budget available (from client's marketing plan)

Media Objectives

- Who (is the target market)
- What (is the message)
- When (is the best time to advertise)
- Where (are the priority markets)
- How (important is reach, frequency, and continuity)

Note: Media objectives are usually clear, concise statements.

Media Strategy

- Target market matching strategy (shotgun, profile match, rifle)
- Market coverage
- Timing
- Reach considerations
- Frequency considerations
- Continuity considerations
- Media selection rationale
- Media rejection rationale

Note: Media strategies expand upon the objectives and provide details about how the objectives will be achieved.

Media Execution

- Blocking chart (calendar showing timing, weight, and market coverage)
- Budget summary (allocations by media, time, and region)

the current situation a brand finds itself in, and the problem that the advertising plan must resolve. Such issues are part of the background information included in the media brief. For example, a plan may have a national focus, regional focus, or it may simply run in a few urban markets that are given priority.

Media objectives typically deal with the following issues:

- **Who:** Who is the target market? The target market profile is defined in terms of demographic, psychographic, and geographic characteristics. Media planners use this profile to match the target with a compatible media profile. For example, magazines know their readership profile, radio stations know their listener profile, and television networks know who watches specific shows. Refer to the media strategy section of this chapter for detailed discussion about target market matching strategies.

- **What:** What is the nature of the message to be communicated? Media planners must be informed about the message strategy. For example, is the message strategy information intensive (lots of copy) or image intensive (lots of visuals)? Does the budget permit television, and if so, is the creative team giving television due consideration? Issues such as these strongly suggest that basic creative and media decisions be made at the same time. Clients should provide guidance in this area. If certain media are mandatory, the client should say so.

- **Where:** Where are the market priorities geographically? The budget plays a key role in this decision. Typically, a brand has regions of strength and weakness. A media plan could be devised to correct a situation in a problem region. In such cases, a decision could be made to reduce media spending in a strong region and allocate more to a weaker region. In other situations, regions may be treated equally with media funds allocated based on population patterns. If this is to be a key market plan only, what key markets are given priority? The number of markets that must be reached and the level of intensity (media investment) are factors largely based on the budget.

- **When:** When is the best time to reach the target market? For example, is the product a seasonal product, such as suntan lotion or ski boots? If so, the media strategy will consider a heavier schedule of advertising in the pre-season, a time when consumers are starting to think about summer or winter activities. Knowledge of the target's daily schedule also plays a role in timing decisions. For instance, a busy executive who rises early and arrives home late may not have much time to spend with the media. How and when is the best time to reach this person? When is the best time to reach a student? Knowledge of media consumption patterns by the primary target is essential.

- **How:** The question of how conjures up all kinds of media issues. How many people to reach, how often to reach them, and for what length of time? These are strategic issues that are best left to the media planners at the ad agency. However, some basic guidance from the client is provided. For example, if the plan is for a new product, the absolute number of people reached and how often they are reached may be given priority. If a product is firmly established and the goal of the plan is to simply remind the target, then length of time may be given priority. Refer to the discussion about reach, frequency, and continuity in the next section for more details.

Media Strategy

Media strategy
A plan for achieving the media objectives stated in the media plan; typically justifies the use of certain media.

Media strategy focuses on how media objectives will be achieved while outlining how to reach the target market as effectively and efficiently as possible. Given the scarcity of clients' financial resources and their demands for accountability, having the right media strategy is crucial. Clients want to see a reasonable return for their investment. A media strategy addresses how often to advertise, how long to advertise, where to advertise, what media to use, and will rationalize why only certain media are recommended. Strategic decisions are linked directly to the media objectives. The various factors that influence media strategy are discussed below.

Target Market Profile

For some products and companies, the target description may be broad in scope. For example, a newspaper's primary readers include adults of all ages and income groups. In contrast, the primary buyer for a Lexus automobile may be described as a male business executive, 35 to 49 years of age, earning $75 000 annually, living in an urban market of 1 million plus. The extent of the target's description directly influences media strategy decisions.

The task of the media planner is to match the profile of the target market as closely as possible with the profile of the medium (e.g., the readership profile of a magazine or the listener profile of a radio station). The more compatible the match, the more efficient the strategy will be. For example, to reach that Lexus buyer, executive-oriented business magazines such as *Financial Post Business*, *Canadian Business*, and *Report on Business* are good matches. Figure 5.3 illustrates a readership profile. The same executive may watch television, but to place an ad in prime-time hours would reach people well beyond the target description. This would not be efficient. There are three basic target market matching strategies: shotgun, profile matching, and rifle.

FIGURE **5.3** **Readership Profile of *Canadian Business* Magazine**

Characteristic	Audience	
Circulation	88 900	
Readers per copy	11.6	
Total readership	1 031 000	
Male readers	703 000	
Female readers	328 000	

Demographics	Readers	Index
HHI $75 000+	533 000	170
HHI $100 000	388 000	221
Senior managers/Owners	88 000	315
Other managers	197 000	155
Professionals	128 000	237
Sales/Tech/Teaching	160 000	169
MOPEs	413 000	198

Business Purchase Involvement		
$50 000+	94 000	273
$100 000+	79 000	339

Financial		
Savings/Securities $100 000+	108 000	168
Own RRSPs	507 000	131
Own mutual funds	399 000	128
Own stocks or bonds	244 000	165

Travel		
Taken 5+ business trips in past 12 months	109 000	206
Spent 15+ nights away on business	61 000	257

Notes

1. Circulation multiplied by the number of readers per copy equals total readership.

2. MOPEs are managers, owners, professionals, and executives.

3. The index in the right column shows how *Canadian Business* readers compare to the Canadian average. The index is calculated by dividing the percentage of *Canadian Business* readers by the percentage of Canadian adults in the various categories being measured. The *Canadian Business* readers are well above average in all categories.

INTERPRETATION

Based on the above readership statistics, *Canadian Business* magazine is a good profile match for advertisers wanting to reach individuals with above-average incomes, including senior managers, professionals, and business owners. These individuals are decision makers in their places of employment.

Source: Adapted from *Canadian Business* Media Kit.

Shotgun strategy

A tactic involving the use of mass media to reach a loosely defined target audience.

Radio TV Ad Spot.com
www.radiotvadspot.com

Profile-matching strategy

A media tactic that involves matching the demographic profile of a product's target market with a specific medium that has a similar target profile.

Rifle strategy

A strategy that involves using a specific medium that effectively reaches a target market defined by a common characteristic.

- If a **shotgun strategy** is used, the target market's profile has a broad scope. The message is placed in media that reach a broad cross-section of the population. For example, television reaches all ages, although viewing by certain age groups varies by time of day. To reach teenagers and adults, prime-time television does the job. In the United States, the cost of placing one 30-second spot on *CSI: Crime Scene Investigation*, CBS's most popular drama show, is US$478 000.[2] The same spot simulcast on the CTV Network in Canada would cost approximately C$50 000. Television is an expensive medium.

  For advertisers on a tighter budget but with a diverse target market, options such as daily newspapers and out-of-home advertising are attractive. Out-of-home options include billboards, transit shelters, and subway stations. They reach a diverse population but generally cost less than television.

- If a **profile-matching strategy** is used, the target market profile is carefully defined by demographic, psychographic, and geographic variables. For example, assume a target profile described as follows: female head of household, working or stay-at-home mother, college or higher education, $50 000 household income, suburban lifestyle, with interests that include home decorating, entertaining, and travel. Several magazines are good possibilities for reaching such a woman: *Chatelaine, Canadian Living, Canadian Home & Country*, and *Homemakers*. The primary reader of each magazine is reasonably close to the description of the target. In contrast, *Canadian Business* magazine appeals to upper-income males and females commonly referred to as MOPEs (managers, owners, professionals, and entrepreneurs).

  Profile matching can extend to television as well. Conventional networks such as CTV and Global have been losing viewers to specialty networks like TSN (sports), YTV (youth), and the Outdoor Life Network (OLN), among others. Specialty networks offer programming that is tailored to specific demographics. OLN caters to 20-something males and females with programs that have an action and adventure orientation. YTV reaches children and tweens (kids 11 to 14 years of age) with appropriate program content.

- In the **rifle strategy**, a common characteristic such as an activity or interest binds a target market together. For example, golfers are golfers, whether they play at a public club, an exclusive private club, or anywhere in between. All golfers look for similar equipment. They cross both genders and most income groups. Therefore, a publication such as *Score Golf* or *Golf Canada* offers a means of reaching the target directly. Enthusiasts look to these kinds of publications for information about the products that are advertised there. Business publications target specific industries; therefore, to target decision makers within a particular industry, its trade publications are attractive. To reach people employed in the hospitality industry, for instance, a publication such as *Hotel & Restaurant* is an option.

In Chapter 1, the concepts of database marketing and customer relationship management were discussed. A rifle strategy is ideally suited for organizations that practise these concepts. Non-traditional media such as the Internet, direct mail, and cell phones can reach customers on an individual basis. These media are discussed in more detail in appropriate chapters of this textbook.

To demonstrate the relationships between media objectives and target market media strategies and to show how difficult it can be to reach a target audience, read the IMC Highlight **BMW MINI's Lifestyle Media Plan**. A good plan always reaches the target and produces desirable results.

Nature of the Message

Creative strategy and media strategy should be developed simultaneously to generate a synergistic effect in the marketplace. Planners should cooperate to ensure that the right message is delivered by the right medium. If a rational appeal technique is used with fac-

BMW MINI'S LIFESTYLE MEDIA PLAN

The BMW MINI is a cool-looking vehicle and was an absolute success in its first year of sales. To sell even more vehicles, BMW needed to expand its target market. The company named various psychographic profiles that would play a key role in identifying appropriate targets and selecting the right media to reach the target. The targets were described as Opinion Leaders and Influencers, Coupe Performance (under-the-hood guys), and Modern Mainstreams.

For the media planners at Gaggi Media Communication, the challenge was how to plan effective media against a philosophical target group. Using a variety of media research sources as guides, a lifestyle media plan was devised. Demographics such as adults 25 to 49 with a male skew were identified, but would not play a key role in the plan.

The key to the plan was to understand the typical day in the life of the target group. They were extremely active and only interacted with the media when they chose to—a sound bite here and there. Selling cars to older targets involves heavy television advertising. Such a strategy wouldn't work here.

A multimedia approach was recommended, embracing selective television, out-of-home, magazines, cinema, and special installations. Television in the form of specialty channels and local market stations using 15-second spots developed by Taxi (another ad agency) effectively delivered the image message to influencers. Only programs that fit the appointment-style viewing habits of the audience were

selected. Handpicked "cops hide here" outdoor boards in high-traffic locations delivered an interesting message. Washroom ads in fitness clubs and hip restaurants and bars delivered the message in a relevant environment.

Lifestyle magazines associated with the varied interests of the MINI buyer were selected. Among the magazines were *Maxim*, *Azure*, and *Canadian Art*. DVD-format full-motion slides were introduced at Famous Players theatres. To round out the campaign and to generate some real buzz, custom-made installations were used in various formats. One such installation was a MINI in a cage, which kicked off the Toronto Auto Show and then travelled to the Montreal and Vancouver shows as well. The installation concept was so successful it was picked up in MINI countries around the world.

Radio and print were used corporately and at the dealer level. This effort was designed to get those people considering buying a MINI into the showrooms for test drives. Radio was leveraged to the hilt to allow dealer visits, live cut-ins from MINI events, and ongoing partner-based promotions.

This plan made innovative use of media through research. The media selected surrounded the target in ways that allowed the message to break through the clutter. With creative and media planners working together, the medium became the message in some non-traditional applications. The plan was very hip and cool, just like the image of the MINI.

Adapted from "MINI chases 'cool' without a true demo in sight," *Strategy*, April 19, 2004, p. 7.

---

tual information to be communicated, then print media options take precedence. If emotional appeals are used and if action and adventure are prominent in the message, television is good. If sales promotion incentives are part of the message, a combination of media may be called for. Television may be used to generate awareness of a contest, for example, while print media and in-store communications provide more details.

Geographic Market Priorities

With regard to where to advertise, strategic decisions must be made on how to divide a budget among the areas where advertising will be scheduled. A company or brand rarely advertises nationally on a continuous basis. It is common for some national advertising to occur during the course of a plan, but it is supplemented by additional advertising in markets where specific problems need to be resolved. In other instances, a brand might decide just to advertise in key urban markets. The top five Canadian markets reach about 40 percent of the total population—and much of the success (or failure) in Canada is governed by how successful the brand is in those five markets. Usually, the budget determines the extent of market coverage. Some of the coverage options include the following.

National Coverage Such a strategy assumes widespread availability of the product with all geographic areas figuring equitably in the success of the product. For example, if product sales as expressed as a percentage of total sales by region are close to population splits by region, a national strategy is an option. Funds can be allocated across media that reach the national market. Network television shows in prime time (*CSI: Crime Scene Investigation*, *The Amazing Race*, *Without a Trace*, etc.) and national magazines such as *Maclean's* are good alternatives. Of course, the precise description of the target audience and the budget also influence this kind of strategy. Prime-time television and general-interest magazines reach a broad cross-section of the population and the cost in absolute terms (the actual cost per ad) is high.

Regional Coverage A regional strategy involves an evaluation of each region's contribution to a brand's (or company's) success. Funds are allocated so that no particular region has an advantage or disadvantage—at least, that's the theory. The reality is different. Some regions will over-contribute to sales while others will under-contribute. An organization might assess the value of a region by analyzing two different indexes. The first index is called a **market development index** or **category development index (CDI)** and is a percentage of category sales (e.g., a category like instant coffee) in an area in relation to the population in that area compared to the sales throughout the entire country in relation to the total population. For example, if the sale of instant coffee in British Columbia represents 10 percent of total sales and BC represents 12 percent of the population, the CDI is 83.3 (10 divided by 12). BC would be considered an underdeveloped region. Conversely, if Ontario represents 42 percent of instant coffee sales and Ontario represents 38 percent of the population, the CDI would be 110.5 (42 divided by 38). Ontario would be described as an overdeveloped instant coffee market.

A **brand development index (BDI)** works the same way. It is a percentage of a brand's sales in an area in relation to the population in that area compared to the sales throughout the entire country in relation to the total population. For example, if Maxwell House instant coffee has 15 percent of its Canadian sales in BC and only 12 percent of the population lives there, the BDI for BC would be 125. This would indicate that BC is an important area for the brand; the brand is very popular there. Refer to Figure 5.4 for some additional calculations of the brand development index, which help explain why certain regions get disproportionate funds. There is only so much money to be allocated. For example, in a market where a brand is underdeveloped but potential for growth is present, that brand may temporarily receive additional funds that will be taken away from a region where the brand is doing well. The BDI is commonly used when determining regional media budgets.

In terms of media selection, a planner will focus on regional media opportunities to reach the target market. Television networks offer regional packages (e.g., all stations within a region) and national magazines such as *Chatelaine*, *Canadian Living*, and *Reader's Digest* offer numerous regional editions.

Key Market Coverage A third alternative is to give priority to those members of the target market residing in key urban markets. Usually there are predetermined criteria to establish what markets will receive media support. If population is the criterion, a planner will consider other strategic factors first and then go down the market list until the media budget is exhausted. Canada's top five cities (Toronto, Montreal, Vancouver, Ottawa-Hull, and Calgary) account for 40.6 percent of the population, while the top 10 cities account for 52.2 percent.[3] Given that the population is migrating steadily toward cities in Canada, a key market plan is a good option.

While this strategic approach seems equitable, smaller cities may never receive media support. For example, no city in the Atlantic region is among the top ten. If the Atlantic region doesn't receive media support, expectations for the brand should be lowered appropriately. In terms of media selection, key market plans offer the most flexibility and

Category development index (CDI) or market development index

The percentage of category sales in a geographic area in relation to the total population of that area; determines if a category is underdeveloped or overdeveloped in a particular region.

Brand development index (BDI)

The percentage of a brand's sales in an area in relation to the population in that area; determines if the brand is underdeveloped or overdeveloped in each area.

FIGURE **5.4**   **Considerations for Allocating Budgets by Region**

One method of determining the importance of a region for a brand (company) is to compare actual sales volume (as a percentage of total sales) to the region's population (as a percentage of Canada's population). Such an analysis is called a **brand development index (BDI)**. The BDI is determined by dividing the sales volume percentage by the regional population percentage.

Region	Sales Volume %	Population %	BDI
Atlantic Region	7.6	7.6	100.0
Quebec	21.5	23.9	89.9
Ontario	42.5	38.5	110.4
Prairie Region	13.4	16.8	79.8
British Columbia	15.0	13.2	113.6
Total	**100.0**	**100.0**	—

Example: The BDI in Ontario is 110.4. The BDI was determined by dividing 42.5 by 38.5

Analysis: Based on the BDI in each region, Ontario and BC over-contribute to sales while Quebec and the Prairies under-contribute. The media planner can concentrate advertising dollars in areas where the brand enjoys most usage. Another option is to transfer some funds from Ontario and BC to Quebec and the Prairies to help improve sales in those regions. Other factors can influence such a decision.

choice. Local market television stations, daily newspapers, outdoor and transit advertising, and radio are attractive alternatives. The combination of media to recommend depends on the media preferences of the target market and the budget available in the plan.

Timing of Advertising

Information about the target market and cyclical patterns in sales influence decisions about when to schedule advertising. The best time could refer to the time of day, day of week, or time of year. For products with a cyclical sales pattern, the media schedule may follow the ebb and flow of sales. If the media plan is for a new product, the planners may decide to hit the market heavy and frequently in a short period. Lower levels of advertising are scheduled later in the plan cycle. Typically, a media schedule is planned in flights. A **flight** is a period of time in which advertising is scheduled. Rarely is advertising scheduled continuously—creative scheduling just makes it seem like it is. There are many options available for planning the timing of a media schedule, all based on unique situations a brand (company) faces. Refer to Figure 5.5 for an illustration of the media schedules discussed below.

Flight
A period of time in which advertising is scheduled.

- A **skip schedule** calls for scheduling advertising on an alternating basis. For example, ads are scheduled one week and not the next, or one month and not the next. This cyclical pattern is maintained for the duration of the campaign. A skip schedule strategically stretches a budget over an extended period while maintaining the effect of the advertising in the marketplace.

Skip schedule
The scheduling of media advertising on an alternating basis, such as every other week or every other month.

FIGURE **5.5**   **Media Scheduling Alternatives**

Effective scheduling patterns improve the efficiency of the media plan. Each of these media schedules serves a unique purpose and meets specific media objectives.

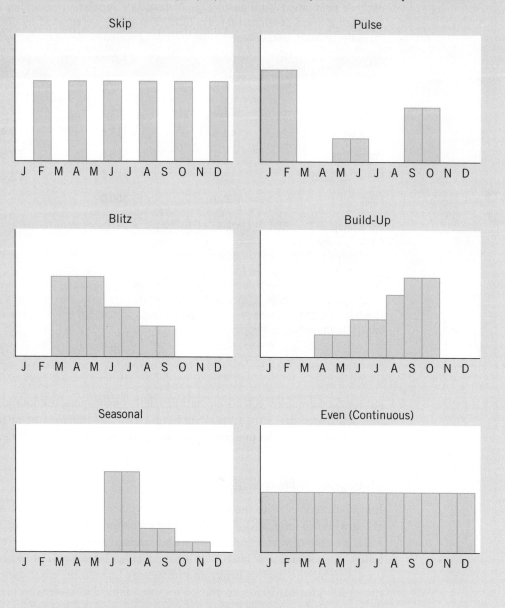

Pulse schedule

A scheduling of media advertising in flights of different weight and duration.

- A **pulse schedule** involves scheduling advertising in flights but with different weights (the amount invested in media) and durations (the length of time). Such a schedule looks random, but the weight and frequency of the spending patterns are carefully rationalized. To demonstrate, assume a schedule has three flights. The first is four weeks long and heavy, the second is six weeks long at a low level, and the third flight is four weeks long and heavy. There is a period of four weeks with no advertising between each flight. The variation in flights creates a "pulsing" effect.

Seasonal schedule

Scheduling media advertising according to seasonal sales trends; usually concentrated in the pre-season or the period just prior to when the bulk of the buying occurs.

- Many products are seasonal in nature so media advertising follows a **seasonal schedule,** with most of the advertising in the pre-season to create awareness and interest prior to the beginning of the seasonal purchase cycle. Banks and financial institutions have a heavy schedule of RRSP advertising in January and February, for example, as the tax-deduction deadline for contributions is the end of February.

Blitz schedule

The scheduling of media advertising so that most spending is front-loaded in the schedule; usually involves a lot of money spent in a short period.

- A **blitz schedule** is best suited for new products that want to hit the market with a bang—a multimedia strategy at a heavyweight level. Lots of money is spent in a very short period. Once the blitz is over, media spending tapers off considerably, and some media are dropped from the schedule.

Build-up schedule

The scheduling of media advertising so that the weight of advertising starts out light and gradually builds over a period of time; also called a teaser campaign.

- Frequently referred to as a teaser strategy, in a **build-up schedule** media advertising is scheduled at low levels initially and gradually builds (as more weight is added) as time passes. Often a teaser campaign is launched well before the product is available on the market (hence the name). The advertising creates a pent-up demand for the product when it becomes available. Hollywood movie releases and manufacturers of video game hardware and software use this strategy frequently.

Even schedule

The uniform schedule of media advertising over an extended period; also referred to as a continuous schedule.

- Often referred to as a continuous schedule, the **even schedule** involves the purchase of advertising time and space in a uniform manner over a designated period. This schedule is best suited for large advertisers that need to sustain a certain level of advertising spending due to competitive pressures. Such a spending pattern is not very common. Even in markets like the quick-serve restaurant market, where various companies seem to be advertising all of the time, the level of advertising they actually schedule does vary from month to month.

Reach/Frequency/Continuity

Media planners must decide on the reach, frequency, and continuity needed to achieve advertising objectives. Much like a riddle, these three factors interact and, if planned effectively, will have a synergistic effect on the target market. It is unrealistic to have maximum reach, frequency, and continuity at the same time. Priorities are based on the situation and the budget.

Reach

The total unduplicated audience exposed one or more times to a commercial message during a specific period (usually a week).

- **Reach** is the total unduplicated audience (individuals or households) exposed one or more times to an advertiser's schedule of messages during a specific period (usually a week). It is expressed as a percentage of the target population in a geographically defined area. For example, a television ad on Ottawa's CJOH-TV may reach 40 percent of the households in the Ottawa region.

Frequency

The average number of times an audience has been exposed to a message over a period of time, usually a week.

- **Frequency** is the average number of times a target audience has been exposed to an advertising message over a period of time, usually a week. It is calculated by dividing the total possible audience by the audience that has been exposed at least once to the message. Frequency may also refer to the number of times a publication is issued or the number of times a commercial is aired. The media planner must decide what combination of reach and frequency is appropriate for achieving the advertising objectives. In the case of a new product where awareness objectives prevail, the emphasis is on reach (and frequency if there is enough budget). A mature product that is trying to defend its position may opt for more frequency and aim the message at a precisely defined target market.

Gross rating points

An expression of the weight of advertising in a media schedule; calculated by multiplying reach by frequency.

- Media planners use gross rating points as a method of designing a media schedule. **Gross rating points (GRPs)** are calculated by multiplying the total reach (the unduplicated audience) of the proposed schedule by the frequency (the average amount of exposures) in the proposed schedule. It is an expression of the weight of advertising in a market. To illustrate, assume the weekly reach is 50 percent of targeted households in a particular city and the average number of exposures is 3.5. The GRP level would be 175 (50 x 3.5). Depending on how important particular markets are, an advertiser usually varies the weight level (the GRP level) from one market to another. For more detailed illustrations of GRPs, refer to Appendix 1, "Media Buying Principles and Media Information Resources," at the end of the book.

Continuity

The length of time required in an advertising medium to generate the desired impact on the target audience.

- **Continuity** refers to the length of time required to ensure impact has been made on a target market through a particular medium. During that period, a consistent theme is communicated (e.g., "Well Made. Well Priced. Well Dressed," the theme for Moores, a men's clothing chain). Since advertising is scheduled in flights, continuity decisions deal with how long a flight will be. Will the schedule be four weeks, six weeks, or eight weeks?

Media planners must juggle reach, frequency, and continuity throughout a campaign. An increase in any one of these variables will increase the cost of advertising, so there would have to be a corresponding decrease on another variable to stay within budget. In debating the issues related to reach, frequency, and continuity, many media agencies will embrace the media concept referred to as "recency." The idea behind recency is that a single ad impression is most effective as long as it is served to a consumer when they are in the market to buy a product.[4] It is the timing of the message that is important, not the frequency of the message.

In combination with the strategic variables described above, the media planners must recommend what media to use. Their media plan will include reasons why certain media were accepted and certain media were rejected. Knowledge of the target market's media preferences and the budget available has a direct and powerful influence on media selection. The section of this chapter titled "Assessing Media Alternatives" discusses the various media in more detail. Figure 5.6 offers additional information about the relationships between reach, frequency, and continuity.

Media Execution

Media execution

The translation of media strategies into specific media action plans; involves recommending specific media to be used in the plan and negotiating the media buys.

The final stage of the media planning is media execution. **Media execution** is a process of fine tuning the media strategy and translating it into specific action plans. This involves comparing various options within a class of media for cost efficiencies, finalizing a schedule in the form of a calendar or blocking chart, and allocating the budget in detail by specific activity. Then the agency buys the media time and space.

Media Selection

Selecting the right media to resolve the problem at hand is a three-step decision process: selecting the general type of media, selecting the class of media within the type, and selecting the particular medium. Of the media discussed in this chapter, the first decision involves what mix of media to use. Among television, radio, newspapers, magazines, and out-of-home, any combination is possible (direct response and interactive media are discussed in separate chapters). For the second decision, let's assume that magazines and television are the media chosen and that the campaign is national in scope. Will general-interest magazines, men's or women's magazines, or special-interest magazines be chosen? What television networks will be chosen? The characteristics of the target market will influence these decisions.

For the third decision, let's also assume the target market is men and women between 35 and 49, living in major cities across Canada. Magazines that reach both males and females would be selected: *Maclean's*, *Time*, and *Reader's Digest* are good candidates. Conventional television networks such as CTV, CBC, and Global are also good candidates.

Cost per thousand (CPM)

The cost of delivering an advertising message to 1000 people; calculated by dividing the cost of the ad by the circulation in thousands.

When selecting specific media, the cost efficiencies of each alternative are analyzed. To demonstrate, magazines are compared on the basis of **CPM (cost per thousand)**. CPM

FIGURE **5.6** The Relationship between Reach, Frequency, and Continuity

Reach is the number of people potentially exposed to a message in one week.
Frequency is the average number of times a person is exposed to a message in a week.
Continuity is the length of time required to generate impact on a target market.

The relationship among these three variables is dynamic. Since the media budget is usually a fixed amount of money, if one variable is given more priority, then another variable will be given less priority. Otherwise, you will spend beyond the budget. Examine the numbers in the chart. Each plan is different but they achieve the same number of gross impressions.

Gross impressions are calculated by multiplying reach x frequency x continuity.

Variable	Reach	Frequency	Continuity	Impressions
Plan 1	500 000	4	6 weeks	12 000 000
Plan 2	250 000	8	6 weeks	12 000 000
Plan 3	125 000	8	12 weeks	12 000 000

INTERPRETATION
Each plan is different. The first plan stresses reach, the second stresses frequency, and the third stresses continuity. The costs of each plan would be about the same. It's all in the numbers!

is the cost incurred in delivering a message to 1000 readers. It is calculated by dividing the cost of the ad by the circulation of the publication in thousands. Therefore, if an ad cost $20 000 and the circulation was 500 000, the CPM would be $40 ($20 000 divided by 500). When comparing publications that reach the same target market, the ones with the lowest cost per thousand are the most efficient at reaching the target.

Media planners also assess media alternatives qualitatively. In other words, do numbers tell the complete story? Factors such as editorial content, quality of reproduction, and demographic selectivity can lead the media planner to prefer one magazine over another, even if the preferred magazine has a higher CPM. Perhaps there are more pass-along readers of one publication than another. If more people are exposed to the ad, then the real costs of reaching the target are lower than the CPM. Daily newspapers, television networks, and radio stations can be compared on a similar basis. The actual cost of advertising varies from one medium to another (see Figure 5.7). **Appendix 1, "Media Buying Principles and Media Information Resources,"** has additional information about media selection and how various alternatives are compared when making decisions about what media to use.

Media Schedule and Budget Allocations

Media calendar (blocking chart)

A document that shows allocation of a brand's media budget according to time of year and type of medium; shows coordination of various media recommendations.

The final stage for the media planners is developing the media calendar and assigning estimated costs to all activities. A **media calendar** or **blocking chart**, as it is also referred to, summarizes in a few pages all the details of the media execution (e.g., media usage, market coverage, weight levels, reach and frequency, and the timing of the campaign). Accompanying the calendar is a detailed budget. Typically, the media budget classifies spending by medium, region or key market, and time of year. Because plans change during the course of the planning cycle, clients and agencies must know how much money

FIGURE **5.7** **Comparing Media Alternatives for Efficiency**

Magazine	Cost (1P, 4-color)	Circulation (000)	CPM
Report on Business	$15 876	336.5	$47.18
Financial Post Business	$18 770	222.6	$84.32
Canadian Business	$15 410	82.8	$186.11
Newspaper	Cost (1000 lines)	Circulation (000)	CPM
Globe and Mail	$31 890	313.4	$101.75
National Post	$15 280	255.5	$59.80
Toronto Star	$19 160	442.8	$43.27

Rates from *CARD*, January 2005. Magazine ads are full colour; newspaper ads are black and white. *Report on Business Magazine* is distributed free with the *Globe and Mail* and *Financial Post Magazine* is distributed free with the *National Post* newspaper.

Analysis: Based on CPM, the cost of reaching 1000 readers, *Report on Business* is the most efficient of the magazines. The cost of reaching the *Globe and Mail* reader is much higher than the other two newspapers. The *Globe and Mail* is an established, trusted newspaper that reaches an upscale reader. Advertisers are willing to pay more to reach this type of reader. The *Toronto Star* is cost-efficient for reaching a broad cross-section of the population in Toronto, but it does not have national reach.

is committed at any point in time, in case there is a need to cancel activities. Taking the axe to the budget while the plan is in midstream is both common and frustrating for managers.

Media Buying

Once the client approves the media plan, media buyers execute the plan. Buyers work with media representatives to negotiate final prices for the various activities. If the required elements of the plan are unavailable, buyers are responsible for making replacement buys that will achieve the same objectives. The demand for key time periods in television and preferred spaces in magazines and newspapers mean that good timing and effective negotiations skills on the part of the buyer are critical elements of the media buy. In the role of negotiator, the media buyer seeks favourable positions and rates to maximize efficiency and achieve the objectives set out in the plan.

Appendix 2 includes an example of a media plan that shows applications of the various media strategy and execution principles discussed in this chapter.

ASSESSING MEDIA ALTERNATIVES

Media planners choose between traditional media alternatives and non-traditional alternatives. The former category includes television, radio, newspapers, magazines, and out-of-home advertising. The latter includes the Internet, mobile communications through cell phones and personal digital assistants, and video games, all of which are interactive forms of media. Typically, a planner will include several media in the plan, as people refer to more than one medium for information. In the hectic world of today's consumers, the simultaneous use of media is popular. Teens, for example, are online or chatting on their cell phone while watching television. Adults frequently read the newspaper or a magazine while watching television. Knowing the right combinations for various age groups will influence media decisions.

Because consumers refer to so many different media, media planners usually recommend a **primary medium**, which will be allocated most of the budget, and support it with **secondary media**, which complement the primary medium and receive less of the budget. As mentioned earlier, a medium such as television is ideal for creating awareness quickly, whereas print media are good for communicating detailed information over a longer period. The combination of the two media is usually effective. This section will analyze the major mass media alternatives and highlight the pros and cons of each. Chapters 6 and 7 will focus on direct response and interactive forms of advertising.

Primary medium

A medium that receives the largest allocation of an advertiser's budget; the dominant medium in a media plan.

Secondary media

Media alternatives used to complement the primary medium in an advertising campaign; typically less money is allocated to these media.

Television

For what seems like forever, television has been the preferred medium for advertisers, assuming sufficient funds are available. To create brand awareness across a wide cross-section of the population, no medium has traditionally done it better than television. But television as we know it could change drastically in the coming years when one considers the impact of technology and changing media habits among viewers.

Many advertisers are questioning the value of television advertising and are actually shifting money away from TV in favour of other media such as the Internet and video games. On the technology front, personal video recorders (PVRs) are devices that threaten the very economics of television advertising because they allow viewers to opt-out of watching commercials. Already, more that 80 percent of PVR users say they skip the commercials, so advertisers and broadcasters are understandably worried.[5] Fortunately, only 4.5 percent of Canadian homes presently have a PVR, according to BBM data (2005).

BBM Canada
www.bbm.ca

As well, the rise of the Internet, video on demand, and the bleeding of viewers from conventional network television to cable and digital channels has caused many an expert to believe the 30-second TV commercial is dead.[6] PepsiCo relaunched Pepsi One without any television advertising—a sign of the times, perhaps.

Generally, the number of hours a person spends viewing television each week has been drifting downward. The public's preoccupation with the Internet is one reason for this decline. There is a correlation between the two media, however, as people are multitasking—using both media at the same time. An Ipsos Reid study among 2000 Internet users found that Canadians spend 12.7 hours a week online, while Internet-using Canadians average 14.3 hours viewing television each week. Figures like these suggest that television is not dead but in transition. Technology is changing the way people consume the mass media. Television shows can now be accessed by computers and cell phones.

Ipsos Canada
www.ipsos.ca

With the TV universe changing so rapidly it is difficult to reach targets effectively. The biggest threat to television is fragmentation arising from the 300-channel universe that exists today. Conventional network television such as CBC, CTV, and Global account for just 43 percent of the hours watched, down from 79 percent in 1985.[7] Viewers have migrated to specialty channels that account for 44 percent of all viewing compared to just 2 percent in 1985. Among the specialty channels are TSN, YTV, MuchMusic, Discovery Channel, Showcase, Outdoor Life Network, Rogers Sportsnet, and many more. Channels like these are tailored to special interests and attract a particular audience, which can be a benefit to advertisers.

More recently, new digital channels have been added to the mix. Channels such as ESPN Classic Canada, Leafs TV, Lonestar TV, and SexTV attract very narrow audiences. Many of these channels are still searching for an audience.

Budget permitting, however, advertisers are still magically drawn to television. It is a multi-sense medium that is ideal for product demonstrations and appeals to consumers on an emotional level. As well, the reach potential is incredibly high. On an average day, 86 percent of Canadians view television at least once, and 38.5 percent of adults watch television at least once in prime time.[8] With television, media planners have four options: network advertising, selective-spot advertising, local spot advertising, and sponsorships.

Network advertising
Advertising from one central source broadcast across an entire network of stations.

- **Network advertising** on networks such as CTV and Global is suitable for products and services that are widely distributed and have large media budgets. When a spot is placed on the network, the message is received in all network markets. The CTV network, for example, comprises 21 stations and reaches 99 percent of English-speaking Canadians. Popular prime-time shows such as *CSI: Crime Scene Investigation*, *The OC*, *Canadian Idol*, and *Corner Gas* attract big-budget advertisers.

Selective spot
Commercial time during a network show that is allocated back to regional and local stations to sell; advertisers buy spots on a station-by-station basis.

- At the regional or local level, stations fill the balance of their schedules with non-network programs and sell **selective spots** directly to interested advertisers. Local stations are also allocated a certain portion of a network program to sell directly to advertisers. That's why you may see an ad for a local restaurant on *Hockey Night in Canada*.

    Strategically, selective spots benefit advertisers using a key market media strategy. For a large-budget advertiser, there is an opportunity to increase the level of advertising in local markets that are judged as priorities. Small-budget advertisers can simply choose the markets they wish to advertise in. Ads for national spots and selective spots are negotiated and scheduled by an advertising agency as part of the overall media buy.

Local spot
Advertising bought from a local station by a local advertiser.

- With **local spots**, local advertisers like independent retailers and restaurants buy time from local stations. Since local market advertisers don't usually work with an advertising agency, the stations usually provide assistance in the development and production of commercials for local clients.

Sponsorship
The act of financially supporting an event in return for certain advertising rights and privileges.

- **Sponsorship** allows an advertiser to take "ownership" of a property that is targeted at its consumer audience. If the fit is right, the advertiser can leverage the sponsorship by extending the relationship to include consumer and trade promotions, and alternate media exposure. To illustrate, consider Bell Canada's investment in a "hockeymentary" called Making the Cut. Making the Cut was a 13-week series that followed 7000 Canadian hockey hopefuls who had the opportunity to make the cut, go to an NHL team training camp, and get a legitimate chance to live their dream of playing in the big league. Bell Canada paid for the entire production of the program.

Bell Canada
www.bell.ca

What was the benefit for Bell? Alek Krstajic, chief marketing officer, knew right away that *Making the Cut* was a perfect and timely fit because hockey had already been identified as a major focus of its marketing efforts. Sports programming serves the company's objective of winning the fiercely competitive Canadian broadband market with a variety of telecom services: voice, video, and Internet. "A program like *Making the Cut* puts the Bell brand in the hearts and minds of Canadians all over, because hockey is Canada's sport," says Krstajic.[9]

Secondary sponsors of *Making the Cut* included Samsung, Kelsey's restaurants, Scotiabank, Schick, and Nike Bauer. Nike Bauer outfitted all of the players with equipment. The branded equipment was clearly visible during the show.

Television provides advertisers a means of reaching huge numbers of people in a short space of time with a compelling message. Companies that can afford to advertise in prime time on shows like *Survivor*, *ER*, and *Law & Order* or on sports programming like *Hockey Night in Canada* or *NHL Playoffs* have high reach almost instantaneously. Television is an expensive medium, so to save money many advertisers are opting for 15-second commercials.

If reaching a well-defined target is a priority, television is not a good option. The audience in prime time, for example, spans all ages. You will reach your target, but you're also paying for everyone else who is watching. Furthermore, clutter is a problem on television;

FIGURE **5.8** **Advantages and Disadvantages of Television Advertising**

ADVANTAGES

Impact—sight, sound, motion; demonstration; emotion
Reach—high reach in short space of time
Some targeting—sports and specialty cable channels reach niche targets
Coverage flexibility—local, regional, and national options

DISADVANTAGES

High cost—desired frequency (message repetition) increases absolute cost
Clutter—too many spots in a cluster negates potential impact
Audience fragmentation—abundance of channels lowers audience size (reach potential)
Technology—electronic equipment records programs and edits out commercials

Cluster

Ads Grouped in a block of time during a break in a program or between programs.

there are simply too many ads. Given that ads are scheduled in a **cluster**, does an advertiser want to be the third or fourth commercial in a cluster of six? Refer to the discussion about CPM in the "Media Execution" section for more details, and consult Figure 5.8 for a summary of the advantages and disadvantages of television advertising.

New Strategies for Reaching a Television Audience

Television and television advertising is not about to disappear, but new solutions for reaching viewers must be found to retain the economics of the system. Many advertisers have already found more compelling ways of delivering advertising messages on television. A few new alternatives include product placement, branded content, and shorter TV commercials.

Product placement

The visible placement of brand name products in television shows, movies, radio, video games, and other programming.

Product placement refers to the visible placement of branded merchandise in television shows, films, or video games. Hollywood has been doing product placement in movies for years, but television is now catching on to the practice fast. In the first quarter of the 2005 television season, Coca-Cola Classic appeared 1931 times on US television shows. It was a dominant brand on *American Idol*, the most-watched program that season.[10] Visa utilizes product placement on the hit show *Corner Gas*. The Visa logo appears on the gas station's door and at the cashier stand. Exposure such as this has more credibility with the audience than regular advertising.

Branded content (product integration)

The integration of brand name goods and services into the script (storyline) of a television show or movie. The brand name is clearly mentioned and sometimes discussed.

Branded content or **product integration** takes product placement a step further by integrating the brand into the script of the television show. Kia Canada joined forces with the CBC in the hockey "mockumentary" series *The Tournament* as fully integrated partners. The Kia brand and products were integrated into the story, with real characters, real Kia dealerships, and real Kia products as a central part of the story. To promote the sponsorship, a five-week national contest invited viewers to tune into the show and then log on to cbc.ca/television for a chance to win a Kia Killer Sports Weekend with Doug Gilmour. Kia and other sponsor brands were also included on rink board advertising in the arenas where the show was filmed.[11]

Kia Canada
www.kia.ca

In the United States, many of *The Apprentice* shows featuring Donald Trump have focused entirely on branded products. Among them have been Dove Body Wash and Pontiac. Pontiac saw instant results for its effort. On *The Apprentice*, teams were challenged to create a brochure for the sleek new Pontiac Solstice, a two-seat sports convertible. During the show, traffic to pontiac.com rose by 1400 percent with close to 1 million unique visitors going to the site. In just 41 minutes, 1000 people placed orders for the vehicle at the website. It is estimated that GM paid about $2 million to have the Pontiac Solstice embedded in the show.[12]

Shorter commercials are another option for effectively delivering television ads. In fact, a double-edged strategy involving short commercials and websites offers great promise. The shorter TV ads are used primarily as a vehicle to drive viewers to a website, where a more thorough job of message delivery is accomplished. A recent Mott's Clamato campaign used a teaser TV ad claiming an intended ad was taken off the air (it was too hot!) and gave a website where viewers could get the full story. The "big idea" was a spicy campaign for a spicy drink—but not all of it could be shown on television. The website attracted 150 000 new visitors in its first week.[13] The short ad attracted attention and at a much lower cost than a standard 30-second commercial.

The changes occurring in the television industry have direct implications for advertisers. Essentially, advertisers have two basic options: they can reduce investment in television advertising, making it less important in the mix than previously, or they can shift their investment entirely. While the latter option seems radical, many large advertisers are doing a lot of soul searching about their TV budgets. Other advertisers firmly believe that television will remain the dominant medium and that it's mandatory if the goal is to build brand image. For some additional insight into this issue, read the IMC Highlight **Is TV Losing Its Luster?**

Mott's Clamato
www.mottsclamato.com

IMC HIGHLIGHT

IS TV LOSING ITS LUSTER?

Many advertisers are taking a closer look at the media habits of their customers and reallocating media budgets in accordance with the latest trends. Television—specifically network television—seems to be the medium that has been hit the hardest as advertisers move in the direction of magazines, outdoor advertising, cable TV, online communications, direct mail, and event marketing.

Mitsubishi Motors North America has perhaps taken the boldest step by totally abandoning network television and newspaper advertising. According to Ian Beavis, senior vice-president of marketing at Mitsubishi, "We are targeting consumer segments based on psychographic rather than demographic information, and it's leading to more integrated communications programs." He says he must fish where the fish are, and since they are leaving network television in big numbers, he has no choice but to reallocate his budget.

Even such traditional TV advertisers like Procter & Gamble and Unilever have reduced their presence on conventional television in favour of specialty cable networks. Similar to Mitsubishi, it's a media strategy based more on psychographics than demographics. Procter & Gamble has instructed its agencies to adopt an approach that calls for media-neutral planning so that each brand uses the best

channel to reach consumers. At P&G there is no such thing as one size fits all—each brand requires a unique marketing mix.

Like other companies, P&G is finding new ways to use television. It leveraged the popularity of reality TV with a product placement deal that embedded some brands, such as Crest, Ivory, and Pantene, as rewards on the program *Survivor: All Stars*.

When Mazda launched the new Mazda5, a sporty-looking family vehicle aimed at 25 to 35 year olds who don't want to give up the "zoom zoom" in their life, television was excluded from the mix. Convinced that this age group didn't sit in front of the TV, the media plan went in a new direction. The media mix included an aggressive magazine push, online ads, direct mail, and cinema-screen advertising. Other Mazda models continue to use television advertising, and television still receives the largest portion of the company's media budget.

Is TV advertising losing its luster? Are these companies making the right decisions or could they be making a huge mistake? You be the judge by investigating the situation further.

Adapted from Patti Summerfield, "Casting for a better net," *Strategy*, August 2004, pp. 24, 28, and Jean Halliday, "Mazda switches off TV, stays out of out-of-home for new-model launch," *Advertising Age*, June 20, 2005, p. 4.

Radio

As of 2005, 1998 radio stations operated in Canada: 425 AM stations and 1573 FM stations. Collectively these stations reach 93 percent of the population, with FM stations being far more popular than AM stations. All radio stations are self-regulating, with no restrictions on the number of commercial minutes or on the placement of those minutes.[14]

Generally, Canadians are listening to the radio less today than they did 10 years ago. On average, people listen to the radio for 19 hours a week, about 1.5 hours less than a decade earlier. Where people listen to the radio is also changing. The proportion of time spent listening to the radio in the home is now 49 percent (down from 55 percent 10 years ago), and listening to the radio in cars is now up to 27 percent (21 percent 10 years ago).[15]

As a medium, radio has little appeal for teenagers. They only listen to radio for about 8.5 hours a week. Teens have shifted their allegiance to new technologies, such as iPods and MP3 players, video games, music file-sharing, and music downloading. Radio, therefore, is at a disadvantage as many advertisers lust at reaching teen consumers just starting to form brand loyalties.

One of the major advantages of radio is its ability to reach selective target markets. In fact, radio is a one-on-one medium more in tune with the lives of its listeners than tele-vision or newspapers, which appeal to the masses. Radio's ability to personally connect with listeners helps explain why it can be effective. For advertisers, this means that messages need to speak to listeners as individuals, not as a group.[16]

Format

The type and nature of the programming offered by a radio station.

The audience reached depends on the format of the station. **Format** refers to the type and nature of the programming offered by a station. Basically, the content is designed to appeal to a particular target group, usually defined by age and interests. In radio, everything is based on demographics.

The most popular radio station formats among adults are adult contemporary, gold, and rock. Adult contemporary (AC) stations play popular and easy-listening music, current and past, and generally appeal to an audience in the 25- to 49-year-old range. Adult contemporary is the top format, commanding a 25 percent market share.[17]

Most listeners tune into FM stations, which hold 75 percent market share. The preference for FM is largely due to the better sound quality and the transfer of many stations from the AM band to the FM band. The news/talk format has been a renaissance for AM stations that moved in that direction. The news/talk format encourages interactivity with listeners and has attracted active rather than passive listeners. This format has been extended further to all-sports stations like THE FAN 590 in Toronto. THE FAN 590 is a niche station popular with sports-minded males who like to talk about sports news and rumours.

Because of its ability to reach precisely defined demographic targets in local markets, radio can be an ideal component of a "key market" media plan. As well, it is a relatively inexpensive medium. An advertiser can achieve high frequency on a weekly basis. In fact, radio is often referred to as the "frequency medium." If frequency is the strategic priority, then radio is a good fit.

While reach potential is high, a radio audience is fragmented in major urban markets. If several stations compete for the loyalty of the same demographic, an advertiser would have to buy spots on all the stations to reach the target. That would drive the cost of advertising up. Unlike TV, which is an evening medium, radio is a morning medium. In fact, breakfast time—between 8 am and 9 am—is the highest daily period for tuning by all demographics. There is a downward drift in listening as the day progresses, with a slight blip upward in the afternoon drive-home period (4 pm to 6 pm). Listening trends such as these can influence the placement (timing) of an advertiser's message.

For additional information about the advantages and disadvantages of radio advertising, refer to Figure 5.9.

FIGURE **5.9** **Advantages and Disadvantages of Radio Advertising**

ADVANTAGES

Target selectivity—station format attracts a defined audience (profile matching possible)
Frequency—reach plans rotate messages through entire audience weekly
Cost—very favourable compared to other media
Flexibility—stations and markets selected according to priority (key market strategy)

DISADVANTAGES

Audience fragmentation—multiple stations competing for the same demographic reduces station's audience potential
Message retention—sound-only medium; clever creative required

---

Internet radio
Listening to radio broadcasts via the Internet.

Podcasting
Audio programming that is downloadable to iPods and other portable digital media devices; allows the listener to tune in when it is convenient for them to do so.

Satellite radio
A radio service that offers commercial-free programming for a monthly fee.

Several new technologies will influence the direction of the radio industry in the near future. Among these technologies are Internet radio, podcasting, and satellite radio. As the name suggests, **Internet radio** involves listening to audio broadcasts via the Internet. The broadcasts are streamed and played by a software media player in the computer. The broadcasts come from a myriad of different organizations as well as traditional radio stations. Since the signal is relayed over the Internet, it is possible to access stations from anywhere in the world.

The second and already popular technology is called podcasting. **Podcasting** describes audio programming that is downloadable to iPods and other portable digital media devices. It allows listeners to tune in when it is convenient for them to do so. Radio shows are recorded, posted to a website as an MP3 file where they can be downloaded to the player. Podcasting is unlikely to make conventional radio obsolete, but it does offer huge commercial potential for sponsors and specially packaged programming once podcasting becomes easier to navigate.[18]

The third technology is satellite radio. **Satellite radio** offers commercial-free programming and is available through two suppliers: XM Canada and Sirius Canada. Both services require a special radio that costs between $70 and $90 and a subscription to one of the service suppliers for $14.99 a month.[19] Despite its name, satellite radio doesn't carry a selection of the best stations from around the world. In fact, they are stations operating solely for their respective services, not traditional stations at all. The question remains: are Canadians willing to pay for commercial-free radio? Satellite radio in the United States has attracted 4 million subscribers since its inception in 2001.[20]

Newspapers

Circulation
The average number of copies per issue of a publication sold by subscription, distributed free to predetermined recipients, carried with other publications, or made available through retail distributors.

Broadsheet
A large newspaper with a fold in its middle.

Canada has 108 daily newspapers, with a total average daily circulation of 5.2 million copies. **Circulation** is defined as the average number of copies per issue of a publication that are sold by subscription, distributed free to predetermined recipients, carried within other publications, or made available through retail distributors.

Industry research indicates that 53 percent of Canada's adult population reads a daily newspaper on any given weekday. On the weekend, readership increases to 58 percent. Newspapers are a popular medium among advertisers. Net advertising revenue generated by newspapers rank second in Canada, behind only television.

Newspapers are produced in two formats: broadsheets and tabloids. A **broadsheet** is a large newspaper with a fold in the middle. Most Canadian dailies are published as broadsheets, including circulation leaders such as the *Toronto Star,* the *Globe and Mail,* and the

Tabloid
A smaller newspaper that is sold flat (not folded).

Retail advertising
Advertising by a retail store; involves advertising the store name, image, location, and the re-advertising of branded merchandise carried by the store.

Classified advertising
Print advertising in which similar goods and services are grouped together in categories under appropriate headings.

Insert
A preprinted, free-standing advertisement (e.g., a leaflet, brochure, or flyer) specifically placed in a newspaper or magazine.

Clutter
The amount of advertising in a particular medium.

National Post. A **tabloid** is a smaller newspaper in terms of surface area. It is sold flat and resembles an unbound magazine. The Sun newspaper chain (*Toronto Sun, Ottawa Sun, Calgary Sun,* and so on) publishes all of its newspapers in tabloid format.

Several "free" daily newspapers have been launched recently in Canada. *Metro* and *24 Hours* are targeted directly at commuters in selected markets and are distributed at or near transit facilities. The free dailies continue to eat into the readership pie. In Toronto they presently account for 25 percent of newspaper readers; in Montreal 20 percent.[21]

Community newspapers are small-circulation newspapers usually published weekly. The community paper is the voice of the community. As such, it is well read. Among English Canadians, community papers are read by 71 percent of the population. Among French Canadians, readership is 63 percent. The readership of community newspapers parallels the demographics of the community. For that reason, they are an excellent advertising medium for local businesses.

Newspapers generate revenues from different types of advertising:

- **National Advertising:** National ads are sold to advertisers and ad agencies by a national sales department. Advertisers in this category include products and services marketed nationally or regionally. Brand name food and beverages, automobiles, airlines, banks and financial institutions, computers, and telecommunications products and services fall into this category.

- **Retail Advertising:** Retail advertisers include department stores, supermarkets, drug stores, restaurants, and a host of other independent retailers. These retailers usually advertise sales or re-advertise the nationally branded merchandise they sell. Retail advertising generates a majority of revenue for a newspaper. It truly is a local market medium.

- **Classified Advertising:** Classified ads provide an opportunity for readers and local businesses to buy, sell, lease, or rent all kinds of goods and services. Typically, the classified section is well read and in many large dailies is a separate section of the newspaper, a testament to its significance.

- **Preprinted Inserts:** The preprinted **insert** (often referred to as a free-standing insert) is a dedicated piece of advertising inserted into the fold of a newspaper. Large users of inserts include department stores (Sears, Wal-Mart, and others), drugstore chains (Shoppers Drug Mart and others), large general merchandisers (Canadian Tire and Home Depot), and electronics retailers (Best Buy, Future Shop, and The Brick).

Preprinted inserts are catching on with marketing organizations, but they are not yet a staple item in a media planner's recommendations to clients. According to Wayne Clifton, vice-president of advertising at the *Toronto Star*, "It's a steadily growing business." He cites Dell Computer and Sprint Canada as clients that frequently use inserts.[22] Perhaps it's the perception of inserts held by media planners that is holding them back.

For advertisers, newspapers offer geographic selectivity and high reach in local markets. Furthermore, newspapers and readers have a relationship with each other. Readers have a tendency to read the entire newspaper in their own unique and sequential manner. For this reason, they are likely at least to see an ad in the paper. Newspapers are an effective choice for reaching broadly defined adult target markets. Unfortunately, the papers' life span is very short (one day for dailies). As the old saying goes, "There's nothing as stale as yesterday's news." Newspapers also suffer from a clutter problem. **Clutter** refers to the amount of advertising in a medium. About 60 percent of newspaper space is devoted to advertising, so standing out in the crowd is a design challenge for the creative team. See Figure 5.10 for a summary of the advantages and disadvantages of newspaper advertising.

FIGURE **5.10** | Advantages and Disadvantages of Newspaper Advertising

ADVANTAGES

Targeting capability—reaches a diverse adult audience in key geographic markets
Reach—ideal for reaching consumers in local markets frequently
Media environment—readers engage with paper based on editorial content; they are receptive to messages
Merchandising—national advertisers have cooperative advertising opportunities with local market retailers

DISADVANTAGES

Life span—daily; exposure to message reduced if paper not read on day of publication
Audience diversity—not suitable if target market profile is precisely defined (exception may be the *Globe and Mail*)
Clutter—lots of space devoted to advertising (many ads on one page)
Reproduction quality—primarily a black and white medium; speed of presses reduces colour quality

Magazines

Magazines Canada
www.cmpa.ca

Paid circulation
The circulation of a newspaper or magazine that is generated by subscription sales and newsstand sales.

Controlled circulation
The circulation of a publication that is distributed free to individuals in a specific demographic segment or geographic area.

Currently, more than 1600 magazines are published and distributed in Canada, 730 of which are classified as consumer magazines. Business magazines are another large category.

Canadian consumer magazines are distributed on the basis of paid circulation or controlled circulation. **Paid circulation** refers to subscriptions and newsstand sales. Magazines such as *Maclean's*, *Chatelaine*, and *Canadian Business* are paid circulation magazines and rely on subscriptions, newsstand sales, and advertising space to generate revenues. Canada's most popular consumer magazines sold by subscription or at newsstands include *Reader's Digest* (957 300 circulation), *Chatelaine* (670 500), and *Canadian Living* (533 300).

Some magazines are distributed free to a predetermined target audience based on demographic, geographic, job function, or some other characteristic. These are **controlled circulation** magazines. Typically, receivers of the magazines are in a unique position to influence sales, so they are attractive to advertisers wanting to reach them. City-oriented lifestyle magazines such as *Toronto Life*, *Ottawa Life*, and *Vancouver Magazine* are examples of controlled circulation magazines. Much of their circulation is based on distribution to selected households, hotels, and motels in their respective markets. Entertainment magazines distributed free in movie theatres also fall in this category.

Business magazines are divided into various industry categories: food manufacturing and distribution, hardware trade, hotels and restaurants, telecommunications, engineering and construction, and so on. These magazines are very specialized, their content appealing to people employed in a certain industry or a particular job function. Some magazine titles include *Canadian Grocer*, *Hotel & Restaurant*, *Modern Purchasing*, and *Marketing Magazine*. The profile of readers is based on a common interest or function, so these magazines are an efficient means of reaching prospects with a business-to-business advertising message.

Magazines are ideal for advertising purposes. For advertisers using a profile-matching strategy or rifle strategy, they serve a useful role. Magazines are often referred to as a "class" medium rather than a "mass" medium. In other words, readership is well defined on the basis of demographic and psychographic variables (profile matching), and there are all kinds of magazines devoted to a particular interest or activity (rifle strategy). As well, many large-circulation consumer magazines offer regional editions, so if geography is a factor influencing the media strategy, magazines can be part of the solution. Magazines are read for their editorial content; therefore, advertisers' messages benefit from the prestige of being associated with the magazine and the quality it represents. Many studies have proven that readers are more engaged with magazines, and they consider advertising in magazines to be more acceptable and enjoyable than in other media.[23]

Clutter remains a problem in most consumer magazines. The clustering of ads at the beginning of a publication, for example, may mean that a reader skips over an entire section of ads on the way to reaching editorial content. Advertisers combat the problem by requesting specific locations in a magazine. Covers, for example, are preferred positions and command a higher price. If frequency is a key objective, magazines are not a viable option. Most are published monthly or every two months, so they are good for achieving reach among a defined target audience and delivering continuity of message from month to month. More information about the advantages and disadvantages of magazine advertising appears in Figure 5.11.

Out-of-Home Advertising

Out-of-home advertising represents a highly visible and effective alternative for advertisers. Think about it: if you drive a car, travel by transit, or stroll through shopping malls, you are constantly exposed to out-of-home advertising messages. Advertising investment in out-of-home advertising is increasing at a much greater rate than other media. In 2004, outdoor advertising revenue in Canada totalled $303 million, a 7 percent increase over 2003.[24] Advertisers' concerns about the fragmentation of television audiences and the tuning out of broadcast messages have driven demand for out-of-home delivery.

If the goal of an advertising campaign is to reach as many people as possible, then out-of-home should be the medium of choice. Although considered by some to be "pollution on a stick," outdoor boards are a proven way to reach an increasingly mobile

FIGURE **5.11** **Advantages and Disadvantages of Magazine Advertising**

ADVANTAGES

Targeting capability—good reach based on readers' demographic (profile-matching strategy) and psychographic (rifle strategy) characteristics
Coverage flexibility—city, regional, and national magazines available
Life span—magazines tend not to be discarded right away; opportunity for multiple exposures to message
Quality—excellent colour reproduction
Environment—message benefits from the prestige of association with the magazine's quality and image
Pass-along readership—actual readership goes beyond the subscriber (added reach)

DISADVANTAGES

Clutter—abundance of ads appearing in the initial section (advertising domination in some magazines)
Cost—colour is an added cost in production of ad
Frequency—distribution is usually monthly or bi-monthly

population.[25] The major classifications of out-of-home media include outdoor advertising and transit advertising.

Outdoor Advertising

Poster (billboard)

A common form of outdoor advertising; usually a picture-dominant advertisement with a minimum of copy.

Posters or **billboards**, as they are commonly referred to, are large sheets of poster paper mounted on a panel of some kind. To maximize reach potential, they are strategically located on major travel routes leading to or within a community's business and shopping districts. To maximize the frequency of message and to extend daily viewing by consumers, posters are often illuminated. A powerful light beams upward from the bottom of the poster.

Trident Splash, a new gum, used outdoor advertising to add reach to its television advertising. TV ads showed unsuspecting people in a bar and at a bus stop being drenched with splashes of water. A gum-chewing male wearing a bathing suit was ready for the splash. Posters were viewed as a means of reaching time-strapped consumers who don't watch as much television as they used to. See the illustration in Figure 5.12.

Backlit poster

A luminous outdoor sign printed on polyvinyl material.

A step up in quality is the **backlit poster**. On a backlit, the advertising message is printed on translucent polyvinyl material. When the posters are erected, lights shine through the material from behind the sign. The primary advantage is the image enhancement offered by this lighting; there is strong visual impact in the day and night. Backlits

FIGURE 5.12 **Trident Splash Expands Reach by Adding Outdoor Posters to Its Media Mix**

Source: Courtesy of Keith Tuckwell.

FIGURE **5.13** **Backlit Posters are Ideal for Day and Night Viewing**

Source: Courtesy of Keith Tuckwell.

are strategically located at major intersections and on high-volume traffic routes. For the advertiser, they cost more. For an illustration see Figure 5.13.

A **superboard** or **spectacular** is an extremely large display unit positioned at the highest-volume traffic locations. It is created to the advertiser's specifications and can include space extensions, flashing lights, louvres, and electronic messaging. Since superboards are one-of-a-kind structures that are illuminated and frequently include moving objects, they require a long-term commitment from the advertiser due to the high expense of designing and constructing them. Spectaculars are beyond the budgets of most advertisers.

Banners are large vinyl banners framed and mounted on the outside of a building. They can be moved and re-used. **Mural advertisements** are hand-painted outdoor extravaganzas placed on the sides of buildings. They are very large—often the entire height of the building. If size really matters, these kinds of ads are real attention grabbers.

Technology is providing a means for outdoor advertising to be interactive. At one time all outdoor posters were static in nature, but now they can display multiple messages at the same time. **Electronic signs** display electronic messages on a rotating basis (typically 10 to 15 seconds in length). Electronic signs are proving to be a medium that helps build frequency of message on a weekly basis. Thus far, they are only available in major urban markets, usually in high-traffic downtown areas.

Transit shelter advertising is located in structures in downtown and surrounding areas to provide shelter for public transit riders. Each shelter has two faces that are back-lit from dusk to dawn. These shelters offer high levels of exposure to motorists, pedestrians, and transit riders. Transit shelter advertising offers the advertiser strong visual impact, as the colour reproduction is of superior quality.

Mall posters differ from the posters described above because they rely only on pedes-

Superboard (spectacular)

Outdoor advertising that is larger than a normal poster and much more expensive to produce; can include extensions beyond borders and electronic messaging.

Banner

In outdoor advertising, a large-sized print ad that is framed and mounted on the exterior of a building.

Mural advertisement

A hand-painted outdoor ad seen on the side of a building.

Electronic signs

Advertisements that are displayed on electronic billboards that rotate about every 10 to 15 seconds so multiple messages can be displayed at the same time.

Transit shelter advertising

Street-level advertisements incorporated into the design of the glass and steel shelters located at a bus stop.

trian traffic and aren't exposed to vehicle traffic. Located in shopping malls, they are directed at consumers who are actually shopping; therefore, they are a useful medium for the mall's retailers. Mall posters are good for supplementing other media and for reinforcing a brand's primary selling message.

The various forms of outdoor advertising are ideal for advertisers using a shotgun strategy. Posters reach a large cross-section of a market's population in a short period. Frequently outdoor boards are included in a blitz or build-up schedule because they are good for launching new products where creating awareness for the brand name, brand logo, and package are important. Outdoor posters are also ideal for advertisers who want geographic flexibility; the advertiser selects only those urban areas that are given priority.

There are a few drawbacks as well. The message must be brief, considering the circumstances in which people view outdoor boards. Since they reach a wide cross-section of the population, they are not a targeted medium. The message reaches people well beyond the target, which will increase the cost of reaching an actual target customer.

Transit Advertising

People who use public transit are a captive audience for advertising messages. To relieve the boredom of travelling, ads offer a form of visual stimulation. I know from personal experience that passengers read the same ad over and over again while riding a subway car or bus.

Interior cards are print advertisements contained in racks above the windows of transit vehicles (buses, street cars, subway cars, and rapid transit cars). The average time spent travelling is approximately 30 minutes, offering the advertiser the flexibility of including longer messages—not an option in other forms of outdoor advertising.

Two different posters are available on the outside of buses. The **king poster** is a very large poster that stretches along the side of a bus. A **seventy poster** is smaller and located on the tail end of the vehicle. The unique characteristic of bus posters is their mobility. They move through the city and are seen by lots of motorists and pedestrians.

Superbus advertising involves painting the outside of a bus to carry one advertising message. Due to the costs, the advertiser must commit to a long-term contract (26 or 52 weeks) with the transit company. As part of the package, the advertiser gets all of the interior cards as well. **Bus murals** are also available and appear on the driver's side or the tail of the bus, or both. These are applied using vinyl products and are sold for commitments of 12 weeks or more.

Station posters are advertisements located on platforms and at the entrances and exits of subway and light rail transit systems. They are available in a variety of sizes and are either paper posters or backlit posters. Passengers waiting on platforms are exposed to the advertising message. A variety of new and innovative concepts have recently been introduced. Among them are *stair risers* (ads that appear on the sides of steps that can be read from a distance), *ceiling decals* in vehicles, and *floor decals* on walkways and platforms. Another concept called *station domination* gives a single advertiser control of all advertising space in a subway station. These are good options for advertisers looking for new ways of standing out amid the clutter of out-of-home advertising.

From an advertising perspective, transit offers continuous exposure. That 30-minute commute provides ample opportunity to deliver an advertising message. In terms of advertising objectives, transit achieves both reach and frequency. Transit riders cut across all demographics, with the heaviest concentration being adults. Factors such as the increasing cost of operating a car and the increasing numbers of commuters travelling to and from a city each day have a positive effect on the reach potential of the medium. Like outdoor advertising, transit advertising is suited for media strategies designed to reach a diverse audience in key markets. Refer to Figure 5.14 for additional details about the benefits and drawbacks of the various forms of out-of-home advertising.

FIGURE **5.14** **Advantages and Disadvantages of Out-of-Home Advertising**

OUTDOOR POSTERS

Advantages

Reach and frequency—reach a large general audience daily
Coverage flexibility—markets selected geographically (key market plan)
Compatibility—a good complementary medium to reinforce a message
(name, logo, slogan)
Awareness—often included in teaser and blitz campaigns for new products due to
reach potential

Disadvantages

Creative limitations—message must be concise; good visuals mandatory
Targeting—not suitable for reaching precisely defined targets
Cost—absolute costs high compared to other media (minimum four-week cycles)
Image—often referred to as "urban clutter"

TRANSIT

Advantages

Reach and frequency—riders receive same message daily, weekly, and monthly
Continuous exposure—trapped riders view same ad many times
Coverage flexibility—markets selected geographically, based on priority
(key market strategy)

Disadvantages

Targeting—a diverse cross-section of population, therefore some circulation wasted
Environment—cluttered and crowded environment in peak periods makes message
less visible

Other Forms of Out-of-Home Advertising

It's everywhere! It's everywhere! There are all kinds of unique opportunities to reach consumers when they least expect it. Among the more popular options with advertisers are washroom advertising, elevator advertising, and cinema advertising.

Washroom advertising involves the placement of mini-posters in public washrooms, usually above urinals in men's washrooms and on the backs of stall doors. They are located in colleges and universities, sporting facilities, hospitals, restaurants, and bars. Levi's and Budweiser are two brands that use this form of advertising. According to Gino Cantalini, marketing manager for Budweiser, "They are innovative and offer a certain degree of targeting."[27] Budweiser is reaching its audience in a location close to where purchase decisions are made.

Elevator advertising is available in two forms: posters contained in display frames on the walls of elevators and slim-line televisions usually mounted in the top corner and tilted downward toward the passengers. The Elevator News Network (ENN) delivers up-to-date news and information along with ads on TV screens in office towers in major cities.

Arena and stadium advertising opportunities extend across North America and offer targeted reach for advertisers. In arenas that are home to professional hockey teams, advertising starts right above the front door, with companies paying megabucks to have an arena adorned with their name. GM Place in Vancouver, Air Canada Centre in Toronto, Scotiabank Place in Ottawa (formerly the Corel Centre), and Bell Centre in Montreal are just some examples. In hockey arenas, there is also on-ice advertising, usually ads painted in the neutral zone between the blue lines. Signs can also be installed

Washroom advertising
A mini-poster ad located in a public or institutional washroom; usually placed above the urinal or on the back of the stall door.

Budweiser
www.budweiser.com

Elevator advertising
Advertising in display frames on elevator walls or on televisions mounted in the corner or above the door.

behind the player's benches and in the penalty box. At ballparks, rotating signs behind home plate are popular, and there are courtside signs on basketball courts. These signs receive additional exposure when a game is broadcast on television.

Cinema advertising
Print advertising inside film theatres and broadcast advertising on screens; options include television-style ads on screen, slides, posters, and ads printed on tickets.

Cinema advertising offers a variety of options, everything from 30- and 60-second commercials, on-screen slides, lobby posters, theatre promotions, ads printed on movie tickets, and more. Cinema advertising is growing in popularity with Canadian advertisers. Cinema advertising is somewhat controversial as theatre patrons have paid to see the movie—many dislike the intrusion of advertising. Nonetheless, a captive audience and engaging content (a full-motion commercial that is entertaining and in Dolby sound) make the cinema a powerful advertising medium. Lifestyle products such as automobiles, telecommunications devices, and beverages find cinema advertising attractive.

Summary

Media planning is the process of developing a plan of action for communicating messages to the right people at the right time. The end result is a media plan prepared by an advertising agency that covers all relevant media strategies and tactics. It is a document that is presented to the client for approval, and, once approved, is put into action.

The key elements of the plan are media objectives, media strategies, and media execution. Media objectives deal with five key issues: who to reach, what and how to present the message creatively, where to advertise, when to advertise, and how often to advertise. Media objectives establish priorities for the plan and provide guidance for developing media strategies.

Media strategy deals with the selection of appropriate media to accomplish the objectives. Strategies are influenced by variables such as the characteristics and behaviour of the target market; the nature of the message; the degree of market coverage desired; the best time to reach the target; competitive activity; reach, frequency, and continuity; an assessment of the benefits and drawbacks of the various media options; and the available budget.

The advertising agency makes specific recommendations regarding the media a client should use. Depending on the assessment of the situation, and assuming the client wants to use traditional mass media, there are numerous alternatives: television, radio, newspapers, magazines, outdoor advertising in a variety of forms, and transit advertising. Some unique and newer options are also considered: washroom advertising, elevator advertising, advertising in arenas and stadiums, and advertising in cinemas. To meet the challenge, the advertising agency usually recommends a combination of media. Typically, there is one primary medium (a medium that receives a significant portion of the budget) supplemented with secondary media.

Media execution is the section of the media plan that outlines the specific tactics for achieving the media objectives. These include the specific media usage recommendations and summaries of how media funds will be allocated. Once the plan is approved, the agency's media buyers negotiate the best possible prices with media representatives. The plan is then put into action.

Key Terms

backlit poster, 158

banner, 159

billboard, 158

blitz schedule, 145

blocking chart, 147

brand development index (BDI), 142

branded content, 151

broadsheet, 154

build-up schedule, 145

bus murals, 160

category development index (CDI), 142

cinema advertising, 162

circulation, 154

classified advertising, 155

cluster, 151

clutter, 155

continuity, 146

controlled circulation, 156

cost per thousand (CPM), 146

electronic signs, 159

elevator advertising, 161

even schedule, 145

flight, 143

format, 153

frequency, 145

gross rating points (GRPs), 145

insert, 155

interior card, 160

Internet radio, 154

king poster, 160

local spot, 150

mall poster, 160

market development index, 142

media brief, 134

media calendar, 147

media execution, 146

media objective, 136

media plan, 136

media strategy, 138

mural advertisement, 159

network advertising, 150

paid circulation, 156

podcasting, 154

post-buy analysis, 136

poster, 158

primary medium, 149

product integration, 151

product placement, 151

profile-matching strategy, 140

pulse schedule, 144

reach, 145

retail advertising, 155

rifle strategy, 140

satellite radio, 154

seasonal schedule, 145

secondary media, 149

selective spot, 150

seventy poster, 160

shotgun strategy, 140

skip schedule, 143

spectacular, 159

sponsorship, 150

station poster, 160

superboard, 159

superbus advertising, 160

tabloid, 155

transit shelter advertising, 159

washroom advertising, 161

Review Questions

1. What are the essential differences among media objectives, media strategies, and media execution?

2. Identify and briefly describe the key issues usually covered by media objective statements.

3. What is the difference between a profile-matching strategy, a shotgun strategy, and a rifle strategy? What media are best suited for each strategy?

4. What is the difference between the following market coverage strategies: national coverage, regional coverage, and key market coverage? What media are best suited for each strategy?

5. Briefly describe how the timing and amount of spending vary in the following media schedules: pulse, skip, blitz, and build-up.

6. Briefly describe the impact of reach, frequency, and continuity on strategic media planning.

7. What role does CPM play in media selection? How is it calculated?

8. Identify two key strengths and weaknesses for each of the following media: television, radio, magazines, newspapers, outdoor boards, and transit.

9. In television advertising, what is the difference between a network spot and a selective spot?

10. What is the difference between product placement and branded content?

11. Briefly describe the following media terms:
    a) format (of a radio station)
    b) broadsheet and tabloid
    c) paid circulation and controlled circulation
    d) clutter and cluster
    e) posters and backlit posters (outdoor)

Discussion and Application Questions

1. How will technological advances affect media strategy and media execution in the future?

2. Should the budget determine the media plan or should the media plan determine the budget? Briefly explain and establish an opinion on this issue.

3. Read the IMC Highlight **Is TV Losing Its Luster?** Do you think television advertising will continue to play a key role in the future, or will advertisers shift their preference to other media? Investigate the situation further by examining any other external trends that may influence such a decision and provide sound arguments for your opinion.

4. Is it possible to implement a rifle media strategy by using television advertising? Justify your position by providing branded advertising campaigns that are scheduled effectively or ineffectively on television networks and channels.

5. Assuming you can't have both high reach and high frequency, under what circumstances should reach take precedence? Under what circumstances should frequency take precedence? Be specific and provide examples.

6. Given the nature of Canada's population and where the bulk of the population is located, when is it practical to implement a national media campaign? When do regional media campaigns or key market media campaigns make economic sense?

7. Using resources that are available in your library or online, compare the CPMs for three different magazines that compete with each other. They must be magazines that reach a similar target audience and attract similar advertisers. Which magazine is the most efficient at reaching the target audience?

8. Assume you are about to devise a media plan to launch a new luxury automobile (such as a BMW, Audi, Lexus, or Infiniti). The new model is a very sleek-looking sporty car. The target market is males aged 35 to 49 living in urban markets. What magazines and newspapers would you use to reach this target and why would you recommend them? What target-market media-matching strategy would you use? Is there any other medium you would recommend? Justify your position.

Endnotes

[1] Jean Halliday, "Study claims TV advertising doesn't work on car buyers," *Advertising Age*, date not available.

[2] "Ad Age's 05-06 Price Chart," *Advertising Age*, September 19, 2005.

[3] Canadian Media Directors' Council, *Media Digest*, 2005–06, p. 5.

[4] Joe Mandese, "Commercial data zaps 'effective frequency,' supports recency," Media Post, June 29, 2004, **www.mediapost.com.**

[5] Matthew Fraser, "TiVo, PVRs begin to worry advertisers, broadcasters," *Financial Post*, January 20, 2003, p. FP3.

[6] Keith McArthur, "Is it the death of the 30-second spot?" *Globe and Mail*, July 9, 2005, p. B4.

[7] Ibid.

[8] Canadian Media Directors' Council, *Media Digest*, 2005–06, p. 16.

[9] Patti Summerfield, "Beyond the 30-second spot," *Strategy*, September 2004, p. 26.

[10] "*American Idol* curmudgeon gives boost in visibility to Coke Classic," *National Post*, June 11, 2005, p. FP5.

[11] Pia Musngi, "KIA and Subway sit rink-side for season two of The Tournament," November 24, 2005, **www.mediaincanada.com.**

[12] Jean Halliday and Marc Graser, "GM's 'Apprentice' task reaps eye-popping ROI," *Advertising Age*, April 25, 2005, p. 8.

[13] Danny Kucharsky, "The spots next shot," *Marketing*, August 15/22, 2005, pp. 19, 21.

[14] Canadian Media Directors' Council, *Media Digest*, 2005–06, p. 33.

[15] Eric Beauchesne, "Canadians less plugged in to radio at home," *Financial Post*, July 9, 2005, p. FP3.

[16] Patti Summerfield, "Radio connects with consumers," *Strategy*, September 2, 2004, **www.mediaincanada.com.**

[17] Eric Beauchesne, "Canadians less plugged in to radio at home," *Financial Post*, July 9, 2005, p. FP3.

[18] Alexandra Gill, "Radio blogs get great reception," *Globe and Mail*, March 23, 2005, p. R3.

[19] Guy Dixon, "Satellite radio: Do you really want to pay for it?" *Globe and Mail*, December 6, 2005, p. R2.

[20] Grant Robertson, "It's show time for this year's hot music machines," *Globe and Mail*, December 20, 2005, **www.globeandmail.com.**

[21] Patti Summerfield, "NADbank 2004: Post continues decline, Globe stays stable," *Strategy*, April 5, 2005, **www.mediaincanada.com.**

[22] Chris Powell, "Insert your ad here," *Marketing*, November 11, 2002, pp. 32–34.

[23] "10 top reasons to advertise in magazines," *Advertising Age*, September 26, 2005, p. M22.

[24] David Chilton, "The great (well, pretty great) outdoors," *Marketing*, May 16, 2005, p. 15.

[25] John Heinzl, "Billboards enjoy boom times," *Globe and Mail*, June 16, 1999, p. M1.

[26] "McCain Crescendo campaign rises to using outdoor advertising," *Viacom Outdoor Insight*, Spring 2005.

[27] David Carr, "Pinning down the young folk," *Marketing*, November 27, 2000, p. 25.

PLANNING FOR DIRECT RESPONSE COMMUNICATIONS

After studying this chapter you will be able to

1. describe the direct response marketing communications planning process

2. describe the various forms of direct response communications

3. assess the role of database management techniques in the design and implementation of direct response strategies

4. evaluate various external sources of list information and evaluate the role of these lists in building an effective direct response campaign

5. explain the advantages and disadvantages of the various forms of direct response communications

It was only a few decades ago that a mass marketing approach dominated the marketplace. Today, companies have the capability to deal with customers on an individual basis. In Chapter 1, the concepts of customer relationship management (CRM) and database marketing were introduced. Both concepts influence the development of programs that are designed to attract, cultivate, and maximize the return for each customer with whom the company does business. The end result is that companies are combining mass communications and marketing techniques with micro-marketing techniques. Database management and its influence on integrated marketing communications programs are discussed in more detail in this chapter. Information—that is, quality information—is the backbone of a direct response communications strategy.

Direct response communications involves direct mail, direct response communications in the mass media (mainly television, magazines, and newspapers), telemarketing, and catalogue marketing. Direct mail is the most common means of delivering messages directly to consumers, but advances in technology and database management techniques offer great potential for telemarketing and catalogues to become more important in the mix. Using database management techniques, a company can look at a customer over an entire lifetime and plan appropriate strategies to encourage good customers to buy more often or in larger quantities. Communicating directly with customers makes the entire process much more personal.

DIRECT RESPONSE COMMUNICATIONS AND DIRECT MARKETING

Just how important are direct response communications and other direct marketing practices in Canada? Recent statistics suggest direct response communications and direct marketing have a significant impact on advertising expenditures and sales revenues for goods and services. Direct mail advertising alone accounts for $1.5 billion, or 13 percent, of net advertising revenues in Canada. As an advertising medium, it ranks third, just behind television and daily newspapers and ahead of magazines, radio, and outdoor advertising.[1] If investments in direct response television, telemarketing, and catalogue marketing were included, the percentage of total media expenditures would be much higher.

Direct response communications are playing a more prominent role in the overall media mix of Canadian companies. Some of Canada's largest corporations have successfully integrated direct response communications with traditional forms of communications. These companies see the real value to be gained by managing customer relationships. Among these companies are Bell Canada, Rogers Communications, and financial institutions such as RBC Financial Group and BMO Bank of Montreal.

Direct marketing and direct response communications will continue to grow for several reasons. First, companies want managers to be more accountable for the expenditures they oversee. Executives are looking for more immediate sales returns for the dollars they invest. Direct response advertising can be measured for success quickly. Second, the trend toward niche marketing and micro-marketing suggests the importance of forming good relationships with customers. Because direct response communications can be personalized, they constitute an ideal medium for nurturing relationships. Third, the availability of database management techniques provides the fuel that direct response communications run on. Specific message strategies for individual customers are now a possibility—if the organization can effectively analyze the information in its database. Advantages such as these clearly indicate why prudent marketing organizations include direct response as part of their communications mix.

It is important to remember that direct response communications is a subset of direct marketing. In other words, the communications program is a component of a much larger

Direct marketing

A marketing system for developing products, sending messages directly to customers, and accepting orders through a variety of media, and then distributing the purchase directly to customers.

Direct response advertising

Advertising placed in a medium that generates an immediate and measurable response from the intended target.

direct marketing program. What is the distinction between the two practices? In **direct marketing**, products are developed, messages about the products are sent directly to customers (B2C and B2B) through a variety of media, orders are accepted, and then distributed directly to customers. In true direct marketing, all wholesale and retail intermediaries are eliminated.

In contrast, **direct response advertising** is advertising placed in any medium that generates an immediate and measurable response from the intended target. A direct response advertising plan involves the design and development of appropriate messages and the placement of messages in appropriate direct response media to encourage immediate action by the intended target. Alternatively, direct response advertising may be designed to build brand image, alter a perception, or attract a new target, much like other forms of advertising. Therefore, direct response advertising can be part of a fully integrated marketing communications campaign. Figure 6.1 illustrates the direct response planning process and its relationship with other components of marketing communications.

FIGURE **6.1** **The Direct Response Planning Process**

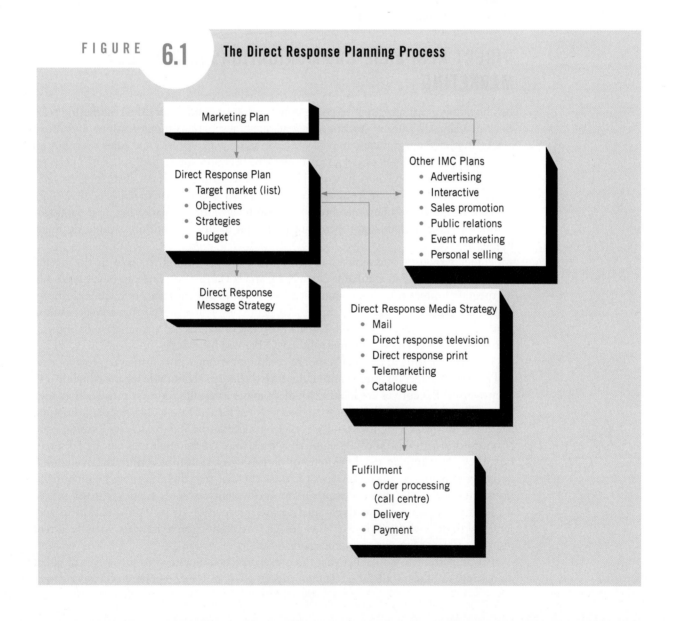

If traditional mass media are used (newspapers, magazines, radio, and television), the message includes a return mail address, 1-800 number, or website address where more information can be obtained or an order can be placed. Direct response advertising is capable of making a sale. Assuming adequate order taking and fulfillment strategies are in place, the entire transaction process from creating awareness to delivering the product is possible, and in a very short span of time.

Direct response communications can be divided between online communications and the more traditional forms. Online communications are presented in Chapter 7. The traditional forms of direct response communications are direct mail, direct response in the mass media (TV or print), telemarketing, and catalogue marketing:

- **Direct mail** is a printed form of communications distributed to prospective consumers by Canada Post or independent delivery agents (e.g., leaflets and flyers that may be dropped at a doorstep). Refer to the illustration in Figure 6.2.

- **Direct response television (DRTV)** or **direct response print** refers to ads that appear in television commercials, extended commercials commonly referred to as infomercials, and print ads in newspapers and magazines. In each case, there is a direct call to action via a 1-800 number, return mail address, or website.

- **Telemarketing** refers to outbound sales calls (a company calls the customer) or inbound sales calls (the customer contacts the company) to secure an order. All calls are usually handled through a central call centre.

- **Catalogues** are important communications vehicles among retail organizations. Typically, they are mailed or hand delivered by independent agents to existing customers. New customers may request catalogues through some form of direct response communication. Catalogues promote the sales of goods the retailer carries. They are also useful tools for communicating information about goods in B2B situations. In fact, many such catalogues are published on CD-ROMs and mailed directly to prospects.

It has taken considerable time for direct response communications to be accepted by blue-chip marketing organizations. For years, traditional advertising agencies resisted using direct response; they were unfamiliar with this aspect of communications and saw it as a last-minute strategy when things weren't working well. How the times have changed! Today, marketing organizations stress accountability and measurability. They want to know what they are getting for their investment. Consequently, most large full-service agencies now offer direct response expertise or have access to it. Many traditional advertising agencies have acquired direct response agencies. Such progression reinforces the importance of direct response communications in today's competitive business environment.

THE ROOTS OF DIRECT RESPONSE COMMUNICATIONS: DATABASE MANAGEMENT

Whether it's mail or telephone communications, there needs to be a convenient and efficient means of contacting customers. As experts in direct response communications often state, it's the list that makes or breaks the campaign. By list, they mean the list that will be used to contact current customers or prospective customers directly. That list is the backbone of the entire campaign; the quality has a direct impact on the success or failure of the campaign.

Companies recognize that it costs about six times as much to acquire a new customer as it does to keep an existing customer. Consequently, companies are compiling databases to keep track of existing customers and are forming relationships with them through mail and electronic means. Obviously, the best list is a well-maintained and well-managed

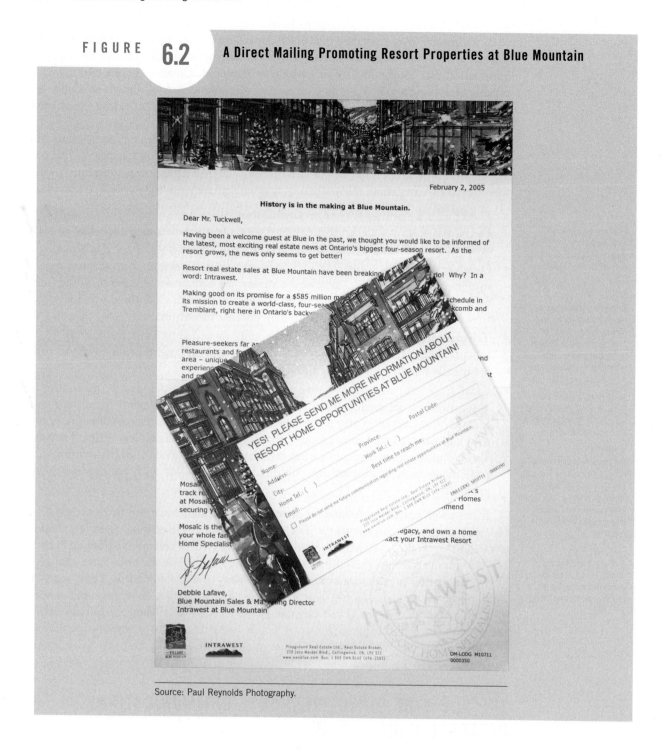

FIGURE **6.2** A Direct Mailing Promoting Resort Properties at Blue Mountain

Source: Paul Reynolds Photography.

House list
An internal customer list.

internal list of customers. Such a list is referred to as a **house list**. Since the best customers are current customers, it is much easier to get them to buy more of something than it is to attract a new customer. If the goal is to generate new business from new customers, then lists can be obtained from external sources.

Internal Data Sources

A good database management system collects and maintains relevant information about customers. The information is stored in such a manner that managers have easy access to it when developing marketing strategies. For example, managers should be able to manipulate the data so that customer profiles will emerge, and future purchase patterns can be forecast from those profiles. In other words, a thorough understanding of a customer's past purchasing behaviour should provide ammunition for predicting his or her future buying patterns.

Collecting Data

The names and addresses of customers are the most common forms of internal data, but simply knowing who the customers are offers little perspective when developing a strategic plan. Factor in technology, and all kinds of information about customers can be combined. Keeping track of purchasing behaviour and then linking it to a name and address is very meaningful. Therefore, the database should identify what a customer purchases, how often the customer purchases, how much the customer spends on average, what brands of goods the customer prefers, and so on.

Sophisticated retail organizations update this information automatically as goods are scanned through checkouts. From this information, buying behaviour profiles of a customer can be developed. Once the behaviour information is linked to the name and address, and perhaps also other demographic information, it is then possible to develop specific offers for specific types of customers. Plus, the offer can be sent to each customer individually. Such profiles can also be used to search for new customers in external databases.

Adding external information to the database rounds out the profile of the customer. Information about customers using credit cards for purchases is readily available. Credit card companies such as Visa and MasterCard are sitting on nest eggs of information that marketing organizations can purchase. Statistics Canada makes census data available that are updated every five years. This information is available at reasonable cost to the marketing organization.

Demographic and psychographic information can also be obtained from commercial research companies like Millward Brown, or a company can hire an independent research company to conduct primary research to uncover such information. The combination of information dealing with age, gender, education, income, marital status, and household formation along with information about attitudes, lifestyles, interests, and hobbies form an arsenal of information ready for use in strategic planning. Procter & Gamble, for example, maintains a database of 50 000 studies and conducts 4000 to 5000 consumer studies a year in North America.[2]

Statistics Canada
www.statcan.ca

Accessing Data

The second step in database management is devising a storage system that allows managers to access information easily when it is needed. In the realm of marketing communications, sales representatives and sales managers need instant access to customer sales records as they prepare for sales calls. Customer service personnel need access to historical information to handle complaints or simply serve customers better. Marketing managers and marketing communications managers need to clearly identify target customers and their behaviour to design special offers and communicate directly with them. To accomplish these kinds of tasks, relevant information must be convenient and accessible to all those who work with the database.

The electronic era has resulted in an information explosion that now allows for the storage and transfer of a great amount of business data in a short time. What has emerged is a new concept called data mining. **Data mining** is the analysis of information that establishes relationships among pieces of information so that more effective marketing strategies are identified and implemented. Rather than looking at an entire data set, data mining techniques attempt to locate informational patterns and nuggets within the database.[3]

Data mining
The analysis of information to determine relationships among the data and enable more effective marketing strategies to be identified and implemented.

Wal-Mart Canada
www.walmart.ca

The goals of data mining are to produce lower marketing costs and to increase efficiency by identifying prospects most likely to buy in large volume. A firm's competitive advantage in the marketplace will depend increasingly on knowing the situation better than the competition and being able to take action rapidly, based on knowing what is going on. Look no further than your local Wal-Mart to see data mining at work. Wal-Mart is the acknowledged leader in data mining with the capability of tracking sales on a minute-by-minute basis. It can also quickly detect regional and local market trends. Such knowledge allows Wal-Mart to customize each store's offerings while keeping suppliers abreast of how well their products are selling.[4]

Data mining offers an organization two essential benefits. First, it provides a means of profiling the "best" customers and the "worst" customers. Clearly, in these times, greater emphasis must be placed on customers who produce sales and high profit margins for an organization. As well, consideration can be given to dumping customers who are costing more than they generate in profit. Why keep customers if they are not profitable? Second, data mining techniques give an organization a means to predict future sales. Continuous compiling and analysis of data about current customers' sales histories should result in more accurate forecasts about what the future holds. As well, when a company wants to expand its business by attracting new customers, it can use the internal customer profile information as a guideline and then rent names from lists that have similar profiles.

For some insight into how a database system is used in a marketing communications program, read the IMC Highlight **Shoppers Optimum Strategy Benefits Claritin**.

IMC HIGHLIGHT

SHOPPERS OPTIMUM STRATEGY BENEFITS CLARITIN

Sales of Claritin were dropping at Shoppers Drug Mart, Canada's largest pharmacy retailer. To solve the problem, Shoppers offered a solution that involved its extensive database of Optimum card customers. The Optimum card is one of Canada's most successful loyalty programs with over 8 million members.

Unlike any other loyalty program, Shoppers tailors its program in a manner that benefits its marketing partners—the companies they buy products from. In this case, the goal was to sell more Claritin, a brand of Schering Canada. Since the Optimum card traces all purchases a particular consumer makes, Shoppers was able to mine its Optimum database to extract specific customer segments (in this case, allergy sufferers). For Schering Canada, being able to speak directly to consumers who want to hear about allergy products provided a distinct competitive advantage.

The cost of the program is shared between Shoppers Drug Mart and any supplier who wants to participate. In this case, Claritin is taking advantage of a loyalty program for its brand without having to invest in the development of the program—a savings of literally millions of dollars.

Shoppers benefits financially from the partnership. It charges a fee to partners who want customized direct marketing solutions and benefits from the additional sales the program generates for the advertised brand. Such an affordable, leading-edge opportunity is difficult for suppliers to pass up. In Claritin's case, Shoppers delivered an outdoor-themed direct mail piece to 180 000 allergy sufferers who were culled from the Optimum database based on their purchasing behaviour. The mailing included information about allergies and an offer of 3000 bonus points toward the next purchase of Claritin. Claritin did not have to discount the price to make the sale. Instead, it was a value-added offer for the consumer.

Other companies, such as Procter & Gamble, Gillette, and Unilever, are taking advantage of the Optimum program as well. Unilever targeted female Optimum members with a direct mail piece offering product samples and Optimum points toward the purchase of Dove face care products. The redemption rate for the Dove offer was above average compared to other direct marketing initiatives, and there was positive trial and repurchase as a direct result of this program.

Schering was very pleased with the results it achieved from the Claritin promotion, citing how measurable the program is. Every purchase is traceable to the offer. Schering plans to invest further in the program with other company brands.

Adapted from Chris Daniels, "Vendor bender," *Marketing*, April 5/12, 2004, p. 15.

External Sources

People who have a history of responding to mail offers tend to be attractive prospects for new offers. Buying by mail or from offers seen on television is part of their behaviour. Therefore, the challenge is to find prospects that have a similar demographic profile, and perhaps a psychographic profile that is close to the profile of current customers. A **list broker** can assist in finding these prospects. The buyer provides the broker with a profile of the target customer, and the broker supplies a list of potential prospects. Generally, a high-quality list is developed through a **merge/purge** process on a computer, whereby numerous lists are purchased, combined, and stripped of duplicate names. Names are purchased (actually rented) on a cost-per-thousand basis. List brokers charge a base rate for names and charge more if additional requests are made. Additional requests, called *selects*, are usually demographic variables, interest or lifestyle variables, or geographic variables.

One of the biggest suppliers of external data about households is Canada Post. Working from postal codes that isolate a neighbourhood or a city block, prospective households are identified when census data is added. For example, relevant statistics regarding the ages and incomes of homeowners in the area and the presence of children in those households could be attractive information for marketing organizations. There are three types of lists available:

Response Lists A **response list** is a list of proven direct response buyers. It's a "hot" list so the price is high on a cost-per-thousand basis. Such lists include book-of-the-month buyers, CD music buyers, and people who routinely place orders with cooperative direct marketing firms. ICOM Information & Communications Inc., a large provider of response lists in North America, charges an additional $15/M (cost per thousand) for proven mail order buyers.[5]

Circulation Lists The word "circulation" indicates these lists are obtained from newspaper and magazine sources. **Circulation lists** can target consumers demographically, psychographically, and geographically. A publishing company, such as Rogers Communications, sells its list of subscribers to any other business that is interested in a similar target. A list management company is usually responsible for managing and renting all of the lists made available by the publisher.

For instance, *Chatelaine* magazine reaches women aged 25 to 49, with children, and busy with careers and family. The *Chatelaine* list has a base cost of $125/M, which rises as certain characteristics are added. There are also additional costs for requesting specific formats for the list, such as tape, disk, email, and so on. *Canadian Business* magazine reaches upper income entrepreneurs and executives. Its list is available for a base cost of $130/M.[6] Additional information about list costs appears in Figure 6.3.

Compiled Lists **Compiled lists** are assembled from government, census, telephone, warranty, and other publication information. Less expensive than circulation lists and response lists, these lists are very common in B2B marketing. Names of prospects can be assembled from various print sources, such as *Fraser's Canadian Trade Index* and *Scott's Industrial Index*. Provincial and national associations like the Canadian Medical Association provide lists of their physicians, as do other associations: accountants, engineers, purchasing managers, teachers, and so on.

Online Databases

Due to advancing technology, there has been a surge in developing online databases. Information from commercial sources can now be transferred to an organization almost instantly. An **online database** is an information database accessible to anyone with proper communications facilities. For example, census data from Statistics Canada are readily

List broker

A company specializing in finding or developing lists for direct response purposes; finds prospect lists based on target market criteria established by marketing organizations.

Merge/purge

A process in which numerous mailing lists are combined and then stripped of duplicate names.

Canada Post
www.canadapost.ca

Response list

A list of direct mail buyers who have previously bought based on direct response offers.

Circulation list

A publication's subscription list that targets potential customers based on specified demographic characteristics, interests, or activities.

Chatelaine
www.chatelaine.com

Compiled list

A direct mail list prepared from government, census, telephone, warranty, or other publication information.

Online database

An information database accessible online to anyone with proper communications facilities.

FIGURE **6.3** The Costs Involved in Renting a Direct Response List

Requirement	Canadian Living	Cottage Life
List Size	335 833	61 229
Minimum Order	5000	5000
Base Cost	$130/M	$160/M
Selects		
Male	$10/M	$10/M
Female	$10/M	$10/M
Key Records	$7/M	$7/M
Province	$10/M	$10/M
Other Selects		
Age	$20/M	N/A
Age/Income	$30/M	N/A
Direct Mail Sold	$10/M	$10/M
Rural	$10/M	N/A
Urban	$10/M	N/A
Cottage Location	N/A	$20/M

There are additional costs that depend on the format of the label required (e.g., peel-off, tape, email, and disk).

CANADIAN LIVING READERSHIP PROFILE

- Household income $59 000
- 68% are 18 to 49 years old
- 64% are 25 to 54 years old
- 42% have children
- 77% are homeowners
- 233 157 identifiable females on list

COTTAGE LIFE READERSHIP PROFILE

- Household income $85 000
- 50% are MOPEs (managers, owners, professionals, and executives)
- Combined value of house and cottage is $670 000
- 70% have two vehicles

Adapted from Cornerstone List Management, www.cornerstonewebmedia.com/CStoneWeb/Lists/CLMLists.aspx (accessed November 2003).

available online. Most of Statistics Canada data are based on census data collected every five years. The nature of the information and reporting of the information is very detailed, covering dozens of demographic and socioeconomic topics such as family and household structures, income, occupation, education, ethnic background, and marital status. For a marketing organization, knowledge about and understanding trend data are essential skills for planning effective marketing strategies.

From commercial sources like Dun & Bradstreet (D&B), marketing organizations can access information through directory databases. A **directory database** provides a quick picture of a company and its products (e.g., ownership, size in terms of sales revenue, company locations, number of employees, key management personnel, and profitability). Examples of business directories that are available electronically include the *Canadian Key Business Directory* and the *Canadian Trade Index*. For businesses marketing goods and services to other businesses, the information contained in these directories helps identify real prospects.

Directory database
A commercial database that provides information about a company (e.g., size, sales, location, number of employees).

THE TOOLS OF DIRECT RESPONSE COMMUNICATIONS

Essentially, five primary media compose the direct response tool kit: direct mail, direct response television, direct response print media, telemarketing, and catalogues. At one time, direct mail marketing and direct marketing were often confused with one another, mainly due to the domination of mail in the direct response mix. Now that more organizations are implementing direct response programs more frequently, they are looking at the other alternatives as a means of solving marketing problems. Direct mail still dominates, but the other options are growing in importance. Let's examine each option in more detail.

Direct Mail

The use of direct mail is widespread thanks to its ability to personalize the message by using names secured from internal databases or rented from external databases. As well, direct mail provides an opportunity to target customers demographically and geographically. For example, an organization might choose to do a mailing to a fairly general audience by distributing a magazine subscription leaflet to all households in Ontario, or by delivering a message to a very selective upper-income household in a concentrated area of a city. Moreover, direct mail provides an opportunity to "tell a story." Since the average mailing includes several pieces, an expanded story can be told about the product or service. Unlike the traditional mass media, the advertiser is not restricted by time (30-second commercials on TV or radio) or space (one page or less in a newspaper or magazine). Benefits such as these make direct mail an attractive option.

A typical direct mailing has several components, each designed to serve a specific purpose:

Envelope The envelope is a critical component of the mailing. Since direct mail is usually unsolicited, the envelope has to suggest strongly why the recipient should read the contents. A recent envelope from Petro-Canada posed a question: Afraid of fuel card fraud? Such a question invokes curiosity and gets the reader to open the envelope.

Letter The letter introduces the prospect to the product or service and encourages the receiver to read more about the offer in the other pieces included in the mailing. The letter may be unaddressed (delivered to the householder) or addressed (with the person's name and address). Addressed mail offers a certain degree of personalization and produces a higher response. Typically, the language used in the letter is persuasive, because the goal is to generate interest and desire and, ultimately, get the receiver to respond to the offer.

Leaflet
A one-page flyer that offers relevant information about a direct mail offer.

Folder
A direct response sales message printed on heavy stock that can be mailed with or without an envelope; may be several pages in length.

Leaflets and Folders These types of inserts can vary in size and structure. By definition, a **leaflet** is one page (though it may not be a full page), printed front and back, and containing vital information about the offer: here's what the product is and here's why you should buy it. Again the language is persuasive in nature. Visuals frequently support the copy. A **folder** can be larger in size and contain multiple pages. For example, a double page folded once results in a four-page layout. That amount of space gives the marketer

Incentive
A free gift or offer included in a direct mail package.

ample room to sell. When an offer is put together, an **incentive** is often included to stimulate a more immediate response. An incentive might nudge a recipient interested in buying closer to taking action. The objective is to get that person to fill in the order form.

Order Form A well-designed order form is essential. It must be easy to read, and it must communicate all details regarding price, additional costs such as shipping and handling charges, and means of payment (usually credit card information). The recipient must be able to place the order effortlessly.

Postage-Paid Return Envelope Eliminating the need for postage is another means of encouraging the recipient to take action. The combination of a clear and concise order form with a postage-paid return envelope makes it a no-hassle process from start to finish.

Figure 6.4 shows a direct mail offer, including several of the components described above.

FIGURE **6.4**   **The Various Components of a Direct Mail Offer**

Source: Paul Reynolds Photography.

Statement stuffer (bounce back)

An ad or offer distributed in monthly statements or with the delivery of goods purchased by some form of direct response advertising.

Solo direct mail (selective direct mail)

A unique advertising offer mailed directly to a target audience by a marketing organization.

Statement Stuffers A **statement stuffer** or **bounce back** is an additional offer that rides along with the delivery of another offer or with the delivery of a monthly statement. Capitalizing on the ease of purchasing by credit or on the knowledge that the customer uses related products or services, such mailings make it convenient for the customer to take action. Bounce backs commonly arrive with Sears, Visa, and MasterCard bills, or with utility statements like those from Enbridge Gas Distribution.

Direct Mail Strategies

There are two basic options for delivering direct mail. The first is to deliver the mailing as a standalone piece. In this option, the organization bears all of the costs associated with developing the offer and distributing it to the target market. The second option is to deliver the offer as part of a package that includes offers from other companies. In this option, the distribution costs are shared equally among all participants. That is the difference between solo direct mail and cooperative direct mail.

Solo Direct Mail Also known as **selective direct mail**, with **solo direct mail** the organization prepares a unique offer and mails it directly to the target market. It is a standalone offer, much like the offer illustrated in Figure 6.4. As discussed earlier, today's technology makes it very convenient for organizations to assess buying information, devise unique offers for existing customers, and deliver offers directly to the customers. Such a plan of action sounds much more efficient than delivering a message blindly to all consumers on prime-time television, or through daily newspapers or national magazines. Furthermore, solo direct mail can play a key role in an organization's CRM program. It is an effective means of keeping the channel of communication open.

According to Nielsen Media Research, the median response rate for selective direct mailings is 12.5 percent.[7] If 100 000 letters were mailed to consumers, 12 500 would be returned, either to request more information or to take advantage of the offer. Statistics such as these are one reason direct mail has become more popular. Marketers can predict the return on investment with reasonable accuracy.

Personalization is an important element of solo direct mail. According to Canada Post, 84 percent of Canadians open direct mail if their name is on it and marketers experience an increase in response and conversion rates as a result of personalization. For more details, refer to Figure 6.5.

Nielsen Media Research
www.nielsenmedia.com

FIGURE **6.5**   **Consumers Are Receptive to Personalized Direct Mail**

According to Canada Post, 84 percent of Canadians open direct mail if it has their name on it. Marketers experience a significant increase in response and conversion rates as a result of personalization. Canada Post also reports that

- 89% of Canadians open direct mail if it comes from a company they know
- 86% open it if it looks intriguing or interesting
- 79% open it if it has their address on it
- 66% open it if it has a postage stamp
- 52% open it if it mentions a free draw

Marketers should have confidence in direct mail because consumers like receiving it.

- 26% of Canadians welcome addressed direct mail advertising, compared to 5% who welcome banner advertising, and 2% who welcome telemarketing.
- 57% enjoy receiving direct mail for products and services that interest them.

Source: Canada Post Research as reported in "How to get the most out of your direct mail," Direct Marketing Resource Guide, *Marketing*, November 14, 2005, p. 4.

Cooperative direct mail

A mailing containing specific offers from non-competing products.

Cooperative Direct Mail **Cooperative direct mail** refers to packages containing offers from non-competing products and services. Consumer goods companies commonly use this method; they are attracted to it because the costs are shared among all participants. A typical mailing might include coupons for packaged goods items, magazine subscription forms, order forms for direct mail offers, and so on. For packaged goods marketers in the food and drug industries, cooperative direct mail has proven to be an effective means of generating trial purchase. Response rates to coupon offers in direct mail are significantly higher (5 percent) than for similar offers in newspapers (1 percent) and magazines (1 percent).[8]

In deciding how and when to use direct mail a manager evaluates the benefits and drawbacks of the medium. Figure 6.6 summarizes what direct mail has to offer.

Direct Response Television

Direct response television (DRTV) is gaining in popularity with advertisers. How so? If mass media advertisers such as Procter & Gamble and the RBC Financial Group are using the medium, then it clearly has something to offer other companies. Their leadership in DRTV will pave the way for others to follow. Essentially, there are three forms of direct response television: the 30- or 60-second commercial that typically runs on cable channels and sells gadgets and music products, the infomercial (a program-like commercial), and direct home shopping (as in The Shopping Channel).

Infomercial

A long commercial (e.g., 10 to 30 minutes) that presents in detail the benefits of a product or service; usually includes a call to action (e.g., a 1-800 number).

The nature of direct response television advertising has changed over time. Once it was regarded as the "domain of schlock"; mainstream marketing organizations would not go near it. It was perceived as a last-resort tactic when all else failed. DRTV is now looked at in a more positive light due to the acceptance of infomercials and their improved level of quality. An **infomercial** is usually a 30-minute commercial that presents, in detail, the benefits of a product or service.

FIGURE **6.6** **Direct Mail as an Advertising Medium**

ADVANTAGES

Audience Selectivity—Targets can be precisely identified and reached based on demographic, psychographic, and geographic characteristics. It is possible to secure external lists that closely match internal lists.

Creative Flexibility—Unlike other media, the message can be copy oriented, visually oriented, or a combination of both. Because a mailing includes several components, there is ample time to expand on the benefits of the product.

Exclusivity—Mail does not compete with other media or other ads upon receipt. In contrast, magazines and newspapers include clusters of ads and create a cluttered environment to advertise in.

Measurability—Direct mail response is measured by the sales it generates. A sale can be directly linked to the mail offer (e.g., receipt of a phone call or order form in the mail). The success of a campaign is determined in a relatively short period.

DISADVANTAGES

Image—Direct mail is not a prestigious medium. Often perceived as junk mail, it can be easily discarded by the recipient.

Cost per Exposure—When all costs are included (e.g., printing, securing list, mail delivery, and fulfillment), total cost can be higher than an ad placed in another print medium, although selective targeting reduces waste circulation.

Lack of Editorial Support—As a standalone medium, compared to newspapers or magazines, it can't rely on editorial content to get people to read the message.

Infomercials today are presented in a more entertaining manner; there is less "hard sell." The transfer of information is less intrusive. Consumers can simply evaluate the message and take action if they so desire. Some experts suggest that their acceptance is due to the success of TV shows like *The Apprentice,* where consumers are willing to be entertained while they're being pitched to. *The Apprentice* develops entire shows around branded products and services.

Well-produced and highly informative infomercials are now being run by serious mainstream marketing organizations. Included in the mix are pharmaceutical companies, banks and financial institutions, packaged goods companies, and automotive companies. First movers into this arena include companies like Ford, Bell, TD Canada Trust, Procter & Gamble, and L'Oréal. These organizations evaluated the returns from their respective investments in mainstream advertising and decided that direct response communications would play a more vital role. Ontario Place, Toronto's downtown waterfront playground, experimented with infomercials in 2004 and it was the attraction's best year ever financially. The infomercial thoroughly showed the experience that a family would have by visiting Ontario Place; a message that could not be adequately conveyed in a 30-second commercial.[9]

Ontario Place
www.ontarioplace.com

Direct response commercials do not always have to sell something. In fact, a good infomercial can serve many different marketing communications objectives: it can establish leads, drive retail traffic, launch new products, create awareness, and protect and enhance brand image. Procter & Gamble, for example, is not selling direct to consumers, but uses infomercials to promote products sold by retailers. The infomercial gives consumers all of the information they need and raises interest in the product; when the customer visits the store they feel assured that they know all about the product.

Some companies are even referring to the medium as "BRTV," or "brand response television." What this means is that advertisers are pursuing a dual benefit—they are combining a branding message with a DRTV technique. The ad builds the brand attributes and generates an immediate response through a 1-800 number and website. Its ability to do both is what excites the advertiser.

Getting into direct response television, however, is not cheap. Experts say it costs at least $150 000 to produce a 30-minute infomercial, with prices going as high as $500 000 depending on locations used and whether celebrity spokespersons are hired.[10]

For additional insight into how Procter & Gamble uses DRTV, read the IMC Highlight **Infomercials Are Catching On**.

Direct home shopping is a service provided by cable television, for example The Shopping Channel. Messages to prospects are presented in the form of close-up shots of the product or, in the case of clothing and accessories, by models wearing the goods. Items such as home gym equipment usually involve a full-scale demonstration. Details on how to place an order are broadcast frequently and a 1-800 number is usually shown continuously on the edge of the TV screen along with a description of the product.

Direct home shopping
A shopping service provided by cable television stations that offers products or services for sale by broadcast message (e.g., The Shopping Channel).

Home shopping offers the shopper convenience. George Foreman, a former boxing champion, markets his cooking grill on The Shopping Channel. The Shopping Channel has annual sales in the $150 million range and sold 90 000 Foreman grills over a two-year period.[11] Now that's effective marketing communications!

Generally, the United States is well ahead of Canada in terms of direct response television and home shopping penetration. American companies embraced these techniques more quickly. The trend, however, suggests that the boom years for direct response television in Canada lie ahead.

Direct Response Print Media

The print media—mainly newspapers and magazines—are good choices for communicating direct response offers or for fielding leads for future marketing programs. Given the

INFOMERCIALS ARE CATCHING ON

Who says packaged goods marketers aren't changing their ways? The list of blue-chip companies now using infomercials as part of their media mix include Ford, Procter & Gamble, Scotiabank, RBC Financial Group, and a host of other companies.

While DRTV counts for only a fraction of P&G's total television budget, the company now uses the strategy across a number of business units, including fabric and home care (Swiffer, Downy, and Mr. Clean), beauty care, and oral care. P&G is experimenting with short infomercials and a web address that people can follow to get more information and a money-saving coupon for the advertised product. P&G believes in DRTV because they can measure the effectiveness of every dollar spent.

DRTV advertising rates are considerably lower than general ad rates for off-peak periods like late-night and mornings, giving marketers a cost-effective means pf pre-selling customers on their products. That's Procter & Gamble's strategy—present useful information that the customer can go to the store with.

Recently, P&G tried a bare-bones direct response ad for Dryel, a home dry-cleaning kit, in addition to traditional 30-second ads. The pitch was to have consumers make the call to request coupons for the product. According to a P&G spokesperson, "The strategy has been effective and the brand is doing well. There are increases in sales, shipments, and awareness. Success is attributed to the overall marketing communications effort of which DRTV is a piece."

Some marketers can even use DRTV to target customer segments directly. For example, golf equipment manufacturers are a natural for using infomercials on The Golf Channel. A manufacturer like TaylorMade can reach people who are predisposed to their product. Through The Golf Channel, the latest and greatest gizmos to improve one's game can be clearly demonstrated, and when endorsed by professional golfers, the message is effectively delivered.

So what does a good infomercial cost? The air time may be relatively cheap, but the production costs are considerable—anywhere from $150 000 to $500 000. The higher range would include things like distant locations and the inclusion of celebrities.

Adapted from Chris Powell, "From Flowbees to Fords," *Marketing*, April 25, 2005, pp. 15, 16, and Jack Neff, "Direct response getting respect," *Advertising Age*, January 20, 2003, pp. 4, 35.

local nature of daily newspapers, an organization can target prospects geographically. If the size of the budget restricts activity, then markets can be assigned priorities until the budget is exhausted. Local market retailers that want to take advantage of direct response techniques have a good option in newspapers.

A majority of magazines are targeted at specific audiences based on demographic and psychographic characteristics, so the direct response message can be sent to specific audiences based on criteria established by the advertiser. For example, a company marketing floating docks or cottage designs might want to reach cottage owners. A direct response ad placed in *Cottage Life* magazine will reach that target market. The basic point is that it is possible to identify magazines that closely match the profile of a company's best customers. If a direct response is the objective, the print ad should include a toll-free telephone number and a mailing address or website that facilitates the response. Viceroy, a designer and builder of modular homes, for example, uses direct response print ads to get potential customers to order a catalogue or to visit a dealer. The catalogue contains colourful pictures and the floor plans for all of the models. A video about the company and how it constructs the cottages is also sent to the prospective customer. This is a good example of an effective, integrated direct response campaign (see Figure 6.7).

Another option to consider is the insert, which was briefly discussed in Chapter 5 in the discussion of newspapers. An **insert** can be a single-page or multiple-page document that is inserted into the publication (see Figure 6.8). In some cases, the insert is actually glued onto a page (rubber-like glue that is easily removed when the insert is removed from the page). This type of insert is referred to as a **tip-in**. Advertisers pay the publication insertion fees on a cost-per-thousand basis. A single-page insert in the *Toronto Star*, for

Insert

A preprinted, free-standing advertisement (e.g., a leaflet, brochure, or flyer) specifically placed in a newspaper or magazine.

Tip-in

An insert that is glued to a page in the publication using a removable adhesive.

FIGURE **6.7** **An Illustration of Direct Response Print Advertising**

Source: Courtesy of Viceroy.

example, costs $38.00/M, and a 16-page insert costs $54.00/M.[12] Preprinted inserts can be used for other communications purposes—they are good handouts at trade shows and other promotional events and can be used to draw attention to products at the point-of-purchase. They can also be mailed directly to customers in the company's database.

Telemarketing

Why are people so rudely interrupted during their supper by a telemarketer—can't telemarketers call at a more suitable time? Doesn't that sound like a common complaint? To a telemarketer, it's simply a fact of life. The best time to call is when the prospect is at home, and that's suppertime or shortly thereafter. Despite the negative feelings consumers have about telemarketing practices, it is a growing in popularity with marketers as a means of communicating with customers. Telemarketing communications are often directly linked to direct response television and direct mail campaigns. Working together, they are a potent combination for achieving all kinds of marketing objectives.

Most telemarketing activities are conducted by call centres. A **call centre** is a central operation from which a company operates its inbound and outbound telemarketing programs. In Canada, telemarketing generated $16 billion in sales revenues in 2004 alone.[13] There are two forms of telemarketing: inbound and outbound. **Inbound telemarketing** refers to the calls received by an order desk, a customer inquiry, and calls generated from toll-free telephone numbers promoted on direct response television commercials.

Call centre
A central operation from which a company operates its inbound and outbound telemarketing programs.

Inbound telemarketing
The calls received by a company from consumers whether to place an order, inquire about products or services, or in response to a toll-free telephone number promoted on a direct response television commercial.

FIGURE **6.8**   **Inserts Are Flexible and Can Be Used in Print Media, Direct Mail, and at Point-of-Purchase**

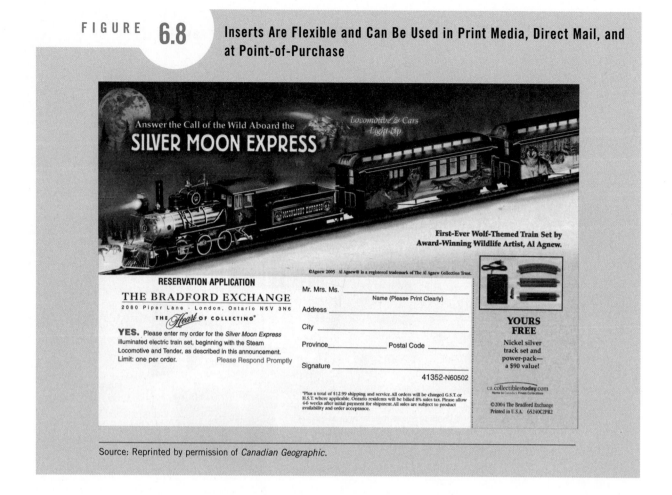

Source: Reprinted by permission of *Canadian Geographic*.

Outbound telemarketing

Calls made by a company to customers to develop new accounts, generate sales leads, and even close a sale.

Outbound telemarketing refers to calls made by a company to customers to develop new accounts, generate sales leads, and even close a sale.

The call centre is a vital link in the database management system, because the telephone is a quick and convenient method of capturing information about customers. Any information that is obtained can be added instantly to the database. Cost-effective software is available to manage this task.

In direct response communications, much emphasis is placed on message and media decisions. For example, how will the offer be communicated to entice the target market and what media will it be placed in? Managing the inbound sales calls generated by commercials has traditionally been a weak link. Therefore, an organization must effectively plan its activities to meet call volume, capture data, present selling opportunities, and handle closing calls. The better a company can do these things, the better the economics of the direct response campaign. To illustrate, consider that a national TV spot on a cable network for a direct response lead generation campaign can easily generate 500 or more inbound inquiries, 85 percent of which will occur within the first three minutes of airing.[14] The call centre has to be ready! If it has to dump the call, or if the consumer hears a busy signal and hangs up, the marketer's return on investment is undermined.

In the pursuit of direct response success, smart marketers understand there is more to it than simply extending the offer. The ability to manage an inbound call requires precision planning to maximize returns. It could be the start of a very fruitful customer relationship.

The primary advantage of telemarketing is cost. Compared to traditional forms of mass advertising and the cost of sending a salesperson into a business call, telemarketing

FIGURE **6.9** **Telemarketing Performs Many Marketing Roles**

FUNDRAISING

- Inbound (donations)
- Outbound (solicitations)

SALES SUPPORT

- Generating leads
- Qualifying prospects
- Securing appointments
- Marketing research

PERSONAL SELLING

- Opening new accounts
- Selling existing accounts
- Selling marginal accounts

FULFILLMENT

- Accepting orders
- Maintaining customer records
- Invoicing and payment processing

CUSTOMER SERVICE

- Handling inquiries and complaints
- Help lines

offers considerable savings. In comparison to direct mail, the response rate for telemarketing is about 100 times higher, so even though direct mail may appear to be cheaper than telephone solicitation it is actually more costly in the long run. To be effective, however, the telemarketing call must be carefully planned. There must be proper training and preparation for telemarketing representatives, just as there is for field sales representatives. Figure 6.9 summarizes the activities that can involve telemarketing.

Earlier in this section, the negative image of telemarketing was mentioned. Image is perhaps telemarketing's biggest drawback. A Canadian research study conducted by Ernst & Young found that 75 percent of Canadians consider marketing calls unwelcome and intrusive; they are ranked as one of the least-liked sales techniques.[15] People who react negatively to the calls simply hang up. Despite this behaviour, marketing organizations persist. To them, it's a game of averages. How many calls does it take to convert one customer? It's inexpensive to make those calls, and economies of scale rule the day!

Catalogues

Sears Canada
www.sears.ca

Catalogues are reference publications, often annual, distributed by large retail chains and other direct marketing organizations. Catalogue marketing involves the merchandising of products through catalogue sales. When someone thinks of catalogues, the Sears catalogue comes to mind immediately, and for good reason. The Sears catalogue is the largest in Canada and is distributed to more than 4 million households. Sears publishes

F I G U R E **6.10** Sears Effectively Integrates Retail, Catalogue Marketing, and Web Marketing

Source: Sears Canada Inc. and Dick Hemingway.

two semi-annual catalogues (Fall & Winter and Spring & Summer) as well as numerous seasonal catalogues such as the Christmas Wish Book and sale catalogues.

Sears is now a fully integrated marketing communications organization that generates $6.5 billion in sales in Canada annually. Much of their business is generated from catalogue sales. Sears also operates one of the busiest commercial websites in Canada. When retail locations and pick-up locations are included, Sears reaches 93 percent of Canadians.[16] The company accepts orders by fax, email, and online. Its 1-800 number is the most frequently called toll-free number in Canada.[17] Refer to Figure 6.10 for an illustration.

The Canadian catalogue market is underdeveloped, yet it offers great potential in the future. One of the leading catalogue marketers in the Unites States is L.L. Bean. Based in Freeport, Connecticut, Bean is the nation's largest outdoor catalogue company, generating $1.2 billion in annual sales. Customers receiving their catalogue can place orders through inbound telemarketing 24 hours a day, 365 days a year. On average, Bean's telephone rings 50 000 times a day. Catalogue-based companies like Bean operate effective fulfillment programs. At Bean, logistics and order fulfillment are the heart of the operation. The Bean warehouse contains three and a half miles of conveyor belts, stores 4 million items, has 25 shipping docks, and a built-in Federal Express shipping system.[18]

Canadian Tire
www.canadiantire.ca

Canadian Tire is another leading catalogue marketing organization. Its catalogue is extremely popular and is referred to frequently. Eight out of ten Canadian households keep their old catalogue until a new one arrives.[19] Both Sears and Canadian Tire see the value in catalogue and online marketing activities. Sales through catalogues definitely take away from store sales, but both companies are responding to their customers' demand for convenience. Customers today are into multi-channel shopping. Both companies effectively combine media advertising (television, print, and flyers) with non-traditional marketing communications (Internet, direct mail, and catalogues). Canadian Tire also has one of the most popular loyalty programs in existence with its Canadian Tire 'Money.' The ongoing discounts that are based on dollars spent at Canadian Tire keep the customers coming back for more.

There are many types of catalogues. In some industries, the catalogue is the dominant means of making sales. For example, more than 50 percent of gardening supplies are sold through catalogues. My household recently received a catalogue from Ashton Green, marketing "Cooking Tools that Work!" The 68-page catalogue includes almost every cooking utensil and accessory you could think of. Goods are shipped direct to consumers from the company's Ottawa location (see Figure 6.11 on the next page). Catalogues are also widely used in business-to-business marketing. These catalogues are used by sales representatives and contain a complete listing and description of all products sold by the company. B2B marketers now put their catalogues on CD-ROMs so that customers can quickly access information about products they are interested in.

Rather than distribute catalogues, some companies have taken the concept a step further and are publishing their own magazines for distribution to current customers. The purpose is to stay in touch with customers after the sale. The Ford Motor Company distributes *My Ford* magazine, and General Motors has a catalogue called *Vision* targeted directly at its Cadillac customers. Both companies believe their investment in these magazines, while unprofitable now, will influence buying decisions down the road. In the automotive industry, loyalty is increasingly crucial as competition swells and the quality gap among vehicle brands closes. Therefore, any effort that builds rapport and keeps customers coming back is well worth the investment.

FIGURE **6.11** Catalogues Provide Consumers with Shopping Convenience

Source: Courtesy of Ashton Green Limited.

Summary

Direct response advertising is the third-largest advertising medium in Canada and is growing at a pace faster than traditional mass media. Several factors are contributing to this growth: companies are looking for tangible returns for the money they invest in communications, direct response communications are a natural extension of database management programs, and direct response is a personalized medium that is ideal for enhancing customer relationships.

The foundation of direct response communications is the organization's database. An organization collects and analyzes data from internal and external sources. Customer or house lists record data about purchase transactions made by customers. This information is combined with demographic and psychographic information to form profiles of an organization's best customers. These customers are then targeted and reached through direct response communications. The analysis and manipulation of data constitute a process called data mining. The goal of data mining is to lower marketing costs and increase efficiency by identifying those customers most likely to buy in large volume.

The success of a direct response campaign depends on the quality of the list used by the advertiser. Lists are available from list brokers and other secondary sources such as directories and trade indexes. Lists provided by brokers are rented on a cost-per-thousand basis. Advertisers can choose between response lists (the most expensive), circulation lists, and compiled lists.

Direct mail is the most common form of direct response advertising. A direct mailing usually includes an envelope, letter, leaflet or folder, order form, and postage-paid return envelope. Each component performs a specific role in trying to get the recipient to take action. Advertisers choose between solo direct mail and cooperative direct mail. Solo distribution is more expensive but produces a higher response rate than cooperative distribution.

In recent years, direct response television has captured the attention of blue-chip marketing organizations. An advertiser can choose between 30- and 60-second direct response commercials and infomercials, which are much longer and are more like a program than a commercial. Direct response commercials are effective if an organization wants to establish leads, build image, and launch new products. Infomercials are effective in situations where there are lots of details to communicate or for explaining complex products. By definition, direct response ads are capable of completing a transaction with the recipient.

Direct response ads in the print media are another option. Advertisers frequently use the print media to encourage prospective customers to call 1-800 numbers or to visit websites to get more information. As well, print is a good medium for distributing inserts. By selecting the right newspaper or magazine, the advertiser can target its primary customer.

There are two types of telemarketing. Inbound telemarketing refers to calls made by customers to an order desk. Outbound telemarketing refers to calls made by a company to prospective customers to generate leads and even close a sale. Telemarketing programs are usually outsourced to a call centre. Companies are attracted to telemarketing because of its low costs. It is much less expensive than face-to-face personal selling and mass advertising. Its major drawback is the negative perception people hold about this form of communication.

Catalogues are an underdeveloped alternative in direct response communications in Canada. However, companies such as Sears and Canadian Tire see the value of producing annual catalogues. As well, there are all kinds of specialty companies that produce catalogues that include descriptions, pictures, and prices of the products they market. Time-pressed consumers appreciate the convenience of catalogue shopping.

Key Terms

bounce back,   177

call centre,   181

catalogue,   169

circulation list,   173

compiled list,   173

cooperative direct mail,   178

data mining,   171

direct home shopping,   179

direct mail,   169

direct marketing,   168

direct response advertising,   168

direct response print,   169

direct response television (DRTV),   169

directory database,   175

folder,   175

house list,   170

inbound telemarketing,   181

incentive,   176

infomercial,   178

insert,   180

leaflet,   175

list broker,   173

merge/purge,   173

online database,   173

outbound telemarketing,   182

response list,   173

selective direct mail,   177

solo direct mail,   177

statement stuffer,   177

telemarketing,   169

tip-in,   180

Review Questions

1. What is the difference between direct marketing and direct response advertising?

2. What are the major forms of direct response advertising?

3. Explain the concept of data mining. What impact does data mining have on marketing and marketing communications?

4. What is the role of the list broker in direct response advertising?

5. In the context of mailing lists, what does merge/purge refer to?

6. What are the differences among a response list, a circulation list, and a compiled list?

7. Briefly explain two advantages and two disadvantages of direct mail advertising.

8. Identify and briefly explain the components of a typical direct mail piece.

9. What is a statement stuffer?

10. What is the difference between a solo direct response campaign and a cooperative direct response campaign?

11. Identify and briefly explain the various direct response television alternatives.

12. What is the difference between an insert and a tip-in?

13. What is the difference between inbound telemarketing and outbound telemarketing?

Discussion and Application Questions

1. Will direct response communications play a more significant role in the marketing communications mix in the future? Through secondary research, identify those factors that will encourage or discourage the use of direct response communications and formulate your position on the issue.

2. Direct mail advertising remains a popular medium for many profit-based and not-for-profit organizations. Why? What are the benefits and drawbacks of using direct mail? Identify some organizations that successfully use direct mail advertising to help achieve their marketing goals.

3. Collect two or three direct mail pieces that have been delivered to your household address. Did the mailing reach the appropriate target market? What components did the mailing include, and how effective were they in communicating the message? Is the message convincing enough to act upon?

4. Assume you are about to develop a direct response advertising campaign to launch a new and improved version of the George Foreman Grill. The target market is male and female heads of households, with a family income of $50 000 or more, living in markets of over 100 000. The campaign will be national in scope. What direct response media would you use in the campaign? Assuming direct mail will be a component of the campaign, how would you find names for the mailing?

5. Conduct some research to find a company that has successfully used direct response advertising as part of an integrated marketing communications campaign (such as a major bank, financial services company, or not-for-profit fundraising campaign). What role did direct response communications play? Describe the successes that resulted from the direct response effort.

6. Is direct response advertising a viable option for Canadian packaged goods companies? Provide appropriate examples to illustrate your point of view.

Endnotes

1 Canadian Media Directors' Council, *Media Digest*, 2005–06, p. 10.

2 Emily Nelson, "P&G wants the truth: Did you really brush your teeth?" *Globe and Mail*, June 1, 2002, p. M2.

3 Ross Waring, "The promise and reality of data mining," *Strategy*, June 7, 1999, p. D9.

4 Susan Pigg, "Diapers, drinking, and data," *Toronto Star*, August 16, 2002, pp. E1, E10.

5 ICOM Target Source Database, Spring/Summer 2004, p. 10.

6 Costs obtained from Cornerstone List Management.

7 *A Special Presentation on Consumer Promotion Fundamentals*, NCH Promotional Services, 1998.

8 Ibid.

9 Chris Powell, "From Flowbees to Fords," *Marketing*, April 25, 2005, p. 17.

10 Ibid., p. 18.

11 Paul Brent, "Brawn = Brains = Bucks," *Financial Post*, March 29, 1999, pp. C1, C7.

12 *Canadian Advertising Rates and Data*, Rogers Media, January 2005.

13 Sarah Dobson, "Wake-up call," *Marketing*, November 14, 2005, p. 20.

14 Maria Eden, "One call, multiple sales opportunities," *Marketing Direct*, November 4, 2002, p. 16.

15 Mary Gooderham, "Level of antipathy a wake-up call for telemarketers," *Globe and Mail*, May 7, 1997, p. C11.

16 Dana Flavelle, "Sears Canada turns 50 while seeking to rejuvenate itself," *Toronto Star*, January 5, 2003, pp. E1, E11.

17 "Sears Canada this year's directors' choice," *Strategy Direct Response*, November 22, 1999, p. 10.

18 Kate Kane, "L.L. Bean delivers the goods," **www.fastcompany.com/online/10/llbean.html**.

19 Stephen Theobald, "Canadian Tire's flyer grows up," *Toronto Star*, March 15, 2001, p. E1.

PLANNING FOR ONLINE AND INTERACTIVE COMMUNICATIONS

After studying this chapter you will be able to

LEARNING OBJECTIVES

1. assess strategies for delivering effective messages using online advertising

2. describe the various roles played by online communications in a marketing and marketing communications environment

3. evaluate the various advertising alternatives that are available online

4. assess the potential of the Internet as an advertising medium

5. assess the role of mobile media alternatives in integrated marketing communications campaigns

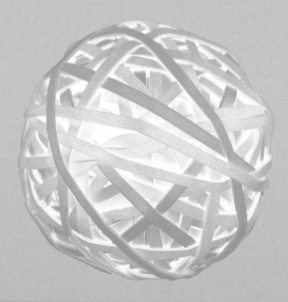

Online communications offer a high degree of personalization. Since personalization is one of the cornerstones of customer relationship management (CRM) programs, the Internet should be attractive to marketers. The medium also offers the ability to listen to customers and learn from them, and to deliver content and services tailored to their responses and actions. Such an advantage must be made the most of. Since the medium is still new, however, companies are still trying to figure things out. Once they do, for certain it will play a more important role.

Automotive companies are among the first to start figuring things out. General Motors, Ford, and Chrylser are among the leading advertisers in North America, and all have repositioned their marketing budgets to put more money into relationship marketing, including sponsorships and the Internet. In such a competitive market, each company is looking for more efficient ways to target customers, and the combination of online advertising and company websites does just that. Automotive advertising online is growing at double-digit rates. Marketers now recognize that they need to be where the people are—and they are online searching for information about products.[1]

Apparently, young, first-time car buyers turn to the Internet more than their parents to research their car purchase. A full 35 percent of respondents in a recent survey said the Internet was their most important source of information. The implication is clear: Generation Y is turning away from traditional media, meaning that companies will have to forge relationships with this group through emerging media such as cell phones, iPods, and video games.[2] If research in the automotive sector applies to other sectors, more companies will be migrating to online advertising in the near future.

Toyota
www.toyota.ca

The spectrum of digital communications is literally exploding, particularly among organizations wanting to reach the youth market and adults 18 to 34 years old. To reach these "tech-savvy" targets an advertiser must be where they are. To demonstrate, consider the strategy that Toyota planned and implemented when it launched the Yaris model in 2006. The target market was 18 to 34 year olds. Message strategy portrayed Yaris as having a cheeky and mischievous personality. To effectively reach the target, a combination of digital media were used, including

- 10-second ads preceding cell phone mobisodes (a mobisode is a downloadable program to a cell phone).
- Contest sponsorship on Current TV's website, which enabled consumers to create their own Yaris commercial. (Current TV is an interactive cable channel where viewers send in video stories they've created to be aired on the network.)
- A Yaris profile page on MySpace.com, a social networking site.
- Title sponsorship of the Evolution Game Fighting Championships.
- Product placement on Fox TV's comedy show *MADtV*.

Note the absence of traditional mass media in this plan. Clearly, Toyota is embarking on a new communications direction with this product launch.[3]

INTERNET PENETRATION AND ADOPTION

More than 70 percent of Canadians have Internet access at home, a penetration rate that strongly suggests the potential influence of the medium. Being more specific, 82 percent of households in the highest income group (the top quarter of households based on income) have a member using the Internet from home. Education is also a factor affecting Internet penetration. The higher the level of education achieved, the more likely someone at home is accessing the Internet. By geographic location, the highest rates of usage are in British Columbia, Alberta, and Ontario, where roughly 7.5 of every 10 households are connected to the Internet.[4]

FIGURE **7.1** Some Facts and Figures on Internet Usage by Canadians

When asked, a majority of respondents to a media research survey agreed with the statement: "The Internet is an integral part of my lifestyle."

Here are some other highlights from the study:

- Usage is higher in English-speaking households (64%) than French-speaking households (49%).

- 72% of Canadians have Internet access at home; 65% have high-speed access.

- 34% of Canadians made an online purchase in the last 12 months.

- The top five online shopping categories are tickets (42%), books (41%), travel (39%), software (32%), and music/audio CDs (27%).

- The Internet is the third most time-consuming medium amongst Canadian adults, behind television and radio (first and second, respectively).

- Average weekly time spent online is 5.2 hours for Canadians with home access.

- The most popular online activities are email (96%), information search (94%), browsing (84%), accessing specific product information (78%), and accessing current news (66%.

- Ads in conventional media (the need for integration) are far more likely to directly influence an online purchase.

Source: ComQUEST Research data published as "Canucks love their net: Study," *Media in Canada*, March 10, 2005, and "BBM media snapshot: Canadians online," *Media in Canada*, March 1, 2005, www.mediaincanada.com, and "Web advertising in Canada," Canadian Media Directors' Council, *Media Digest*, 2005–06, p. 61.

From the data above, it is clear that the Internet is an ideal medium for reaching middle- to upper-income households and households with post-secondary education. Further, the Internet is taking on mass media status to the point where it must be integrated with traditional media campaigns. And just around the corner is the emerging wireless communications market. Mobile media such as iPods, PDAs, and cell phones represent the third screen that consumers are exposed to (television and computer screens are the first two). Soon, wireless communications will be the preferred method of connecting to the Internet and it will enable consumers to be exposed to advertising messages anywhere and any time.

A recent research study by ComQUEST Research observed that the number of Canadians connected to the Internet has doubled in the past five years. Researcher Pamela Herrington says, "The role that the Internet plays in most Canadian's daily lives has grown from a convenience to an absolute necessity. Many Canadians have become reliant upon products and services which are delivered via the Internet."[5]

ComQUEST Research
www.comquest.ca

For additional insight into how and why Canadians refer to the Internet so often and what they actually do online, see Figure 7.1.

ONLINE AND INTERACTIVE MARKETING COMMUNICATIONS

As with any new medium, it takes time to establish a presence in the marketplace. The Internet has been an overwhelming success among consumers who search for information online, but the commercial side of the Internet, particularly the advertising side, has met with consumer opposition and advertiser skepticism.

In the online environment, advertising is perceived by many to be an intrusion; it is something that is there to stall them from doing what they want to do online. Slowly, however, consumers are starting to realize that what they have begun to take for granted comes at a cost, and that cost involves the placement and acceptance of advertising.

Due to the infancy of the medium, most companies are exploring the Internet while trying to figure out ways to blend traditional media (what they know best) with new or non-traditional media (what they know little about). As discussed elsewhere in this textbook, the media landscape is changing: newspaper consumption is down, satellite radio allows people to listen to music free of advertising, television audiences are highly fragmented, and technologies allow TV viewers to delete commercials while recording and watching prerecorded shows. The winds of change are blowing, and advertisers have no choice but to change with them.

Thus far, most companies that have embraced the Internet for advertising purposes have included it as a supplementary or complementary medium. To be successful in the future a more progressive attitude toward the medium is needed. No longer will it simply be an add-on. Instead, it will be an equal partner in the integrated marketing communications mix—and for some very good reasons. Unlike any of the traditional mass media, online advertising provides immediate feedback to advertisers regarding how effectively their message reached the target; it automatically gears ads to personal viewer's tastes, and it generally reaches receptive consumers—they want to see the ads they click on![6]

In Canada, online advertising only accounts for 4 percent of all advertising expenditures, but the rate of growth in online spending is much higher than any other medium. Several factors are contributing to online advertising growth:[7]

- The Internet delivers on the corporate mandate for marketers to be more accountable; since online investment is measurable, it is attractive to marketing organizations.
- Expansion of broadband capabilities allows for high-speed video downloading, an attractive option for both viewers and advertisers.
- Search advertising continues to evolve and draw more dollars.
- The shear number of people online continues to grow.

The Internet and online communications isn't the only game in town. The fast pace of Canadian society and the persistent development of new technologies has created other interactive advertising opportunities. Video games, for example, are very popular with youth and young adult males. Cell phones are the foundation of social interactivity among young people, and iPods and other MP3 players are popular with a wide cross-section of the population. As consumers continue to embrace the Internet and other interactive media as an integral part of their everyday lives, marketers have little choice but to acknowledge that anything interactive is a critical medium to engage consumers and create deeper brand experiences.[8]

This chapter will explore the various opportunities available to companies and show how the Internet can play a significant role in the integrated marketing communications mix. The reality is that the Internet can do a host of things that other media simply can't. For example, it helps create brand awareness and build brand image. Further, when online advertising is combined with other media in an integrated campaign, better results are obtained, especially in the areas of aided and unaided brand awareness and brand loyalty.

**Interactive Advertising
Bureau**
www.iabcanada.com

Research studies conducted by the Interactive Advertising Bureau (IAB) show the benefits of adding an online component to the communications mix. In one study for Dove Sensitive Essentials line of skin care products, advertising targeted women 18 to 49 using a combination of television, online, print, and outdoor media. The online component lifted aided brand awareness by 33 percent even though it only accounted for 6 percent of the dollars spent on media. Online advertising outperformed TV alone in terms of raising purchase intent for face care products (by about 18 percent), but for consumers who saw television, print, and online ads, purchase intent skyrocketed 47 percent.[9]

For additional insight into the benefits of adding online advertising to the marketing communications mix, see the IMC Highlight **Integrated Campaign Delivers Results at Canadian Tire**.

IMC HIGHLIGHT

INTEGRATED CAMPAIGN DELIVERS RESULTS AT CANADIAN TIRE

Canadian Tire is a very successful company. It is a company that prides itself on being a leader in the area of integrated media campaigns, for it saw the benefits of integration long before many of its competitors.

Terry Yakimchick, manager of media integration at Canadian Tire, says "We strongly believe in the integration of consistent themes and branding through all of our communications as well as our in-store customer experience. We have increased our investment in online spending and believe that online plays an important role in our overall media mix."

The impact of Canadian Tire's investment in online communications has been proven through a research study conducted by the Interactive Advertising Bureau. The study, referred to as CMOST (Canadian Media Optimization Study), examines the impact of integrated campaigns on factors such as brand awareness, favourability, intent to purchase, and, ultimately, return on investment.

A two-week Father's Day campaign was tested at Canadian Tire. The campaign included 30-second radio spots, online banner ads, flyers (nationally delivered print flyers and eflyers), along with the promotion of a contest and price promotional offers communicated at the Canadian Tire website.

The findings of the research study were as follows:

- The combination of online advertising and radio advertising increased awareness by an additional 6 percent.

- The combination of radio and online advertising increased scores for a variety of Canadian Tire brand attributes from 6 to 10 percentage points above that delivered by radio alone.

- The combination of online and radio had an impact on the female target, whose unaided brand awareness increased by 16 percent.

- The combination of online and radio produced the highest percentage of unique visitors to the Canadian Tire website in two years.

These results indicate the impact that online communications offers advertisers. Clearly, online communications have become an effective medium that must be given due consideration when planning an integrated campaign. A company must deliver their message where their customers are, and clearly they are online!

Adapted from "Fourth CMOST Study demonstrates online's ability to influence behavior in short period of time," *IAB News Letter*, www.iabcanada.com.

At the same time, online communications can go further than many other media because they can secure a purchase and make arrangements to have goods delivered. They are capable of closing the loop, from initial awareness to a buying decision, in a very short period, assuming a website has ecommerce capabilities. Figure 7.2 illustrates how Internet communications link with traditional advertising and ecommerce. For these reasons, the Internet is an exciting medium, and its potential must be exploited.

The Internet and Online Marketing Communications

Internet
A worldwide network of computers linked together to act as one in the communication of information; like a global mail system in which independent entities collaborate in moving and delivering information.

World Wide Web
A system of Internet servers that publish websites, which are specially formatted documents that contain graphics, audio, and video files and links to other websites.

The **Internet** is a network of computer networks (independent, interconnected networks) linked together, like a global mail system in which independent entities collaborate in moving and delivering information. The **World Wide Web** is the collection of websites, which are documents that contain graphics, audio, and video files as well as links to other websites, on the Internet. Users of the Internet go to the websites that interest them and browse through the material for as long as they like. Along the way, they can be exposed to various forms of online advertising.

The reality of the Internet is that consumers voluntarily visit specific websites. To get what they want, they also give up valuable information about themselves. Smart companies use the Internet as a means of obtaining information for their database. It is a way to build a stockpile of information that can be mined at a later date. Once the information is analyzed, it can be translated into specific messages, and marketing offers can be tailored to specific customer needs.

FIGURE **7.2**   **The Links among Online Communications, Traditional Communications, and Ecommerce**

Traditional forms of advertising drive customers online. Online communications provide detailed information. The information could lead to an online purchase (ecommerce) or an offline purchase. Online communications strategies must complement offline communications strategies.

```
┌──────────────────┐
│  Corporate Plan  │
└──────────────────┘
         │
         ▼
┌──────────────────┐      ┌──────────────────┐
│  Marketing Plan  │─────▶│  Ecommerce Plan  │
└──────────────────┘      └──────────────────┘
         │                         ▲
         ▼                         │
┌──────────────────┐   ┌───────────────────────────┐   ┌──────────────────┐
│ Advertising Plan │──▶│ Online Communications Plan│──▶│ Offline Purchase │
│ (Traditional     │   └───────────────────────────┘   └──────────────────┘
│  Media)          │
└──────────────────┘
```

Behavioural targeting

A means of delivering online ads based on a consumer's previous surfing patterns.

Cookie

An electronic identification tag sent from a web server to a user's browser to track the user's browsing patterns.

Volkswagen
www.vw.com

The Internet is a medium that allows marketers to target customers on the basis of their behaviour. In its simplest form, **behavioural targeting** means delivering ads based on a consumer's previous surfing patterns.[10] An individual's surfing behaviour is tracked by placing a **cookie**, which is a small text file uploaded to a consumer's web browser and sometimes stored on their hard drive. The cookie can be used to remember a user's preferences. By tracking preferences, an organization can directly tailor messages to reach specific consumers.

Behavioural targeting is ideal for reaching consumers when they are researching a purchase. A recent Volkswagen campaign invited consumers to visit vw.com and configure a Jetta. Consumers were asked to interact with car features, like colour and model. Volkswagen believed that if consumers interacted with the features they would be more likely to buy. If they visited the Volkswagen site and did not interact, they were served another Jetta ad when they returned to the AOL network. The strategy worked, as 28 percent of the original visitors who did not configure a car eventually did visit the site to do so after the exposure to the second ad.

The sheer amount of research done online by consumers is reason enough for a company to be actively engaged with consumers through online communications. A user who sees something of interest (that is, an advertising message that creates awareness) can obtain information immediately by clicking the ad and visiting the website. Therefore, well-designed, well-placed, and well-targeted messages are useful tools for consumers who engage in online product research.

Online communications differ from traditional media communications. Traditional media are passive by nature, and the Internet is interactive by nature. Traditional media target an audience, whereas on the Internet consumers target the content they are interested in and, in the process, are exposed to messages that should be of interest (the concept of behavioural targeting discussed earlier). The potential of the Internet is huge—it will become the medium of choice for companies wanting to reach large numbers of people in a cost-efficient manner.

The Internet offers three significant marketing and marketing communications opportunities. First, from a communications perspective, it is an excellent medium for telling a story. The medium is ideally suited for extended copy and loads of visuals.

FIGURE **7.3** Dell Operates One of the Highest-Value Commercial Websites in the World

Second, from a marketing perspective, an organization can complete a sale online. In terms of securing action, the Internet is very similar to direct response advertising (discussed in Chapter 6). Online storefronts such as those for Sears and Canadian Tire fall into this category. Third, the Internet deals with the concept of mass customization. **Mass customization** refers to the capability of personalizing messages and ultimately products to a target audience of one. The marketer deals with each customer individually. For example, Dell Computer does not produce a computer until it hears directly from a customer. Once the exact specifications are determined through a process of interaction at the Dell website, a unique computer is produced and shipped directly to the consumer. See the illustration in Figure 7.3.

Mass customization

The development, manufacture, and marketing of unique products to unique customers.

Interactive communications

The placement of an advertising message on a website, usually in the form of a banner, pop-up ad, rich media ad, sponsorship at a website, or an ad delivered by email.

ONLINE AND INTERACTIVE COMMUNICATIONS PLANNING

Interactive communications refers to the placement of an advertising message on a website, usually in the form of a banner, pop-up ad, rich media ad, sponsorship at a website, or an ad delivered by email. Advertising messages may also be communicated through other electronic devices such as cell phones, personal digital assistants, MP3 players, and video games.

When devising an interactive communications plan, decisions about which medium to use are largely based on the communications objectives and the budget available. Refer to Figure 7.4 for a visual review of the interactive planning process. The first step in the process is to establish the objectives. The second step is to evaluate the various media options strategically. Will it be an online campaign, a mobile media campaign, a video game campaign, or any combination of alternatives? What interactive media are best suited for effectively delivering the message? Once the strategy is determined the next step is execution. Here, decisions are made on specific media, how much to spend, and how to schedule media activities during the year.

ONLINE AND INTERACTIVE COMMUNICATIONS OBJECTIVES

Online advertising performs the same or similar roles as traditional media advertising. It can help create brand awareness, build or enhance brand image, generate sales leads, provide a means to make a purchase, improve customer service and communications

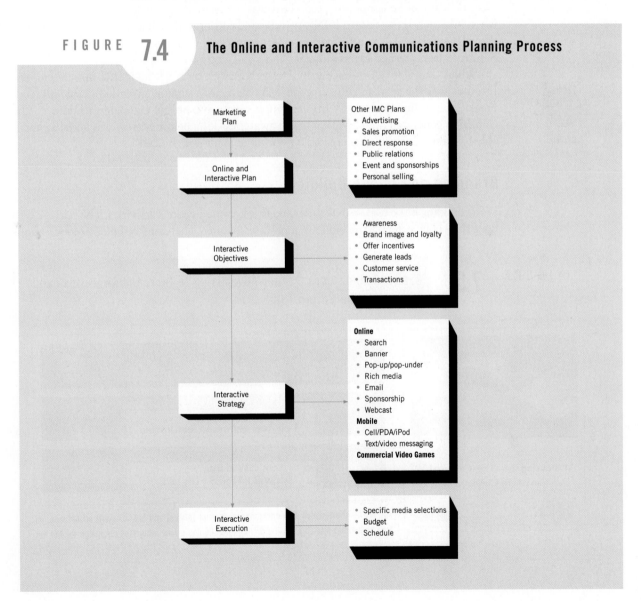

FIGURE **7.4** **The Online and Interactive Communications Planning Process**

between customers and the company, and acquire meaningful data about potential customers (as in database management).

Creating Awareness

Given the amount of time and the frequency with which consumers go online, there is ample opportunity for a company or brand to develop advertising that will generate awareness. The most obvious way to achieve awareness is to advertise on a web portal. A **portal** is a website featuring several commonly used services, such as news or searching, and serves as a starting point or gateway to other services, such as shopping, discussion groups, and links to other sites. Examples of such sites include Yahoo!, Google, Canoe, Canada.com, Sympatico, AOL, and MSN. These are sites that people are automatically routed to when they launch their browser.

A variety of advertising alternatives, including banners and rich media (discussed later in this chapter), are available on most search engine sites. While the standard banner cannot communicate much information, it can help create brand name awareness (see Figure 7.5). When the user clicks on the ad, he or she is routed to a website where more details can be communicated. This was precisely the strategy Saturn Canada used when it launched the Saturn ION. As indicated earlier in the chapter, new car buyers surf the web extensively for information when in car-buying mode, a compelling reason for Saturn to use Internet advertising.[11]

Chrysler
www.chrysler.com

When Chrysler reintroduced the Dodge Charger in 2005, its iconic muscle car, the Internet was the lead medium in the campaign. In a campaign called "Unleash Your Freak," the online push was Chrysler's most aggressive online campaign to date.[12] The campaign generated high levels of brand awareness long before the car was actually available for sale, which in turn created a pent up demand for the car.

Branding and Image Building

Brand building is the responsibility of marketing communications activities. The purpose is to have the public perceive the brand in a positive manner. Therefore, online communications

---

F I G U R E **7.5**   **Saturn Canada Uses Banner Advertising to Increase Awareness and Interest in the Saturn ION**

Introducing the all-new Saturn ION
See where it takes you.

The online effort—which also encompasses banner (above) and big box (left) advertising, as well as a micro-site (top)—is the driving force behind a new integrated campaign for the Ion

Source: Courtesy of General Motors of Canada.

must present a message and image consistent with and comparable to any traditional form of communication. Consumers actively seek out product information on company websites, so it is important that the site project an image in keeping with overall company image.

It is common for consumers to be routed to sub-pages on a website (e.g., a brand page) as they search for the information they are after. Therefore, the brand page must comply with the brand's image and persona. The messages communicated through online advertising or on a website should be consistent with traditional media advertising. Since it is common practice to include website addresses on traditional forms of advertising, it makes good sense to have an integrated message in terms of look, appearance, and style across all media. Such a practice helps produce a synergistic effect for the total communications effort.

Companies in the telecommunications, automotive, and financial services industries are masters at matching message strategies among traditional and non-traditional forms of media. Automotive sites in particular do an excellent job of creating and building an image for a new car model. When an interested consumer or tempted car buyer first sees a new car in a print ad or on television, he or she almost automatically migrates to the Internet for more information (see Figure 7.6).

Offering Incentives

The Internet is a good medium for implementing a variety of sales promotion activities. To encourage consumers to make their initial online purchase, price discounts are commonplace. Canadian Tire, for instance, offers unique and special deals online as a means of getting people comfortable with online buying. Once they realize it is a safe and convenient way to buy, they go back for more. Online coupon offers are available from companies that specialize in this business. One example is Save.ca, which identifies offers available from various manufacturers and services, takes requests for the coupons online, and then mails the coupons to consumers (see Figure 7.7).

Contests and sweepstakes are popular online promotions. Typically they encourage consumers to buy for the first time or they encourage brand loyalty (repeat purchases). Regardless, the true benefit to the company is the names and information that are collected through entry forms. For the chance of winning a prize, it is surprising how much personal information an individual will divulge to a marketing organization. This information can be used either to start or expand a database.

Generating Leads

In a business-to-consumer or business-to-business marketing situation, the Internet is a useful medium for generating leads. As already indicated, consumers willingly disclose information when entering contests. Consumers and business people will also leave the same vital information when they are searching for information online. The stumbling block in retrieving the information they want is the transfer of personal or business information. However, online visitors are known to give out more details about themselves, or the business they are part of, so that they may retrieve the information they are searching for. Business sites often request information such as company size, number of employees, type of business, location, postal code, email address, and so on. It's a fact of life in doing business online. This type of information, once analyzed and mined (data mining), can be used to identify potential targets (one-to-one marketing) and to customize messages and products that are suited to that target. It's the start of CRM.

Providing Customer Service

In any form of marketing, offering good customer service is crucial. Satisfied customers hold positive attitudes about a company and are likely to return to buy more goods.

FIGURE **7.6**   **An Integrated Approach to Message Strategy across All Media Has Greater Impact**

Source: Courtesy of Mazda Canada.

Again, the Internet plays a pivotal role. It can be an efficient and cost-effective way of providing service, assuming a company's website is well organized. Service demands by customers tend to be high. Therefore, any frustration a customer experiences when searching for service on a website will only compound the problem. Speed of service is a primary benefit offered by the Internet. It goes without saying that customers should have

FIGURE **7.7** **The Internet Is a Useful Medium for Distributing Incentives to Prospective Customers**

Source: Save.ca

quick and open access to service information. Carefully indexed FAQs (frequently asked questions) or key word searches are common ways to access online information quickly.

For specific questions and concerns, email is another good option. Of course, response time for handling email has unfortunately become a real issue. Making customers wait a few days for a response is not the type of service they expect. Successful online businesses don't forget that online activities must be backed up by a human component. They must pay close attention to inbound sales, order tracking, out-of-stock issues, deliveries and returns, and all the service issues associated with these tasks. All of these activities are part of a good CRM program.

Conducting Transactions

The business-to-business market is booming with online transactions, and the business-to-consumer market is growing steadily each year. A total of 34 percent of Canadians have made an online purchase in the last 12 months (March 2004 to April 2005), approximately triple the percentage from five years ago.[13] Considering this statistic and the fact that consumers use the Internet for researching purchases, it is very important that the message being delivered is both interesting and informative.

Having a website with ebusiness capabilities is important today. While shoppers are concerned about security aspects of the Internet, they are willing to use their credit cards online. Companies such as Canadian Tire, Sears, and Chapters-Indigo use the Internet to communicate effectively with shoppers, and they have combined emarketing and ebusiness with their traditional methods of conducting business. More businesses will follow their lead. If they don't, they will be watching their competitors take business away from them.

ONLINE AND INTERACTIVE COMMUNICATIONS STRATEGIES

As indicated by the increase in advertising revenues from year to year and the amount of time consumers spend online each week, advertisers now embrace online communications from a more strategic perspective. They know they have to use online communications, but based on limited exposure to the medium and its costs and benefits, they remain puzzled about how to use it. Therefore, today's media planners must be technologically savvy; they must recognize the value of online communications and other forms of interactive communications and make appropriate recommendations when necessary. Anything less is unacceptable in today's fast-paced and rapidly changing marketplace.

This section examines the various online and interactive opportunities available to advertisers and provides some success stories that potential advertisers can learn from. There are a variety of opportunities available to online advertisers: search advertising; banner advertising; pop-up and pop-under ads; rich media ads; sponsorships; websites; and email advertising.

Prior to examining the various online advertising alternatives, some basic terminology should be understood. All terms relate to how Internet ads are measured for effectiveness:

Ad views (impressions)
An ad request that was successfully sent to a visitor. This is the standard way of determining exposure for an ad on the web.

Ad clicks (clickthroughs)
The number of times users click on a banner (clicking transfers the user to another website).

Ad click rate (clickthrough rate)
The percentage of ad views that resulted in an ad click; determines the success of an ad in attracting visitors to click on it.

Visitor
A unique user of a website.

Visit
A sequence of page requests made by a visitor to a website; also called a session or a browsing period.

Stickiness (sticky)
A website's ability to keep people at the site for an extended period or to have them return to the site frequently.

Search advertising (pay-per-click advertising)
An advertiser's listing is placed within or alongside search results in exchange for paying a fee each time someone clicks on the listing.

- **Impressions (Ad Views):** An ad request that was successfully sent to a visitor. This is the standard way of determining exposure for an ad on the web.

- **Ad Clicks (Clickthroughs):** This refers to the number of times that users click on a banner ad. Such a measurement allows an advertiser to judge the response to an ad. When the viewer clicks the ad, they are transferred to the advertiser's website or to a special page where they are encouraged to respond in some way to the ad.

- **Clickthrough Rate (Ad Click Rate):** This indicates the success of an advertiser in attracting visitors to click on their ad. For example, if during one million impressions, there are 20 000 clicks on the banner, the clickthrough rate is 2 percent. The formula is *clicks* divided by *ad views*.

- **Visitor:** Any individual who accesses a website within a specific time period.

- **Visit:** A sequence of page requests made by one user at one website. A visit is also referred to as a *session* or *browsing period*.

A site's activity is described in terms of visits and visitors, the former always being larger than the latter because of repeat visitors. A site that can report, for example, that it had 8 million page views, 100 000 visitors, and 800 000 visits last month would be doing very well. It means that the average visitor returns to the site 8 times each month and views 10 pages on each visit. That's incredible "stickiness" (most sites don't do that well)! **Stickiness** refers to the notion that the website has a compelling reason for users to stay for a longer visit or to come back frequently for more information.

Search Advertising

With **search advertising**, the advertiser's listing is placed within or alongside search results in exchange for paying a fee each time someone clicks on the listing. This is also known as **pay-per-click advertising**. Many experts perceive search advertising as the preferred form of online advertising, and as such, investment in search advertising should be given priority before considering other online advertising alternatives.

Most search engines like AOL, Google, and Yahoo! set advertisers against one another in auction-style bidding for the highest positions on search results pages.[14] For example,

Google Advertising
www.google.com/ads

Google offers a service called AdWords, which allows companies, for a small fee, to have a link to their website featured when a user searches a specific key word that the company specified.[15] To illustrate, if a user types in the phrase "investments" and TD Waterhouse has bought that key word, an advertisement for TD Waterhouse appears on the screen.

It is literally a war of words among advertisers in the search marketplace. When General Motors launched the Pontiac Solstice, a compact sports car that would compete with the Mazda MX-5 (Miata in Canada), television ads encouraged viewers to "Google Pontiac." What General Motors did not know was that Mazda bought the words "Pontiac" and "Pontiac Solstice" as part of its search engine strategy to launch the redesigned Mazda MX-5. Googlers saw ads for both products. In explaining the ambush, Don Romano, vice-president of marketing for Mazda says, "This is one of those great rivalries—two sports cars coming out—and we thought the best way to get our message out was to offer a comparison."[16]

Banner Advertising

Banner

Online, an ad that stretches across a webpage; the user can click on the ad for more information.

A **banner** refers to advertising on a website, usually placed by a third party. A standard banner ad resembles an ad on an outdoor board or an ad that stretches across the bottom of a newspaper. Not much copy can be included on a static banner. The combination of brand name, short message, and visual must convince the user to click on the ad, which links to another website. Another option is the animated banner, which typically includes movement of some kind or a message that is looped in predetermined time intervals. Generally, response rates or click rates for animated banners are higher than for static banners.

The industry, through the Interactive Advertising Bureau (IAB), has established standard ad sizes to reduce costs and inefficiencies associated with planning, buying, and creating online media. The size of an ad is based on Internet Measurement Units (IMU), an expression of the width and depth of an ad.

Four banner sizes were established in the initial standardization phase. Refer to Figure 7.8 for a visual illustration of the ad sizes.

Rectangular ad

A large ad, slightly wider than it is tall, on a webpage.

Big box ad

An online ad shaped like a large rectangle that offers greater width and depth to an ad.

Leaderboard (super banner)

An ad that stretches across the entire top of a webpage.

Skyscraper

A vertical box-shaped ad that appears on a webpage.

- **Rectangle:** A larger box-style ad (180 x 150 IMU) that offers more depth than a standard size banner.
- **Big box:** A large rectangle (300 x 250 IMU) that offers greater width and depth to an ad.
- **Leaderboard (Super Banner):** An ad that stretches across the entire top of a webpage (728 x 90 IMU).
- **Skyscraper:** A tall, slim, oblong-shaped ad that appears at the side of a webpage (160 x 600 IMU).

Advertising research conducted by the IAB has concluded that larger formats that are naturally more visible and provide more creative freedom are significantly more effective than smaller, standard-sized banners across all campaigns. Larger ads make it more difficult for users to avoid them and provide an opportunity to deliver a more complete message, even if the user doesn't click on the ad. Because of their size and better performance, they command a higher price. Cost must be factored into the equation when an advertiser decides to use online advertising. For insight into the effects of ad size on brand awareness and message association, refer to Figure 7.9.

Given the interactive nature of the medium and the behaviour of Internet users who like to avoid ads if possible, the results achieved from banner ads have fallen short of expectations. Consequently, advertisers are experimenting with more animated forms of advertising, television-style online advertising, sponsorships, and email advertising.

FIGURE **7.8** **Universal Ad Package Sizes for Internet Advertising**

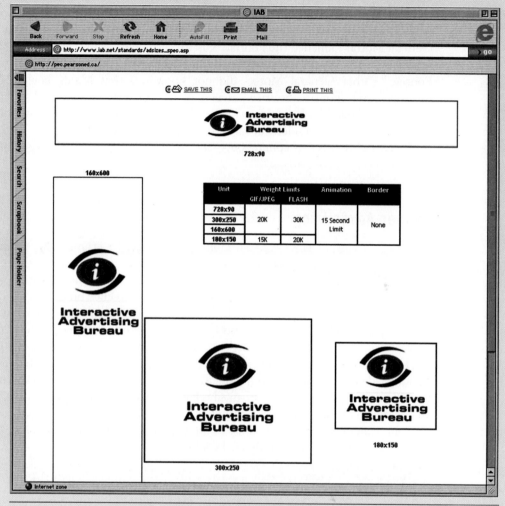

Source: Courtesy of IAB.

FIGURE **7.9** **The Impact of Ad Size on Brand Awareness and Other Advertising Measures**

Size of Ad	Brand Awareness	Message Association	Brand Favourability	Purchase Intent
Banner	1.8	2.4	0.3	0.2
Skyscraper	2.7	3.9	1.4	1.4
Large Rectangles	3.1	8.5	2.5	3.3

Large rectangles seem to offer the greatest benefit to advertisers. This information represents the point above the statistical baseline that helped increase the brand measure in absolute terms and is based on an aggregate of all online campaigns tested.

Reprinted with permission from the January 13, 2003, issue of *Advertising Age*. Copyright, Crain Communications Inc. 2003.

Pop-up and Pop-under Ads

A pop-up or pop-under appears in a separate window on top of or beneath content already on the computer screen. Pop-under ads remain concealed until the top window is closed or minimized. Generally, consumers object to these types of ads due to their nuisance factor; they are perceived negatively, much like an unsolicited telemarketing call. Therefore, advertisers must use them at their own peril. Despite the negative perceptions held by consumers, advertisers like pop-ups and pop-unders because they achieve higher click rates than banner ads. Some web publishers have banned their use due to the negative feedback by their customers.

Rich Media

Rich media are a form of online communication that includes animation, sound, video, and interactivity. An **interstitial** is a rich media message contained in a pop-up window (described above) while the requested content loads in the background. It is an intrusive message that is delivered automatically without being requested by the user. A **superstitial** is similar to an interstitial but is more elaborate, usually incorporating multimedia and interactive elements. A superstitial is displayed in the active browser and to view it usually requires special software such as Flash or Shockwave.

A superstitial closely resembles a television commercial and is delivered by a process called streaming media. **Streaming media** involve the continuous delivery of small packets of compressed data that are interpreted by a software player and displayed as audio and full-motion video. The creativity aspect of rich media options makes online advertising sexy, fun, and something new to try. Figure 7.10 contains an animated banner ad and rich media ad for the Suzuki Vitari. When the banner is clicked on the user is transferred to a page containing a full-motion ad for the vehicle.

The similarity to television advertising makes rich media attractive to traditional advertisers. Consequently, this is a high-growth area of Internet advertising. More to the point, rich media ads lend themselves well to branding, so they have quickly become the domain of the big consumer brands such as Coca-Cola, Nike, Ford, and many others. Rich media are often sold as part of a package that includes other types of online advertising like banners.

ESPN.com now runs web commercials in a video format bundled with video content the user has requested. The TV-style ads are embedded in sports highlight clips that are readily available at the website. Viewers see the video clip, followed by an ad, followed by another video clip, and so on. The strategy ensures the ad is viewed. The clickthrough rates for rich media ads are higher than for banner ads. The rate for rich media averages 3.5 percent, whereas banners average only 0.5 percent.[17]

While use of rich media ads is growing right now, they will become increasingly common as users adopt high-speed Internet access in greater numbers. These kinds of ads grab the viewer's attention more quickly and can deliver the message on a more emotional level. An organization's ability to adapt its messages to rich media technology could be the key to online advertising success. For more insight into the use of TV-style ads online and their growing popularity, read the IMC Highlight **General Motors Goes Online**.

Sponsorships

An online **sponsorship** is a commitment to advertise on a third-party website for an extended period. Advertisers are attracted to sponsorships on the basis of web content. If the content of a site is particularly interesting to an advertiser's target market, visitors are apt to visit the site frequently. For example, investors in the stock market frequently visit ROBTv.com, which broadcasts business news online. Business and recreational travellers visit theweathernetwork.ca, and sports junkies frequently visit tsn.ca and other sports sites. Brands that are closely linked to the content of these networks pursue sponsorships.

Rich media
Streaming video, audio, and special effects similar to television and used online.

Interstitial (pop-up or pop-under)
An online ad that appears in a separate browser window while another webpage is loading; a pop-up appears in a window in front of the active window, and a pop-under appears in a window behind the active window.

Superstitial
Elaborate online advertising that usually incorporates multimedia and interactive elements.

Streaming media
Audio or video delivered online in small, compressed packets of data that are interpreted by a software player as they are received.

ESPN.com
www.espn.go.com

Sponsorship
When a company or brand commits to advertise for an extended period on a third-party website or sponsors a webpage.

Source: Courtesy of Suzuki.

Quarto Communications Ltd., publisher of *Cottage Life* magazine and broadcaster of Cottage Life TV, offers sponsorships at its cottagelife.com website. TIM-BR Mart advertises in the magazine and sponsors a web page titled "What's New." The page usually features projects involving lumber—docks, decks, and fences—a natural tie-in for a lumber retailer. See Figure 7.11 for an illustration. Similarly, a product like Claritin, which helps

IMC HIGHLIGHT

GENERAL MOTORS GOES ONLINE

How effective is any form of online advertising? General Motors, Canada's largest advertiser, has discovered it is quite effective when used in conjunction with traditional media. When online advertising and television advertising were used together in a GM campaign versus television alone, there was a 28 percent increase in brand awareness among the sample group.

GM has long been a believer in the value of online advertising, but the research study that produced the above awareness scores helped the company further understand the synergies between the different media and provided actionable ways to create better creative plans, allocate media funds, and schedule execution. Canadians are changing their media habits, so marketers must follow their customers.

Very likely, GM will start to cash in on the latest craze in online advertising—video advertising. TV-style ads delivered over the Internet are exploding in popularity. The ads appear in small windows or full screen. Some are user initiated while others are interspersed within video content or appear on screen when users surf from page to page.

The TV-style ads offer several benefits to advertisers. They can minimize their creative costs, as they can simply convert commercials into digital files for the web. Couple that with the high level of broadband Internet adoption in Canada and you've got an appealing format. At the very least, it gives advertisers that are skeptical about the effectiveness of web advertising an incentive to at least dabble in it.

Inevitably, there will be a downside to video ads. For starters, web surfers have notoriously short attention spans. Advertisers also risk a backlash against unexpected video among online users who are still fuming about persistent pop-up ads. And with people now paying less attention to television ads, it stands to reason that TV-style ads online will eventually get the same response from consumers. However, since consumers are spending more and more time online, and less time with other media, advertisers have little choice but to jump on the online-video-ad bandwagon.

Adapted from Tessa Wegert, "On-line video ads grow more popular," *Globe and Mail*, November 11, 2004, p. B10, and Carl Bialik, "TV commercials go online, but will surfers tune in?" *Yahoo! Finance*, July 8, 2004, www.yahoo.com.

FIGURE **7.11**   **TIM-BR Mart Takes Advantage of a Sponsorship Opportunity on the Cottage Life Website**

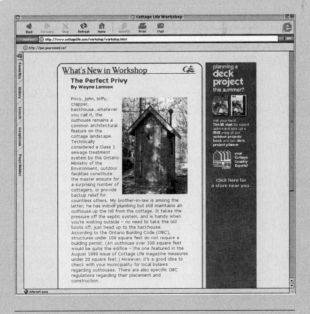

Source: Courtesy of Cottage Life.

allergy sufferers breathe better, is an ongoing sponsor of the pollen report on the Weather Network and theweathernetwork.ca. The report is simply known as the Claritin Pollen Report.

With a sponsorship, the advertiser does not have to drive the viewer to a website. Instead visitors come to the site voluntarily. The sponsor benefits from the status and prestige of the site it is associated with. Consumers trust the sites that they visit frequently on the web, so a brand that is associated with the site could be perceived more positively through the sponsorship association.

Email Advertising

One of the most promising applications in online advertising is email advertising, specifically permission-based email. **Permission-based email** is sent to recipients who agree to receive information in that form. In other words, people actively subscribe to the email service. This form of advertising is relatively inexpensive, response rates are high and easy to measure, and it is targeted at people who want information about certain goods and services. An offshoot of email advertising is sponsored email. With **sponsored email**, the email includes a short message from a sponsor along with a link to the sponsor's website.

Email is an attractive opportunity for businesses of all sizes. According to Statistics Canada, nearly 96 percent of Canadian Internet users access email. It is less expensive than direct mail and allows for greater frequency of distribution and an incredible level of customization. Email is an efficient method of delivering new product information and information about promotional offers. Email campaigns cost $5 to $7 per thousand, compared with $500 to $700 per thousand for direct mail.[18] Further, a company can segment its message based on demographic and psychograhic data.[19]

Email advertising is similar to direct mail advertising, but at the same time it is very different. It does operate the same way insofar as it is based on a list contained in a database and it targets customers specifically interested in something. The difference, though, is that email advertising generates higher responses—and that is attracting advertisers' attention. Unlike any other form of online advertising, sending messages by email in this way seems quite acceptable to Internet users. Users can subscribe and unsubscribe to email lists as they wish.

Similar to direct mail, the success of an email campaign depends on the quality of the list. The lists are called **opt-in lists**, an appropriate name because consumers agree to have their names included. There are two kinds of opt-in lists. A *first-party list* comprises people who have specifically agreed to receive email from an organization. A *third-party list* is composed of names and addresses compiled by one company and sold to another.

In the age of database marketing, the compilation of an in-house list is essential. Sending email to customers and prospects who specifically request it will almost always work better than using a rented list. Online promotions and contests sponsored by companies are another way of securing names and addresses. However, as indicated above, organizations should be careful how they distribute names to other organizations. There's a saying these days: "Permission rented is permission lost."

Although email advertising is attractive, that third-party list is what promotes spam. **Spam** is unsolicited email, even from reputable sources, and third-party lists can result in people receiving mail they do not expect. With a first-party list, subscribers agree to receive messages, but they might not have agreed to have their names sold for marketing purposes. The use of the Internet to send large volumes of email has infuriated many consumers, forced employees in organizations to waste precious time deleting junk email, overwhelmed the server capacities of many Internet service providers, spread viruses as well as the fear of viruses, and hurt the business of legitimate Internet marketers. This issue has to be

Permission-based email
Email sent to recipients who have agreed to accept email advertising messages.

Sponsored email
Email that includes a short message from a sponsor along with a link to the sponsor's website.

Opt-in list
A list of people who have agreed to receive messages via email.

Spam
Unsolicited email.

addressed, for many of the efficiencies gained through the use of email are diminished as consumer suspicion rapidly grows with the flood of unsolicited commercial email.[20]

Email also opens up opportunities for a new communications technique called viral marketing. **Viral marketing** is a situation where the receiver of an online message is encouraged to pass it on to friends. A research study in the United States reports that 89 percent of adult Internet users share content with others via email. Only 5 percent of respondents in the study said they refuse to share content that contains a brand message.[21]

Should an organization pursue a viral campaign, the goal is to create content that people feel compelled to pass around, not because they like the product. As a result, things that tend to spread in a truly viral environment are things that most organizations wouldn't want their brands associated with because they're shocking or risky.[22] Riskier messages tend to create buzz for a brand. To illustrate, beer.com, an adult-oriented site (you must be 19 years old to enter), is engaging to visitors because it shows various exploits of a sexy bartender named Tammy. Word of mouth, or in this case word of mouse, spreads fast!

Viral marketing

Online marketing that encourages the receiver of a message to pass it along to others to generate additional exposure.

Beer.com
www.beer.com

Company Websites

Traditional media communications and online communications encourage users to visit a company or brand website. Clicking on an ad automatically takes you to the website. The purpose of the ad is to attract attention; once the person is at the website, the purpose is to deliver more meaningful and detailed information in an entertaining manner. The website provides an opportunity to tell a story. A company cannot tell or show as much through traditional media as inexpensively as it can on the Internet. Advertising in the traditional media should always provide a website address and encourage potential customers to contact the site for additional information.

Rolex, a very expensive and reputable brand of watches, advertises in upscale publications read by upper-income targets. Typically, the ads feature a close-up of the watch to highlight its elegance and beauty. Detailed information is available at the website (see Figure 7.12).

The nature of information communicated on a website varies from one organization to another. For example, news and information organizations such as the *Globe and Mail* and *Maclean's* magazine provide copy-intensive information (they are online versions of their respective print editions). In contrast, automobile companies provide unique and vivid visual images of their latest makes and models along with technical specifications and related information. Many sites include contests and games to make the experience of visiting more entertaining. A fun experience leads to more frequent visits.

Websites play a role in building brand awareness and preference and provide an opportunity for a brand to engage with its target audience. Axe (a line of male grooming products) effectively interacts with its 18- to 24-year-old male customers via its Axe U website. The brand hosts two events a year across Canada, allowing young men to interact with the fairer sex, including blonde Axe representatives. Users can also download Axe U "course materials," like playbooks and wallpaper, as well as chat. The message board seeds anticipation about events and captures feedback.[23] In a very short time, Axe has become a leading brand, and web communications have contributed to the brand's success. Refer to the illustration in Figure 7.13.

Websites are a common source of information among business decision makers. Nearly 50 percent of business decision makers in a recent poll said the web has influenced them to make a purchase or obtain a service for their business. Related findings indicated that references to television, newspapers, and magazines had declined. In B2B marketing, the web is the place to find out about new products and companies.[24]

FIGURE **7.12** **The Combination of Elegant Print Advertising and a Website Enhances the Image of Rolex Watches**

Model in stainless steel and 18kt. yellow gold.
Oyster bracelet.

Oyster Perpetual Datejust

Also available with a Jubilee bracelet.
Waterproof to 100 metres.

www.rolex.com

ROLEX

For the name and address of your nearest authorized Rolex jeweller,
please contact Rolex Canada Ltd., 50 St.Clair Avenue West, Toronto, Ontario M4V 3B7, 416-968-1100.

Source: Reprinted by permission of Rolex.

FIGURE **7.13**   **Axe Encourages Users to Interact with the Brand through an Online Experience**

Source: ©Unilever Canada Inc.

Webcasting (Webisodes)

Webcasting (webisodes)
The production of an extended commercial presented on the web that includes entertainment value in the communications.

Mercury
www.mercuryvehicles.com

Webcasting or **webisodes** involve the production of an extended commercial that includes entertainment value in the communications. While consumers are using digital video recorders to skip television ads they don't like, they are using the Internet to tune in to commercials they want to see—an interesting phenomenon!

The Ford Motor Company produced a webisode called "Meet the Lucky Ones" that showed the misadventures of a quirky, dysfunctional family. It enticed droves of young, female buyers into its Mercury Mariner SUV. The vehicle is subtly integrated into the webisode with unobtrusive product placement. Ford is very pleased with the results. "This has brought in a new customer [one that is 15 years younger than the average Mercury customer]," says Kim Irwin, Mercury brand manager. More than half of the customers were also new customers to the Mercury brand.[25] BMW North America is also experimenting with extended commercials, some as long as nine minutes, on its website.

While the number of potential viewers of a webcast is much lower than for a conventional television ad, the fact that viewers are there for a reason indicates the benefit of showing commercials online. The behaviour of people watching a commercial on the web is much different from that of people watching a television commercial.

For a summary of the advantages and disadvantages of the various forms of online communications, refer to Figure 7.14. As time progresses, as advertisers and agencies become more familiar with online capabilities, and as consumers become more comfortable with the commercial aspects of the Internet, the true benefits of the medium will be realized. What is known is that younger target audiences—a desirable audience for many advertisers—spend considerable amounts of time online. Since this is a hard-to-reach target through any medium, the Internet represents an opportunity to get to them.

FIGURE **7.14**   **Advantages and Disadvantages of Online Marketing Communications**

Advantages

Targeting capability—Advertiser reaches individuals based on browsing behaviour and preferences

Timing—Messages can be delivered 24 hours a day, 7 days a week

Interactivity—Messages encourage consumers to interact with brands while online (perform a task, play a game, etc.)

Transaction—Assuming ebusiness capability at a website, an online purchase can occur

Disadvantages

Acceptance (lack of)—Consumers continue to reject the notion of online advertising; it gets in the way of what they are doing

Privacy—Concerns about transferring sensitive or personal information online along with misuse of information by marketing organizations

MOBILE MEDIA

The screen is small, the audience's attention span is short, and the environment—a park bench or a busy subway station—is variable. Yet the possibilities of mobile marketing are capturing the attention of advertisers. Opportunities to communicate with consumers exist through text messaging, video messaging, and online video games. Electronic devices such as cell phones, personal digital assistants, and iPods now allow advertisers to reach customers in a targeted manner.

Text Messaging

Text messaging
The transmission of short text-only messages using wireless devices such as cell phones and personal digital assistants.

Canadian Wireless Telecommunications Association
www.cwta.ca

It may be a generational thing, but people under the age of 35 are into **text messaging**, the transmission of short text-only messages on wireless devices such as cell phones and PDAs. According to the Canadian Wireless Telecommunications Association, roughly half of all Canadians—or just over 15 million people—use a cell phone. While making voice calls remains the primary function of cell phones, the popularity of Palm and BlackBerry devices for email has allowed text messaging to emerge as a popular communications tool.[26]

Cell phones are becoming multi-purpose devices as consumers use them to take and send pictures, browse the Internet, and play video games. Such widespread use has to be explored by content providers, but to date the delivery of most content has been subscription based. Even though there is a threat of public backlash, should advertising take hold on cell phones, consumers will gradually adapt to the practice as they have done with the Internet. It will be the younger generations of consumers that make or break the cell phone marketing communications market.

Marketers interested in reaching the youth market are looking seriously at text messaging. It is one of the latest weapons in the arsenal of guerilla marketing tactics used to reach youth. Promotional tours and the distribution of free samples to selected youth markets are other strategies that have proven successful in recent years. Advertisers are asking consumers to take time to text message and interact with their brands. Marketers now add "call-to-action" short codes to their marketing material (outdoor posters, transit ads, bottle caps, and so on). Cell phone users can punch in the codes to participate in contests, download free music, and get ring tones or merchandise.

FIGURE **7.15** **L'Oréal Invited Cell Phone Users to Receive Their Horoscopes through Text Messaging**

Source: Courtesy of Dick Hemingway and Jen Handel.

L'Oréal effectively communicated with 12- to 17-year-old females by promoting a brand called ColourPulse on digital television screens in shopping malls, a notorious teen hangout. The campaign invited cell phone users to text the message "PULSE" (78573) and receive their horoscope delivered to their cell phone on a daily basis (refer to the illustration in Figure 7.15). Consumers were also entered into a contest to win a one-year supply of L'Oréal products. According to Stephanie Angelone, ColourPulse product manager, "Text messaging created a daily interaction with our consumer in an unobtrusive manner, which we can't achieve with television or print advertising."[27] L'Oréal recognizes that text messaging is an ideal format for reaching the fickle teen market since traditional approaches are not as effective as they once were.

All marketers must be careful how they use cell phones. If the messages are overly intrusive, their attempts could backfire. Too much commercialism is not a good thing among today's skeptical youth. It would also be dangerous for wireless carriers to open up their databases to commercial interests without having an opt-in from their customers. The risk of losing customers is strong incentive for carriers to keep down the advertising noise.

Video messaging **Video messaging,** the next generation of cell phone communications, is in its experimental stages. Using a subscription pricing model, consumers can download news and sports clips and selected television shows from major networks. For a monthly fee viewers can go online to watch live streaming of CTV Newsnet and ROBTv. In the United States, viewers who own an iPod can download episodes of selected NBC TV shows (approximate costs are $15.00 for four episodes).[28]

Consumers with video capabilities on their cell phones can download news and sports clips and selected television shows from major networks and watch them on their phones.

Whether or not consumers will enjoy watching shows on such a small screen is a question yet to be answered. Sports channel ESPN already sends highlight clips to cell phone users and has plans to include video clips for advertisers like Visa, Nike, and Hilton Hotels in the near future.

The limiting factor so far is technology—only a fraction of phones on the market are capable of playing video. This is about to change, however. Industry experts are forecasting that as many as 18 million Canadians will own cell phones with video capability within two years (by the end of 2008).[29]

Teens and young adults have been attracted to text messaging because of its portability and low cost. Marketers are excited about text messaging and video messaging due to its intimacy and immediacy. Many cell phones are equipped with global positioning systems so ads can be sent to consumers based on their location. With such information, a retailer could send a message to a consumer when they are in the vicinity of the store.[30]

Online and Commercially Purchased Video Games (Advergaming)

Trident Gum
www.tridentgum.com

Advergaming refers to the integration of brands into video games, either games played online or in games purchased directly by consumers. Integration of brands into games can generate positive brand awareness, higher brand preference ratings, and help achieve purchases. The tactic is seen as being more effective than product placements in TV shows. Video game advertising is popular among male teenagers—research indicates 49 percent of them visit game sites regularly. Video games are also popular with 20- to 34-year-old males, a target that spends more time with games than with television.[31]

Cadbury Adams used branded games to create awareness for some new flavours of Trident gum. Regular television and in-store advertising encouraged consumers to visit the game site to compete in a variety of adventure games. By playing the game, consumers could collect points toward weekly prizes such as MP3 players and a grand prize of $10 000. The average user returned to the site four times and spent 40 minutes interacting with the brand.[32]

Games also attract a female target. Recent research from the Entertainment Software Association has determined that online gamers are 50 percent male, 50 percent female, and 36 years old. Further, 44 percent download games from game-oriented sites, and 53 percent of online gamers play games on their mobile phones. Advertising in games is advertising directed at a family of middle-class technology adopters.[33]

For additional insight into the benefits of video game marketing communications, read the IMC Highlight **Games Reach the Male Target**.

IMC HIGHLIGHT

GAMES REACH THE MALE TARGET

What is the best way to reach a male between the ages of 15 and 34 with an advertising message? You might say television, but the correct answer is video games. Yes, video games are capturing the marketing imagination of all kinds of brands.

A recent study concluded that people who view advertisements in video games have better brand recall, and in some cases are more likely to favourably change their opinion of a brand. Nielsen Interactive Entertainment reports that unaided brand recall scores for in-game advertisers is in the 27 to 35 percent range and that one-third of gamers say the ads influence product purchases. A majority of respondents said, "the ads made the game seem more real." That's good news for advertisers!

The popularity of video games among 20-something males has attracted some luxury brands: TAG Heuer, Bang & Olufsen, and Lacoste, among others. Since this highly coveted age group spends more time with Xboxes and PlayStations than watching prime-time television, in-game advertising is now one of the fastest-growing segments of the entire advertising industry.

Already, video game publishers have waiting lists of brands wanting a piece of the action. Video game maker Electronic Arts only had one game with ads in 2001. In 2006, product placements appeared in 30 new games. The explosion is partly due to improved technology. Brand placements are no longer just static billboards; they are dynamic commercials where the brand is intertwined into the storyline, such as a murder victim who was about to sign a contract with fashion designer Lacoste in the "Law & Order: Justice Is Served" game.

It was only a few years ago that game makers were paying to use brands in their games. Now it's the brands that are paying. And it costs anywhere from $5000 to $500 000, depending on the popularity of the game. That's a lot of money, but for advertisers it's worth it. The 18- to 34-year-old demographic is an important segment for marketers wanting to build brand loyalty.

Advertisers that have jumped on the video game bandwagon include PepsiCo, General Motors, Samsung, Procter & Gamble, and McDonald's. Film studios like Paramount Pictures and Universal also use video games to promote new movies.

Adapted from Jenn Abelson, "Brands line up for roles in video games," *National Post*, December 9, 2005, p. FP8, and Eve Lazarus, "Keep it real," *Marketing*, March 13, 2006, p. 14.

Summary

As advertisers and agencies develop a stronger understanding of the role and importance of the Internet and other forms of interactive media in the daily lives of consumers, they will integrate more interactive communications into the media mix.

Internet penetration continues to rise while significant growth in wireless penetration is also occurring. The combination of online and other forms of interactive communications represents significant opportunities for advertisers. Thus far, the Internet has been employed as a complementary medium, but recent media trends strongly suggest that online communications should be addressed more seriously by advertisers. The interactive nature of the medium allows a brand to engage consumers and create deeper brand experiences. The challenge for advertisers is to create useful and entertaining messages while not alienating Internet users.

The Internet is a medium that allows marketers to target customers on the basis of behaviour, a concept referred to as behavioural targeting. By tracking preferences, unique messages are delivered to consumers on an individual basis. As well, there is the capability to design unique products for customers, a concept referred to as mass customization.

Advertising online plays a key role in achieving specific marketing objectives. Online advertising will help create brand awareness for the launch of new products and is an excellent medium for building brand image. The fact that so much information can be presented visually and in a tone and style comparable to television is a real asset. Companies also find the Internet ideal for distributing buying incentives and for promoting contests. In both cases, information about consumers is collected and added to a database for use at a later date. In a business-to-business context, online advertising is a means of generating leads. It is also a good medium for implementing customer service programs. Furthermore, unlike other media (except direct response advertising), online advertising can complete a transaction.

There are a variety of advertising alternatives to choose from. Among the options are search advertising, banner ads in both static and animated forms, pop-up and pop-under ads, rich media ads that include full audio and video, sponsorships at other websites, and email ads. Gaining in popularity is permission-based email advertising. Using lists generated from in-house databases or from other sources (rented lists), email represents a cost-efficient way to reach prospects and current customers. Rich media ads are gaining in popularity due to their similarity to television ads.

As an advertising medium, the Internet provides targeting capability at a very reasonable cost and also offers tracking capabilities that measure effectiveness in a variety of ways (e.g., clicks, clickthrough rates, leads, and purchases). Because it is available at all hours of the day, seven days a week, there is ample opportunity for brand and company exposure online. Some drawbacks of the Internet include selective reach (higher educated and higher income households are the main users) and the perception among users that advertisers are invading their privacy. Security issues involving the transfer of sensitive information can impede online purchases.

Mobile media represent new opportunities to deliver advertising messages. Electronic devices such as cell phones and personal digital assistants are part of the daily lives of many consumers. Text messaging is a relatively new medium, but it allows for consumers and brands to interact with each other, a definite step toward developing brand loyalty. The next generation of cell phones offers video capabilities, an even stronger way to deliver a message. Marketers are attracted to mobile media based on the immediacy and intimacy they offer.

Finally, video games are proving to be an effective means of reaching youth and young male adults. Both segments are spending more time playing games than they are watching television. Advertisers must capitalize on this trend and adjust their media budgets accordingly.

Key Terms

ad click rate,   202

ad clicks,   202

ad views,   202

advergaming,   214

banner,   203

big box ad,   203

behavioural targeting,   195

clickthrough rate,   202

clickthroughs,   202

cookie,   195

impressions,   202

interactive communications,   196

Internet,   194

interstitial (pop-up or pop-under),   205

leaderboard,   203

mass customization,   196

opt-in lists,   208

pay-per-click advertising,   202

permission-based email,   208

portal,   198

rectangular ad,   203

rich media,   205

search advertising,   202

skyscraper,   203

spam,   208

sponsored email,   208

sponsorship,   205

stickiness,   202

streaming media,   205

super banner,   203

superstitial,   205

text messaging,   212

video messaging,   213

viral marketing,   209

visit,   202

visitor,   202

webcasting,   211

webisodes,   211

World Wide Web,   194

Review Questions

1. What is behavioural targeting and how is it applied in online marketing communications programs?

2. What is mass customization and how do online communications facilitate its practice?

3. What are the primary marketing and marketing communications roles that the Internet can provide marketing organizations? Identify and explain each role briefly.

4. In the context of online marketing communications, briefly explain what viral marketing is. Is it a worthwhile pursuit for marketing organizations?

5. Explain the following terms as they relate to online advertising:
   a) ad impressions
   b) clicks
   c) ad click rate
   d) visits

6. What is banner advertising and how does it work?

7. Identify and briefly describe the various types of banner ads.

8. What is the difference between a pop-up ad and a pop-under ad?

9. What does rich media refer to and how does it work? What does streaming media refer to?

10. Briefly explain how an online advertising sponsorship works. What benefits does it provide? Illustrate the benefits with some examples.

11. Briefly explain the following email advertising terms:
    a) permission-based email
    b) sponsored email
    c) opt-in list
    d) spam

12. What is a cookie and what role does it perform in online communications and marketing?

13. What is a "webisode"? Briefly explain the difference between a webisode and other types of rich media advertising.

Discussion and Application Questions

1. Identify and briefly explain two advantages and two disadvantages of Internet-based advertising.

2. What future lies ahead for email advertising? Will it continue to grow or will consumers and businesses turn away from it? Conduct some online research on the issue and present a brief report on your findings.

3. "Persistent invasions of consumer privacy will be the undoing of online advertising." Is this statement true or false? Conduct some online secondary research on this issue. Report on your findings.

4. How important are websites to companies today? Examine their role in the marketing communications mix and present a position on what lies ahead for marketing organizations.

5. Visit some commercial websites of your choosing. Evaluate these websites in terms of their ability to achieve certain marketing and marketing communications objectives such as building brand image, offering incentives, generating leads, and providing customer service. Are communications on the websites coordinated with any other form of marketing communications?

6. Assess how consumer goods marketing organizations can use web-based communications to their advantage. Can it be an effective medium for building relationships with customers?

7. Will consumers accept or reject the notion of delivering advertising messages via cell phones and other portable devices? Examine the issues surrounding this emerging practice and formulate a position on the matter.

8. Assess the various online advertising alternatives such as banners,

interstitials, and rich media. Which alternative is best at communicating with consumers?

9. Is it possible to launch a new product using online communications as the

primary medium for creating awareness and interest? What strategies would be necessary to make such a plan work?

Endnotes

1 Shankar Gupta, "Automakers shift ad budgets online," *Media Post*, February 17, 2006, **www.mediapost.com**.

2 "First-time car buyers seek out the Internet," *Detroit Free Press*, February 1, 2006, **www.freep.com**.

3 Marc Graser, "Toyota hits touch points as it hawks Yaris to youth," *Advertising Age*, May 1, 2006, p. 28.

4 "Household Internet Usage Survey," 2003, Statistics Canada, **www.statcan.ca**.

5 "Canucks love their net: Study," *Media in Canada*, March 10, 2005, **www.mediaincanada.com**.

6 Kerry Munro, "Online: Be there or be square," *National Post*, March 10, 2006, p. FP9.

7 "What's driving growth?" Internet Advertising Bureau, **www.iab.com**.

8 "Internet advertising revenues estimated to be $12.5 billion for full year 2005," Internet Advertising Bureau, **www.iab.com**.

9 "Mixing it up," *Essential Interactive*, Volume 2, pp. 29, 30.

10 Andrea Zoe Aster, "Tactful targeting," *Essential Interactive*, Volume 2, p. 20.

11 Chris Daniels, "Saturn sets a virtual scene," *Marketing*, April 21, 2003, pp. 8, 9.

12 Jean Halliday and Kris Oser, "Dodge charges online for Charger," *Advertising Age*, July 7, 2005, **www.adage.com**.

13 "Canucks love their net: Study," *Media in Canada*, March 10, 2005, **www.mediaincanada.com**.

14 Dan Grossman, "Pay-per-click search advertising comes first," *Website Goodies*, **www.websitegoodies.com/article/39**.

15 "Search engine marketing," **www.wikipedia.org**.

16 Sharon Silke Carty, "Mazda pulls web-search switcheroo with Pontiac," *USA Today*, January 30, 2006, **www.usatoday.com**.

17 Pamela Parker, "Branding beyond intuition," Streaming Media 101, part V, **www.turboads.com/richmedia_news/2001rmn/mn200110822.sthml** (accessed November 2003).

18 Kevin Marron, "E-mail gets the message across," *Globe and Mail*, September 27, 2002, p. B11.

19 Suzan Bianchi and Dany Roth, "E-Mail marketing," *SOHO Business*, Winter 2006, p. 20.

20 Tyler Hamilton, "Ottawa ponders junk e-mail," *Toronto Star*, January 23, 2003, p. C5.

21 Kris Orser, "Study finds consumers fans of viral e-mails," *Advertising Age*, February 13, 2006, p. 35.

22 Chris Daniels, "Stalk the talk," *Marketing*, May 2, 2005, pp. 16, 17.

23 "Axe U educates marketing department, too," *Strategy*, January 2006, p. 9.

24 Tobi Elkin, "Study: Net best to get at business," *Advertising Age*, September 9, 2002, p. 24.

25 Sarah Webster, "Ford makes more films for web to sell vehicles," *Detroit Free Press*, March 14, 2006, **www.freep.com**.

26 Chris Daniels, "The new frontier," *Essential Interactive*, Volume 2, p. 24.

27 Ibid, p. 26.

28 Michelle Halpern, "Shows on the go," *Marketing*, February 6, 2006, p. 18.

29 Ibid., p. 18.

30 Matt Richtel, "Marketers interested in small screen,"*New York Times*, January 16, 2006, **www.nytimes.com**.

31 Jenn Abelson, "Brands line up for roles in video games," *National Post*, December 9, 2005, p. FP8.

32 Chris Daniels, "The new frontier," *Essential Interactive*, Volume 2, p. 26.

33 Eve Lazarus, "Keep it real," *Marketing*, March 13, 2006, p. 15.

Part 3

Planning for Integrated Marketing

Part 3 looks at non-traditional media choices and a variety of marketing and promotional choices that enhance the communications plan.

Chapter 8 introduces various sales promotion alternatives that are frequently used in integrated marketing communications plans. Discussion is divided between consumer promotions and trade promotions, with each area examined for its ability to achieve marketing and marketing communications objectives.

Chapter 9 describes the role of public relations communications in the marketing communications mix. Various public relations techniques are introduced. The process of planning public relations activities is examined in detail, along with various measurement techniques used to

determine the effectiveness of public relations messages.

Chapter 10 discusses the role of event marketing and sponsorships in contemporary marketing. The criteria for participating in event marketing and the steps and procedures for planning an event are introduced, as are various evaluation techniques that determine the effectiveness of event marketing and sponsorship strategies.

In Chapter 11, the role of personal selling in a variety of business settings is examined. Personal selling adds a human component to the integrated marketing communications mix, and for this reason plays a very important role in an era where customer relationship management practices dominate.

8

SALES PROMOTION

After studying this chapter you will be able to

1. distinguish between consumer promotions and trade promotions

2. describe the steps in the sales promotion planning process

3. assess the role of consumer promotions in achieving specific marketing communications and marketing objectives

4. assess the role of trade promotions in achieving specific marketing communications and marketing objectives

5. outline the nature of various consumer promotion and trade promotion activities

6. assess various criteria for integrating sales promotion strategies with other integrated marketing communications strategies

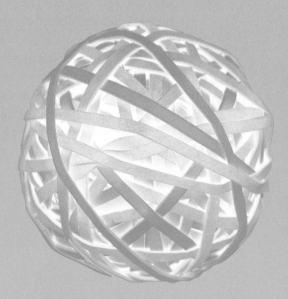

This chapter examines the role of sales promotions in the marketing communications mix. Promotions are activities that focus on making a sale, usually in a short period of time. When planning and implementing promotions, the marketing organization provides an offer to customers in return for something they must do. Because the offer is valid only for a certain period, the impact of the offer—and its success or failure—can be measured quickly.

A wide variety of promotion offers are presented here, all of which are suited to achieving specific marketing and marketing communications objectives. The right promotion must be offered at the right time if the offer is to bring true benefit to the brand or company. In order to create awareness and interest in the promotion, there must also be media advertising to support it, and possibly some publicity generated by a public relations campaign. A coordinated effort is usually required to make a sales promotion a success. This chapter focuses on two distinct yet related areas of sales promotion: consumer promotion and trade promotion. An organization must consider strategies for both if it is to grow and prosper.

SALES PROMOTION

Sales promotion

An activity that provides incentives to bring about immediate response from customers, distributors, and an organization's sales force.

Sales promotion is defined as activity that provides special incentives to bring about immediate response from customers, distributors, and an organization's sales force. It is a strategy that encourages action by the recipient. According to the definition, three distinct groups are considered when planning sales promotion strategies. First, the consumer or final user must be motivated to take advantage of the offer. Second, the distributor (reseller of goods) must be motivated to support the offer by providing merchandising support. Third, the company's sales force must be motivated to sell the promotion to its trade customers. Because the intent of a promotion is to provide some added excitement to the product, an organization's sales representatives must present it enthusiastically to the trade distributors.

Consumer promotion

Incentive(s) offered to consumers to stimulate purchases or encourage loyalty.

Pull

Demand created by directing promotional activities at consumers or final users, who in turn pressure retailers to supply the product or service.

Consumer promotions are designed to stimulate purchases or to encourage loyalty. Among the options readily available are coupons, free samples, contests, rebates, price incentives, and rewards programs. These types of promotions are planned to help **pull** the product through the channel of distribution. An organization creates demand for the product by directing its promotional efforts directly at the consumer. The combination of advertising and promotions, for example, creates demand and causes consumers to look for the product in stores or request a service; by asking for it specifically, they put pressure on the retailer to provide it. Many companies now include experiential marketing activities, often referred to as buzz marketing, in their promotion strategies. These concepts are presented in detail later in the chapter.

Trade promotion

An incentive offered to channel members to encourage them to provide marketing and merchandising support for a particular product.

Push

Demand created by directing promotional activities at intermediaries, who in turn promote the product or service among consumers.

Trade promotions are less visible activities, given that they are offered to members of the channel of distribution. These promotions include options such as discounts and allowances, cooperative advertising funds, dealer premiums and incentives, and point-of-purchase materials. Offering financial incentives to distributors encourages them to support a manufacturer's promotion plans. Such promotions **push** the product through the channel of distribution. Refer to Figure 8.1 for a visual image of pull and push promotion strategies.

To be successful, an organization must determine what type of promotion will contribute the most to achieving its objectives. In most cases, it is a combination of both consumer and trade promotions. The real decision is to determine the extent to which each type of promotion is offered. Such a decision is based on the market analysis that precedes the development of any sales promotion plan. Sales promotion planning is discussed in the following section.

FIGURE **8.1**   **Pull and Push Promotion Strategies**

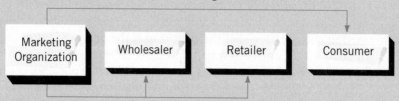

Pull—The promotion strategy is directed at consumers, who in turn request the product or service from distributors, and pull it through the channel.

Push—The promotion strategy is directed at distributors, who resell the product. Incentives help push the product from one distributor to another.

SALES PROMOTION PLANNING

Like any other component of the marketing communications mix, a sales promotion plan is but one component of a much larger plan. It must directly fit into the marketing communications plan and play a role in achieving the specific objectives that are identified in that plan. Whereas advertising plans have a long-term perspective, and longer-term objectives, the sales promotion plan adopts a short-term view and achieves objectives of a more immediate nature. For example, while advertising is building a brand's image, sales promotions are implemented to encourage a spike in sales. All domestic automobile manufacturers, for example, offered employee discount offers to the general public in the summer of 2005—the goal being to increase sales immediately.

Sales promotions are activities that complement advertising. When you consider the primary goals of advertising—awareness, comprehension, conviction, and action—the primary goal of sales promotion is to focus on one specific area—action. A well-timed promotional offer that coincides with an image-building advertising campaign could be just the incentive needed to get the customer's money out of that wallet or purse. Such a relationship suggests that integration of advertising strategies and promotional strategies is essential and, on a larger scale, that their integration with online communications, events and sponsorships, and public relations is what promotes a brand or company with a sense of continuity.

Sales promotion planning involves developing a plan of action for communicating incentives to the appropriate target markets (consumers and trade customers) at the right time. Very often, an external company that specializes in sales promotion will assume responsibility for developing and implementing the consumer promotion plan. As with developing an advertising plan, the specialist must be briefed. The client's role is to provide the necessary background information and then evaluate the promotion concepts put forth by the agency. The promotion agency must assess the information provided by the client and then prepare a strategic plan that will meet the client's objectives (see Figure 8.2). A sales promotion brief typically includes some or all of the following information.

Market Profile

An overview of sales and market share trends provides market perspective to the promotion planners. Knowing if the brand is a leader, challenger, or follower has an impact on the nature of the promotion they will ultimately recommend. It is important to know if the market is growing and what brands are growing in the market.

FIGURE **8.2**   **The Sales Promotion Planning Process**

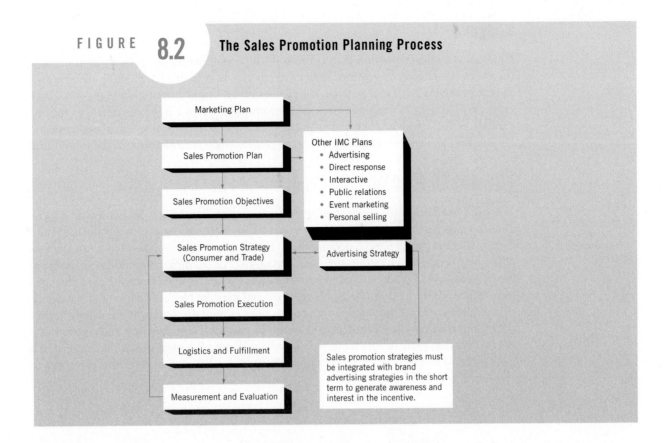

Competitor Activity Profile

In general terms, what marketing communications strategies do key competitors rely upon? The role of the various elements of the mix will vary from one brand to another. What brands dominate the market and what are their mixes? An evaluation of this kind of information may suggest that various combinations of activities have more or less impact on customers. A review of competitors' recent sales promotion activities is essential.

Target Market Profile

Perhaps the most important aspect of planning a promotion is a good understanding of the target customer. As discussed earlier in the text, customers are described according to demographic, psychographic, and geographic characteristics. Additional information about shopping behaviour usually plays a role in developing a sales promotion plan. For example, many of today's consumers are time challenged and value conscious and are looking for good deals they can take advantage of quickly. When planning the promotion, the value must be immediately evident to the consumer.

Sales Promotion Objectives

A variety of background factors will determine the objectives of the promotion campaign. Essentially, sales promotion plans focus on three distinct objectives: generating trial purchases, encouraging repeat or multiple purchases, and building long-term brand loyalty. Objectives for trade promotion plans concentrate on building sales and achieving merchandising support. These objectives are discussed in more detail in the "Consumer Promotion Execution" and "Trade Promotion Execution" sections of this chapter.

Budget

Funds for the sales promotion plan come from the overall marketing budget. In most cases, the client has already determined how much money is available for promotions. Knowing the size of the budget is crucial when the promotion agency is thinking about potential concepts. Will this be a large-scale national promotion, or will it be restricted to specific regions? Will it involve an expensive grand prize, or will there be a series of smaller prizes? How much media advertising support will be needed to create awareness for the promotion?

THE SALES PROMOTION PLAN

Sales promotion plan

An action plan for communicating incentives to appropriate target markets at the right time.

The **sales promotion plan** is a document that outlines the relevant details about how the client's budget will be spent. Objectives are clearly defined, strategies are justified, and tactical details are precisely documented. Similar to direct response communications plans, back-end considerations are very important. For example, if a fulfillment program is part of the package, details about how the offer will be handled from the time the consumer responds to the time the goods are delivered must be precisely planned. Promotions that include coupons, free samples, contests, rebates, and premiums might involve other companies that handle various aspects of the promotion. The structure and content of a sales promotion plan are the focus of this section. Figure 8.3 summarizes the content of a sales promotion plan, but because the content of a plan varies from one company to another, it is only a guideline.

FIGURE **8.3** **The Content of a Sales Promotion Plan**

Situation Analysis

- Market profile
- Competitor activity profile
- Target market profile

Budget

- Funds available

Sales Promotion Objectives

A. Consumer Promotion

- Trial purchase
- Repeat purchases
- Multiple purchases
- Brand loyalty

B. Trade Promotion

- New listings
- Sales volume
- Merchandising support

Sales Promotion Strategy

- Incentive or offer (save, win, or reward)
- Merchandise, cash, or combination
- Balance between consumer and trade

Advertising Strategy

- Broadcast
- Print
- In-store
- Digital and Interactive

Sales Promotion Execution

- Details of consumer offer (coupon, sample, contest, premium, rebate, loyalty promotion)
- Details of trade offer (trade allowance, performance allowance, cooperative advertising funds, dealer premiums, collateral materials, display materials, trade shows)

Logistics and Fulfillment

- Back-end plan to administer and implement the promotion

Budget and Timing

- Activity costs
- Calendar of events

Sales Promotion Objectives

Sales promotion objectives are statements that clearly indicate what the promotion plan is to accomplish. As with other communications plans, objective statements should be realistically achievable, quantitative in nature to facilitate measurement, and directed at a carefully defined target market.

The nature of the promotion plan (that is, consumer promotion versus trade promotion) determines the objectives. Although objectives for both are quite different, they complement each other when implemented. Let's start with consumer promotion objectives.

The most common objective of consumer promotion is to encourage consumers to make a *trial purchase*. When a product is new, for example, an organization wants to establish acceptance as quickly as possible. Therefore, trial-oriented promotions are common (see Figure 8.4). Even when a product is in the growth stage of development there is need to distinguish one brand from another. At that stage, incentives that encourage purchase of a specific brand remain essential. Media-delivered coupons are an excellent promotion tool for encouraging trial purchase.

The second objective is to stimulate *repeat purchases* by existing customers. An extension of this objective is to encourage consumers to make *multiple purchases* at one time (see Figure 8.5). To illustrate, a well-conceived contest will encourage multiple entries by consumers. Persistent purchases of the brand in the contest ties the consumer to the brand for a period of time. Those consumers won't be buying a competitor's brand!

The third objective deals with customer relationship management (CRM). Here, the objective is to encourage *brand loyalty* for an extended period. Traditionally, promotions encourage instant activity, but there are promotion alternatives that can meet both short-term and long-term brand objectives. Something as simple as the loyalty card offered by a local coffee shop helps keep a customer a customer. Rewards bring customers back.

The overall goal of trade promotions is to give sales a jolt in the short run. But such an accomplishment is usually the result of promotion strategies combined with other marketing strategies to influence trade customers and consumers. Therefore, trade promotion objectives must be confined to what they can realistically achieve. Generally speaking, trade promotion plans are designed to encourage distributors to carry a product and then sell it to retailers, and to increase the volume sold for products they already carry.

FIGURE  **A Consumer Promotion Designed to Encourage Trial Purchase**

Source: Reprinted by permission of Yoplait.

A Consumer Promotion Designed to Encourage Multiple Purchases

Source: Courtesy of Parmalat.

Listing

An agreement made by a wholesaler to distribute a manufacturer's product to the retailers it supplies.

In the case of a new product, the first objective is to *secure a listing* with distributors. A **listing** is an agreement made by a wholesaler to distribute a manufacturer's product to the retailer it supplies. For example, when the head office of Canada Safeway or Sobeys agrees to list a product, it is then available to all of their retail outlets. Typically, trade promotions in the form of financial incentives are used to secure listings.

A second objective is to *build sales volume* on either a seasonal basis or a predetermined cyclical basis throughout the year. For example, baking products are promoted in the pre-Christmas season and there are usually displays of such products in retail stores. In other cases, it is common for a company to offer temporary discounts for its key brands on a quarterly basis because they recognize that consistent activity keeps a popular brand in a preferred position with the trade and consumers. The nature of competition often dictates such a strategy.

A third trade objective is to *secure merchandising support* from distributors. Their support is crucial, because once the product leaves the manufacturer's warehouse the manufacturer is no longer in control of how it is sold. Consequently, funds are allocated to activities that get the product out of a distributor's warehouse and into displays on the retail sales floor. As well, the manufacturer will look for a sale price and perhaps a brand mention of the sale price in a retailer's advertising flyer. These activities constitute merchandising support.

SALES PROMOTION STRATEGY

Decisions about sales promotion strategy focus on the selection of the best promotion activity to meet the objectives. Decisions point the organization in a certain direction and, if agreed to, the tactical details are then developed. For example, on the consumer side of things, an organization can choose among coupons, free samples, contests, rebates, premiums, and loyalty programs. Other decisions may involve the selection of prizes. Should they be cash, merchandise, or a combination of both? The organization can use any one of these options or combine several to maximize the potential of the promotion.

Each of these options provides a different kind of incentive. For example, coupons and rebates save people money; contests give people a chance to win something; and samples, premiums, and loyalty programs offer something free with a purchase. As a result, the first decision relates directly to the incentive. Should the promotion program offer savings, a chance to win something, or a reward?

Key decisions about trade promotion strategy involve the allocation of funds among the different alternatives. Depending on the promotion objectives, preference may be given to listing allowances, trade and performance allowances, and cooperative advertising allowances. Alternatively, some combination of several of these allowances may be employed. The manager must also decide about the balance between consumer promotions (pull) and trade promotions (push). Successful promotions use both and are carefully integrated with other forms of marketing communications to maximize impact on the intended target audience.

The second component of the sales promotion strategy involves integration with the advertising strategy. You need to promote a promotion! In many cases, a brand will already be planning a brand-image campaign and several different media may be involved. Is special creative needed for the sales promotion? What media will be used to advertise the sales promotion?

With creative, the ideal situation is to have promotional creative blend effectively with existing brand creative. Therefore, separate but integrated messages must be prepared for the promotion. A promotion is an added incentive, so it temporarily becomes the brand's unique selling point. The combination of a strong ongoing sales message with the added bonus of a special offer will help achieve short-term and long-term objectives.

Resolve Corporation
www.resolvecorporation.com

Marketing research by Resolve Corporation observes that consumers should be able to immediately see that a promotion offer provides significant real value. This means that the savings have to be meaningful in relation to the purchase price of the product and must also make sense in relation to the market strength and purchase frequency of the brand.[1] The lesson here is that the offer must be a good match for the product and the target market.

A sales promotion will only work if it receives the necessary media support, so another decision must be made about allocating funds specifically for promotion-related programs. Once that decision is made, the media strategy will focus on two objectives: creating awareness for the promotion and providing details about how the consumer can take advantage of the promotion (e.g., how to send in order forms for premium offers or entry forms for contests).

Typically, a variety of broadcast, print, and online media is selected. Television is an ideal medium for creating instant awareness of the promotion. High-impact television advertising in a short period (a blitz strategy) is common. In the case of a contest or sweepstakes promotion, television is ideal for creating excitement and for conveying a sense of urgency to consumers. It encourages them to take advantage of the offer right away. Television can also direct consumers to a website where all the details of the promotion are available.

In-store advertising can also assist in achieving awareness objectives while playing a key role in communicating details of the offer. Consumers are conditioned to look for details at point-of-purchase. In conjunction with trade promotion strategies, the ideal situation is to have brand displays in stores supported by posters and shelf cards at the product's regular shelf location to draw attention to the promotion.

Obviously, the nature and size of the promotion will dictate the degree of media support. A contest with a significant grand prize will garner abundant media support (see Figure 8.6). It is common for brands such as Pepsi-Cola, Gillette, and Kellogg's cereals to invest in media advertising to promote contests that offer huge grand prizes. In contrast, a premium offer may simply be announced to the target market on the package itself and by shelf cards at point-of-purchase. The investment in media advertising in this case would be low.

Trade customers must be made aware of consumer promotion offers, a task that falls on the shoulders of the manufacturer's sales representatives. The manufacturer commonly prepares specific sales literature such as brochures, pamphlets, and display material for representatives to use to introduce the promotion. The sales representatives will integrate the consumer promotion offer with their trade promotion plans (a combination of pull and push) to maximize the impact of the dollars being invested in the promotion. A manufacturer will also consider direct mailings to trade customers to create awareness and interest in the promotion. The sales rep-

FIGURE **8.6** **A Contest Promotion Attracts New and Present Users and Helps Build Sales Volume**

Source: © 2003 Maple Leaf Foods Inc. Reprinted with Permission. The Hulk movie: © 2003 Universal Studios. Licensed by Universal Studios Licensing LLLP. The INCREDIBLE HULK and All Related Comic Books Characters: TM & © 2003 Marvel Characters, Inc. All Rights Reserved.

FIGURE **8.7** **Display Activity at Retail Stores Helps Make a Promotion a Success**

Source: Paul Reynolds Photography.

resentatives must sell the promotion to the distributors and show how it will affect their business positively. Their objective may be to secure a listing for a new product or to ensure the distributor orders sufficient inventory of an existing product to cover the anticipated demand and to encourage adequate merchandising support in their stores (see Figure 8.7). If the trade customers are on board, the promotion will be successful. Their support is crucial.

Logistics and Fulfillment

The final phase of planning a promotion campaign involves working out all of the details of the offer. Depending on the nature of the promotion, there is a variety of dates and deadlines, there will be other companies involved in planning and implementing the offer, and a system will need to be put in place to deliver the goods to consumers, if the promotion so dictates. These are only a sampling of the potential decisions that are made.

To demonstrate the fulfillment process, let's assume that a major contest is the sales promotion offer. The grand prize is a trip to Disneyland with a series of smaller prizes to be awarded to runners-up. Answers to the following questions start to create a plan of action for implementing the awareness and fulfillment sides of the promotion:

- When will the promotion be announced to the trade and to consumers?
- Who are the contest prize suppliers and what are the costs?
- How will consumers enter the contest? Who will design the entry form?
- Where will the entry forms be sent?
- What is the deadline for receiving entries?
- Who will draw the prizes?
- How will the prizes be delivered to the winners?
- What costs are associated with contest administration by a third-party organization?
- Who will the third-party organization be?
- Who will prepare in-store promotional materials?
- Who will print the promotional literature and what will it cost?
- How will media advertising be coordinated with the sales promotion offer?

Such a list of questions reveals the logistical implications for running a sales promotion offer. Needless to say, the entire promotion must operate seamlessly from the front end (announcing the promotion) to the back end (delivering prizes to winners). Smart marketing organizations outsource the administration of the promotion to a specialist in this industry.

Measurement and Evaluation

Similar to any other marketing communications program, sales promotion activities must be evaluated for success or failure. As indicated earlier, a boost in sales is the immediate goal of most forms of promotion, but other factors beyond promotion also influence sales. Therefore, a promotion must be evaluated based on the objectives that were established for it. If the objective was to generate trial purchases, how many new users were attracted to the product? If the objective was loyalty, are current customers buying the product more frequently? To answer these questions, some pre- and post-promotion marketing research is necessary.

Specific promotions are also measured by response rates of consumers. For example, a coupon promotion could be assessed by the number of coupons returned. If the average return rate for coupons distributed by magazines is 1 percent and an offer draws a 2 percent response, the promotion could be judged a success. A contest is evaluated on the basis of the number of entries received. If the objective was 10 000 entries and only 7500 were received, the promotion could be judged a failure.

If there is a method of projecting revenues generated by a promotion, then it is possible to estimate some kind of financial payout from the promotion. The difference between revenues and costs would be the return on investment, because the costs of the promotion are known. Figure 8.8 illustrates how to evaluate the financial payout of a coupon offer.

A side benefit of consumer promotions is the collection of names. The names on entry forms from contests and order forms for premium offers and rebate offers can be added to the organization's database. Smart marketers seek additional information about consumers on promotion entry forms to develop more thorough customer profiles and determine who their primary target market is.

Boston Market
www.bostonmarket.com

When Boston Market restaurants entered Canada, consumer promotions played a key role in getting unfamiliar customers to visit. Figure 8.9 shows how Boston Market applied the sales promotion planning process. Their very unique offer generated extremely high response rates.

FIGURE **8.8** **Evaluating the Financial Impact of a Sales Promotion Offer**

This example shows the return on investment for a coupon offer distributed to households by cooperative direct mail. Costs and revenues are estimated to determine the return on investment.

Coupon Plan	
Face value of coupon	$1.00
Handling charge for retailer	$0.15
Handling charge for clearing house	$0.05
Distribution cost	$18.00/M
Distribution	2 million households
Printing cost (digest-sized ad with perforated coupon at bottom)	$12.00/M
Redemption rate (estimated)	5.0%
Retail price of product	$3.89

(Manufacturer receives about 65% of retail price when distributors' mark-ups are deducted)

Costs	Cost Calculation	Total	Grand Total
Distribution	2 000 000 x $18/M	$36 000	
Printing	2 000 000 x $12/M	$24 000	
Coupon redemption	2 000 000 x 0.05 x $1.20	$120 000	
Total cost		**180 000**	**$180 000**
Cost per coupon redeemed	180 000/100 000	$1.80	

Revenues			
Per unit of revenue	$3.89 x.065	$2.53	
Total revenue*	2 000 000 x 0.05 x 0.80 x $2.53	**202 400**	**$202 400**
Return on investment			**$22 400**

*With any coupon offer, there is a risk of coupons being returned without a purchase being made. This is referred to as misredemption. In this example, the misredemption rate is 20%, hence the 0.80 factor in the revenue calculation equation.

FIGURE **8.9** **Summary Example of a Sales Promotion Plan for Boston Market**

SITUATION ANALYSIS

- Canadian consumers totally unaware of Boston Market
- Boston Market is a subsidiary of McDonald's Restaurants
- 650 locations in 28 US states
- Food perceived as very good (home-cooked style); high incidence of repeat visits

SALES PROMOTION OBJECTIVES

- To show how Boston Market can benefit the everyday lives of consumers
- To generate traffic (trial usage)

TARGET MARKET

- Married households; two working adults; with or without children; suburban
- Time starved and searching for home replacement meals

SALES PROMOTION STRATEGY

- An incentive that ties into what the brand stands for: "Home-style meals made easy"
- Free sample offer to designated households in trading area

SALES PROMOTION EXECUTION

- Promotion theme: "Dinner on Us"
- Location: Mystery bag attached to front door knob of designated area households
- Message on bag: "Too much on your plate?" (a question to create curiosity)
- Incentive: Free meal for two (no strings attached)
- Action: Consumer must bring the dinner plate from the bag to the restaurant to get the free meals. Plate inferred a home-cooked meal away from home. The unique promotion would encourage positive word-of-mouth.
- Distribution: Different homes selected each Thursday

MEASUREMENT AND EVALUATION

- The Thursday rollouts created a high level of anticipation among households
- Very positive press coverage by local media (free advertising and endorsements)
- Redemption rate 70% (outstanding)

Adapted from Lisa McGillivray, "Bagging a tasty promo," *Marketing*, December 2, 2002, p. 15.

Consumer Promotion Execution

As indicated earlier, an organization will combine various consumer promotion activities with trade promotion activities so that there is balance between the pull and push strategies. It is that combination of pull and push that creates a synergistic effect in the marketplace. This section will discuss the various forms of consumer promotions that are often included in sales promotion plans.

The major types of consumer promotions include coupons, free samples, contests, cash rebates and related incentives, premiums, and loyalty programs. The popularity of the various alternatives varies from one industry to another. In the packaged goods industry, all alternatives are used, but coupons seem to be the most popular. A survey conducted by NCH Promotional Services ranked coupons as the most important form of promotion for companies in the food, household, and personal care products industries. Following in order of importance were samples, contests, cash refunds, and premiums.[2]

In the automotive industry, rebates are the preferred tactic. Domestic manufacturers such as Ford, General Motors, and Chrysler frequently offer cash-back rebates and extremely low financing terms. Does anyone actually buy a car that doesn't have some kind of incentive offer attached to it? Let's analyze the various consumer promotions and determine the conditions for which each type of promotion is best suited.

Coupons

Coupon

A price-saving incentive offered to consumers to stimulate quick purchase of a specified product.

Coupons are price-saving incentives offered to consumers to stimulate quick purchase of a designated product. The motivation for distributing the coupons is the same across all industries, although the value of the coupons varies considerably. Grocery coupons, for example, may only be valued at $0.75, while a trial coupon for a restaurant may be valued at 50 percent of the cost of the meal. A common offer is "Buy one meal at regular price and save 50 percent off the price of the second meal."

In packaged goods markets, coupons are the dominant form of sales promotion activity. The latest data available from Resolve Corporation, which keeps records on coupon distribution and redemption rates in Canada, reveal that more than 2.93 billion coupons are distributed annually. A total of 99 million are returned, for a total savings on goods of about $118 million. The average value of a redeemed coupon is $1.19.[3]

Coupons are an excellent medium for achieving several marketing objectives at various stages of the product life cycle. First, coupons can encourage *trial purchase* among new users (and encourage competitive brand users to switch brands), and they can encourage *repeat purchases* by current users. In the latter situation, the coupon is a means of building brand loyalty.

Media-delivered coupon

A coupon distributed by traditional media alternatives such as newspapers, magazines, and direct mail.

The method by which the coupons are distributed to consumers is based on the objectives of the coupon offer. When a product is new or relatively new, trial purchase is the marketer's primary objective, so **media-delivered coupons** are popular. Options for delivery include **free-standing inserts (FSI)** in newspapers, magazines, direct mail, in-store distribution, and the Internet. Using the Internet to deliver coupons is a fairly new practice. Websites such as Save.ca distribute coupons on behalf of manufacturers. Many companies distribute coupons to consumers who request them while visiting their website. Samples of free-standing inserts appear in Figure 8.10.

Free-standing insert (FSI)

A booklet featuring coupons, refunds, contests, or other promotional advertising distributed by direct mail or with newspapers, magazines, or other delivery vehicles.

Once a product moves into the late growth and early mature stages of its life cycle, a marketer's attention shifts from trial purchase to *repeat purchase*. By now there are many competing brands, all of which have a certain degree of consumer loyalty. As a defensive measure, it is important to reward current customers in one form or another. The package itself becomes an important medium for distributing coupons. The insertion of a coupon in or on a package, for example, is an incentive for a customer to keep buying the product.

In-pack self-coupon

A coupon for the next purchase of a product that is packed inside the package or under a label.

Coupons contained inside a package are called **in-pack self-coupons**, because they are redeemable on the next purchase. Usually the face panel of the package makes mention of the coupon contained inside. A coupon that appears on the side panel or back panel is called an **on-pack self-coupon**. Another option is the **instantly redeemable coupon**, which is attached to the package in some fashion and can be removed immediately and used on the purchase of the product. Sometimes two different products collaborate on a coupon offer. Too illustrate, Tetley includes an in-pack coupon for Christie cookies, and

On-pack self-coupon

A coupon that is printed on the outside of a package redeemable on the next purchase of the product.

Instantly redeemable coupon

A removable coupon often located on the package or a store shelf that is redeemable on the current purchase of the product.

FIGURE **8.10** Coupons Distributed in Free-standing Inserts Help Achieve Awareness and Trial Purchases

Source: Paul Reynolds Photography.

Christie places a Tetley tea coupon in its package. The relationship between the two brands is obvious. Each brand capitalizes on the other's consumer franchise in its effort to attract new users. This type of coupon is called a **cross-ruff** or **cross-coupon**.

The success or failure of a coupon offer is often determined by the redemption rate that is achieved. The **redemption rate** refers to the number of coupons returned to the manufacturer expressed as a percentage of the total coupons in distribution. If, for example, 1 million coupons were distributed and 45 000 were returned, the redemption rate would be 4.5 percent (45 000 divided by 1 000 000).

For budgeting purposes, it is important to know the average redemption rates for the various methods of delivering coupons. For example, NCH research shows the average redemption rate for addressed direct mail coupons to be 6.5 percent, while the range can be anywhere from 1.9 percent to 22.6 percent. Magazine coupons have a range of 0.1 percent to 7.0 percent with an average of only 0.8 percent. A key factor that influences the redemption rate and causes such variations in the rate is the perceived value of the offer in relation to the regular price of the product. If it is not a worthwhile incentive, it will not be acted upon. Refer to Figure 8.11 for some additional information about coupons in Canada.

Cross-ruff (cross-coupon)
A coupon packed in or with one product that is redeemable for another product. The product the coupon is packed with is the means of distributing the coupon.

Redemption rate
The number of coupons returned expressed as a percentage of the number of coupons that were distributed.

FIGURE **8.11** **Coupon Distribution and Redemption Rates in Canada**

Variable	2003	2004
Quantity distributed	2.6 billion	2.93 billion
Quantity redeemed	97 million	99 million
Average face value of coupons distributed	$1.23	$1.55
Average face value of coupons redeemed	$1.08	$1.19
Consumer savings	$105 million	$118 million

Interpretation: Canadian consumers saved $118 million by redeeming coupons in 2004.

Coupon Distribution and Redemption Rates by Method of Delivery

Media Type	% Distributed 2003	% Redeemed 2003	% Distributed 2004	% Redeemed 2004
FSI	65	13	62	11
In-store	11	45	10	44
In/On package	9	21	7	22
Direct to home	5	7	7	9
Magazine	6	4	6	3
Newspaper/Sample pack	—	1	5	2
Charity	1	6	2	7
Other	3	3	1	2

Sample Interpretation: Freestanding inserts (FSI) account for 62% of all coupons distributed, but only 11% of all coupons actually redeemed. Packages deliver 7% of all coupons and account for 22% of all redemptions. The redemption rate is higher for packages because current users are redeeming the coupons.

Source: Reprinted by permission of Resolve Corporation.

Product Samples and Experiential Marketing

Product sampling is a powerful, yet expensive way to promote a product. It is an effective strategy for encouraging trial purchase, but due to the costs involved, many manufacturers do not select this option. Traditionally, **free sample** programs involved the distribution of trial-size packages (small replicas of the real package) or actual-size packages (see Figure 8.12). The latter option is obviously an expensive proposition.

Free sample
Free distribution of a product to potential users.

In order to implement a sampling program, the marketer must appreciate the true benefit of such an offer. In a nutshell, it is unlike any other form of promotion in that it is the only alternative that will convert a trial user to a regular user solely on the basis of product satisfaction. Essentially, the marketing organization has eliminated any perceived risk the consumer may have about buying the product. That's a compelling reason for using samples. Gillette followed this strategy when it launched the MACH3Turbo, a razor that was targeted at males 16 to 29 years of age. The company provided samples directly to players and coaches of 326 Junior 'A' hockey teams across Canada and handed out 100 000 razors to fans at games.[4]

Gillette
www.gillette.com

There are less expensive ways to implement sample programs, but they lack the impact of household distribution of free goods. A tried and true approach, particularly for food products, is *in-store sampling*. Costco uses this approach extensively by setting up sample stations at the ends of food aisles. A smart shopper can practically have a free lunch while shopping at Costco on a Saturday! When packaged good grocery manufac-

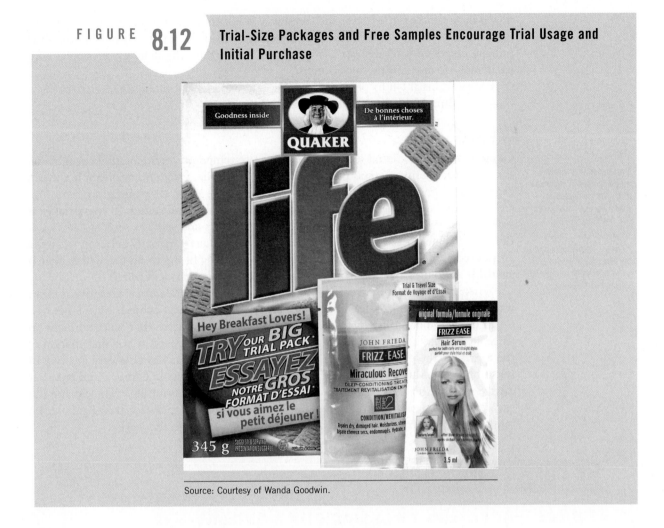

FIGURE **8.12**

Trial-Size Packages and Free Samples Encourage Trial Usage and Initial Purchase

Source: Courtesy of Wanda Goodwin.

turers do sample tasting in local supermarkets, they usually outsource the promotion to an independent company that specializes in this activity. Booths are strategically set up in stores to intercept customers as they shop.

Companies are discovering new ways of delivering samples while at the same time generating positive publicity for the brand involved in the promotion. Some refer to it as **on-site sampling**; others call it **experiential marketing**. To illustrate, consider a recent campaign for Coffee-Mate liquid. Nestlé launched an eight-week sampling program in which street teams handed out over 800 000 cups of free coffee flavoured with Coffee-Mate liquid. The program involved a tease, taste, and reveal approach—consumers weren't told they were tasting Coffee-Mate until after they tried the sample. Apparently, people have preconceived notions about Coffee-Mate as a brand. Following the sample consumers were given a $1.00 coupon toward their first purchase of Coffee-Mate liquid.[5]

Larry Burns, co-chair of US-based Promotion Marketing Association (PMA), says "Targeted, well thought-out sampling programs are the way to go in today's market." He cites research findings to back up his claim. From a survey conducted by the PMA, 94 percent of respondents view sampling as a way of increasing their comfort level when buying a product. A further 68 percent said they were "excited" about receiving the sample.[6]

When deciding whether to use a free sample program, a review of the benefits and drawbacks is essential. Samples are an expensive proposition due to product, package, and handling costs. In spite of these costs, samples rank second to coupons among marketers, so clearly the long-term benefit outweighs the short-term costs. The fact that it eliminates the risk usually associated with new product purchases is a key benefit. On the

Experiential marketing (on-site sampling)
A promotion in which potential customers interact directly with a product (e.g., sample giveaways).

Coffee-Mate
www.coffee-mate.com

downside, a sample is the fastest and surest way to kill an inferior product. In terms of timing, sample programs are best suited to the early stage of the product life cycle when the primary objective is to achieve trial purchase. For certain, the delivery of samples adds excitement to any new product launch.

For more insight into product sampling and experiential marketing, read the IMC Highlight **Buzz Marketing Pays Off for Cadbury**.

Contests

Contest
A promotion that involves awarding cash or merchandise prizes to consumers when they purchase a specified product.

Sweepstakes
A chance promotion involving the giveaway of products or services of value to randomly selected participants.

Contests are designed and implemented to create temporary excitement about a brand. For example, offering a grand prize such as an automobile, vacation, or dream home can capture the consumer's imagination, even though the odds of winning are very low. Contests can be classified into two categories: sweepstakes and games. A **sweepstakes** is a chance promotion involving the giveaway of products and services such as cars, vacations, and sometimes cash. It's like a lottery: winners are randomly selected from the entries received. Typically, consumers enter a contest by filling in an entry form that is available at point-of-purchase, through print advertising, or at a website.

When companies are searching for the right sweepstakes idea, their objective is clear: it must light a fire under sales. Experience reveals that successful contests have longevity.

In the world of promotional contests, experts generally agree that success hinges on three factors: cash, cars, and travel. That said, the prize must capture the imagination of the target for the promotion to be successful. Some marketers are now very creative in selecting prizes. MasterCard Canada recently offered an automobile for a grand prize but discovered younger members of its desired target preferred "gas for life." The car and the gas were bundled as the grand prize. Carlsberg beer offered a one-week travel grand prize but is letting the winner choose the destination—anywhere in the world![7]

IMC HIGHLIGHT

BUZZ MARKETING PAYS OFF FOR CADBURY

One of the latest trends in integrated marketing is buzz marketing. But what is buzz marketing? It seems to combine elements of marketing, promotions, public relations, and event marketing, so it is a bit of a confusing concept. Loosely speaking, buzz marketing uses the power of word of mouth to create excitement and awareness for a product. Some call it guerilla marketing or stealth marketing, but regardless of what it's called, it is an unconventional way of spreading the news.

Cadbury Adams Canada has experimented successfully with buzz marketing. For the launch of Trident Splash, a character known as Splashman carried the message. Wearing nothing but a bathing cap and swimsuit he jumped on and off buses in Vancouver, Calgary, Toronto, and Montreal.

For those who cared to ask what he was doing, he would open his briefcase, revealing a message that read "You've been splashed!" and promptly hand them a pack of the new product. According to David Nichols, VP of marketing at Inventa, the company that developed the promotion, "The effort created lots of buzz." The promotion reinforced the TV commercial that features a Speedo-sporting man getting

splashed at a bus stop, and offered an experience for consumers to connect with the brand beyond receiving a sample.

Nichols estimates 250 000 Canadians saw Splashman on the streets. At least 11 000 had some form of interaction with him and received the free pack of gum. The effort created excellent word of mouth. Splashman showed up in media across the country, including Toronto's *Breakfast Television*, Montreal's *Caféine—le show du matin*, and Vancouver's Shaw Cable.

Cadbury also employed some street-level marketing when it redesigned its chocolate bar packages and launched several new bars. The Cadbury name and logo is now more prominent on all chocolate bars along with the traditional purple colour the brand is strongly associated with.

To promote the new products and packages, Cadbury launched a "Get caught purple-handed" contest that featured street teams that rewarded people "caught" eating a Cadbury bar.

Adapted from Rebecca Harris, "Sweet rebranding," *Marketing*, November 7, 2005, p. 7, and "Spotting Splashman," *Strategy*, September 5, 2005, p. 62.

Games are also based on chance but can be more involving because they often require repeat visits for game pieces. This makes them a good device for encouraging continuity of purchase by consumers. McDonald's is somewhat of an expert in this area. Its "Monopoly" game is a regular feature in annual marketing plans. As the saying goes, "You have to play to win," and the only way to play is to go to a McDonald's restaurant.

An offshoot of the game contest is the **instant-win** promotion, which involves predetermined, pre-seeded winning tickets in the overall fixed universe of tickets. For example, if the promotion is implemented nationally, prize tickets should be regionally dispersed based on population patterns. Pepsi-Cola ran an instant win promotion, "Win an iPod an hour," for several weeks. The contest was extremely popular with young people since gadgets like iPods are such important communications devices today. The connection between Pepsi-Cola and iPod was relevant. Pepsi benefited from the halo effect of being connected to such a hot brand.

Variations of instant-wins include *collect-and-wins* and small instant-wins combined with a grand prize contest. Tim Hortons's annual "Rrroll Up the Rim to Win" is an example of a contest combining instant-wins with a series of grand prizes. Most of the instant-win prizes involve food products available at the organization's restaurants, but it is the roster of bigger prizes that draws the consumer in. "Rrroll Up the Rim to Win" is another example of a longstanding successful promotion. It delivers a consistent theme and has a catchy and memorable slogan. According to Tim Hortons, the promotion is now less of a promotion and more like a brand unto itself: "Rrroll Up the Rim to Win" has become recognized as its own entity, much as a product would. Franchisees indicate that sales increase 10 to 15 percent during the promotion period.[8] This promotion is an integral part of the company's annual marketing plan.

Tim Hortons
www.timhortons.com

Planning any kind of contest is a challenge. Most manufacturers rely on external suppliers to develop and implement a contest. In this regard, there is much upfront discussion with suppliers to ensure proper briefing on objectives and expectations. The success of a contest depends on the consumer's perception of the value and number of prizes being awarded and on the odds of winning. As well, the prizes must match the image of the product and the lifestyle of the target market. Successful contests tend to have a grand prize that captures the imagination of the target market, or have prizes of less value but awarded in large numbers to compensate for the disappointment factor associated with most contests (see Figure 8.13).

A cost–benefit analysis should be done prior to getting involved with a contest. In terms of benefit, a contest is a good device for achieving repeat purchase objectives. A well-designed contest encourages customers to come back or buy more frequently. By returning or buying more goods, consumers exhibit a certain degree of loyalty. As such, contests are ideal promotions for products in the mature stage of the product life cycle. They can boost brand sales in a time of need. According to Tony Chapman, president of Capital C Communications, "Contests have the ability to excite consumers, excite a sales force, sell incredible volume, and build brand equity, and that's a sweet spot every marketer dreams about."[9]

On the cost side of things, a contest requires a significant investment in media advertising to create awareness and interest. Contests such as "Rrroll Up the Rim to Win" are supported by multimedia advertising campaigns. A combination of media advertising and in-store promotional materials tends to be effective. When the cost of prizes and the cost of having an external organization implement the contest are factored in, the amount required for a contest promotion can be a sizeable portion of a marketing budget.

Legal issues are another concern for marketers when they get involved in contests. The manager must be familiar with some of the basic laws that govern contests in Canada. Section 189 of the *Criminal Code* and sections 52 and 59 of the *Competition Act* regulate most contests in Canada, and there are certain fairly standardized rules and regulations for what information must be communicated to participants. The following information must be clearly conveyed:

FIGURE **8.13** An Example of a Promotion that Combines a Coupon and Contest Communicated by In-store Shelf Pads

Source: Courtesy of Gillette.

- the number of prizes and the value of each;
- the odds of winning, if known;
- whether a skill-testing question will be administered;
- whether facsimiles are acceptable in the case of a sweepstakes;
- how to enter, and what proof of purchase is required; and
- the contest's closing date.

For some tips on planning an effective contest, see Figure 8.14.

Rebates

Rebate
A predetermined amount of money returned directly to customers by the manufacturer after the purchase has been made.

A **rebate** is a predetermined amount of money returned directly to the customer by the manufacturer after the purchase has been made. It is an incentive to get consumers to buy in greater volume during the promotion period. Initially, rebates were the promotion of choice among packaged goods marketers, but they are now an integral element of marketing programs for durable goods such as automobiles and major appliances.

FIGURE **8.14** **Tips for Planning an Effective Contest**

Effective contests do not happen by chance. They are carefully planned to spark interest and action and achieve specific marketing objectives. Here are some pointers from those in the business:

- Choose prizes that spark wish-fulfillment fantasies.
- Give consumers a decent chance of winning (low odds of winning create ill will).
- Plan an engaging media component to drive consumer awareness and generate publicity.
- Keep the company name in the contest moniker (again for positive press).
- Use strategic partnerships; co-brand the contest to leverage each other's equity.
- Make sure contest rules are clear and unambiguous.
- Ensure that fulfillment (awarding of prizes) occurs quickly.
- If it ain't broke, don't fix it! Stay with a successful contest if it's producing desired results.

Source: Adapted from "Tips for creating killer contests," Special Report on Premiums and Incentives, *Strategy*, August 26, 2002, p. 24.

Slippage
The situation of a consumer collecting labels in a promotion offer but failing to follow through and request the refund.

The most common type of rebate is the *single-purchase refund*, in which the consumer receives a portion of their money back for the purchase of a specified product. Such an offer is one method of achieving trial purchases. Other variations of rebates include making an offer according to an escalating schedule. For example, an offer could be structured as follows: buy one and get $1.00 back, buy two and get $2.00 back, and buy three and get $5.00 back. The nature of the offer encourages consumers to buy three items at one time, thus helping achieve multiple purchase objectives.

Though many people buy a product because of the possibility of a rebate, many rebates go uncollected due to the hassle of filling out the form and mailing it in with the proof of purchase documentation a manufacturer requires. This phenomenon is referred to as **slippage**, when the consumer collects labels but fails to follow through and request the refund, even for a refund with a $100 value. Time-pressed consumers often forget about the rebate offer. In the retail environment, rebate promotions boost sales since retailers can feature items at lower prices then their manufacturer partners could otherwise afford. They attract more customers and provide opportunities for additional sales.[10]

In recent years, incentives and rebates have become commonplace among automobile manufacturers. Offers such as zero percent (or an incredibly low percentage) financing and cash-back deals of between $1000 and $2500 try to entice consumers to buy now. These types of incentives were first instituted to help car companies reduce inventories, making way for the introduction of new models each year. But, in an uncertain economy, they have become more of an ongoing practice. In fact, so common are they now that many consumers have adopted an attitude that they won't buy a new car unless there is some kind of incentive provided.

Automobile incentives can boost sales in the short term, but in the long term they have made the cost of an automobile higher and have affected the profitability of domestic manufacturers.

Rebate offers are best suited to products in the mature stage of the product life cycle. As indicated above, they are a good incentive for encouraging multiple purchases of inexpensive packaged goods products. Encouraging multiple purchases or building frequency of purchases is a common objective for mature products. At this stage in the life cycle, maintaining customer loyalty is critical. Apart from the rebates offered by automobile companies, which tend to be very high, a rebate promotion is not that expensive to implement. Since it is current users who tend to take advantage of rebate offers, advertising support can be confined to the package and various in-store opportunities, such as shelf cards and product displays.

Premium Offers

Premium

An additional item given free, or greatly discounted, to induce purchase of the primary brand.

A **premium** is an additional item given free, or greatly discounted, to induce purchase of the primary brand. The goal of a premium is to provide added value to tempt consumers to buy. McDonald's frequently uses premiums because they are effective with its primary target market of families with young children. A "Happy Meal" for example, becomes a "Nintendo Happy Meal."

Premiums are offered to consumers several ways: either as a mail-in, by sending in proofs of purchase so the item can be delivered by mail; as an in-pack or on-pack promotion, where the item is placed inside or attached to a package; and by an order form that is usually available at point-of-purchase. Packaged goods companies frequently use their packages to distribute free premiums. Cheerios recently had a very successful in-pack premium offer. Inside marked boxes of Cheerios were CD versions of popular games such as Monopoly, Clue, and Boggle. These games are instantly recognizable by kids and the parents who buy the cereal (see Figure 8.15).

Many marketers firmly believe that there is something to be said for offering a tangible quality gift, which can surprise the consumer and build long-term equity through association. Others see the benefits of premiums as largely misleading, citing large increases in sales followed by an equally large tumble once the giveaway ends. Both Molson and Labatt experienced this feast-and-famine phenomenon when they packed everything from golf balls, to T-shirts, to ball caps in their beer cases. Both companies found the pro-

FIGURE **8.15**   **Cheerios Cereal Offers High-Value Premiums Inside Packages to Attract New and Current Users**

Source: Dick Hemingway.

motions expensive, and rather than create loyalty, they simply encouraged drinkers to switch brands constantly.[11]

Bonus pack
The temporary offering of a larger package size (e.g., 20 percent more) for the same price as the regular size.

An offshoot of a premium offer is the **bonus pack**. The traditional bonus pack offers the consumer more for less. For example, a brand offers a package size that gives the consumer 20 percent more product for the regular price. Another option is to bundle a product in pairs and offer a deal like "Buy One Get One Free." Offers like these, if implemented properly, will attract new users and reward current users. If done wrong, they can cheapen the image or value perception of the brand.

Marketing managers tend to rank premiums lower in terms of popularity, but they do offer some tangible benefits. They achieve several marketing objectives: they can increase the quantity of brand purchases made by consumers during the promotion period; they help to retain current customers, therefore building brand loyalty; and they provide a merchandising tool to encourage display activity in stores.

A good premium offer will help differentiate one brand from another at a crucial point in time, the time when consumers decide which brand to buy. Despite Labatt's objection to premium offers as cited above, one of Labatt Blue's most successful promotions ever was a premium offer. Blue experienced a 300 percent increase in sales when it ran the "NHL Crazy Coldie Program" during the 2002 NHL playoffs. Each case of Blue (24s) included 1 of 30 insulated bottle holders shaped like the jersey of an NHL hockey team. The connection with the number-one sport among young Canadian men was an immediate hit![12] The promotion was supported with television advertising, an online contest, and on-site advertising in bars and pubs across Canada. It was truly an integrated effort!

Labatt Blue
www.labattblue.com

Loyalty Programs

Loyalty programs take the short-term premium offer a step further—they encourage long-term brand loyalty. How many loyalty cards do you have in your wallet? It seems that consumers are collecting points to obtain something for free years from now. In the meantime, we keep going back to the loyalty sponsor to earn more points. By definition, a **loyalty program (frequent buyer program)** offers consumers a small bonus, such as points or play money, each time they make a purchase. The bonus accumulates and can be redeemed for merchandise or some other benefit at a later date.

Loyalty program (frequent buyer program)
A program that offers consumers a small bonus, such as points or play money, each time they make a purchase; the bonus accumulates and can be redeemed for merchandise or some other benefit.

Shoppers Drug Mart has a frequent buyer program that is updated electronically. Member customers swipe their Optimum card each time they make a purchase. Shoppers can cross-reference transaction data electronically and tailor offers and services to specific customers. One such offer included a free Gillette MACH3 razor along with coupons for replacement blades and Gillette shaving foam or gel, an attractive combination offer that promotes a family of branded products (see Figure 8.16). These samples were distributed by mail to a select group of Shoppers's customers. As discussed elsewhere in this book, the true benefit of a loyalty program is the information it collects for database marketing.

Perhaps the longest running and most successful loyalty program in Canada is Canadian Tire 'Money.' It rewards regular shoppers who pay by cash or Canadian Tire credit card with Canadian Tire 'Money' worth up to 5 percent of the value of the purchase. Now at an advanced stage, customers can collect virtual money at Canadian Tire's website. Canadian Tire 'Money' represents the true essence of a loyalty program: customers can actually receive something for free. In contrast, a program like AIR MILES takes considerable time before the consumer can get even the smallest of rewards.

Canadian Tire
www.canadiantire.ca

Given that our wallets are bulging with loyalty cards, it is safe to say that loyalty programs are popular with consumers. In fact, a study conducted by Kubas Consultants revealed that more Canadians participate in loyalty programs (76 percent participate in at least one program) than voted in the last federal election (61 percent of the eligible population).[13] Programs such as AIR MILES and the Safeway Club Card fall into this category. What consumers fail to realize is that while they are chasing a dream vacation or a state-of-the-art, theatre-style television, the cost of the merchandise they are buying

FIGURE **8.16** **Selected Shoppers Drug Mart Customers Receive a Free Sample of the Gillette MACH3 Razor**

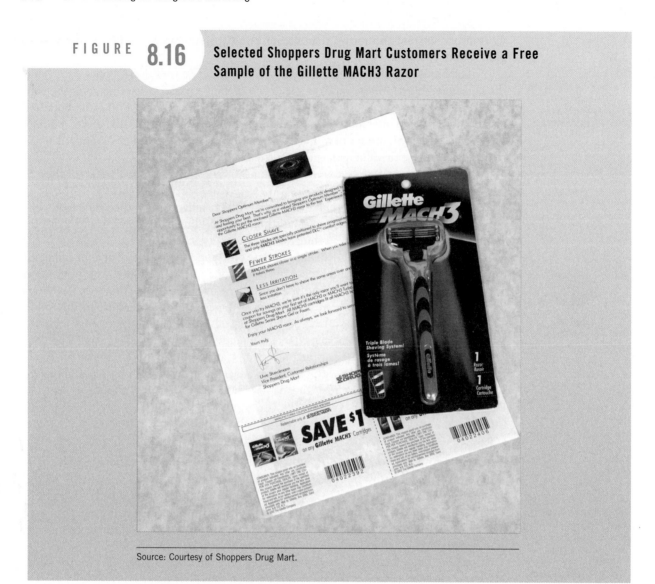

Source: Courtesy of Shoppers Drug Mart.

is going up. Loyalty programs add to the costs of a business in the form of additional employees, call centres, catalogues, and computers. As well, investment in media advertising is needed to draw attention to the loyalty program.

Technology and the desire to manage customer relationships better is the fuel that drives loyalty programs. Electronic cards capable of storing customer data have all but replaced paper cards. SUBWAY restaurants introduced its new loyalty program using plastic cards with magnetic strips. The cards capture purchase information that can be used to present personalized marketing offers at a later date.[14]

Plastic cards can function as both a loyalty card and a gift card. Gift cards are a booming market. In 2003, gift card sales in the United States reached US$45 billion and are expected to reach US$70 billion by 2006. For retailers, gift cards boost sales because consumers tend to spend more than the face value of the card. Apparently, there is a tendency to splurge when you are not spending your own money! A study by Léger Marketing indicates that 18 to 24 year olds spend 55 percent more while those 65 and older spend 40 percent more.[15]

The *Globe and Mail* offers a recognition card to its loyal readers. The card gives subscribers access to exclusive offers from many of its advertising partners and is only offered to readers who have subscribed to the paper for longer than six months. The program

Globe and Mail
www.theglobeandmail.com

focuses on frequency and loyalty instead of trying to generate fleeting new readership—a trap many other newspapers have fallen prey too.[16]

Marketing organizations must carefully consider the decision to use loyalty programs. In some cases, consumers perceive the "free" reward as a real incentive, but they don't realize they are paying for the privilege. Since loyalty programs add costs, customers may eventually tire of paying more for the goods they buy. The true benefit for the organization is the information it is collecting about customer purchase behaviour. The electronic capture of transaction data that will be mined at a later date is extremely useful as organizations move toward individualized marketing programs. Once an organization starts a loyalty program, it is an ongoing program.

Canadian Tire has integrated several promotional offers into an integrated marketing communications campaign. For insight into its campaign, read the IMC Highlight **Canadian Tire Scores Big**.

Trade Promotion Execution

Trade customers are the link between manufacturers and consumers, and in Canada they have incredible control in many markets. In the grocery industry, for example, the combination of two large wholesale/retail operations, Loblaws and Sobeys, controls more

---

IMC HIGHLIGHT

CANADIAN TIRE SCORES BIG

Canadian Tire 'Money'... a simple concept. Yet it is the cornerstone of Canadian Tire's marketing mix. According to Eymbert Vaandering, vice-president of marketing at Canadian Tire, "Canadian Tire 'Money' is the most successful and popular customer reward program and has a 90 percent redemption and participation level. It is the very heart of what Canadian Tire stands for in today's competitive marketplace."

Canadian Tire recently launched a fully integrated marketing communications campaign called the "Big Spender Giveaway." The campaign was born out of an ad campaign called "Big Spender," which marked the first time that Canadian Tire 'Money' was the central focus of advertising. The campaign featured the customers' love of the money and the relationships they have with the company.

Using Canadian Tire 'Money' as the focal point, the integrated campaign included media advertising, an in-store contest supported by flyers, credit card statement stuffers, point-of-purchase display materials in stores and gas bars, and an online contest.

Canadian Tire 'Money' was originally introduced in 1958 to attract customers to the company's new gasoline business and to get more traffic into stores. Today, there is a fully integrated customer rewards program in place that allows the company to leverage a multi-channel approach to increase traffic and loyalty that Canadian Tire 'Money' always delivered. By taking an integrated approach to pro-

mote the contest, the aim was to use a privileged asset—Canadian Tire 'Money'—to leverage the creative equity of the Big Spender TV campaign and to extend the excitement and fun to customers in stores, online, and at gas bars.

The Big Spender contest prize pool featured $250 000 in Canadian Tire 'Money' and merchandise prizes. Entry forms were collected at stores or submitted online. There were three grand prizes of $50 000 in Canadian Tire 'Money.' The online component featured daily prizes of $1000 in Canadian Tire 'Money' and hundreds of draws for prizes.

According to Vaandering, "The focus on Canadian Tire 'Money' held tremendous appeal for customers as it is an important aspect of the shopping experience. People love the money because it is simple to use. It can be redeemed anytime, anywhere, on any item." From a marketing perspective, the program allows the company to further differentiate itself and provides immense competitive advantage. It drives traffic to the stores, and Canadian Tire's website is one of the top three ecommerce sites in Canada.

For the record, Canadian Tire is the most-shopped retailer in Canada: 90 percent of Canadians shop there, 40 percent shop there weekly. There is a very loyal customer base equally split between males and females. The Canadian Tire brand is one of the top five most-recognized brands in the country.

Adapted from Eymbert Vaandering, "Hey, Big Spender," *Marketing*, January 14, 2002, p. 8.

than half of all food store sales. In the hardware market, the combination of Canadian Tire and Home Hardware controls a significant portion of volume. Distributors make money by selling your products, but they are also in business to sell anyone's products. Consequently, their loyalty to any supplier can waver if they do not receive the trade promotion offers they feel they deserve.

Simply stated, the trade looks for the best offers from suppliers and makes buying decisions accordingly. As with consumer promotions, trade promotions must be designed to deliver the highest possible value to the trade while costing as little as possible for the manufacturer. Manufacturers choose between many trade promotion options when developing trade promotion plans. Typically, the options work together to generate a high degree of impact during the promotion period. This section explores the various trade promotion options.

Trade Allowances

Trade allowance
A temporary price reduction that encourages larger purchases by distributors.

A **trade allowance** is a temporary price reduction that encourages larger purchases by distributors. It can be offered several ways: a percentage reduction from the list price, a predetermined amount off the list price, or free goods. A free goods offer may be something like "Buy 10 cases and get one free."

In addition to encouraging larger volume purchases, the manufacturer would like to see a portion of the allowance devoted to lowering the price of the product at retail for a short period. In the grocery industry, products are commonly offered on sale for one week. The manufacturer absorbs the discount offered to consumers. Trade allowances can be deducted from the invoice immediately, and in such cases are called *off-invoice allowances*. Or they can be offered on the basis of a *bill-back*, in which case the manufacturer keeps a record of all purchases shipped to the distributor and, when the deal period expires, reimburses the distributor for the allowances it earned.

Performance Allowances

Performance allowance
A discount offered by a manufacturer that encourages a distributor to perform a merchandising function on behalf of a manufacturer.

A **performance allowance** is a discount that encourages the distributor to perform a merchandising function on behalf of the manufacturer. As indicated above, a trade allowance helps lower prices, but additional incentives are required to make the promotion a real success. It is common for the manufacturer to request automatic distribution of goods to retail stores, displays in stores, and a mention of the sale price in the retailer's weekly advertising flyer. The additional funds provided in the performance allowance help cover the distributor's costs of implementing these activities. The distributor may or may not comply with all of the requests of the manufacturer, but some kind of deal is negotiated and agreed to. Before paying the allowance, the manufacturer requires proof of performance by the distributor.

Given this information, you can now appreciate that many of the advertising flyers and in-store promotional activities that are undertaken by large retail chain stores are actually subsidized by the manufacturers' brands involved in the promotions. The costs of trade promotions are significant and take a considerable portion of a brand's marketing budget each year.

Cooperative Advertising Allowances

Cooperative advertising allowance (co-op)
The sharing of advertising costs by suppliers and retailers or by several retailers.

A **cooperative advertising allowance**, or **co-op** as it is commonly referred to, is a fund allocated to pay for a portion of a distributor's advertising. Marketing organizations often pay a percentage (often 50 percent or more) of the distributor's ad cost, provided the marketer's brand is featured prominently. An example of a co-op campaign that you see frequently is "Intel Inside." By featuring those two words and the logo, the computer manufacturer receives partial funding for its advertising from Intel.

To maximize the effectiveness of allowances offered to the trade, the above allowances are frequently combined to develop an integrated promotion plan. If a bigger plan is in place, the trade promotion plan will be integrated with consumer promotions and brand advertising. Combining the allowances is attractive to the retailers. The financial rewards will be much greater and the funds available are sufficient to support their own advertising and merchandising activities. Financial incentives are a great motivator among distributors.

Dealer Premiums

Dealer premium

An incentive offered to a distributor to encourage the special purchase of a product or to secure additional merchandising support from the distributor.

A **dealer premium** is an incentive offered to a distributor by a manufacturer to encourage the special purchase of a product or to secure additional merchandising support from a retailer. Premiums are usually offered in the form of merchandise and distributed by sales representatives of the company offering the premium. Some common premiums include golfing equipment, cameras, audio equipment, and leisure clothing. The offering of premiums is a controversial issue. Some distributors absolutely forbid their buyers to accept them. They argue that the buyer is the only beneficiary and the buying organization might be purchasing more goods than they really need. Many believe the practice of offering premiums, often referred to as "payola," to buyers is unethical. However, dealings between sellers and buyers sometimes occur under the table.

Spiff

An incentive offered to retail salespeople to encourage them to promote a specified brand of goods to customers.

An offshoot of a premium offer is a **spiff**. Next time you're in a store, ask yourself why that retail sales representative recommended the Canon camera (or any other popular brand name) over the others? It could be that the manufacturer encouraged the sales representative to promote its brand by providing some kind of incentive. The retail sales representative stands to gain if more Canon products are sold. Such a practice is common in product categories where consumers have a tendency to ask for recommendations. In the camera illustration above, the buyer wants a certain type of camera, but choosing the brand to buy always presents risk—there are many good brands to choose from. The seller's job is to help eliminate such risk, but that may not always happen if spiffs are in play.

Clearly, the use of premiums and spiffs achieves certain marketing objectives. Many companies employ them when they are facing unusual circumstances, such as when trying to meet year-end sales objectives and it's a touch-and-go situation. Compared to other forms of sales promotion, though, they are not the kinds of activity that will be used regularly.

Collateral Material

Collateral material

Visual aids used by sales representatives in sales presentations, such as price lists, product manuals, sales brochures, and audiovisual materials.

The role of the sales representative cannot be underestimated, particularly in business-to-business selling situations. Companies invest significant sums in programs that tell consumers about their goods and services, but as indicated above, it is also important to invest in programs that help push the product through the channel. Sales representatives need selling resources, and that's where collateral material comes into play. **Collateral materials** are visual aids that are specific to special promotions or simply ongoing aids for the variety of products being sold. Collateral materials include price lists, catalogues, sales brochures, pamphlets, specification sheets, product manuals, and audiovisual sales aids.

In the age of electronics, it is now common for much of this material to be available in CD or DVD formats or on a company's website. Either medium is capable of communicating lengthy and complex information. From a buyer's point of view, sales information on a CD or DVD can be reviewed at a more leisurely pace and perhaps a more convenient time than during a sales call. Sometimes when a sales representative is selling the goods, the pace can be rapid and there isn't time to really digest the information. Therefore, the use of hard-copy and soft-copy collateral materials is a good combination.

Dealer Display Material

Dealer display material (point-of-purchase material)

Advertising or display materials located in a retail environment to build traffic, advertise a product, and encourage impulse purchasing.

As indicated earlier, one of the objectives of trade promotion is to encourage merchandising support from retail distributors. The manufacturer can assist in this area by providing **dealer display material**, or **point-of-purchase material** as it is often called. Dealer display material includes posters, shelf talkers (mini-posters that hang or dangle from

FIGURE **8.17** **A Shelf Talker Creates Awareness for a New Flavour of Oreo Cookies**

Source: Kraft Canada.

store shelves), channel strips (narrow bands that fit into the side of a store shelf), and advertising pads (tear-off sheets that hang from pads attached to shelves). Figure 8.17 provides an illustration of a shelf talker.

Material of a more permanent nature includes display shippers (shipping cases that convert to display stands when opened and erected properly) and permanent display racks. One of the problems with display material is it frequently goes to waste. In many retail outlets, permission to erect displays must be granted by the store manager and sometimes by the head office of the retailer. Some retailers do not allow manufacturer-supplied display material at all. To be effective, displays must be erected in a visible location. The retailer makes the location decision and it may not be to the liking of the manufacturer. A poor location will diminish the intended impact of the display.

Trade Shows

Trade show
An event that allows a company to showcase its products to a captive audience and generate leads.

Trade shows are an effective way for a company to introduce new products to the marketplace. There is no better opportunity to showcase something special than at a trade show. Where else will a manufacturer find as many customers, all in one place, actively and willingly seeking product information? All industries seem to have trade shows, and in many cases they move around the country to make it more convenient for prospective customers to visit. Depending on the nature of the show, it may attract consumers, trade distributors, or both.

FIGURE **8.18** Trade Shows Bring the Customer to the Marketer

Source: Canadian National Sportsmen's Shows.

The automobile industry and the recreation and leisure products industry are among the largest users of trade shows. Here, all manufacturers gather to show their latest models (see Figure 8.18). Auto shows are magnets for the media, so they generate all kinds of positive press for the participating companies. From a manufacturer's perspective, a trade show provides an opportunity to develop a prospect list that the sales force can follow up on. When visiting a trade show, customers leave a trail of valuable information about themselves, which can be added quickly to a database for analysis and use later. The very nature of a trade show, however, requires considerable planning by participants along with a considerable financial investment. There is a simple rule of thumb about participating in trade shows: "If you are going to do it, do it right." It's a great opportunity to outshine the competition.

ADDITIONAL CONSIDERATIONS FOR SALES PROMOTION PLANNING

Sales promotions are not usually the focal point of a brand's marketing communications strategies but, as mentioned above, play a complementary role in achieving certain objectives. Therefore, sales promotions must be carefully planned so they effectively integrate with advertising, public relations, and any other marketing communications plans. Decisions must be made regarding how frequently promotions are offered, what types of promotions will have a positive effect on brand image, and how they will build brand value in the long term. Let's look at each situation briefly.

Frequency of Promotions

How frequently should a brand offer sales promotions? All kinds of influencing factors contribute to this decision: the type of product, the activities of the competition, the stage of the brand in the product life cycle, and the receptiveness of customers toward promotions. A theme running throughout this chapter is that promotions are complementary in nature, so they should never disrupt the flow of regular and more dominant communications activities. There is a risk that too many promotions could cheapen the image of a brand—short-term gain for long-term pain! In general, coupon activity can be implemented more frequently than cash refunds, premium offers, and contests. It is less disruptive to the regular message expressed through media advertising.

Brand Image and Promotions

Much of the discussion about promotion strategies in this chapter mentioned lowering prices so that consumers get a better deal. In the short run, such a strategy brings positive results. However, if this practice becomes frequent, consumers will perceive the sale price to be more of a regular price. In the long term, such a practice will hurt the brand's image and lower profit margins. Domestic automobile manufacturers are facing this dilemma right now. Advertising is so focused on rebates and low financing packages that much less time is devoted to building an image, the former priority of these companies.

Consumers who are continually exposed to low prices may begin to believe a brand is in trouble. They could desert it for another brand. When you consider the psychology of buying, brands are often a personal statement, and people like winning brands.

Building Brand Equity

The cumulative force of all marketing communications is a key factor in building brand equity. Marketers must be aware that sales promotions are a rather chaotic sequence of deals and events that create noise in the marketplace. They are not a sustaining message. It is preferable to adopt a view about promotions that will pay attention to long-term brand values and a consistent approach that will build good relationships with the trade and consumers. A few of the promotions mentioned in this chapter do just that. Among them are Tim Hortons's "Rrroll Up the Rim to Win" and Canadian Tire's reward money. Promotions like these become a positive part of the brand's heritage and reinforce relationships with customers.

Summary

Sales promotions are incentives offered to consumers and the trade to encourage more immediate and larger purchases. Strategically, consumer promotions are designed to help pull a product through the channel of distribution, while trade promotions help push a product through the channel of distribution. A good sales promotion plan usually balances between pull and push.

Sales promotion planning involves a series of steps or decisions. After an assessment of the situation is made, specific objectives and strategies are established and the appropriate offers or incentives are determined. The plan must also consider fulfillment obligations at the back end, and a means of assessing the effectiveness of the plan must be in place.

A key to a successful sales promotion plan lies in how it is integrated with other marketing communications strategies. For certain, sales promotion strategies must be integrated with advertising strategies. Because sales promotions are short term in nature, they often become the focus of the advertising message while the promotion is in place. When the overall plan is implemented, advertising creates awareness for the promotion while in-store displays and websites provide additional details.

Some specific objectives of consumer promotions are to achieve trial purchase by new users and repeat and multiple purchases by current users. The types of activities commonly used to achieve these objectives include coupons, free samples, contests, rebates, premium offers, and loyalty programs.

Specific marketing objectives of trade promotions are to secure new listings and distribution, build volume on a preplanned cyclical basis, and encourage merchandising support at point-of-purchase. Trade promotion activities that help achieve these objectives include trade allowances, performance allowances, cooperative advertising funds, dealer premiums, point-of-purchase display materials, collateral materials, and trade shows.

The impact of sales promotions are short term in nature and therefore complement other integrated marketing communications strategies. As such, sales promotions should not disrupt regular brand advertising. They must be integrated into advertising strategies to enhance the overall impact on consumers and trade customers. When planning promotions, a manager should guard against running them too frequently so as to not harm the image of the brand. A good sales promotion concept will fit with the brand's image and help build brand equity.

Key Terms

bonus pack,   241

collateral material,   245

consumer promotion,   221

contest,   236

co-op,   244

cooperative advertising allowance,   244

coupon,   232

cross-coupon,   233

cross-ruff,   233

dealer display material,   245

dealer premium,   245

experiential marketing,   235

free sample,   234

free-standing insert (FSI),   232

frequent buyer program,   241

game,   237

in-pack self-coupon,   232

instantly redeemable coupon,   232

instant-win game,   237

listing,   226

loyalty program,   241

media-delivered coupon,   232

on-pack self-coupon,   232

on-site sampling,   235

performance allowance,   244

point-of-purchase material,   245

premium,   240

pull,   221

push,   221

rebate,   238

redemption rate,   233

sales promotion,   221

sales promotion plan,   224

slippage,   239

spiff,   245

sweepstakes,   236

trade allowance,   244

trade promotion,   221

trade show,   246

Review Questions

1. What is the difference between a pull strategy and a push strategy, and how do sales promotions complement both strategies?

2. What are the primary objectives of a consumer promotion plan?

3. What are the primary objectives of a trade promotion plan?

4. Briefly explain how sales promotion strategies are integrated with advertising strategies. Why is such integration essential?

5. In sales promotion planning, what is meant by logistics and fulfillment?

6. Briefly describe the following consumer promotion terms:
   a) redemption rate
   b) in-pack self-coupon
   c) cross-ruff
   d) on-site sampling
   e) instant-win promotions
   f) slippage
   g) bonus pack

7. What types of coupon distribution are appropriate for the early stages of the product life cycle? What distribution is appropriate for the later stages? Why?

8. What are the benefits and drawbacks of a free sample offer?

9. What elements contribute to the success of a contest offer?

10. What is the objective of a consumer premium offer and when is the best time to implement such an offer?

11. What are the benefits and drawbacks of loyalty promotions?

12. How do trade allowances, performance allowances, and cooperative advertising funds complement each other when implementing a trade promotion plan?

13. Briefly describe the following trade promotion terms:
    a) spiff
    b) dealer premium
    c) collateral material
    d) point-of-purchase material

Discussion and Application Questions

1. Assume you are a brand manager launching a new snack food or confectionary product. What balance would you recommend among consumer promotion, trade promotion, and media advertising? What specific sales promotion activities would you recommend? Justify your choices.

2. Conduct some secondary research on consumer and trade promotion budgets and spending patterns in various industries. Is there undue pressure placed on marketing organizations to spend more on trade promotions and less on other

activities? Does the situation vary from one industry to another?

3. A common criticism of consumer premium offers is that they only encourage temporary brand switching. Once the offer is over, consumers switch back to their regular brand. Therefore, in the long run, the promotion will not contribute to sales objectives. Conduct some secondary research on this issue and determine if such a criticism is valid.

4. This chapter suggests that consumers could be suffering from "loyalty pro-

motion fatigue." Conduct some secondary research on loyalty promotions to find out how organizations view loyalty promotions. Do loyalty promotions provide real benefits to consumers and the sponsor? What are the elements that make a loyalty promotion a success?

5. What forms of sales promotion are best suited for the following brands? (Hint: you may want to consider the life cycle stage the brand is in). Justify your position.
   a) Secret deodorant
   b) Quaker Chewy Granola Bars
   c) Goodyear tires (replacement tires)
   d) Valvoline motor oil
   e) Hewlett-Packard laser printer
   f) New Balance running shoes

6. Evaluate the sales promotion strategies employed by Canadian Tire. What marketing and marketing communications objectives do they meet? How effective are the programs? How does Canadian Tire integrate sales promotions with other components of its marketing communications plan?

7. Evaluate the sales promotion strategies used by Tim Hortons. What marketing and marketing communications objectives do they meet? How does Tim Hortons integrate sales promotions with other components of the marketing communications mix?

8. It was stated in the chapter that brands such as Coffee-Mate and Cadbury Adams (see product sampling section and IMC Highlight **Buzz Marketing Pays Off for Cadbury**) had success with on-site sampling. Conduct some secondary research to determine the effectiveness of on-site sampling or experiential marketing. Do you think this form of sales promotion will become more popular in the future? Justify your position.

9. Automobile manufacturers have used rebate programs for years to provide consumers with an incentive to buy (and buy now!). Is this an effective sales promotion strategy? Conduct some secondary research on rebate incentives and develop some kind of cost–benefit analysis for using this form of promotion.

Endnotes

[1] Wayne Mouland, "Coupon convenience," *Marketing*, May 9, 2005, p. 16.

[2] Wayne Mouland, "General information on the coupon industry in Canada," *NCH Promotional Services*, May 2001.

[3] "Couponing takes off," Resolve Corporation, February 2005.

[4] News Line, Gillette Canada, *Marketing*, October 21, 2002, p. 3.

[5] "Coffee-Mate gets street smart," *Marketing*, February 23, 2004, p. 1.

[6] Geoff Dennis, "Sampling growth spurs creativity," *Strategy*, May 20, 2002, pp. 1, 10.

[7] Chris Daniels, "Giving it away," *Marketing*, August 15/22, 2005, p. 3.

[8] Laura Pratt, "Roll up the Rim major player for Tim Hortons," *Strategy*, May 22, 2000, p. 22.

[9] Terry Poulton, "A winner every time," *Strategy*, August 26, 2002, p. 19.

[10] Wayne Mouland, "Rebates rule!" *Marketing*, October 18, 2004, p. 35.

[11] John Heinzl, "Beer firms rethink giveaways," *Globe and Mail*, March 3, 2003, p. B5.

[12] Michelle Halpern, "Labatt's big promo! Score," *Marketing*, October 6/13, 2003, p. 28.

[13] John Heinzl, "You may be loyal, but its costing you," *Globe and Mail*, January 31, 2003, p. B8.

[14] Keith McArthur, "Subway latest eatery to adopt e-loyalty card," *Globe and Mail*, June 3, 2005, p. B3.

[15] Rebecca Harris, "Card party," *Marketing*, April 18, 2005, p. 15.

[16] Ali Rahnema, "Subscriber loyalty is in the card," *Marketing*, October 4/11, 2004, p. 19.

9

PUBLIC RELATIONS

After studying this chapter you will be able to

1. identify and assess the various roles of public relations communications in achieving marketing and business objectives

2. describe the various steps in public relations planning

3. identify and evaluate various public relations execution techniques for potential application in public relations plans

4. identify and assess the various evaluation and measurement techniques that determine the effectiveness of public relations strategies

Public relations are an often misunderstood form of marketing communications. The term often conjures up negative images of a company trying to cover something up or trying to put its own spin on a situation. Certainly, with all the news coverage that companies receive when they are in trouble, there is some truth to such perceptions, but public relations can have a very positive impact on a brand or company's performance, and are responsible for communicating all kinds of positive information.

The theme of this book deals with how messages from various disciplines in communications are integrated and how, whatever the discipline, all must work together to give the consumer a unified message. Most advertising agencies have changed over the past five years or so, recognizing that television commercials are not the answer. Today more than ever before, public relations has a rightful seat at the table. PR's place in the marketing mix and marketing communications mix is growing in importance, and marketing budgets are starting to reflect that.

For example, at BMW Canada, PR is now an equal communications partner. At its head office is a staff of five PR people who actively participate in new product launch meetings with the 23-person internal marketing team. Cara Operations has increased its PR efforts for some of its brands. When Cara launched the Big Harv (a new 6-ounce burger at Harvey's restaurants), the PR campaign generated over 70 media stories with more than half of them showing a picture of the burger. The effort reached more than 25 million Canadians at very little cost.[1] For companies with smaller marketing budgets PR offers good value.

In the age of hypercompetition and advancing electronic technology, marketers are looking for multiple solutions to brand building. This position further suggests the need for the integration of various forms of marketing communications. To rely too much on any one medium or channel of marketing communications could be harmful. This chapter will show how public relations play a role in creating brand awareness and building relationships with customers.

DEFINING PUBLIC RELATIONS

Public relations
A form of communication designed to gain public understanding and acceptance.

Public relations are a form of communication that is primarily directed toward gaining public understanding and acceptance. Unlike advertising, which is a form of communication paid for by the company, public relations use publicity that does not necessarily involve payment. Public relations communications appear in the news media and, as such, offer a legitimacy that advertising does not have. Recently, company's have been using public relations to extol the merits of a product by assisting in new product launches or reporting eventful occurrences of the product.

The practice of public relations is used to build rapport with the various publics a company, individual, or organization may have. These publics are either internal or external. **Internal publics** involve those with whom the organization communicates regularly and include employers, distributors, suppliers, shareholders, and regular customers. **External publics** are more distant and are communicated with less frequently. They include the media, governments, prospective shareholders, the financial community, and community organizations.

Internal publics
The publics with which an organization communicates regularly; can include employees, distributors, suppliers, shareholders, and customers.

External publics
Those publics that are distant from an organization and are communicated with less frequently.

The goal of public relations is to conduct communications in such a way that an organization builds an open, honest, and constructive relationship with its various publics. In comparison to advertising, public relations communications are not controlled by the organization. Instead, the media determine what is said about the company regardless of what information the company provides. In other words, the media act as a "filter" for the information an organization releases.

THE ROLE OF PUBLIC RELATIONS

While all indications suggest PR will play a more strategic role in the future, that role will vary from one organization to another. A survey among senior marketing executives suggests that public relations will be effective for raising awareness (83 percent response), providing credibility (67 percent), reaching influencers (63 percent), and educating consumers (61 percent). Only 22 percent of the executives thought PR could help drive sales, and just 28 percent said PR was effective at prompting trial.[2] While executives seem to recognize the supporting role that PR can play in marketing a product, there is a need for more education at the executive level about the value of public relations.

The role of public relations is varied, but generally falls into six key categories: corporate communications; reputation management; publicity generation; product placement, branded content, and product seeding; community relations and public affairs; and fundraising. The diversity of this list indicates how public relations can be company oriented or product oriented. Let's examine each category in more detail.

Corporate Communications

Corporate advertising
Advertising designed to convey a favourable image of a company among its various publics.

An organization that believes in the benefits of public relations communications will take positive and constructive action to disseminate useful information about itself. This may involve communications that are paid for or not paid for. A good public relations plan strives to maximize communications in an unpaid manner, but there are times when paid communications are necessary. Such communications may be in the form of **corporate advertising**: advertising designed to convey a favourable image of a company among its various publics. It can do so by showing how the resources of the organization resolve customers' problems, by promoting goodwill, or by demonstrating a sense of social responsibility. For example, Shell Canada shows how it integrates economic progress with environmental issues, often a delicate challenge for a company in the oil exploration business (see Figure 9.1). This advertisement is an example of social responsibility marketing and reflects an attitude of corporate conscience that anticipates and responds to social problems. Corporate advertising is quite separate from brand-based integrated marketing communications strategies.

A company can also be active in the area of issue management. In such cases, the company delivers messages to the public to show where it stands on a particular issue, usually an issue that is important to its various publics. The Shell example shows a proactive stance on protecting the environment. Companies also engage in corporate advertising to generate goodwill in the communities they serve. With reference to the ad that appears in Figure 9.2, Shell is letting the public know how it financially supports educational programs and students in order to build a stronger company and country. Shell is investing today to build a better tomorrow.

Reputation Management

Chances are that a company in the headlines is there for all the wrong reasons. Something went wrong and key executives are being called upon to defend the company's position. Public relations play a vital role when a company finds itself in a crisis situation, because the final outcome often depends on how effectively an organization manages its communications during the crisis.

In 2005, CN Rail found itself in such a situation when one of its trains came off the tracks and dumped hundreds of thousands of litres of bunker oil and toxic pole-treating oil into Lake Wabamun (Alberta). The first and most obvious problem was the derailment itself, the worst spill of oil in Canada in 35 years. The derailment became an image

FIGURE **9.1** **An Illustration of Advocacy Advertising: Shell Canada Works toward Finding Environmental Solutions**

Is Shell committed to reclaiming the land being mined in Canada's oil sands?

Rob Seeley says yes, and they're taking the time to do it right.

One of the largest oil deposits on earth is found in northern Alberta's oil sands, competing in size and potential with Saudi Arabia. But this oil is difficult to extract, so Shell employees like Rob Seeley, general manager, oil sands sustainable development, are faced with a demanding challenge - not just separating oil from sand - but also finding socially and environmentally responsible ways to restore the land for generations that follow. So by combining research and science with traditional environmental knowledge learned from their Aboriginal neighbours, Shell won't wait for the mining to finish before reclaiming the land; they'll do it as they go, taking the time to do it right. For more information, visit **shell.ca**

Source: Céline Parisien/*Canadian Geographic*. Reprinted by permission of Shell Canada Limited.

debacle for CN because it did not take positive action initially. CN kept its trains running while nothing was being done about the spill—a fact that infuriated local residents and the media. It took three days for CN to officially notify residents that cancer-causing toxic chemicals had been spilled. Outrage from citizens was the result of communications lapses by CN. While CN did take action, it simply did not impart enough information early on, it did not offer details about the clean-up process, nor did it reveal a full description of what was in the spill.[3]

FIGURE **9.2** An Illustration of Corporate Responsibility: Shell Canada Is Investing to build a Stronger Company and a Better Future

Is a scholarship the only way for a company like Shell to help Canadian students?

McGill University grad Geneviève Savoie says no, and she has the experience to prove it.

Following a student work term at Shell, Geneviève graduated and started her engineering career at the company's Montréal East Refinery. It's a win-win relationship that demonstrates Shell's approach to building tomorrow's workforce. Over the years, Shell has invested millions of dollars in post-secondary institutions across Canada. But it's more than scholarships and recruitment; it's about finding innovative ways to support education, strengthening programs and engaging students in face-to-face dialogue. Because Shell knows that investing in students like Geneviève today will contribute to a stronger company - and country - tomorrow. For more information, visit **shell.ca**

Source: J. W. Thompson, Toronto. Reprinted by permission of Shell Canada Limited.

Another highly publicized case involved Bridgestone/Firestone tires. The tires were linked to more than 200 deaths, and as many as 6.5 million tires were eventually recalled. Bridgestone did not handle the situation effectively. It mishandled concerns about tire safety by not addressing the public's questions and concerns soon enough. Bridgestone/Firestone acted only after being warned by the US government. The public questions the moral values of such a company and demonstrates its anger by not buying its products.

Situations like these clearly show how important it is for organizations to be prepared; having a plan in place to meet disaster head on makes more sense than simply reacting to an unforeseen circumstance. Senior executives must be ready to act instantly and demonstrate they are in control of the situation. All messages sent to the public must be credible and based on fact from the outset. Company executives must be ready to meet the demand of a more sophisticated and more demanding consumer audience, or suffer the consequences of its wrath. Some tips for handling a crisis situation appear in Figure 9.3.

FIGURE **9.3** Tips for Handling a Crisis Situation

An organization never knows when it will be caught off guard. Circumstances can arise quickly and get out of control if an organization is not prepared. Here are some tips for handling a crisis situation properly.

1. Take responsibility. If your name is on the problem you have to take responsibility for it. This is different from accepting blame. The public respects an organization that accepts responsibility.

2. Respond quickly and communicate directly and sincerely. Show the public you are going to resolve the problem.

3. Embrace the three fundamentals of good crisis communication:

   • Communicate very clearly what has gone wrong.
   • Communicate what you are doing about it.
   • Describe the steps you are taking to ensure it doesn't happen again.

4. Have access to a former journalist who knows how to deal with the media (their knowledge of what to expect when the media calls is essential).

5. Offer an apology if an apology is warranted. If the public is satisfied with your efforts in rectifying the problem, they will forgive and move on.

Adapted from David Menzies, "Silence ain't golden: Media crisis dos and don'ts," *Marketing*, August 1/8, 2005, p. 18.

Product Publicity

Publicity
News about an organization, product, service, or person that appears in the media.

Publicity is news about an organization, product, service, or person that appears in the media. There is often a tendency for people to confuse publicity and public relations, thinking they are one and the same. Publicity is but one aspect of many public relations activities. Essentially, publicity is something that a company and the media deem to be newsworthy. When Dunlop Tires wanted to heighten awareness of its brand among young, hip, male consumers, it launched a contest challenging Canadians named Dunlop to officially change their name to Dunlop-Tire. The prize bucket only cost Dunlop $25 000, but the publicity generated was worth hundreds of thousands of dollars.[4] Most of the time, however, reporters don't see things the same way as a company does. Big news for a company is not necessarily big news for the media.

One of the major opportunities for a product or company to generate positive publicity is during a new product launch. Nike, for example, benefited greatly from a seemingly impossible shot by Tiger Woods during the 2005 Masters. With an incredible chip shot, Tiger's ball rolled down the green toward the sixteenth hole only to pause at the lip for about two seconds—the Nike logo in clear view. As luck would have it, it was the new One Platinum ball that Nike was just about to launch on the market. Nike redesigned the launch campaign around this now very famous shot. Winning at the highest level with Nike products is an important mission at Nike. On this day it was The Masters, one of the most prestigious golf tournaments in the world, that was the statement for Nike.[5] The live shot and subsequent replays on CBS and other stations were estimated to be worth $1 million in free advertising exposure.[6]

The Dunlop and Nike examples seem to indicate that a combination of public relations and advertising will work more effectively than either activity working exclusively on its own. When integrated, the impact on the customer is greater. Another example clearly shows how PR can generate lots of interest in a new product. Auto-Ref of Waterloo, Ontario, began marketing a computerized system for tennis capable of determining instantly if a ball is in or out

Nike Golf
www.nikegolf.com

of bounds. Eight cameras located above the court are connected to a computer, and all eight are attached to a central server. With no advertising budget available, the company invested just over $50 000 in a PR campaign that resulted in more than $2 million worth of articles in newspapers and magazines.[7] Perhaps the current reality of advertising clutter enhances the opportunity for public relations to break through by placing effective messages in newspapers, on news broadcasts or shows, and on websites.

Product Placement, Branded Content, and Product Seeding

Product placement

The visible placement of brand name products in television shows, movies, radio, video games, and other programming.

Product Placement
www.productplacement.biz

Product placement refers to the visible placement of branded merchandise in television shows, video games, films, or other programming. With television viewers paying less attention to 30-second commercials, networks and advertisers are fighting back and are relying more on product placements to deliver brand messages.

Ironically, product placement was a popular strategy in the early days of television, as several cigarette companies had their brands included in shows. The theory behind placement is simple: a product featured in a TV show or movie, as opposed to a 30-second spot, will have more credibility with viewers and have a better chance of being noticed and remembered. To illustrate, the Toyota Prius, a hybrid vehicle, was featured in the final six minutes of the finale of the popular show *Six Feet Under*. With more car buyers steering toward hybrid vehicles, Toyota is planning on using entertainment to promote its brands. The Prius, being such a distinctive-looking vehicle, makes a statement about itself simply by appearing in a show.[8]

On *Falcon Beach*, a hit show broadcast on Global Television, various General Motors' brands are featured—Buick, Cadillac, and Pontiac. The young, female lead character is shown driving the sporty Pontiac Solstice while her mother drives a Cadillac SRX. "We saw this as a unique opportunity for a range of GM brands," explains Hugh Dow, president of U2 Universal, the agency behind the deal. "We wanted a seamless, highly visible 'fusion,' aligning various products with certain characters."[9]

A box of Club Crackers was shown with some cheese on an episode of *Yes, Dear*, but the box did not really exist. Technology allows for *virtual product placement*, a process that uses computer graphics and digital editing to put products like potato chips, soft drinks, and shopping bags into television programs. It is estimated that North American advertisers spent $3.5 billion in 2004 on product placement with close to $2 billion being spent on television placements alone.[10]

Branded content

The integration of brand name goods and services into the script (storyline) of a television show or movie. The brand name is clearly mentioned and sometimes discussed.

Branded content takes product placement a step further by weaving the name of the brand right into the storyline of a show. In one episode of *The Sopranos*, Tony is extolling the virtues of a brand new Nissan Pathfinder he has just given Anthony, his son. The car was a bit of a bribe to encourage Anthony to do better in school. In the scene, Tony enthusiastically explains several unique features of the vehicle to Anthony. In the same episode, Tony yells at his wife, "Where's my Dewalt?" (a power drill). He mentioned the brand name three times in a space of 20 seconds. Exposure like this has to benefit the brand!

Product seeding (buzz marketing)

Giving a product free to a group of trendsetters who promote the product to others by word of mouth.

Product seeding is a relatively new activity that involves giving a product free to a group of trendsetters who in turn influence others to become aware of the product and, one hopes, purchase the product. While the product is in the hands of the trendsetters, they are creating "buzz" for the product by chatting it up whenever and wherever they can. For this reason, product seeding is often referred to as **buzz marketing**, though buzz marketing can also mean a host of other things as well.

To illustrate, consider the seeding campaign of Fujifilm Canada when it launched the FinePix F440 digital camera. Fuji and its agency, a company called Matchstick, tracked down appropriate women 25 to 55 years old, middle to high income, and considered a source of information among their friends. Careful scrutiny of various magazine subscriber lists and names from baby shows were helpful in the identification process. These "influencers" received a package containing the camera, an album and photo card for 25 free prints, and an extended memory card. Over a four-week period they were simply asked to

Fuji Canada
www.fujifilm.ca

integrate the camera into their daily lives and to chat it up with other women when asked about it. Fuji opted for this approach based on the knowledge that purchase decisions in this category are based on peer influence, especially from someone deemed as having greater understanding of the product.[11]

Product seeding offers several advantages. First, it is a low-cost strategy that is nowhere near the cost of an advertising campaign. Second, it can reach a narrowly defined target. In the case of Fujifilm, a specific female target was identified. If seeding works, it will attract the attention of the media, and the next thing you know there is a complete story about it in the newspaper or a broadcast feature on the TV news. Now that's good public relations!

Product placement, branded content, and product seeding have expanded opportunities for integration with other forms of marketing communications, particularly advertising campaigns and sales promotions. For more insight into the phenomenon of product placement, branded content, and product seeding, refer to the IMC Highlight **Buzz Pays!**

IMC HIGHLIGHT

BUZZ PAYS!

One of the latest trends in marketing is buzz marketing. Loosely defined, buzz involves using the power of word-of-mouth communications to create excitement and awareness and stimulate sales of a product. There are some variations on the buzz marketing theme. Some refer to it as guerilla marketing, while others call it stealth marketing. Regardless of the name, it refers to unconventional ways for spreading news about a product.

Carefully planned and executed events can catapult brands onto the front pages of newspapers and into the national spotlight of TV news. Such was the case when a throng of scantily clad men and women flashed their underwear emblazoned with the phrase "Booty Call" in front of Grand Central Station in New York City. Pedestrians and car drivers whipped out their digital cameras and photos posted on the Internet soon drew viewers from all over the world. The skivvy sighting had nothing to do with self-expression. It was part of a campaign by the New York Health and Racquet Club to promote a butt-building class for J.Lo wannabes. The racquet club estimates the stunt generated a half a million dollars worth of publicity.

In the wake of changing demographic trends, consumer preferences, and lifestyles, marketers are shifting their way of thinking to be relevant to consumers. Consumers are spending less time with the media (they are time poor), so public relations and buzz are taking on a new role in building and protecting a brand.

Reebok Canada offers another good example of buzz marketing. When it launched the U-Shuffle DMX shoe for women, a trendy black and red sneaker with no laces, the company gave 90 young women from across Canada a free pair ($150 value) and asked them to wear them around town. Reebok's goal was to get the funky cross-trainer on the feet of suburban trendsetters, who in turn would influence others to purchase the new product. It worked! The trendsetters were asked all kinds of questions about the shoes, and women wanted to know where they could buy them. The word-of-mouth network was soon in high gear!

Buzz marketing offers several advantages. The biggest advantage is the low cost—it's nowhere near the cost of an ad campaign to launch a new product. It also has the capability of reaching a narrowly defined target, as in the case of Reebok. If the seeding works, it will attract the attention of the media and next thing you know there is a complete story in the newspaper!

There are a few disadvantages as well. The spreading of buzz cannot be controlled. It will spread, but it cannot be moulded, directed, or stopped. It grows, gains momentum, and eventually fades if it is not refuelled. As well, the message cannot be controlled. The message is distorted and filtered by every transmitter and receptor of buzz. Potentially, the communications could have negative implications on the brand or company.

Do buzz marketing and word-of-mouth communications really work? The jury is still out on this issue, but one thing is certain: buzz is gaining in popularity because consumers are more connected than ever due to cell phones and the Internet. While some marketing managers remain skeptical about its effectiveness, they realize that finding innovative ways of breaking through the clutter of competitive activity is essential for success.

Adapted from Krysten Crawford, "Gotcha! Ads push the envelope," *CNN Money*, August 17, 2004, Karl Moore, "Gotta get that buzz," *Marketing*, July 5, 2004, p. 9, Judy Lewis, "Building buzz," *Marketing*, January 28, 2002, p. 17, and John Heinzl, "If the shoe fits, sell it," *Globe and Mail*, September 7, 2001, p. M1.

Community Relations and Public Affairs

Companies today are operating in an environment where social responsibility is very important. Consequently, they place much higher value on programs that foster a good public image in the communities where they operate. Sponsoring community events, local groups, and sports teams is part of being a good corporate citizen. The effect of such an investment on sales is indirect and long term in nature. Very often, being part of the fabric of a community takes precedence over sales. Leaders of companies that place a high value on public relations will tell you that the public has to "like you before they will buy you." Tim Hortons is a good example of a community-minded company. It supplies sports jerseys to local hockey and soccer teams through its Timbits Sports program, offers free ice skating in local communities during the Christmas break, and sends thousands of needy children to camps each summer through the Tim Horton Children's Foundation (see Figure 9.4).[12]

FIGURE 9.4 **Public Relations Is Key to Building Community Relationships and Enhancing a Company's Image in the Community**

Source: Courtesy of Morgan MacLean.

Public affairs

Strategies to deal with governments and to communicate with governments.

Lobbying

Activities and practices designed to influence policy decisions that will affect an organization or all organizations in a particular industry.

Greenpeace
www.greenpeace.org

Public affairs involve strategies to deal with governments and to communicate with governments. **Lobbying** involves activities and practices designed to influence policy decisions that will affect an organization or all organizations within a particular industry. It is very common for a national association to represent the interests of industry members. Naturally, a company or association wants government policy to conform to what's best for business. For example, the Packaging Association of Canada (PAC) has advocated successfully in all areas of government packaging policy and regulation—from the *Consumer Packaging and Labelling Act*, to the National Packaging Protocol, and the North American Free Trade Agreement. The PAC is the focal point for action on environmental packaging initiatives and competitive measures for Canadian packagers.[13]

Independently funded organizations like Greenpeace actively lobby governments to ensure industry maintains environmental standards. Recently, Greenpeace has been active in trying to ensure that Fortune 500 companies support the Kyoto Protocol (an issue dealing with the long-term effects of climate change largely caused by industry practices). Many leading companies, including oil exploration companies and automobile manufacturers, do not support the protocol and lobby the government from a different angle. The lobbying and counter-lobbying help shape national government policy on such issues. When making policy decisions, governments must balance economic well-being with social and environmental well-being, and that explains the conflict between government, business, and special interest groups.

Fundraising

In the not-for-profit sector, public relations play a key role in fundraising. National organizations such as the Canadian Cancer Society, the Canadian Heart and Stroke Foundation, and the United Way face huge financial challenges each year. For these and similar organizations, public relations help educate the public about how funds are used. The message is designed to predispose people to give, to solicit commitment, and to make people feel good about giving. The overall goal of such campaigns is to create a positive image and secure support by sending a message that clearly states what the organization is all about. Such campaigns use a variety of techniques to deliver the message. Media strategies include direct mail, telemarketing, print advertising (outdoor, newspapers, and magazines), and websites (see Figure 9.5).

PUBLIC RELATIONS PLANNING

As a component of the integrated marketing communications mix, public relations plans are designed to fit directly with the needs of the organization's marketing objectives. They can be active (help support a brand or company positively) or reactive (help out in a crisis situation). Regardless of the situation, as already stated, a plan must be in place.

As with advertising, a good public relations plan can help build an image and assist in developing relationships with customers. Furthermore, a well-timed public relations plan can play a key role in the launch of a new product, especially in times when budget resources are scarce. Advertising is a very expensive endeavour; public relations is much more economical. In companies searching for greater effectiveness at lower cost, public relations look like a better option than advertising, or, at the very least, the two disciplines must work effectively together to achieve objectives efficiently.

Based on the discussion presented so far in this chapter, it is very apparent that the planning of public relations communications is best left to specialists. It is not an area of expertise in most organizations, though many have a senior-ranking officer assigned the responsibility. Typically, the in-house public relations specialist is a liaison with outside agencies that prepare and implement public relations plans. If there is an in-house public relations department, its responsibilities might focus on public affairs and community

FIGURE **9.5** **Public Relations Communications Play a Key Role in Fundraising Campaigns**

FIGURE **9.5** **Public Relations Communications Play a Key Role in Fundraising Campaigns**

Source: Courtesy of ACLC.

relations. For the preparation and implementation of corporate and product public relations plans, there is a tendency to hire an organization that specializes in these areas. Hill and Knowlton and NATIONAL Public Relations are examples of leading public relations agencies in Canada. The specialist is briefed by the organization on its needs and expectations. Then, the specialist assesses the information and prepares a strategic plan that will meet the client's objectives. Figure 9.6 illustrates the public relations planning process. Let's discuss each stage of the planning process in more detail.

FIGURE **9.6** The Public Relations Planning Process

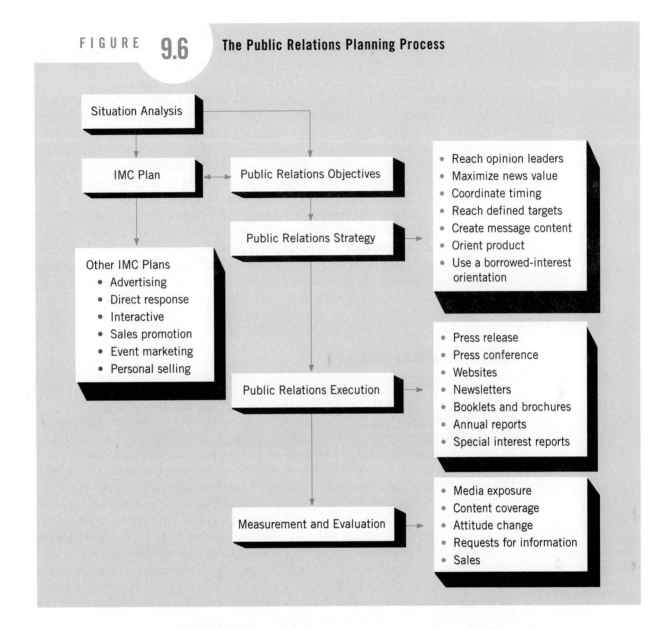

Public Relations Objectives

Public relations objectives typically involve creating awareness, shaping attitudes, and altering behaviour. As marketing campaigns become more integrated and seamless, the ability both to quantify and to measure objectives becomes more difficult. On the surface, public relations objectives are very similar to advertising objectives. Therefore, to try to distinguish between the two is difficult. Increased awareness and predisposition to buy are influenced by numerous factors well beyond the scope of public relations, so trying to evaluate public relations in terms of sales and increased market share is next to impossible.

What can be measured, however, is the level of publicity generated by a public relations plan. Typically, the goal of public relations is to achieve media exposure, so quantifiable objectives can be established in this area. Publicity objectives should consider the media through which the message will be communicated and the target audience reached by the media. Surprisingly, even very targeted public relations plans can catch the attention of the national media, because good stories, no matter where they come from, are good stories on national news broadcasts, in national newspapers, and in general interest magazines.

Media exposure can be measured in terms of *gross impressions*, the number of times an item was potentially seen. If a news story appears in a large-circulation newspaper, what is the circulation or readership (circulation multiplied by the readers per copy) of that newspaper? An objective can be stated in terms of impressions. For example, the objective is to achieve 10 million gross impressions nationally in Canadian daily newspapers.

Another objective could entail matching the message with the appropriate medium. To illustrate, assume you are doing a campaign for TaylorMade golf equipment (drivers, fairway woods, irons, and golf balls). The objective would be to reach golfers in a medium they refer to frequently to communicate to them the latest and greatest technology that has been built into your products. Some options include The Golf Channel and *Golf Digest* as well as a host of other golf-related publications. Reaching your audience in highly targeted media offers several benefits: the message will be read or seen by influencers who will create a word-of-mouth network, and the message could influence the editorial agenda of the publication or station. The media are constantly looking for new and innovative ideas to promote. If they don't find you, you have to find them. Figure 9.7 is an example of a press release announcing a new line of outerwear that offers different kinds of protection for golfers. Golf magazines and a variety of golf shows on The Golf Channel report on stories like this.

Public Relations Strategy

Every form of marketing communications has its strengths and weaknesses. With public relations, the company cannot control the media or dictate the manner in which the message is communicated. Getting past the media gatekeepers is the first challenge; the second challenge is ensuring the message is communicated with reasonable accuracy. On the positive side, public relations messages provide enhanced credibility. When the consumer reads a story in a newspaper or hears and sees something positive on a news broadcast about a product or company, it is much more authentic than an advertisement.

Corporate blogging has put some message control back into the hands of the organization. A **blog** is a website where journal entries are posted on a regular basis and displayed in reverse chronological order. Adding information to a blog is called **blogging**. Consumers and consumer groups have developed blogs that often defame an organization—a situation an organization has little control over. Consequently, organizations are developing their own blogs to distribute favourable information. In this role it is becoming an important communications tool. Blogging is discussed in more detail in the "Public Relations Execution" section of this chapter.

The role of public relations is determined in advance and is outlined in the marketing communications plan. Typically, that role is to reach influential individuals such as industry analysts, key media representatives, and early adopters of products (refer back to the discussion about product seeding).

The strategic role of public relations should be examined based on how best to

- reach the opinion leaders, including professionals, industry analysts, trade audiences, and media, well in advance of the public;
- maximize the news value of new product introductions, new advertising campaigns, and event sponsorships. Messages must be written creatively and visuals must grab attention;
- time public relations events to reinforce advertising and promotion campaigns and to maintain visibility between campaigns;
- reach markets that are defined by demographics, psychographics, or geographic location that might not be targeted by advertising.[14]

A public relations strategy allows an organization to tell a longer story about itself and its products. Strategy deals more with informing and educating rather than motivating someone to buy something. Therefore, when claims are made about a product, proper

Blog
A frequent, chronological publication of personal thoughts at a website.

Blogging
The act of posting new information and thoughts on a blog.

FIGURE **9.7** **A Press Release that Presents a New Product Favourably to the Media**

THE BEST PERFORMANCE GOLF BRAND IN THE WORLD

To download high-resolution visuals,
please go to http://www.tmag.com/media
(please use the password provided to you by the TMaG PR department.)

adidas Golf Announces New Outerwear Line

CARLSBAD, Calif. (January 13, 2006) - TaylorMade-adidas Golf announces a new range of outerwear to be introduced at the 2006 PGA Merchandise Show.

The range features garments that fall into five different levels of protection categories. Categories include ClimaProof® Wind in three levels, ClimaProof Rain, ClimaProof Storm, ClimaWarm®, and ClimaCompression, available in a lightweight and thermal version. Just as ClimaCool® is designed to keep a player comfortable in the heat, adidas outerwear is designed to protect the golfer from the elements, whether it is a light wind or driving rain, keeping the golfer dry and warm.

Integrating leading technologies in fabrications, laminates, and constructions allows adidas to produce outerwear garments that are comfortable, lightweight, and extremely quiet. In ClimaProof Wind, ClimaWarm, and ClimaProof Storm, adidas introduces both two and four way stretch applications for additional comfort.

The new outerwear range can be seen at adidas Golf's display at booth location #14037 within the apparel section of the Orange County Convention Center during the PGA Merchandise Show January 26-29, 2006. Also on display will be the full-line of adidas footwear and apparel. Daily fashion shows will also present the opportunity to explore the new range of outerwear.

The full line of outerwear by adidas will be available at retail starting May 15, 2006.

About Taylor Made Golf Company, Inc. dba TaylorMade-adidas Golf Company
TaylorMade Golf has led the golf industry's technological evolution since being founded in 1979. adidas Golf footwear and apparel is the choice of hundreds of professional golfers around the world. Consumers can find more information on TaylorMade-adidas Golf at (800) 888-CLUB or www.tmag.com, www.taylormadegolf.com, www.adidasgolf.com, www.maxfli.com or www.rossaputters.com.

For more information contact:
TaylorMade-adidas Golf
John Steinbach
Tel: 760.918.6330
eMail: john.steinbach@tmag.com

| 5545 fermi court carlsbad california 92008 | phone 760.918.6000 fax 760.918.6014 |
| www.taylormadegolf.com | www.adidasgolf.com |

Source: Courtesy of TaylorMade-adidas Golf.

substantiation should be provided. Unlike advertising, where time and space are often restricted, public relations communications can spend additional time expanding on something of importance. News editors might edit the length of the story, but they will strive to maintain the credibility of the message.

A company may employ a **borrowed-interest strategy** to generate publicity. A borrowed-interest strategy will typically promote a newsworthy marketing activity that is related to the product. For example, participation and sponsorship of a community event or national event is news, as is the launch of a national sales promotion offer designed to stimulate sales. An Olympic sponsorship involving significant sums of money is certainly

Borrowed-interest strategy
A plan to promote a marketing activity that is related to a product.

FIGURE **9.8** **A Press Release Using a Borrowed-Interest Strategy to Promote a Company**

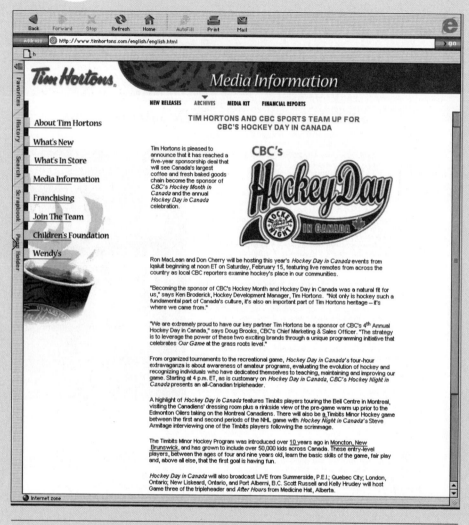

Source: Courtesy of The TDL Group Corp.

a newsworthy item for companies like Coca-Cola, McDonald's, and Visa. The PR wheels at Tim Hortons start rolling well before its annual "Rrroll up the Rim to Win" promotion that runs every March. Refer to Figure 9.8 for an illustration.

Public Relations Execution

The tools available to execute public relations programs are diverse. Some are used routinely to communicate newsworthy information and some are brought out periodically or only on special occasions. This section examines some of the more routinely used media tools.

Press Release

Press release

A document prepared by an organization containing public relations information that is sent to the media for publication or broadcast.

A **press release** is a document containing all the essential elements of the story (who, what, when, where, and why). Editors make very quick decisions on what to use and what to discard, so the release must grab their attention quickly. Copies of the release are delivered to a list of preferred editors, for example those with whom an organization has a good relationship. Alternatively, the release could be distributed to a national wire service as well as posted on the company's website. Figure 9.9 is an illustration of a press release. Note that contact information is provided should the media require any additional information. The objective of this press release is to secure media support in advising the public of a recall on travel mug lids.

FIGURE **9.9** **The Essential Elements of a Good Press Release: Who, What, When, and Where**

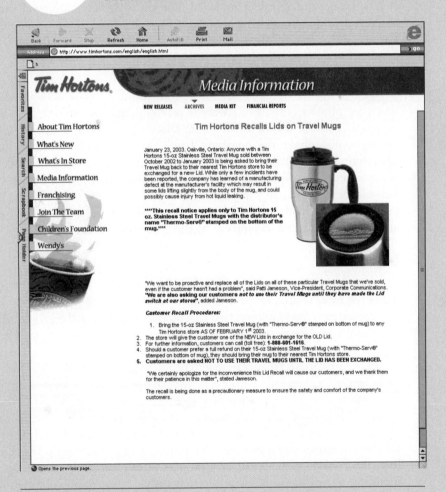

Source: Courtesy of the TDL Group Corp.

Press Conference

A **press conference** is a meeting of news reporters invited to witness the release of important information about a company or product. Because a conference is time consuming for the media representatives, it is usually reserved for only the most important announcements. A crisis, for example, is usually handled by an initial press conference. When a professional sports team is about to announce a new star player entering the fold, a press conference is very common. A conference allows the media to interact by asking questions, which results in the transfer of additional and perhaps more meaningful information for the story they will publish or broadcast.

A media kit is usually distributed at a press conference. A **media kit** can include a schedule of conference events, a list of company participants including biographical information, a press release, historical fact sheets if applicable to the situation, a backgrounder that tells something about the character of the organization and the nature of what it does, a page of standalone facts about the company, photographs, copies of speeches, videos, and any other relevant information. Depending on need, any combination of these materials can be included. The key to developing a good media kit is to evaluate who will use it and what that person is likely to need. For example, a media kit for a special event or new sales promotion activity would be very different in tone, style, and content from one needed for a crisis situation.

Websites

Since the primary purpose of a website is to communicate information about a company or brand, it can be a very useful public relations tool. Visitors to a website quickly form an impression about the company based on the experience they have at the site. Therefore, the site must download quickly and be easy to navigate. Providing some kind of entertainment or interactive activity also enhances the visit. Unlike other media, the web can be updated easily and quickly, so the very latest news about a company and its products can be made available for public consumption. It is now very common to post all press releases about a company on the corporate website.

Newsletters

The **newsletter** is a very common public relations tool. By nature, it is a concise reporting of the news related to the organization and is very clear and to the point. A successful newsletter conveys information in a unique way so that the people who receive it pay attention to it. Newsletters are distributed regularly to their intended audience, so they are an efficient method of conveying information.

There are various types of newsletters, but most are published by companies that want to communicate regularly with employees and customers, by recreation and sports clubs that wish to keep in touch with their members, and by professional associations that regularly publish information to members who are geographically dispersed. Typically, a newsletter is distributed by internal or external mail or email, and relies on an accurate database of names and addresses. The frequency of publication is based on budget, time-lines, and serialization. Small budgets may dictate quarterly distribution as opposed to monthly; if timeliness is an issue, then more frequent distribution is required. See Figure 9.10 for an illustration.

A newsletter is a useful tool for communicating company policies to employees, for announcing social and recreational events, and for acknowledging individual and team success within the organization. As well, a newsletter is useful for informing employees of news (good or bad) about the company before it is announced to the general public. The newsletter often assumes this role. *Special interest newsletters* are distributed by a wide variety of lifestyle clubs and organizations, and by professional associations. Investors in the stock market, for instance, often receive newsletters from a bank or other financial institutions.

FIGURE **9.10** **A Newsletter Published Quarterly by the TDL Group Keeps Tim Hortons Employees and Customers Informed of Recent Activities**

Source: Paul Reynolds Photography.

Booklets and Brochures

Booklet (brochure)

A multiple-page document distributed to consumers and other interested stakeholders.

A **booklet** or **brochure** is a brand-sponsored, multiple-page document that is distributed to consumers and other interested stakeholders. The information in a booklet is usually related to a product or service. For example, it may promote usage of a product in a variety of ways or it may appeal to the lifestyle of the target audience it is intended for. Campbell's Soup is well known for distributing recipe booklets in food stores, through

Campbell's Soup
www.campbellsoup.com

Annual report

A document published annually by an organization primarily to provide current and prospective investors and stakeholders with financial data and a description of the company's operations.

direct mail, and through its website. These booklets encourage consumers to use Campbell's products more frequently in cooking recipes as well as in other non-traditional ways. Greater usage equals greater sales.

Annual Reports and Special Interest Reports

The primary purpose of an **annual report** is to provide current and prospective investors and stakeholders with financial data and a description of an organization's operations. But it can do much more to promote the company. In terms of public relations, it is a good opportunity for the organization to tell the public how it stands on social and environmental issues, for example. In fact, the annual report is often seen by audiences beyond the primary target—such as the media, community leaders, and employees. Word can spread fast about what a company stands for.

Special interest reports can be integrated into an annual report or can be standalone documents. For companies that want to portray to the public that there is more to business than a healthy bottom line, a special interest report is an ideal vehicle to get a different message out. Special interest reports are designed to appeal to a very selective audience—usually opinion leaders—and focus on issues that affect the organization and the target audience. To illustrate, RBC Financial Group issues the *First Principles* Corporate Responsibility Report each year. The report documents the social responsibility practices of the company and goes a long way in building trust with employees, customers, and clients. The report focuses on issues such as integrity in business, commitment to clients and employees, commitment to diversity, commitment to the environment, and policies regarding governance, compliance, and ethics (see Figure 9.11). How RBC supports local communities all across Canada is also profiled in the publication. The latest report shows RBC contributing $59 million to community causes worldwide.[15]

Blogs

As stated earlier, a blog, also called a weblog, is a frequent, chronological publication of personal thoughts at a website. Blogs are the property and works of everyday people who like to rant about things they don't like, and very often they will challenge the integrity of an organization in their blog. While an organization cannot control this situation, it must live with the reality that negative things are being said about them.

The growing popularity of blogs must be viewed positively from both a public relations and corporate communications perspective. A corporate blog can be an effective tool to fight back. It offers an opportunity to present relevant information in a positive manner. The popularity of blogs has changed the nature of public relations. Today, consumer-generated content contained in a blog has just as much weight as information presented by corporations and traditional media outlets. "Consumers are in control, and consumers are the media. It's a paradigm shift that's going to change PR forever."[16]

This viewpoint is shared by Burson-Marsteller, a public relations agency. It says that the news-making process has become a collaborative process between the media and publics. "To participate in this process with immediate, accurate, and continuous information, companies need to designate resources, establish policies, train staff, and communicate with online audiences who are readers, producers, journalists and publishers simultaneously."[17]

Some companies have already benefited from blogs. Before Procter & Gamble launched Mr. Clean AutoDry, a car washing product that dries spot-free, auto enthusiasts were trading notes about the product in auto blogs and chat rooms. To seed more discussion, P&G gave away AutoDry kits to bloggers, asking for their honest review. Some 80 percent gave the item a thumbs-up. Before the product reached the store shelves, brand awareness was 25 percent among consumers and 45 percent among car aficionados. Already a hit, prominent retailers had no choice but to carry the product.[18]

Mr. Clean AutoDry
www.autodry.com

FIGURE **9.11** **RBC Financial Group Publishes a Corporate Responsibility Report to Document its Contribution to Communities**

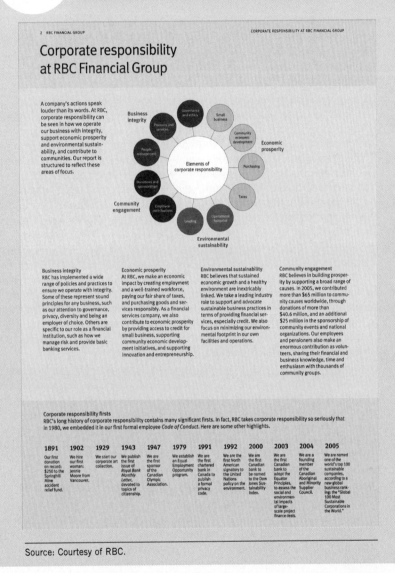

Source: Courtesy of RBC.

Blogs enable companies to speak directly to consumers, and as a result are pushing the news media out of their central role in public relations. Richard Edelman, president and CEO of Edelman Public Relations Worldwide, believes "PR practitioners must become more like journalists and rely less on the media to get the message out. If we are putting information online and people are reading it and accepting it as truth, then we should have a journalist-level quality as our objective."[19] Instead of persuading the media to report a story, the practitioner must speak directly to the public, or try to influence bloggers to post messages on their behalf.

Figure 9.12 offers some insight into additional and unique public relations techniques appropriate for special occasions.

Timeline and Budget

A timeline is essential so that all activities are carefully coordinated with other marketing communications activities. In the case of a new product launch, for example, public

FIGURE **9.12**   **Some Unique and Innovative Public Relations Techniques**

With so much advertising out there, it is increasingly difficult to get a product message through the clutter. Companies are turning to public relations techniques that simply approach customers a different way in order to catch their attention. Sometimes, the customers don't even realize they're being sold something!

THE CELEBRITY PITCH

Drug companies are hiring Hollywood stars to discuss illnesses and treatments on the talk show circuit. Lauren Bacall speaks openly about Visudyne (a drug that treats macular degeneration, an eye disease). Bacall is financially rewarded by Novartis, the drug's manufacturer. Kathleen Turner plugs Enbral, an anti-arthritis drug marketed by Wyeth, and Rob Lowe promotes Neulesta, a drug that treats febrile neutropenia (a kind of fever condition often related to cancer). It all sounds technical, but these stars speak to the issues when interviewed on talk shows.

THE LOCAL ACTOR PITCH

Marketers hire local actors to pose as tourists in a bid to generate buzz about a new product. Sony Ericsson's undercover operatives ask strangers at tourist destinations across the United States to snap their picture with the new camera/cell phone device. The purpose is to create the illusion of a spontaneous encounter with someone who bought the gadget. The actors talk up the gadget once they are asked questions about it.

CEOS

A company's top executive could be the company's most effective spokesperson. His or her presence in the media can have a significant impact on a company's financial performance. Some great ones past and present include Lee Iacocca at Chrysler, Bill Gates at Microsoft, and Dave Thomas at Wendy's. Dave Thomas's personality reflected the personality of the entire organization. Since his death in 2002, his sense of humour and warm demeanour are no longer part of Wendy's television advertising.

ROAD SHOWS

A brand hits the road with a decorated vehicle as a means of attracting attention. Product samples can be given away at each stop. Red Rose Tea reshaped a Volkswagen Beetle to look like a teapot (handle on the back hood and spout on the front hood). Other popular brands that use this technique include Microsoft Xbox, Sony Music, and Pepsi-Cola. In the case of Microsoft, the vehicle was a travelling gaming arcade that encouraged experiential contact. In the sky, there's the Goodyear blimp, the Met Life Blimp with Snoopy, and the Fuji blimp.

relations programs can be put in place well before the product is actually available. One strategy is to start the public relations communications in a small way, slowly building credibility, and proceed with a slow rollout. This strategy creates demand in such a manner that the public is eager to buy the product once it is launched. The Mr. Clean AutoDry example cited in the preceding section followed this strategic approach.

Public relations programs cost much less than advertising programs, but they are nonetheless costs that must be accounted for. If a company employs corporate advertising, the costs are similar to brand advertising programs. There are costs associated with producing print and broadcast materials and with buying time in the broadcast media, space in the print media, and in developing and maintaining websites and blogs. A company might also employ newsletters, brochures, annual reports, and media kits, and the costs of producing these materials must also be included in the public relations budget.

Measurement and Evaluation

Ketchum Public Relations
www.ketchum.com

To justify a financial investment in any form of marketing communications, certain expectations and results must be delivered. There must be some kind of financial return, increase in awareness, or change in behaviour. Walter K. Lindenmann, senior vice-president and director of research at Ketchum Public Relations, has identified levels for measuring public relations effectiveness: outputs, outgrowths, and outcomes.

- *Outputs* measure the transmission, that is, the amount of exposure in the media, the number of placements and audience impressions, and the likelihood of reaching the target audience.
- *Outgrowths* measure message reception by the target audience. Did the target pay attention to, understand, and retain the message?
- *Outcomes* measure attitude and behavioural change. Was there a change in attitude and did the recipient do something as a result of the message?[20]

Output measures are the most common means of evaluating public relations effectiveness. There are companies that specialize in tracking everything that is written and broadcast about a company and its brands. For example, if an article appears in the front section of the *Toronto Star*, a newspaper with a weekday circulation of more than 400 000, how many impressions will be made? If there are 2.5 readers for every newspaper, the potential number of impressions is 1 million (400 000 x 2.5). If a similar story appears in other newspapers, the total impressions accumulate.

It is also possible to attach an *equivalent advertising value* to such an article. The tracking firm examines the size of the article, the location in the publication, the number of brand mentions, and so on, and through the magic of mathematical calculations, determines the value in terms of advertising. While this may not be exact science, it does appease senior executives who are looking for some kind of return on their investment. While there is no real agreement on such matters, public relations experts believe that a good article about a product is worth anywhere from three times as much to ten times as much as an equivalent size ad in the same publication.

Measuring for outgrowths involves determining if the target audience received and understood the message. Collecting this information involves a combination of qualitative and quantitative research methodologies, so it is much more costly. Since creating awareness is the primary objective of most public relations campaigns, many firms do not proceed with research in this area.

Marketing research is required to measure for outcomes such as a shift in behaviour. As with research conducted for any other marketing activity, this form of evaluation involves pre-campaign and post-campaign research. The initial research firmly establishes a benchmark. For example, the research identifies how consumers perceive and use a product or company before being exposed to the public relations message. The initial research group is then divided into a test group and a control group. The test group receives the public relations message and the control group does not. Post-campaign research determines the differences between the two groups in terms of what they know and if their attitudes have changed.

More detailed information about specific procedures for measuring and evaluating public relations activities is included in Chapter 12, "Evaluating Marketing Communications Programs."

PUBLIC RELATIONS AS A COMMUNICATIONS MEDIUM

Senior executives today are starting to have a better understanding of the role played by public relations in achieving their organization's marketing objectives. As a communications discipline, the status of public relations has been considerably elevated. The examples in this chapter show how public relations can play a key role in specific situations, and it will certainly continue to grow in terms of its contribution to marketing communications strategies and the achievement of an organization's objectives. Those responsible for corporate and brand communications should be aware of the basic benefits and drawbacks of public relations communications.

For some insight into some recent successful PR campaigns, see the IMC Highlight **PR Brings Results for Lee and Labatt.**

Advantages of Public Relations

If public relations is done properly, it can be a *credible source* of information. Unlike advertising, public relations messages are delivered by third parties who have no particular interest in the company or product. They are communicating information that they deem useful to their readers, listeners, viewers, and so on. Consumers reading or viewing such messages perceive those messages to be more objective than they do advertisements. If a company can win favourable press coverage, its message is more likely to be absorbed and believed.[21]

60 Minutes
www.cbsnews.com

Third-party endorsements by trusted media personalities can have a *positive impact on sales*. To illustrate, consider what happened when the CBS news program *60 Minutes*

IMC HIGHLIGHT

PR BRINGS RESULTS FOR LEE AND LABATT

Senior marketing executives want results. They look for tangible benefits gained from their investment in any form of marketing communications. Public relations are no different. In planning a PR program, specific objectives are established; the campaign is implemented and then evaluated. Here are a few campaigns that really clicked.

When Lee Jeans returned to Canada, Strategic Objectives, the PR agency hired by Lee, created a multi-faceted communications program that included street events and sampling in Toronto and Montreal; media partnerships; video productions; a sexy, standing-room-only media and retail trade fashion show; and national business and consumer media relations. All were conceived to build brand image, demand, and sales for Lee Jeans in Canada.

The results: One prominent retailer ordered 75 000 pairs of jeans immediately following the fashion show. Audience impressions from the media effort generated 22 million consumer impressions. There was more than 75 minutes of television coverage and newspaper, magazine, and online coverage from coast to coast.

Labatt Breweries used a PR campaign to launch Labatt Sterling, a low-carb beer. The objective of the campaign was trial purchase by presenting Sterling as a beer suited for healthier lifestyle choices.

A seasonally focused campaign featuring fitness and lifestyle experts as spokespersons were prominent in the media materials. On launch day, media materials and product samples were delivered to key print and broadcast media outlets in Ontario's major markets. An aggressive follow-up plan encouraged interview opportunities with Labatt spokespeople and the fitness experts.

The results: There was sustained coverage in a variety of lifestyle and business media with product visuals appearing in almost 75 percent of the coverage. More than half the coverage delivered messages directly from the spokespeople. Without any traditional advertising support, demand for the product resulted in it being virtually sold out at liquor and beer outlets within one week of its availability.

Adapted from "Public relations ROI: Lee's jean pool and Sterling's debut," *Marketing*, January 31, 2005, pp. 13, 14.

FIGURE **9.13**   **Successful Public Relations Campaigns Have a Positive Impact on Sales**

This public relations plan for Dunlop Tires demonstrates how a carefully planned public relations campaign can increase brand sales.

CLIENT

Goodyear Canada and its Dunlop Tire brand

AGENCY

Environics Communications, Toronto

PUBLIC RELATIONS OBJECTIVE

To increase consumer awareness for the Dunlop Tire brand and drive sales.

PUBLIC RELATIONS CAMPAIGN

The campaign theme revolved around the Dunlop name. Dunlop challenged people whose last name was Dunlop to change their name to Dunlop-Tire for a cash reward. It was promoted as the "Tired of Your Name Challenge."

The story received prominent coverage across Canada and the United States, including front-page stories, television features, and radio interviews.

MEASUREMENT AND EVALUATION

- 100% of media stories mentioned the name Dunlop Tire.
- Many stories were front-page or top stories reported on television news.
- The tone of all news coverage was positive and/or humorous.
- Forty-nine people named Dunlop inquired about changing their name.
- Four people legally changed their name to Dunlop-Tire.
- Sales increased 59 percent over two years in a market only growing by 3 percent.
- Canadian Tire (the largest distributor of tires) agreed to sell Dunlop tires, a decision attributed to the public relations support received by the brand.

Adapted from Sara Minogue, "Proving value," *Strategy*, November 18, 2002, p. 18.

announced that drinking a moderate amount of wine each day could prevent heart attacks by lowering cholesterol. The effect was so astonishing that red wine sales in the United States jumped 50 percent after the broadcast. Figure 9.13 illustrates how good public relations can increase sales.

Indirectly, public relations also play a role in developing sound *customer relationships*. Public relations campaigns offer a means to build rapport through ongoing dialogue with consumers and other stakeholders. Such a benefit is important, considering the rising costs of media advertising, the fragmentation of the media, and the clutter of commercial messages. A good public relations campaign can cut through the clutter faster and may encourage the desired attitude or behaviour change to occur more immediately.

Disadvantages of Public Relations

One of the biggest drawbacks of public relations is the *absence of control* experienced by the sponsoring organization. Through press releases and press conferences, the company does its best to ensure that factual information is available and presented accurately to the public. In the process of communicating the information, however, the media might add their own opinions, which detract from the intent of the original message. Companies facing crisis situations often see stories in the media that misrepresent the company or mislead the public. In the case of blogs, consumers act as publishers and control what is said about your product or company, be it good, bad, or indifferent.

A second disadvantage deals with the sheer *waste* of time, energy, and materials that goes into a public relations campaign. This is not to say that the effort isn't worthwhile, but the challenge of catching the attention of editors (the media gatekeepers) is an onerous one. Enormous amounts of material flow into media newsrooms daily, so standing out in the crowd is part of the public relations challenge. Senior management must recognize the waste factor and be prepared to absorb the costs that go along with it. Finally, what is important to management may not be perceived as important by the media. End of story!

Summary

Public relations are a form of communications directed at gaining public understanding and acceptance. They are used by organizations to change or influence attitudes and behaviour. Unlike advertising, which is a very costly means of communications, public relations go largely unpaid for. The organization presents information to the media in the hopes they will publish or broadcast it in a news story.

The primary roles of public relations are diverse. They constitute a useful channel for communicating corporate-oriented messages designed to build the organization's image. Public relations are also the most important form of communications when an organization finds itself in a crisis situation. In such times, an organization must be honest and forthright with the public. Public relations specialists help prepare organizations to handle crisis situations.

At the product level, public relations help generate positive publicity by distributing news releases and holding press conferences when there is newsworthy information to announce. As well, relatively new communications alternatives, such as product placement, branded content, and product seeding, fall under the umbrella of public relations. Product placement and branded content are proving to be an effective alternative to regular television advertising, and product seeding offers a means of getting the product in the hands of trendsetters who influence the public's attitudes and behaviour.

Public relations planning begins with a situation analysis. Usually, the client organization provides a brief containing all relevant background information to a public relations agency. Public relations are a form of communications that does require external expertise. The public relations firm establishes the goals and objectives, develops the communications strategy, selects the best execution techniques, and after receiving the client's approval, implements the plan.

The primary objectives of public relations programs tend to dwell on creating awareness, altering attitudes, and motivating a change in behaviour. The public relations strategy focuses on reaching opinion leaders, maximizing the news value of the story, and reinforcing other communications campaigns such as advertising, sales promotions, and event marketing activities. There are several techniques for getting a story into distribution. The most commonly used options include the press release, press conferences, websites, newsletters, booklets and brochures, and blogs.

Once the public relations plan is implemented, research is necessary to determine the effectiveness of the campaign. Output measurements are the most common evaluation technique. They measure message transmission—that is, the amount of exposure in the media, the number of placements and audience impressions, and the likelihood of the message reaching the intended target audience. If pre-campaign and post-campaign research is conducted (budget permitting), an organization can measure the impact of public relations messages in terms of influencing attitudes and altering behaviour.

Public relations communications offer several benefits: they help build credibility for a product or company with its various publics, and they help build brand awareness and interest and indirectly have an impact on brand sales. There are some drawbacks to public relations communications. For one, the organization has little control over the message that is delivered by the media. Also, a company often views the effort as wasteful as so little is actually reported by the media in comparison to the amount of information distributed to the media.

Key Terms

annual report, 270

blog, 264

blogging, 264

booklet, 269

borrowed-interest strategy, 265

branded content, 258

brochure, 269

buzz marketing, 258

corporate advertising, 254

external publics, 253

internal publics, 253

lobbying, 261

media kit, 268

newsletter, 268

press conference, 268

press release, 267

product placement, 258

product seeding, 258

public affairs, 261

public relations, 253

publicity, 257

Review Questions

1. What are the essential differences between media advertising and public relations communications?

2. Identify and briefly explain the role of public relations in the following areas:
   a) corporate communications
   b) reputation management
   c) product publicity
   d) product seeding
   e) community relations

3. What is the difference between product placement, branded content, and product seeding?

4. What is lobbying and why is it necessary for an organization to conduct such a practice?

5. What are the key elements of a public relations strategy?

6. What is a borrowed-interest public relations strategy? Provide an example of this strategy that isn't in the text.

7. What is a media kit and what role does it serve?

8. What are the roles of special interest newsletters and special interest reports that are distributed by companies, organizations, and associations?

9. Public relations effectiveness is measured based on outputs, outgrowths, and outcomes. Briefly explain each form of measurement.

10. What are the advantages and disadvantages of using public relations as a marketing communications medium? Briefly explain.

Discussion and Application Questions

1. Considering the nature of the business environment today, do you think that public relations will play a more significant role or less significant role in future marketing communications strategies? State your position and justify it based on your vision of the future business environment.

2. What is your opinion of product placement? Is it a fad or will it continue to grow in importance? Is it really more effective than regular forms of brand

advertising? Review the IMC Highlight **Buzz Pays!** for essential insights about product placement.

3. How important will blogs be in future public relations communications campaigns? Provide some examples of organizations that are successfully employing blogs in their public relations strategies.

4. Conduct some secondary research that involves an organization facing a crisis situation. How did it handle the situation from a public relations perspective? Were its strategies effective?

5. Conduct some secondary research that involves an organization using public relations strategies to launch a new product. How important was public relations in the marketing communications mix? What were the objectives of the public relations effort? Was the plan effective in achieving its goals?

6. Find some examples of organizations that are involved in advocacy advertising. Can you determine why that organization is involved in communicating that specific message?

7. Identify two different companies that compete with each other in the same industry or markets. Analyze the information they provide on their websites in terms of public relations value. Are these companies maximizing the potential of the web for communicating vital information to customers? Sample sites to visit include Procter & Gamble and Colgate-Palmolive, Coca-Cola and Pepsi-Cola, Bell and TELUS, Hudson's Bay Company and Sears, etc.

8. Visit a company website of your choosing. Usually, there is a link to the press release section of the site. Review that company's five latest press releases. What subject matter did they deal with? Try to determine how the company uses public relations to its advantage.

Endnotes

1. Chris Daniels, "An increased profile," *Marketing*, July 26/August 2, 2004, pp. 13, 14.

2. Paul Holmes, "Senior marketers are sharply divided about the role of PR in the overall mix," *Advertising Age*, January 24, 2005, p. C1.

3. Patrick Brethour, "PR 101: How CN botched damage control," *Globe and Mail*, date unknown.

4. "Public relations: Branding's secret weapon," **www.profitguide.com/sales/article. jsp?content=1073.**

5. Gigi Suhanic, "Once-in-a-decade shot," *Financial Post*, April 12, 2005, p. FP10.

6. "Nike, Tiger on the ball," *Advertising Age*, April 18, 2005, p. 3.

7. Keith McArthur, "How Auto-Ref scored a PR ace," *Globe and Mail*, March 22, 2005, p. B3.

8. Marc Graser, "Toyota's Prius hybrid finds favor in Hollywood," *Advertising Age*, September 12, 2005, p. 14.

9. Pia Musngi, "Falcon Beach to boast bods, and now, brands," *Media in Canada*, January 5, 2006, **www.mediaincanada.com.**

10. Sam Lubell, "Advertising's twilight zone: The signpost up ahead may be a virtual product," *New York Times*, January 2, 2006, **www.nytimes.com.**

11. "Un-flashy: Fuji's subtle approach to word of mouth," *Strategy*, September 5, 2005, p. 63.

12. Tim Hortons, **www.timhortons.com.**

13. Packaging Association of Canada, "Lobbying," November 2003, **www.pac.ca/services/lobbying.html.**

14. Thomas L. Harris, *Value-Added Public Relations* (Chicago: NTP Publications, 1998), p. 243.

15. *First Principles*, 2004 Corporate Responsibility Report, RBC Financial Group.

16. Kevin Newcomb, "MWW debuts blog marketing practice," **www.clickz.com/news/print.php/3454471.**

17. Dil Cakim, "Measuring the blogosphere and beyond," *DM News*, July 18, 2005, **www.dmnews.com.**

18. Kris Oser, "More marketers test blogs to build buzz," *Advertising Age*, September 13, 2004, pp. 3, 49.

19. Keith McArthur, "Online era leaves media out of the loop: PR expert," *Globe and Mail*, March 21, 2005, p. B5.

20. Walter K. Lindenmann, Ketchum Public Relations, "It's the hottest thing these days in PR," a presentation at PRSA Counselors Academy, Key West, Florida, April 25, 1995.

21. Kevin Goldman, "Winemakers look for more publicity," *Wall Street Journal*, September 29, 1994, p. 53.

EVENT MARKETING AND SPONSORSHIPS

After studying this chapter you will be able to

1. explain the importance of event marketing and sponsorships in contemporary marketing

2. differentiate among the various forms of event sponsorships

3. evaluate the role of event marketing and sponsorships in the marketing communications mix

4. assess the criteria that a marketing executive considers before participating in event marketing and sponsorships

5. identify and assess the various evaluation techniques that deter-

mine the effectiveness of event marketing and sponsorship activities

6. describe the steps in event marketing planning

7. evaluate various marketing strategies for making an event successful

8. identify and explain the key elements of event marketing execution

Event marketing and sponsorships are fast becoming important elements of the marketing communications mix, and for very good reasons. According to David Lackie, public relations manager for Harry Rosen, "Events can build loyalty that's steadfast and unshakeable. They take time, are an investment, and quite often do not show immediate results. But if you are consistent and commit to it for a number of years, the payoff in customer loyalty can be tremendous."[1] This chapter explores the exciting world of event marketing and shows how a variety of companies reap the benefits of event and sponsorship participation.

AN INTRODUCTION TO EVENT MARKETING

Event marketing

The process, planned by a sponsoring organization, of integrating a variety of communications elements with a single event theme.

There is a distinct difference between event marketing and event sponsorship. **Event marketing** is the process, planned by a sponsoring organization, of integrating a variety of communication elements with a single event theme. For example, Nike plans and executes road races in large urban markets and supports the event with advertising, public relations, and sales promotion activities to achieve runner participation and buzz for the event. In other words, the costs of developing or participating in an event are only part of the costs. To maximize the true benefit of event marketing, a significant investment must be made in other forms of marketing communications. Such investments are necessary to generate awareness of the event, sell tickets to it, and generate publicity for it.

Event sponsorship

The financial support of an event in exchange for advertising privileges associated with that event.

Event sponsorship is the financial support of an event, say a sports event, theatre production, or cause marketing effort, in return for advertising privileges associated with the event. Bell Canada was recently announced the communications sponsoring partner for the Vancouver 2010 Winter Olympics. Bell is giving the organizing committee $200 million: $90 million in cash; $60 million in communications equipment; and $50 million in games-related marketing. As the games get closer, the Olympic logo will be all over everything Bell does in Canada. One might question such a large investment in only one event, but the CEO of Bell, Michael Sabia, says, "Just a one percent increase in market share will generate $300 million worth of improved shareholder value. Further, there is no better brand than the Olympic Games with which to associate our company. It is the perfect platform to enhance Bell's brand as the leading national provider of communications services."[2]

Usually, an event marketer offers sponsorships on a tiered basis. For instance, a lead sponsor or sponsors would pay a maximum amount and receive maximum privileges. Bell is lead sponsor of the 2010 Olympics in Vancouver and will maximize the benefits of that association. Other sponsors will pay less and receive fewer privileges.

Event marketing is big business! According to IEG Consulting, a Chicago-based sponsorship measurement firm, the North American sponsorship market is valued at $11.14 billion (2004).[3] Growth in event marketing is being fuelled by deals with traditional broadcast properties that include a sponsorship element. In the age of TiVo (US) and PVRs (Canada), advertisers and TV programmers are developing alternatives to the 30-second commercial that are less about buying media and more about interaction and experiential marketing.

A recent survey among North American marketing executives indicates that events deliver the greatest return on investment over other customary tools, including advertising. As indicated in the Bell example above, Bell expects considerable financial return for its Olympic investment. Executives (82 percent of respondents in the survey) now perceive event marketing to be a strategic and efficient business tool. It will play a greater role in their marketing mix and be allocated more dollars. Executives hold similar views on other integrated marketing communications components, particularly public relations and online communications. Event marketing often includes a public relations and online communications component through news and feature articles, employee communications, advertising, and promotions.[4]

FIGURE **10.1**   **Leading Sponsorship Investors in North America**

Rank	Company	Amount ($ million)
1	PepsiCo. Inc.	$250M–$255M
2	Anheuser-Busch	$240M–$245M
3	General Motors Corp.	$185M–$190M
4	The Coca-Cola Compnay	$180M–$185M
5	Nike Inc.	$160M–$165M
6	Miller Brewing Company	$155M–$160M
7	DaimlerChrysler Corp.	$125M–$130M
8	Ford Motor Company	$100M–$105M
9	McDonald's Corp.	$ 95M–$100M
10	Eastman Kodak Company	$ 95M–$100M

Source: IEG Sponsorship Report, Chicago 2003.

General Motors
www.gm.ca

Given that Canada is 10 percent the size of the United States in almost everything (our population is 10 percent of that of the US), the Canadian market size is traditionally estimated at 10 percent of the US market for everything from toothpaste to beer. So why not also apply the 10 percent rule to investment in sponsorship? Given this percentage, sponsorships here could be worth as much as $1.1 billion annually.

Investment in event marketing and sponsorships is mainly divided among five areas: sports; entertainment; festivals, fairs, and annual events; causes; and the arts. A list of the leading event marketing and sponsorship companies in North America appears in Figure 10.1. Among the leaders are PepsiCo, General Motors, and the Coca-Cola Company. In Canada, GM sponsors the Canadian national ski team as well as numerous national and international ski and snowboarding events held here each year. Among GM's entertainment sponsorships are the annual Juno Awards and the Montreal Jazz Festival. GM also has a philanthropic side, making annual contributions to educational, civic, social, and environmental causes. GM is a lead sponsor of the Women's Health Matters Forum and Expo held each year in Toronto.[5]

Sports Marketing Sponsorship

Sports sponsorship occurs at amateur and professional levels and can be subdivided into classifications from local events to global events (see Figure 10.2). Among the various categories of sponsorships, sports sponsorship is by far the largest in terms of dollars invested by marketing organizations. It presently accounts for about 65 percent of all sponsorship investments, or approximately $7.2 billion.

Sports sponsorships tend to be dominated by certain industries and manufacturers. In Canada, for example, the automobile industry is well represented by General Motors and Ford, the brewing industry by Molson and Labatt, and the financial industry by RBC Financial Group, BMO Financial Group, Visa, and MasterCard.

Sponsorships are a key component of BMO's marketing mix. BMO partners with organizations that help create brand exposure nationally while also building regional visibility. BMO is a proud sponsor of women's golf in Canada on several levels: the BMO Financial Group Women's Open, the only LPGA event in Canada; BMO Financial

FIGURE **10.2**   The Various Levels of Sports Event Marketing

The investment in sports sponsorship increases at each level moving upwards on the chart. Organizations choose between spending locally to support community events at relatively low cost to investing in national and international sponsorships at significantly higher cost. Such decisions are based on how sponsorships fit with other marketing communications strategies and the overall marketing strategy of the organization.

Level	Example
Global	Olympic Games and World Cup Soccer
International	Ryder Cup Golf, Tour de France, Grand Prix
National	Canadian track and field championships
Regional	Provincial summer and winter games, Ontario Hockey League, Quebec Major Junior Hockey League, etc.
Local	Minor sports programs, road races, walks, etc.

Group Future Links, a junior golf development program; and BMO Financial Group Women's Tour, a three-event series for Canadian women golfers on their way to the bigger LPGA tour. See Figure 10.3 for an illustration. BMO is also a lead sponsor of various Skate Canada events (figure skating) and BMO Financial Group Nations' Cup, an international equestrian event held each year in Calgary. BMO was recognized as Canada's Corporate Citizen of the Year in 2004.[6]

As noted in Figure 10.2, an organization's involvement in sports sponsorship does not have to be extravagant. The extent of involvement and the financial commitment depends upon the organization's marketing objectives and its overall strategy. To illustrate, Visa associates with national and international events, a reflection of the card's status around the world. In contrast, Tim Hortons prefers to sponsor local sports programs all across Canada. The company's Timbits Minor Sports Program provides team jerseys for community-based youth soccer and hockey leagues. The initiative stems from the local franchisees and their desire to be involved with local market events. The sponsorship program fits nicely with the target audience the company is trying to reach.

A recent phenomenon associated with event sponsorship is the practice of ambush marketing. **Ambush marketing** is a strategy used by non-sponsors to capitalize on the prestige and popularity of an event by giving the false impression they are sponsors. Such a strategy works especially well if people are confused about who the real sponsors are. To illustrate, consider what happened in the 2002 Winter Olympic Games in Salt Lake City. Labatt was a major advertising sponsor on the CBC network (which held the broadcast rights in Canada). During the Olympic period, Molson placed Olympic-themed television ads (showing Canada's Olympic hockey opponents as being afraid to face our national team) on competing networks—a classic case of ambush marketing.[7]

Tim Hortons
www.timhortons.com

Ambush marketing

A strategy used by non-sponsors of an event to capitalize on the prestige and popularity of the event by giving the false impression they are sponsors.

FIGURE **10.3** **BMO Financial Group Actively Sponsors Junior Golf and Women's Golf in Canada**

®/TM Trademarks of Bank of Montreal.

We're helping young golfers recognize their potential.

Since 1996, the Future Links junior golf development program has introduced nearly 200,000 kids to the game of golf. As well, we've also given them the chance to witness the true artistry of the game by sponsoring the BMO Financial Group Canadian Women's Open. At BMO Financial Group, we're proud to bring the spirit of the game to all Canadians.

BMO Financial Group
For the world you live in.

Source: Courtesy of BMO.

Venue marketing (venue sponsorship)

Linking a brand name or company name to a physical site, such as a stadium, arena, or theatre.

Venue marketing or **venue sponsorship** is another form of event sponsorship. Here, a company or brand is linked to a physical site, such as a stadium, arena, or theatre. In Canada, there is the Air Canada Centre (home of the Toronto Maple Leafs and Raptors), GM Place (home of the Vancouver Canucks), and Rexall Place (home of the Edmonton Oilers). Pre-eminent title positions like these break through the clutter of other forms of advertising, but it does come at a cost. Air Canada spent $20 million for a 20-year agreement for the naming rights to the Leaf's home rink. Hummingbird, a software development company, paid a flat fee of $5 million to have its name on a performing arts theatre in Toronto.[8]

Besides their name on the building, most naming rights partners receive a luxury box plus a selection of regular seat tickets, rights to use the team's trademark in advertising, and coach or player appearances. Companies may also receive in-arena display areas for their products.[9] It's all a matter of negotiating the right deal. Venue marketing is illustraed in Figure 10.4.

At the Air Canada Centre, an arena owned by Maple Leaf Sports and Entertainment, there are also sponsors within the building—platinum, gold, and silver—depending on the desired scope of the association. Platinum members pay $2 million a contract for the best advertising inventory and title rights to special timeout segments during the games. IBM is a platinum sponsor and places high value on other intangibles. They can entertain clients in the Hot Stove Lounge, have access to special rooms for business presentations, and then attend a Raptors or Leafs game. Schmoozing like that can help move a potential sale further down the pipeline.[10]

For a more detailed list of corporations involved in venue marketing, see Figure 10.5.

What's thriving in sports marketing is the concept of **value-added sponsorships**, where hefty doses of public relations and media exposure accompany a marketer's sponsorship

FIGURE **10.4** **The Branding of Sports Venues Helps Improve Brand Awareness**

Source: Courtesy of Dick Hemingway.

FIGURE **10.5** **Venue Marketing Is Popular among North American Corporations**

AIR CANADA CENTRE ($20 MILLION, 20-YEAR DEAL)

Sponsor: Air Canada
Toronto Maple Leafs (hockey), Toronto Raptors (basketball), Toronto Rock (lacrosse)

PEPSI CENTRE ($68 MILLION, 20-YEAR DEAL)

Sponsor: PepsiCo.
Colorado Avalanche (hockey), Denver Nuggets (basketball)

CONTINENTAL AIRLINES ARENA ($29 MILLION, 12-YEAR DEAL)

Sponsor: Continental Airlines
New Jersey Devils (hockey), New Jersey Nets (basketball)

COORS FIELD ($15 MILLION OVER INDEFINITE PERIOD)

Sponsor: Adolph Coors Co.
Colorado Rockies (baseball)

DELTA CENTRE ($25 MILLION, 20-YEAR DEAL)

Sponsor: Delta Air Lines
Utah Jazz (basketball)

FIRST UNION CENTRE ($40 MILLION, 30-YEAR DEAL)

Sponsor: First Union Corp.
Philadelphia Flyers (hockey), Philadelphia 76ers (basketball)

HEINZ FIELD ($57 MILLION, 20-YEAR DEAL)

H.J. Heinz Company
Pittsburgh Steelers (football)

STAPLES CENTRE ($116 MILLION, 20-YEAR DEAL)

Sponsor: Staples
Los Angeles Clippers (basketball), Los Angeles Lakers (basketball), Los Angeles Kings (hockey)

Source: Reprinted with permission from the October 28, 2002, issue of *Advertising Age*, Special Report on Sports Marketing, "Naming rites," p. S7. Copyright, Crain Communications Inc., 2002.

agreement. The key in this strategy is a lucrative player endorsement. Reebok International was quick to strike an endorsement deal with young hockey sensation Sidney Crosby—a 5-year deal worth $2.5 million, more money than any hockey company has ever paid established stars. Crosby is considered by many experts to be the heir apparent to Wayne Gretzky, hockey's all-time leading scorer. Crosby is included in Reebok's global advertising campaign that uses the slogan "I am what I am." Reebok is investing heavily in Crosby's ability to help build its hockey business, and for marketing purposes Reebok sees him as "the total package." When interviewed by the media Crosby is always seen wearing Reebok clothing and equipment (see Figure 10.5). As part of the deal, Crosby will participate in a variety of company business-building functions throughout the life of the deal.[11]

Why do corporations invest in sports marketing and how effective is the investment? The true benefits of event marketing are discussed later in the chapter. For now, simply consider that key indicators of success are brand awareness and brand association with the event. For example, which credit card sponsors the Olympics? Which company sponsors the men's national curling championships each year, an event called the Brier? If you can or can't answer these questions, it helps a company justify the benefits and drawbacks of investing in sports sponsorships.

Entertainment Sponsorships

Coca-Cola
www.coca-cola.com

Canadian corporations invest huge amounts of money to sponsor concerts and secure endorsements from high-profile entertainment personalities in the hopes that the celebrity-company relationship will pay off in the long run. Companies like Molson and PepsiCo, which are interested in targeting youth and young adult segments, use entertainment sponsorship as a vehicle for developing pop-music and youth-lifestyle marketing strategies. Pepsi-Cola recently decided to end its sponsorship of the *Academy Awards* because it is not a distinct enough platform for reaching younger people. Typically, shows such as the *Academy Awards* present opportunities to launch a big-event commercial or a new campaign. Coca-Cola replaced Pepsi on the broadcast, citing the "continuing marketing power" of the show and the "diverse audience" it reaches as reasons to get involved.[12] Coca-Cola is also a lead sponsor of the hit show *American Idol*; branded product placements for Coca-Cola are common on *American Idol*.

Film Festivals

Film festivals are enticing because they reach a cross-section of adult target audiences. At a top film festival, a corporate sponsor hitches a ride on the most glamorous coattails of all—movie stars! For two prominent film festivals, the Toronto International Film Festival and the Festival des Films du Monde in Montreal, there are waiting lists for platinum sponsorships. These events showcase branded products not only to filmgoers, but also to the thousands of deep-pocketed domestic and international wheeler-dealers who do business at festivals. Key clients get to hobnob with the movie stars.

Toronto International Film Festival
www.bell.ca/filmfest

Sponsorship revenue for the Toronto International Film Festival averages $4 million annually, with top sponsor spots occupied by Bell Canada, Visa, Motorola, and FedEx Express (notice that the film festival's URL contains Bell's website address—a true indication of Bell's role as leading sponsor). Visa leverages its sponsorships of film festivals in Toronto, Montreal, and Vancouver in several ways. There are exclusive ticket packages that include advance purchase opportunities to Visa cardholders, and there are "Visa Screening Rooms": posh, branded lounges where purchasers of special passes can avoid long lines and enjoy a relaxing environment with refreshments for up to one hour before a screening (see Figure 10.6). Pass holders enter the theatre before other patrons and have first choice of seats. As for corporate hosting, Visa entertains its best clients at film festival events.[13]

Film and other types of theatre festivals are now popular with marketing decision makers as organizers are offering customized packages better suited to sponsor's unique needs. The Toronto International Film Festival approaches sponsorships as true partnerships. It offers a broad spectrum of associations: from corporate entertaining to marketing exposure and product sampling opportunities.[14] As the saying goes, these types of sponsorships reach a "class" audience rather than a "mass" audience.

Television

Due to the waning impact of the 30-second TV commercial, the television industry and programs are offering branded sponsorship opportunities. The poker craze has swept over North America in recent years, largely due to television exposure on cable channels such as TSN and Rogers Sportsnet. Branded products are capitalizing on this trend. Degree, a unisex deodorant brand, had been suffering double-digit sales declines for years and

FIGURE **10.6** **Visa Capitalizes on Entertainment Sponsorships to Reach a More Exclusive Audience**

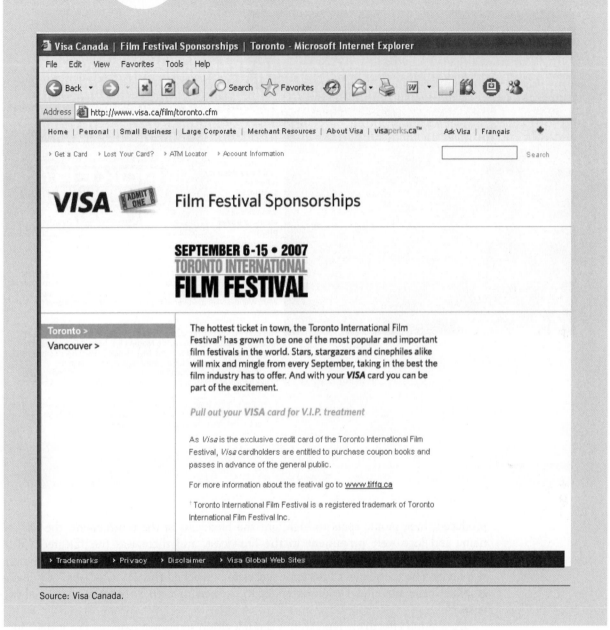

Source: Visa Canada.

decided to relaunch with distinct male and female product lines. The package was redesigned, new masculine-named scents were introduced, and a new ad campaign hit the airwaves. Splashy television poker tournaments, a non-traditional opportunity, would play a key role in the relaunch. Refer to Figure 10.7 for an illustration.

For Degree, poker was a perfect fit—it was seen as a metaphor to help position Degree as "the thinking man's deodorant" and for the man who takes "calculated risks." By partnering with TSN, the Degree Poker Championship was broadcast nationally. TSN

FIGURE **10.7** A Sponsorship Association with TSN Helps Relaunch Degree

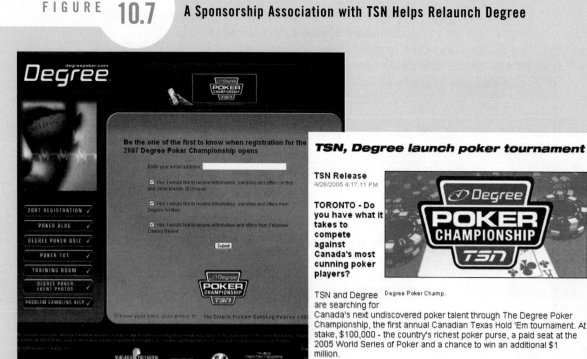

Source: Unilever Canada Inc.

produced three promo spots to highlight the broadcast of the tournament, the Degree name and logo were prominent in the broadcast, and there was the "Degree All-in Moment" that was mentioned and flashed on the screen at the critical moment in a high-risk hand. The tournament broadcast successfully reached the 25- to 40-year-old demographic Degree was after. Degree extended its partnership with TSN for an additional two years.[15]

L'Oréal has effectively tapped into the television sponsorship arena. For insight into its activities and success, read the IMC Highlight **L'Oréal Sponsors Canadian Idol: Because It's Worth It**.

Culture and the Arts Sponsorships

Arts and cultural event opportunities embrace such areas as dance, film, literature, music, painting, sculpture, and theatre. What separates cultural events from sports and entertainment events is the audience size. Depending on the sponsor, this is an advantage or a disadvantage. A company such as Molson might prefer the mass audience reach of a sports event, whereas Mercedes-Benz and BMW might prefer to reach a more selective and upscale audience through an arts event. Perhaps only 2500 people attend the arts event, but those people can be powerful. Typically, their education level would be above

L'ORÉAL SPONSORS *CANADIAN IDOL*: BECAUSE IT'S WORTH IT

One of the most-watched television shows in Canada in recent years has been *Canadian Idol*—in excess of 3 million viewers when the show gets into its final stages and the Idol is announced. L'Oréal Canada has benefited greatly from its sponsorship association with the show. In fact, the integrated marketing strategy is the most significant mass media effort the company has ever undertaken in Canada.

L'Oréal's marketing objective was to reach a younger demographic and to alter the image of the brand—to make it more of a hip brand. The sponsorship strategy was a package that included opening and closing billboards, a major presence on the *Canadian Idol* website, and sponsorship announcements during on-air promotion of the show. As well, L'Oréal products were included in several show segments. For example, one segment encouraged viewers to go to L'Oréal's website, upload pictures of themselves, and create new looks, an activity that resulted in lots of traffic to the site.

What are the results of the sponsorship? Sales growth in the first year of sponsorship was up 30 percent during the *Idol* promotion. In terms of brand awareness and brand association, more than half of *Canadian Idol* viewers directly linked L'Oréal to the show. As well, 75 percent of viewers sincerely appreciated the beauty tips that were integrated into the show.

The targeting objective was achieved as awareness and interest in the brand among younger females rose considerably. *Canadian Idol* proved to be an ideal vehicle for promoting the brand in English Canada. In the past, L'Oréal concentrated most of its efforts in Quebec. Dominique De Celles, vice-president and general manager of L'Oréal Canada, says "Sponsorships are at the heart of L'Oréal's communication strategies because they allow the brand to build an emotive link with consumers."

L'Oréal evaluates its sponsorships on the basis of the ratio of investment to media value, its pertinence, and short-term impact on sales and medium-term impact on brand awareness. L'Oréal leveraged the *Idol* association through a contest and special displays in Shoppers Drug Mart stores. The sale of L'Oréal products increased 20 percent at Shoppers Drug Mart during the promotion period.

As a result of this success, L'Oréal is looking at other sponsorship opportunities and is expanding its distribution into other drug retailers. Traditionally, the brand has been sold in department stores. Further, inspired by the success of L'Oréal Canada's *Canadian Idol* campaign, the Australian subsidiary of L'Oréal has decided to sponsor *Australian Idol*.

Adapted from Danny Kucharsky, "Because you're worth it, L'Oréal," *Marketing*, February 9, 2004, p. 8.

average, as would their income. Such an audience profile would be a good match for promoting a new luxury car. A financial services company such as RBC Financial Group or MasterCard may sponsor both large-audience and small-audience events given the diversity of age and income of its customers.

The primary benefit these companies gain by sponsoring the arts is goodwill from the public. Most firms view this type of investment as part of their corporate citizenship objectives; that is, they are perceived as a good, contributing member of society. Bell Canada has always invested in the communities it serves and has a varied sponsorship portfolio that includes major cultural and sporting events that enable it to be present in the community throughout the year. Some of the cultural events sponsored by Bell include the Stratford Festival, the Shaw Festival, and the *Just for Laughs* Festival in Montreal.

Cause Marketing Sponsorships

Cause-related marketing is relevant in the minds of consumers, corporations, and not-for-profit organizations that mean something to consumers. This feeling, when associated with a brand or company, can have a positive effect on the consumer's perception of the brand. Such is the benefit that the CIBC derives from its ongoing title sponsorship of the Canadian Breast Cancer Foundation CIBC "Run for the Cure," where the overall goal is to raise funds to help find a cure for breast cancer. Other sponsors of this cause include Kimberly-Clark

FIGURE **10.8** **Kimberly-Clark Is an Ongoing Sponsor of the Canadian Breast Cancer Foundation**

Sometimes the best way to dry someone's tears is to offer your support.

HELPING TO CREATE A FUTURE WITHOUT BREAST CANCER.

Source: Courtesy of john st. advertising.

BMO Financial Group
www.bmo.com

Worldwide, Air Canada, and the Ford Motor Company of Canada (see Figure 10.8).

In today's competitive business world brands drive marketing, but as brand loyalty diminishes, marketing executives are searching for new ways to connect with consumers emotionally. Not-for-profit organizations are proving to be good business partners for achieving this goal. The right combination produces a win-win situation for both parties. BMO Financial Group, for example, makes a significant investment in civic and community causes to help build vibrant, safe, and tolerant communities. BMO sponsors the United Way, a Take Our Kids to Work program, and Fashion Cares, a program to help fight against AIDS and HIV. BMO also makes financial contributions to hospitals and various foundations. Among them are the Cystic Fibrosis Foundation, University Health Network, and the Foundation for Fighting Blindness. In 2004, BMO's total corporate donations were $37 million, of which $12.8 million was in charitable donations.[16]

Other organizations develop and foster their own causes. Tim Hortons recognizes the benefits of touching their audience on an emotional level and does so through the Tim Horton Children's Foundation. The Foundation is a not-for-profit charitable organization committed to providing a fun-filled camping experience for children from economically disadvantaged homes and is dedicated to fostering within children the quest for a bright future.[17] It raises funds from donation containers at point-of-purchase, donations from other organizations, and an annual fundraiser where franchisees donate all monies raised from the sale of coffee one day each year. The program is fully supported by media advertising that encourages consumers to visit Tim Hortons on the fundraising day.

Experiential Marketing: Product Promotional Tours and Tour Sponsorships

Experiential marketing

A promotion in which potential customers interact directly with a product (e.g., sample giveaways).

Growing in popularity is a concept called experiential marketing, although some refer to the practice as guerilla marketing. **Experiential marketing** is about finding ways for a target audience to interact directly with a product. Product promotional tours and tour sponsorships fall into this category of activity. The use of tour vehicles such as the Hershey's Kissmobile used to be common, but today marketers are moving in the direction of street teams as a means of achieving face-to-face interaction with the target audience. Experiential marketing was initially presented in Chapter 8 (refer to that chapter for additional details).

Global Television
www.canada.com/globaltv

Global Television effectively used street marketing to pump up the buzz for new shows such as *Prison Break* and *E-Ring*. The network used traditional media advertising like television promotional ads, subway, and outdoor advertising to raise awareness. To further catch the public's attention, however, street teams were employed. Individuals known as the Pixmen were outfitted in prison-like outfits (a la *Prison Break*). Attached to the Pixmen were flat screen television monitors (attached to their bodies but above their heads) that played trailers of the new shows. As the Pixmen roamed the streets of downtown Toronto and Vancouver, the effort created quite a bit of buzz.[18]

Wakestock
www.wakestock.com

Tour events and sponsorships of extreme (or fringe) sports events are popular with younger age groups. Fringe sporting events now attract bigger crowds and therefore have captured the marketing attention of mainstream sponsors. Wakestock, a wakeboarding event held in Toronto each summer, attracts 30 000 spectators who are encouraged to interact with marketers—Coors Light, TELUS, and Levi Strauss among them. While many people now wakeboard, it is its growing popularity as a spectator sport that is causing marketing momentum; wakeboarding is an extremely popular sport on ESPN's *X Games*. Wakestock happens over several days and its festival-type atmosphere creates a strong interaction between advertisers and the audience. This type of sponsorship is much more affordable than high-profile, mass-audience sports sponsorships. Levi's objective was to achieve a "cool-but-not-to-cool" cachet from the event.[19]

CONSIDERATIONS FOR PARTICIPATING IN EVENT MARKETING

Companies enter into events and sponsorships in an effort to create a favourable impression with their customers and target groups. For this to be accomplished, the fit between the event and the sponsor must be a good one. For instance, Nike sponsors national and international track and field events as well as community-based events, such as fun runs. Much of the company's success has been based on event sponsorship and the distribution of merchandise that bears Nike's trademark logo—the swoosh. Generally, event sponsorship is a vehicle for building brand awareness and enhancing the reputation of a company or brand. The most effective sponsors generally adhere to the following principles when considering participation in event marketing:

- **Select Events Offering Exclusivity:** If a company needs to be differentiated from its competition within the events it sponsors, it calls for exclusivity so direct competitors are blocked from sponsorship. Also, sponsors are often concerned about the clutter of lower-level sponsors in non-competing categories that reduce the overall impact of the primary sponsor. There is a lot of clutter, for example, in sports events such as NASCAR (brand logos seem to be everywhere).

PepsiCo
www.pepsico.com

- **Use Sponsorships to Complement Other Promotional Activities:** The roles that advertising and promotion will play in the sponsorship must be determined first. Sponsoring the appropriate event will complement the company's other promotional activities. For example, Pepsi-Cola and Frito Lay (both PepsiCo brands) sponsor the Super Bowl and place several ads during the broadcast. To leverage the association with the Super Bowl, both brands combine to advertise a Super Bowl contest (game tickets and other major prizes) in the months preceding the game. Huge in-store displays further promote the Super Bowl connection and a mail-in rebate offer ($10.00 back for various purchase combinations of Pepsi and Tostitos products) encourages consumers to buy. Pepsi's integrated strategy embraces advertising, sales promotion (consumer and trade promotion), and event marketing across key company brands.

- **Choose the Target Carefully:** Events reach specific targets. For example, while rock concerts attract youth, symphonies tend to reach audiences that are older, urban, and upscale. As suggested earlier, it is the fit—or matching—of targets, that is crucial, not the size of the audience.

- **Select an Event with an Image That Sells:** The sponsor must capitalize on the image of the event and perhaps the prestige or status associated with it. For example, a luxury car such as the Mercedes-Benz may be a suitable sponsor for a significant art or cultural event, or a major national golf championship. Mercedes-Benz sponsors the Mercedes Championships in Hawaii, the opening event of the PGA Tour, each year. The prestigious image and status of such events have an impact on the sale of products that project a comparable image; the image and status that come with ownership of a Mercedes-Benz automobile.

- **Establish Selection Criteria:** In addition to using the criteria cited here, companies should consider the long-term benefit that sponsorship offers compared with the costs in the short term. For example, being associated with an event that is ongoing, popular, and successful is wise because there is less risk for the sponsor. Before committing financial resources to an event, a company should also consider whether it is likely to receive communications exposure through unpaid media sources and whether the event organizers will be able to administer the event efficiently. The company must establish objectives in terms of awareness and association scores, image improvement, sales, and return on investment so it can properly evaluate its participation in the activity.

MEASURING THE BENEFITS OF EVENT MARKETING AND SPONSORSHIP

One reason many companies are reluctant to enter into sponsorship programs is that results are difficult to measure. Large sums of money are spent at one time for a benefit that may be short lived. The basic appeal of event marketing is that it provides an opportunity to communicate with consumers in an environment in which they are already emotionally involved. Beyond this, companies conduct marketing research to determine the impact of the sponsorship association. The following indicators, many of which are obtained from research, are used to measure the benefits of sponsorship.

- **Awareness:** How much awareness of the event is there within each target group? How well do people recall the brand or product name that sponsored the event?

- **Image:** What change in image and what increase in consumer perception of leadership or credibility result from the sponsorship?
- **New Clients:** How many new clients were generated as a result of the company's sponsoring an event? Entertaining prospective clients in a luxury box at an event goes a considerable way in building a relationship.
- **Sales:** Do increases in sales or market share occur in the period following the event? Be aware that the real sales benefit may take years. It takes time for a sponsor to become closely associated with an event.
- **Specific Target Reach:** Do the events deliver constituency? Carefully selected events reach specific targets that are difficult to reach by conventional communications. For example, pre-teens and teens are difficult to reach through conventional media but can be reached effectively through sponsorship of concerts and music tours. As discussed earlier, events need not be big in terms of attendance to attract constituency.
- **Media Coverage:** What value was derived from editorial coverage? Did the sponsorship result in free publicity for the sponsor? The industry benchmark for sports sponsorship is currently four to one, meaning $4 in exposure (e.g., free air time) for every $1 spent on sponsorship and its marketing support.

For sponsorships to be successful they must be seamlessly integrated into corporate marketing and marketing communications plans. All forms of communications must be complementary. The organization must leverage the use of its website and incorporate the sponsorship into public relations campaigns as well as run thematic promotions to get all customer groups (trade and consumers) involved. Above all, it has to make a financial commitment above and beyond the rights fees. A general ratio for spending should be three to one: $3 should be spent to promote the relationship to the event for every dollar spent on securing the rights.[20]

For smaller events, success or failure is determined by the financial outcome of the event. Key indicators of success would be the profit the event generated. The event planner and perhaps a financial executive would scrutinize all the revenues and costs associated with planning and operating the event to determine if a profit or loss was ultimately generated. In the pre-planning stage, the budget statement and profit-and-loss statement are based on anticipated revenues and cost estimates, but after the event it is time to compare plan figures to actual figures.

An organization must choose between event marketing (planning and implementing its own event) and event sponsorships (providing financial support in return for advertising privileges). Either option presents challenges and opportunities. For more insight on how companies decide on which approach to take, see the IMC Highlight **Hooking Up with the Right Event**.

PLANNING THE EVENT

Should an organization decide to develop its own event, it must be comfortable with an exhaustive planning process. Putting the plan into place is one thing—executing it is quite another! As in the case of many other forms of marketing communications, a more prudent approach may be to outsource the activity, allowing experts in this field to do the job.

An organization's marketing team carefully considers the role of an event or sponsorship to ensure it is an appropriate opportunity for achieving the company's business objectives. The organization's primary role is to identify the overall goal and marketing objectives, identify the target audience and timing, consider the financial implications (revenues, costs, and profit), and evaluate the results. Working with the client organization, the event planner develops the event theme, identifies the best venue, and establishes the marketing strategy and implementation plan. The event planner's role is tactical in nature at the implementation stage, as all kinds of concerns need to be addressed.

IMC HIGHLIGHT

HOOKING UP WITH THE RIGHT EVENT

Companies approach sponsorships from different angles. Some companies like to develop their own events while others like to sponsor ongoing, popular events that effectively reach their target market. Such is the difference between Nike Canada and TELUS.

Nike likes to launch its own youth-oriented events and each year creates events from scratch. TELUS, on the other hand, is not in the event marketing business, so it supports established events. According to John Mikkelsen, assistant vice-president of corporate partnerships at TELUS, "We receive about five or six sponsorship proposals every week and choosing which ones to be involved with is a daunting task."

Nike develops its own events because of the "ownership" factor. Its events can resonate directly with the consumers it chooses to target. Nike Canada created the Nike Hockey Training Program, an event that featured Calgary Flames star Jarome Iginla and Rick Hesketch, Calgary's strength and conditioning coach. The program included on-ice instruction and off-ice conditioning programs run in Vancouver and Toronto and attracted 2000 young hockey

players and parents—a prime audience for Nike hockey products.

TELUS likes the benefits of sponsoring established events. According to Mikkelsen, "Supporting existing and well-known events helps build corporate citizenship, and being a premier corporate citizen is one of our goals." The company will provide financial support to events that need it—for example, TELUS is the lead sponsor of the TELUS World Ski & Snowboard Festival. Mikkelsen does acknowledge one disadvantage of sponsoring ongoing events, and that's the clutter of brand sponsors wanting to be seen and heard at an event. For that reason, TELUS only gets involved if it can be the lead sponsor.

The association with the Ski & Snowboard Festival has paid off for TELUS on two key measures: brand awareness and brand association with the event. Mikkelsen says that in popular blogs and chat rooms, participants and spectators just call the competition the 'TELUS.'"

Adapted from Chris Daniels, "Show time," *Marketing,* January 16, 2006, pp. 16, 17.

Among these are staging the event, having adequate and trained staff, operations and logistics planning, and safety and security. Successful events run smoothly, moving like clockwork from one activity to another. To do so requires careful planning down to the minutest of details (see Figure 10.9).

Event Concept Development

The initial stage of planning is developing the concept. In determining the nature of the event, the planner considers the event's purpose, the audience it will reach, available resources, potential venues, and timing. In terms of *purpose*, an event that is designed to transfer information to prospective clients would be much different from one intended to entertain an audience. The former might have a business tone and style, while the latter would be much more upbeat and participative. To illustrate, an event with a trade show orientation (e.g., some kind of business fair where new products are introduced to the market) is much different from the annual Calgary Stampede. The Calgary Stampede is a community event that is presented with all the enthusiasm and passion that the people of Calgary and all of Alberta can muster. The Stampede represents the historical and cultural fabric of the West.

The Calgary Stampede
http://calgarystampede.com

The **theme** of the event should be linked to the purpose and consider the needs of the audience. Events tend to adopt a colour scheme and a tagline that tie various components of the event together. For example, tickets, programs, promotional literature, and signs are usually designed to look like they are all part of a package. Key influences on theme development are one's imagination and money. The latter always brings a sense of reality to one's imagination! Potential themes could involve history (the organization's history), geography and culture (the location of the organization or the event), sports (being part

FIGURE **10.9** The Event Marketing Planning Process

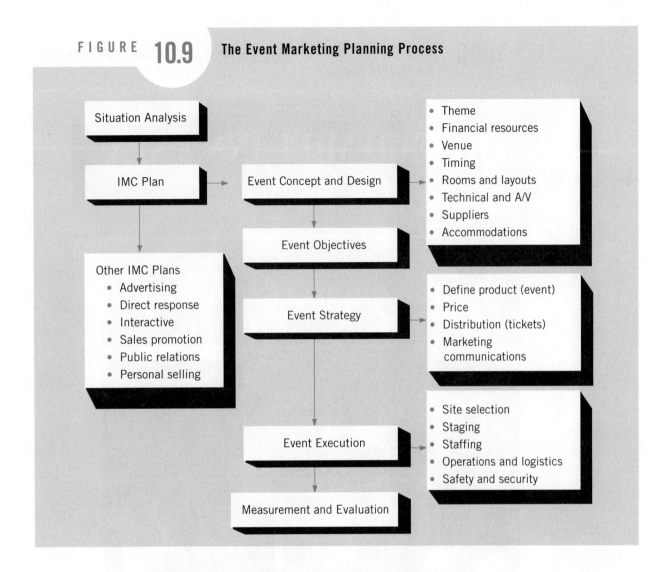

of a sports event that fits with the product), music and entertainment (offers significant appeal for younger audiences), and so on.

Once the theme is determined, the next decision is *venue*. Will the venue be a traditional setting such as a hotel, convention centre, arena, or stadium (see Figure 10.10)? Or will it be something unusual such as a parking lot or a site at a company facility? Or will it move from location to location, as in the case of product promotional tours? Regardless of the venue, the planner must carefully consider factors such as sound, lighting, and other technical issues, and availability of parking and public transportation. And of course, there's always the unpredictability of the weather. Should the event be inside or outside?

The **financial resources** must be considered immediately. Much like an advertising budget, where a relatively small budget precludes the use of television advertising, an event's budget quickly determines the degree of extravagance. What an event planner would like to do and what the planner can actually do are usually quite different—a good idea is only a good idea if it is financially viable. Therefore, the event planner must carefully balance creative instincts with the financial resources of the organization.

The **timing** of an event is often linked to the season or weather. For example, the Canadian Home Show, an annual show held at Exhibition Place in Toronto, is held in early April each year. The show is timed to coincide with the public's interest in home improvements and renovations, which tends to peak in the early spring. Essentially, there

FIGURE **10.10** **Hotels and Conference Centres Actively Market Their Facilities to Conference Planners**

Source: Reprinted by permission of The Old Mill Inn & Spa.

are four time-related factors to consider: season, day of the week, time of day, and duration of the event. Business trade shows, for example, are usually scheduled on weekdays. In contrast, home and leisure shows cover weekends as well as weekdays, with traffic at the show peaking on the weekends.

Designing the Event

Once the concept decisions have been made, the next stage is *design*. For the purpose of illustration, let's assume we are planning a two-day business conference at which several prominent business speakers will make presentations about various aspects of marketing communications. Attendees will include advertising agency personnel, marketing executives, as well as managers employed in sales promotion and public relations. The theme of the conference is "How to Communicate Effectively with Youth," a hot topic among marketing communications practitioners.

In designing this conference, key decision areas include venue, room layout, technical requirements, food and beverage requirements, material suppliers, and hotel room availability. Regarding *venue*, a downtown hotel location in a major city would likely be a logical choice because the target audience works in that environment. The hotel's banquet room facilities will be considered, because a room for 250 to 300 attendees is required, and an additional banquet room will be needed for some of the meals. For example, it is common for keynote speakers to make their presentations after a meal in the main banquet room. Meals without keynote speakers are often in an adjacent room where the atmosphere is less formal.

The **layout** of the banquet room has a bearing on how well the audience and speakers interact with each other. A common layout at this type of conference includes carefully spaced round tables with eight people seated at each. Attendees usually like this arrangement because a table can be reserved for a large group from one company. Such an arrangement encourages collegiality at the table even if the people did not know each other initially. The speakers usually address the audience from an elevated podium at the front of the room.

In today's technologically driven world, the use of proper and effective *technology* is crucial. Most speakers today use slides or video presentations as their primary visual aid to illustrate the key points. Therefore, an event planner must consider all possible audiovisual needs in advance. Typically, the audiovisual aspect of the conference is outsourced to an expert company in this field. This company brings in the equipment (sets it up and tears it down) and is responsible for coordinating the visual aspect of the presentation with the speaker. For extremely large conferences where attendees are distant from the speaker, it is common to have additional screens that display the speaker making the presentation.

Attending a marketing communications conference involves a considerable investment in time and money. Therefore, the attendee expects *good-quality food* and *efficient service* by hotel staff. A poor experience in this area can negate any other positive experiences the attendee has at the conference. Buffet-style meals, for example, seem efficient, but only if there are enough serving stations so the lineups aren't too long. If the meal is served directly to tables, adequate staff must be on duty so that the meal is served within the time allocated. Conferences must stick to their schedule. Light snacks and beverages must be readily available in convenient locations during the break periods.

Dealing with **suppliers** behind the scenes is another key decision area. At our example of the marketing communications conference, print materials were prepared and copied by a printing company to be distributed at registration. It is quite common to have a booklet containing an event schedule, profiles of the various speakers, information about the host sponsor, and copies of the various presentations. As indicated earlier, audiovisual supply requirements must also be confirmed in advance. Food and beverage supplies are the responsibility of the hotel, but all meal requirements must be confirmed ahead of time between the event planner and catering manager.

The final decision area involves having adequate **hotel rooms** available for the anticipated number of attendees. Hotels usually block off rooms until a specified date before the conference. If there aren't enough rooms at the host hotel, additional rooms should be reserved nearby. All promotional materials should include hotel information and indicate the key dates and reservation procedures.

Setting Objectives

As indicated earlier in the chapter, an organization must establish concrete objectives to justify any financial investment in event marketing. Therefore, quantitative objectives are identified—objectives that are realistic, achievable, and measurable. They must be within the realm of what event marketing is capable of achieving. A direct link to sales is not possible, but it may be possible to measure changes in awareness about a company's product as a result of event participation.

Other objectives might relate to the size of audience reached, the ability to reach a specific target audience (e.g., the quality of reach), sponsor recognition levels, sales of sponsor products, the economic impact of the event, and profit. In the example of the marketing communications conference, the event's objective may have been to attract 300 participants (perhaps any number above 200 participants would produce a profit for the event). Since the event will attract a quality target audience of marketing communications practitioners, it could attract additional sponsors who will help defray the costs of planning and executing the conference.

Planning Tools

Run sheet
A schedule of daily events that shows the various dates, times, and locations of activities at an event.

The initial stage of planning is the preparation of an event proposal. The *proposal* should include the objectives of the event as well as details about organization, layout, venue, technical requirements, and any other key considerations such as those discussed above (see Figure 10.11). Certain planning tools are essential in the planning stages. Most important is a *timeline chart* that indicates when various planning activities start and finish. As well, a schedule of daily events, often called a **run sheet**, is essential to list the various dates, times, and locations of activities (see Figure 10.12). The importance of the timeline chart will become clear in the discussion of execution issues later in this chapter. With so many logistical things to consider, it is important to identify a critical path for those elements of the plan that are essential for a successful outcome.

MARKETING THE EVENT

Marketing an event is no different from marketing a product; an integrated plan is needed. The key decisions involve carefully defining the product (event) and then positioning it in the minds of the target audience in a favourable way. Motivating people to attend the event depends on the quality and quantity of marketing communications activities. This section examines some of the essential strategic planning elements.

Product Strategy: Defining the Event

In defining the event, the planner must identify the essential features and benefits of the event that can ultimately be used in messages directed at the target audience. For example, is the purpose to entertain, to provide a learning experience, or to simply have fun with friends? The marketing communications conference cited earlier in the chapter offers a learning experience for participants, who gain from the success and expertise of others. In contrast, attending the Molson Grand Prix of Toronto brings race car enthusiasts together to cheer and celebrate racing excellence. Clearly, the nature of communications to motivate attendance for these two events would be very different. Promotional information for the Molson Grand Prix stresses words such as speed, thrill, and emotion.

In contrast, promotional information for a business conference is quite different. A recent conference planned and implemented by *Strategy* magazine used the theme "Metro versus Retro: How well do you understand the male market?" The conference was officially titled: Understanding Men: Metro versus Retro. The following pitch was used to attract marketing and marketing communications practitioners to attend:

Strategy
www.strategymag.com

This exploration of the evolving state of masculinity around the world will help marketers understand the opportunities and challenges in reaching men today. Advertisers will miss

FIGURE **10.11** **Key Elements of an Event Proposal**

An event proposal is drafted in the preliminary stages of planning to highlight key elements. As planning progresses, the proposal becomes more detailed and execution oriented.

EVENT DESCRIPTION

- Type of event and event name
- Location
- Timing
- Event concept (including goals and objectives)

EVENT MANAGEMENT

- Management responsibilities
- External supplier requirements
- Facility requirements (venue, rooms, layout, etc.)
- Identification of target audience

MARKETING

- Assessment of audience needs
- Competitor analysis (similar events, timing, etc.)
- Product (event definition)
- Price strategy (price ranges, ticket availability, etc.)
- Marketing communications strategy (media advertising, web, public relations)
- Distribution strategy (registration procedures, methods, etc.)

FINANCIAL

- Budget (consideration of all associated costs)
- Profit and loss statement

STAGING

- Theme
- Decor
- Layout
- Sound and lighting

- Catering
- Services (parking, transportation, vehicle requirements, electricity, etc.)

STAFFING

- Recruitment of staff
- Staff training (roles and responsibilities)
- Recruitment of volunteers
- Volunteer training

SAFETY AND SECURITY

- Risk identification and management
- Safety strategy (audience, presenters, entertainers, etc.)
- Security strategy (premises, equipment, cash, etc.)
- Reporting procedures and communications
- First aid

OPERATIONS AND LOGISTICS

- Bump-in (setup)
- Room layout
- Technical execution (sound, lighting, computers, projectors, etc.)
- Attendee traffic flow (venue layout, room locations, meeting rooms, etc.)
- Contingencies (weather, technology failure, accidents, etc.)
- Bump-out (teardown)

EVALUATION

- Actual versus plan (based on objectives)
- Profitability

real men unless they tune in to the ways in which they are adapting to the changing environment. The conference provides pointers for getting it right. The secrets behind some recent and successful campaigns will be presented.[21]

In defining the product (event) and understanding the motivation of the target audience, the event planner discovers what buttons to press to motivate participation.

FIGURE **10.12** **A Sample Run Sheet**

A run sheet is an indispensable planning tool that is updated as needed during planning. It is particularly useful for hotels and conference centres at the execution stage of an event. The schedule below was used at the Ambassador Resort Hotel and Conference Centre, Kingston, Ontario, when it hosted the Ontario Colleges' Marketing Competition in 2002.

THURSDAY, NOVEMBER 14, 2002

2:00–4:00 p.m.	Registration and Team Photographs *(Atrium)*
5:30–7:00 p.m.	Complimentary Buffet Dinner *(Ballroom)*
7:00–7:15 p.m.	Opening Ceremonies *(Ballroom)*
7:15–9:30 p.m.	Marketing Quiz Bowl *(Ballroom)*
10:00–11:30 p.m.	Faculty Social *(Prime Minister's Suite)*

FRIDAY, NOVEMBER 15

7:00–8:00 a.m.	Judges' Breakfast *(East Ballroom)*
7:00–8:00 a.m.	Continental Breakfast, Students and Faculty *(West Central Ballroom)*
8:00 a.m.	First Participants Enter Prep Rooms *(refer to event schedules)*
8:00 a.m.–12:00 p.m.	Judging Begins for Cases, Job Interview, and Sales Presentation
12:00–1:00 p.m.	Judges' Lunch and Faculty Lunch *(East Ballroom)*
1:00–4:00 p.m.	Competition Continues
6:30–7:30 p.m.	Reception *(Ballroom)*
7:30–10:00 p.m.	Awards Banquet *(Ballroom)*

All activities take place at the Ambassador Resort Hotel and Conference Centre.

Pricing Strategy

Price also plays a role in motivating attendance. Literature promoting professional seminars and conferences is easily discarded if the price-value relationship is incongruent. Charge too much for a conference and the value is questioned. Charge too little and people may think they won't learn anything important by attending. All things considered, the pricing decision is a delicate one. To put things in perspective, the registration fee for the one-day "Understanding Men: Metro versus Retro" conference mentioned earlier was $600, not including hotel and travel costs. Such an event might attract 200 people and could prove to be profitable for the sponsoring organization. However, if the price was lowered to less than $500 (say $495), would it attract a larger audience? Pricing an event is much like pricing a product—a lot of psychology is involved.

In contrast, ticket prices for the Molson Grand Prix of Toronto (formerly the Molson Indy) are based on location at the track. A three-day pass that includes a Gold Grandstand seat (near Pit Row and the start and end of the race) goes for $250. Corporate customers wishing to use the event for hospitality purposes have numerous options available: reserved seats in the Champ Club go for $580; corporate suites in Pit Lane are priced at

Molson Grand Prix
www.grandprixtoronto.com

$36 950 (for 50 guests per day); and for those looking for more privacy there's the Pavilion, a tiered, tented, private viewing and dining area overlooking Pit Row at a cost of $45 950 (50 guests per day). It is either the degree of thrill that consumers are looking for or how corporate Canada might use the event for marketing purposes that determines how much they will pay. Over three days, attendance at this event exceeds 100 000 people.

A second pricing consideration involves a plan for purchasing tickets. The sale and distribution of tickets for an event or the registration process for a business conference must be convenient for the participant. As well, the planning organization must decide if it will sell the tickets directly or outsource this task to a specialist, such as Ticketmaster. Consumers now find online ticket buying and event registration very convenient. Therefore, registration could be handled by an organization's website, or handled by the website of a ticket intermediary.

Marketing Communications Strategy

The success of any event is often dictated by the effectiveness of the marketing communications strategy. What message will be delivered to the target audience to motivate participation, and what media will be used to efficiently reach that audience? A separate budget must be drawn up for marketing communications, because it may take a considerable portion of the event's overall budget.

The initial marketing communications decisions are basically **branding** decisions. Typically, an event will adopt a distinctive name, logo, colour scheme, and image. Every component of the communications mix, including tickets, will bear the same logo and colour scheme. Such consistency of presentation gives the event a branded look. For the Tim Hortons Brier (a national men's curling championship) all forms of marketing communications have a common look. The Tim Hortons logo also appears in the centre ring on the ice for maximum exposure during television broadcasts. Refer to the illustration in Figure 10.13.

Among the various elements of the marketing communications mix, advertising, public relations, and Internet communications frequently play key roles in promoting an event. The *advertising strategies* for the event are based on the target market profile and how best to reach the target given the financial resources available. The content of the message and the style of delivery must combine effectively to meet the motivational needs of the audience. Media alternatives include television and radio advertising, magazine and newspaper advertising, direct mail (letters, brochures, and pamphlets), and the Internet.

The size of the media budget obviously dictates media decisions. An event like the Molson Grand Prix of Toronto that attracts a broad cross-section of ages will adopt a multimedia strategy to create awareness and relies heavily on the Internet to communicate specific information and sell tickets. In contrast, an event like the "Understanding Men: Metro versus Retro" conference will use targeted media such as direct mail, email, and business-oriented print media to effectively reach business executives.

Public relations are also essential in generating positive publicity for an event. Organizers of large events frequently hold press conferences, timed appropriately, to build some pre-event publicity. Organizers may also issue press releases, as in the case of the Tim Hortons Brier, held in Regina in 2006, to stimulate interest in the community where the event is taking place. Refer to Figure 10.14 for an illustration. Smaller and more local events send a press release to all local media and then hope for the best—and take care to invite the press to the actual event.

EVENT MARKETING EXECUTION

Execution involves dealing with specific details about an event. A planner usually works from a checklist to ensure that all details are taken care of in the planning stage and the

FIGURE **10.13**   **An Event Is a Brand with a Branded Look**

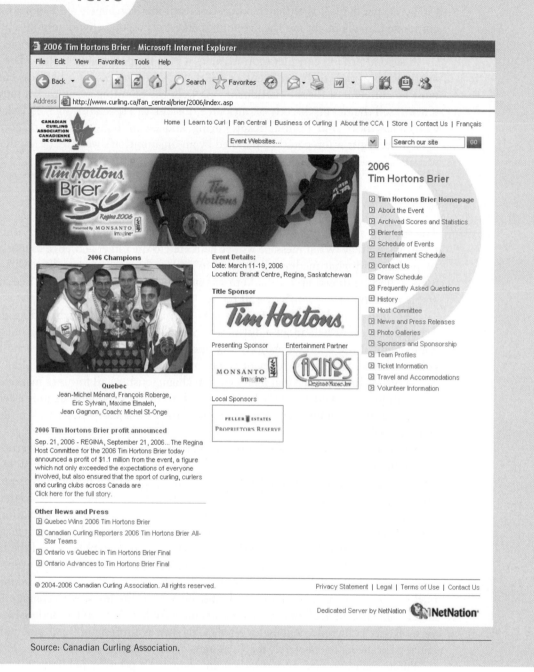

Source: Canadian Curling Association.

execution stage of an event. For the purpose of illustrating event execution, this section assumes that a planner is planning a marketing conference. Discussion will focus on several key areas, including site selection and staging, staffing, operations and logistics, and safety and security. Event execution is complex and a full discussion of such a topic is beyond the scope of this textbook.

Site Selection and Staging

In the theatre, the *stage* is the scene of action. The same is essentially true in event marketing. The scene of action for an event involves a site selected according to consid-

FIGURE **10.14** **A Press Release Announcing Details of the Tim Hortons Brier**

Source: Canadian Curling Association.

erations such as theme development, sound and lighting, and availability of essential services. The venue chosen should be consistent with the event's purpose and theme, and it should provide all of the essential services that are required. Some of the key factors influencing site selection include

- the size of the event (e.g., the number of participants);
- the suitability of the site for planned activities (e.g., formal and informal activities);

- the primary field of play (e.g., the theatre or conference room where the main event will be held);
- the availability of or proximity to accommodation, food, and attractions; and
- the availability of on-site technical support and venue management experience.

Theme development was discussed earlier in the chapter. At the event, the theme should be supported in every aspect, including sound and lighting, decor, and special effects. For example, the theme at a marketing conference could be very subtle and communicated only by signage and colour schemes. At much larger events of a longer duration, music and entertainment (e.g., specific acts revolving around the theme) could be included, along with special props appropriately placed around the venue. If the latter is the choice, an event planner is wise to seek advice from staging and rental companies that offer specialized services in this area.

For the purpose of illustration, let's assume for our one-day marketing conference we need a hall that can accommodate 150 people. The conference theme will be billed as "Marketing in the Future: What Lies Ahead?" The purpose of the conference is to educate and inform concerned marketing managers about what trends and external environments will influence marketing strategies over the next decade. Influential guest speakers from the ranks of industry, government, and the services sectors will present their views on what the future holds and provide insights into how they are already responding.

At this type of conference, most of the speaker's presentations involve computer-generated shows, so a planner must be concerned about room layout—the stage where the speakers are positioned, sound, lighting, and vision. Let's start with **room layout**. Since a standard, rectangular-shaped banquet room is the theatre, the speakers will be placed at one long side of the room, reducing the distance between the front and back of the room. The seating will be laid out in a way conducive to taking notes. For this type of a presentation, there are four basic seating layouts: cabaret, banquet, classroom, and theatre (see Figure 10.15). Of the options available, the cabaret layout seems most appro-

FIGURE **10.15** **An Event Planner Can Choose from a Variety of Room Layouts**

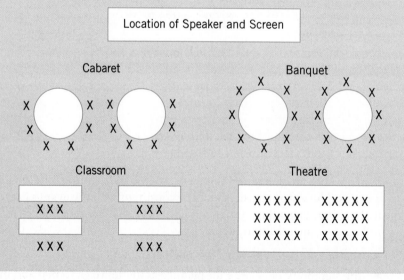

An event planner chooses the room layout based on such factors as ease of serving meals, note taking by participants, audience participation, subgroup activities, and entertainment.

priate, because it allows for good eye contact for all participants and encourages communication among participants at each table.

The guest speakers will be on an elevated platform at one side of the room. The height of the platform considers the sight lines of the audience. The audience must be able to see the speaker and the screen clearly. Appropriate backdrops should be on stage to isolate the presentation area and create a more intimate feeling. At such a conference, the speaker rarely controls the slide presentation—technical coordination is usually the responsibility of an audiovisual expert who is located at the side of the room.

Proper **sound** and **lighting** are essential to create mood and ambience. Professional advice from a sound and lighting expert is recommended. Such advice is usually readily available at conference centres. If audience communication is going to be important, microphones should be strategically situated throughout the conference room.

With all details addressed, the final aspect of staging is **rehearsal**. The rehearsal is an opportunity for everyone to integrate their efforts and to ensure that all technical glitches are remedied. Contingency plans should be established in case the unexpected occurs, which it often does! For example, there should be a plan in place in case a speaker falls sick at the last minute or the projector breaks down.

Additional staging considerations include making arrangements for **catering** and **accommodations**. Since the marketing conference is being held at a conference centre, food and beverages are readily available. Decisions involve the style of service (e.g., buffet or set menu with table service), the timing and availability of snacks and beverages (e.g., during planned breaks), and choosing the menu for each meal. Hotels and conference centres usually offer food and beverage packages that are available in a range of prices (see Figure 10.16). Of course, the planner must negotiate room rates with the host hotel or conference centre. Typically a group rate is negotiated based on number of rooms that will be booked.

Staffing

Planning and executing an event are complex undertakings and, depending on the size and scope of the event, the human resources required can vary considerably. Can you imagine the number of people that would be required (paid and volunteers) when a city hosts the Olympic Games or a national sports championship? For large-scale events the roles and responsibilities of all individuals must be spelled out in detail. Therefore, organization charts are needed for various stages of event planning: pre-event, event, and post-event. In the pre-event stage, the focus is on planning, so anyone connected with marketing, financial, and human resource planning is involved. During the event itself, human resources capacity expands to its fullest, so it is essential that reporting relationships for all operations are delineated. After the event, only those people involved with evaluation and financial planning play a key role.

Operations and Logistics

Canadian Open
www.rcga.org/cdnopen

To illustrate the importance of operations and logistics, consider the planning required to get a major golf championship such as the Bell Canadian Open up and running. For the participants alone, a plan is needed to ensure that

- all golfers, their entourage, and their equipment arrive on time;
- golfers are settled in the correct accommodation and that all equipment is safe and secure;
- the golf course is in immaculate condition (a process that starts months before the competition) and that spectator stands, scoreboards, and crowd barriers are in place; and
- golfers arrive in time for their tee-off each day.

FIGURE **10.16**   **A Sample of a Meal Package Offered by a Conference Centre**

Sample American Plan Menus

Country Buffet Breakfast
7 am to 9:30 am Monday to Saturday

Assorted chilled juices
Fresh fruit slices
Choice of cold cereals
Farm fresh scrambled eggs
Canadian bacon and country sausages
Chef's choice of:
Buttermilk pancakes, waffles or French toast
Selection of freshly baked pastries with jams, jellies and Alliston creamery butter
Coffee and tea

Lunch Buffet
11:30 am to 1:30 pm*

Tossed field greens and market salad selections
Carved roast of the day
Three hot entrées including fresh pasta and a custom grilled specialty
Seasonal country vegetable and potato
Bakery fresh rolls and Alliston creamery butter
Assorted dessert display
Fresh fruit assortment
Coffee and tea

*On Sunday, lunch is replaced with a Buffet Brunch
10 am – 2 pm. An upgrade charge applies.

Dinner - Table d'hôte
Mon to Thurs. 6 pm to 9 pm
Fri.& Sat 5 pm or 8 pm to 10 pm*
Sunday 5 pm – 9 pm**

Market fresh field greens with Italian balsamic vinaigrette

Slow Roasted Prime Rib au jus with garlic potatoes and fresh seasonal vegetables

Bay of Fundy Fillet of Salmon brushed with hoisen glaze and Asian vegetables

Penne Pasta with roasted garlic and spinach cram sauce, topped with parmesan and fresh herbs

Seared Supreme of Chicken with roast corn and tomato salsa, tortilla crisps and oven roast potatoes

Chocolate Cappuccino Torte

Coffee and Tea

*On Friday and Saturday, maximum group size is 40 guests. Larger groups can be accommodated as a private banquet.
**From May to October, dinner is from a Gourmet International Buffet
We suggest groups allocate a minimum of 11/2 hours for Dinner Service

Table d'hôte selections change daily in our non-smoking Riverview Dining Room. It is recommended that groups of over 40 people pre-select a set dinner menu in advance.

Source: Nottawasaga Resort, www.nottawasagaresort.com.

Bump-in (setup)

The setting up of structures and other equipment at an event.

Bump-out (teardown)

The process of dismantling everything after an event.

This set-up process is referred to as the bump-in. **Bump-in**, or **setup**, involves setting up structures and facilities required for an event.[22] For an event such as our marketing conference example, tasks such as installing sound and lighting equipment, computers, projectors, and screens involve the services of a specialist. Regardless of how the bump-in occurs, it is essential that all facilities and equipment are in place and in good working condition prior to the official start of the event. Simply stated, logistics is about getting equipment and people into the right place at the right time so that things run smoothly, and then, once the event is complete, taking everything down. The process of dismantling is referred to as **bump-out**, or **teardown**.

Safety and Security

Imagine the potential safety and security concerns for an event like the Molson Grand Prix of Toronto. For this and similar events that involve large crowds in arenas and stadiums, safety and security issues must be given priority. There must be a plan in place that considers potential crowd behaviour and methods proposed for controlling crowds should the need arise.

At an event everyone must feel safe, including the audience, the staff, and the subcontractors (e.g., technical crews). At large events, accidents can occur, people might fall ill, or something completely unexpected happens. Potential risks include fires, bomb threats, gas leaks, overzealous fans (even riots), and so on. A few years back some NBA basketball players and fans were involved in an ugly brawl, a situation that threatened the safety of both fans and players. Crowd management—the orderly flow of spectators in and out of the venue—is very important. Signage indicating direction and staff barking out commands where necessary play a key role in moving audience pedestrian traffic smoothly.

Disasters can strike in a flash. On September 5, 1972, terrorists invaded the Olympic Village in Germany, killing Israeli athletes and taking hostages. In an ensuing shootout, nine athletes, five guerillas, and one policeman were killed. On May 9, 2001, 120 people were killed in a stampede at a soccer match in Accra, Ghana.[23] People were literally crushed to death against barricades at the side of the field. An inquiry into the disaster concluded "there was an appalling lack of event pre-planning, preparation, risk assessment, and an arrogant indifference to public safety by crucial organizations involved in a highly anticipated championship match."[24] Gross underestimation of the possible crowd attendance at the match was cited as the fundamental cause of the tragedy.

Proper security measures for property, equipment, and cash must also be planned for. As well, the planner must ensure that only certain people have access to specific areas and must act responsibly in case of emergency. Typically, people in positions of authority or special responsibility wear badges identifying their role at the event. Vehicles may be necessary to transport security personnel to areas where emergencies occur. Event planners have a choice of hiring private security firms or members of the local police force.

Summary

Event marketing and sponsorships are now an important element of a firm's marketing communications mix. Sponsorships tend to be concentrated in four areas: sports; entertainment, tours, and attractions; causes; and the arts. Events and sponsorships can be local in nature or they can be expanded to become regional, national, or international in scope. Sports sponsorships and events draw the majority of the sponsorship pie, but interest is now growing faster in the other areas. Organizations that are involved in sports marketing are now pursuing opportunities such as venue marketing and value-added sponsorships.

Prior to getting involved with sponsorships, an organization should establish specific criteria for participation. Factors to consider include product category exclusivity, relationships with other marketing communications programs, the event's ability to reach the desired target market effectively, and the image-building potential offered by the event.

Once the event is over, attention turns to evaluation. In relation to objectives that were established for the event, measures are determined for criteria such as awareness, image enhancement, new business clients, product sales, target market reach, and media coverage. There will be an assessment of all revenues and costs to determine profitability, and to make recommendations for improvements should the event be planned for another occasion.

Should an organization decide to plan its own event, it must be comfortable with a rather exhaustive planning process. The first decision is to evaluate the role of the event or sponsorship to ensure it offers a good opportunity for achieving business objectives. An organization often works with an event planner (a specialist in this area). The organization is responsible for establishing goals and objectives, identifying the target audience, determining the best time for the event, providing adequate financial resources, and evaluating the event for effectiveness. The event planner develops strategies for staging the event, making available properly trained staff to execute the event, planning operations and logistics to make sure everything runs smoothly, and preparing for safety and security issues that could arise during an event.

The first stage in developing an event is to determine the event's concept and design. This involves decisions about the type of event, the name, and theme of the event. Once these decisions are made, attention focuses on issues such as venue alternatives, financial resources required, timing, room layouts, and technical requirements. To secure proper technical advice and support, a planner usually works with a specialist. Technical support is commonly outsourced.

As with other forms of marketing communications planning, qualitative and quantitative objectives are established. Typically, event marketing objectives focus on quality and quantity of target audience reach, potential new business and product sales, the economic impact of the event, and profit. Event marketing strategies involve carefully defining the product (the event) and then positioning it in the minds of the target audience. A good event title and theme become the foundation for building an effective communications strategy for motivating attendance at the event. An effective price strategy is also crucial, because prospective participants evaluate the potential benefits against the cost of attending. To promote the event, a combination of media advertising, web-based communications, and public relations is an effective mix. All communications must have a branded look and present a similar message to the target audience.

At the execution stage, concerns focus on specific details in the following areas: site selection and staging, staffing, operations and logistics, and safety and security. All details must be checked and rechecked to ensure a smooth flow of activities and people.

Key Terms

ambush marketing, 282

bump-in, 306

bump-out, 306

event marketing, 280

event sponsorship, 280

experiential marketing, 291

run sheet, 298

setup, 306

teardown, 306

venue marketing, 283

venue sponsorship, 283

Review Questions

1. What is the difference between event marketing and event sponsorship?

2. What is ambush marketing and what benefits does it offer?

3. Identify and briefly explain the main classifications of event marketing.

4. What is experiential marketing and what benefits does it offer?

5. Briefly explain the criteria an executive considers before pursuing an event marketing opportunity.

6. What are the measures commonly used to evaluate the effectiveness of event marketing participation?

7. Identify the basic steps in the event marketing planning process.

8. Developing the event concept is the initial stage of planning an event. What are the key decision areas in this stage? Briefly explain each.

9. Designing the event is the second stage of event planning. What are some of the key decision areas in this stage? Briefly explain each.

10. Briefly explain the purpose of the following planning tools:
    a) proposal
    b) run sheet

11. A key element of event marketing strategy is defining the event. What decisions are associated with defining the event?

12. Briefly explain the following stages of event marketing execution:
    a) site selection and staging
    b) staffing
    c) operations and logistics
    d) safety and security

Discussion and Application Questions

1. Marketers seem to be growing wary of sports event marketing, particularly at the professional level. Can you suggest any reasons why this is so?

2. Why are companies becoming more actively involved in cause-related event sponsorships? Conduct some secondary research on this issue and formulate a position on the matter.

3. Do value-added sponsorships such as the one between Reebok and Sidney Crosby offer significant benefits to the sponsoring organization? If so, what are the benefits? Discuss.

4. What classification of event sponsorship is appropriate for the following companies or brands? (More than one can apply.) Justify your decision.
    a) Becel margarine
    b) Michelin tires
    c) Perrier water
    d) BMW automobiles
    e) McDonald's

5. Assume you are responsible for planning an event such as a marathon/half-marathon race to raise funds for the Alzheimer's Association of Canada or some similar not-for-profit organization. What are your objectives? Consider both qualitative and quantitative objectives. Provide examples of a few objective statements. What marketing strategies will you employ to create awareness and interest in the event? Provide details of the activities you recommend.

6. Provide some examples of companies and brands that are involved with "experiential marketing." Based on your observations of their activities, identify the strengths and weaknesses of this form of event marketing.

Endnotes

1 Justin Smallbridge, "The main (retail) event," *Financial Post*, November 25, 2002, p. FP7.

2 "Vancouver 2010 Selects Bell Canada as premier national partner," press release, Bell Canada Enterprises, November 18, 2004.

3 "Sponsorship spending in North America," *IEG Sponsorship Report*, 2004.

4 "Event marketing tops list of marketing tactics for ROI," based on research from the George P. Johnson Company and MPI Foundation, Meeting Professionals International, **www.mpiweb.org**.

5 General Motors, **www.gmcanada.com**.

6 BMO Financial Group, **www.bmo.com**.

7 Chris Zelkovich, "Corporations love games," *Toronto Star*, January 23, 2002, p. C6.

8 "Your name here," *Report on Business Magazine*, May 2002, p. 31.

9 Rick Westhead, "What's in a name? $$$," *Toronto Star*, August 19, 2003, p. E3.

10 Paul-Mark Rendon, "Hot properties," *Marketing*, June 27, 2005, p. 11.

11 Robert Thompson, "The next one sets record off the ice," *National Post*, March 9, 2005, p. A3

12 Kate McArthur, "Pepsi is out, Coke is in as 2006 Oscars sponsor," *Advertising Age*, June 2, 2005, **www.adage.com/news.cms?newsId=45205**.

13 Terry Poulton, "Basking in the starlight," *Strategy*, September 9, 2002, pp. 21–24.

14 Toronto International Film Festival, **www.tiff.ca/content/support/sponsoropps.asp** (website no longer active).

15 "Trend: Degree taps into poker craze," *Strategy*, August 2005, p. 30.

16 BMO Financial Group, **www.bmo.com**.

17 Tim Hortons, "Children's Foundation," **www.timhortons.com**.

18 Pia Musngi, "Global goes guerilla," *Strategy*, September 2005, p. 57.

19 Chris Daniels, "Going to extremes," *Marketing*, October 31, 2005, p. 4.

20 Wendy Cuthbert, "Sponsors pump ROI with experimental approach," *Strategy*, March 12, 2001, p. B7.

21 "Metro versus Retro: How well do you understand the male market?" Brunico Communications, Toronto.

22 Lynn Van Der Wagen, *Event Management* (Elsternwick, Australia: Hospitality Press, 2001), p. 196.

23 Fact Monster, **www.factmonster.com**.

24 John Van Stan, *The Ellis Park Stadium Soccer Disaster Interim Report*, 2001.

PERSONAL SELLING

After studying this chapter you will be able to

1. understand the role of personal selling in retail, business-to-business, and direct selling environments and its relationship to integrated marketing communications

2. describe the evolution of personal selling strategies and evaluate the role that relationship selling plays in integrated marketing communications programs

3. identify the human variables that contribute to the successful application of personal selling strategies

4. learn how to apply this knowledge to a variety of personal selling situations

5. identify the fundamental roles and responsibilities of a sales representative

6. identify the essential steps in the selling process and the key elements required for preparing a successful sales presentation

7. assess how selling strategies need to adapt to a changing business environment

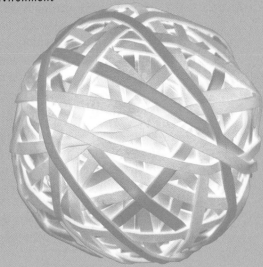

Among the various components of the integrated marketing communications mix, personal selling differentiates itself due to its personal nature. Advertising and promotions rely on the media to spread the word, public relations uses various tools to seek the media's support in spreading the word, and direct response communications rely on the mail, telemarketing, the Internet, and mobile communications. All these forms of communications are impersonal. In spite of all of the changes that have occurred in the marketplace, and in spite of the fact that industry has come to rely on technology as a means of communication, personal selling still remains a vital component. Organizations continue to sell—they just sell differently than they used to.

To demonstrate, customer relationship management (CRM) practices affect all forms of communication, but none more than personal selling. The human contact and the ability to negotiate form the foundation of CRM practices. Furthermore, all of the technical wizardry in the world can only go so far. Once the show is over, someone has to ask for the order. And that's the responsibility of the sales representative. This chapter examines the role of personal selling in the context of integrated marketing communications.

PERSONAL SELLING AND INTEGRATED MARKETING COMMUNICATIONS

Personal selling

Face-to-face communication involving the presentation of features and benefits of a product or service to a buyer; the objective is to make a sale.

Personal selling is a personalized form of communications that involves sellers presenting the features and benefits of a product or service to a buyer for the purpose of making a sale. It is an integral component of marketing communications, because it is the activity that in many cases clinches the deal. Advertising and promotions create awareness and interest for a product; personal selling creates desire and action. In creating desire and action, the interaction between the seller and buyer is crucial.

Personal selling can be divided into three main areas: retail selling, business-to-business (B2B) selling, and direct selling, either to consumers or other businesses (see Figure 11.1). In all these areas, personal selling is connected to other aspects of integrated marketing communications planning. For example, a sales representative for Kraft Foods who calls on the head office of a grocery chain such as Safeway or Sobeys does more than just communicate the benefits of various product lines. If the salesperson's presentation involves a new product launch, the objective is to get the product listed by the chain's head office so that retail stores in the chain can order it. Buyers want to know what kind of marketing support will be provided by Kraft. Therefore, at the very least, the salesperson must include information about advertising plans and sales promotion plans (both consumer and trade promotions) that will help create demand for the new product. Details about when advertising is scheduled, what markets it will run in, and what incentives will be offered to the consumer and the trade are all critical factors that influence the buying decision. Similar situations exist in other industries. Personal selling is directly linked to other communications strategies.

Retail Selling

Transactions occur on the sales floor of a department store, in a checkout line of a grocery store, at an insurance agent's office, and at the service desk of an automobile maintenance shop, to name just a few examples of retail selling. In these situations, the nature of the sale is defined as a single transaction or a repeat transaction. The quality of service offered at the point of sale and the degree of satisfaction the customer receives usually influence repeat transactions. In fact, the retail salesperson is the face of the organization, and how that person deals with customers affects the buyer's experience.

FIGURE **11.1** **Classifications of Personal Selling**

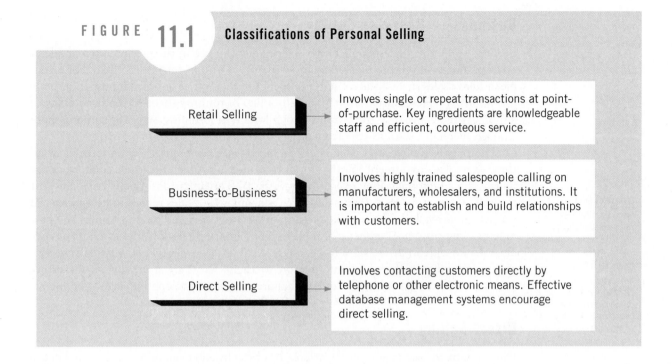

Retail Selling	Involves single or repeat transactions at point-of-purchase. Key ingredients are knowledgeable staff and efficient, courteous service.
Business-to-Business	Involves highly trained salespeople calling on manufacturers, wholesalers, and institutions. It is important to establish and build relationships with customers.
Direct Selling	Involves contacting customers directly by telephone or other electronic means. Effective database management systems encourage direct selling.

Single transaction

A retail sales situation where a salesperson spends time with a customer and closes the sale on the spot.

Order taking

In retail sales, a floor clerk provides product information and shows goods to the customer who then goes to the checkout counter to pay for purchases.

Repeat transaction

A retail sales situation that involves a relationship between the buyer and the seller; the customer returns to the same store for similar goods and services.

A **single transaction** occurs when a salesperson spends time with a customer and eventually closes the sale on the spot. In many organizations, **order taking** is becoming popular. Stores such as Canadian Tire, Wal-Mart, Home Depot, IKEA, and other large retailers have popularized the concept of self-serve. In these stores, floor personnel assist customers in locating the goods they need and provide useful information, but the customer simply passes through the checkout when purchasing the goods.

In situations where **repeat transactions** occur, there is an ongoing relationship between the buyer and seller. For example, a customer will return to the same automobile repair shop after getting to know the people who are working on his or her car. The customer wants to avoid potential risk in dealing with different repair shops. The relationship between the buyer and seller is usually based on factors such as trust, respect, and satisfaction with the goods or services provided. These factors must be present if the retailer is to profit in the long run.

Successful retailers continuously stress the importance of customer contact at point-of-purchase. How a retail salesperson interacts with the customer has a significant impact on how the customer perceives the retailer and helps determine if that individual will make a purchase. It is the seller's responsibility to clarify what the customer actually needs, usually by politely asking a few questions. The seller must then offer some product suggestions and demonstrate knowledge by presenting the essential benefits of the products to the customer.

When the purchase decision is made, the seller should look for opportunities for add-on sales or suggest service warranties to protect the customer's long-term interests. In retail stores where single transactions are the goal, high-pressure sales tactics are often applied. Although these kinds of tactics may work in the short term, many customers react negatively to them, and simply leave the store feeling frustrated. Generally speaking, a low-key approach involving positive customer contact in a pleasant and courteous manner is the main ingredient for retail selling success. In retail, the salespeople are the most essential point of contact in the purchasing process—integral to a well-planned integrated marketing communications program.

Business-to-Business Selling

Business-to-business salespeople either sell products for use in the production and sale of other products, or sell products to channel members who in turn resell them. For example, a Xerox sales representative sells photocopiers to another business for use in its daily operations; a representative from Nike sells a line of running shoes to the head office of a specialty retailer such as the Forzani Group, which in turn distributes the running shoes through its retail locations (Sport Chek).

Thoroughly trained and adequately prepared sales representatives are crucial in all these examples. Investment in other forms of marketing communications could be all for naught if the personal selling execution is weak. B2B organizations usually have different types of sales personnel. A **field sales force** is composed of sales representatives who call on customers regularly. They make presentations to existing and new customers and provide ongoing customer contact to establish a good business relationship. A company may also operate with an **inside sales force**, often referred to as order takers, who seek out new customers and provide useful information to them. Working from the organization's premises, an order taker handles orders that are received by telephone, fax, or online.

Direct Selling

Direct selling to customers either by telephone or the Internet can be accommodated in the retail selling and B2B selling situations described above. **Telemarketing** involves using the telephone as an interactive medium for a marketing response. It uses highly trained people and database marketing techniques to seek and serve new customers. Figure 11.2 summarizes the role that telemarketing can play in the selling process. Telemarketing improves productivity by reducing direct-selling costs, specifically the costs associated with keeping sales representatives on the road (automobiles, accommodations, and related travel expenses). It is also useful in screening and qualifying incoming leads, generating leads from various database directories and mailing lists, calling on current customers to secure additional orders, and determining the level of customer satisfaction.

Online selling refers to the use of websites to conduct sales transactions. Consumers who are looking for convenience now include the web as part of their shopping experience. Figure 11.3 shows how Grocery Gateway, an online supermarket, provides its consumers convenience. Websites like Grocery Gateway's are capable of accepting and processing orders, receiving payment, and arranging for the delivery of goods and services directly to consumers

Field sales force

An organization's external sales representatives who regularly call on customers to pursue orders.

Inside sales force

An internal group of sellers, often referred to as order takers, who accept orders from customers by telephone or other means.

Telemarketing

The use of telecommunications to promote the products and services of a business; involves outbound calls (company to customer) and inbound calls (customer to company).

Online selling

Using the Internet to conduct sales transactions.

FIGURE **11.2**   **Some of the Roles Played by Telemarketing in Personal Selling**

Sales Support
- Generate leads
- Qualify leads
- Schedule appointments
- Collect market intelligence

Selling
- Open new accounts
- Call marginal accounts
- Sell to existing customers

Customer Service
- Operate customer help lines
- Handle inquiries and complaints
- Offer after-sales service
- Conduct satisfaction surveys

FIGURE **11.3** **Online Selling Offers Convenience to Consumers**

Source: Grocery Gateway Inc., Mississauga, Ontario.

and businesses. Indigo Books & Music, operators of Chapters and Indigo stores, sells goods in a similar fashion. Since all transactions are electronically recorded, companies accumulate huge databases of information that can be used for marketing purposes in the longer term.

THE EVOLUTION OF SELLING

Over the years, the nature of selling has changed. Since the 1970s, personal selling has passed through three distinct stages: consultative selling, strategic selling, and relationship selling.[1] Relationship selling has been extended a step further as companies adopt electronic data interchange practices. For these companies, partnership selling is now the name of the game (see the next section for details).

Consultative selling stresses open two-way communication between sellers and buyers. The initial task of the seller is to discover a need or set of needs by asking questions and listening carefully. The seller then uses that information to formulate appropriate product recommendations—acting as a consultant. Once the sale is complete, the seller gets involved with after-sales service and customer care programs. A satisfied customer remains a customer!

Changes in the marketplace have dictated changes in selling strategies. Products are now more sophisticated and complex, competition is more intense and occurs on a broader (global) scale, and customer expectations of quality, price, service, and individualized solutions have increased considerably. Similar to other components of the marketing communications mix, strategic selling strategies are influenced by an organization's strategic marketing plan. The marketing plan acts as a guide for the strategic selling plan. Refer to Figure 11.4 for an illustration of the planning model.

Consultative selling
A form of selling that stresses open two-way communication between a buyer and seller.

FIGURE **11.4**   **Personal Selling Planning Model**

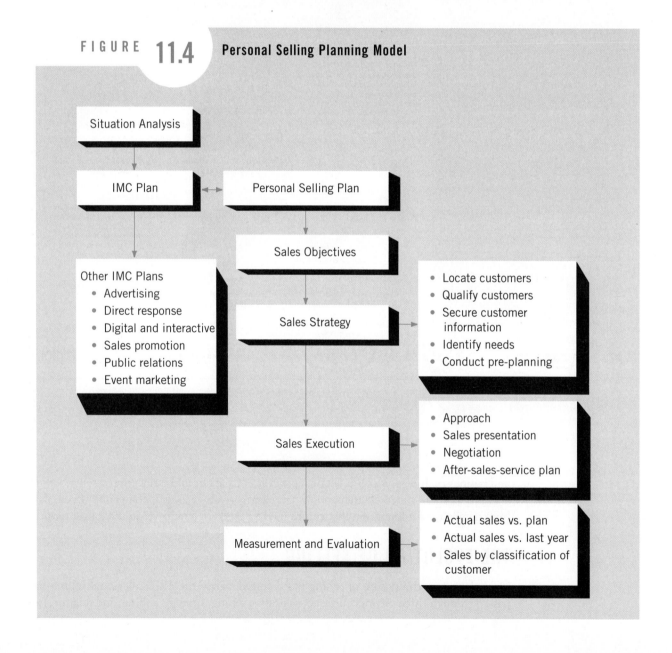

Strategic selling
A form of consultative selling that involves dealing with each customer as an individual, stressing that in the transfer of product information.

Strategic selling takes consultative selling to the next level. It considers the most recent yet continuously changing conditions in the marketplace, adds technology to enhance the methods of presenting products to buyers, and focuses on serving customers one customer at a time. The goal is to remain flexible while providing solutions that are unique to each customer. There are three key factors to be considered when formulating a strategic sales strategy. First, the seller must do what is necessary to form a good relationship with the customer. Second, the seller must effectively match products and position them so that they meet customer needs. And third, the seller must develop a compelling presentation that will clearly portray the usefulness of a product in resolving a customer's problem.

Relationship selling
A form of selling with the goal of developing a plan of action that establishes, builds, and maintains a long-term relationship with customers.

In **relationship selling**, the goal is to develop a plan of action to establish, build, and maintain customers. In involves taking a long-term perspective on selling and considers the fact that good relationships don't necessarily form very quickly. Instead, a seller must take the necessary steps to form a relationship, such as establishing rapport and building trust and respect, over a long period of time. Having a positive attitude, projecting a good image, and being able to get along with all kinds of different people and personalities are key factors that contribute to a sales representative's ability to build a solid relationship with customers.

Establishing a good relationship depends on how well the seller positions products in the minds of customers, how effectively (persuasively) the product's benefits are presented, and how well the seller guards the relationship in the long run. The latter requires ongoing customer contact and the implementation of customer care programs. Figure 11.5 reviews the key aspects of relationship selling.

Apple Computer
www.apple.com

With relationship selling, it is the seller's responsibility to match the right product to the customer and then develop the communications strategy that will position it appropriately in the customer's mind. A sales representative for Apple Computer, for example, will capitalize on the user-friendly positioning strategy that Apple uses in other forms of marketing communications to sell computers. The representative differentiates Apple from other brands based on benefits such as uniqueness, degree of innovation, performance capabilities (speed of performing functions), and reliability.

FIGURE **11.5** **The Key Elements of Relationship Selling**

Overall Goal	To establish, build, and maintain customers.
Personal Strategy	The seller must initiate steps that will build rapport with customers. The seller must earn the trust and respect of the customer. The salesperson must have a strong and positive self-image and be flexible when dealing with many different people and personalities.
Selling Strategy	The salesperson must effectively position the product (a solution) in the customer's mind by relating the right benefits to a unique problem or situation that the customer presents. The benefits should be related to the rational needs of the buying organization and the emotional needs of the buyer. A salesperson must make a convincing presentation and be flexible enough to adapt to the unexpected while the presentation is in progress. A persuasive presentation should lead the buyer to the right decision.
Building Relationships	Customers not only want good products, but also want good relationships. Selling today is not about selling products—it's about selling solutions!

The formation of the right positioning strategy depends largely on the seller's knowledge of the customer. The more knowledge the seller has going into the presentation, the easier it is to structure the presentation. A good salesperson continuously updates his or her files with customer information. In the age of technology, such a practice is easy to do and vital to success. People in organizations move around, so it is very important to be constantly on top of who is responsible for what.

A good salesperson formulates a **presentation strategy** that focuses on what to say to customers when presenting the product. A good plan is based on the seller's knowledge of the customer and his or her immediate needs; it summarizes potential benefits that will be stressed (often prioritized from most important to least important) and considers potential objections that the buyer might raise. As with most marketing communications strategies, a sales strategy must remain flexible. The seller, for example, must be able to adapt the presentation based on new information that surfaces during a presentation, or to rephrase relevant benefits if the buyer introduces the benefits of a competitor's product. The importance of knowledge in a variety of areas and the key elements of a presentation are discussed in more detail later in this chapter.

Presentation strategy
A plan of what to say to a customer in a sales presentation to identify customer needs, summarize benefits, and prepare for potential objections.

Partnership Selling

Partnership selling
A strategically developed long-term relationship that involves selling products and providing comprehensive after-sales service and effective two-way communications to ensure complete customer satisfaction.

Partnership selling is an extension of relationship selling. It involves a strategically developed, long-term relationship to sell products, provides comprehensive after-sales service, and encourages effective two-way communications to ensure complete customer satisfaction. The goal is to form partnerships with customers in a manner that fosters prosperity among partners.

Changing conditions in the marketplace have fostered the concept of partnership selling. There was a time when companies could rely on the strength of their company, product, and service components to secure stability and growth. Now, however, the intensity of competition, the availability of copycat products, the need to constantly reduce costs, and the speed in which innovative products are introduced necessitates strong buyer-seller partnerships. Therefore, sellers are transforming their selling procedures and methods to build formal relationships with other organizations in the channel of distribution.[2] It is all part of the CRM philosophy discussed earlier in this book.

Selling organizations today must be willing to invest time and money into finding good solutions. It's not about selling products any more—it's about selling solutions! To illustrate, consider that UPS has moved from a courier service to become a supply chain management company with the goal of assisting customers with their long-range growth needs (see Figure 11.6). The company has evolved with changes in the marketplace and with the changing needs of its customers.

PERSONAL SELLING: THE HUMAN COMMUNICATIONS ELEMENT

If establishing and building effective relationships are the keys to modern-day success, what strategies must the salesperson use to form a good working relationship with his or her customers? To be successful, a salesperson must focus on three primary areas: personal characteristics, verbal communications, and non-verbal communications. A well-prepared and energetic salesperson knows how to communicate effectively both verbally and non-verbally, and as a result, will be successful. Let's examine each area briefly.

Personal Characteristics

To survive in selling, certain personal characteristics are required. Typically, successful salespeople are self-confident, motivated, flexible, optimistic, and project a good image

FIGURE **11.6** Sophisticated Marketing Organizations such as UPS Offer Business Solutions to Current and Prospective Customers

Source: Courtesy of UPS and The Martin Agency.

when confronted with social and business situations. These characteristics can be learned and practised, and given time and proper training, poorly performing salespeople can be transformed into prosperous salespeople. All that is required are dedication and a desire to confront the challenges of selling.

Self-image

One's own idea about oneself and one's relationship with others.

Self-image is a psychological term referring to one's attitude and feelings about oneself and one's roles in relation to others. It certainly plays a key role in selling. Perhaps the most important aspect of self-image is one's confidence. For example, an individual who approaches a challenge with enthusiasm, or possesses that "I'm going to win" attitude, is likely to succeed. In contrast, an individual who tends to forecast failure, or has a "doom and gloom" attitude, will almost certainly get disappointing results. To succeed, therefore, you have to think you can succeed.

Among all the theories about building self-confidence that exist, three essential strategies stand out. First, a positive self-image will exist if a person does not dwell on past mistakes. Instead, people must learn from those mistakes and move forward. Second, a salesperson should develop some expertise in a certain area because there is special status in being an expert. Others will call upon you for advice. Third, a salesperson should develop a positive outlook. For example, taking courses that reinforce the principles of success and simply associating with other positive and successful people are both good practices to follow.

Typically, a good salesperson has good *verbal skills*. They are generally comfortable when addressing a buyer, buying committee, or even a larger audience. When one thinks of a salesperson the stereotype of the fast-talker often comes to mind, but the reality is that listening skills are just as important. A salesperson who listens carefully to what the buyer says can respond better. Communications in a selling situation is a two-way street.

Non-verbal communication
(body language)

The expression of thoughts, opinions, or information using non-verbal cues such as body movement, facial expressions, and eye contact.

Non-verbal communication or **body language** is another essential aspect of self-confidence. Non-verbal communication refers to the imparting of thoughts, opinions, or information without using spoken words. An observer (in this case the buyer) will notice non-verbal cues such as body movement, facial expressions, and eye contact.[3] A buyer's perceptions of a salesperson are often determined by body language. For example, does the seller squirm in the chair while conversing or does the seller fidget with a small object while speaking? Such body language could be perceived as a lack of confidence. Alternatively, does the seller make direct eye contact? Was that handshake firm and friendly? Such body language suggests positive self-confidence. For a summary of some essential characteristics and traits for successful selling, refer to Figure 11.7.

Other non-verbal characteristics that influence buyers' perceptions include facial expressions, personal appearance, and manners. The old expression that "the lips say one

FIGURE 11.7 **Personal Characteristics and Planning Lead to Selling Success**

Considerations for Developing a Positive Self-Image

- Atention to personal appearance and hygiene
- Suitable style of dress
- Positive attitude
- Good manners
- Confident handshake and voice
- Appropriate gestures and facial expressions
- Eye contact
- Enthusiatic approach and presentation

Some Preparation Tips

- Learn from mistakes and move forward.
- Become an expert (in the product, company, the competition, and the customer).
- Maintain a positive outlook.
- Personalize the presentation.
- Speak clearly and emphasize important points.
- Use clear, economical language.
- Follow a structured plan but remain flexible.
- Practise to ensure all aspects of the presentation blend together.

thing, but the eyes say another" applies to selling situations. Facial gestures can communicate confidence, as does a smile; boredom, as does a grin; or evaluation or judgment, as in a frown or perplexed expression. Given that the goal in selling is to express confidence, successful salespeople always wear a sincere and winning smile when they approach customers and when they present information to them.

Dress codes have changed drastically in recent years. The business world moved away from formal attire (business suits) and toward informal attire (business casual) for a period of time. The "Casual Friday" concept spread to the entire week. Recently, however, there has been a return to more formal dress. Wardrobe experts believe clothing makes a significant difference in building one's credibility and likeability with customers. Experts offer different opinions on how to dress, but generally there is one common theme: the situation (or appropriateness) dictates the style of dress. For example, if you are meeting your customer in a business office or boardroom setting, formal dress is appropriate. If the meeting is in a factory or at a construction site, less formal attire is suitable. Other traditional guidelines for wardrobe focus on simplicity, quality, and the selective use of accessories. Accessories such as earrings, necklaces, and facial jewellery could be a distraction for the buyer and anything causing a distraction should be avoided.

There is a relationship between verbal communication and non-verbal communication in a selling situation. Successful salespeople effectively blend together verbal and non-verbal communications. They communicate the message in a positive and enthusiastic manner and reinforce it with body language that is consistent with what they say. Such a combination builds confidence in the buyer and gives the buyer the impression you can be trusted. Such perceptions certainly go a long way in building and maintaining a business relationship.

For additional insight into the habits of successful salespeople, see the IMC Highlight **Great Salespeople Take Care of Business.**

IMC HIGHLIGHT

GREAT SALESPEOPLE TAKE CARE OF BUSINESS

Being prepared for a sales presentation is essential; dealing effectively with people is essential; asking for the order is essential. These are the things a good salesperson does every day. Beyond essential skills like these, though, are a host of little things a successful salesperson does, and it's these things that often separate a good salesperson from a great salesperson.

Highly successful sales people have a few things in common:

They maintain an accurate customer contact file—Since selling is about finding people that need your product, keeping in touch with people is essential. The successful salesperson uses his or her entire network of contacts as sources of potential leads.

They apply technology—Great sellers use technology to manage information, and they have the right information readily available in a time of need. They spend time selling with information rather than searching for information.

They are curious—Asking customers "why" questions brings out the necessary information the salesperson needs to adequately prepare a sales presentation. They know that information is more powerful if the reason behind it is known.

They love what they do—Selling is an attitude, an attitude of optimism and belief in the value of their work. They are enthusiastic about the challenges that lie ahead and show a "passion" for the job that can be infectious. Maintaining the passion is one of the most difficult challenges a salesperson faces.

They are very creative—Successful salespeople have vision to come up with new ideas to solve business problems. The word "no" is just the beginning. Using their "creativity," they eventually turn that "no" into a "yes." Creativity is a cornerstone of selling and is useful for questioning, presenting, and strategizing.

Adapted from Maura Schreier-Fleming, "Habits of highly successful salespeople, March 27, 2005, www.surefirewealth.com.

Preparation and the Importance of Knowledge

In a nutshell, the primary task of a salesperson is to provide a customer with a solution to a problem by matching the right product or service at a price that is agreeable to the customer. It sounds so simple! But it requires much advance preparation, and that preparation is divided into three primary areas: product knowledge, company knowledge, and competitor knowledge. With regard to product knowledge, the salesperson must become an expert and know exactly what benefits to stress with any particular customer. For example, two different customers might require the same product, but one customer is motivated by quality, the other by service. The salesperson would have to adapt the presentation to offer different perspectives based on each buyer's unique needs and priorities. In complex situations, such as when various products must be combined to form a solution, the salesperson must be capable of bringing the right products and services together. This process is called **product configuration**.

Product configuration
The bringing together of various products and services to form a solution for the customer.

Product Knowledge

Essentially, product knowledge can be classified into four key areas: product development and quality improvement processes, performance data and specifications, maintenance and service, and price and delivery. The various combinations of this information make up the essential elements of a planned sales presentation. To grow, companies develop new products to solve new needs. It is important for a salesperson to know how a product was developed, how much it cost to develop, and why it was developed. This sort of information strongly suggests to a customer that the company takes research and development seriously and strives to build better products for its customers. In terms of performance and quality, a salesperson should be familiar with quality control standards so that information regarding product claims can be substantiated and compared with claims made by competitors. Knowing that a product meets or exceeds certain standards often provides competitive advantage in a sales presentation.

A buyer usually poses questions or raises objections about performance data and specifications in the middle of a sales presentation. To illustrate, assume you are considering various conference centres for a business conference you are planning. What kinds of questions would you ask the sales managers? Here are a few examples:

- Does the conference centre offer technical support if we need it?
- Is there an Internet connection available to delegates and at what cost?
- Is there sufficient accommodation available for 200 delegates?
- How efficient is the catering department in serving a buffet dinner to 200 people?

Certainly the list could be longer and much more diverse. And that is the key point. A good salesperson must be ready to respond to the expected and unexpected.

If the competing products are similar, it could be that information about maintenance and service provide product differentiation. If service is provided as part of a package deal, all specifications regarding additional services must be part of the sales presentation. Specifications must be agreed upon about who is responsible for what service, when it will happen, how often it will happen, and so on. It is very common for selling companies to draw up official service contracts based on specific requirements provided by the buying organization. Such contracts play a vital role in the relationship building process.

Other knowledge that helps differentiate one product from another is knowledge about price and delivery. The easiest and most common objection that buyers raise is price: "Your price is too high!" Knowing how to respond appropriately is crucial to closing the sale. If your price is higher than the competition, that fact must be acknowledged, and additional and tangible product benefits must be presented to justify the higher price. In such situations, the buyer simply wants more information; the salesperson must show good product knowledge.

Company Knowledge

Since the salesperson is the customer's primary source of contact, the salesperson is the company. The perceptions formed by a customer or prospective customer about a company depend largely on the attitude, style, behaviour, and communications ability of the salesperson. If perceptions are positive there is a stronger likelihood of making the sale and for developing a long-term business relationship. A salesperson, therefore, should integrate essential information about the company into a sales presentation.

Business organizations exist to serve their customers, and all employees must recognize that they contribute to this effort. This attitude, often referred to as **corporate culture**, is defined as the values, norms, and practices shared by all employees of an organization. A good corporate culture always puts the customer first. A successful and diversified organization such as 3M thinks "customer" all the time. All employees are part of a marketing team and consider themselves to be in the customer care business. In fact, 3M uses the phrase "From need to...3M Innovation" as its advertising slogan. At the 3M website there are other phrases such as "From Imagination to Innovation" and "Leading through Innovation." 3M identifies customer needs and develops innovative products to satisfy those needs. Such information should be passed on to prospective customers by sales representatives, because it sends out a clear signal about the type of company 3M is: a company willing to develop new products and to respond to new challenges in an ever-changing marketplace. Figure 11.8 provides some insight into the innovations of 3M in the consumer marketplace and the B2B marketplace.

What services a company provides after the sale is also crucial information to provide to customers. As many experts say, "The relationship begins once the sale is made." Therefore, after-sales service, which is a function that is usually implemented by other departments of a company, must be integrated into a sales presentation. It is important for a company to track the level of satisfaction that customers are experiencing, so it is quite common for organizations to contact customers directly by telephone or mail. The results of surveys, for example, can be passed on to sales representatives for follow-up.

Competitor Knowledge

A good salesperson knows the competitor's products almost as well as his or her own. In a sales presentation, comparisons inevitably crop up, making it essential to know the benefits and weaknesses of competing products and adapt the selling strategy accordingly. If a seller cannot respond to the challenges posed by a buyer, the chances of making a sale are lost.

Talking about competing products is usually awkward. Obviously, a salesperson does not want to acknowledge a competitor's strengths, but at the same time a seller cannot be too critical of what is being offered. The customer may already be doing business with the competition. Here are a few basic guidelines for dealing with competing products:[4]

- Do not deliberately include reference to competitors in your presentation as it shifts the focus off your own product. Do, however, respond to questions about the competition.
- Do not make statements about the competitor if you are uncertain of the facts. Your credibility will suffer if you make inaccurate statements.
- Do not criticize the competition. State the facts as you know them and avoid emotional comments if you have to make a comparison.

Remember, prospective customers are forming perceptions of you and your company when you are making the sales presentation. How you handle competing products goes a long way in creating a favourable or unfavourable impression.

Corporate culture
The values, beliefs, norms, and practices shared by all employees of an organization.

3M
www.3m.com

FIGURE **11.8** **3M Responds to the Challenge of Developing New and Innovative Products for a Changing Marketplace**

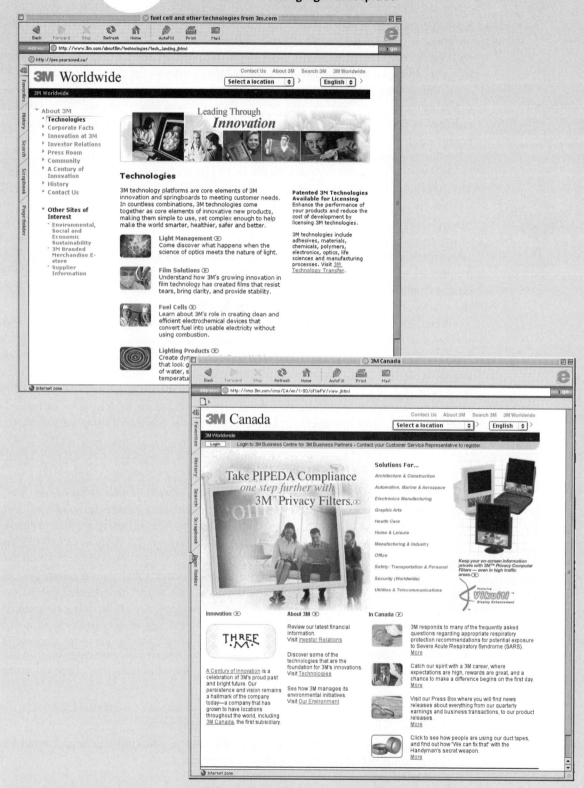

Source: © 3M 2003.

ROLES AND RESPONSIBILITIES OF SALESPEOPLE

The primary tasks of a salesperson, particularly in a business-to-business environment, are to gather market intelligence, solve customers' problems, locate and maintain customers, and provide follow-up service. This section examines each key responsibility.

Gathering Market Intelligence

In a competitive marketplace, salespeople must be attuned to the trends in their industry. They must be alert to what the competitor is doing, to its new product projects, and to its advertising and promotion plans, and they must listen to feedback from customers regarding their own products' performances. As indicated earlier, competitive knowledge is important when the salesperson faces questions involving product comparisons. Data collected by a salesperson can be reported electronically to the company's head office. Managers can retrieve the information and use it appropriately at a later date.

Problem Solving

The only way a salesperson can make a sale is to listen to what a customer wants and ask questions to determine his or her real needs. Asking, listening, and providing information and advice that is in the best interests of the customer are what relationship selling is all about. The seller must demonstrate a sincere concern for the customer's needs.

Locating and Maintaining Customers

Salespeople who locate new customers play a key role in a company's growth. A company cannot be satisfied with its current list of customers, because aggressive competitors are always attempting to lure them away. To prevent shrinkage and to increase sales, salespeople actively pursue new accounts. Their time is divided between finding new accounts and selling and servicing current accounts.

Follow-up Service

The salesperson is the first point of contact should anything go wrong or should more information be required. Maintenance of customers is crucial and, very often, it is the quality of the follow-up service that determines if a customer will remain a customer. Since the salespeople are the company's direct link to the customer, it cannot be stressed enough how important it is that they handle customer service well. The sale is never over! Once the deal has closed, numerous tasks arise: arranging for delivery, providing technical assistance, offering customer training, and being readily available to handle any problems that might emerge during and after delivery. The personalized role of the sales representative is instrumental in building relationships.

PERSONAL SELLING STRATEGIES

Feature
Tangible aspects of a product, such as durability, design, and economy of operation.

Benefit
The value a customer attaches to a brand attribute.

Before discussing the various steps involved in successful personal selling, let's first explore the difference between features and benefits. A product feature is anything that can be felt, seen, or measured. **Features** include such things as durability, design, and economy of operation. They provide a customer with information, but do not motivate a customer to buy. A **benefit** provides the customer with advantage or gain, and shows how a product will help resolve a specific problem. Benefits provide motivation! To demonstrate, consider all of the technical features usually associated with a laptop or desktop computer. The list seems endless and includes much technical jargon. Assuming the customer wants quick access to information when using the computer (information the seller would seek out by asking a few questions), the seller can quickly zoom in on the appropriate features and translate them into benefits that are appropriate for and meaningful to the customer.

Regardless of the sales situation—whether retail selling, business-to-business selling, or direct selling—the steps in the selling process are similar. They are simply adapted to each situation. This section covers the seven essential steps in the selling process (see Figure 11.9).

Prospecting

Prospecting
A procedure for systematically developing sales leads.

The first step is **prospecting**, which is a procedure for systematically developing sales leads. If salespeople do not allocate enough time to finding new customers, they risk caus-

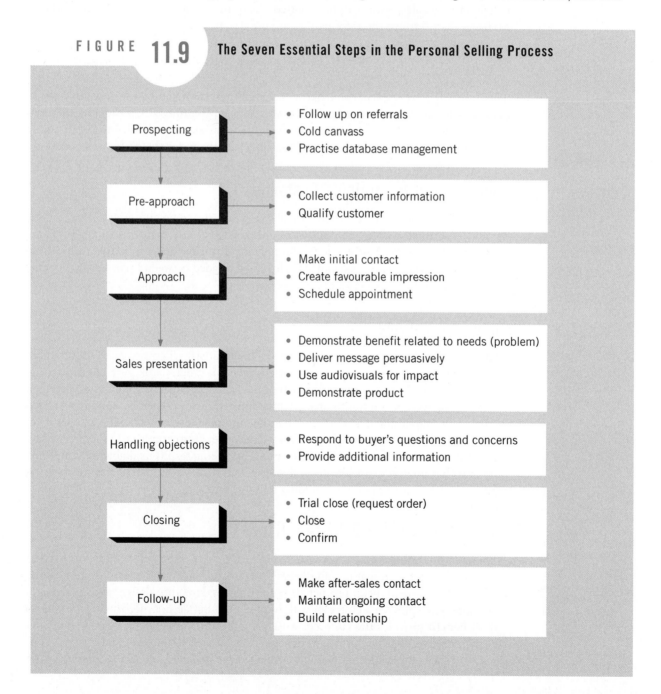

FIGURE **11.9** **The Seven Essential Steps in the Personal Selling Process**

Prospecting
- Follow up on referrals
- Cold canvass
- Practise database management

Pre-approach
- Collect customer information
- Qualify customer

Approach
- Make initial contact
- Create favourable impression
- Schedule appointment

Sales presentation
- Demonstrate benefit related to needs (problem)
- Deliver message persuasively
- Use audiovisuals for impact
- Demonstrate product

Handling objections
- Respond to buyer's questions and concerns
- Provide additional information

Closing
- Trial close (request order)
- Close
- Confirm

Follow-up
- Make after-sales contact
- Maintain ongoing contact
- Build relationship

ing a decline in sales for their company. If their income is geared to the value of the business they produce, they risk the loss of personal compensation as well. Prospecting is also important because of attrition. Attrition refers to the loss of customers over a period of time. Even with extensive CRM programs in place as a means of retaining customers, buyers switch suppliers when better products and services become available.

Potential customers, or prospects, are identified by means of published lists and directories, such as Scott's Industrial Directories, the *Frasers Trade Index*, and the *Canadian Key Business Directory*. Another strategy for seeking new customers is the referral. A **referral** is a prospect that is recommended by a current customer. The salesperson also seeks new customers by **cold canvass**, the process of calling on people or organizations without appointments or advance knowledge of them. Other sources of leads include names obtained from trade shows, advertising, direct response communications, telemarketing and online communications, sales promotion entry forms, and channel members.

Pre-approach

The **pre-approach** involves gathering information about potential customers before actually making sales contact. During the pre-approach stage, customers are **qualified**, which is the procedure for determining if a prospect needs the product, has the authority to buy it, and has the ability to pay for it. There is little sense in pursuing customers who lack the financial resources or have no need to make the business relationship successful. In the process of qualifying customers, the seller also gains insights that can be used in the sales presentation: information such as the buyer's likes and dislikes, personal interests and hobbies, buying procedures, and special needs and problems.

Approach

The **approach** is the initial contact with the prospect, often in a face-to-face selling situation. Since buyers are usually busy, little time should be wasted in the approach. In the first few minutes of a sales interview, the salesperson must capture the attention and interest of the buyer and create a favourable first impression so that there is an effective environment for the presentation of the product's benefits.

Sales Presentation

As discussed in Chapter 1, it is common for a salesperson to make presentations to individuals (one-on-one selling) or to buying teams (one-on-group selling). Buying teams were classified as buying centres (an informal grouping of people in the buying group) or buying committees (a formal group with a structured buying procedure in place). In dealing with buying committees, the salesperson must listen attentively and observe body language to determine which members of the group are the real influencers and decision makers.

The actual **sales presentation** consists of a persuasive delivery and demonstration of a product's benefits. An effective sales presentation shows the buyer how the benefits of the product satisfy his or her needs or help resolve a particular problem. In doing so, the seller focuses on the benefits that are most important to the buyer. Critical elements usually focus on lower price, the durability of the product, the dependability of supply, the performance of the product, and the availability of follow-up service.

At this stage, asking proper questions and listening attentively are particularly important to uncover real needs. A salesperson listens to and analyzes what buyers are saying, then uses what has been discovered when presenting the appropriate benefits. Being flexible and adapting a presentation in mid-stream could be the difference between making a sale and not making a sale.

Referral
A recommendation by a current customer of a potential new customer to a sales representative.

Cold canvass
The process of calling on people or organizations without appointments or advance knowledge of them.

Pre-approach
The gathering of information about customers before actually making sales contact.

Qualifying (customers)
Assessing if a prospect needs a product, has the authority to buy it, and has the ability to pay for it.

Approach
The initial contact with a customer.

Sales presentation
A persuasive delivery and demonstration of a product's benefits; shows buyers how the product's benefits will satisfy their needs.

Demonstration
A sales technique that involves showing the product in action to portray its benefits to a buyer.

Demonstrations play a key role in a sales presentation. A **demonstration** is an opportunity to show the product in action and substantiates the claims being made about the product. A good demonstration (something the buyer can see) adds to the convincing nature of the presentation. It helps hold the buyer's attention and create interest and desire. It is wise to rehearse the demonstration so that what the salesperson says and what the salesperson demonstrates are in harmony with each other. Laptop computers and changing technology now allow for multimedia presentations and very effective demonstrations.

While technology certainly helps put the spotlight on the product, it is important not to get carried away with it—the content of the presentation is always what is most important. A useful tactic in the presentation is to involve the prospect by letting him or her handle the product and the materials relevant to it. This action results in a feeling of ownership and helps in the decision-making process. In situations where technology is part of the presentation, the salesperson must be certain all equipment is in good working condition. A failure with the technology is embarrassing for the salesperson and costly in terms of potential time lost for the presentation. Figure 11.10 lists useful reminders for planning a sales presentation.

Handling Objections

Objection
An obstacle that a salesperson must confront during a sales presentation.

An **objection** is an obstacle that the salesperson must confront during a presentation and resolve if the sales transaction is to be completed. An objection is a cue for more information. The buyer is suggesting that the presentation of a product has not revealed how the product will satisfy a particular need. The objection, therefore, is feedback to be analyzed and used. It may enable the salesperson to discover another benefit in the product, a benefit that can then be presented to the buyer.

Typical objections involve issues related to the following: product quality and the level of service and technical assistance; the price or the level of discounts suggested, for example the price may be too high, discount too low, or credit terms unacceptable; and sourcing issues such as how the buyer feels about the company in comparison to other potential suppliers. Objections are a normal response from buyers, so salespeople should not take them personally. Instead, the salesperson should ask questions of the buyer to confirm his or her understanding of the situation, answer the objection, and then move on to the next benefit or attempt to close the sale. A good salesperson develops effective strategies for handling objections; being prepared for the expected and unexpected is essential. When responding to objections, the salesperson can call upon the product itself, testimonials and case histories of success, test results shown in a variety of formats (e.g., graphs and charts), and other forms of audiovisual support.

FIGURE **11.10**   **Useful Reminders for Planning a Sales Presentation**

- Ask the buyer questions and listen attentively to the responses.
- Include useful information about the company.
- Watch for cues by observing body language.
- Include a product demonstration (rehearse to make sure it works).
- Involve the buyer in the presentation.
- Remain flexible throughout the presentation and adapt it based on feedback.
- Add technology where appropriate to enhance the presentation.
- Respond to objections pleasantly (be prepared for the expected and unexpected).
- Ask for the order (always be closing).

Closing

Closing
Asking for the order at the appropriate time in a sales presentation.

Trial close
A failed attempt at closing a sale; the buyer said no.

Closing cue
An indication that the buyer is ready to buy; can be expressed verbally or nonverbally.

Does the buyer voluntarily say "Yes, I'll buy it"? The answer is "rarely"! Getting the buyer to say "yes" is the entire purpose of the sales interview, but this task is only accomplished if the salesperson asks for the order. **Closing** consists of asking for the order, and it is the most difficult step in the process of selling. Salespeople are reluctant to ask the big question, even though it is the logical sequel to a good presentation and demonstration. In fact, a good salesperson attempts a close whenever a point of agreement is made with the buyer. If the buyer says "no," the close is referred to as a **trial close**, or an attempt to close that failed. The salesperson simply moves on to the next point in the presentation.

The close can occur at any point in a sales presentation. Knowing when to close is essential. Therefore, as the sales presentation progresses, the salesperson must be alert to closing cues. A **closing cue** is an indication that the buyer is ready to buy. The cue may be verbal or non-verbal. If a cue is detected, a close should be attempted. Verbal cues include statements such as "What type of warranty do you provide?" Such a statement shows that the buyer is thinking ahead. Another cue is "The delivery and installation schedule fits well with our factory conversion schedule." Such a statement suggests confirmation of a key benefit. Or another: "We need the product in one week." In other words, if you can supply it, we'll buy it! Statements such as these are closing cues that must be acted upon.

Positive non-verbal communications include changing facial expressions, a change in buyer's mood (e.g., buyer becomes more jovial), or the buyer nods in agreement or reads the sales information intently. Good salespeople do not miss such opportunities, even if they are not finished their presentation. The buyer is telling you it is time to close—do it!

Timing a close is a matter of judgment. Good salespeople know when to close—it is often referred to as the "sixth sense" of selling. The salesperson assesses the buyer's verbal and non-verbal responses in an effort to judge when that person has become receptive, and at the right moment, asks the big question with a high degree of self-confidence. A list of commonly used closing techniques appears in Figure 11.11.

FIGURE **11.11** **Successful Closing Techniques**

The objective of the sales presentation is to get the order. To do so, the seller must close the sale by asking for the order. Asking for the order can be accomplished in a variety of ways.

Assumptive Close
The seller assumes the buyer has already decided to buy. The seller says, "I'll have it delivered by Friday," or "What is the best day for delivery?" An agreement or answer confirms the seller's assumption.

Alternative-Choice Close
The seller assumes the sale is made but asks for clarification on another point. He or she may say, "Would you prefer metallic blue or cherry red?"

Summary-of-Benefits Close
At the end of the presentation the seller calmly reviews the key points the buyer has already agreed to (price, service, quality, reliability, etc.). Once the summary is complete the seller says, "When would you like it delivered?"

Direct Close
No beating around the bush here. The seller confidently says, "Can I deliver it on Friday?" then stops talking and awaits the response.

Take-Away Close
It is human nature to want what one can't have. The seller says, "This product isn't for everyone. It's a certain kind of person who can appreciate the finer qualities of this product."

Once the sale has been closed, it is time to reassure the customer that a good decision has been taken and to confirm that you will provide all the essential services that were promised in the presentation. Parting on a positive note is crucial, because buyers very often experience cognitive dissonance. **Cognitive dissonance** refers to a feeling of doubt or regret once the buying decision has been made. The buyer wants to be reassured that the best choice has been made. This is the start of the relationship-building process.

Cognitive dissonance
A feeling of doubt or regret in a consumer's mind once a buying decision has been made.

Follow-up

There is an old saying: "The sale never ends." There is truth to this statement, because a new sale is nothing more than the start of a new relationship. Keeping current customers satisfied is the key to success. Effective salespeople make a point of providing **follow-up**; that is, they keep in touch with customers to ensure that the delivery and installation of the goods were satisfactory, that promises were kept, and that the expectations of the buyer were met. When problems do occur, the salesperson is ready to take action to resolve the situation.

Follow-up
Maintaining contact with customers to ensure that service has been satisfactory.

In the current competitive business environment, good follow-up strategies help reduce customer attrition. Companies realize that a satisfied customer is a long-term customer. Furthermore, research shows that it is four or five times more costly to attract a new customer than it is to retain a current customer.[5] Larry Rosen, president of upscale clothier Harry Rosen, firmly understands this concept. Harry Rosen has implemented programs that ensure the utmost in customer service and care. "We don't look at a person in terms of an immediate sale. We look at him in terms of potential lifetime value."[6]

Harry Rosen
www.harryrosen.com

Success in selling requires dedication, determination, and discipline. What separates the successful salesperson from the unsuccessful one usually boils down to how well an individual follows an established set of principles. While the wording of these principles might vary from one source to another, the intent behind them is consistent. See Figure 11.12 for some pointers on what separates the professionals from the average salespeople.

An effective salesperson should possess knowledge in three key areas: the customer and the industry they operate in, their own company and products, and the competition. The salesperson should follow the essential steps in the selling process if they are to be successful. Unfortunately, it is not that easy. Personal motivation also plays a key role in one's success. For additional insight into how to be successful in selling, read the IMC Highlight **Some Succeed While Many Fail. Why?**.

SELLING IN A CHANGING BUSINESS ENVIRONMENT

The nature of selling is changing rapidly. To be successful in the future, a salesperson and his or her company must consider the importance of teamwork in communicating with customers (another aspect of integration), the importance of building long-term relationships, and the importance of adapting to technologies that directly influence the selling process.

Selling Is a Team Effort

Traditionally, selling has been thought of as an individual effort (e.g., the salesperson calling on the customer and presenting a product to an individual or to a committee of buyers). Today, selling is a team effort involving everyone in an organization, spearheaded by the salesperson. For example, selling sophisticated technical equipment in a B2B environment requires a team of experts, including research and design specialists, engineers, and other marketing personnel in addition to the salesperson. They all bring different expertise to the presentation and make the customer feel more at ease with the decision-making process.

FIGURE **11.12** **Tips for Successful Selling**

1. SELLING SKILLS ARE LEARNED SKILLS

Successful salespeople take the time to develop their skills. They ask meaningful questions, listen attentively, and observe buyer behaviour. Through learning, they can relate appropriate product benefits to the customer's needs. Knowledge of the product, company, customer, and competition is essential.

2. THE SALESPERSON IS THE MOST IMPORTANT PRODUCT

Successful salespeople sell themselves. They project a positive image about themselves and their company. If the customer isn't sold on you, he or she won't buy your product.

3. EMOTIONS, FEELINGS, AND RELATIONSHIPS ARE IMPORTANT

Successful salespeople present more than just facts. They create positive emotions about themselves, their products and services, and their company. Through effective communications, they bring the buyer into the relationship, showing how their problems will be resolved.

4. PREPARATION IS CRUCIAL

Be prepared! A sales presentation is like a stage performance. You may not get a second chance. Command the buyer's attention immediately and encourage participation throughout the presentation. Through participation, the buyer will discover the product's benefits. Ensure that all components of the presentation are coordinated and all electronic aids are in working condition.

5. NEGOTIATION SKILLS ARE IMPORTANT

A successful salesperson can deal with any and all concerns raised by the buyer. Be prepared to meet challenges by offering additional information and package together all points of agreement in order to close the sale.

6. ALWAYS BE CLOSING

Closing begins at the start of a presentation. The challenge is to build agreement and help the prospect decide how to buy, not whether to buy. When the prospect agrees, ask for the order. If the buyer refuses, continue with the presentation and ask for the order again when the prospect agrees. Persistence pays off!

Buyers also form teams to better evaluate the product offerings of sellers. From a buying perspective, the team approach helps eliminate financial risks and other risks that are associated with large and complex buying decisions. As well, the personalities of people on both sides of the relationship are put to a test. If the chemistry is good, it is a good sign that the business relationship will grow and prosper.

Companies Sell Relationships, Not Products

Organizations abiding by contemporary corporate culture—that is, those that believe in relationship marketing—actively pursue relationships in the selling process. Making a sale or getting the order is simply one step in the sales continuum. It symbolizes the start of a new relationship or the solidification of an existing one.

The key for the seller is to determine how the company's resources can give the customer an edge. It is a consultative process in which the seller proves to the buyer that

IMC HIGHLIGHT

SOME SUCCEED WHILE MANY FAIL. WHY?

Reducing sales to a set of knowledge and a series of essential steps diminishes the role that sales play in any organization. As indicated in this chapter, it is the salesperson who is the face of the company, so how the salesperson presents him or herself to the customer plays a key role in how the customer ultimately reacts to a company and its products.

Many an expert in selling will tell you that attitude and motivation determine success. Many a salesperson will ask,

"Why am I not closing the sale?"

"Why am I losing sales to competitors?"

"Why don't prospects return my calls?"

"Why can't I reach the real decision maker?"

These kinds of questions need answers. Ineffective salespeople will find excuses, perhaps by blaming others or situations beyond their control for their lack of success. They won't take responsibility or admit that they are the problem!

While some moan and complain, others make the sale. In every market there is a sales leader. And more often than not it isn't the seller with the lowest price. Simply put, good salespeople don't complain. Instead they channel their energies into creative thought to find solutions.

Jeffery Gitomer, an expert in sales and author of *The Sales Bible* and *The Little Red Book of Selling*, offers a success theory he calls "red selling." Why red? Red is the colour of passion. Red is the colour of love. Red is the brightest colour. Red is the most visible colour. And red is fire. His analogy: salespeople need to love what they do, be passionate about what they do, believe in what they sell, be bright about the selling process, and salespeople have to be on fire. If you don't possess this kind of attitude but your competitor does, the competitor will prevail even if he or she does not have the lowest price.

Gitomer goes on to state that if there is a secret ingredient to selling it lies within the individual, not in the techniques. At the very heart of sales success is how deeply one believes in the validity of the company, the product, and oneself. Blame rests on one's own shoulders and to artificially blame things on others or external conditions is an indication that the salesperson lacks passion, dedication, understanding, and belief in what he or she is doing.

He does offer one secret: "People don't like to be sold, but they love to buy." If you know how to sell and why people buy you will win every time. A full understanding of that simple truth, that simple strategy, will change a salesperson's outlook forever.

Adapted from Jeffrey Gitomer, "The secret ingredient of sales success: Add red!" *The Competitive Advantage*, www.competitiveadvantage.net.

---

there is an advantage in doing business together. The search for a good fit between sellers (suppliers) and buyers stems from customers' relentless search for value in everything they purchase.

Technology Is Changing Selling

The nature of selling is changing in many industries due to the advances in communications technology. Members of a channel of distribution that includes raw material suppliers, manufacturers, wholesalers and retailers, and end users are working cooperatively on supply chain management programs. By electronically transferring information among the participants in the supply chain—a cornerstone of true CRM programs—basic buying decisions are automated. Therefore, the challenge facing creative sellers is how to get their products into such a system. The practice of online marketing is a threat to the traditional ways of selling. Companies that do not pursue relationship and partnership selling strategies risk losing sales.

Technology-based CRM programs and a company's ability to sell goods online also have consequences for salespeople and the way they communicate with customers. Technology makes it possible to use fewer people in personal selling, and these sellers find themselves spending less time in personal contact with customers and more time in electronic contact with them. Companies using technology to help market goods and services are finding that geographical boundaries are being eliminated as buyers search for the best value in what they require. Because customers contact companies in a variety of ways, such as by telephone, in person, by email, or through websites, it is important to send out a consistent and integrated marketing communications message.

Summary

Personal selling refers to personal communications between sellers and buyers. Typically, personal selling is divided into three main areas: retail selling, business-to-business selling, and direct selling. In all forms, the immediate goal is to complete a sales transaction, and then adopt appropriate strategies to encourage repeat transactions, thus building a relationship with the customer that will last for an extended period.

The nature of selling has evolved with the changing marketplace. Since the 1970s, selling has moved from consultative selling to strategic selling to relationship selling. Relationship selling involves strategies to establish, build, and maintain customers. It approaches selling from the perspective of the lifetime value of a customer and the concept that retaining satisfied customers is much more profitable than constantly finding new ones. In many cases, relationship selling has extended into partnerships between sellers and buyers. Partnership selling is but one aspect of customer relationship management programs and is strategically developed to encourage a profitable long-term relationship.

There are several essential attributes for successful selling today. A good salesperson possesses the right combination of personal characteristics (characteristics that can be learned and practised) and communication skills (both speaking and listening). A good self-image and positive approach to selling are essential—a successful outlook breeds success! The ability to read a customer is also necessary. Observing and interpreting verbal and non-verbal cues from the customer allow the salesperson to adapt a presentation while in progress and to close the sale at the appropriate time.

Adequate advance preparation is another key to successful selling. A good salesperson possesses sound knowledge in four key areas: product, company, competition, and customer. The task of the salesperson is to match the right product or combination of products and services with the customer's needs. In doing so, the salesperson plans a presentation strategy that shows how the products meet customer needs better than the competition's products. Other essential roles of the salesperson include gathering market intelligence, solving problems, locating and maintaining customers, and providing follow-up service.

The selling process involves seven distinct steps: prospecting, pre-approach, approach, sales presentation, handling objections, closing, and follow-up. Contemporary selling strategies involve the presentation of appropriate product benefits to meet customer needs. A benefit provides the customer with a gain or advantage and shows how the product will resolve a specific problem. Product benefits that are identified as important for a particular buyer are built into a pre-planned presentation designed to resolve a unique problem. During the presentation, a seller's negotiation skills are called upon to respond to the buyer's objections and concerns. Once those are answered, the seller closes the sale by asking for the order. Assuming a satisfactory response, the sale is confirmed and follow-up strategies are implemented. This is the start of the CRM process that, if nurtured carefully, will be profitable for both parties.

Advancements in technology are changing the nature of personal selling. Less time is now spent in personal contact while more time is devoted to electronic contact and activities designed to service and retain customers. As in other forms of marketing communications, the challenge is to develop effective strategies to solidify relationships.

Key Terms

approach, 327

benefit, 325

body language, 320

closing, 329

closing cue, 329

cognitive dissonance, 330

cold canvass, 327

consultative selling, 316

corporate culture, 323

demonstration, 328

feature, 325

field sales force, 314

follow-up, 330

inside sales force, 314

non-verbal communication, 320

objection, 328

online selling, 314

order taking, 313

partnership selling, 318

personal selling, 312

pre-approach, 327

presentation strategy, 318

product configuration, 322

prospecting, 326

qualifying (customers), 327

referral, 327

relationship selling, 317

repeat transaction, 313

sales presentation, 327

self-image, 319

single transaction, 313

strategic selling, 317

telemarketing, 314

trial close, 329

Review Questions

1. What are the distinctions between single transactions and repeat transactions?

2. What are the fundamental differences among consultative selling, strategic selling, and relationship selling?

3. In relationship selling, what is meant by the phrase "positioning the product in the customer's mind"?

4. Briefly define partnership selling and explain its importance.

5. What personal and non-personal characteristics are essential for successful selling?

6. Advance preparation is crucial to successful selling. Briefly describe the importance of knowledge in the following areas: product, company, and competition.

7. Briefly explain the roles and responsibilities of a salesperson.

8. List and briefly describe the seven steps in the selling strategy process.

Discussion and Application Questions

1. "Advances in communications technology will dramatically change the role and nature of selling in the future." Discuss this statement and provide examples of changes that are already influencing selling strategies or will have an influence on them in the future.

2. Conduct some secondary research on the concept of partnership selling. How prevalent is partnership selling in business today? Provide some examples of organizations that have adopted this strategy.

3. Conduct an interview with a salesperson involved in business-to-business selling. Ask if he or she has a relationship strategy for working with customers. How are the relationship strategies adapted to the changing conditions in the marketplace? Present a brief outline of what those strategies are and if they are effective.

4. Assess the role of follow-up in the context of customer relationship management practices. How important is it, and how much emphasis do sales representatives place on this aspect of selling?

5. Evaluate the personal selling strategies of the following retail businesses: Future Shop, The Brick, and Canadian Tire. Do the style and nature of personal selling vary from one business to the other? Which approach is more effective at selling goods at retail? Justify your opinion.

6. Conduct a brief interview with a business-to-business sales representative for a company in your area. Inquire about his or her role in the context of integrated marketing communications. Are there links to other aspects of marketing communications that offer assistance in selling goods and services? Explain the various links as best you can.

7. Conduct some secondary research on telemarketing practices in Canada. Is telemarketing an effective form of personal selling? What are the strengths and weaknesses of this type of selling? Will new privacy laws hamper the development of telemarketing programs?

8. Pre-planning is an essential step in making a sales presentation. Assume you are working for Apple Computer (or any other marketer of desktop and laptop computers) and plan to make a sales presentation to your school. The school is going to purchase or lease desktop computers for a new 50-station lab and is in the process of securing information from various computer suppliers. What questions would you ask to determine your prospect's specific needs? What benefits would you stress when planning the sales presentation and why? What objections do you foresee being raised by the buyer? You may wish to discuss this question with the individual responsible for information technology at your school.

Endnotes

1 Gerald Manning, Barry Reece, and H. F. MacKenzie, *Selling Today* (Toronto: Prentice Hall, 2001), pp. 9–16.

2 Terrence Belford, "Re-arm your sales force," *National Post*, May 5, 2003, p. BE1.

3 *Dictionary of Marketing Terms* (Barron's Educational Series Inc., 1994), p. 367.

4 Gerald Manning, Barry Reece, and H. F. MacKenzie, *Selling Today* (Toronto: Prentice Hall, 2001), p. 110.

5 Geoffrey Brewer, "The customer stops here," *Sales and Marketing Management*, March 1998, pp. 31, 32.

6 "Relationship marketing," *Venture* (Canadian Broadcasting Corporation), broadcast on April 7, 1998.

Part 4

Measuring Plan Performance

Part 4 takes a look at the role of marketing research in evaluating the effectiveness of marketing communications programs. Because so much of the evaluation process relies on the collection of qualitative and quantitative data, it is essential to develop an appreciation of the various research techniques and procedures available.

Chapter 12 introduces some fundamental methodologies for collecting primary research data and distinguishes between qualitative and quantitative data. It discusses the relationship between data analysis and interpretation, and their impact on the development and evaluation of marketing communications strategies and executions.

EVALUATING MARKETING COMMUNICATIONS PROGRAMS

LEARNING OBJECTIVES

After studying this chapter you will be able to

1. define the role and scope of marketing research in contemporary marketing organizations

2. describe the methodologies for collecting primary research data

3. distinguish between qualitative data and quantitative data

4. determine the influence of primary data and information on the development of marketing communications plans

5. assess a variety of marketing research procedures and methodologies that measure and evaluate behavioural responses to communications messages

6. identify the unique methods that measure the effectiveness of individual components of marketing communications

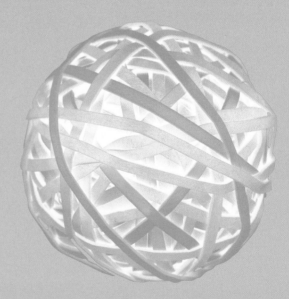

Because a considerable amount of money is invested in marketing communications activities, a marketing organization is very concerned about protecting its investment. In addition, its desire to remain competitive and be knowledgeable about consumers' changing needs makes it necessary to collect appropriate information before and after critical decisions are made. Certainly, a firm understanding of relevant and contemporary consumer behaviour will play a major role in the development of a marketing communications campaign (refer to Chapter 1 for details). Carefully planned and well-timed marketing research is the tool that provides organizations with the insight necessary to take advantage of new opportunities. This chapter will discuss some fundamental concepts about the marketing research process and present various specific research techniques that are used to measure and evaluate the effectiveness of marketing communications programs.

THE ROLE AND SCOPE OF MARKETING RESEARCH

Research provides an organization with data. The data do not guarantee that proper decisions and actions by the firm will be taken, because data are always open to interpretation. The old saying that "some information is better than no information" puts the role of marketing research into perspective. A vital marketing tool, it is used to help reduce or eliminate the uncertainty and risk associated with making business decisions. Of course, this principle applies to marketing communications decisions as well.

In many ways, marketing research is a form of insurance. It ensures that the action a company might take is the right action. For a multi-million dollar advertising decision, a manager would want to have good information (a foundation, so to speak) available to make sure the right decision is made. To demonstrate, consider a marketing communications problem once faced by Molson Canadian, a popular brand of beer. When Brett Marchand, vice-president of marketing, first showed senior executives a commercial called "Rant," it wasn't greeted with overwhelming applause. The ad showed a young guy working himself into a feverish pitch over what it means to be a Canadian. In fact, the ad zeroed in on things that separate Canadians from Americans. From marketing research, however, Molson had discovered a pent-up sense of patriotism among young Canadians. "Rant" ended up touching a nerve with Canadians, who related to "this proud Canadian message," says Marchand.[1] The ad generated much publicity, even in the United States, and helped Molson Canadian recover some lost market share. The moral of the story is simple: research provided useful information to develop an effective advertising strategy.

Marketing research links the consumer/customer/public to the marketer through information—information used to define marketing opportunities and problems, to generate, refine, and evaluate marketing actions, to monitor marketing performance, and to improve the understanding of marketing as a process. It designs the method for collecting information, manages and implements the information collection process, analyzes the results, and communicates the findings and their implications.[2]

The scope of marketing research seems endless. In a marketing communications setting, research is useful for identifying consumer insights that can be considered when developing message strategies, for measuring the impact and effectiveness of message and media strategies, for tracking brand awareness during the life of a campaign, for pre-testing and post-testing advertising strategies, and for measuring changes in behaviour based on the effects of all forms of marketing communications. Regardless of the nature of the research study, the information obtained will assist managers in their decision making.

The very nature of marketing research, however, requires significant investment by a marketing organization. Due to the diversity of marketing communications and the complementary ways in which the various components blend together, it is difficult to isolate one communications component and state definitively that it determined success or failure. Wise marketing managers also rely on their own experience and intuitiveness when making decisions. When the situation so dictates, marketing research should be undertaken.

Molson
www.molson.com

Marketing research

A marketing function that links the consumer/customer/public to the marketer through information; the information is used to define marketing opportunities and problems, generate marketing strategies, evaluate marketing actions, and monitor performance.

How do managers go about collecting information? Prudent marketing decision makers combine their intuition and judgment with all other information sources available. They use the scientific method, which implies that the data generated are reliable and valid. **Reliability** refers to the degree of similar results being achieved if another study were undertaken under similar conditions. **Validity** refers to the research procedure's ability to measure what it was intended to measure.

Reliability (of data)
Degree of similarity of results achieved if another research study were undertaken under similar circumstances.

Validity (of data)
A research procedure's ability to measure what it is intended to measure.

RESEARCH TECHNIQUES FOR MARKETING COMMUNICATIONS

When an organization attempts to measure the potential impact of its advertising messages on consumers, it implements a variety of primary research techniques. Students should be aware of the basic steps involved in planning various research procedures to appreciate the value of the data. Essentially, the evaluation of advertising messages or any other form of marketing communications involves the collection of primary data.

Primary Research

Once the organization decides it requires input from customers and potential customers before making a decision, the research process moves to the stage of collecting primary data. **Primary research** refers to the process of collecting and recording new data, called **primary data**, to resolve a specific problem, usually at a high cost to the sponsoring organization. Primary research is custom designed and focuses on resolving a particular question or obtaining specified information. A procedure is developed and a research instrument designed to perform the specific task. Figure 12.1 summarizes the steps involved in collecting primary data.

Primary research
The collection and recording of primary data.

Primary data
Data collected to resolve a problem and recorded for the first time.

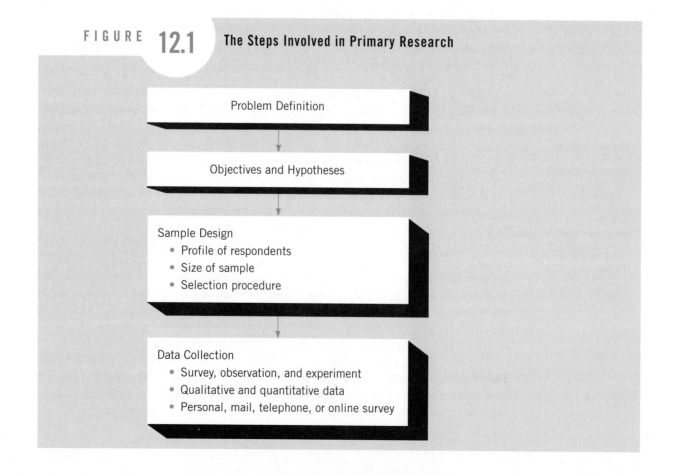

FIGURE **12.1** **The Steps Involved in Primary Research**

Problem Definition

Objectives and Hypotheses

Sample Design
- Profile of respondents
- Size of sample
- Selection procedure

Data Collection
- Survey, observation, and experiment
- Qualitative and quantitative data
- Personal, mail, telephone, or online survey

In directing the primary research, the marketing organization identifies the precise nature of the problem, the objectives of the study, and the hypotheses associated with it. **Research objectives** are statements that outline what the research is to accomplish, while **hypotheses**, which are statements of predicted outcomes, are confirmed or refuted by the data collected. The outcome of the research often leads to certain actions being taken by the marketing organization. Refer to Figure 12.2 for an illustration of research objectives, hypotheses, and action standards.

Conducting a marketing research study is beyond the scope and expertise of most marketing organizations in Canada. Consequently, independent market research firms such as Millward Brown are hired to perform the task. For example, Millward Brown conducts a considerable amount of research on advertising campaigns under consideration by General Motors of Canada. Usually, a marketing research manager from the sponsoring organization is responsible for supervising the research study and works directly with the marketing research firm in designing the project.

Sample Design

Prior to implementing a research study, the researchers identify the characteristics of the people they would like to participate in the study. This process is referred to as sample design. A **sample** is defined as a portion of an entire population used to obtain information about that population and must form an accurate representation of the population if the information gathered is to be considered reliable. Some basic steps must be taken to develop a representative sample:

- **Define the Population (Universe):** A **population (universe)** is a group of people with specific age, gender, or other demographic characteristics. It is usually the description of the target market or audience under study. For the purposes of primary research, a description of a population might be "single or married females between the ages of 21 and 34 years living in cities with more than 500 000 residents." A proper research procedure will screen potential respondents for these characteristics.

- **Identify the Sampling Frame:** The **sampling frame** refers to a list that can be used for reaching a population. The telephone directory could be used as a sampling frame for the population described above. If Sears wanted to conduct research among its current customers about the style of advertising it uses, it could use its credit card account holder list as a means of access.

- **Determine the Type of Sample:** The researcher has the option of using a probability sample or a non-probability sample. If a **probability sample** is used, the respondents have a known or equal chance of selection and are randomly selected from across the population. For example, the researcher may use a predetermined and systematic procedure for picking respondents through a telephone directory. The known chance of selection enables statistical procedures to be used in the results to estimate sampling errors and determine the reliability of the data collected. In a **non-probability sample**, the respondents have an unknown chance of selection, and their selection is based on factors such as convenience for the researcher or the researcher's judgment. The researcher relies on experience to determine who would be most appropriate. For example, Sears could randomly stop shoppers inside its stores to seek their input on a variety of marketing concerns. Factors such as cost and timing are other reasons for using non-probability samples.

- **Determine the Sample Size:** Generally, the larger the sample, the greater the accuracy of the data collected and the higher the cost. The nature of the research study is a determining factor in the number of participants required. Some researchers use a 1 percent rule (1 percent of the defined population or universe), while others state absolute minimums of 200 respondents. The accuracy of the sample is usually calculated statistically and stated in the research report. Therefore, a researcher considers the margin of error that is acceptable and the degree of certainty required.

Research objective
A statement that outlines what the marketing research is to accomplish.

Hypothesis
A statement of outcomes predicted in a marketing research investigation.

Sample
A representative portion of an entire population that is used to obtain information about that population.

Population (universe)
In marketing research, a group of people with certain age, gender, or other demographic characteristics.

Sampling frame
A list used to access a representative sample of a population; it is a means of accessing people for a research study.

Probability sample
A sample of respondents who are known to have an equal chance of selection and are randomly selected from the sampling frame.

Non-probability sample
A sample of respondents who have an unknown chance of selection and are chosen because of factors such as convenience or the judgment of the researcher.

FIGURE **12.2** **A Sample of Research Objectives, Hypotheses, and Sample Design for a Marketing Communications Study**

PRODUCT

Labatt Blue

PROBLEM

Labatt Blue has been using a humorous appeal technique in its "Cheers to Friends" advertising campaign. The brand manager is less than satisfied with the impact of this campaign on current customers and would like to evaluate alternative appeal techniques.

OBJECTIVES

1. To determine the potential impact of a lifestyle appeal technique on current Labatt Blue drinkers.
2. To determine the potential impact of a sexual appeal technique on current Labatt Blue drinkers.

HYPOTHESES

1. The communication of lifestyle appeals may have impact initially but over the long term will not be viewed as unique and distinctive because so many competing brands use lifestyle imagery.
2. The communication of sexual appeal will break through the clutter of competitive beer advertising and separate Blue from other leading brands.

ACTION STANDARD

Given the assumption that research results indicate a preference for either the lifestyle appeal technique or the sexual appeal technique, and preference can be sustained for an extended period, then a new creative campaign will be devised for Labatt Blue. The implementation date for a new campaign will be May 2005.

SAMPLE DESIGN

Population

Input will be sought from Blue's primary target market, described as males, 19 to 29 years old, living in urban markets.

Sampling Frame

Current Blue drinkers will be recruited by telephone and by using telephone directories in three cities: Toronto, Edmonton, and Vancouver. A series of qualifying questions will be asked of potential respondents to determine their degree of brand loyalty.

Type of Sample

A probability sample is essential to ensure accurate and reliable data. A systematic procedure will be devised to recruit respondents in each city.

Sample Size

It is anticipated that a mixture of qualitative research and quantitative research will be employed. A focus group will be conducted in each city to derive qualitative information. Survey research will require a minimum of 200 respondents in each city to secure accurate quantitative data.

The above is a hypothetical example and is intended for illustration purposes only.

Figure 12.2 contains a sample design. It should be noted that errors in the design and implementation of a research sample could distort the validity and reliability of the data collected.

Data Collection Methods

There are three primary methods a researcher can use to collect data: surveys, observation, and experiments (see Figure 12.3). The data collected can be qualitative or quantitative in nature.

For **survey research**, data are collected systematically through some form of communication with a representative sample by means of a questionnaire that records responses. Most surveys include predetermined questions and a selection of responses that are easily filled in by the respondent or the interviewer. This technique is referred to as **fixed-response (closed-ended) questioning**. Surveys will also include **open-response (open-ended) questions**, a situation where space is available at the end of a question where verbatim comments by the respondent are recorded. Survey research can be conducted by personal interview, telephone, mail, or online.

Most surveys are designed with a high degree of structure. The questionnaire follows a planned format: screening questions at the beginning, central issue questions (dealing with the nature of the research) in the middle, and classification (demographic) questions at the end. In survey research, closed-ended or fixed-response questions (questions that include predetermined answers that a person simply checks off) are most popular. They permit the data to be easily transferred to a computer for tabulation and subsequent analysis.

In **observation research**, the behaviour of the respondent is observed and recorded. In this form of research, participants do not have to be recruited; they can participate in a study without knowing it. In other situations, respondents are usually aware of being observed, perhaps through a two-way mirror, by a hidden camera while being interviewed, or by electronic measurement of impulses. All of these techniques can be used when consumers are asked to evaluate advertising messages. Electronic observation over the Internet is achieved through cookies. A **cookie** is a file that websites store on a user's

Survey research
The systematic collection of data by communicating with a representative sample by means of a questionnaire.

Fixed-response (closed-ended) questioning
Questions that are predetermined with set answers for the respondents to choose from.

Open-response (open-ended) questioning
A situation where space is available at the end of a question where the respondents can add their comments.

Observation research
A form of research in which the behaviour of the respondent is observed and recorded; may be by personal or electronic means.

Cookie
An electronic identification tag sent from a web server to a user's browser to track the user's browsing patterns.

FIGURE **12.3** **Data Collection Methods**

SURVEYS

- Data are collected systematically by communicating with a representative sample, usually using a questionnaire.
- Questionnaires can be disguised (purpose hidden) or undisguised (purpose known), and structured (fixed responses provided) or unstructured (open-ended question format).

OBSERVATION

- The behaviour of the respondent is observed by personal, mechanical, or electronic means.

EXPERIMENTS

- Variables are manipulated under controlled conditions to observe respondents' reactions.
- Experiments are used to test marketing influences such as product changes, package changes, and advertising copy tests.

computer (browsers contain features that allow users to control whether cookies are stored). The contents of those files can contain information about a user's preferences—and that information is a valuable resource to marketers.

In **experimental research**, one or more factors are manipulated under controlled conditions, while other elements remain constant so that respondents' reactions can be evaluated. Test marketing is a form of experimental research. In a marketing communications context, **test marketing** involves placing a commercial or set of commercials in a campaign (could be print ads as well) in one or more limited markets, representative of the whole, to observe the potential impact of the ads on consumers. Do the ads generate the desired level of awareness and preference? Do they provide sufficient motivation so that consumers take the desired action? Good test marketing provides valuable experience prior to an expensive regional or national launch of the campaign. If the test market proves the campaign to be less than effective, a pending disaster can be avoided.

For more insight into how observational research influences creative strategies, read the IMC Highlight **Scott Paper and P&G Dig Deep for Clues**.

Experimental research

Research in which one or more factors are manipulated under controlled conditions while other elements remain constant so that the respondent's actions can be evaluated.

Test marketing

Placing a commercial, set of commercials, or print ad campaign in one or more limited markets that are representative of the whole to observe the impact of the ads on consumers.

IMC HIGHLIGHT

SCOTT PAPER AND P&G DIG DEEP FOR CLUES

"Seek and ye shall find." Perhaps that's the mantra of marketing research practices today. Many companies now hire anthropologists to gather deeper consumer insights. What they discover can enhance positioning strategies and offer guidance for the development of effective message strategies. They will go shopping with people, follow them around, and watch how they interact with others.

Scott Paper placed an anthropologist in selected homes to observe their primary target, women 25 to 54 years old. The objective was to discover a central brand idea by finding out what goes on in the bathroom. Scott discovered that women view the bathroom as a place of solitude and privacy. For many women it is a shrine. An idea was born! Cashmere toilet paper (formerly known as Cottonelle) would be positioned as a "luxury" brand, a step up from all others. It was aligned with the idea that solitude can be a luxury in a hectic life. One of Cashmere's print ads showed a roll of toilet paper unfurling into a cashmere scarf.

Procter & Gamble designed a completely new campaign for Tide based on what it learned from spending a week with consumers in two American cities. The visitors from P&G and its advertising agency literally tagged along with the family. The objective was to learn more about the role of laundry in their life. While that may sound ridiculous, Tide is a global brand that contributes significantly to P&G's sales and profits.

Instead of asking questions related directly to laundry, the executive visitors asked questions about their lives, what their needs were, and how they felt as women. In doing so, they discovered how unimportant laundry was in people's lives today and that Tide wasn't the most important thing on a woman's mind. The executives quickly determined that Tide needed to be repositioned in the minds of women. Tide had always been about cleaning power; simply stated, the brand performs better than competing brands. In repositioning the brand, the new emphasis would be on fabric protection.

After the new insights were assessed, the agency developed a new advertising campaign with the theme "Tide knows fabric best." The ads rely on music, rich visual imagery, and emotional benefits—quite a departure from the traditional demonstration and side-by-side comparisons with other brands that Tide had been using for years. In one commercial for Tide with Febreze, Tide's laundry-odour removal benefit gets an emotional heft, billed as "the difference between smelling like a mom and smelling like a woman" amid shots of mom with baby and then mom with husband cuddling, all to the tune of "Be My Baby."

P&G is pleased with the results. Tide is once again building its market share in a very competitive product category. Tide holds a 43 percent share and has been climbing gradually since the new campaign was launched. Any new products that come on stream will undoubtedly adopt a similar style of advertising.

Adapted from Jack Neff, "Five years in the making, Tide gets a new ad campaign," *Advertising Age*, February 8, 2006, www.adage.com/news, and Andrea Zoe Aster, "Digging deeper," *Marketing*, November 22, 2004, p. 31.

Qualitative Data versus Quantitative Data

According to the nature of the information sought, research data are classified as either qualitative or quantitative. There are significant differences between these two classifications.

Qualitative data are usually collected from small samples in a controlled environment. They result from questions concerned with "why" and from in-depth probing of the participants. Typically, such data are gathered from focus group interviews. A **focus group** is a small group of people (usually eight to ten) with common characteristics (e.g., a target market profile), brought together to discuss issues related to the marketing of a product or service. A typical qualitative project consists of four to six groups representing various regions or urban areas of Canada.

The word "focus" implies that the discussion concentrates on one topic or concept. A trained moderator usually conducts the interview over a period of a few hours. The role of the moderator is to get the participants to interact fairly freely to uncover the reasons and motivations underlying their remarks. Probing uncovers the hidden interplay of psychological factors that drive a consumer to buy one brand rather than another. With regard to advertising evaluations, it provides a multitude of favourable and opposing views on how effective a message might be. Consumers' reactions to the message, the characters that present the message, the campaign theme and slogan, and their general likes and dislikes of the ad can be discussed at length.

The major drawback of using focus groups concerns the reliability of the data. The sample size is too small to be representative of the entire population, and most people in a focus group do not like to show disagreement with a prevailing opinion. For that reason, interviews are usually held in several locations.

Marketing decisions involving considerable sums of money are very risky if based on such limited research. One of the most spectacular focus group failures, the launch of new Coke in the 1980s, came about because the soft drink maker was not asking the right questions. Worried that archrival PepsiCo had a better-tasting product, Coca-Cola asked consumers if they liked its new formulation without ever asking if they wanted its tried-and-true beverage changed.[3] The new version of Coke failed miserably when it was launched, and the public backlash was so significant that Coca-Cola had to reintroduce the original Coke as Coca-Cola Classic.

The Coca-Cola example shows the potential weakness of focus groups—they are exploratory in nature. A follow-up quantitative survey is often required to establish numbers, which costs organizations additional money and time. On the positive side, attitudes that are revealed in a focus group can be used as a foundation for forming questions and questionnaires if and when quantitative research is required. The attitudes uncovered can be expressed as answers for closed-ended questions in a questionnaire.

Quantitative data provide answers to questions concerned with "what," "when," "who," "how many," and "how often." This research attempts to put feelings, attitudes, and opinions into numbers and percentages. The data are gathered from structured questionnaires and a large sample to ensure accuracy and reliability. The interpretation of the results is based on the numbers compiled, not on the judgment of the researcher. Quantitative research will statistically confirm the attitudes and feelings that arose in qualitative research. Therefore, a manager will have more confidence in the decisions that are based on the research. Figure 12.4 briefly compares qualitative and quantitative research.

With so much risk involved in major decisions about marketing communications, the wise organization should use both forms of data collection. Molson, for example, has a vice-president accountable for marketing research. Molson does focus groups and qualitative research, but it also does quantitative research on all television ads before production of the ad takes place. Each ad must hit a specific persuasion level. "We do not shoot ads until we know they will persuade beer drinkers to drink that brand," says Michael Downey, Molson's senior vice-president of global marketing.[4]

Qualitative data

Data collected from small samples in a controlled environment; it describes feelings and opinions on issues.

Focus group

A small group of people with common characteristics brought together to discuss issues related to the marketing of a product or service.

Coca-Cola
www.coca-cola.com

Quantitative data

Measurable data collected from large samples using a structured research procedure.

FIGURE **12.4** **A Comparison of Qualitative and Quantitative Data**

QUALITATIVE DATA

- Collected from a small sample, usually in a focus-group environment.

- Unstructured questions.

- Questions seek attitudes, feelings, and opinions.

- Data not always reliable because of small sample.

QUANTITATIVE DATA

- Collected from a large, representative sample of target market.

- Structured questions with predetermined responses.

- Deals with who, what, when, how many, and how often.

- Statistically reliable, with calculated degree of error.

Survey Methodology

Personal interview

In marketing research, the collection of information in a face-to-face interview.

There are four primary means of contacting consumers when conducting surveys to collect quantitative data: telephone, personal interview, mail, and the Internet. **Personal interviews** involve face-to-face communication with groups (e.g., focus groups) or individuals and are usually done through quantitative questionnaires. Popular locations for interviews are busy street corners, shopping malls, and the homes of respondents.

Telephone interview

In marketing research, the collection of information from a respondent by telephone.

Telephone interviews involve communication with individuals over the phone. Usually, the interviews are conducted from central locations (i.e., one location that can reach all Canadian markets), and, consequently, there is supervised control over the interview process. Telephone technology is now so advanced that research data can be transferred from the telephone directly to a computer. However, there is a very high refusal rate for telephone surveys. A recent study by the Professional Marketing Research Society observed that 78 percent of people contacted refuse to participate.[5]

Mail interview

In marketing research, the collection of information from a respondent by mail.

Mail interviews are a silent process of collecting information. Using the mail to distribute a survey means that a highly dispersed sample is reached in a cost-efficient manner. The main drawbacks are the lack of control and the amount of time required to implement and retrieve the surveys.

Online survey

In marketing research, using an online questionnaire to collect data from people.

Online surveys allow an organization to be much less invasive in collecting information. Some companies have found that consumers seem more willing to divulge information over the Internet compared with the more traditional means of surveying. Furthermore, compared to traditional data collection methods, online research offers results quickly and at much lower cost. In a paper environment, a company like P&G would spend $25 000 and get results in two months. Online, the same test costs $2500 and results are available in two weeks.[6] On the downside, recruiting participation can be a lot like fishing—participation is left up to the fish. Therefore, the validity of the information is questionable.

The decision about which technique to use is based on three primary factors:

- **Nature of Information Sought:** The amount of information to be collected and the time it will take to complete the survey are considerations. For example, if discussion is necessary to get the answers, personal interviews in a focus group may be best. If large amounts of information are required, the best option may be the mail.

- **Cost and Time:** When time is critical, certain options are eliminated. The telephone and the Internet are the best means of obtaining quick, cost-efficient information. Costs must also be weighed against benefits. The net financial gains expected to result from the research may determine which method is used.
- **Respondents:** The selection of a survey method can be influenced by the location of the respondents and how easily they can be reached. For example, if the participant is to be reached at home, any method—personal interview, telephone, mail, or online—can be used. Responding online is very convenient for people. In contrast, if the participant is to be reached in a central location, such as a shopping mall, a personal interview is the only choice.

Figure 12.5 summarizes the advantages and disadvantages of each survey method.

E.D. Smith, a jam manufacturer, wanted to get closer to its consumers. To understand the primary customer better and to get insight into how to advertise to them some unique research was undertaken. E.D. Smith markets jams, spreads, and pie fillings in a variety of flavours. See Figure 12.6 on page 349. For details, read the IMC Highlight **E.D. Smith: Passionate about Jam**.

FIGURE **12.5** **The Advantages and Disadvantages of Various Survey Methods**

	ADVANTAGES	DISADVANTAGES
Personal Interview		
	• High rate of participation	• Higher cost due to time needed
	• Visual observations possible	• Respondents reluctant to respond to certain questions
	• Flexible (can include visuals)	• Interviewer bias possible
Telephone Interview		
	• Convenient and allows control	• Observation not possible
	• Costs less	• Short questions and questionnaires
	• Timely responses	• Privacy concerns (bad time of day)
Mail Surveys		
	• Cost efficient	• Lack of control
	• Large sample obtainable	• Potential for misinterpretation by respondent
	• Relaxed environment	• Time lag between distribution and return
	• Impersonal nature produces accurate responses	• Low response rates
Online Surveys		
	• Efficient and inexpensive	• Immature medium compared to alternatives
	• Less intrusive (respondent driven)	• Limited sample frame (Internet users only)
	• Convenient for respondent	• Image concerns associated with spam
	• Fast response time (days)	• Reliability of information suspect

E.D. SMITH: PASSIONATE ABOUT JAM

At E.D. Smith, changes in marketing and marketing communications were necessary if the brand was going to survive in the very competitive jam market. New insights into consumer shopping behaviour were urgently needed. Rather than follow a traditional approach to collecting such information, the company embarked upon a very intensive research study that took them right to the supermarket aisles. The objective was to discover the consumer dynamics for buying something as simple as a jar of jam. When the research was complete, the company had polled more than 3000 consumers from coast to coast.

Brand Leadership Marketing, a research company, conducted the surveys. Typically, this kind of information would be collected from focus groups and through surveys, but in this case the recommendation was to collect information right on the spot, at a time when consumers were actually making the buying decision. The company invaded the supermarket aisles to seek the responses they needed. According to Dennis Barham, chairman of Brand Leadership, "You get more genuine comments from people. At that moment the product is top of mind, and it's a true-to-life scenario that no survey or focus group can replicate."

CEO Michael Burrows of E.D. Smith says further, "If you are looking for the big idea, you will find it using such one-on-one interfacing. You catch the customer at just the right moment." And what did E.D. Smith learn? "The main insight surrounded the taste of jam," says Barham. Most respondents stated that jam was too sweet. As a result of these findings E.D. Smith took action. The company reduced the sugar content of all lines, redesigned the labels, and introduced 23 new flavours of jam. See Figure 12.6 for an illustration.

The nature of marketing communications also changed. The company added a new focus on point-of-purchase communication to draw attention to the new products and product changes. The company provided retailers with standalone shelves with signage, employed coupons to encourage trial purchases of new products, and put more dollars into public relations and advertising messages that used third-party endorsements. Apparently, endorsements resonate well with the primary target, the female head of household.

Media advertising also played a key role in communicating the changes. The media chosen focused on female-friendly publications like *Chatelaine*, *Canadian Living*, and *Homemakers*. These publications effectively reached the primary target audience.

Adapted from "For the love of jam," *Strategy*, July 2005, p. 26.

Data Transfer and Processing

Editing
In marketing research, the review of questionnaires for consistency and completeness.

Data transfer
In marketing research, the transfer of answers from the questionnaire to the computer.

Tabulation
The process of counting various responses for each question in a survey.

Frequency distribution
The number of times each answer in a survey was chosen for a question.

Cross-tabulation
The comparison of answers to questions by various subgroups with the total number of responses.

Data analysis
The evaluation of responses question by question; gives meaning to the data.

Once the data have been collected, then editing, data transfer, and tabulation take place. In the **editing** stage, completed questionnaires are reviewed for consistency and completeness. Whether to include questionnaires with incomplete or seemingly contradictory answers is left to the researcher to decide. In the **data transfer** stage, answers from questions are transferred to a computer. Answers are pre-coded to facilitate the transfer. In the case of telephone surveys, it is now common to enter the responses directly into the computer as the questions are being asked.

Once the survey results have been entered into a computer, the results are tabulated. **Tabulation** is the process of counting the various responses for each question and arriving at a frequency distribution. A **frequency distribution** shows the number of times each answer was chosen for a question. Numerous cross-tabulations are also made. **Cross-tabulation** is the comparison and contrasting of the answers of various subgroups or of particular subgroups and the total response group. For example, a question dealing with brand awareness could be analyzed by the age, gender, or income of respondents.

Data Analysis and Interpretation

Data analysis refers to the evaluation of responses question by question, a process that gives meaning to the data. At this point, the statistical data for each question are reviewed, and the researcher makes observations. Typically, a researcher makes comparisons between responses of subgroups on a percentage or ratio basis.

FIGURE **12.6** **Customer Insight Obtained from Marketing Research Leads to New Product Lines at E.D. Smith**

Source: Courtesy of Dick Hemingway.

Data interpretation
The relating of accumulated data to the problem under review and to the objectives and hypotheses of the research study.

Data interpretation, on the other hand, involves relating the accumulated data to the problem under review and to the objectives and hypotheses of the research study. The process of interpretation uncovers solutions to the problem. The researcher draws conclusions that state the implications of the data for managers.

Recommendations and Implementation

The recommendations outline suggested courses of action that the sponsoring organization should take in view of the data collected. Once a research project is complete, the research company will present its findings in a written report. Frequently, an oral presentation of the key findings is also made to the client. Very often, senior management is informed of the information when it becomes known so that the managers are better prepared for possible actions or changes in strategic direction.

These days, thanks to changing technology and fast turnaround times, market research is more streamlined, with clients expecting solid decision-making results—yesterday. It is quite common for research companies to present their findings in personal presentations, using PowerPoint or the like to display succinct objectives, results, and recommendations.

For a more complete look at how marketing research influences the direction of marketing strategy refer to Figure 12.7. It identifies a problem faced by Kraft Dinner, outlines the research procedures used to obtain information, and shows how Kraft used the information to develop a new advertising campaign.

FIGURE **12.7**   **Psychological Profiling Leads to New Advertising for Kraft Dinner**

BACKGROUND
Kraft Dinner is the country's number-one selling grocery item with a 75 percent share of its category and Kraft Canada's biggest volume business. Despite such a lofty status, sales were flat and had been for some time.

PROBLEM
To discover just what was ailing this powerhouse brand. It was hypothesized that erosion in brand confidence among consumers was due to the fact there was no communication with people about what they love about Kraft Dinner.

MARKETING RESEARCH PROCEDURE
A methodology was employed that would create a personality profile for the brand. There would be an exclusive focus on the emotional aura around the brand. The notion of a brand carrying human traits is nearly as old as advertising itself, but it is only lately that psychiatric profiling has been gaining momentum.

To determine Kraft dinner's personality profile, *two specific exercises* were undertaken by research participants:

1. "Kraft Dinner has died. You have to write the obituary that goes in your local newspaper."
2. "You're a psychiatrist and Kraft Dinner has come to see you. Analyze the problem and tell him a solution."

THE RESEARCH FINDINGS
From the obituary pages:

- "Tragically yesterday the hero of many a Canadian meal died accidentally."
- "He was affectionately known as KD by his many friends."
- "There was an easy way about him that was both knowing and comforting."
- "KD valued his time with friends."

From the psychiatrist's couch:

- "Kraft has low self-esteem and insecurity."
- "Kraft Dinner is feeling guilt and anxiety about his image."
- "Kraft has low self-esteem, is old, lethargic, and withdrawn."

ANALYSIS AND INTERPRETATION
Kraft Dinner is

- dependable
- comfortable
- a friend
- nonjudgmental
- easy-going
- unpretentious
- trustworthy
- loved by all

RECOMMENDED THERAPY

- Build self-confidence.
- Remember and promote the immortal place he holds in our hearts.
- Raise self-esteem.
- Get across the point that you are worth more.

ACTIONS TAKEN
Kraft raised the price of Kraft Dinner, redesigned the packaging, launched a new KD website, and created a series of television commercials targeting young people who grew up eating the product. The ads touched on a person's relationships with Kraft Dinner.

RESULTS
Testing of the commercials revealed that the spots outperformed all others in the category in North America. Although the product was already the biggest seller on the grocery shelves, base brand sales experienced a significant increase.

Adapted from Peter Vamos, "Psychological profiling gets inside a brand's head," *Strategy*, August 27, 2000, p. 2.

MEASURING AND EVALUATING ADVERTISING MESSAGES

One of the first steps in measuring advertising messages is an evaluation of agency creative ideas by the client. It seems that a creative idea is just that—an idea—until it is sold to the client for approval. Very often, these kinds of evaluations are subjective in nature because they rely on opinions put forth by brand managers, marketing directors, and presidents of companies. The chain of command for approving advertising creative and media expenditures can go very high in an organization.

Client Evaluation

Creative can be tested at several stages of the development process. The first step is usually a qualitative assessment by the client to determine if the message conforms to the strategic direction that was provided to the agency. This evaluation is conducted by means of a managerial approach. In this evaluation, a client needs to resist the impulse to assess the creative on personal, subjective bases. However, if a "to proceed or not to proceed" decision must be made, the client reserves the right to conduct consumer research prior to making the decision.

Clients using the **managerial approach** for evaluating creative may apply some or all of the criteria listed below:

1. **In terms of content, does the advertisement communicate the creative objectives and reflect the positioning strategy of the brand (company)?** The client reviews the creative for its ability to communicate the key benefit and support claims that substantiate the benefit. All creative objectives would have been outlined in the creative brief. As well, the client would determine if the message strategy and execution conform to the overall positioning strategy of the brand. If it is off strategy, the ad will be rejected.

2. **In terms of how the ad is presented (strategy and execution), does it mislead or misrepresent the intent of the message? Is it presented in good taste?** The client must be concerned about the actual message and any implied message since it is responsible for the truthfulness of the message. Legal counsel often has the final say regarding message content. Consumers frequently lodge complaints about ads they find offensive or that encourage risky behaviour. Consumer complaints forced the Ford Motor Company to pull an ad for the Ford Focus. There were complaints about a scene in which a female shopper pushes a male clerk into the hatchback of her car. For some reason the ad was perceived to condone violence, which clearly wasn't the intention.

3. **Is the ad memorable?** Breaking through the clutter of competitive advertising is always a challenge, and a lot of advertising that is approved doesn't quite cut it. Is there something that stands out that customers will remember—what will they take away from the ad? For instance, Bell Canada introduced a multi-division campaign featuring two computer-generated beavers named Frank and Gordon during the 2006 Super Bowl and during CBC's coverage of the Turin Winter Olympics. The personality of the life-like beavers and the humour they brought to the commercials made them memorable; consumers wanted to see more of the beavers. Brand recognition of the various Bell services increased significantly as a result of the Frank and Gordon campaign.[7]

4. **Is the brand recognition effective?** There must be sufficient brand registration in the ad. Some companies go as far as to stipulate how many times the package should be shown in a television commercial or how many times the brand name should be mentioned. The creativity of the commercial or print ad should not outweigh the product—it should complement the product. For example, people often recall funny ads and they can talk at length about the humorous situations that were presented. Sometimes, however, they are unable to recall the name of the product that appeared in the ad. So much for the laughs!

Bell Canada
www.bell.ca

5. **Should the advertisement be researched**? When it comes to assessing the impact and effectiveness of the advertisement, subjective judgments by the client have the disadvantage of not being quantifiable. Prior to spending money on production, the client may decide to conduct consumer research to seek quantifiable data that will help the decision-making process. Better safe than sorry!

The evaluation process can occur at any stage of the creative development process. A television commercial, for example, could be evaluated by consumers at the storyboard, rough-cut, or finished commercial stage. Although it is not practical to test commercials at all stages, if the quality or effectiveness of the commercial is ever in question, the client should conduct research to avoid costly and embarrassing errors in judgment.

It is difficult to isolate any particular form of marketing communications and state categorically that it had an impact on sales. There are simply too many factors that influence buying decisions by consumers and business customers. The source of motivation to take action could be any combination of product quality, services offered, price, availability, advertising, public relations, sales promotions, and so on. As this book reiterates time and time again, it is the integrated effort of all forms of marketing communications that ultimately influences the customer's buying decision. It is very difficult to measure the direct effect of any single communications element on sales.

When evaluating the impact of advertising messages, the objectives of the advertising plan must be considered. What did the brand set out to achieve? As discussed in Chapter 2 on strategic planning and Chapter 4 on creative planning, common objectives of advertising are to create and increase awareness, attract new target markets, encourage trial purchase by including incentives with advertising, create brand preference in the consumer's mind, and alter consumers' perceptions about the brand. Various primary research techniques can be used to evaluate whether or not advertising achieved these kinds of objectives.

External Research Techniques and Procedures

Creative evaluation involves a variety of research techniques. The objective of most creative research is to measure the impact of a message on a target audience. Creative research is conducted based on the stage of creative development. It is either a pre-test or a post-test situation. **Pre-testing** is the evaluation of an advertisement, commercial, or campaign before it goes into final production or media placement to determine the strengths and weaknesses of a strategy and execution. By getting input from the target market at an early stage, a company will have more confidence in the creative once it is placed in the media. **Post-testing** is the process of evaluating and measuring the effectiveness of an advertisement, commercial, or campaign during or after it has run. Post-testing provides information that can be used in future advertising planning.

Common techniques used to measure the effectiveness of creative are *recognition* and *recall testing*, *opinion-measure testing*, and *physiological-response testing*. Procedures such as inquiry tests and controlled experiments used in post-testing also measure the effectiveness of the message.

Recognition and Recall Testing

In **recognition tests**, respondents are tested for awareness. They are asked if they can recall an advertisement for a specific brand or any of the points made in the advertisement. For example, consumers who have read a publication in which an ad has appeared are asked if they remember what brand was advertised and what the basic message being communicated was. Typically, an individual is asked a series of questions to determine what they know about an ad.

Several factors affect the level of recognition of an ad. For example, a large print ad occupying a full page usually has a higher level of recognition than an ad occupying only

Pre-testing
The evaluation of commercial messages prior to final production to determine the strengths and weaknesses of the communications.

Post-testing
The evaluation and measurement of a message's effectiveness during or after the message has run.

Recognition test
A test that measures a target audience's awareness of a brand, copy, or of the advertisement itself after the audience has been exposed to the message.

a portion of a page. The inclusion of a celebrity might draw more attention to an ad simply because consumers like the celebrity. The amount of text in the ad may also be a factor. Ads with lots of copy might get lower recognition simply because consumers don't read all of the copy.

Recall test
A test that measures an ad's impact by asking respondents to recall specific elements (e.g., the selling message) of the advertisement; can be aided (some information provided) or unaided.

In **recall tests**, respondents are tested for comprehension to measure the impact of advertising. The test can be an *aided* situation (some information is provided the respondent to stimulate thinking) or an *unaided* situation (no information is provided). In either situation, respondents are asked to name or recall ads and asked to recall specific elements of an advertisement or commercial, such as its primary selling points, the characters in it as presenters, and its slogan. Test scores are usually higher when some form of aid is provided. For that reason, researchers tend to prefer the unaided recall technique, citing it as a truer test of an ad's impact on people.

Recognition and recall both help develop a brand's image with consumers over a period of time. Therefore, once an advertiser finds an ad or advertising campaign that is performing well, it must resist the temptation to make changes. In the long run, effective advertising plays a role in building sales and market share. A summary of some specific recall and recognition test procedures offered by Gallup & Robinson, a marketing research company, is included in Figure 12.8.

Two of the most common methods for collecting recognition and recall information are Starch readership tests and day-after recall tests. A **Starch readership test** is a post-test recognition procedure applied to both newspaper and magazine advertisements. The objectives of the test are to measure how many readers saw an ad an how many actually read the ad.

Starch readership test
A post-test recognition procedure that measures readers' recall of an advertisement (noted), their ability to identify the sponsor (associated), and whether they read more than half of the written material (read most).

In a Starch readership test, a consumer is given a magazine to read, after which an interviewer goes through it ad by ad with the respondent. For each advertisement in the magazine (the entire magazine is "starched"), responses are divided into three categories:

- **Noted:** the percentage of readers who remember seeing the ad in this issue.
- **Associated:** the percentage of readers who saw any part of the ad that clearly indicated the brand or advertiser.
- **Read Most:** the percentage of readers who read half or more of the written material.

The Starch readership test offers several benefits. The client can measure the extent to which an ad is seen and read, the extent of clutter breakthrough can be determined by reviewing the results of other ads that were tested, and various layout and design options can be evaluated for effectiveness by reviewing scores obtained by other products in previous tests.

Day-after recall (DAR) test
Research conducted the day following the respondent's exposure to a message to determine the degree of recognition and recall of the advertisement, the brand, and the selling message.

In the broadcast media, particularly television, the use of **day-after recall (DAR) testing** is common. As the name implies, research is conducted the day after an audience has been exposed to a commercial message for the first time. By means of a telephone survey technique, a sampling of the client's target market is recruited and asked a series of questions to determine exposure to and recall of particular commercials. Respondents who saw the commercial are asked what the ad actually communicated. The test seeks specific information about the primary selling message, what the respondent likes and dislikes about the ad, areas of disbelief or confusion, and purchase motivation.

Related recall
The percentage of a test commercial audience who claims to remember the test commercial and can provide as verification some description of the commercial.

The actual quantified measures obtained in a DAR test are described as total related recall levels. Total related recall measures two dimensions of the test commercial: intrusiveness and impact. **Related recall** refers to the percentage of the test-commercial audience who claim to remember the test execution, and who are also able to substantiate their claim by providing some description of the commercial.[8] The higher the percentage is, the more intrusive the message with respect to the audience. For measuring the impact of a commercial on an audience, the total related recall score is broken down into categories: unaided (by brand name mention) versus aided, specific versus non-specific, communication-objective or selling-message playback, and central-situation playback.

FIGURE **12.8** **A Selection of Research Services Offered by Gallup & Robinson**

COPY TESTING

Tests for the performance of individual advertising executions and campaigns, their strengths and weaknesses in the context of other alternatives, past experience, and category norms. Among the services are

- *InTeleTest*—Commercials are exposed using an at-home, in-program context via VCR cassettes or DVDs among widely dispersed samples.
- *InView*—Respondents are invited to view a show in which the commercial is aired for testing. Recall and persuasion scores are obtained from the test.
- *Magazine Impact Research Service (MIRS)*—Ads are tested using an in-home, in-magazine context. The system offers standardized measures. Test ads may naturally appear or are inserted for testing.
- *FasTrac*—A pre-testing service yielding qualitative and quantitative analysis in a mall-intercept environment. FasTrac provides a full range of measures for clients operating on a tight time frame.

TRACKING STUDIES

Assesses the aggregate effect of a company's advertising in terms of creating awareness, building knowledge, enhancing attitudes, and generating purchase intent.

CONCEPT TESTING

Gauges the potential of the concept or idea behind new advertising before time and material are invested in it.

CLAIMS SUBSTANTIATION

Determines reaction to advertising messages claims, usually to support or challenge possible actions by media review bodies, regulatory agencies, or courts.

SPOKESPERSON OR ICON TESTING

Assesses how the use of spokespersons, celebrities, and icons in advertising influences attitudes toward the brand.

MEDIA INFLUENCES RESEARCH

Explores how people think about and use media content and how the medium itself influences the value of the advertising to help determine which media choices are more effective than others for communicating the message.

Adapted from Gallup & Robinson, "Services," www.gallup-robinson.com (accessed November 2003).

Opinion-Measure Testing

Opinion-measure testing
A form of research yielding information about the effect of a commercial message on respondents' brand name recall, interest in the brand, and purchase intentions.

Measuring attitudinal components is another means of evaluating advertising effectiveness. Attitudes and opinions can be gathered from surveys or focus groups. The intent of attitude surveys is to delve a bit deeper with consumers to determine their true feelings about an ad and the product. Marketing research organizations use a combination of closed-ended and open-ended questions to uncover attitudes and opinions.

With television commercials, **opinion-measure testing** exposes an audience to test-commercial messages in the context of special television programs. In a research setting, respondents view commercials on a large screen (theatre) or on television monitors. Once all of the ads are viewed, participants respond to a series of questions.

The test commercial is usually presented twice during the program, in cluster situations. Also included in the cluster is a set of control commercials against which the test commercial or commercials (sometimes more than one commercial is being tested) can be compared. The position of the test commercial is different in each cluster. The test measures three key attributes: the audience's awareness of the commercial based on brand name recall, the extent to which the main idea of the ad is communicated, and the effect the commercial could have on purchase motivation—that is, the likelihood of the respondent buying the brand. This final measure is based on a comparison of pre-exposure brand purchase information and post-exposure brand preference data.

This procedure is often referred to as a *forced exposure test*, a name that suggests its potential weakness: the artificial environment in which it occurs. However, the results for commercials are compared to results from previous tests, and since the procedure remains constant, the data should provide reasonable direction to advertisers. Millward Brown, a marketing research company, uses a procedure it calls TVLink™ to predict how well an ad will perform.

Physiological-Response Testing

Advertisers also have access to a variety of physiological testing methods that measure involuntary responses to a specific element of an advertisement. In an **eye movement–camera test**, consumers read an advertisement while a hidden camera tracks their eye movements. Such a test gauges the point of immediate contact, how a reader scans the various components of an ad, and the amount of time spent reading it. The **pupilometer test** measures the dilation of a person's pupil to see how it changes based on emotional arousal. For example, a person's pupils widen when frightened or excited and are smaller when the response is negative. In a **voice-pitch analysis test**, a person's voice response is recorded. It measures changes in voice pitch caused by emotional responses. The change in pitch indicates how strongly a person is affected.

These types of tests are popular with researchers because emotions trigger physiological responses that can be measured. Physiological responses to something a person sees or hears are difficult to mask. In two of the tests mentioned above, reactions are monitored with no words being spoken. Sometimes respondents try to hide their true feelings by saying something that contradicts their physiological reaction. For example, a person might respond in the desired way physiologically to a print ad with sexual imagery but might state that the ad should not be shown in a magazine. In such a case, physiological reactions speak louder than words.

Testing procedures and the need for them are controversial issues in the industry, particularly among advertising agencies whose work is being tested. Many creative directors argue that too much testing defeats the creative process (because it stifles creativity) and that what people say in research and do in the real world can be completely different. These same creative directors also realize it is the client's money at stake, so if the client is inclined toward research, the ad agency must deal with the situation as best it can.

For additional insight into how research influences the development of advertising messages, refer to the IMC Highlight **Branding Oregon**.

Eye movement–camera test

A test that uses a hidden camera to track eye movement to gauge the point of immediate contact in an advertisement, how the reader scans the ad, and the amount of time spent reading.

Pupilometer test

A device that measures pupil dilation (enlargement) of a person's eye when reading; it measures emotional responses to an advertisement.

Voice-pitch analysis test

A test that uses a recording of a person's voice response to measure change in voice pitch caused by emotional responses to the communications.

MEASURING AND EVALUATING SALES PROMOTIONS

The overall goal of sales promotions is to produce an increase in sales in the short term and to build brand loyalty in the long term. As discussed in Chapter 8, promotions are classified as consumer promotions and trade promotions. Consumer promotions embrace activities such as coupons, contests, free samples, cash rebates, premium offers, and loy-

IMC HIGHLIGHT

BRANDING OREGON

How consumers perceive a brand and how an organization would like consumers to perceive a brand can be two different things. The latter is the ideal situation, because it suggests that the marketing and marketing communications strategies actually had an effect on people. A primary role of marketing communications is to influence or alter perceptions. The state of Oregon and the Pacific Northwest are well known as outdoors region. The area has the beautiful Pacific coastline, majestic mountains, great camping, and scenic vistas. People instantly think of its natural beauty, but they generally know little else about the region.

Ten years ago, the Oregon Tourism Commission implemented a branding campaign to portray the state as having a special quality of life where nature and the built environment coexist, where "fresh" and "clean" permeate everything, where culture is alive and the heritage showcased. The slogan for the campaign was "Oregon. Things Look Different Here." Wieden+Kennedy, an ad agency renowned for its Nike advertising, created the campaign.

To determine how well the campaign was working, a three-tiered research program was devised and implemented by Longwoods International, a US marketing research company. The research involved an overnight visitor profile, an advertising effectiveness study, and an image study. The primary goal was to determine how well Oregon compared to other regional and national norms for tourism communications.

The commission found that the campaign did encourage new visitors to the region, but that Oregon's image did not compare well to Washington, British Columbia, and California in terms of excitement, unique opportunities, and entertainment. Looking critically at its advertising, it determined that there was too much focus on the pristine environment. There was little emphasis on things to do.

The commission also discovered that visitors rated their experiences very highly, and that Oregon's actual tourism product is rated much higher than its image. In other words, Oregon's image did not live up to the product! Oregon recognized that a good communications solution would correct this problem. New advertising was developed to build Oregon's image in specific areas such as being exciting, showing cultural amenities, and being a real adventure. The new campaign focused on "capturing the moment" and "people having fun."

To supplement media advertising, the commission also formed partnerships with cultural organizations and destinations to launch a cultural tourism campaign, with public relations and other marketing communications elements. High-end resorts, world-class golf courses, regional cuisine, and historic trails serve as backdrops for advertising. It's culture packed with beauty!

The commission's investment in research demonstrates the importance of crafting a message that communicates what life in Oregon is really like. The research helped to identify information that really helped develop an effective marketing communications campaign.

Adapted from Julie Curtis, "How research shapes a message," *Longwoods International*, www.longwoods-intl.com/case-study-Oregon.htm (accessed November 2003).

alty card programs. These activities are designed to encourage trial purchase by new customers, repeat purchases by existing customers, and, generally, brand loyalty. Therefore, consumer promotions are measured against these objectives.

Trade promotions include activities such as trade allowances, performance allowances, cooperative advertising allowances, dealer premiums, and dealer display materials. These activities are designed to secure listings of new products with distributors, build sales volume in the promotion period, and secure merchandising support from distributors. Trade promotions are measured against these objectives.

Specific sales promotion measures include response rates to coupon offers, the number of entries received for a contest, and the number of cash rebate forms returned to the company. A marketing manager typically compares response rates for current promotions to response rates received for past and similar promotions. For example, some brands may run a major contest each year in the peak season. Brands like Pepsi-Cola and Coca-Cola usually run a summer contest. If a particular contest generates significantly more entries than usual, the manager will attempt to isolate the elements of the promotion that lead to the higher degree of interest.

Coupon offers are usually evaluated based on the redemption rate, which is defined as the number of coupons returned, expressed as a percentage of the number of coupons distributed. The higher the redemption rate, the more successful the coupon promotion. For example, if a magazine coupon draws a 2 percent return rate and the norm for magazine coupons is only 1 percent, the offer is an overwhelming success.

Historical redemption rates for coupon offers are used to develop budgets for new coupon offers. Again, should response to a particular coupon offer be significantly higher than past offers, the manager would try to identify the elements of the offer that contributed to the increase in redemptions. Was it the face value of the offer? Was it the timing of the offer? Are consumers generally more price sensitive than they previously were? Marketing managers have the necessary information available to forecast coupon redemptions. Actual redemptions received are compared to forecasted redemptions to determine the success or failure of the coupon promotion. For an illustration of such a calculation, refer to Figure 12.9.

The absolute number of entry forms received from contests and rebate offers are a means of measuring the effectiveness of these types of offers. The names collected provide an additional marketing benefit, as they can be added to the company's database. Smart marketers seek additional information about consumers on the contest or rebate entry form such as demographic and psychographic information that can be used to plan direct response communications programs.

The use of dealer display materials affects the success of sales promotions. Point-of-purchase advertising helps create awareness for promotion offers and reminds consumers about a product at precisely the right time—the purchase decision time. This medium provides a good finishing touch to a well-integrated advertising and promotion program.

Figure 12.10 shows that a significantly higher purchase response is achieved if various combinations of in-store merchandising activities are implemented. The importance of these activities is highlighted by the fact that 70 percent of brand purchase decisions are made in-store.[9]

MEASURING AND EVALUATING DIRECT RESPONSE AND INTERNET COMMUNICATIONS

One method of measuring direct mail and direct response television messages is to include a toll-free telephone number or website address. The number of inquiries received or the actual sales that result from a particular offer can be compared to those of offers in the past. From this, an observation can be made about the effectiveness of a new offer. As well, a great deal of information can be collected about consumers responding to phone calls. Sales data can be recorded and demographic information gathered. Sales data can be tied to demographic information to determine who is actually buying the product. Knowing who is responding to each offer helps a firm better understand its customers and provides insight into how to develop better marketing communications strategies to reach particular targets.

Response cards are another means of assessing impact and collecting information about customers. Typically, these cards are filled in at the time of purchase. Any information that is collected can be added to the organization's database and be combined with other information that may be available on a particular customer.

In an online environment, cookies enable an organization to track online responses. The Internet is a unique communications medium that has built-in technology unlike any other medium. That technology allows for all communications to be measured for effectiveness. In fact, Internet communications are much easier to measure in terms of hard numbers than any other form of media advertising.

Response card
A card filled in, usually at the time of purchase, that collects information about customers that can be added to the organization's database.

FIGURE **12.9**   **Measuring the Effectiveness of a Coupon Promotion**

ASSUMPTION

A manufacturer offers a $1.00 coupon on a branded box of cereal that has a regular retail price of $4.09. The coupon is distributed through a cooperative direct mail package. For the purposes of budgeting, an average coupon redemption rate for cooperative direct mail will be used. A misredemption rate of 20% is considered, because on average only 80% of coupons redeemed are on valid purchases. The manufacturer receives about 65% of the retail price when wholesale and retail profit margins are considered.

COUPON INFORMATION

Face value:	$1.00
Handling charge (retailer)	$0.10
Handling charge (clearing house)	$0.03
Distribution cost	$15.00/M
Printing cost	$10.00/M
Total coupons in distribution	2.5 million
Redemption rate	5.0%

COSTS

Distribution	2 500 000 x $15.00/M	$37 500
Printing	2 500 000 x $10.00/M	$25 000
Redemption	2 500 000 x 0.05 x $1.13	$141 250
Total cost		**$203 750**

REVENUES

Revenue from each purchase	$4.59 x 0.65	$2.98
Total revenue	2 500 000 x 0.05 x 0.80 x $2.66	**$266 000**

PAYOUT

Total revenue minus total cost	$266 000 – $203 750	**$62 250**

From the total revenue line, it can be determined that the coupon offer generated 100 000 purchases (2 500 000 x 0.05 x 0.80).

Ad clicks (clickthroughs)
The number of times users click on a banner (clicking transfers the user to another website).

Ad views (impressions)
The number of times a banner is downloaded to a user's screen.

Hit
Each time a server sends a file to a browser.

Online observation is a common form of recording and analyzing usage patterns. Banner advertising, for example, is measured in terms of **ad clicks** (the number of times users click on a banner) and **ad views** (the number of times a banner ad is downloaded). Every time a server sends a file to a browser, it is recorded in that organization's server log. This statistical information, frequently referred to as **hits**, is readily available for analysis and interpretation. A high number of hits can be attributed to the effectiveness of the message.

The number of visitors to a website and the number of visits that each visitor makes over a period of time are factors that measure a website's ability to communicate. A

FIGURE **12.10** **Measuring the Effectiveness of Point-of-Purchase Communications**

FORM OF COMMUNICATION	INCREMENTAL RESPONSE RATE
Brand signage	+2%
Sign plus base wrap	+12%
Display stand and sign	+27%
Display stand, sign, and mobile	+40%
Display stand plus sign about sports tie-in	+65%

On average, point-of-purchase communication generates incremental sales ranging from +2% to +65%, independent of any price reductions. The above figures were based on research in 250 stores in 22 cities, and 94 brands in eight different product categories (beer, salty snacks, cold and allergy products, dog food, soft drinks, laundry detergent, shampoo, and conditioner).

Adapted from "Initial results from supermarket phase of POPAI/ARF study reveal Iinsights into POP advertising," *Point-of-Purchase Advertising International*, March 27, 2000.

Visitor

A unique user of a website.

Visit

A sequence of page requests made by a visitor to a website; also called a session or a browsing period.

Stickiness (sticky)

A website's ability to keep people at the site for an extended period or to have them return to the site frequently.

visitor is a unique user who comes to a website. A **visit** is a sequence of page requests made by a visitor at a website. Websites are evaluated based on their **stickiness**—how long visitors stayed at the site. Sticky sites are ones that people are interested in, as shown by their tendency to revisit favourite sites frequently. A plethora of factors influence visits: site design, navigation speed and ability to move from page to page conveniently, site content, and more.

As indicated earlier in the chapter, many organizations are experimenting with online surveys. They have discovered that online consumers are more responsive and generous with the information they provide. The use of structured surveys where predetermined responses are provided offers several advantages: results are obtained quickly and at much lower cost than traditional research methods.

MEASURING AND EVALUATING PUBLIC RELATIONS COMMUNICATIONS

There are several ways to evaluate public relations communications: counting clippings, calculating the number of impressions based on the numbers of clippings, and employing a mathematical model that equates public relations to an advertising value. The latter is referred to as an *advertising equivalency*.

Clipping service

An organization that scans the print and broadcast media in search of a company's or brand's name.

Many organizations that are active in public relations subscribe to a **clipping service**, which scans the print and broadcast media in search of a company's name. Each time the name is found it is recorded and compared to the number of press releases that were issued. For example, if 500 press releases were issued and there were 50 clippings, the return rate would be 10 percent. The success of the campaign would be based on historical comparisons of return rates.

The number of *impressions* generated is based on the circulation of the medium in which the organization's name is mentioned. For example, if an article appears in the *Toronto Star* on a Tuesday and the circulation that day is 450 000, the total number of

Toronto Star
www.thestar.ca

impressions is 450 000. A company may also "gross up" the number of impressions by considering the actual readership of the paper. If the average number of readers is 2.5 per copy, the gross impressions would be 1 125 000 (450 000 x 2.5).

There is a problem associated with counting clippings and impressions. Such a procedure ignores the nature of the article written or broadcast about the organization. Was it positive or negative? There is a presumption that an article that is critical of a company is of equal value to one that praises a company. It could be argued that positive articles and negative articles should be separated. For certain, companies receive a lot of negative publicity when they face a crisis situation, and such publicity negates much of the positive publicity that is generated by planned public relations communications. On the other hand, there are also those that believe that any publicity is good publicity.

Trying to equate public relations to a corresponding advertising value is an attempt to eliminate the problems associated with clippings and impressions. A technique called **advertising equivalency** involves an evaluation of the space occupied by a public relations message and relating it to a similar amount of advertising space. To demonstrate, assume that a one-page article about a company appeared in *Canadian Business* magazine. If a one-page ad costs $25 000, then that is the value of the public relations to the organization. Similar calculations can be made for the broadcast media. Based on this type of calculation, the sum total of a public relations campaign can be considerable. Specialist companies exist to provide this service.

Ideally, some form of evaluation in relation to specific public relations objectives would be preferable, but rarely does a company have sufficient funds to perform pre-campaign and post-campaign research—the techniques required for such an evaluation. For instance, if the objective of public relations were to increase awareness of a company's name, the pre-campaign research would establish a benchmark figure. Once the campaign is over, a second research study would determine how the level of awareness increased. Justifying such an investment for so many different types of communications programs is often difficult. Again, it is the combination of marketing communications activities that determines true success or failure.

Advertising equivalency
A mathematical model that equates public relations to an advertising value by evaluating the space occupied by a public relations message in relation to advertising space.

MEASURING AND EVALUATING EVENT MARKETING AND SPONSORSHIPS

Among all of the integrated marketing communications components, event marketing and sponsorships are the most difficult to evaluate, particularly on a quantitative basis. At their best, sponsorships are a high-profile way to increase sales and improve brand recognition. At their worst, they're a haphazard form of promotion. It is difficult to tell which is which.[10]

Event marketing is attracting a bigger piece of the marketing communications pie each year, but it doesn't get the respect it deserves because there aren't any widely accepted, standardized methods of measuring its results. Examples of proposed event measurement systems include adopting accepted methods of measuring attendance, total number of consumer contacts, and the level of consumer immersion in an event. Despite measurement flaws, event marketing and sponsorship programs continue to be a valued element in a good many marketing plans.

The most common measure of an event's success is **how well the event reaches the target audience**. If some form of return on investment can be added to the evaluation mix, so much the better. But, unless you are establishing leads or selling something at the event, the true impact of the sponsorship won't be felt immediately. Nowhere are sponsorships more visible than in the world of sports. In professional football, basketball, and hockey leagues, there is no shortage of sponsors willing to jump in. The Olympics are also a hot ticket, resulting in a sponsorship battle among bidding advertisers. At this level,

Imperial Oil
www.imperialoil.ca

however, an organization has to evaluate the costs versus the benefits. Once the Olympic flame faded in Nagano in 1998, Imperial Oil said goodbye to Olympic sponsorship. The company switched to sponsoring national sports federations in Canada that support athletes on their way to the games.[11]

Most managers rely on less concrete evidence to justify investing in event marketing and sponsorships. Having Tiger Woods walking around a golf course wearing a Nike hat, for example, has a positive impact for all kinds of Nike products that extends well beyond golf products. Seeing Tiger Woods driving a Buick Rendezvous adds an element of prestige to the automobile; it also has a halo effect on the image of General Motors. But to measure the direct impact of such an association on the sales of that automobile is next to impossible because of the influence of other forms of communication.

How beneficial are naming rights on a building? As of 2006, Scotiabank has the name rights to the building where the Ottawa Senators play, which is now called Scotiabank Place. Will it enhance their brand image? As part of the bank's overall marketing strategy, sponsorship marketing plays a key role; the bank believes sponsorships provide "more bang for the buck." Scotiabank is also involved with the Canadian Football League and the Giller Prize, the most lucrative Canadian literary award.

Industry experts believe Scotiabank will get lots of media exposure for its $20-million investment at Ottawa's Scotiabank Place. Media exposure is a true benefit of event marketing, since hockey games are broadcast and covered by newspapers. But it may not get the halo effect in the community that Corel did when it put its name on the building in 1996.[12]

As discussed in Chapter 10, certain indicators are commonly used to measure the benefits of sponsorship. For example, an organization might look at **awareness** and association measures as well as changes in **image perceptions** among its customers. However, to measure for changes in awareness and image, pre-event and post-event marketing research is necessary. Is the organization willing to invest further to get some measure of how well an event is contributing to achieving certain marketing objectives? Many managers presume that if an event effectively reaches the desired target audience, then measures for awareness, event association, and image will be positively affected and no investment in research is necessary.

Another common measure is the impact on **brand sales**. Is it immediate, during the event period, or will it happen after the event? The sale of Roots Olympic clothing rose considerably during the Olympic period and the few months that followed the Olympics. The clothes were so popular that they remained a staple item commanding their own section in stores for extended periods, a clear indication that the association with Canada's Olympic team paid dividends.

Scotiabank
www.scotiabank.com

Roots
www.roots.com

MEASURING THE INTEGRATED MARKETING COMMUNICATIONS EFFORT

Because integrated marketing communications is a coordinated and collaborative effort among many different individuals and organizations and many different communications disciplines, perhaps the best form of measurement and evaluation is to look at the big picture. In other words, how healthy is a particular brand or the company as a whole based on all of the marketing and marketing communications strategies that have been implemented over the past year (a typical planning cycle)?

Some typical indicators of success or failure include market share, productivity, sales and profitability, customer satisfaction levels, and social responsibility. As in most evaluation systems already discussed in this chapter, the organization should look back at the corporate objectives it established in these areas to see how well it performed.

Market share
The sales volume of one product or company expressed as a percentage of total sales volume in the market the company or brand is competing in.

An increase in **market share** would indicate greater acceptance by more customers, a higher degree of brand loyalty among current customers, and a strong competitive position. A well-planned integrated marketing communications program would have contributed to such an outcome. **Productivity** measures are more difficult to come by, but where tangible results can be attributed to a specific communications activity, it should be noted. Did the IMC program generate new customers? Was brand awareness higher than it was previously? Was the company's or brand's image altered in a positive way? These kinds of measures indicate whether or not a plan is working.

Marketing managers are responsible for producing sales while keeping marketing and marketing communications investments at reasonable levels. *Sales* must generate an adequate level of **profit** for the company to thrive and survive in the long term. Most brands in an organization have their own profit and loss statement, which is reviewed continually to ensure that sales, costs, and profit targets are always within sight. Alterations and adjustments to a marketing plan or marketing communications plan will occur during the year when necessary.

As discussed elsewhere in the text, every employee of an organization plays a role in providing **customer satisfaction;** all employees must adopt a marketing attitude. Therefore, it is very important for all employees to be aware of the marketing and marketing communications strategies. Informed employees play a key role in implementing the strategies; they thus directly influence how customers perceive the organization.

With regard to **social responsibility** objectives, planned public relations programs play a key role. An organization must promote its positive contributions while eliminating, as best it can, the negative outcomes. Brand equity and company image are directly influenced by the quality of social programs and ethical behaviour that a company and its employees demonstrate to the public.

In summary, the real challenge for an organization is to develop an integrated marketing communications strategy that will communicate clearly and effectively with the organization's various publics. The company that does so stands a very good chance of achieving both short-term and long-term success.

Summary

Marketing research must be viewed as a tool that assists the manager in the decision-making process. It is a systematic procedure that, if used properly, will produce reliable and valid data.

The research process begins with a firm becoming aware of a problem situation. Problems associated with evaluating marketing communications typically involve primary research. Primary research is the gathering of new data from a representative sample. Primary data are collected from surveys, observation, and experiments. Survey data are either qualitative or quantitative in nature. Qualitative data are collected by focus group or one-on-one interviews and answer the question "why." Quantitative data are obtained by questionnaires through personal interview, telephone, mail, or online surveys and involve translating thoughts and feelings into measurable numbers. Once the data are secured, they are processed for analysis and interpreted by the researcher.

Experimental research involves testing a marketing mix activity within a controlled situation to measure the effectiveness of the activity. Test marketing is an example of experimental research. In a test market involving marketing communications, an advertisement, a commercial, or set of ads in a campaign is placed in designated geographic markets to evaluate the potential impact on consumers. Knowledge gained from such tests allows an organization to make changes to a campaign before it is launched in additional markets.

In order to measure the effectiveness of marketing communications programs, various research procedures are implemented. In advertising, several pre-test and post-test techniques are available. If recognition and recall are a concern, a Starch readership test, a day-after recall test, and opinion-measure tests can be applied. These tests generate data on brand identification and message comprehension. If there is a desire to measure emotional responses, various physiological tests that evaluate eye movement, pupil dilation, and analyze voice pitch are available.

Sales promotion measures include response rates to coupon offers and the number of entries received for contest and cash rebate offers. Response rates for current promotions are compared to response rates of previous promotions. The manager will evaluate the various elements of the promotion to determine what elements contributed to success or failure.

Direct response communications and online communications are easier to evaluate quantitatively. Direct response communications usually include a toll-free telephone number, a website address, or response cards. Inquiries can be tracked, and any sales that occur can be attributed to specific customers. With Internet communications, the use of cookies allows an organization to track responses. Other forms of Internet measures include ad clicks, impressions, hits, numbers of visitors to a website, and time spent while at a website.

The most common ways of measuring public relations communications include counting actual clippings that appear in the print and broadcast media, calculating the number of impressions that the press clippings generate, and converting the press coverage (the size of space or amount of time it occupies) to some kind of advertising equivalency. The latter places a monetary value on public relations and is a popular means of justifying investment in public relations.

Event marketing and sponsorships remain difficult to measure. Nonetheless, events and sponsorships are popular among marketing executives because they are perceived as a high-profile way to increase sales and improve brand recognition. The most common measure of an event's success is determined by how well the event reaches the target audience. Other commonly used measures include changes in brand awareness levels and image, both of which are based on how well a brand associates with an event.

When measuring the success of an integrated marketing communications campaign, an organization looks at the bigger picture. Typical indicators of success or failure include shifts in market share, productivity, sales and profitability, employee performance and attitude, and the public's perceptions of an organization's social responsibility. A carefully planned marketing communications program contributes to achieving objectives in all of these areas.

Key Terms

ad clicks,   358

ad views,   358

advertising equivalency,   360

clickthroughs,   358

clipping service,   359

closed-ended questioning,   343

cookie,   343

cross-tabulation,   348

data analysis,   348

data interpretation,   349

data transfer,   348

day-after recall (DAR) test,   353

editing,   348

experimental research,   344

eye movement–camera test,   356

fixed-response questioning,   343

focus group,   345

frequency distribution,   348

hit,   358

hypothesis,   341

impressions,   358

mail interview,   346

market share,   362

marketing research,   339

non-probability sample, 341

observation research, 343

online survey, 346

open-ended questioning, 343

open-response questioning, 343

opinion-measure testing, 354

personal interview, 346

population, 341

post-testing, 352

pre-testing, 352

primary data, 340

primary research, 340

probability sample, 341

pupilometer test, 356

qualitative data, 345

quantitative data, 345

recall test, 353

recognition test, 352

related recall, 353

reliability of data, 340

research objective, 341

response card, 357

sample, 341

sampling frame, 341

Starch readership test, 353

stickiness, 359

sticky, 359

survey research, 343

tabulation, 348

telephone interview, 346

test marketing, 344

universe, 341

validity of data, 340

visit, 359

visitor, 359

voice-pitch analysis test, 356

Review Questions

1. In the context of marketing research, what is the relationship between the following sets of terms?

   a) secondary data and primary data

   b) research objectives and hypotheses

   c) observational and experimental techniques

   d) population and sampling frame

   e) qualitative data and quantitative data

   f) probability sample and non-probability sample

   g) frequency distribution and cross-tabulation

   h) tabulation and cross-tabulation

   i) data analysis and data interpretation

2. What is the problem-awareness stage of the marketing research process?

3. Briefly explain the four steps in the sample design process.

4. What is a focus group? What are the benefits of focus group research?

5. Under what circumstances would you use the telephone for collecting survey data? When would you use the personal interview?

6. In terms of measuring the effectiveness of advertising, what is the difference between pre-testing and post-testing? What benefits does each form of research provide?

7. What is the difference between a recognition test and a recall test?

8. What are the three categories of measurement in a Starch readership test? Briefly explain each category.

9. What does opinion-measure testing refer to?

10. What are the three primary ways of measuring the effectiveness of public relations campaigns? Briefly discuss each form of measurement.

11. What are the primary ways of measuring the effectiveness of event marketing and sponsorship participation? Briefly discuss each form of measurement.

Discussion and Application Questions

1. Compare and contrast the nature of qualitative data and quantitative data. Is it essential to have both types of information prior to investing in a new advertising campaign? Prepare a position and provide appropriate justification for it.

2. You are about to devise a new advertising strategy (a message strategy) for the Porsche Boxster. You do not know how to present the automobile to potential customers and would like to find out more about them. What information would you like to obtain, and what procedure would you recommend to obtain it?

3. "Too much information obtained from marketing research ultimately stifles creative thinking and the production of innovative creative." Many creative directors have expressed this opinion. Conduct some secondary research on this issue and present an opinion on the issue. Justify your position with appropriate examples.

4. Companies are now using online surveys to learn more about their customers and how they feel about the company's products. What are the benefits and drawbacks of using online research? Is it as useful and effective as traditional survey methodologies? Briefly discuss the key issues.

5. If event marketing and sponsorships are so difficult to measure for tangible business results, why do so many large and prosperous companies pursue such associations? What are the advantages and disadvantages of being involved in this form of marketing communications? Is it a worthwhile investment? Present an opinion supported with appropriate justification.

Endnotes

1 Chris Daniels, "Canuck vs. Yanks," *Marketing*, May 22, 2000, p. 26.

2 "New definition for marketing research approved," *Marketing News*, January 22, 1987, p. 1.

3 "Managers should rethink the power and limitations of focus groups," *Financial Post*, December 14, 1999, p. C4.

4 Wendy Cuthbert, "Hold the numbers," *Strategy*, June 4, 2001, pp. B6, B7.

5 Colin Flint, "Marketing researchers facing a lot of hang-ups," *Financial Post*, March 26, 2004, p. FP4.

6 Jack Neff, "P&G weds data, sales," *Advertising Age*, October 23, 2000, pp. 76–80.

7 Paul Marck, "Canadians heed call of the wild," *National Post*, February 24, 2006, p. FP7.

8 Cherie Hill, "In defense of DAR testing," *Marketing*, June 1984, p. 28.

9 "In-store merchandising, the power of P.O.P.," insert in *Marketing*, n.d., p. 1.

10 Patrick Maloney, "Do sponsorships measure up?" *Marketing*, July 8, 2002, p. 13.

11 Keith McArthur, "Olympic strategy key to branding gold," *Globe and Mail*, February 13, 2006, p. B3.

12 Keith McArthur and Sinclair Stewart, "Scotiabank Place? Oh, don't you mean the Corel Centre?" *Globe and Mail*, January 12, 2006, **www.globeanmail.com**.

Media Buying Principles and Media Information Resources

This appendix presents the essential aspects of media buying and acquaints the student with a variety of media rate cards and how to read them. The rate cards used in this section have been gathered from online sources and *Canadian Advertising Rates and Data* (*CARD*). Rate cards are usually posted on a media company's website under a title like "Advertise with Us" or "Media Kit." Students can refer to *CARD*, a publication usually available in the reference section of college and university libraries. *CARD* contains summary rate cards for all media in Canada except television.

In addition, this section exposes the student to a variety of media information sources often referred to by marketing organizations and communications agencies. In most cases, specialized software available by subscription is required to access specific data. However, students are encouraged to visit the various websites listed under "Media Information Resources" to gain exposure to basic information that is available for free.

A set of review questions dealing with various media calculations is included at the end of the appendix.

MEDIA BUYING PRINCIPLES

Newspaper Advertising

Agate line
A non-standardized unit of space measurement, equal to one column wide and 1/14" deep, used in newspaper advertising.

Broadsheet
A large newspaper with a fold in its middle.

Tabloid
A smaller newspaper that is sold flat (not folded).

Modular agate line (MAL)
A standardized unit of measurement used in newspaper advertising equal to one column wide and 1/14" deep.

Newspaper space is sold on the basis of agate lines or modular agate lines. An **agate line** is a non-standardized unit of space measurement, equal to one column wide and 1/14" deep. For **broadsheets**, a standard page is 11 1/2" wide with column widths of 1 1/16". The number of columns ranges from 7 to 10, so full-page lineage ranges from 1800 to 3150 agate lines. In **tabloids**, the number of columns range from 6 to 10, and full-page lineage ranges from 1134 to 2000 agate lines. Most broadsheets and tabloids use agate lines to determine the size of an advertisement.

A **modular agate line (MAL)** is a standardized unit of measurement equal to one column wide and 1/14" deep. Standard column widths are 2 1/16" in broadsheets. An MAL is wider than an agate line. For a broadsheet, the full-page lineage ranges from 1800 to 1848 MALs. For a tabloid, the full-page lineage ranges from 890 to 1050 MALs.

Note that in this context "lines" and "columns" are not physical lines and columns. They are invisible lines and columns that the newspaper industry uses to measure the size of an ad.

The basic procedure for buying newspaper space is to determine the size of the ad either in agate lines or modular agate lines. In either case, the cost is calculated by multiplying the width of the ad (number of columns) by the depth of the ad (inches of depth). One column inch of depth equals 14 agate lines. Other factors that influence costs include the number of insertions, creative considerations such as the use of colour, and position charges, if applicable.

Some newspapers offer standard-size ads that are easier to understand in terms of size. With reference to the *Globe and Mail* (see Figure A1.1), some of the standard-size options include full page (1800 agate lines), 1/2 page (900 agate lines), magazine page (616 agate lines), and 1/4 page (453 agate lines).

FIGURE **A1.1** **Some Standard-Size Page Options in Newspapers**

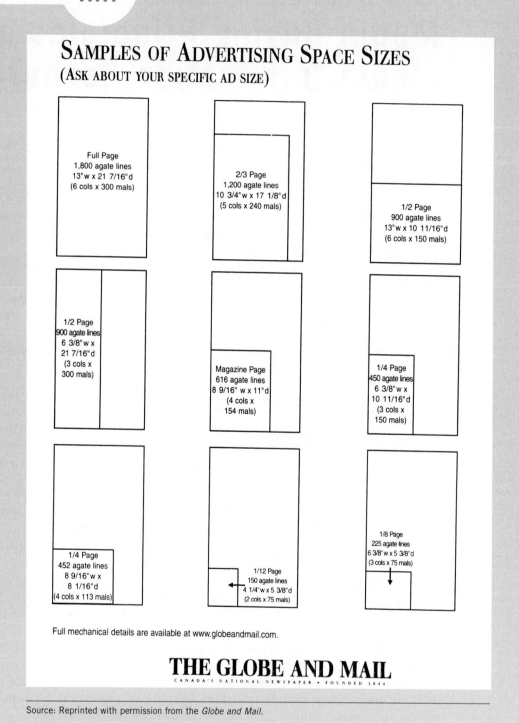

SAMPLES OF ADVERTISING SPACE SIZES
(ASK ABOUT YOUR SPECIFIC AD SIZE)

Full Page
1,800 agate lines
13"w x 21 7/16"d
(6 cols x 300 mals)

2/3 Page
1,200 agate lines
10 3/4"w x 17 1/8"d
(5 cols x 240 mals)

1/2 Page
900 agate lines
13"w x 10 11/16"d
(6 cols x 150 mals)

1/2 Page
900 agate lines
6 3/8"w x
21 7/16"d
(3 cols x
300 mals)

Magazine Page
616 agate lines
8 9/16" w x 11"d
(4 cols x
154 mals)

1/4 Page
450 agate lines
6 3/8"w x
10 11/16"d
(3 cols x
150 mals)

1/4 Page
452 agate lines
8 9/16"w x
8 1/16"d
(4 cols x 113 mals)

1/12 Page
150 agate lines
4 1/4"w x 5 3/8"d
(2 cols x 75 mals)

1/8 Page
225 agate lines
6 3/8"w x 5 3/8"d
(3 cols x 75 mals)

Full mechanical details are available at www.globeandmail.com.

THE GLOBE AND MAIL
CANADA'S NATIONAL NEWSPAPER • FOUNDED 1844

Source: Reprinted with permission from the *Globe and Mail*.

Determining Space Size

To illustrate the concept of agate lines, let's assume the size of the ad is 4 columns wide by 10 column inches deep. Considering that each column inch of depth equals 14 agate lines, the size of the ad would be calculated by the following formula:

$$\text{Number of columns wide} \times \text{Inches of depth} \times 14$$

$$4 \times 10 \times 14 = 560 \text{ agate lines}$$

If the size of the advertisement is 5 columns wide by 8 inches deep, the size of the ad in agate lines will be:

$$5 \times 8 \times 14 = 560 \text{ lines}$$

These two examples illustrate that different configurations of ads (combinations of width and depth) can produce the same size of ad in terms of space occupied and rates charged.

The calculations above would be the same for modular agate lines. The only difference is that the modular agate line is slightly wider than the agate line. Before calculating the costs of an ad, the planner must be aware of what system the newspaper is using: agate lines or modular agate lines.

Modular agate unit

A standardized unit of measurement in which a newspaper page is divided into equal-sized units, each 30 modular agate lines deep.

Newspaper space can be sold on the basis of **modular agate units**, though only a few daily newspapers use this system. In this system, the size of the ad is expressed in terms of units of width and units of depth (e.g., 4 units wide by 6 units deep). In effect, the page is sectioned off into equal size units with each unit being 30 modular agate lines deep. Therefore, to calculate the actual size of an ad that is 4 units wide by 6 units deep, the calculation would be as follows:

$$\text{Number of columns wide} \times \text{Units deep} \times 30 = \text{Modular agate lines}$$

$$4 \times 6 \times 30 = 720 \text{ MAL}$$

Rate Schedules

Line rate

The rate charged by newspapers for one agate line or one modular agate line.

Line rate is defined as the rate charged by newspapers for one agate line or one modular agate line. With regard to rate schedules, several factors must be noted. First, rates charged by line go down as the volume of the lineage increases over a specified period. Second, costs for the addition of colour or preferred positions are quoted separately. Third, the line rates may vary from one section of the paper to another. For example, the transient rate (the highest rate paid by an advertiser) for advertisers in the *Globe and Mail's* News and Report on Business sections is higher than in other sections of the newspaper. Fourth, line rates may vary by day of the week. The *Toronto Star*, for example, charges more per line for its Saturday edition, since the circulation is significantly higher that day.

Transient Rate (casual rate)

A one-time rate, or base rate, that applies to casual advertisers.

In the chart in Figure A1.2, the rates quoted start with a **transient rate**, which is defined as a one-time rate, or base rate, that applies to casual advertisers. *Discounts* are offered to advertisers as the number of lines purchased increases. Lines accumulate over a period of time, usually a year. The volume discount scale is clearly indicated on Figure A1.2.

To illustrate how costs are calculated in newspapers, let's develop a hypothetical plan using the rate card for the *Globe and Mail*. For the illustration assume the *Globe and Mail* uses the agate line format.

Newspaper: *Globe and Mail*—Wednesday Edition, National Section

Size of ad: 4 columns wide x 10 column inches deep

Rate: Transient Rate

Frequency: Once

The first calculation determines the total number of modular agate lines:

$$4 \text{ columns wide} \times (10 \text{ column inches deep} \times 14) \times 1 = 560 \text{ lines}$$

The next step is to multiply the number of lines by the line rate by the frequency to determine the cost of the insertion. In this case, the *casual rate* applies because there is not enough lineage to earn a discount.

$$560 \times \$40.34 = \$22\,590.40$$

FIGURE **A1.2** The Globe and Mail Rate Card

THE GLOBE AND MAIL

2006

GENERAL RATES

Canada's largest and leading national newspaper is, without a doubt, the No. 1 choice for reaching affluent and educated Canadians from coast to coast*.

Industry studies repeatedly confirm that The Globe and Mail dominates the national newspaper market in Canada – and by a wide margin.

The Globe and Mail is a unique medium with the most educated, influential, affluent readership in Canada – a loyal and important audience you can't find anywhere else.

No matter what you need to advertise, The Globe and Mail delivers more of your best prospects in numbers too significant to ignore.

When quality prospects with money to spend and intent to purchase matter to your media buy, buy The Globe and Mail.

NEWS, REPORT ON BUSINESS, TORONTO

News appears daily, in all editions.
Report on Business appears daily in the National Edition.
Toronto appears Monday through Friday within News, Saturday as a stand-alone in the Metro edition only.

SPORTS, REVIEW/'7', STYLE FOCUS AND BOOKS

Sports appears daily in the Metro and National editions.
Review appears daily in the Metro and National editions ('7' tabloid replaces Review on Friday in Metro and B.C. editions).
Style appears Saturday in the Metro and National editions.
Focus appears Saturday in the National edition.
Books Tabloid appears Saturday in the National edition.

Advertising Rates effective April 1, 2006

Monday to Friday

	National	Ont/Que	Metro
Transient	$40.34	$34.69	$31.87
$25,000	34.29	29.49	27.09
$50,000	33.28	28.62	26.29
$100,000	32.27	27.75	25.49
$150,000	31.26	26.89	24.70
$250,000	30.26	26.02	23.90
$350,000	29.04	24.98	22.95
$500,000	27.83	23.94	21.99
$750,000	26.62	22.90	21.03
$1,000,000	25.41	21.86	20.08
$1,500,000	24.20	20.82	19.12
$2,000,000	22.99	19.77	18.17
$2,500,000	21.78	18.73	17.21

Saturday

	National	Ont/Que	Metro
Transient	$44.37	$38.16	$35.06
$25,000	37.72	32.44	29.80
$50,000	36.61	31.48	28.92
$100,000	35.50	30.53	28.04
$150,000	34.39	29.58	27.17
$250,000	33.28	28.62	26.29
$350,000	31.95	27.48	25.24
$500,000	30.62	26.33	24.19
$750,000	29.29	25.19	23.14
$1,000,000	27.96	24.04	22.08
$1,500,000	26.62	22.90	21.03
$2,000,000	25.29	21.75	19.98
$2,500,000	23.96	20.61	18.93

Monday to Friday

	National	Metro
Transient	$18.96	$14.98
$25,000	16.12	12.73
$50,000	15.64	12.36
$100,000	15.17	11.98
$150,000	14.69	11.61
$250,000	14.22	11.23
$350,000	13.65	10.78
$500,000	13.08	10.33
$750,000	12.51	9.89
$1,000,000	11.94	9.44
$1,500,000	11.38	8.99
$2,000,000	10.81	8.54
$2,500,000	10.24	8.09

Saturday

	National	Metro
Transient	$20.86	$16.48
$25,000	17.73	14.00
$50,000	17.21	13.59
$100,000	16.68	13.18
$150,000	16.16	12.77
$250,000	15.64	12.36
$350,000	15.02	11.86
$500,000	14.39	11.37
$750,000	13.76	10.87
$1,000,000	13.14	10.38
$1,500,000	12.51	9.89
$2,000,000	11.89	9.39
$2,500,000	11.26	8.90

Advertising rates shown are per line, based on annual dollar volume contract commitment.

All rates are gross. Prices in Canadian dollars.

TORONTO
tel 416.585.5111
toll-free 1.800.387.9012
fax 416.585.5698

EASTERN CANADA
(Ottawa region, Quebec and Atlantic Canada)
tel 514.982.3050
toll-free 1.800.363.7526
(from NFLD, NS, PEI, NB, PQ)
fax 514.982.3074

WESTERN CANADA
tel 604.685.0308
toll-free 1.800.663.1311
(from BC, AB, SK, NT)
fax 604.685.7549

UNITED STATES AND INTERNATIONAL ADVERTISING REPRESENTATIVES
Publicitas, New York, NY
tel 212.599.5057
fax 212.599.8298

* SOURCE: NADbank 2005, 50 National Markets.

YOU ALSO NEED TO KNOW:
Any advertising published by The Globe and Mail in the newspaper or any of its other publications may, at our discretion, be published, displayed, retained and archived by us and anyone authorized (including any form of licence) by us, as many times as we and those authorized by us wish, in or on any product, media and archive (including print, electronic and otherwise).

All advertising must meet Globe and Mail terms and conditions – ask for a printed copy from your Globe and Mail advertising representative.

THE GLOBE AND MAIL
CANADA'S NATIONAL NEWSPAPER • FOUNDED 1844

continued

GENERAL RATES

TRAVEL

Travel appears Wednesday and Saturday in the Metro, Ontario/Quebec and National editions.

Monday to Friday

	National	Ont/Que	Metro
Transient	$25.01	$21.51	$19.76
$25,000	21.26	18.28	16.79
$50,000	20.63	17.75	16.30
$100,000	20.01	17.21	15.81
$150,000	19.38	16.67	15.31
$250,000	18.76	16.13	14.82
$350,000	18.01	15.49	14.23
$500,000	17.26	14.84	13.63
$750,000	16.51	14.20	13.04
$1,000,000	15.76	13.55	12.45
$1,500,000	15.01	12.91	11.86
$2,000,000	14.26	12.26	11.26
$2,500,000	13.51	11.62	10.67

Saturday

	National	Ont/Que	Metro
Transient	$27.51	$23.66	$21.73
$25,000	23.39	20.11	18.47
$50,000	22.70	19.52	17.93
$100,000	22.01	18.93	17.39
$150,000	21.32	18.34	16.84
$250,000	20.63	17.75	16.30
$350,000	19.81	17.04	15.65
$500,000	18.98	16.33	15.00
$750,000	18.16	15.62	14.34
$1,000,000	17.33	14.91	13.69
$1,500,000	16.51	14.20	13.04
$2,000,000	15.68	13.49	12.39
$2,500,000	14.86	12.78	11.74

COLOUR CHARGES

National	Ont/Que	Metro
$8,873	$8,068	$7,424

NOTICES

Appointment Notices	$59.48
Financial Notices/Tombstones	43.41

GLOBE CAREERS

Includes 3 insertions – Wednesday, Friday and Saturday or Monday	43.56

RESERVATIONS AND CLOSINGS

Issue Day	Camera Ready	Pub-set Material
News, Report on Business, Sports	Thurs. 4:30pm	Wed. 4:30pm
Mon.	Thurs. 4:30pm	Wed. 4:30pm
Tues.	Fri. 4:30pm	Thurs. 4:30pm
Wed.	Mon. 4:30pm	Fri. 4:30pm
Thurs.	Tues. 4:30pm	Mon. 4:30pm
Fri.	Wed. 4:30pm	Tues. 4:30pm
Sat.	Thurs. 4:30pm	Wed. 4:30pm
Mon. Careers	Thurs. 2:00pm	Wed. 2:00pm
Wed. Careers	Mon. 2:00pm	Fri. 2:00pm
Fri. Careers	Wed. 2:00pm	Tues. 2:00pm
Sat. Careers	Thurs. 2:00pm	Wed. 2:00pm
Wed. Travel	Fri. 4:30pm	Fri. 4:30pm
Sat. Travel	Tues. 4:30pm	Tues. 4:30pm
Sat. Style/Focus	Tues. 2:30pm	Mon. 4:30pm
Fri. Review/7	Wed.12:00pm	Tues. 4:30pm
Saturday Review	Thurs.10:00am	Wed. 4:30pm
Saturday Toronto	Wed.10:00am	Tues. 4:30pm

All deadlines are based on Eastern Standard Time.

Complete deadlines listed on our Web site:
globeandmail.com/advertise

Colour advertising
4 business days in advance for space booking and material.

Double truck
4 business days in advance for space booking and material.

Colour and double truck advertising is subject to availability.

COPY CHANGES

News, Report on Business, Sports, Globe Review
2:00pm day prior to publication date.

Wednesday Travel:
Monday 2:00pm.

Style/Focus: Thursday 12:00pm.

Review: Monday - Thursday 12:00pm day prior.

Friday '7': Wednesday 4:30pm.

Saturday Travel/Review:
Thursday 2:00pm.

ADDITIONAL INFORMATION

- Deadlines and specifications available separately.
- There is a $74 production charge for ads under 50 MAL that are not camera-ready.
- Minimum display space in News, Style, and Report on Business is 30 MAL; unless specified, it is 15 MAL in other sections.
- Advertising columns 251 MAL or more in depth are charged full depth.
- Double Trucks: Gutter is charged as full column.
- Regional copy changes: $540 per plant.
- Position charge: +25 per cent.
- Front News Banner: +50 per cent and must be colour.
- Page 3, News: +40 per cent.
- Front ROB banner: +25 per cent and must be colour.
- Pages 2 & 3, ROB: +40 per cent.
- Charge for Globe and Mail box number: $74.
- Charge for affidavits: $74.
- Cancellation charge: 50 per cent for ads cancelled after deadline. No cancellations for colour advertising two days prior to publication. No cancellations accepted the day prior to publication.

- The Publisher shall not be liable for errors in advertisements beyond the actual space paid. No liability for non-insertions of any advertisement.
- Not responsible for return of advertising material.

NEWSPAPER SPECIFICATIONS

Complete mechanical and digital specifications available at http://adforward.globeandmail.ca.

Number of columns: 6.

Column width: 50mm
11.9 picas
1.96"

Column depth: 300 modular agate lines for full page ads (1,800 lines per 6 column page).

THE GLOBE AND MAIL
CANADA'S NATIONAL NEWSPAPER • FOUNDED 1844

Advertisers earn discounted line rates based on annual dollar volume line commitment. To demonstrate, assume an advertiser commits to $100 000. At that level, the line rate drops to $32.27 if the ads are placed in the News section or Report on Business section. Therefore, if the dollar commitment is divided by the line rate ($100 000/$32.27), the advertiser can place ads in various sizes totalling approximately 3100 lines. From the previous example, the total line space was 560 lines for one ad, which means that this ad could run six times (560 lines × 6) for a total of 3360 lines. This lineage earns the discounted line rate and on a dollar basis is just over the $100 000 discount plateau:

$$560 \text{ lines} \times 6 \times 32.27 = \$108\ 427.20$$

If the advertiser only has $100 000 to spend, one option would be to marginally reduce the size of the ad so there are fewer total lines.

Position Charges

Since one disadvantage of newspaper advertising is clutter, advertisers and agencies normally request positions in the newspaper that are deemed to be favourable. The request may be for a particular section, or it could be for the first few pages of the newspaper. With reference to Figure A1.2, the *Globe and Mail* charges more for preferred locations. A general request for a specific section will increase rates by 25 percent, while a request for an ad to appear on page 3 (news section) will increase the rates by 40 percent.

Position charge
The cost of requesting a preferred position in a newspaper.

The privilege of having a preferred position in a newspaper at a higher cost incurs a **position charge**. An advertiser usually justifies the additional expense of a position request by referring to the improved recognition and recall that will result from the better position.

Colour Charges

Although newspapers are often referred to as the black-and-white medium, colour is available to advertisers willing to pay for it. With reference to the *Globe and Mail*'s rate schedule in Figure A1.2, a separate cost of $8873 is added if the ad runs in colour. The colour charge applies each time the ad is run. Other newspapers quote cost increases for each additional colour that is added. The addition of 1-colour is often referred to as **spot colour**. A newspaper will also indicate if there is a minimum size requirement for ads running in colour. Make sure you read the fine print on the rate cards!

Spot colour
The addition of one colour to an otherwise black-and-white newspaper or magazine ad.

Generally speaking, there is higher recognition and recall of ads that appear in colour, but given the constraints of most budgets, the use of colour in newspaper advertising is reserved for very large advertisers.

Preprinted Inserts

Preprinted inserts, such as advertising supplements for supermarkets, drug stores, and mass merchandisers, are inserted into most newspapers and distributed by them. Rates are usually quoted on CPM (cost per thousand). As the size of an insert increases (number of pages) or the delivery circulation increases, the rates on a cost per thousand basis also increase. For example, a 24-page catalogue insert would cost more than a four-page folded insert. Insert rates are quoted separately on newspaper rate cards. In many cases, there is only a reference to the rates on the rate card. Advertisers must contact the newspaper for details.

Comparing Newspapers for Efficiency

In large metropolitan markets where several newspapers compete for advertising revenue, advertisers must decide which papers to place advertising with. If using a shotgun strategy, the advertiser may use all newspapers. Conversely, if the budget is limited and the target market is more precisely defined, the advertiser might be more selective.

Since the circulation and the cost of advertising (line rates) vary among newspapers, the advertiser must have a way of comparing the alternatives. To make this comparison, the

Cost per thousand (CPM)
The cost of delivering an advertising message to 1000 people; calculated by dividing the cost of the ad by the circulation in thousands.

advertiser may use a standard figure called the **cost per thousand (CPM)**. CPM is the actual cost of reaching 1000 readers in a market. The formula for calculating CPM is as follows:

$$\frac{\text{Cost}}{\text{Circulation (in thousands)}} = \text{CPM}$$

To illustrate the concept of CPM, assume an advertiser that wants to reach adults in the Toronto market is considering both the *Toronto Star* and the *Toronto Sun*. Refer to Figure A1.3 for specific details on how the newspapers are compared.

As shown by Figure A1.4, the newspaper CPM is strictly a quantitative figure and the results vary considerably. If the advertiser bases the decision of which newspaper to use solely on this principle, the decision is an easy one—the *Toronto Sun* has a much lower CPM than the *Toronto Star*. However, to reach the adult population of Toronto effectively, the advertiser will realize that the circulation of both newspapers will be needed. Even though the *Toronto Star* costs more, it reaches a larger segment of the adult population than the *Toronto Sun*. Advertisers wanting to reach a more upscale segment of Toronto's adult population will have to consider the *Globe and Mail*, a paper that targets a higher income executive and professional-type audience.

Magazine Advertising

The procedure for buying magazine space begins with deciding on the size of the ad, which involves choosing from among the variety of page options sold by the magazines under consideration. The rates quoted are based on the size of page requested. Other factors that influence the cost of advertising in magazines include the frequency of insertions and appropriate discounts, the use of colour, guaranteed-position charges, and the use of regional editions.

Size of an Advertisement and Rate Schedules

Magazines offer a variety of page options or page combinations. For example, *Canadian Geographic* sells space in the following formats: double-page spread, double 1/2-page spread, one page, 2/3 page, 1/2-page digest, 1/2-page horizontal, and 1/3 page. See Figure A1.4 for illustrations of various magazine ad sizes. The size selected for the advertisement determines the rate to be charged. Magazine rates are typically quoted for all page combinations.

FIGURE **A1.3**   **Comparing Newspapers for Efficiency**

The CPM, or cost per thousand, is used to compare newspaper alternatives. It is calculated by dividing the cost of the advertisement by the circulation (in thousands) of the newspaper.

Specifications	Toronto Star	Toronto Sun
Ad size	1000 lines	1000 lines
Cost per line	$20.65	$7.33
Ad cost (rate x lines)	$20 650	$7330
Circulation	454 529	199 766
CPM	$45.43	$36.70

Interpretation: Both newspapers reach adult males and females in Toronto, but the *Toronto Sun* reaches the audience in a more cost-efficient manner. An advertiser would have to place ads in both newspapers to effectively reach an adult target in Toronto.

Adapted from rate card information published by the *Toronto Star*, www.torontostar.com, and the *Toronto Sun*, www.torontosun.com.

FIGURE **A1.4** **Various Sizes of Magazine Ads**

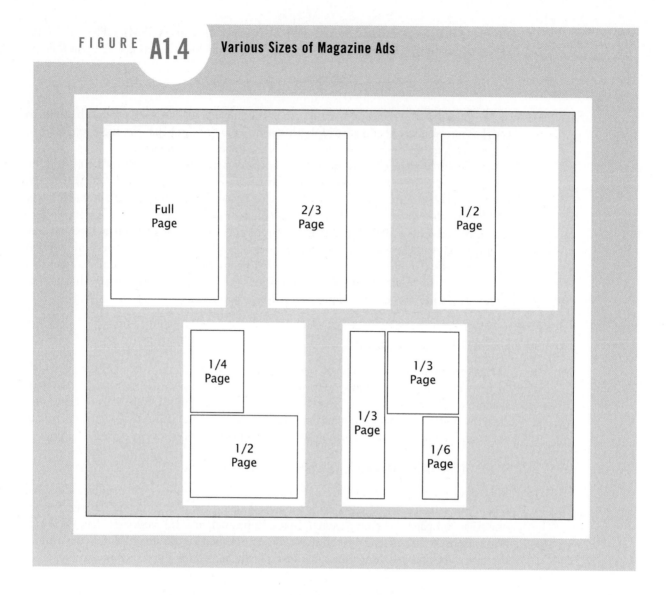

To illustrate how costs are calculated, let's consider a simple example. Assume an advertiser would like to purchase a one-page, four-colour ad in *Canadian Geographic* for January/February and March/April (see Figure A1.5 for rate card details). *Canadian Geographic* is issued eight times a year. The column headings on the rate card: 1X, 3X, 6X, and so on, refer to frequency (1 time, 3 times, 6 times). In this example, the frequency is only two. Therefore, the rates in the 1X column are used to calculate the campaign. A discount does not apply until the advertiser commits to three advertisements. The cost calculation would be as follows:

One-page rate × Number of insertions = Total cost

$$\$15\ 740 \times 2 = \$31\ 480$$

Discounts

Advertisers that purchase space in specific magazines with greater frequency will qualify for a variety of discounts. The nature of these discounts varies from one publication to another. Some of the more common discounts include frequency, continuity, and corporate discounts. In magazines, a **frequency discount** refers to a discounted page rate, with the discount based on the number of times an advertisement is run. The more often the

Frequency discount
A discounted page rate based on the number of times an advertisement runs.

FIGURE **A1.5** Canadian Geographic Rate Card

Geographic
canadiangeographic.ca
8x PER YEAR!

RATES AND DATA

PUBLISHING SCHEDULE 2006

ISSUE	FEATURES AND SUPPLEMENTS	CLOSING DATES (insertion orders & material)	ON NEWSSTAND (subs. may arrive earlier)
Jan/Feb 2006	Theme Issue: Canada's Musical Landscape	November 23, 2005	December 22, 2005
Mar/Apr 2006	Travel	January 25, 2006	February 23, 2006
	Travel & Adventure — Spring/Summer	January 25, 2006	
May/June 2006	Annual Report on the Environment	March 29, 2006	April 27, 2006
	Canadian Environment Awards	n/a	
July/Aug 2006	TBA	May 24, 2006	June 22, 2006
Sept/Oct 2006	Livable Cities — Regional Profile, includes Poster Map	July 26, 2006	August 24, 2006
November 2006	Travel (NEW 7TH ISSUE!)	September 20, 2006	October 19, 2006
December 2006	TBA	October 25, 2006	November 23, 2006
Jan/Feb 2007	TBA	November 29, 2006	December 28, 2006
Mar/Apr 2007	TBA	January 24, 2007	February 22, 2007
May 2007	Travel (NEW 8TH ISSUE!)	March 21, 2007	April 19, 2007
June 2007	Annual Report on the Environment	April 25, 2007	May 24, 2007

2006 ADVERTISING RATES

NATIONAL	1X	3X	6X	9X	12X
IFC spread	32,235	31,260	30,325	29,410	28,525
OBC	18,785	18,220	17,675	17,140	16,630
IBC	18,010	17,460	16,940	16,430	15,930
Double-page spread	28,025	27,185	26,365	25,580	24,810
Full page	15,740	15,305	14,840	14,390	13,960
Double 1/2-page spread	18,440	17,880	17,175	16,820	16,320
2/3 page	12,515	12,140	11,770	11,420	11,080
1/2-page digest	11,435	11,095	10,760	10,430	10,115
1/2-page horizontal	11,180	9,730	9,435	9,150	8,860
1/3 page	7,500	7,290	7,060	6,835	6,635
EAST/WEST SPLIT RUNS	1X	3X	6X	9X	12X
DPS	21,020	20,395	19,780	19,190	18,620
Full Page	11,835	11,480	11,130	10,800	10,480

Source: Courtesy of *Canadian Geographic*.

ad is run, the lower the unit cost for each ad. In the *Canadian Geographic* rate card, the unit rate is reduced when the ad is run three times, six times, nine times, and twelve times.

Continuity discount
A discount offered to advertisers that purchase space in consecutive issues of a publication.

A **continuity discount** is an additional discount offered to advertisers that agree to purchase space in consecutive issues of a magazine (such as buying space in 12 issues of a monthly magazine). When continuity discounts are combined with frequency discounts, lower unit costs per page of advertising result.

Large advertisers that use the same magazine to advertise a variety of products (note that such an advertiser would likely be a multi-product firm with products that share similar target markets) may qualify for corporate discounts. A **corporate discount** involves consideration of the total number of pages purchased by the company (all product lines combined), and a lower page rate for each product. Companies such as Procter & Gamble or Unilever that advertise extensively in women's magazines such as *Chatelaine* and *Canadian Living* would earn preferred rates for the advertising pages they buy in those magazines.

Corporate discount
A discount based on the total number of pages purchased by a single company (all product lines combined).

Colour and Position Charges

Most magazines publish in colour. Therefore, rates for black and white ads or ads that only include spot colour are usually quoted separately. Additional costs for requesting a guaranteed position are also quoted separately on the rate card. For a guaranteed position, such as the outside back cover (OBC) or the inside front cover (IFC) and inside back cover (IBC), the additional costs are usually in the +20 percent range. With reference to the *Canadian Geographic* rate card, the rate for the outside back cover is $18 785, compared to a full-page ad inside the magazine at $15 740. The difference is about 20 percent.

To illustrate the cost calculations of buying magazine space, let's develop a couple of examples based on the *Canadian Geographic* rate card (see Figure A1.5) and the following information:

Example 1:

Magazine:	*Canadian Geographic*
Size of ad:	one-page, 4-colour ad
Number of insertions:	one-page ad to run in 4 consecutive issues

The calculation for this buying plan will be as follows:

Costs for one page, 4 colour:

Base rate	3X rate applies
$15 305 x 4	= $61 220

Example 2:

Magazine:	*Canadian Geographic*
Size of ad:	double-page spread, 4-colour ad
Number of insertions:	6 issues

The calculation for this buying plan will be as follows:

Costs for DPS, four colour:

Base rate	6X rate applies
$26 365 x 6	= $158 190

Comparing Magazines for Efficiency

Let's assume the advertiser has decided to use magazines because they usually have a well-defined target audience based on demographic variables. The advertiser still must choose particular magazines in which to advertise. Because costs and circulation figures vary, the advertiser needs a way to compare alternatives. As with newspapers, CPM is an effective quantitative means of comparing competing magazines.

In most magazine classifications, there is usually a group of publications competing for the same market. For example, *Chatelaine*, *Homemaker's*, and *Canadian Living*, among others, compete against each other in the women's classification. Although the editorial content varies from one magazine to another, each reaches a similar target, so advertisers must look at the efficiencies of each.

Figure A1.6 contains the comparative calculations for two of the magazines in the women's classification. In terms of a purely quantitative measure, both magazines are almost equal, which is why they attract the same types of advertisers. Advertisers wanting to reach the demographic profile of readers of these magazines have little choice but to allocate dollars to both. They reach different readers, but readers with the same profile. Therefore, to advertise in both increases the reach of the magazine campaign. The question to be answered is, how much weight does each magazine receive?

Television Advertising

As indicated earlier, stations and networks tend not to publish a rate card. There are a variety of factors that influence the costs of television advertising: the supply of advertising time available and the demand for that time, the type of program, the time of day the ad will appear, and the length of the commercial.

Supply and Demand

For major networks such as CTV, CBC, and Global, fundamental economic principles rule the cost of advertising. Advertising space is restricted to 12 minutes per hour, so the network has to maximize advertising revenues on shows that are popular. Top-rated shows like *CSI* (CTV), *American Idol* (CTV), *Desperate Housewives* (CTV), *Survivor* (Global), and the *NHL Playoffs* (CBC) attract advertisers willing to pay a premium price for being on a popular (highly watched) show. The low supply and high demand for the space

FIGURE **A1.6** **Comparing Magazines for Efficiency**

Similar to newspapers, CPM (cost per thousand) comparisons are made between magazines that reach similar target markets. In this case, *Chatelaine* and *Canadian Living* compete head-to-head for advertisers.

Specifications	*Chatelaine*	*Canadian Living*
1 time, 4-colour rate	$46 505	$35 500
Circulation	586 136	527 694
CPM	$79.34	$67.27

Both magazines charge different rates and have different circulations. In this comparison it appears that Canadian Living is more efficient at reaching female adults. If the objective were to maximize reach, an advertiser would have to include both magazines in the media mix. Similar CPM comparisons can be made on the basis of total readership for each magazine (circulation x the number of readers = total readership) drives the rates upward. National ads on a popular show like *CSI: Crime Scene Investigation* can be as high as $80 000. By comparison, *Hockey Night in Canada* sells for about $25 000. Canada's top-rated shows are determined weekly by research organizations such as the BBM and Nielsen Media Research. A sample of their research appears in Figure A1.7.

The rates ultimately paid for popular shows depend largely on their advertising agency's ability to negotiate with the networks. To illustrate, the quoted 30-second spot on *CSI: Miami* in 2003 was $49 500, an indication of the show's popularity. The negotiated rate, typically given to larger year-round advertisers after negotiations, packaging strategies, and agency agreements was $34 000.[1] Again, negotiation skills play a key role in the rates an advertiser actually pays.

Types of Programs

Special programs such as drama specials, sports events, and miniseries are usually distinguished from regular programming. They are designated as special buys and are sold separately from regular programs. In the case of sports programs, for example, hockey and baseball broadcasts tend to appeal to a particular demographic: males between 18 and 49. They are attractive shows for certain types of advertisers. For these shows, networks need sponsors that are willing to make a long-term commitment, and there are separate rates and discount schedules for those that make such a commitment. Canadian Tire, for example, is a committed advertiser for *Hockey Night in Canada* and the *NHL Playoffs*. Labatt Blue is a prominent advertiser on Toronto Blue Jays' broadcasts on Rogers Sportsnet.

Rates for one-time annual sports programming are usually separate from regular programming because they also attract a particular audience. The Masters Golf Tournament, one of the PGA's most prestigious championships, is broadcast (simulcast) on Global each year. The cost of a spot in the final two rounds averages $30 000 (for a day-time spot), well beyond the rate for an average spot in prime time on the same network.[2]

Time of Day

Television is divided into three time categories: *prime time*, *fringe time*, and *day time*. Prime time is usually between 7 pm and 11 pm, fringe time between 4 pm and 7 pm, and day time from sign-on to 4 pm. Because television viewing is highest in prime time, the advertising rates are higher for that time period. Rates vary from show to show and are based solely on the size of viewing audience each show reaches. As indicated above, shows like *CSI* and *Survivor* reach a very large audience, so their rates are among the highest. Other shows in prime time with a smaller audience have rates that are adjusted downward proportionately. The difference is based on the popularity of the show and the size of the audience.

Television viewing in fringe time and day time is much lower, so the advertising rates are adjusted downward. Program content is of a different nature: talk shows, children's shows, reruns of popular programs, and so on. CKCO-TV does publish a rate card, which illustrates how rates fluctuate based on time of day and the popularity of the show (see Figure A1.8).

Length of Commercial

Most advertisers run 30-second commercials, so rates are normally quoted based on that length. Due to the rising costs of television advertising, however, advertisers are starting to use 15-second commercials more frequently. There is a slight premium for using 15-second commercials; rates are normally about 65 percent of the cost of a 30-second commercial on the same network or station. A 60-second commercial is normally twice the cost of a 30-second commercial. If an advertiser can accomplish creatively what it desires

FIGURE   **A1.7**   Canada's Top TV Shows

Measuring Audiences. Delivering Intelligence.

Auditoires mesurés. Décisions éclairées.

Top Programs - Total Canada
March 27 - April 2, 2006
Based on preliminary program schedules and audience data, Demographic: All Persons 2+

Rank	Program	Broadcast Outlet	Weekday	Start	End	Total 2+ AMA(000)
1	CSI	CTV Network	...T...	21:00	21:59	3448
2	American Idol 5 AP	CTV Network	.T.....	20:00	21:00	3330
3	American Idol 5 AR	CTV Network	..W....	21:00	21:30	2449
4	Survivor 12	Global Network	...T...	20:00	21:00	2441
5	Grey's Anatomy	CTV Network	......S	22:01	23:00	2411
6	Desperate Housewives	CTV Network	......S	21:00	22:01	2368
7	Amazing Race 9	CTV Network	.T.....	22:00	23:00	2259
8	ER	CTV Network	...T...	21:59	23:00	2186
9	CSI:New York	CTV Network	..W....	22:00	23:00	2041
10	CSI:Miami	CTV Network	M......	22:00	23:00	1952
11	House	Global Network	.T.....	21:00	22:00	1949
12	Law & Order:SVU	CTV Network	.T.....	21:00	22:00	1770
13	SP:CTV At The Junos	CTV Network	......S	19:00	21:00	1720
14	Lost	CTV Network	..W....	20:00	21:00	1584
15	CSI:New York	CTV Network	M......	21:00	22:00	1515
16	News: CTV Evening News	CTV Network	MTWTF..	18:00	19:00	1488
17	Prison Break	Global Network	M......	20:00	21:00	1364
18	Without a Trace	Global Network	...T...	22:00	23:00	1217
19	Ghost Whisperer	CTV Network	....F..	20:00	21:00	1198
20	CSI	CTV Network	M......	20:00	21:00	1184
21	Apprentice 5	Global Network	M......	21:00	22:00	1140
22	Simpsons	Global Network	......S	20:00	20:30	1138
23	Hockey Night Canada	CBC Network	.....S.	19:00	22:00	1134
24	OC	CTV Network	...T...	20:00	21:00	1079
25	Jeopardy/Access Hollywood	CTV Network	MTWTF..	19:30	20:00	1071
26	News: CTV Weekend News	CTV Network	.....SS	18:00	19:00	1025
27	Close To Home	CTV Network	....F..	21:00	22:00	1013
28	24	Global Network	M......	22:00	23:00	1011
29	Las Vegas	Global Network	....F..	21:00	22:00	995
30	News:Global National	Global Network	MTWTF..	17:30	18:00	951

Understanding this report ...

This chart shows the Top 30 TV programs for all Canadian national networks and specialty stations for the week indicated. Programs are ranked based on their AMA(000). AMA(000) is the average minute audience in thousands. The chart also indicates the broadcast outlet on which the program aired and the program's start and end time (shown in Eastern Time).

© 2005 BBM Canada

BBM Canada
1500 Don Mills Road, 3rd Floor
Toronto, ON M3B 3L7
416 445 9800 Tel
416 445 8644 Fax

Sondages BBM
2055, rue Peel, 11' etage
Montréal, PQ H3A 1V4
514 878 9711 Tál.
514 878 4210 Téléc.

BBM Canada
10991 Shellbridge Way, Suite 208
Richmond, BC V6X 3C6
604 249 3500 Tel
604 214 9648 Fax

www.bbm.ca

Source: Courtesy of BBM Canada.

FIGURE **A1.8** CKCO-TV Rate Card

2005-2006 RATE CARD

REVISED EFFECTIVE: June 6/05
30 SECOND - PUBLISHED RATE (GROSS)
FOR INTERNAL USE ONLY
RATES ARE PROTECTED FOR 5 WORKING DAYS

PRIME

DAY	TIME	PROGRAM		GROUP #	FALL SEP 12/05-DEC 11/05	WINTER DEC 12/05-FEB 19/06	SPRING FEB 20/06-JUN 4/06	SUMMER JUN 5/06-SEP 17/06	52 WEEK SEP 12/05 - SEP 17/06
M-F	557-7P	CTV NEWS AT 6PM	O	015	$1,140	$970	$1,140	$970	$1,010
SA-SU	558-7P	CTV NEWS AT 6PM	O	162	$690	$590	$690	$590	$610
M-F	7-730P	ETALK DAILY	O	153	$600	$510	$600	$510	$530
M-F	730-8P	JEOPARDY	SIM	001	$820	$690	$820	$690	$720
MO	8-830P	CORNER GAS	O	198	$930	$790	$930	$790	$820
MO	9-10P	MEDIUM	PRE	157	$1,600	$1,360	$1,600	$1,360	$1,420
MO	10-11P	CSI MIAMI	SIM	192	$3,400	$2,890	$3,400	$2,890	$3,020
TU	8-9P	AMERICAN IDOL	SIM	057		$3,150	$3,700		
TU	8-9P	CLOSE TO HOME	PRE	071	$1,140	$970	$1,140	$970	$1,010
TU	9-10P	THE AMAZING RACE	SIM	073	$4,010	$3,410	$4,010		
TU	10-11P	LAW & ORDER SVU	SIM	092	$1,880	$1,600	$1,880	$1,600	$1,670
WE	8-9P	LOST	PRE	096		$1,070	$1,260		
WE	8-9P	INVASION	PRE	075	$910	$770	$910	$770	$810
WE	9-10P	LOST	SIM	146	$1,890			$1,610	
WE	9-10P	AMERICAN IDOL	SIM	084		$2,690	$3,160		
WE	10-11P	CSI NEW YORK	SIM	052	$2,160	$1,840	$2,160	$1,840	$1,920
TH	8-9P	THE O.C.	SIM	167	$1,580	$1,340	$1,580	$1,340	$1,400
TH	9-10P	C.S.I.	SIM	068	$4,940	$4,200	$4,940	$4,200	$4,380
TH	10-11P	ER	SIM	049	$3,700	$3,150	$3,700	$3,150	$3,280
FR	8-9P	GHOST WHISPERER	SIM	185	$690	$590	$690	$590	$610
FR	9-10P	NIP/TUCK	O	137	$1,220	$1,030	$1,220	$1,030	$1,080
FR	10-11P	INCONCEIVABLE	SIM	061	$910	$770	$910	$770	$810
SA	7-8P	W-FIVE	O	039	$420	$350	$420	$350	$370
SA	8-9P	COLD CASE	PRE	128	$690	$590	$690	$590	$610
SA	9-10P	CRIME TIME SATURDAY	SIM	035	$690	$590	$690	$590	$610
SA	10-11P	SOPRANOS	O	104	$690				
SA	10-11P	SUE THOMAS F.B.EYE	O	172		$660	$780	$660	
SU	7-8P	LAW & ORDER CI	PRE	103	$1,010	$860	$1,010	$860	$900
SU	8-9P	THE WEST WING	SIM	042	$1,540	$1,310	$1,540	$1,310	$1,370
SU	9-10P	DESPERATE HOUSEWIVES	SIM	025	$4,010	$3,410	$4,010	$3,410	$3,560
SU	10-11P	GREYS ANATOMY	SIM	066	$2,240	$1,900	$2,240	$1,900	$1,990

Source: Courtesy of CKCO-TV.

by using 15-second commercials, it will cost less to advertise in absolute dollars. This is an important budget consideration.

Gross Rating Points

Gross rating points (GRPs)
An expression of the weight of advertising in a media schedule; calculated by multiplying reach by frequency.

The weight of advertising in a market is determined by a rating system referred to as gross rating points. **Gross rating points (GRPs)** are an aggregate of total ratings in a schedule, usually in a weekly period, against a predetermined target audience. GRPs are based on the following formula:

$$\text{GRPs} = \text{Reach} \times \text{Frequency}$$

To illustrate how GRPs work, assume a message reaches 40 percent of target households three times in one week. The GRP level would be 120 (40 x 3). If the message reaches 35 percent of households with an average frequency of 3.6 per week, the GRP level would be 126 (35 x 3.6). The reach of a television show is referred to as a **rating**. For example, if *CSI: Crime Scene Investigation* reaches 40 percent of households during its weekly time slot, the show has a 40 rating. Therefore, another way to calculate GRPs is to multiply a show's rating by the frequency of messages on that show. See Figure A1.9 for an illustration of this calculation.

Rating
Television and radio audience estimates expressed as a percentage of a population in a defined geographic area.

Decisions about reach and frequency are difficult. Traditional wisdom suggests frequency is the more important variable because it is necessary to drive the message home before people take action. Traditional models are based on achieving awareness, attitude, and action. But there is a threshold at which an advertiser starts to turn the consumer off.[3] Consequently, many advertisers buy into a relatively new concept called recency. **Recency** is a model that suggests advertising works best by reminding consumers about a product when they are ready to buy; this model suggests the timing of an ad is the crucial decision.[4] The debate goes on!

Recency
A model that suggests advertising works best by reminding consumers about a product when they are ready to buy.

Since reach, frequency, and GRPs are discussed in the negotiation process, along with a host of other factors, it is next to impossible to illustrate its application in this book. However, to illustrate the basic use of a television rate card, let's look at a few examples. The rate card for CKCO-TV included in Figure A1.8 will be used as reference for these illustrations.

FIGURE A1.9   **Calculating GRPs for Television**

The weight of advertising in a market or on a particular show is determined by a rating system. Media weight is expressed in terms of gross rating points (GRPs). GRPs consider two key variables: the size of the audience reached and frequency with which the ad is run against that audience. The chart shows some sample calculations to arrive at total GRPs.

Audience Demographic	Rating	Number of Spots	GRPs
18–49	30	2	60
18–49	25	2	50
18–49	20	2	40
18–49	23	2	46
Total		**8**	**196**

If the eight spots were scheduled in a one-week period, the weight level for the advertising would be expressed as 196 GRPs for the week.

Example 1:

CSI: Miami:	2 spots per week
The OC:	1 spot per week
eTalk Daily:	3 spots per week

All ads are scheduled over a 12-week period between September 19 and December 2.

Cost Calculations:

Based on the time period, the Fall rates would apply from Figure A1.8 (see the rate card for details).

CSI: Miami:

$3400 × 2 spots per week × 12 weeks = $81 600

The OC:

$1580 × 1 spot per week × 12 weeks = $18 960

eTalk Daily:

$600 × 3 spots per week × 12 weeks = $21 600

Total cost: $122 160

Example 2:

Grey's Anatomy:	2 spots per week (13 weeks from February 20 to May 19)
CSI:	1 spot per week (13 weeks from February 20 to May 19)
American Idol:	1 spot per week (8 weeks from Feb 20 to April 14)

Cost Calculations:

Based on the timing of this campaign, the Spring rates would apply from Figure A1.8 (see the rate card for details).

Grey's Anatomy:

$2240 × 2 spots per week × 13 weeks = $58 240

CSI:

$4940 × 1 spot per week × 13 weeks = $64 220

American Idol:

$3700 × 1 spot per week × 8 weeks = $29 600

Total cost: $152 060

A variety of discounts are usually available to television advertisers. A *frequency discount* is usually earned by purchasing a minimum number of spots over a specified period. A **volume discount** is linked to the dollar volume purchased over an extended period, usually 52 weeks. The greater the volume purchased, the greater the discount. A *continuity discount* is earned when advertisers purchase a minimum number of spots over an extended period (also usually 52 weeks). With reference to Figure A1.8, note that the average rates for a spot are lower in the 52-week column. This reflects the continuity discount offered by the station. Generally, discounts are not published. Instead, they are part of the discussion when buyers and sellers are negotiating with each other.

Volume discount

A discount linked to the dollar volume purchased over an extended period; the more volume purchased, the higher the discount.

Radio Advertising

The rates paid by radio advertisers are affected by several factors: the season or time of year in which commercials are placed, the time of day at which the commercials are scheduled, the use of reach plans, and the availability of discounts offered by individual stations.

Seasonal Rate Structures

Radio stations use grid-rate schedules that reflect seasonal listening patterns and reach potential. Refer to Figure A1.10 for an illustration of specific grid-level rates. Generally, radio rates fluctuate with the seasons as follows:

Time Period	Rate
May–August (summer) and December	Higher
September–October	Mid-range
March–April	Mid-range
January–February	Lower

Dayparts

Daypart
A broadcast time period or segment on radio or television.

Since the size and nature of the audience vary according to the **daypart** (a broadcast time period or segment), different rates are charged for each. Generally, the dayparts are classified as follows:

Classification	Time
Breakfast	6 to 10 am
Midday	10 am to 4 pm
Drive	4 to 7 pm
Evening	7 pm to midnight
Nighttime	Midnight to 6 am

Dayparts vary from one station to another, with some stations having more or fewer classifications than those listed above. In addition, weekend classifications are often different from weekday ones, as the listening patterns of the audience change on weekends.

Reach Plans

Rotation plan
The placement of commercials in time slots purchased on radio; can be vertical according to the time of day or horizontal according to the day of the week.
Vertical rotation
The placement of radio commercials based on the time of day (within various dayparts).
Horizontal rotation
The placement of radio commercials based on the day of the week (same daypart on different days).
Reach plan
Rotation of commercials in various dayparts on radio according to a predetermined frequency.

Radio advertisers can purchase specific time slots and schedule a particular rotation plan during the length of the media buy, or they can purchase a reach plan. For the first option, a **rotation plan**, the advertiser specifies the time slots and pays the rate associated with it. Two types of rotation plans are available:

- *Vertical Rotation:* the placement of commercials based on the time of day (within various dayparts)
- *Horizontal Rotation:* the placement of commercials based on the day of the week (same daypart on different days)

Radio stations sell reach plans so that advertisers can maximize reach. In a **reach plan**, commercials are rotated through the various dayparts according to a predetermined frequency to reach different people with the same message. As shown in Figure A1.10, the reach plan divides spots equally between breakfast, daytime, drive time, and evening/Sunday dayparts. For the advertiser, the benefit of the reach plan is twofold. First, the reach potential is extended, and second, the rates charged for the reach plan collectively are lower (because of the discounts) than those that would result from the individual purchase of similar time slots. Reach plans do require a minimum spot purchase on a weekly basis (16 spots per week is common).

Discounts Offered by Radio

Advertisers that purchase frequently from specific stations qualify for a variety of discounts.

FIGURE **A1.10**   **CJAZ-FM Rate Card**

CJAZ-FM Radio
101.7 JAZ-FM
Jazz that Rocks!

30-sec spot rates

Daypart/Grid	1	2	3	4	5
Breakfast 6:00 to 10:00 am	300	275	250	225	200
Daytime 10:00 am to 3:00 pm	245	225	205	185	165
Drive 3:00 to 7:00 pm	250	230	210	190	170
Evening and Sunday	220	200	180	160	140

Reach Plan - 30 sec spots

	1	2	3	4	5
Breakfast 25% Daytime 25% Drive 25% Evening and Sunday 25%	250	225	200	175	150

Discount Schedule

Contract Buy (Continuity)		*Volume (Spots)*	
14 to 26 weeks	Grid 3	250	Grid 3
27 to 39 weeks	Grid 4	450	Grid 4
40 to 52 weeks	Grid 5	700	Grid 5

A *frequency discount* is a discounted rate earned through the purchase of a minimum number of spots over a specified period of time, usually a week. Having earned such a discount, advertisers are referred to a lower-rate grid schedule, or could be quoted a percentage discount, such as 5 percent for 15 to 20 spots per week, 8 percent for 21 to 30 spots per week, 10 percent for over 31 spots, and so forth. With a *volume discount*, the advertiser is charged a lower rate for buying a large number of spots; the discount might be 5 percent for 260 spots, for example, or 10 percent for 520 spots. A *continuity discount* applies when an advertiser agrees to place ads over an extended period such as intervals of 26, 39, and 52 weeks.

Advertisers can increase reach by buying a *reach plan*. The reach plan offers a minimum number of weekly spots across all dayparts in return for a packaged discount rate. Refer to Figure A1.10 for examples of discounts.

Buying Radio Time

A strategic plan guides the purchase of radio commercial time. To get the best possible rate from a station or network of stations, all details of the plan must be known by the radio station. Factors such as volume and frequency (the total number of spots in the buy), the timing of the schedule (in terms of time of day or season in which the plan is scheduled), and continuity (the lengths of the plan) collectively affect the spot rate that is charged the advertiser. It places an advertiser on a particular grid with the station. Refer to Figure A1.10 for a listing of grid rates and how an advertiser arrives at a certain grid. For advertisers that purchase large amounts of time, the discounts described above usually apply.

To illustrate some basic cost calculations used in buying radio time, let's develop some examples based on the CJAZ-FM rate card in Figure A1.10.

Example 1:

30-second spots

10 breakfast spots per week

15 drive spots per week

12-week schedule

Cost Calculations:

The advertiser does not qualify for a continuity discount. Therefore, the first calculation is to determine the total number of spots in the buy to see if a volume discount applies.

Total number of spots	= Spots per week × Number of weeks
Breakfast	= 10 per week × 12 weeks = 120
Drive	= 15 per week × 12 weeks = 180
Total spots	= 300

Based on the total number of spots (300), the rate charged will be from Grid 3. In this case, the 30-second rate is $250 for breakfast and $210 for drive time. The cost calculations are as follows:

Total cost = Number of spots × Earned rate	
Breakfast	= 120 spots × $250 = $30 000
Drive	= 180 spots × $210 = $37 800
Total cost	= $67 800

Example 2:

The advertiser would like to evaluate a reach plan (involving 16 commercials per week) against a specific buying plan. Details of each plan are as follows:

Plan A: Reach Plan (30-second spots)

16 spots per week (reach plan)

Rotated between breakfast, drive, day, and evening/Sunday

Schedule over 16 weeks, June through September

Plan B: Specific Plan (30-second spots)

8 breakfast spots per week

8 drive spots per week

16-week schedule

Cost Calculations for Plan A:

The advertiser qualifies for a continuity discount because of the 16-week schedule. The rate would be in Grid 3 in the reach plan. The earned rate is $200 per spot.

Total Cost	= Total number of spots × Earned rate
	= (16 spots per week × 16 weeks) × $200
	= $51 200

Cost Calculations for Plan B:

The total number of spots is as follows:

Breakfast	= 8 spots per week × 16 weeks = 128 spots
Drive	= 8 spots per week × 16 weeks = 128 spots
Total spots	= 256

Based on this calculation, the advertiser does not qualify for a volume discount, but since the contract runs for 16 weeks, a continuity discount does apply. The advertiser is charged the rate from Grid 3.

Breakfast	= 128 spots × $250 = $32 000
Drive	= 128 spots × $210 = $26 880
Total cost	= $58 880

In conducting a comparative evaluation of Plan A and Plan B, the advertiser must weigh the more selective reach potential of Plan B against the savings of Plan A. Perhaps the advertiser wants to reach business commuters in drive time to and from work. With Plan A, the advertiser can reach a somewhat different audience by means of a daypart rotation of spots. The net result is a cost difference of $7680 in favour of Plan A. Should the advertiser decide to go with the cost savings of Plan A, or with the more selective reach of Plan B at greater cost?

Out-of-Home Advertising

Out-of-home advertising offers a variety of outdoor poster options, street-level advertising, wall murals, transit shelters, and transit vehicle and station advertising. Regardless of the alternative, the media buying procedure is similar. Out-of-home rates are based on GRPs, so factors such as reach and frequency are built into the rate cards.

Referring to Figure A1.11, a rate card for Viacom transit shelters, let's assume an advertiser wants to buy 50 GRPs in Toronto. That means the advertiser will reach the equivalent of 50 percent of Toronto's population. The word "equivalent" is important because vehicle and pedestrian traffic in a city is habitual, that is, people tend to travel the same routes each day. Therefore, in the Toronto example, the advertiser might reach 25 percent of the population twice a day for a total of 50 daily GRPs.

All out-of-home advertising rates are quoted on a four-week basis and are sold on a market-by-market basis. Posters and transit shelters are sold on the basis of a four-week minimum purchase. The other options (backlits, mall posters, and superboards) usually have a 12-week minimum purchase requirement. To illustrate outdoor cost calculations, let's consider a couple of media buying examples. Rates and data from Figure A1.11 (transit shelter rates) and Figure A1.12 (outdoor poster rates) are used to calculate costs.

Example 1: Outdoor Buying Plan

Medium:	Transit shelters (Viacom)
Markets:	Toronto/Hamilton (CMA), Montreal District, Calgary (CMA), and Edmonton (CMA)

FIGURE **A1.11**   **Outdoor Rate Card for Transit Shelters**

VIACOM
O U T D O O R

Viacom Outdoor - Street Level

Audited by
COMB

Owned and operated by Viacom Outdoor, 377 Horner Ave., Toronto, ON M8W 1Z8. Phone: 416-255-1392. Fax: 416-255-2063.
Nick Arakgi, General Manager

TRANSIT SHELTERS

	Pop.	25 Daily GRPs			50 Daily GRPs			75 Daily GRPs		
		min. panels	max. panels	4 wk. rate	min. panels	max. panels	4 wk. rate	min. panels	max. panels	4 wk. rate
St. John's CMA	162,700	—	6	3,180	—	11	5,214	—	17	8,058
Mount Pearl, C (NL)	23,600	—	1	510	—	2	1,020	—	3	1,530
Halifax CMA	351,200	9	10	4,871	18	20	9,279	28	30	13,918
Cape Breton CA (Sydney)	98,400	—	3	1,794	4	5	3,416	6	7	5,124
Annapolis Valley ESA	95,000	—	3	1,134	—	6	2,172	—	9	3,213
Saint John CMA	113,100	—	3	1,442	—	6	2,748	—	8	4,121
Quebec City CMA	651,800	14	16	10,562	28	30	20,118	41	45	30,176
Chicoutimi-Jonquiere (Saguenay) CMA	145,100	4	5	2,109	8	9	4,018	12	14	6,026
Trois Rivieres CMA	129,000	4	5	1,673	8	9	3,186	13	15	4,779
Sherbrooke CMA	147,900	—	3	2,020	5	6	3,848	8	9	5,771
Montreal CMA	3,308,100	52	58	38,387	104	114	73,118	159	169	109,676
Hull C & District	196,100	—	7	2,660	—	14	5,068	—	19	7,600
Shawinigan CA & District	53,100	—	3	2,040						
Toronto CMA/Hamilton CMA	5,403,800	80	88	66,780	162	172	127,200	245	255	190,800
Toronto CMA	4,761,100	70	76	68,117	140	150	129,746	212	222	194,619
Hamilton CMA	642,500	16	18	9,987	31	35	19,024	47	51	28,536
Stratford CA	28,400	—	4	2,193	—					
London CMA	416,200	7	8	5,264	14	16	10,026	21	23	15,039
Windsor CMA	305,100	7	8	4,386	15	17	8,355	22	24	12,533
Leamington CA	46,500	2	3	1,097	—					
Sarnia CA	80,900	—	3	2,295	5	6	4,371	7	8	6,557
Owen Sound CA	29,400	—	3	910	—					
Barrie CA	171,200	5	6	1,685	11	13	3,210	17	19	4,815
Sault Ste. Marie CA	70,200	—	2	876	—	4	1,752	—	5	2,190
Timmins CA	39,400	—	2	1,090	—	4	2,016	—	6	2,622
Sudbury CMA	137,900	—	3	1,875	—	6	3,600	—	9	5,130
Winnipeg CMA	625,500	8	9	6,544	16	18	12,465	24	26	18,698
Calgary CMA	978,300	18	20	13,351	36	40	25,431	54	60	38,147
Grande Prairie C	152,500	—	—	260						
Edmonton CMA	904,700	18	20	13,351	35	39	25,431	52	58	38,147
Vancouver CMA	2,051,300	31	35	29,901	62	68	56,954	93	101	85,431

	100 Daily GRPs		
	min. panels	max. panels	4 wk. rate
St. John's CMA	—	23	10,534
Mount Pearl, C (NL)	—	4	2,040
Halifax CMA	36	40	18,558
Cape Breton CA (Sydney)	8	9	6,833
Annapolis Valley ESA	—	11	3,872
Saint John CMA	—	11	5,495
Quebec City CMA	54	60	40,235
Chicoutimi-Jonquiere (Saguenay) CMA	17	19	8,035
Trois Rivieres CMA	17	19	6,373
Sherbrooke CMA	11	13	7,695
Montreal CMA	213	223	146,235
Hull C & District	—	25	10,550
Shawinigan CA & District	—	—	—
Toronto CMA/Hamilton CMA	328	338	254,400
Toronto CMA	284	294	259,493
Hamilton CMA	62	68	38,048
Stratford CA	—	—	—
London CMA	28	32	20,053
Windsor CMA	29	33	16,710
Leamington CA	—	—	—
Sarnia CA	9	10	8,743
Owen Sound CA	—	—	—
Barrie CA	—	—	—
Sault Ste. Marie CA	—	7	3,066
Timmins CA	—	7	2,961
Sudbury CMA	—	12	6,420
Winnipeg CMA	31	35	24,930
Calgary CMA	73	79	50,863
Grande Prairie C			
Edmonton CMA	71	77	50,863
Vancouver CMA	124	134	113,908

MECHANICAL SPECIFICATIONS:
TRANSIT SHELTERS - ALL MARKETS
Live Area: 3' 6-1/2" x 5' 4-11/16"
Visible Area: 3' 9" x 5' 6-1/4"
Trim Size: 3' 11-1/4" x 5' 8-1/4"
Prod. costs extra. Replacement/renewal material required. Viacom Outdoor has full production facilities.
Contact rep or see web site for product and art specs.
Data confirmed 11/03/2005

Source: Canadian Advertising Rates and Data, 2005 data.

FIGURE **A1.12** **Rate Card for Outdoor Posters**

Viacom Outdoor - Posters

	Pop.	25 Daily GRPs min. panels	25 Daily GRPs max. panels	25 Daily GRPs 4 wk. rate	50 Daily GRPs min. panels	50 Daily GRPs max. panels	50 Daily GRPs 4 wk. rate	75 Daily GRPs min. panels	75 Daily GRPs max. panels	75 Daily GRPs 4 wk. rate
St. John's CMA	162,500	—	4	4,200	—	7	7,140	—	11	9,350
Charlottetown CA	77,600	—	3	2,808	—	3	2,808	—	3	2,808
Amherst C & District	30,000	—	4	3,264	—	4	3,264	—	4	3,264
Halifax CMA	347,000	6	7	6,444	12	14	12,275	18	20	18,413
Acadian Peninsula	48,800	—	4	2,400	—	6	3,330	—	6	3,330
Sydney C	44,200	1	2	1,553	2	3	2,958	3	4	4,437
Bathurst CA	39,600	—	2	1,400	—	4	2,600	—	4	2,600
Miramichi & District	34,200	—	2	1,400	—	4	2,600	—	4	2,600
Fredericton C	44,800	2	3	1,925	4	5	3,667	5	6	5,500
Moncton C	113,700	3	4	1,656	6	7	3,155	8	9	4,733
Saint John C	63,800	2	3	1,869	4	5	3,560	6	7	5,340
TOTAL ATLANTIC	1,006,200	—	—	28,919	—	—	47,357	—	—	62,375
St. Lawrence Basin/Matapedia	145,300	9	11	6,837	18	20	13,023	18	20	13,023
Charlevoix North Shore	68,900	4	5	3,647	8	9	6,946	12	14	10,419
Beauce District	61,200	6	7	6,381	11	12	12,154	15	17	18,231
Thetford Mines/Victoriaville CA & District	77,600	5	6	5,013	9	10	9,549	12	14	14,323
Quebec City CMA	649,700	9	11	19,512	18	20	37,165	27	29	55,748
Chicoutimi/Jonquiere District	157,800	5	6	3,723	10	12	7,091	15	17	10,637
Trois Rivieres CMA & District	182,800	4	4	4,441	8	9	8,459	13	15	12,688
Granby/Drummondville CA	127,600	3	4	5,653	3	4	5,653	3	4	5,653
Sherbrooke CMA	148,600	3	4	4,495	6	7	8,563	9	10	12,844
Montreal District	3,067,100	24	26	62,442	47	53	118,936	72	78	178,404
Montreal ESA	3,175,200	26	28	64,243	51	57	122,368	76	84	183,551
Northwestern Quebec	54,300	4	5	3,375	7	8	6,430	7	8	6,430
Gatineau/Hull C	220,700	6	7	5,579	12	14	10,626	12	14	10,626
TOTAL QUEBEC	5,069,700	—	—	132,899	—	—	248,027	—	—	354,173
Kingston/Belleville/Brockville CA & District	308,800	7	8	8,254	14	16	15,723	22	24	23,584
Kingston CA	139,500	3	4	5,279	6	7	10,054	9	11	15,081
Ottawa ESA	798,800	21	23	31,554	41	45	60,104	61	67	90,155
Peterborough CA	96,500	5	6	3,582	10	12	6,805	10	12	6,805
Peterborough/Lindsey CA	130,700	7	8	4,390	15	17	8,341	15	17	8,341
Toronto/Hamilton/Oshawa CMA	5,587,700	72	78	93,958	145	155	178,968	215	235	268,451
Toronto CMA	4,854,300	58	64	97,447	116	126	185,613	177	187	278,419
Oshawa CMA	297,700	8	9	7,568	16	18	14,415	25	27	21,623
Hamilton CMA	635,700	14	16	14,546	28	30	27,708	41	45	41,561
Kitchener CMA	404,600	7	8	10,127	15	17	19,290	15	17	19,290
Kitchener CMA/Brantford CA	486,300	10	12	12,280	21	23	23,391	21	23	23,391
St. Catharines/Niagara CMA	354,500	10	12	9,772	20	22	18,614	30	34	27,921
Brantford CA	81,700	3	4	3,859	3	4	3,859	3	4	3,859
Woodstock CA	31,700	—	1	879	—	2	1,340	—	2	1,340
London CMA	412,700	7	8	9,387	15	17	17,880	22	24	26,820
Windsor ESA	452,100	9	10	8,965	19	21	17,076	28	30	25,614
Sarnia CA	81,200	2	3	2,259	4	5	4,303	4	5	4,303
Owen Sound/Collingwood CA & District	202,500	12	14	11,000	24	26	20,953	35	39	31,429
Barrie CA/Orillia CA/Central Ontario	319,900	10	11	16,552	18	20	31,528	27	29	47,291
Barrie CA	162,200	5	6	9,737	10	12	18,546	15	17	27,819
Sault Ste. Marie CA	77,600	—	2	1,620	—	4	3,240	—	6	4,860
Sudbury CMA/North Bay CA/North Shore & District	235,000	—	8	7,400	—	15	13,125	—	23	19,665
Thunder Bay CMA	113,200	3	4	2,303	5	6	4,386	8	9	6,579
TOTAL ONTARIO	9,700,500	—	—	224,163	—	—	425,892	—	—	620,200
Winnipeg CMA	624,400	7	8	9,869	13	15	18,799	19	21	28,198
Brandon CA	38,300	2	3	2,028	2	3	2,028	2	3	2,028
Yorkton CA	16,000	2	3	1,648	3	4	2,318	3	4	2,318
Regina CMA	178,100	3	4	3,500	6	7	6,668	9	10	10,001
North Battleford CA	15,900	2	3	1,245	3	4	1,556	4	5	2,334
Rural Saskatchewan	437,000	—	1	820						
Moose Jaw CA	30,400	2	3	1,189	3	4	2,265	4	5	3,398
Saskatoon CMA	212,900	4	5	4,001	7	8	7,620	10	11	11,430
Calgary CMA	950,500	16	18	20,608	31	35	39,254	31	35	39,254
Edmonton CMA	893,600	14	16	18,332	28	30	34,918	41	45	52,376
Vancouver CMA	1,998,800	33	37	71,225	33	37	71,225	33	37	71,225
TOTAL PRAIRIES/B.C.	5,395,900	—	—	133,645	—	—	186,651	—	—	222,562
TOTAL CANADA	21,172,300	—	—	519,626	—	—	907,927	—	—	1,259,318

Source: Canadian Advertising Rates and Data, 2005 data.

Weight: 25 GRPs weekly in Toronto/Hamilton and Montreal; 50 GRPs weekly
                                 in Calgary and Edmonton

Contract length: 16 weeks in all markets

Cost Calculations:

The costs for a four-week period for each market would be as follows:

Toronto/Hamilton $66 780

Montreal $38 387

Calgary $25 431

Edmonton $25 431

Total   **$156 029**

Because the contract is for 16 weeks, the costs are multiplied by four (16 weeks divided by
four-week rates). The gross cost would be as follows:

$156 029 × 4 = $624 116

Although not shown in this particular illustration and rate card, outdoor media usually offer advertisers volume discounts (e.g., a reduced rate based on dollar volume purchased) and continuity discounts (e.g., a reduced rate for extended buys such as 12 weeks,
16 weeks, etc.).

Example 2: Outdoor Buying Plan

Medium: Outdoor posters (Viacom)

Markets: Toronto (CMA), Montreal (ESA), and Ottawa (ESA)

Weight: Toronto and Montreal at 50 GRPs and Ottawa at 25 GRPs

Contract length: 16 weeks in Toronto; 12 weeks in Montreal and Ottawa

Cost Calculations:

Using the data from Figure A1.12, the appropriate costs for each market over a four-week period would be as follows:

Toronto $185 613 x 4 = $742 452

Montreal $122 368 x 3 = $367 104

Ottawa $31 554 x 3 = $94 662

Gross cost   **= $1 204 218**

Because the length of the contract in Toronto is 16 weeks, the costs are multiplied by four (16
weeks divided by the four-week rate). In Montreal and Ottawa, the contract is 12 weeks.
Therefore, the costs are multiplied by a factor of three (12 weeks divided by the four-week rate).
Should volume and continuity discounts apply, they would be deducted from the gross amount
shown in this illustration.

Direct Mail Advertising

Three basic steps are involved in buying direct mail: obtaining a proper prospect list, con-
ceiving and producing the mailing piece, and distributing the final version.

Obtaining Direct Mail Lists

The direct mail list is the backbone of the entire campaign. Both the accuracy and definition of the list can have a significant bearing on the success or failure of a campaign.

Since it is much less expensive to keep a current customer than to find a new one, a company should compile accurate lists of customers in their database and form relationships with customers through mail and electronic means. Internal lists compiled from a database management system are referred to as **house lists**.

Prospective names are also gathered from external sources. People with a history of responding to mail offers tend to be attractive prospects for new offers. Buying by mail is part of their behaviour. Therefore, the challenge is to find prospects that have a demographic profile and, perhaps, a psychographic profile that mirror the profile of current customers. A **list broker** can assist in finding these prospects. The buyer provides the broker with the profile of the target customer, and the broker supplies a list of possible prospects on a cost-per-name basis. Generally, a high-quality list is developed through a **merge/purge** process on a computer, whereby numerous lists are purchased, combined, and stripped of duplicate names.

Cornerstone Group of Companies, a database management company, compiles lists for various consumer, business, and professional targets. A consumer list can be compiled based on predetermined criteria such as income, home ownership, marital status, and type of dwelling. Business lists can be developed based on the type or size of business (e.g., small, home-based businesses). Professional lists are available for medical, legal, and engineering practitioners, among many others.

Canada Post also supplies information vital to the accurate targeting of messages. For example, a postal code can isolate a small geographic area—say, a city block—and can then be combined with census data to provide relevant statistics regarding the ages and incomes of homeowners in the area and whether children are present in the households.

A few types of lists are available: *response lists, circulation lists,* and *compiled lists.* A **response list** is a list of proven mail-order buyers. Such lists include book-of-the-month-club buyers, CD music buyers, or people who order from cooperative direct mailing firms. Because these lists include proven mail-order buyers, they tend to cost more. For example, customers of Time Life Products (an established direct mail marketing company) rent for $365/M. The list includes buyers of books, videos, and children's products. A minimum purchase of 5000 names is required.[5]

Circulation lists are magazine subscription lists that target potential customers according to an interest or activity. A publishing company, for example, might sell its list of subscribers to another business interested in a similar target. Rogers Media offers a consumer database composed of unduplicated active subscribers to a host of its publications, including *Maclean's, Chatelaine,* and *Flare.*

Compiled lists are prepared from government, census, telephone, warranty, and other publication information. These are the least expensive of the lists and are not always personalized. Provincial and national associations, such as the Canadian Medical Association, commonly provide mailing lists of their members. A list broker, for example, could compile a list of a cross-section of professionals from various occupations, if required by a client.

Production

Direct mail packages are usually designed by a specialist agency. Once the mailing package is designed, it is ready for printing. Various factors that influence cost include size, shape, number of pieces, use of colour, and so on. Costs are usually quoted CPM, with larger runs incurring lower unit costs. Once printed, the mailing pieces are turned over to a letter shop that specializes in stuffing and sealing envelopes, affixing labels, sorting, binding, and stacking the mailers. Once this task is complete, the mailing units are sent to the post office for distribution.

House list
An internal customer list.

List broker
A company specializing in finding or developing lists for direct response purposes; finds prospect lists based on target market criteria established by marketing organizations.

Merge/purge
A process in which numerous mailing lists are combined and then stripped of duplicate names.

Response list
A list of direct mail buyers who have previously bought based on direct response offers.

Circulation list
A publication's subscription list that targets potential customers based on specified demographic characteristics, interests, or activities.

Compiled list
A direct mail list prepared from government, census, telephone, warranty, or other publication information.

Distribution

Distribution costs of direct mail replace placement costs in traditional forms of media advertising. The most common means of delivery is Canada Post. Several options are available through the postal system: first-class mail, third-class mail, and business-reply mail. Obviously, the quicker the means of delivery the higher the costs will be. Most direct mail pieces—whether single pieces, bulk items, catalogues, or cooperative mailings—are delivered third class. The advantage over first class is the cost savings.

Direct Mail Buying Illustration

The procedures for estimating the cost of solo direct mail and cooperative direct mail are similar. However, with a solo direct mail campaign, the advertiser absorbs all the costs rather than sharing them with other advertisers. Taken into consideration are factors such as costs of renting a mailing list, distribution costs, printing costs, mailing costs, and costs associated with fulfillment. For this example, we will assume a cooperative direct mail program will be undertaken in the Open & Save Cooperative Mailing package (see Figure A1.13). The Open & Save mailer is distributed to a predetermined list of households across Canada and contains offers from non-competing brands in various product categories.

Buying Information:

Open & Save Cooperative Mailings (Transcontinental Publications)

The offer:	one-page folded ad that includes a $1.50 coupon
Redemption rate:	3 percent
Distribution:	3 000 000 households

Cost Calculations:

Distribution costs (cost for inclusion in envelope)	3 000 000 x $12/M	= $36 000
Printing costs (estimated at 3/4 cost of mailing)	3 000 000 x $9.00/M	= $27 000
Redemption costs (based on a 3 percent redemption rate)	3 000 000 x 0.03 x $1.50	= $135 000
Total cost		**= $198 000**

Depending on how the coupon offer is returned, there could be additional costs for the advertiser. For example, there is a handling fee provided to the retailer for conducting the coupon transaction. As well, coupons are usually sent from the retailer to a clearing house for processing. The clearing house pays the retailer and provides periodic reports to the advertiser about how many coupons are being redeemed. The advertiser pays a fee for this service.

Internet Advertising

The most common model for quoting advertising rates on the Internet is CPM. Other pricing models include pay for performance (pay per click) and flat fees.

CPM Model

CPM is the price charged for displaying an ad one thousand times. The calculation for CPM is cost divided by impressions (number of impressions divided by 1000). For online advertising, an organization pays a rate for every 1000 impressions made. Therefore, if the

FIGURE **A1.13** Open & Save Cooperative Mail Rate Card

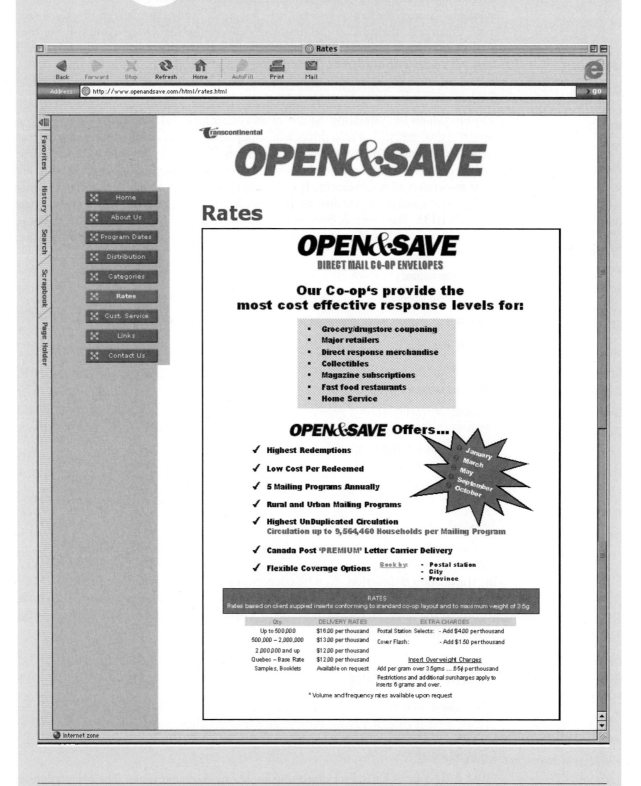

Source: Courtesy of Open & Save.

FIGURE **A1.14** **Online Advertising Rate Card for Canada.com**

AD TYPE

Banners: $13 CPM

- 468 × 60 pixels/GIF format and rich media
- Placement: Headers on all pages of Canada.com

Buttons: $10 CPM

- 120 × 90/GIF format
- Placement: near right hand top of most Second Level Pages

Skyscraper Ads: $20 CPM

- 120 × 240, 120 × 600, or 160 × 600 pixels
- GIF format and Rich Media
- Placement: fourth column

Pop-up and Pop-under Windows: $35 CPM

- File size limits: GIF format – 15K/Rich Media formats – 15K Initial download/25K in total
- Placement available on most Canada.com pages

Big Box Ads (In Story): $30 CPM

- 250 × 250 pixels
- GIF format and Rich Media
- Placement: within editorial content

CONTESTS

Regional: Starting at $10 000
National: Starting at $20 000

OTHER ADVERTISING OPTIONS

Interstitials and Superstitials: $60 CPM
All pricing is based on Run of Network rotation.
A 10% premium is charged for each applied target specification.

DOLLAR VOLUME DISCOUNTS

$15 000–25 000	5%
$25 000–50 000	10%
$50 000–75 000	12%
$75 000–100 000	15%
$100 000+	20%

Adapted from CanWest Media Sales, a division of CanWest Interactive Inc.,
canada.com/aboutus/advertising/rate_card.html (accessed June 2003). By permission of CanWest
Interactive.

total number of impressions is 500 000 and the CPM was $30, the total cost of the advertising campaign will be $15 000 (500 000 impressions/1000) x $30.

CPM rates vary according to the level of targeting desired by the advertiser, and they range anywhere from $10 to $100. Typical options include *run of site*, *run of category*, and *keyword targeting*. With reference to the rate card for Canada.com shown in Figure A1.14,

Run of site (run of network)
Ad rate for placements anywhere on a website.

Targeting request
An ad placed to reach a specific target audience of a website, for which a premium is usually paid.

if **run of site** or **run of network** is selected, the rates charged are those quoted for the various sizes and styles of advertising for ads that will appear anywhere on the website. For example, a banner ad rate is $13/M, a skyscraper is $20/M, and big box ad (in a story) is $30/M. The difference in rates is indicative of the effectiveness of the different sizes of ads—bigger ads are more effective.

If **targeting requests** are applied, a 10 percent premium is charged for each targeted request. Volume discounts might be offered based on the total dollar value of the advertising space that is purchased.

CPM rate cards vary from one site to another, but the high-traffic sites of course charge a higher CPM. Popular portal sites like MSN, Canoe, Sympatico.ca, Yahoo!, Google, and various sports and media sites (TSN and Rogers Sportsnet) attract significant traffic and price their CPMs accordingly.

Here are a few illustrations to show how online advertising costs are calculated. Rate information is obtained from Figure A1.14.

Example 1:

Type of ad:	Banner
Impressions desired:	3 000 000
CPM:	$13

Cost Calculation:

(3 000 000/1000) × $13 = $39 000

Once the ad achieves the desired number of impressions it would be removed from the website.

Example 2:

Type of ad:	Pop-up
Impressions desired:	5 000 000
CPM:	$35
One target request	+ 10%

Cost Calculation:

(5 000 000/1000) × $35 × 1.10 = $192 500

In this example, the advertiser earns a 20 percent volume discount (refer to the dollar volume discount scale in Figure A1.16). Therefore, the additional calculation would be:

$192 500 – ($192 500 × 0.20) = $192 500 – $38 500 = $154 000

Although these rates are those quoted, the reality of the situation is similar to offline advertising. CPM rates are negotiable and depend on factors such as length of the campaign, season, and relationship between client and vendor. Effective negotiation skills in the media buying process could result in lower CPM rates.

Pay for Performance Model

Advertisers must remember that the purpose of online advertising is to create interest so that the viewer clicks the ad for more information. Once clicked, the viewer sees the ad in its entirety, usually via a link to a page at the advertiser's website. Since clicking is the desired action, many advertisers feel they should pay on a **cost-per-click** basis instead of CPM. The benefit of such a system is clear: the degree of clicking achieved by an ad indicates the effectiveness of the ad.

Cost-per-click
An Internet advertising pricing strategy where advertisers pay based on the number of ad clicks received.

If the success of an ad is based on the clickthrough rate, then many current campaigns are not doing very well. In fact, latest industry surveys peg the average click rate at about 0.5 percent. The quality of the creative (e.g., its cleverness, its animation, and so on) along with a certain degree of targeting can improve the clickthrough rate.

From a publisher's perspective, the clickthrough system has several drawbacks. First, the publisher has to rely on the quality of the advertiser's message (the banner) for advertising revenue. If it does not stimulate clicks, it will not generate revenues for the website. A web publisher provides an audience to deliver the message to; they don't believe they are responsible for the quality of the advertising message itself. Second, such a model completely discounts what a banner can do to build brand image. There has to be an advertising cost associated with this benefit. Pricing models based on cost-per-click are becoming more popular, but they are plagued with all kinds of click fraud that is costing advertiser's money unnecessarily. Tighter restrictions and controls are needed for this pricing model to be applied successfully.

Flat-Fee Model

Some websites charge a flat fee for advertising—typically, it is a set amount for the length of time the ad appears on the site. Sponsorships, for example, are usually sold on a flat-rate basis rather than on the number of impressions. The *Maclean's* website, for example, charges $1000 net per week (net means the agency commission has been deducted) for one banner ad at the top of the home page with two rotations. Rates on other pages on the site are lower. Contract advertisers that commit to periods longer than 13 weeks earn significant discounts.[6] Fee structures vary considerably from site to site. Lower traffic sites are more likely to use the flat-fee system.

MEDIA INFORMATION RESOURCES

Media planners rely on secondary research data provided by specialist media organizations. **Secondary research** refers to data compiled and published by others for purposes other than resolving a specific problem. In advertising, secondary sources are frequently used to gain access to media information that benefits media analysis and planning. This information is available through various media associations, specialized media research companies, and individual media outlets (e.g., a daily newspaper, national magazine, or a local television station).

Most organizations that provide media data also provide appropriate software for users to sift through the data (e.g., data can be cross-tabulated with product and service consumption data to determine the best way of reaching a specific target audience). Much of the information is made available through the media research companies and organizations mentioned above, or through specialist companies that develop software for use with database information provided by these organizations. Agencies pay for the data provided by the various media research organizations.

Television Resources

The organizations that compile television media data on a continuous (year-to-year) basis include BBM Bureau of Measurement, Nielsen Media Research, and the Television Bureau of Canada.

BBM Bureau of Measurement

The BBM Bureau of Measurement is divided into two divisions for recording and analyzing data: BBM TV and BBM Radio. BBM TV collects audience data through a combination of electronic observation and diaries that are returned by mail. The BBM employs three commercially available methodologies: paper diaries, picture matching technology (PMT), and portable people meters (PPM).

When the **diary system** is used, participants complete a seven-day log by recording the television viewing for all television sets in the household for each quarter hour of the

---

Secondary research
Data compiled and published by others for purposes other than resolving a specific problem. In advertising, secondary sources are frequently used to gain access to media information that benefits media analysis and planning.

Diary system
A system to collect audience data where participants complete a seven-day log by recording the television viewing for all television sets in the household for each quarter hour of the day from 6 am to 2 am.

day from 6 am to 2 am. Information from returned diaries is keyed into computers for processing and verification.

In the case of the **portable people meter (PPM)** a form of electronic observation is employed. Electronic metering devices are installed in approximately 2100 households across Canada. The meter registers what is being watched every minute of every day in every metered household. The data is sent back to the BBM at the end of each day. Because the households are a representative sample, extrapolations are made about how people view programs on local, regional, and national bases.

Picture matching technology (PMT) is relatively new. It determines what viewers are watching by periodically "sampling" the video image on their television screens, and then comparing this time-stamped video "fingerprint" with a library of all television sources that are available at that time. It measures minute-by-minute viewing behaviour in 5000 households across Canada. PMT meters help determine the Top 30 programs broadcast each week.[7]

BBM data focus on national and local markets. The BBM conducts its surveys three times a year—fall, winter, and spring—in 40 television markets. Their reports contain current audience ratings and share data, as well as full coverage data for local market stations. The data are presented in four sections: time block, program, time period, and trend.

The BBM also conducts a "sweep" survey in the fall and spring that covers the national market (television viewers two years of age and older). The data collected during the ratings period are used to estimate the audiences of programs on individual stations and networks. *Ratings* are audience estimates expressed as a percentage of a population in a defined geographic area. For example, if a show has a rating of 20, it reaches 20 percent of that market's population. For some examples of basic trend data available from the BBM, visit **www.bbm.ca**.

Nielsen Media Research

The data available from Nielsen refer to channels watched and audience composition. The Nielsen Television Index (NTI) network reports cover audiences for all programs, 52 weeks a year, for national and regional networks and for four local markets: Toronto, Vancouver, French Montreal, and Calgary.

Network reports provide viewing information 24 hours a day for the entire year. Data are organized according to age, education, income, and occupation of audience members. Nielsen electronically collects information from a sample panel of 3300 households across Canada. Respondents indicate their viewing responses using a remote-control device. Among the data recorded are program rankings, audience composition, and average weekly cable television and VCR penetration.

Advertisers and agencies use Nielsen data to estimate the future performance of TV shows, to execute TV buys, and to measure the performance of campaigns after they have aired. Nielsen's software can be used to perform reach/frequency, duplication, and quintile delivery analyses.[8]

Nielsen Media Research also offers a variety of competitive tracking services that provide the quantitative information necessary for strategic determination and tactical execution of communications plans. Nielsen provides estimates of media expenditures by measuring advertising activity in the traditional mass media: television, daily newspapers, magazines, and out-of-home advertising. The information observed is translated into advertising dollars using published rates in *Canadian Advertising Rates and Data (CARD)*. Nielsen also receives information from billing statements from the broadcast representative companies and information from the broadcasters themselves. For additional information about Nielsen Media Research, visit **www.nielsenmedia.ca**.

Portable people meter (PPM)

A form of electronic observation where electronic metering devices are installed in households that register what is being watched on television every minute of every day.

Picture matching technology (PMT)

A relatively new way to collect television audience data; determines what viewers are watching by periodically "sampling" the video image on their television screens, and then comparing this time-stamped video "fingerprint" with a library of all television sources that are available at that time.

www.bbm.ca

www.nielsenmedia.ca

Television Bureau of Canada

www.tvb.ca

The Television Bureau of Canada (TVB) is a sales and marketing resource centre for the commercial television industry. Its mandate is to promote television as an effective advertising medium. Each year, this organization publishes a booklet, "TV Basics," that contains the latest data on television trends. It covers viewing trends by demographic and geographic variables, programming preferences by demographic variables, and television-station circulation by gender and age for all station markets. The TVB provides such data as viewing by time of day, day of week, and by time of year. For additional information about the data provided by the TVB, visit **www.tvb.ca**.

Radio

The organizations that compile radio consumption data on a continuous basis are the BBM Bureau of Measurement and the Radio Marketing Bureau.

BBM Bureau of Measurement

BBM Radio conducts three surveys per year in more than 130 radio markets across Canada using a seven-day personal diary. In addition to collecting tuning data, the diary contains questions collecting product usage and lifestyle data. Market reports are published three times a year in the nine largest markets. Regional reports (Atlantic, Quebec, Ontario, Manitoba/Saskatchewan, Alberta, and British Columbia) are published twice a year to supplement the market reports. Tuning data are reported in the market and regional reports on up to 22 demographics for more than 30 dayparts.

The data compiled by the BBM include demographic audience profiles based on hours tuned per week, listening by daypart, and listening by location (e.g., home, automobile, and other locations). Other standard data include market share and audience profiles and listening locations tuning. For some samples of basic trend data published by the BBM, visit **www.bbm.ca**.

Radio Marketing Bureau

The Radio Marketing Bureau is the marketing, sales development, and resource centre for radio advertising in Canada. It provides statistical data while seeking to educate advertisers and agencies on the effective use of the medium. In conjunction with the BBM, the Bureau conducts a Radio Product Measurement (RPM) study in selected major markets. This study is designed to generate information about product usage and media consumption of radio, television, magazines, and newspapers. For more information about the Radio Marketing Bureau, visit **www.rmb.ca**.

Magazines

The companies and organizations involved in magazine research and data collection include the Audit Bureau of Circulations, PBA Worldwide, and the Print Measurement Bureau.

Audit Bureau of Circulations

Publisher's statement
A statement published by the Audit Bureau of Circulations twice a year that is the authority on which advertising rates are based.

The Audit Bureau of Circulations (ABC) issues standardized statements verifying circulation statistics for paid-circulation magazines (consumer and business publications) and most daily newspapers in Canada. All publications that are members of ABC receive an audited **publisher's statement**. This statement is the authority on which advertising rates are based (verified circulation is used to establish the advertising rate base as shown in the publication's rate card). The statement is issued twice each year. A publisher's statement includes the following information: average paid circulation for the past six months, paid circulation for each issue in the last six months, an analysis of new and renewal subscriptions, paid circulation by county size, and geographic analysis of total paid circulation. For a selection of sample data published by ABC, refer to **www.access-abc.com.**

Each year the ABC publishes the Canadian newspaper *Circulation Fact Book* that outlines circulation data for all daily newspapers by market, county, and province. Five-year circulation trend data are included in the report. ABC also publishes the magazine *Trend Report*, an annual report providing circulation and advertising rate trends for five years for all Canadian magazines.

BPA Worldwide (formerly Canadian Circulations Audit Board—CCAB)

The CCAB division of BPA Worldwide (a global provider of audited data) audits all paid, all controlled, or any combination of paid and controlled circulation for over 425 business and farm publications, consumer magazines, and community and daily newspapers throughout Canada.

www.bpaww.ca
www.ccab.ca

Statements include type of circulation (e.g., paid or controlled circulation), recipient qualification (e.g., distribution to a predetermined target based on demographic data), circulation for the past six months, average paid circulation per issue, and a geographical breakdown of the circulation. Additional information about the CCAB is available at **www.bpaww.com** or **www.ccab.ca.**

Print Measurement Bureau

The Print Measurement Bureau (PMB) provides standardized readership information for members, a group that includes advertisers, agencies, publishers, and other related companies in the Canadian media industry. The PMB publishes Canada's leading single-source multimedia study.

The major data component of the annual PMB study is the detailed readership data for more than 110 magazines and newspapers and the linking of those data with information on readers' product usage patterns, their usage of brands, their retail shopping habits, and their lifestyles.

The product usage section of the PMB study provides usage data on more than 2500 products and brands as well as retail shopping categories, including over 400 individual stores. Information is also available on consumer lifestyles, leisure habits and psychographics, and extensive demographic data.

The annual PMB study is released in March each year and is based on a two-year rolling sample of 24 000 respondents. Readership data is collected via in-home interviews. Product data is retrieved from a leave-behind, self-completed questionnaire.

www.pmb.ca

Data provided by the PMB study benefit advertisers and agencies in the media planning process. Based on cross-tabulations of data concerning media, product, brand, and lifestyle, the information can be used to identify target markets more precisely, to assist in budget allocation, and to make better decisions regarding media selection and placement. PMB information is available to clients electronically and requires special software to access it. For additional information about the PMB, visit **www.pmb.ca.**

Newspapers

As stated in the magazine section, newspaper circulation and readership data are available from the Audit Bureau of Circulations and BPA Worldwide. Readership information is also compiled by an industry-sponsored measurement organization known as NADbank.

NADbank—Newspaper Audience Databank

www.nadbank.com

NADbank provides advertisers, advertising agencies, and daily newspapers with accurate and credible information on newspaper readership, retail data, and consumer behaviour. NADbank is an annual survey among 31 000 adults 18 years and older that compiles relevant data about newspaper circulation and readership. NADbank members have access to readership data for 74 daily newspapers in 52 markets and 55 community newspapers in 29 markets.

The nature of information produced by NADbank includes weekday and weekend readership, demographic profiles of readers, product ownership and purchase intentions, media habits (e.g., other media referred to), and shopping habits (e.g., malls visited and frequency of visits). Additional information and some sample data published by NADbank are available at **www.nadbank.com**.

Out-of-Home Media

Canadian Outdoor Measurement Bureau

The Canadian Outdoor Measurement Bureau (COMB) audits the circulations of outdoor posters, superboards, mall posters, backlit posters, and street-level advertising (e.g., transit shelter ads). Audience data are location specific, full coverage, and in-market in nature. Circulation data concerning all outdoor media except mall posters are based on municipal and provincial traffic counts and converted to circulations according to an established traffic-variation factor. COMB currently uses an average occupancy factor of 1.75, which represents the average number of people in an automobile.[9] Mall counts are based on observation (head counts) in each location by an independent research firm.

www.comb.ca

COMB publishes the *Market Data Report* on a semi-annual basis. The report contains daily and weekly audience averages for each product in each market. Verification reports are also provided. These reports verify that suppliers are delivering what they are contracted to deliver and compare the percentage of audience delivered to what was contracted. For more information about COMB, visit **www.comb.org**.

Internet Data Sources

Measuring the number of people who notice web-based advertising has been a difficult and controversial task, but a few organizations have emerged to provide useful information on Internet traffic and related activities: the Interactive Advertising Bureau, comScore Media Metrix, and TNS Media Intelligence.

Interactive Advertising Bureau (IAB)

The Interactive Advertising Bureau (IAB) is a national organization of Internet publishers, advertisers, and agencies acting as the collective voice to represent companies engaged in selling advertising on Internet-based media. IAB promotes the value of Internet advertising to advertisers and agencies and serves as an educational resource through which advertisers can increase their knowledge and gain a competitive edge in the marketplace.

IAB reports that spending on Internet advertising will continue to grow at an annual rate much higher than any other medium. Such a claim is based on increased penetration rates of the medium year to year and the amount of time people spend online on a daily and weekly basis. The Internet is the third most time-consuming medium among Canadian adults, accounting for 16 percent of per capita share. Television accounts for 35 percent and radio 31 percent.[10]

Research studies conducted by independent organizations for IAB show the effectiveness of online advertising. When online is added to the media mix, scores for various brand measurements increase. Tests among many leading brands in various product categories are the foundation of the research findings. Details of these studies are available at the IAB website. For more information about the IAB, visit **www.iab.net.**

comScore Media Metrix

comScore Media Metrix Canada is an Internet audience measurement service that reports details of website usage, visitor demographics, and online buying behaviour. The company collects data from a nationally representative panel of Internet users.

Media Metrix 2.0 is a service that combines technology, reporting capability, and sample sizes to offer a comprehensive audience measurement. Media Metrix 2.0, a service provided by comScore, provides reliable estimates for the following measures: a website's unique visitors; reach; average usage days per user; average unique pages per user per month; average minutes spent per person per page per month; and age, gender, and other demographic characteristics of visitors.

Other services offered by comScore Media Metrix include online buying power metrics based on actual consumer purchases made online, local audience measurement for major Canadian markets, and detailed measurements of online search behaviour. With the Internet growing in importance as a medium, the research that supports it is becoming more sophisticated. For more information, go to **www.comscore.com.**

TNS Media Intelligence—Evaliant Services

Evaliant Services provides online advertising data for brands and products sold in North America. The company provides data on the following issues: who is advertising on the web; where brands are advertising; when advertising is occurring and how much is being spent; what the media dollar value is (ad spending); what new ads are running; and what the ads actually look like. Trend data is compiled for advertising spending by product category and brands within categories, so it is a good source of competitive advertising information. For more information, visit **www.tns-mi.com.**

RESEARCH DATA BY INDIVIDUAL MEDIA

The specific media vehicles often conduct their own marketing research, or use research data provided by independent sources such as those just described. These data provide advertisers and agencies with objective, reliable information showing the relative strengths of the given medium as an advertising vehicle. In local market situations, a daily newspaper or a local radio station provide advertisers and agencies with data to assist them in the decision-making process. Here, local media compete with each other for advertising revenue, so comparisons on criteria such as reach, readership, number of people listening and watching, and so on are inevitable. When assessing this type of data, the advertiser should ensure that it is audited data and that it has been verified by an independent organization. Much of this data is available at the website of the particular magazine, newspaper, radio station, and so on.

The same situation exists for magazines and newspapers. All magazines and newspapers have their circulation and readership data readily available for review by advertisers and agencies. The viewer of such information should ensure it is audited data, as in audited by the various research organizations cited in this appendix.

Key Terms

agate line, 367

broadsheet, 367

casual rate, 369

circulation list, 390

compiled list, 390

continuity discount, 376

corporate discount, 376

cost-per-click, 394

cost per thousand (CPM), 373

daypart, 383

diary system, 395

frequency discount, 374

gross rating points (GRPs), 381

horizontal rotation, 383

house list, 390

line rate, 369

list broker, 390

merge/purge, 390

modular agate line (MAL), 367

modular agate unit, 369

picture matching technology (PMT), 396

portable people meter (PPM), 396

position charge, 372

publisher's statement, 397

rating, 381

reach plan, 383

recency, 381

response list, 390

rotation plan, 383

run of network, 394

run of site, 394

secondary research, 395

spot colour, 372

tabloid, 367

targeting request, 394

transient rate, 369

vertical rotation, 383

volume discount, 382

Review Questions

1. Calculate the cost of the following newspaper campaign. Refer to Figure A1.2 for rate card information.

Newspaper:	Globe and Mail, National Edition, Sports Section
Ad Size:	4 columns wide by 6 column inches deep
Colour:	All ads are black and white
Frequency:	2 ads per week (Wed. and Fri.)
Continuity:	8 weeks
Rate:	Transient

2. Calculate the total cost of the following magazine campaign. Refer to Figure A1.5 for rate card information.

Magazine:	*Canadian Geographic*
Ad Size:	Double-page spread
Frequency:	4 insertions

3. Calculate the total cost of the following magazine campaign. Refer to Figure A1.5 for rate card information.

Magazine:	*Canadian Geographic*
Ad Size:	1/2 page horizontal
Frequency:	8 insertions

4. Calculate the total cost of the following television campaign. Refer to Figure A1.8 for rate card information.

Station:	CKCO-TV Kitchener
Type of Ad:	Selective spot

Shows and Frequency:
Law & Order: SVU, 2 spots per week
The Amazing Race, 1 spot per week
Close to Home, 1 spot per week
Continuity: 15 weeks between February 20 and June 4

5. Calculate the total cost of the following radio campaign. Refer to Figure A1.10 for rate card information.

Station:	CJAZ-FM
Nature of Plan:	Specific times requested during breakfast and drive periods
Breakfast:	8 spots per week
Drive:	8 spots per week
Continuity:	6 weeks

6. Calculate the total cost of a 16-spot weekly reach plan for the same period of time as in Question 6 on CJAZ-FM radio. Refer to Figure A1.10 for rate card information. When the total costs of the reach plan are compared to the total costs of the specific request plan in Question 6, how much does the advertiser save by using the reach plan?

7. Calculate the total cost of the following outdoor campaign. Refer to Figure A1.11 for rate card information.

Medium:	Viacom Transit Shelters
Markets and GRPs:	Toronto CMA, 25 GRP
	Calgary CMA, 50 GRP
	Halifax CMA, 50 GRP
	Vancouver CMA, 25 GRP
Continuity:	24 weeks in all markets

8. Calculate the total cost of the following outdoor campaign. Refer to Figure A1.12 for rate card information.

Medium:	Viacom Outdoor Posters
Markets and GRPs:	St. John's, 50 GRP
	Moncton, 50 GRP
	Halifax, 50 GRP
	Edmonton, 75 GRP
	Winnipeg, 50 GRP
	Calgary, 75 GRP
	Regina, 50 GRP
Continuity:	Atlantic markets 16 weeks; Western markets 12 weeks.

9. Calculate the total cost of delivering a $2.00 coupon to 4 million Canadian households using the Open & Save direct mail envelope. Printing costs on a CPM basis are estimated to be half of the distribution costs. The estimated redemption rate for the offer is 2.5 percent. Refer to Figure A1.14 for rate card information.

10. Calculate the total cost of the following online banner campaign. Refer to Figure A1.15 for rate card information.

Medium:	Canada.com website
Ad Type:	Big box
Impressions:	10 million

Endnotes

1 Chris Powell, "Rate hikes confound media buyers," *Marketing*, June 30/July 7, 2003, p. 4.

2 Rick Westhead, "Ad rates par for the course," *Toronto Star*, April 8, 2004, p. D13.

3 Andrea Zoe Aster, "How much is way too much?" *Marketing*, August 16, 1999, p. 14.

4 Chris Daniels, "Media buying gets scientific," *Marketing*, July 31, 2000, pp. 11, 12.

5 Based on costs obtained from Accountable List Brokers, **www.listbroker.com**, direct responders *Time Life*.

6 *Maclean's* Online Media Kit, November 2003.

7 Canadian Media Directors' Council, *Media Digest*, 2005–06, p. 70.

8 Ibid., p. 71.

9 *Market Data Report*, Canadian Outdoor Measurement Bureau, 1986, p. 4.

10 Canadian Media Directors' Council, *Media Digest*, 2005–06, p. 61.

Integrated Marketing Communications Plan: Mr. Sub[1]

MARKET BACKGROUND

Market Analysis

The quick-serve restaurant (QSR) market is a mature market. The degree of competition among the various banners is intensive and extensive.

- The restaurant industry is growing only marginally (+2% a year).
- Quick-serve segment sales totalled $11.2 billion in Canada (2004).
- The quick-serve segment is saturated and offers limited growth potential over the next five years.
- The casual dining segment, composed of mid-range establishments like Montana's and Kelsey's, is experiencing higher growth (+8% a year).
- The sandwich segment of the market is presently worth $1.3 billion and accounts for about 10 percent of the quick-serve restaurant market.
- The sandwich segment is growing at the rate of +2.5% a year.

External Influences on the Market

Economic Trends

The cyclical nature of the economy influences the volume of business in the QSR market segment. Generally, the Canadian economy is growing at a moderate rate, as is the restaurant industry. There is a variation in trends within the various segments of the restaurant industry.

Demographic Trends

- With the population aging, restaurants must reposition themselves to maintain customers.
- Youthful generations who are influenced less by traditional marketing methods are the next generation of customers.
- Ethnic Canadians are creating a demand for ethnic dishes in QSR establishments.

Social Trends

- The health boom associated with the late 1990s appears to be over, but in general terms, a healthier lifestyle is an ambition for many people.

---

[1]This marketing communications plan was created for illustrative purposes only. It is designed to show the relationship between various components of the marketing communications mix and how they interact with each other to achieve marketing and marketing communications objectives.

- People are maintaining an active lifestyle, but are subject to indulgences.
- Youthful generations favour non-traditional methods for learning about products; peer influences are very important.
- Time-pressed consumers are constantly searching for products and services offering convenience.

Technology

- Non-traditional methods of communications are popular with younger generations of consumers.
- Multi-tasking consumers refer to several media at the same time, so reaching consumers is now more challenging for marketing organizations.

Consumer Data

Consumers indicate that the following criteria are important when selecting a quick-serve restaurant:

- value (in terms of food quality at competitive prices);
- reduced wait times;
- convenience (location in time of need is important); and
- food served "their" way.

Competitive Analysis

Mr. Sub competes directly with SUBWAY and Quizno's in the fresh sandwich segment. Quizno's is somewhat different as it specializes in hot-served or toasted sandwiches.

SUBWAY dominates the sandwich segment. Much of its strength can be attributed to the number of restaurant locations it operates across Canada.

McDonald's and Tim Hortons compete in the sandwich segment, but sandwiches account for only a portion of their business. Both restaurants offer only a limited selection of fresh and toasted sandwiches, but are very popular destinations for quick meals.

Market shares for the national chains (in the sandwich segment *only*) are as follows:

Chain	Share	Locations
SUBWAY	25.0	2100
Tim Hortons	8.0	2000
Mr. Sub	6.5	500
McDonald's	3.5	1375
Quizno's	3.0	350

SUBWAY

As the commercials say, "SUBWAY...Eat Fresh." SUBWAY is positioned as the premier destination for fresh sandwiches. SUBWAY's success in the QSR market is due to the following factors:

- The brand name is synonymous with fresh food.
- High-quality and healthy food products are available.
- It has an association with social responsibility causes such as childhood obesity.
- It has an ability to react quickly to consumer preferences (e.g., introducing healthier breads).

- Financial resources are available for marketing and marketing communications.
- The "Jared" ad campaign (weight-loss message) was a success.
- It has extensive distribution with over 2000 restaurants coast to coast.
- Its successful rewards program encourages loyalty.

Quizno's

The market share for Quizno's has tripled in the past two years. The Company's success is based on the following factors:

- It claims to own the "toasted" and "grilled" segment (even though other brands offer similar items).
- An advertising campaign that included celebrities such as Don Cherry and Tie Domi helped establish the brand.
- A focus on quality justifies higher prices; consumers seem willing to pay more for a sandwich.

Brand Analysis (Mr. Sub)

Mr. Sub was the original submarine sandwich retailer in Canada, but over the years it has not maintained marketing and marketing communications support at a sufficient level to build the brand. Mr. Sub has lost considerable market share to SUBWAY. Mr. Sub's present position in the marketplace is a result of the following factors:

- It is a popular destination for former generations of young people.
- Quality products are offered at competitive prices.
- Its product range includes popular items such as sandwiches, wraps, salads, and hot and cold beverages.
- Its present positioning fits with customer expectations and is based on "quality, freshness, and quantity."
- It has a loyal following among older age groups (40+ years).
- The brand is not well-known among younger age groups.
- Only 500 locations (1:4 ratio of stores compared to SUBWAY) exist coast to coast, with more than 60 percent of locations in Southern Ontario.
- Investment in advertising and marketing communications is much lower than that of its competitors.

SWOT Analysis

Brand Strengths

- Products offered are as good as the leading brand.
- The brand is well known with older consumers (a sense of loyalty exists).
- Its good reputation will enhance new marketing initiatives.

Brand Weaknesses

- Young consumers are unfamiliar with the brand and its offerings.
- It has low visibility among primary targets due to lack of marketing communications activity.

- Lack of availability (convenience); its key competitor has a significant distribution advantage.

Marketing Opportunities

- Fit the brand into healthier and contemporary lifestyles.
- Take a fresh marketing approach to attract a younger target audience.
- Appeal to consumer demand for value (a combination of convenience and quality).

Threats

- The marketing and financial resources of direct competitors are extensive.
- Taste preferences among consumers (less demand for fresh) shift.
- Further encroachment from other fast food restaurants and casual dining establishments is possible.

MARKETING COMMUNICATIONS PLAN

Target Market

To rebuild/rejuvenate Mr. Sub requires that greater attention be given to younger generations of consumers, for they are the primary consumers of QSR establishments.

Primary Target

Demographic
- Males and females 15 to 29 years old
- Secondary and post-secondary education level
- Students and newly employed graduates
- Income not important

Psychographic
- Time-pressed and fast-paced daily routines
- Socially active (peer groups are influencers)
- Technologically savvy (online and mobile communications generation)
- Active with a healthy outlook

Geographic
- All across Canada, with emphasis on major urban markets

Secondary Target

- Males and females 35+ years old
- Young families
- Active lifestyles
- Located in major urban markets
- More inclined to refer to traditional media for information

Marketing Objectives

1. To increase market share from 6.5 percent to 7.5 percent.
2. To position Mr. Sub as a restaurant offering healthy and hearty sandwiches at reasonable prices.

Marketing Communications Goal (Challenge)

- To create more top-of-mind awareness for Mr. Sub among younger generations of consumers and secure a place on their "consideration list."
- To associate Mr. Sub with a contemporary urban lifestyle that will appeal to the primary and secondary targets.

Marketing Communications Objectives

1. To achieve a 70 percent brand awareness level among the primary target market.
2. To achieve a trial purchase rate of 20 percent among the primary target market.
3. To communicate the quality, variety, and freshness of the various menu items offered by Mr. Sub.
4. To create an image for Mr. Sub that is in keeping with contemporary lifestyles.
5. To build buzz for Mr. Sub among a new generation of consumers currently unfamiliar with the brand.

Marketing Communications Strategy

Budget

For the first year of the campaign, a budget of **$3.0 million** is available to cover all marketing communications expenditures. The budget will cover a multimedia campaign and will include various integrated marketing communications activities.

Positioning Strategy Statement

The current positioning strategy will be retained and is described as follows:

> "Mr. Sub is a restaurant that offers the best in terms of fresh, healthy food served quickly. Mr. Sub prides itself on giving the customer a little bit more for their money."

Marketing Communications Mix

A mix of marketing communications elements will combine to create a synergistic impact on the primary and secondary target markets. The various elements of the mix will each contribute to achieving the marketing communications objectives. The marketing communications mix will include traditional media advertising, sales promotions, event marketing, and online and interactive communications. The rationale for this combination of media is as follows:

- **Advertising**—Traditional forms of media advertising are needed to make a "visual impression" in key urban markets and to achieve the awareness objective.
- **Sales Promotion**—A variety of "incentives" are needed to achieve the trial purchase objectives. Some street-level activities will help achieve the "brand buzz" objective.

- **Event Marketing**—A significant event will be staged in Toronto that will start an association between Mr. Sub and basketball (a popular and growing sport). Basketball appeals directly to the primary male target, and the street-level marketing event will create buzz for Mr. Sub.
- **Online Communications**—The primary target audience is the biggest user of online and mobile technologies; therefore, these media are both effective and efficient for delivering Mr. Sub's message.

Advertising Plan—Creative

Creative Objectives

1. To communicate that Mr. Sub offers quality sandwiches, wraps, and salads.
2. To portray Mr. Sub as an appealing restaurant destination suited to a contemporary urban lifestyle.

Creative Strategy

Mr. Sub does not have the physical presence of its primary competitor; therefore, the message will focus on the quality of the food (scrumptious shots of sandwiches and wraps) and people (teens and 20-somethings) enjoying the food. It's worth searching a little harder for!

Selected messages in various media will also include members of the secondary target enjoying the Mr. Sub experience.

Central Theme All messages, regardless of media, will show the sandwich being created or the finished product; a mouth-watering selection of sandwiches that will satisfy any type of hunger will be visually presented in advertisements.

Appeal Technique The message will combine a *positive* appeal (with an emphasis on the product and what it looks like) with a *lifestyle* appeal (the target will be shown enjoying the food).

Tone and Style A straightforward approach will be used. All messages will be clear, product focused, and easy to understand. Print media will stress visual imagery by showing the "scrumptious" aspect of the sandwiches.

Tagline Some options to summarize the message strategy include

"Mr. Sub. More than enough"

"Mr. Sub. Enough and then some"

"Mr. Sub. It's all about the sandwich."

Creative Execution

The campaign will include 30-second television spots, 4-colour print advertising, 4-colour newspaper inserts, outdoor posters, online banner ads, and an interactive component. Selected messages will encourage consumers to visit the Mr. Sub website to participate in a selection of new video games.

Print and outdoor media will be product focused, while broadcast media will feature consumer enjoyment and the fun associated with the Mr. Sub experience.

Integrated aspects of the campaign will include trial incentives delivered by newspaper inserts, a contest, a street-level marketing program in Toronto, and a television and online sponsorship element. Creating awareness for the brand and tagline will be a priority throughout the campaign.

Advertising Plan—Media

Budget

A budget of approximately **$2.0 million** has been allocated for media advertising to cover a one-year period from January 2007 to December 2007.

Media Objectives

Who As described earlier, the primary target is teens and 20-somethings residing in urban locations. The secondary target is adults 35+ years residing in urban markets.

What The message to be communicated will focus on the scrumptious quality of the food and people enjoying the Mr. Sub experience.

When The launch phase of the plan will be given heavier support to set the new campaign in motion. Spending will be slightly higher than normal in the summer when promotions are in progress. A steady spending pattern will be implemented at other times of the year.

Where The campaign will be national in scope with additional emphasis placed on key urban markets.

How Creating awareness and developing a new image for a brand takes time; therefore, reach and frequency will be a priority in the initial phase of the campaign (the first three months). Continuity will be more important as the campaign progresses.

Media Strategy

Target Market Strategy In the initial phase of the campaign, a shotgun strategy is recommended to reach the primary and secondary target markets. A multimedia approach will be employed to achieve reach objectives. As the campaign progresses, there will be a shift to a profile-matching strategy to effectively reach the primary target.

Market Coverage Since this is a national campaign, media that reach the national market will be used. Supplementary media will be added in urban markets to increase reach and frequency against the primary and secondary target. The budget available will determine the extent of key market coverage.

Timing Spending will be heavier in the initial phase (first three months), reflecting a blitz strategy. Spending will then taper off for a few months but rebound upward during the summer months when various integrated marketing activities are scheduled. For the remaining months of the campaign, spending will follow a moderate but steady pattern.

Reach/Frequency/Continuity The initial phase of the campaign is devoted to attracting a new target market to Mr. Sub. Therefore, reach and frequency are the priorities. Various media will be employed to reach the target market in different ways. As the campaign progresses, continuity of message will be more of a priority. Media advertising will be scheduled in flights to ensure maximum impact, regardless of the media employed.

Media Selection Rationale

A multimedia campaign that embraces network television, specialty television stations, national (targeted) magazines, key market daily newspapers (for inserts), out-of-home advertising, and online media is recommended.

Television Television reaches the national target audience with a strong visual message (the message emphasis on food and friends is best delivered by television). Prime-time ad placements will ensure a high level of brand recognition. A television sponsorship opportunity will associate Mr. Sub with basketball, a popular and growing sport in Canada.

Print A combination of targeted lifestyle magazines, newspapers, and inserts in selected daily newspapers will assist in creating brand awareness and distributing trial incentives. Inserts will be used exclusively to announce discounted meal combinations and special coupon offers to encourage trial visits.

Out-of-Home   In major markets, outdoor posters will deliver the message while people are "on the move." The decision about where to dine is often made when people are in transit, presenting an ideal opportunity to remind them about Mr. Sub.

Online Since the primary target market spends a lot of time online, there is an opportunity for consumers to interact directly with the brand. In conjunction with messages delivered by other media, the target will be encouraged to visit a new Mr. Sub website to play a selection of new sports games. Banner ads will also appear on two third-party sites that will move viewers to the Mr. Sub website.

Media Execution

The CTV Network and TVA Quebec are recommended to reach a broad cross-section of the population. TSN and The Score are recommended to reach the primary target market.

Outdoor posters will complement television ads and reach a broad cross-section of the population in 12 major markets across Canada.

Both *Tribute* and *Inside Entertainment* magazines are recommended as they effectively reach males and females in the primary target. *Maclean's* is also recommended since it effectively reaches a cross-section of the adult population regardless of age.

For a summary of all media activity (timing and expenditures), refer to Exhibits 1 to 3.

EXHIBIT **1**   **Television Advertising**

Network	# of Spots	Cost/Spot	Total Cost
CTV	40	$16 500	$660 000
TVA	30	$3 000	$90 000
TSN	50	$3 500	$175 000
The Score	65	$300	$19 500
Total	**185**		**$944 500**
The Score TV Sponsorship			$25 000
Total TV Costs			**$969 500**

Note: All ads are 30-second spots.

EXHIBIT **2** **Outdoor Advertising**

Market	GRPs	Weeks	Total Cost
Toronto/Hamilton	25	12	$295 800
Vancouver	25	12	$223 500
Ottawa	25	12	$108 600
Calgary	25	12	$64 800
Edmonton	25	12	$57 600
Quebec City	25	8	$40 800
Winnipeg	25	8	$20 800
London	25	8	$19 600
Kitchener	25	8	$22 200
Halifax	25	8	$13 400
Regina	25	8	$7 200
St. John's	25	8	$8 600
Total Cost			**$882 900**

Note: All ads are horizontal outdoor posters.

EXHIBIT **3** **Magazine Advertising**

Magazine	# Inserts	Cost/Insert	Total Cost
Maclean's	4	$25 400	$101 600
Tribute	4	$18 900	$75 600
Inside Entertainment	4	$15 000	$60 000
Total	**12**		**$237 200**

Note: All ads are 1-page, 4-colour

Sales Promotion Plan

Promotion Objectives

1. To encourage trial purchase among primary and secondary targets.
2. To secure interactivity between the consumer and the brand by encouraging consumers to visit the Mr. Sub website.

Promotion Strategy

Trial coupons offering a discounted price for any sandwich or wrap will be distributed by daily newspapers in major urban markets. In many cases, the daily newspapers offer reach well beyond their designated market area.

Consumers visiting a Mr. Sub restaurant during the first two months of the campaign will receive a coded entry form for a contest. Consumers must visit the Mr. Sub website to enter their contest code.

Sales Promotion Execution

Trial Coupon   A $1.50 coupon for the purchase of any sandwich or wrap (with a two-month expiry date) will be circulated. The initial coupon drop is timed for February/March.

Contest   A grand prize and two secondary prizes will be awarded:

- Grand Prize: $25 000 cash
- 2nd Prize: One of three all-expenses-paid ski trips for two to Whistler/Blackcomb (value: $5000 each)
- 3rd Prize: One of five Sony HDTV flat screen televisions (value: $2000 each)

The contest is open to all residents of Canada with winners randomly drawn from all entries received. Winners will be announced at the Mr. Sub website the day following the closing date of the contest. Complete contest details are available at the Mr. Sub website and all restaurant locations.

Trial Coupon   A second wave of $1.50 coupons (with a two-month expiry date) will be distributed by national daily newspapers in the August/September period.

The coupon inserts will be distributed via daily newspapers in the following markets: Toronto, Hamilton, Vancouver, Ottawa, Calgary, Edmonton, Quebec City, Winnipeg, London, Kitchener, Halifax, Regina, Saskatoon, St. John's, and Windsor.

Coupon inserts will be distributed by community newspapers in the following markets: Oshawa/Whitby/Clarington, St. Catharines, Niagara Falls, Cambridge, Barrie, Kingston, Peterborough, and Sudbury.

For cost details on these sales promotion activities see Exhibits 4 and 5.

EXHIBIT **4**   **Sales Promotion Costs for Coupon Inserts**

Component	Circulation	Cost/M	Frequency	Total Cost
Distribution	2 785 000	$40	2	$222 800
Printing	2 785 000	$10	2	$55 700
Coupon Redemption*				$83 500
Total Cost				**$362 000**

* Circulation × Redemption Rate × Value of Coupon × Frequency = Coupon Cost

2 785 000 × .01 × $1.50 × 2 = $83 500

EXHIBIT **5** Sales Promotion Costs for Coupon Inserts

Prize	# Winners	Prize Cost	Total Cost
Cash Grand Prize	1	$25 000	$25 000
Ski Trip	3	$5 000	$15 000
Sony HDTV Flat Screens	5	$2 000	$10 000
Total Cost			**$50 000**

Online and Interactive Plan

Objectives

1. To increase brand awareness among teens and 20-something males.
2. To associate the Mr. Sub brand with a sporting activity popular with young urban males.

Strategy

A combination that involves online banner advertising, a combination television and online sponsorship, and a brand new website will help build awareness among the primary target and help associate the brand with an urban lifestyle.

Execution

Banner Ads Banners will be scheduled on the TSN and The Score sports websites that are popular with a younger male audience.

Sponsorship In conjunction with The Score television channel, Mr. Sub will sponsor a highlight segment shown once a week. Each Wednesday night during the last four months of the basketball season, The Score broadcasts a show called *NBA Court Surfing*. During the show, Mr. Sub will sponsor a segment called "Dunks of the Week" that features all of the exciting dunks from the previous week's NBA action. The same video clip sponsored by Mr. Sub will be available on The Score's website, **www.thescore.ca**.

Mr. Sub Website An entirely new and exciting website will be constructed. The new site will offer essential product information and provide opportunities for consumers to engage in some entertaining activities. A selection of sports and action video games will be available for play at the site.

Refer to Exhibit 6 for online and interactive cost details.

Event Marketing Plan

To further develop the association between Mr. Sub and basketball, a street-level marketing event is planned in conjunction with the Toronto Raptors basketball team. This event fits with the Raptors objective of being "more visible in the community" and provides an opportunity to generate positive publicity for the Raptors in the off-season.

EXHIBIT **6**   **Online and Interactive Costs**

Site	Impressions/Month	CPM	# Months	Total Cost
TSN.ca	500 000	$40	6	$120 000
thescore.ca	125 000	$20	6	$15 000
Mr. Sub website				$200 000
Total Cost				**$335 000**

Note: Mr. Sub website costs include development and maintenance costs of the site.

Objectives

1. To encourage members of the primary target market to participate in a "3-on-3" basketball tournament.
2. To create buzz for Mr. Sub in a key urban market.

Strategy

To associate Mr. Sub with the growing sport of basketball (playground, high school, college, and university level) in a key urban market.

To associate Mr. Sub with the Toronto Raptors (an exciting team that is creating its own "buzz" in Toronto based on recent player acquisitions and performance).

Execution

- The Mr. Sub Toronto Raptors 3-on-3 Tournament (straight elimination) will be held on half-size courts at Exhibition Place, Toronto, over one weekend in July.
- A predetermined number of teams (128 teams) will compete against each other in four age categories: 8 to 12 years; 13 to 16 years; 17 to 21 years; and 21 to 30 years. The youngest age category will attract the children of Mr. Sub's secondary target, while the older categories will attract the primary target. A total of 32 teams will be entered in each age category.
- Toronto Raptors players will participate in a skills competition to determine "the most skilled Raptor."
- Prizes will be awarded to each member of the winning team (five members on each team) in each category.
- Mr. Sub kiosks will be set up at the event to serve meals.
- The general public will be invited to the event, though all viewing of the games and Raptor skills competition will be on a "stand and watch" basis.
- A one-month outdoor ad campaign just prior to the event will create awareness and recruit teams for the event. A press release will also be issued to the media outlining all event-related details.

Cost details for this event marketing activity are included in Exhibit 7.

EXHIBIT **7** **Event Marketing Costs**

Item or Activity	Estimated Cost
Equipment Rental	$50 000
Site Rental	$25 000
Bump-in (Setup)	$10 000
Staffing	$10 000
Security	$8 000
Bump-out (Teardown)	$10 000
Administration Costs	$15 000
Prizes	$40 000
Miscellaneous Costs	$10 000
Total Cost	**$178 000**

Note: 3-on-3 Basketball Tournament, Exhibition Place, Toronto

For summary details of all marketing communications expenditures and the timing of all activities, refer to Exhibits 8 through 11.

EXHIBIT **8** **Marketing Communications Budget Allocation**

Activity	Expenditure	% of Total
Television	$969 500	32.2
Outdoor	$882 900	29.3
Magazine	$237 200	7.8
Sales Promotions (Coupons and Contest)	$412 050	13.7
Online and Interactive	$335 000	11.1
Event Marketing	$178 000	5.9
Total	**$3 014 650**	**100.0**

EXHIBIT **9**   **Marketing Communications Expenditures by Month**

Month	Expenditure	% of Total
January	$211 300	7.0
February	$708 900	23.5
March	$426 850	14.2
April	$169 150	5.6
May	$117 000	3.9
June	$398 700	13.2
July	$264 000	8.8
August	$261 050	8.7
September	$100 500	3.3
October	$144 300	4.8
November	$118 500	3.9
December	$94 400	3.1
Total	**$3 014 650**	**100.0**

EXHIBIT **10**   **Plan Budget vs. Estimated Budget**

Estimated Budget (Based on Activities)	$3 014 650
Plan Budget	$3 000 000
Expenditure Over Budget	$(14 650)

The marketing communications budget will be reviewed quarterly. Adjustments to the budget will be made when necessary.

EXHIBIT 11 Marketing Communications Calendar

Activity	Jan.	Feb.	Mar.	Apr.	May	June	July	Aug.	Sept.	Oct.	Nov.	Dec.
Television												
CTV	8	8	8	4	4				4	4		
TVA	5	5	5	5						5	5	
TSN	10	10					10				10	10
The Score	15	15	10	10					5	10		
The Score Sponsorship	←——————————→											
Outdoor												
Top 5 Markets		←——→				↔						
Remaining Markets		↔				↔						
Magazines												
Maclean's				1		1		1		1		
Tribute						1		1		1		1
Inside Entertainment					1		1		1		1	
Sales Promotions												
Coupon Insert		←——→						←——→				
Contest		←——→										
Online												
TSN.ca					←————————→						←——→	
thescore.ca	←————————→										←——→	
Mr. Sub Website	←———————————————————————————————→											
Event Marketing												
3-on-3 Basketball						↔						

Notes:

Television: Figures represent the number of spots on each network each month. All spots are 30-seconds long and run in prime time.

Outdoor: Top five markets include Toronto/Hamilton, Vancouver, Ottawa, Calgary, and Edmonton. Remaining markets include Quebec City, Winnipeg, London, Kitchener, Halifax, Regina, and St. John's. All ads are outdoor posters.

Magazines: Figures indicate one insertion in each month scheduled (*Maclean's* is a weekly magazine; others are monthly). All ads are 1P, 4-colour

Online: 500 000 impressions monthly on TSN.ca and 125 000 impressions monthly on the thescore.ca.

Coupon Insert: Coupons will be distributed in key market daily newspapers or community newspapers. Dailies include: *Toronto Star, Toronto Sun, Vancouver Sun, Vancouver Province, Ottawa Citizen, Ottawa Sun, Calgary Herald, Calgary Sun, Edmonton Journal, Edmonton Sun, Regina Leader Post, Saskatoon Star Phoenix, Winnipeg Free Press, Hamilton Spectator, Kitchener Record, London Free Press, Windsor Star, Halifax Chronicle Herald,* and *St. John's Telegram.* Community newspapers include: *Oshawa/Whitby/Clarington This Week, St. Catharines News, Niagara This Week, Cambridge Times, Barrie Examiner Complimentary, Kingston This Week, Peterborough This Week,* and *Sudbury Northern Life.*

Glossary

Acquisition strategy – A plan of action for acquiring companies that represent attractive financial opportunities.

Ad click rate (clickthrough rate) – The percentage of ad views that resulted in an ad click; determines the success of an ad in attracting visitors to click on it.

Ad clicks (clickthroughs) – The number of times users click on a banner (clicking transfers the user to another website).

Ad views (impressions) – An ad request that was successfully sent to a visitor. This is the standard way of determining exposure for an ad on the web.

Advergaming – The integration of brands into video games, either games played online or in games purchased directly by consumers.

Advertising – A form of marketing communications designed to stimulate a positive response from a defined target market.

Advertising equivalency – A mathematical model that equates public relations to an advertising value by evaluating the space occupied by a public relations message in relation to advertising space.

Advocacy advertising – A form of advertising paid for by a sponsor that promotes a particular view on a recognized, controversial issue.

Agate line – A non-standardized unit of space measurement, equal to one column wide and 1/14" deep, used in newspaper advertising.

Ambush marketing – A strategy used by non-sponsors of an event to capitalize on the prestige and popularity of the event by giving the false impression they are sponsors.

Annual report – A document published annually by an organization primarily to provide current and prospective investors and stakeholders with financial data and a description of the company's operations.

Approach – The initial contact with a customer.

Attitude – An individual's feelings, favourable or unfavourable, toward an idea or object.

Attribute – A descriptive feature of a product.

Backlit poster – A luminous outdoor sign printed on polyvinyl material.

Banner – In outdoor advertising, a large-sized print ad that is framed and mounted on the exterior of a building. Online, an ad that stretches across a webpage; the user can click on the ad for more information.

Behavioural targeting – A means of delivering online ads based on a consumer's previous surfing patterns.

Benefit – The value a customer attaches to a brand attribute.

Big box ad – An online ad shaped like a large rectangle that offers greater width and depth to an ad.

"Big idea" – See **Central theme**.

Billboard – see **Poster**.

Blitz schedule – The scheduling of media advertising so that most spending is front-loaded in the schedule; usually involves a lot of money spent in a short period.

Blocking chart – See **Media calendar**.

Blog – A frequent, chronological publication of personal thoughts at a website.

Blogging – The act of posting new information and thoughts on a blog.

Body language – See **Non-verbal communication**.

Bonus pack – The temporary offering of a larger package size (e.g., 20 percent more) for the same price as the regular size.

Booklet (brochure) – A multiple-page document distributed to consumers and other interested stakeholders.

Borrowed-interest strategy – A plan to promote a marketing activity that is related to a product.

Bounce back – See **Statement stuffer**.

Brand – An identifying mark, symbol, word or words, or combination of mark and words that separates one product from another product; can also be defined as the sum of all tangible and intangible characteristics that make a unique offer to customers.

Brand development index (BDI) – The percentage of a brand's sales in an area in relation to the population in that area; determines if the brand is underdeveloped or overdeveloped in each area.

Brand equity – The value (monetary or otherwise) of a brand to its owners; determined by the success of marketing activities; influenced by brand name awareness, degree of customer loyalty, perceived quality, etc.

Brand insistence – A situation where the consumer searches the market for the specific brand.

Brand loyalty – The degree of attachment to a particular brand expressed by a consumer. There are three stages of brand loyalty: brand recognition, brand preference, and brand insistence.

Brand manager – An individual assigned responsibility for the development and implementation of marketing programs for a specific product or group of products.

Brand name – That part of a brand that can be spoken.

Brand preference – The situation where a brand is perceived as an acceptable alternative by a customer and will be purchased if it is available.

Brand recognition – Customer awareness of the brand name and package.

Branded content (product integration) – The integration of brand name goods and services into the script (storyline) of a television show or movie. The brand name is clearly mentioned and sometimes discussed.

Brandmark or logo – A unique design, symbol, or other special representation of a brand name or company name.

Broadsheet – A large newspaper with a fold in its middle.

Brochure – See **Booklet**.

Build-up schedule – The scheduling of media advertising so that the weight of advertising starts out light and gradually builds over a period of time; also called a teaser campaign.

Bump-in (setup) – The setting up of structures and other equipment at an event.

Bump-out (teardown) – The process of dismantling everything after an event.

Bus murals – Advertisements that appear on the driver's side or the tail of a bus, or both.

Business-to-business (B2B) market – A market of goods and services needed to produce a product or service, promote an idea, or operate a business.

Buying centre – An informal purchasing process in which individuals in an organization perform particular roles but may not have direct responsibility for the actual decision.

Buying committee – A formal buying structure in an organization that brings together expertise from the various functional areas to share in the buying decision process.

Buzz marketing – See **Product seeding**.

Call centre – A central operation from which a company operates its inbound and outbound telemarketing programs.

Casual rate – A one-time rate, or base rate, that applies to casual advertisers.

Catalogue – A reference publication, usually annual or seasonal, distributed by large retail chains and direct marketing companies.

Category development index (CDI) or market development index – The percentage of category sales in a geographic area in relation to the total population of that area; determines if a category is underdeveloped or overdeveloped in a particular region.

Central theme ("big idea") – The glue that binds various creative elements of a campaign together; transferable from one medium to another.

Channel positioning – A marketing strategy based on an organization's position in its distribution channel and its market coverage.

Cinema advertising – Print advertising inside film theatres and broadcast advertising on screens; options include television-style ads on screen, slides, posters, and ads printed on tickets.

Circulation – The average number of copies per issue of a publication sold by subscription, distributed free to predetermined recipients, carried with other publications, or made available through retail distributors.

Circulation list – A publication's subscription list that targets potential customers based on specified demographic characteristics, interests, or activities.

Classified advertising – Print advertising in which similar goods and services are grouped together in categories under appropriate headings.

Clickthrough rate – See **Ad click rate**.

Clickthroughs – See **Ad clicks.**

Clipping service – An organization that scans the print and broadcast media in search of a company's or brand's name.

Closed-ended questioning – See **Fixed-response questioning**.

Closing – Asking for the order at the appropriate time in a sales presentation.

Closing cue – An indication that the buyer is ready to buy; can be expressed verbally or nonverbally.

Cluster – Ads grouped in a block of time during a break in a program or between programs, or in a section of a publication.

Cluster profiling – See **Geodemographic segmentation**.

Clutter – The amount of advertising in a particular medium.

Cognitive dissonance – A feeling of doubt or regret in a consumer's mind once a buying decision has been made.

Cold canvass – The process of calling on people or organizations without appointments or advance knowledge of them.

Collateral material – Visual aids used by sales representatives in sales presentations, such as price lists, product manuals, sales brochures, and audiovisual materials.

Communication – The transmission, receipt, and processing of information between a sender and a receiver.

Compiled list – A direct mail list prepared from government, census, telephone, warranty, or other publication information.

Consultative selling – A form of selling that stresses open two-way communication between a buyer and seller.

Consumer behaviour – The combined acts carried out by individuals choosing and using goods and services, including the decision-making processes that determine these acts.

Consumer promotion – Incentive(s) offered to consumers to stimulate purchases or encourage loyalty.

Contest – A promotion that involves awarding cash or merchandise prizes to consumers when they purchase a specified product.

Contingency plan – The identification of alternative courses of action that can be used to modify an original plan if and when new circumstances arise.

Continuity – The length of time required in an advertising medium to generate the desired impact on the target audience.

Continuity discount – A discount offered to advertisers that purchase space in consecutive issues of a publication.

Controlled circulation – The circulation of a publication that is distributed free to individuals in a specific demographic segment or geographic area.

Cookie – An electronic identification tag sent from a web server to a user's browser to track the user's browsing patterns.

Co-op – See **Cooperative advertising allowance**.

Cooperative advertising allowance (co-op) – The sharing of advertising costs by suppliers and retailers or by several retailers.

Cooperative direct mail – A mailing containing specific offers from non-competing products.

Core values – The primary attributes and benefits a brand delivers to the customer.

Corporate advertising – Advertising designed to convey a favourable image of a company among its various publics.

Corporate culture – The values, beliefs, norms, and practices shared by all employees of an organization.

Corporate discount – A discount based on the total number of pages purchased by a single company (all product lines combined).

Corporate objective – A statement of a company's overall goal; used to evaluate the effectiveness or ineffectiveness of a company's strategic plan.

Corporate plan – A strategic plan formulated at the executive level of an organization to guide the development of functional plans in the organization.

Corporate strategy – see **Strategic planning**.

Cost-per-click – An Internet advertising pricing strategy where advertisers pay based on the number of ad clicks received.

Cost per thousand (CPM) – The cost of delivering an advertising message to 1000 people; calculated by dividing the cost of the ad by the circulation in thousands.

Coupon – A price-saving incentive offered to consumers to stimulate quick purchase of a specified product.

Creative brief – A document developed by a client organization that contains vital information about the advertising task at hand; it is a useful tool for discussions between the client and its advertising agency.

Creative objective – A statement that clearly indicates the information to be communicated to the target audience; usually involves a key benefit statement and a support claims statement.

Creative plan – A plan that outlines the nature of the message to be communicated to the target audience; involves the development of creative objectives, creative strategies, and creative execution.

Creative strategy – A plan of action for how the message will be communicated to the target audience, covering the tone and style of message, the central theme, and the appeal techniques.

Cross-coupon – See **Cross-ruff**.

Cross-ruff (cross-coupon) – A coupon packed in or with one product that is redeemable for another product. The product the coupon is packed with is the means of distributing the coupon.

Cross-tabulation – The comparison of answers to questions by various subgroups with the total number of responses.

Customer relationship management (CRM) – A process that enables an organization to develop an ongoing relationship with valued customers; the organization captures and uses information about its customers to its advantage in developing the relationship.

Data analysis – The evaluation of responses question by question; gives meaning to the data.

Data interpretation – The relating of accumulated data to the problem under review and to the objectives and hypotheses of the research study.

Data mining – The analysis of information to determine relationships among the data and enable more effective marketing strategies to be identified and implemented.

Data transfer – In marketing research, the transfer of answers from the questionnaire to the computer.

Database management system – A system that collects information about customers for analysis by managers to facilitate sound business decisions.

Database marketing – The use and analysis of accumulated information on customer buying behaviour to develop more effective marketing strategies.

Day-after recall (DAR) test – Research conducted the day following the respondent's exposure to a message to determine the degree of recognition and recall of the advertisement, the brand, and the selling message.

Daypart – A broadcast time period or segment on radio or television.

Dealer display material (point-of-purchase material) – Advertising or display materials located in a retail environment to build traffic, advertise a product, and encourage impulse purchasing.

Dealer premium – An incentive offered to a distributor to encourage the special purchase of a product or to secure additional merchandising support from the distributor.

Demographic segmentation – The identification of target markets based on characteristics such as age, income, education, occupation, marital status, and household formation.

Demonstration – A sales technique that involves showing the product in action to portray its benefits to a buyer.

Diary system – A system to collect audience data where participants complete a seven-day log by recording the television viewing for all television sets in the household for each quarter hour of the day from 6 am to 2 am.

Direct competition – Competition from alternative products and services that satisfy the needs of a target market.

Direct (customized) segmentation – The identification of a target audience at the level of the individual; marketing programs designed for and communicated to individual customers.

Direct home shopping – A shopping service provided by cable television stations that offers products or services for sale by broadcast message (e.g., The Shopping Channel).

Direct mail – A printed form of direct response advertising distributed by Canada Post or independent delivery agents.

Direct marketing – A marketing system for developing products, sending messages directly to customers, and accepting orders through a variety of media, and then distributing the purchase directly to customers.

Direct response advertising – Advertising placed in a medium that generates an immediate and measurable response from the intended target.

Direct response communications – The delivery of a message to a target audience of one; the message can be distributed by direct mail, direct response television, or telemarketing.

Direct response print – An ad in print media that issues a direct call to action via a toll-free number, return mail address, or website.

Direct response television (DRTV) – Advertising that appears on television and encourages viewers to respond by telephoning a toll-free number, by mail, or online; often referred to as infomercials.

Directory database – A commercial database that provides information about a company (e.g., size, sales, location, number of employees).

Editing – In marketing research, the review of questionnaires for consistency and completeness.

Electronic signs – Advertisements that are displayed on electronic billboards that rotate about every 10 to 15 seconds so multiple messages can be displayed at the same time.

Elevator advertising – Advertising in display frames on elevator walls or on televisions mounted in the corner or above the door.

Encoding – The transformation of a message into a meaningful format, such as an advertisement, a mailing piece, or an article in a newspaper.

Endorsement – A situation where a celebrity speaks highly of an advertised product.

Eprocurement – An online, business-to-business marketplace through which participants can purchase goods and services from one another.

Even schedule – The uniform schedule of media advertising over an extended period; also referred to as a continuous schedule.

Event marketing – The process, planned by a sponsoring organization, of integrating a variety of communications elements with a single event theme.

Event sponsorship – The financial support of an event in exchange for advertising privileges associated with that event.

Experiential marketing (on-site sampling) – A promotion in which potential customers interact directly with a product (e.g., sample giveaways).

Experimental research – Research in which one or more factors are manipulated under controlled conditions while other elements remain constant so that the respondent's actions can be evaluated.

External publics – Those publics that are distant from an organization and are communicated with less frequently.

Eye movement–camera test – A test that uses a hidden camera to track eye movement to gauge the point of immediate contact in an advertisement, how the reader scans the ad, and the amount of time spent reading.

Feature – Tangible aspects of a product, such as durability, design, and economy of operation.

Field sales force – An organization's external sales representatives who regularly call on customers to pursue orders.

Fixed-response (closed-ended) questioning – Questions that are predetermined with set answers for the respondents to choose from.

Flight – A period of time in which advertising is scheduled.

Focus group – A small group of people with common characteristics brought together to discuss issues related to the marketing of a product or service.

Folder – A direct response sales message printed on heavy stock that can be mailed with or without an envelope; may be several pages in length.

Follow-up – Maintaining contact with customers to ensure that service has been satisfactory.

Format – The type and nature of the programming offered by a radio station.

Free sample – Free distribution of a product to potential users.

Free-standing insert (FSI) – A booklet featuring coupons, refunds, contests, or other promotional advertising distributed by direct mail or with newspapers, magazines, or other delivery vehicles.

Frequency – The average number of times an audience has been exposed to a message over a period of time, usually a week.

Frequency discount – A discounted page rate based on the number of times an advertisement runs.

Frequency distribution – The number of times each answer in a survey was chosen for a question.

Frequent buyer program – See **Loyalty program**.

Game (including instant-win) – A promotional contest that includes a number of pre-seeded winning tickets; instant-win tickets can be redeemed immediately.

Geodemographic segmentation (cluster profiling) – The identification of target markets according to dwelling areas defined by geographic and demographic variables; based on the assumption that like people seek out residential neighbourhoods in which to cluster with their lifestyle peers.

Geographic segmentation – The identification of a target market based on the regional, urban, or rural location of the customers.

Gross rating points (GRPs) – An expression of the weight of advertising in a media schedule; calculated by multiplying reach by frequency.

Head-on positioning – A marketing strategy in which one product is presented as an equal or better alternative than a competing product.

Hit – Each time a server sends a file to a browser.

Horizontal rotation – The placement of radio commercials based on the day of the week (same daypart on different days).

House list – An internal customer list.

Hypothesis – A statement of outcomes predicted in a marketing research investigation.

Image positioning – See **Lifestyle positioning**.

Impressions – See **Ad views**.

Inbound telemarketing–The calls received by a company from consumers whether to place an order, inquire about products or services, or in response to a toll-free telephone number promoted on a direct response television commercial.

Incentive – A free gift or offer included in a direct mail package.

Indirect competition – Competition from substitute products that offer the same benefit as another type of product.

Infomercial – A long commercial (e.g., 10 to 30 minutes) that presents in detail the benefits of a product or service; usually includes a call to action (e.g., a 1-800 number).

Innovation positioning – A marketing strategy that stresses newness (based on a commitment to research and development) as a means of differentiating a company or a brand from competing companies and brands.

In-pack self-coupon – A coupon for the next purchase of a product that is packed inside the package or under a label.

Insert – A preprinted, free-standing advertisement (e.g., a leaflet, brochure, or flyer) specifically placed in a newspaper or magazine.

Inside sales force – An internal group of sellers, often referred to as order takers, who accept orders from customers by telephone or other means.

Instantly redeemable coupon – A removable coupon often located on the package or a store shelf that is redeemable on the current purchase of the product.

Instant-win – See **Game**.

Integrated marketing communications – The coordination of all marketing communications in a unified program that maximizes the impact on the intended target audience.

Interactive communications – The placement of an advertising message on a website, usually in the form of a banner, pop-up ad, rich media ad, sponsorship at a website, or an ad delivered by email.

Interior card – A transit ad in the rack above the window or near the door of a bus or subway car.

Internal publics – The publics with which an organization communicates regularly; can include employees, distributors, suppliers, shareholders, and customers.

Internet – A worldwide network of computers linked together to act as one in the communication of information; like a global mail system in which independent entities collaborate in moving and delivering information.

Internet radio – Listening to radio broadcasts via the Internet.

Interstitial (pop-up or pop-under) – An online ad that appears in a separate browser window while another webpage is loading; a pop-up appears in a window in front of the active window, and a pop-under appears in a window behind the active window.

Key benefit statement – A statement of the basic selling idea, service, or benefit promised the consumer by the advertiser; appears in the creative plan section of an advertising plan.

King poster – An oversized poster attached to the side of a bus.

Leaderboard (super banner) – An ad that stretches across the entire top of a webpage.

Leadership positioning – A marketing strategy in which a product presents itself as a preferred choice among customers.

Leaflet – A one-page flyer that offers relevant information about a direct mail offer.

Lifestyle (image) positioning – A marketing strategy based on intangible characteristics associated with a lifestyle instead of tangible characteristics.

Line rate – The rate charged by newspapers for one agate line or one modular agate line.

List broker – A company specializing in finding or developing lists for direct response purposes; finds prospect lists based on target market criteria established by marketing organizations.

Listing – An agreement made by a wholesaler to distribute a manufacturer's product to the retailer it supplies.

Lobbying – Activities and practices designed to influence policy decisions that will affect an organization or all organizations in a particular industry.

Local spot – Advertising bought from a local station by a local advertiser.

Logo – See **Brandmark**.

Loyalty program (frequent buyer program) – A program that offers consumers a small bonus, such as points or play money, each time they make a purchase; the bonus accumulates and can be redeemed for merchandise or some other benefit.

Mail interview – In marketing research, the collection of information from a respondent by mail.

Mall poster – A form of advertising located inside shopping malls; relies on pedestrian traffic only.

Market development index – See **Category development index (CDI).**

Market segmentation – The division of a large market into smaller homogeneous markets based on common needs and characteristics.

Market share – The sales volume of one product or company expressed as a percentage of total sales volume in the market the company or brand is competing in.

Marketing communications plan – A plan that identifies how the various elements of marketing communications will be integrated into a cohesive and coordinated plan.

Marketing control – The process of measuring and evaluating the results of marketing strategies and plans and of taking corrective action to ensure marketing objectives are achieved.

Marketing objective – A statement that identifies what a product will accomplish in a one-year period, usually expressed in terms of sales, market share, and profit.

Marketing plan – A short-term, specific plan of action that combines strategy and tactics.

Marketing planning – The analysis, planning, implementing, and controlling of marketing initiatives to satisfy target market needs and achieve organizational objectives.

Marketing research – A marketing function that links the consumer/customer/public to the marketer through information; the information is used to define marketing opportunities and problems, generate marketing strategies, evaluate marketing actions, and monitor performance.

Marketing strategy – A plan of action that shows how the various elements of the marketing mix will be used to satisfy a target market's needs.

Mass customization – The development, manufacture, and marketing of unique products to unique customers.

Media brief – A document that contains essential information for developing a media plan; used to stimulate discussion between a client and agency.

Media calendar (blocking chart) – A document that shows allocation of a brand's media budget according to time of year and type of medium; shows coordination of various media recommendations.

Media execution – The translation of media strategies into specific media action plans; involves recommending specific media to be used in the plan and negotiating the media buys.

Media kit – A package of relevant information associated with a product or organization that is distributed at a press conference.

Media objective – A statement that outlines what a media plan is to accomplish (who, what, when, where, or how).

Media plan – A strategy that outlines the relevant details about how a client's budget will be spent; involves decisions about what media to use and how much money to invest in the media chosen to reach the target audience effectively and efficiently.

Media strategy – A plan for achieving the media objectives stated in the media plan; typically justifies the use of certain media.

Media-delivered coupon – A coupon distributed by traditional media alternatives such as newspapers, magazines, and direct mail.

Merge/purge – A process in which numerous mailing lists are combined and then stripped of duplicate names.

Micro-segmentation (micro-marketing) – The identification of very small yet profitable market segments.

Mission statement – A statement of an organization's purpose and operating philosophy; provides guidance and direction for the operations of the company.

Modular agate line (MAL) – A standardized unit of measurement used in newspaper advertising equal to one column wide and 1/14" deep.

Modular agate unit – A standardized unit of measurement in which a newspaper page is divided into equal-sized units, each 30 modular agate lines deep.

Monopolistic competition – A market in which there are many competitors, each offering a unique marketing mix; consumers can assess these choices prior to making a buying decision.

Motive – A condition that prompts an individual to take action to satisfy a need.

Mural advertisement – A hand-painted outdoor ad seen on the side of a building.

Need – The perception of the absence of something useful.

Network advertising – Advertising from one central source broadcast across an entire network of stations.

New product development strategy – A marketing strategy that calls for significant investment in research and development to develop innovative products.

Newsletter – A document sent to a predetermined audience that contains news about an organization (e.g., a newsletter sent to alumni of a school or to all employees of an organization).

Noise – Any potential form of disruption in the transmission of a message that could distort the impact of the message; competitive advertising or the clutter of advertising messages in a medium are forms of noise.

Non-probability sample – A sample of respondents who have an unknown chance of selection and are chosen because of factors such as convenience or the judgment of the researcher.

Non-verbal communication (body language) – The expression of thoughts, opinions, or information using non-verbal cues such as body movement, facial expressions, and eye contact.

Objection – An obstacle that a salesperson must confront during a sales presentation.

Observation research – A form of research in which the behaviour of the respondent is observed and recorded; may be by personal or electronic means.

Oligopoly – A market situation in which only a few brands control the market.

Online database – An information database accessible online to anyone with proper communications facilities.

Online selling – Using the Internet to conduct sales transactions.

Online survey – In marketing research, using an online questionnaire to collect data from people.

On-pack self-coupon – A coupon that is printed on the outside of a package redeemable on the next purchase of the product.

On-site sampling – See **Experiential marketing**.

Open-ended questioning – See **Open-response questioning**.

Open-response (open-ended) questioning – A situation where space is available at the end of a question where the respondents can add their comments.

Opinion-measure testing – A form of research yielding information about the effect of a commercial message on respondents' brand name recall, interest in the brand, and purchase intentions.

Opt-in list – A list of people who have agreed to receive messages via email.

Order taking – In retail sales, a floor clerk provides product information and shows goods to the customer who then goes to the checkout counter to pay for purchases.

Outbound telemarketing – Calls made by a company to customers to develop new accounts, generate sales leads, and even close a sale.

Overall goal – The objective of an advertising campaign.

Paid circulation – The circulation of a newspaper or magazine that is generated by subscription sales and newsstand sales.

Partnership selling – A strategically developed long-term relationship that involves selling products and providing comprehensive after-sales service and effective two-way communications to ensure complete customer satisfaction.

Pay-per-click advertising – See **Search advertising**.

Peer group – see **Reference group**.

Penetration strategy – A plan of action for aggressive marketing of a company's existing products.

Perception – The manner in which individuals receive and interpret messages.

Performance allowance – A discount offered by a manufacturer that encourages a distributor to perform a merchandising function on behalf of a manufacturer.

Permission-based email – Email sent to recipients who have agreed to accept email advertising messages.

Personal interview – In marketing research, the collection of information in a face-to-face interview.

Personal selling – Face-to-face communication involving the presentation of features and benefits of a product or service to a buyer; the objective is to make a sale.

Personality – A person's distinguishing psychological characteristics that lead to relatively consistent and enduring responses to the environment in which that person lives.

Picture matching technology (PMT) – A relatively new way to collect television audience data; determines what viewers are watching by periodically "sampling" the video image on their television screens, and then comparing this time-stamped video "fingerprint" with a library of all television sources that are available at that time.

Podcasting– Audio programming that is downloadable to iPods and other portable digital media devices; allows the listener to tune in when it is convenient for them to do so.

Point-of-purchase material – See **Dealer display material**.

Population (universe) – In marketing research, a group of people with certain age, gender, or other demographic characteristics.

Pop-up or pop-under – See **Interstitial**.

Portable people meter (PPM) – A form of electronic observation where electronic metering devices are installed in households that register what is being watched on television every minute of every day.

Portal – A website that serves as a gateway to a variety of services such as searching, news, directories, email, online shopping, and links to other sites.

Position charge – The cost of requesting a preferred position in a newspaper.

Positioning – The selling concept that motivates purchase, or the image that marketers desire a brand to have in the minds of consumers.

Positioning strategy statement – A summary of the character and personality of a brand and the benefits it offers customers.

Post-buy analysis – An evaluation of actual audience deliveries calculated after a specific spot or schedule of advertising has run.

Poster (billboard) – A common form of outdoor advertising; usually a picture-dominant advertisement with a minimum of copy.

Post-testing – The evaluation and measurement of a message's effectiveness during or after the message has run.

Pre-approach – The gathering of information about customers before actually making sales contact.

Premium – An additional item given free, or greatly discounted, to induce purchase of the primary brand.

Presentation strategy– A plan of what to say to a customer in a sales presentation to identify customer needs, summarize benefits, and prepare for potential objections.

Press conference – A meeting called by an organization to present information to representatives of the media.

Press release – A document prepared by an organization containing public relations information that is sent to the media for publication or broadcast.

Pre-testing – The evaluation of commercial messages prior to final production to determine the strengths and weaknesses of the communications.

Price positioning – A marketing strategy based on the premise that consumers search for the best possible value given their economic circumstances.

Primary data – Data collected to resolve a problem and recorded for the first time.

Primary medium – A medium that receives the largest allocation of an advertiser's budget; the dominant medium in a media plan.

Primary research – The collection and recording of primary data.

Probability sample – A sample of respondents who are known to have an equal chance of selection and are randomly selected from the sampling frame.

Problem statement – A brief statement that summarizes a particular problem to resolve or an opportunity to pursue and serves as the focus of a marketing strategy.

Product advertising – Advertising that provides information about a branded product to help build its image in the minds of customers.

Product as hero – A creative execution technique in which the advertised product is shown coming to the rescue (e.g., of a consumer in a difficult situation).

Product configuration – The bringing together of various products and services to form a solution for the customer.

Product differentiation strategy – A plan of action for communicating meaningful attributes and benefits of a product to a target market.

Product integration – See **Branded content**.

Product placement – The visible placement of brand name products in television shows, movies, radio, video games, and other programming.

Product seeding (buzz marketing) – Giving a product free to a group of trendsetters who promote the product to others by word of mouth.

Profile-matching strategy – A media tactic that involves matching the demographic profile of a product's target market with a specific medium that has a similar target profile.

Promotional advertising – Advertising that communicates a specific offer to encourage an immediate response from the target audience.

Prospecting – A procedure for systematically developing sales leads.

Psychographic segmentation – The identification of a target market according to lifestyle characteristics such as activities, interests, and opinions.

Public affairs – Strategies to deal with governments and to communicate with governments.

Public relations – A form of communications designed to gain public understanding and acceptance.

Publicity – News about an organization, product, service, or person that appears in the media.

Publisher's statement – A statement published by the Audit Bureau of Circulations twice a year that is the authority on which advertising rates are based.

Pull – Demand created by directing promotional activities at consumers or final users, who in turn pressure retailers to supply the product or service.

Pulse schedule – A scheduling of media advertising in flights of different weight and duration.

Pupilometer test – A device that measures pupil dilation (enlargement) of a person's eye when reading; it measures emotional responses to an advertisement.

Push – Demand created by directing promotional activities at intermediaries, who in turn promote the product or service among consumers.

Qualifying (a customer) – Assessing if a prospect needs a product, has the authority to buy it, and has the ability to pay for it.

Qualitative data – Data collected from small samples in a controlled environment; it describes feelings and opinions on issues.

Quantitative data – Measurable data collected from large samples using a structured research procedure.

Rating – Television and radio audience estimates expressed as a percentage of a population in a defined geographic area.

Reach – The total unduplicated audience exposed one or more times to a commercial message during a specific period (usually a week).

Reach plan – Rotation of commercials in various dayparts on radio according to a predetermined frequency.

Rebate – A predetermined amount of money returned directly to customers by the manufacturer after the purchase has been made.

Recall test – A test that measures an ad's impact by asking respondents to recall specific elements (e.g., the selling message) of the advertisement; can be aided (some information provided) or unaided.

Recency – A model that suggests advertising works best by reminding consumers about a product when they are ready to buy.

Recognition test – A test that measures a target audience's awareness of a brand, copy, or of the advertisement itself after the audience has been exposed to the message.

Rectangular ad – A large ad, slightly wider than it is tall, on a webpage.

Redemption rate – The number of coupons returned expressed as a percentage of the number of coupons that were distributed.

Reference group (peer group) – A group of people who share common interests that influence the attitudes and behaviour of its members.

Referral – A recommendation by a current customer of a potential new customer to a sales representative.

Related recall – The percentage of a test commercial audience who claims to remember the test commercial and can provide as verification some description of the commercial.

Relationship selling – A form of selling with the goal of developing a plan of action that establishes, builds, and maintains a long-term relationship with customers.

Reliability (of data) – Degree of similarity of results achieved if another research study were undertaken under similar circumstances.

Repeat transaction – A retail sales situation that involves a relationship between the buyer and the seller; the customer returns to the same store for similar goods and services.

Research objective – A statement that outlines what the marketing research is to accomplish.

Response card – A card filled in, usually at the time of purchase, that collects information about customers that can be added to the organization's database.

Response list – A list of direct mail buyers who have previously bought based on direct response offers.

Retail advertising – Advertising by a retail store; involves advertising the store name, image, location, and the re-advertising of branded merchandise carried by the store.

Rich media – Streaming video, audio, and special effects similar to television and used online.

Rifle strategy – A strategy that involves using a specific medium that effectively reaches a target market defined by a common characteristic.

Rotation plan – The placement of commercials in time slots purchased on radio; can be vertical according to the time of day or horizontal according to the day of the week.

Run of network – See **Run of site**.

Run of site (run of network) – Ad rate for placements anywhere on a website.

Run sheet – A schedule of daily events that shows the various dates, times, and locations of activities at an event.

Sales presentation – A persuasive delivery and demonstration of a product's benefits; shows buyers how the product's benefits will satisfy their needs.

Sales promotion – An activity that provides incentives to bring about immediate response from customers, distributors, and an organization's sales force.

Sales promotion plan – An action plan for communicating incentives to appropriate target markets at the right time.

Sample – A representative portion of an entire population that is used to obtain information about that population.

Sampling frame – A list used to access a representative sample of a population; it is a means of accessing people for a research study.

Satellite radio – A radio service that offers commercial-free programming for a monthly fee.

Search advertising (pay-per-click advertising) – An advertiser's listing is placed within or alongside search results in exchange for paying a fee each time someone clicks on the listing.

Seasonal schedule – Scheduling media advertising according to seasonal sales trends; usually concentrated in the pre-season or the period just prior to when the bulk of the buying occurs.

Secondary media – Media alternatives used to complement the primary medium in an advertising campaign; typically less money is allocated to these media.

Secondary research – Data compiled and published by others for purposes other than resolving a specific problem. In advertising, secondary sources are frequently used to gain access to media information that benefits media analysis and planning.

Selective direct mail – See **Solo direct mail**.

Selective spot – Commercial time during a network show that is allocated back to regional and local stations to sell; advertisers buy spots on a station-by-station basis.

Self-image – One's own idea about oneself and one's relationship with others.

Setup – See **Bump-in**.

Seventy poster – A small poster usually affixed to the back of a bus.

Shotgun strategy – A tactic involving the use of mass media to reach a loosely defined target audience.

Single transaction – A retail sales situation where a salesperson spends time with a customer and closes the sale on the spot.

Skip schedule – The scheduling of media advertising on an alternating basis, such as every other week or every other month.

Skyscraper – A vertical box-shaped ad that appears on a webpage.

Slippage – The situation of a consumer collecting labels in a promotion offer but failing to follow through and request the refund.

Slogan – A short phrase that captures the essence of an entire advertising campaign; reflects the positioning strategy of the brand and is shown in all ads in all media.

Solo direct mail (selective direct mail) – A unique advertising offer mailed directly to a target audience by a marketing organization.

Spam – Unsolicited email.

Spectacular – see **Superboard**.

Spiff – An incentive offered to retail salespeople to encourage them to promote a specified brand of goods to customers.

Sponsored email – Email that includes a short message from a sponsor along with a link to the sponsor's website.

Sponsorship – The act of financially supporting an event in return for certain advertising rights and privileges.

Spot colour – The addition of one colour to an otherwise black-and-white newspaper or magazine ad.

Starch readership test – A post-test recognition procedure that measures readers' recall of an advertisement (noted), their ability to identify the sponsor (associated), and whether they read more than half of the written material (read most).

Statement stuffer (bounce back) – An ad or offer distributed in monthly statements or with the delivery of goods purchased by some form of direct response advertising.

Station poster – An advertisement located on the platform or at the entrance or exit of subways and light rail transit systems.

Stickiness (sticky) – A website's ability to keep people at the site for an extended period or to have them return to the site frequently.

Strategic alliance – The combination of separate companies' resources for the purpose of satisfying their shared customers; the companies have strengths in different areas.

Strategic planning (corporate strategy) – The process of determining objectives (setting goals) and identifying strategies (ways to achieve the goals) and tactics (specific action plans) to help achieve objectives.

Strategic selling – A form of consultative selling that involves dealing with each customer as an individual, stressing that in the transfer of product information.

Streaming media – Audio or video delivered online in small, compressed packets of data that are interpreted by a software player as they are received.

Super banner – See **Leaderboard**.

Superboard (spectacular) – Outdoor advertising that is larger than a normal poster and much more expensive to produce; can include extensions beyond borders and electronic messaging.

Superbus advertising – An advertisement painted on the exterior of a bus; the advertiser also has exclusive use of interior cards.

Superstitial – Elaborate online advertising that usually incorporates multimedia and interactive elements.

Support claims statement – A substantiation of the promise made in the key benefit statement; appears in the creative plan.

Survey research – The systematic collection of data by communicating with a representative sample by means of a questionnaire.

Sweepstakes – A chance promotion involving the giveaway of products or services of value to randomly selected participants.

SWOT analysis – An analysis procedure that involves an assessment of an organization's strengths, weaknesses, opportunities, and threats; strengths and weaknesses are internal variables, whereas opportunities and threats are external variables.

Tabloid – A smaller newspaper that is sold flat (not folded).

Tabulation – The process of counting various responses for each question in a survey.

Tactics (execution) – Action-oriented details that outline how a strategic plan will be implemented.

Tagline – A short phrase that captures the essence of an advertised message.

Target market profile – A description of a customer group based on demographic, psychographic, and geographic variables.

Targeting request – An ad placed to reach a specific target audience of a website, for which a premium is usually paid.

Teardown – See **Bump-out**.

Telemarketing – The use of telecommunications to promote the products and services of a business; involves outbound calls (company to customer) and inbound calls (customer to company).

Telephone interview – In marketing research, the collection of information from a respondent by telephone.

Test marketing – Placing a commercial, set of commercials, or print ad campaign in one or more limited markets that are representative of the whole to observe the impact of the ads on consumers.

Text messaging – The transmission of short text-only messages using wireless devices such as cell phones and personal digital assistants.

Tip-in – An insert that is glued to a page in the publication using a removable adhesive.

Torture test – A creative execution technique in which the product is subjected to extreme conditions to demonstrate its durability.

Trade allowance – A temporary price reduction that encourages larger purchases by distributors.

Trade promotion – An incentive offered to channel members to encourage them to provide marketing and merchandising support for a particular product.

Trade show – An event that allows a company to showcase its products to a captive audience and generate leads.

Trademark – A brandmark or other brand element that is granted legal protection so that only the owner can use it.

Transit shelter advertising – Street-level advertisements incorporated into the design of the glass and steel shelters located at a bus stop.

Transmission– The sending of a message through a medium such as television, radio, newspapers, magazines, outdoor advertising, Internet, and so on, or through personal selling.

Trial close – A failed attempt at closing a sale; the buyer said "no."

Unique selling point (USP) – The primary benefit of a product or service that distinguishes it from its competitors.

Universe – See **Population**.

Validity (of data) – A research procedure's ability to measure what it is intended to measure.

Venue marketing (venue sponsorship) – Linking a brand name or company name to a physical site, such as a stadium, arena, or theatre.

Venue sponsorship – See **Venue marketing**.

Vertical rotation – The placement of radio commercials based on the time of day (within various dayparts).

Video messaging – Consumers with video capabilities on their cell phones can download news and sports clips and selected television shows from major networks and watch them on their phones.

Viral marketing – Online marketing that encourages the receiver of a message to pass it along to others to generate additional exposure.

Visit – A sequence of page requests made by a visitor to a website; also called a session or a browsing period.

Visitor – A unique user of a website.

Voice-pitch analysis test – A test that uses a recording of a person's voice response to measure change in voice pitch caused by emotional responses to the communications.

Volume discount – A discount linked to the dollar volume purchased over an extended period; the more volume purchased, the higher the discount.

Washroom advertising – A mini-poster ad located in a public or institutional washroom; usually placed above the urinal or on the back of the stall door.

Webcasting (webisodes) – The production of an extended commercial presented on the web that includes entertainment value in the communications.

Webisodes – See **Webcasting**.

Wordmark – The stylized treatment of the brand name; serves the same function as a symbol.

World Wide Web – A system of Internet servers that publish websites, which are specially formatted documents that contain graphics, audio, and video files and links to other websites.

Index

A

ACCA model, *102*
accessing data, *171–172*
accommodations, *305*
accountability, *12*
acquisition strategy, *45*
action, *103*
ad click rate, *202*
ad clicks (clickthroughs), *202, 358*
ad views, *202, 358*
advergaming, *214–215*
advertising
    advocacy advertising, *254–256f*
    corporate advertising, *254*
    defined, *1, 105*
    evaluation, *351–355*
    famous advertising slogans, *87f*
    measurement, *351–355*
    online. *See* interactive communica-
      tions strategies; Internet
    out-of-home advertising, *157–162*
    outdoor advertising, *158–160*
    product advertising, *4–5*
    promotional advertising, *6*
    timing of, *143–145*
advertising equivalency, *359, 360*
advertising measurement and efficiency
    client evaluation, *351–352*
    day-after recall (DAR) testing, *353*
    external research, *352–355*
    opinion-measure testing, *354–355*
    physiological testing, *355*
    post-testing, *352*
    pre-testing, *352*
    recall tests, *353*
    recognition tests, *352–353*
    related recall, *353*
    Starch readership test, *353*
advertising objectives, *109*
advertising plan, *59–62*
advertising planning
    creative planning. *See* creative
      planning
    media planning. *See* media plan-
      ning
advocacy advertising, *254–256f*
agate line, *367*
allowances

cooperative advertising allowance,
    244
    performance allowance, *244*
    trade allowance, *244*
altering perceptions, *112*
ambush marketing, *282*
annual reports, *270*
appeal techniques
    comparative appeals, *123–125*
    emotional appeals, *122–123*
    factual appeals, *125*
    humorous appeals, *120–121,*
      120f–121f
    lifestyle appeals, *123, 123f*
    negative appeals, *119, 119f*
    positive appeals, *118–119*
    sexual appeals, *121–122, 122f*
approach, *327*
arena advertising, *161*
the arts, *288–289*
attitudes, *15–17*
attribute, *76, 78f*
Audit Bureau of Circulations (ABC),
    397–398
automated teller machines (ATMs), *40*
awareness, *103, 198, 292, 361*

B

baby boomer, *19*
backlit poster, *158–159, 158f–159f*
banners, *159, 203, 205f*
BBM Bureau of Measurement,
    395–396, 397
behavioural targeting, *195*
benefit, *76, 325–326*
big box ad, *203*
"big idea," *117*
bill-back, *244*
billboards, *158*
blitz schedule, *145*
blocking chart, *147*
blog, *264, 270–271*
blogging, *264*
BMW MINI, *141*
body language, *320–321*
bonus pack, *241*
booklets, *269–270*
borrowed-interest strategy, *265*
bounce back, *177*

brand awareness, *109, 109f, 204f*
brand-building process, *76–78, 76f*
brand development index (BDI), *142*
brand differentiation, *78f, 78*
brand equity, *75–76, 75f, 248*
brand identification, *89f*
brand image, *248*
brand insistence, *74*
brand leadership positioning, *82–83*
brand loyalty, *74–75, 74f, 208f, 225*
brand management, *71*
brand manager, *76*
brand name, *69, 70–71, 73*
brand positioning. *See* positioning
brand preference, *74*
brand recognition, *74, 351*
brand sales, *361*
branded content, *3, 151–258*
branding, *198–199*
branding by design, *93–95*
branding strategy
    benefits of branding, *73–76*
    brand equity, *75–76, 75f*
    brand loyalty, *74–75, 74f*
    brand positioning, establishment of,
      76–78
    brand positioning concepts, *78–88*
    branding by design, *93–95*
    building the brand, *76–78, 76f*
    core values, establishment of,
      76–78
    defining the brand, *69–73*
    packaging and brand building,
      88–92
brandmark, *70*
brands
    see also branding strategy
    components of, *69–71*
    decision-making process, role in,
      73
    defined, *69*
    intangible dimensions, *71*
    retail organizations, *73*
    superbrands, *88*
    world's top ten brands, *75f*
broadsheet, *154, 367*
brochure, *269*
browsing period, *202*

budget
  media budget. *See* media budget
  public relations, *271–273*
  sales promotion, *224*
build-up schedule, *145*
bump-in, *306*
bump-out, *306*
bus murals, *160*
business buyer behaviour
  buying centre, *29, 29f*
  buying committee, *29*
  criteria, *29*
business market. *See* business-to-business (B2B) market
business-to-business (B2B) market
  defined, *29*
  integration, *29–31*
  partnering, *29–31*
  strategies employed, *29–31*
  vs. consumer market, *29*
business-to-business selling, *314*
business-to-consumer (B2C) market, *201*
buying centre, *29, 29f*
buying committee, *29*
buzz marketing, *236, 258, 259*

C

Cadbury Adams Canada, *236*
call centre, *181*
Canadian Advertising Rates and Data (CARD), *396*
Canadian Circulations Audit Board (CCAB), *398*
Canadian Code of Advertising Standards, *40*
Canadian Outdoor Measurement Bureau (COMB), *399*
Canadian Tire, *194, 243*
casual rate, *369*
catalogues, *169, 183–185f*
category development index (CDI), *142*
catering, *305*
cause marketing sponsorships, *289–291*
ceiling decals, *160*
cell phones, *12*
  see also mobile media
central theme, *117*
channel positioning, *85*
Chrysler 300 sedan, *94*
cinema advertising, *162*
circulation, *154*
circulation lists, *173, 390*
classified ads, *155*
clickthrough rate (ad click rate), *202*
clickthroughs, *202*

client evaluation, *351–352*
clipping service, *359*
closed-ended questioning, *343*
closing, *329–330, 329f*
closing cue, *329*
cluster profiling, *28, 151*
clustering, *157*
clutter, *155, 157*
co-op, *244*
cognitive dissonance, *330*
cold canvass, *327*
collateral material, *245*
collection of data, *171*
colour charges, *372, 376*
commercials. *See* television
communications
  defined, *101*
  encoding, *101*
  essentials of, *101–112*
  FCB Grid, *103–104, 103f*
  involvement, degree of, *103–104*
  marketing communications planning process, *104–105*
  online communications, *194f–195f*
  process, *101–102, 102f*
  traditional communications, *194f–195f*
  transmission, *101*
community newspapers, *155*
community relations, *260–261, 260f*
company knowledge, *323*
company websites, *209*
comparative appeals, *123–125*
comparative positioning, *83*
competing products, *102*
competition, *37–38*
Competition Act, *237*
competitor activity profile, *223*
competitor analysis, *50*
competitor influence, *37–38*
competitor knowledge, *323*
competitor media strategy, *134*
compiled lists, *173, 390*
comprehension, *103*
comScore Media Matrix, *400*
conference centres, *296f*
consultative selling, *316*
consumer behaviour
  see also consumers
  attitudes, *15–17*
  consumer data, *49*
  defined, *12*
  family influences, *17–18*
  motive, *13–14*
  needs, *13–14*
  perception, *17*

  personality, *15*
  reference groups, *17*
  self-concept, *15*
consumer data, *49*
consumer promotions
  bonus pack, *241*
  contests, *236–238, 237f, 239f*
  coupons, *232–233, 238f*
  defined, *221*
  execution, *231–243*
  experiential marketing, *235–236*
  frequent buyer program, *241–243*
  loyalty programs, *241–243*
  multiple purchases, *225*
  premium offers, *240–241*
  product samples, *234–236*
  rebates, *238–240*
  trial purchase, encouragement of, *225f*
consumers
  see also consumer behaviour
  involvement, *103–104*
  multi-tasking, *9*
  qualifying, *327*
  target markets, *19*
contests, *227f, 236–238, 237f, 239f*
contingency plan, *45*
continuity, *146*
continuity discount, *376, 382, 384*
controlled circulation, *156*
conviction, *103*
cookie, *195, 343*
cooperative advertising allowance, *244*
cooperative direct mail, *178*
core values, *76–78*
corporate advertising, *254*
corporate communications, *254*
corporate culture, *323*
corporate discount, *376*
corporate objectives, *43*
corporate plan, *41, 42–45*
corporate responsibility, *254, 254f–255f*
corporate strategy. *See* strategic planning
cost-per-click, *394*
cost per thousand. *See* CPM (cost per thousand)
costs. *See* media buying principles
coupons
  combined with contest, *237f*
  cross-ruff, *233*
  defined, *232*
  described, *232*
  distribution, *233f*
  free-standing inserts (FSI), *232, 232f*

in-pack self-coupons, *232*
instantly redeemable coupons, *232*
and the Internet, *232*
measurement of effectiveness, *357,*
357f–358f
media-delivered coupons, *232*
on-pack self-coupon, *232*
redemption rate, *233, 233f*
coverage strategies
key market coverage, *142*
national coverage, *142*
regional coverage, *142*
CPM (cost per thousand), *146–180,*
372–373
CPM model, *391–394*
creative brief, *106–107, 106f, 107f*
creative execution
described, *126*
endorsement, *128*
product as hero, *126*
product demonstrations, *126*
slogans, *128, 129f*
taglines, *128*
testimonials, *126*
torture test, *126*
creative objectives, *114–115*
creative plan, *59–61*
creative planning
advertising objectives, *109*
altering perceptions, *112*
appeal techniques, *117–125*
attraction of new target markets,
110–111
brand awareness, creating or
increasing, *109, 109f*
creative brief, *106–107, 106f, 107f*
creative execution, *126–129*
creative objectives, *114–115*
creative strategy, *115–119*
illustration of, *104f, 105f*
key benefit statement, *114*
overall goal, *107*
positioning strategy statement,
112–113
preference, encouragement of,
111–112
problem identification, *107*
problem statement, *107*
support claims statement, *114–115*
trial purchase, encouragement of,
109–110
creative strategy
"big idea," *117*
central theme, *117*
defined, *116*
style, *117–119*

tone, *117–119*
Criminal Code, 237
crisis situations, *257f*
cross-coupon, *233*
cross-ruff, *233*
cross-tabulation, *348*
cultural events, *288–289*
customer relationship management
(CRM), *6, 10–11*
customer relationships, *275*
customer satisfaction, *362*
customer service, *199–201*
customers. *See* consumers
customized segmentation, *26–28*

D
DAGMAR model, *102*
data. *See* database management
data analysis, *348*
data collection methods, *343–344,*
343f
data interpretation, *349*
data mining, *27, 171–172*
data processing, *348*
data transfer, *348*
database management
accessing data, *171–172*
and call centres, *182*
circulation lists, *173*
collection of data, *171*
compiled lists, *173*
data mining, *171–172*
demographic information, *171*
directory database, *175*
external sources, *171, 173*
house list, *170*
internal data sources, *170*
list broker, *173*
merge/purge process, *173*
need for, *169–170*
online databases, *173–174*
opt-in list, *208*
psychographic information, *171*
response list, *173, 173f*
database management systems, *11*
database marketing, *27*
day-after recall (DAR) testing, *353*
day time, *378*
dayparts, *383*
dealer display material, *245–246*
dealer premiums, *245*
debit cards, *40*
demand, *377–378*
demographic influences, *38*
demographic information, *171*
demographic profile, *52*

demographic segmentation
aging population, *19–20, 19f–20f*
defined, *19*
ethnic diversity, *21*
gender economics, *21–23*
household formations, *21*
urban growth, *20*
demographic trends, *49*
demonstration, *328*
design, *93–95*
designing the event, *296–297*
diary system, *395*
digital communications technologies,
11–12
digital screen advertising, *213, 213f*
direct competition, *37*
direct (customized) segmentation, *26–28*
direct home shopping, *179*
direct mail
as advertising medium, *178, 178f*
bounce back, *177*
buying, illustration, *391*
components of, *175–177, 176f*
cooperative direct mail, *178*
defined, *169*
distribution costs, *391*
envelope, *175*
example of, *170f*
folder, *175*
incentive, *176*
leaflets, *175*
letter, *175*
media buying principles, *389–391*
obtaining lists, *389–390*
order form, *176*
personalization, *177, 177f*
postage-paid return envelope, *176*
production costs, *390*
selective direct mail, *177*
solo direct mail, *177*
statement stuffer, *177*
strategies, *177–178*
use of, *175*
direct marketing, *167*
direct response advertising
defined, *168*
evaluation of, *357–359*
measurement of, *357–359*
direct response communications
acceptance of, *169*
catalogues, *169, 183–185f*
database management, *169–175*
defined, *6*
described, *6*
direct mail, *169, 169f, 175–177*

direct response print, *169, 179–180, 180f*

direct response television (DRTV), *169, 178–179*

forms of, *169*

planning process, *168f*

roots of, *169–175*

telemarketing, *169, 181–183*

tools of, *175–185*

traditional forms of, *169*

direct response list, *173, 173f*

direct response plan, *62*

direct response print, *169, 179–180, 180f*

direct response television (DRTV)

advertising rates, *180*

changes in, *178*

costs, *180*

and customer segments, *180*

defined, *169*

described, *178*

direct home shopping, *179*

infomercial, *178–179, 180f*

direct selling, *314*

directory database, *175*

discontinuous innovation, *83*

discounts

magazine advertising, *374–383*

radio advertising, *383–384*

television advertising, *382*

display activity, *228f*

distribution, *50*

distribution costs, *391*

dress codes, *321*

E

the Echo, *119*

echo boom, *19*

ecommerce, *194f–195f*

economic influences, *36–37*

economic trends, *49*

E.D. Smith, *348*

editing, *348*

efficiency, *12*

electronic signs, *159*

elevator advertising, *161*

email advertising

brand loyalty, *208f*

described, *208–209*

opt-in list, *208*

permission-based email, *208*

spam, *208*

sponsored email, *208*

viral marketing, *209*

emotional appeals, *122–123*

encoding, *101*

endorsement, *128*

entertainment sponsorships

described, *286*

film festivals, *286*

television, *286–288*

envelope, *175*

eprocurement, *30*

equivalent advertising value, *273*

ethnic diversity, *21*

Evaliant Services, *400*

evaluation

advertising messages. *See* advertising measurement and efficiency

client evaluation, *351–352*

direct response advertising, *357–359*

event marketing, *360–361*

event sponsorship, *360–361*

Internet communications, *357–359*

of marketing communications, *64–65*

public relations, *359–360*

sales promotions, *355–357*

even schedule, *145*

event concept development, *294–296*

event marketing

see also event sponsorship

considerations for participation, *291–292*

defined, *8, 280*

described, *8–9, 280–281*

evaluation, *360–361*

event as brand, *301f*

exclusivity, *292*

execution. *See* event marketing execution

image of event, *292*

investment in, *281*

marketing communications plan, *64*

measurement of benefits, *292–293*

measurement of effectiveness, *360–361*

planning the event. *See* event marketing planning

selection criteria, *292*

sports event marketing levels, *281f–282f*

target, choice of, *292*

event marketing execution

described, *301–302*

logistics, *305–306*

operations, *305–306*

safety, *307*

security, *307*

site selection, *302–305*

staffing, *305*

staging, *302–305*

event marketing planning

advertising strategies, *301*

defining the event, *298–299*

described, *293–294*

designing the event, *296–297*

event concept development, *294–296*

financial resources, *295*

marketing communications strategy, *301*

marketing the event, *298–301*

objectives, *297–298*

planning tools, *298*

pricing strategy, *300–301*

process, *293f–295f*

product strategy, *298–299*

proposal, *298, 298f*

purpose, *294*

run sheet, *298, 300f*

theme, *294–295*

timeline chart, *298*

timing of event, *295*

event proposal, *298, 298f–299f*

event sponsorship

see also event marketing

the arts, *288–289*

cause marketing sponsorships, *289–291*

as complement to other activities, *292*

cultural events, *288–289*

defined, *280*

described, *8–9*

entertainment sponsorships, *286–288*

evaluation, *360–361*

experiential marketing, *291*

integration with other communications forms, *293*

investment in, *281*

leading investors in North America, *281f*

marketing communications plan, *64*

measurement of benefits, *292–293*

measurement of effectiveness, *360–361*

online, *205–208*

product promotional tours, *291*

sports marketing sponsorship, *281–286*

television advertising, *150–151*

value-added sponsorships, *284*

venue sponsorship, *283*

execution, *54*

experiential marketing, *235–236, 291*

experimental research, *344*

external data sources, *173*

external influences, *49*
external publics, *253*
external research, *352–355*
eye movement-camera test, *355*

F

factual appeals, *125*
family influences, *17–18*
FCB Grid, *103–104, 103f*
features, *325*
field sales force, *314*
film festivals, *286*
financial summary, *55–56*
first-party list, *208*
fixed-response questioning, *343*
flat-fee model, *395*
flight, *143*
floor decals, *160*
focus groups, *345*
folder, *175*
follow-up, *330*
follow-up service, *325*
forced exposure test, *355*
format
    newspapers, *155*
    radio, *153*
free dailies, *155*
free sample, *234, 234f–235f*
free-standing inserts (FSI), *232, 232f*
French-Quebec market, *24–27f*
frequency, *145*
frequency discount, *374–382, 384*
frequency distribution, *348*
frequency of promotions, *248*
frequent buyer program, *241–243*
fringe time, *378*
fulfillment, *229*
full-motion ad, *205f*
fundraising, *261*

G

games, *236–237*
gender economics, *21–23*
General Motors, *207–207*
Generation X, *19*
Generation Y, *19*
geodemographic segmentation, *28*
geographic market priorities
    described, *141*
    key market coverage, *142*
    national coverage, *142*
    regional coverage, *142*
geographic profile, *52*
geographic segmentation, *24–26*
gift cards, *242*

grid-rate schedules, *383*
gross rating points (GRPs), *145–382, 381f*

H

handling objections, *328*
head-on positioning, *83*
hierarchy of needs, *13, 13f*
hits, *358*
hiving, *38*
home shopping, *179*
horizontal rotation, *383*
hotels, *295f–296f, 297*
house list, *170–390*
household formations, *21*
human communications element, *318–323*
humorous appeals, *120–121, 120f–121f*
hypotheses, *341*

I

ideal self, *15*
image, *293*
image building, *198–199*
image perceptions, *361*
image positioning, *85*
implementation, *349*
impressions, *202, 358, 360*
in-pack self-coupons, *232*
inbound telemarketing, *181*
incentive, *62f, 176, 199, 245*
indexes
    brand development index (BDI), *142*
    category development index (CDI), *142*
    market development index, *142*
indirect competition, *37*
infomercial, *178–179, 180f*
information resources. *See* media information resources
innovation positioning, *83*
inserts, *155, 180, 180f*
inside sales force, *314*
instant-win, *237*
instantly redeemable coupons, *232*
integrated approach, *200*
integrated marketing communications
    see also integrated marketing communications mix; specific elements
    accountability, *12*
    customer relationship management, *10–11*
    database management systems, *11*
    defined, *3*
    digital communications technolo-

gies, *11–12*
    efficiency, demand for, *12*
    factors encouraging, *9–12*
    measurement, *361–362*
    media consumption trends, *9–10*
    and personal selling, *312–314*
integrated marketing communications mix
    advertising, *4–6*
    described, *3f, 4f*
    direct response communications, *6*
    event marketing, *8–9*
    interactive communications, *6*
    personal selling, *8*
    public relations, *8*
    sales promotion, *6–7*
    sponsorship, *8–9*
integrated marketing communications plan (sample), *404–418*
integration, *29–31*
Interactive Advertising Bureau (IAB), *399*
interactive communications
    see also Internet; online communications
    awareness, creation of, *198*
    branding, *198–199*
    customer service, *199–201*
    defined, *196–197*
    described, *6*
    image building, *198–199*
    incentives, *199*
    leads, *199*
    mobile media. *See* mobile media
    objectives, *197–202*
    planning, *196–197, 197f*
    strategies. *See* interactive communications strategies
    transactions, conduct of, *201–202*
interactive communications plan, *62*
interactive communications strategies
    advantages and disadvantages, *211f–212f*
    banner advertising, *203*
    company websites, *209*
    email advertising, *208–209*
    interstitial, *205*
    pay-per-click advertising, *202–203*
    pop-under ads, *205*
    pop-up ads, *205*
    rich media, *205*
    search advertising, *202–203*
    sponsorships, *205–208*
    streaming media, *205*
    superstitial, *205*

webcasting, *211*
interior cards, *160*
internal data sources, *170*
internal publics, *253*
Internet
    see also interactive communications
    ad clicks (clickthroughs), *202, 358*
    ad size, impact of, *203f*
    ad views, *358*
    adoption, *191–192*
    advertising alternatives, *198*
    behavioural targeting, *195*
    big box ad, *203*
    browsing period, *202*
    clickthrough rate (ad click rate), *202*
    comScore Media Matrix, *400*
    cookie, *195*
    cost-per-click, *394*
    coupons and, *232*
    CPM model, *391–394*
    customer communications, *40*
    defined, *194*
    eprocurement, *30*
    Evaliant Services, *400*
    evaluation of effectiveness, *357–359*
    flat-fee model, *395*
    hits, *358*
    impressions, *202, 358*
    incentives and, *199f*
    Interactive Advertising Bureau (IAB), *399*
    keyword targeting, *393*
    leaderboard (super banner), *203*
    marketing opportunities, *194–196*
    mass customization, *196*
    measurement of effectiveness, *357–359*
    media buying principles, *391–395*
    media information resources, *399–400*
    as new medium, *11–12*
    online selling, *314–314f*
    pay for performance model, *394–395*
    penetration, *191–192*
    pop-under ads, *205*
    pop-up ads, *205*
    portal, *198*
    rate card, *394f*
    rectangular ad, *203*
    research, *195*
    run of category, *393*
    run of network, *394*
    run of site, *394*

session, *202*
skyscraper, *203*
stickiness, *202, 359*
targeting requests, *394*
transactions, *40*
universal ad package sizes, *204f*
usage by Canadians, *192f*
visit, *202, 358*
visitor, *202, 358–359*
websites, *209, 268*
World Wide Web, *194*
Internet radio, *154*
interstitial, *205*
interviews
    mail interviews, *346*
    personal interviews, *346*
    telephone interviews, *346*
involvement, *103–104*

K
key benefit statement, *114*
key market coverage, *142*
keyword targeting, *393*
king poster, *160*
knowledge
    company knowledge, *323*
    competitor knowledge, *323*
    product knowledge, *322*

L
Labatt Breweries, *274*
layout, *297, 304f*
leaderboard (super banner), *203*
leadership positioning, *82–83*
leads, *199*
leaflets, *175*
Lee Jeans, *274*
legal influence, *40*
letter, *175*
lifestyle appeals, *123, 123f*
lifestyle imagery, *24f–26f, 85f–86f*
lifestyle positioning, *85, 85f*
lifestyle segments, *25f*
lighting, *305*
line rate, *369*
list broker, *173, 390*
listing, *226*
lists
    circulation lists, *173, 390*
    compiled lists, *173, 390*
    direct response list, *173, 173f*
    first-party list, *208*
    house list, *170–390*
    obtaining, *389–390*
    opt-in list, *208*
    response list, *390*

third-party list, *208*
lobbying, *261*
local spots, *150*
logistics, *229, 305–306*
logo, *70, 70f*
looking-glass self, *15*
L'Oréal, *289*
loyalty programs, *241–243*

M
magazines
    advantages and disadvantages, *157f*
    advertisement size, *373–374, 373f*
    Audit Bureau of Circulations (ABC), *397–398*
    as "class" medium, *156–157*
    clustering, *157*
    clutter, *157*
    colour charges, *376*
    comparisons, for efficiency, *376–377*
    controlled circulation, *156*
    discounts, *374–383*
    industry categories, *156*
    information resources, *397–398*
    media buying principles, *373–377*
    paid circulation, *156*
    PBA Worldwide, *398*
    position charges, *376*
    Print Measurement Bureau (PMB), *398*
    publisher's statement, *398*
    rate schedules, *373–374, 374f*
mail interviews, *346*
mail posters, *160*
managerial approach, *351*
market
    growth, *49*
    regional markets, *49*
    size, *49*
market analysis, *49*
market background, *47–50*
Market Data Report, *399*
market development index, *142*
market intelligence, *325*
market opportunities, *45*
market profile, *134, 222*
market segment analysis, *49*
market segmentation
    defined, *19*
    demographic segmentation, *19–23*
    direct (customized) segmentation, *26–28*
    geodemographic segmentation, *28*
    geographic segmentation, *24–26*
    micro-marketing, *19*

micro-segmentation, *19*

millennials, *28*

psychographic segmentation, *23–24*

market share, *362*

market share trends, *50*

marketing

ambush marketing, *282*

buzz marketing, *236, 258, 259*

database marketing, *27*

direct marketing, *167*

the event, *298–301*

experiential marketing, *235–236, 291*

micro-marketing, *19*

the product, *90–92*

test marketing, *344*

venue marketing, *283–285f*

viral marketing, *209*

and women, *23*

marketing budget, *55–56, 54f–56f*

marketing communications

defined, *50*

evaluation, *64–65*

measurement of, *64–65*

marketing communications objectives, *59*

marketing communications plan

advertising plan, *59–62*

defined, *58*

described, *57*

direct response plan, *62*

evaluation of marketing communications, *64–65*

event marketing, *64*

interactive communications plan, *62*

marketing communications objectives, *59*

marketing communications strategy, *59–64*

measurement of marketing communications, *64–65*

model, *57f*

personal selling plan, *64*

public relations plan, *64*

sales promotion plan, *62*

sponsorships, *64*

marketing communications planning process, *104–105*

marketing communications strategy

advertising plan, *59–62*

creative plan, *59–61*

described, *59*

direct response plan, *62*

event marketing, *64, 301*

interactive communications plan, *62*

media plan, *62*

personal selling plan, *64*

public relations plan, *64*

sales promotion plan, *62*

sponsorships, *64*

marketing control, *56*

marketing objectives, *52–54*

marketing plan

budget, *55–56*

defined, *41*

evaluation, *56*

financial summary, *55–56*

formats, *46*

marketing control, *56*

marketing objectives, *52–54*

marketing strategies, *54*

positioning strategy, *50–51*

tactics (execution), *54*

target market profile, *52*

marketing plan model, *48*

marketing planning

competitor analysis, *50*

contingency plan, *45*

and control process, *46f*

defined, *45*

external influences, *49*

market analysis, *49*

market background, *47–50*

marketing plan, *50–56*

product (brand) analysis, *50*

SWOT analysis, *47–48*

target market analysis, *49*

marketing programs

management of, *46*

planning and implementation, *46*

marketing research

data analysis, *348*

data collection methods, *343–344, 343f*

data interpretation, *349*

data transfer and processing, *348*

defined, *339*

experimental research, *344*

focus groups, *345*

hypotheses, *341*

implementation, *349*

Internet, *273*

mail interviews, *346*

observation research, *343*

online surveys, *346*

personal interviews, *346*

primary research, *340–349, 340f*

qualitative data, *345, 345f*

quantitative data, *345, 345f*

recommendations, *349*

reliability, *340*

research objectives, *341, 341f*

role of, *339–340*

sample design, *341–343*

scope of, *339–340*

secondary research, *395*

survey methodology, *346–347, 347f*

survey research, *343*

techniques, *340–349*

telephone interviews, *346*

test marketing, *344*

validity, *340*

marketing strategies, *54*

marketing strategy assessment, *50*

mass customization, *27, 196*

Mazda, *71*

measurement

advertising messages. *See* advertising measurement and efficiency

coupons, effectiveness of, *357, 357f–358f*

direct response advertising, *357–359*

event marketing, *360–361*

event sponsorship, *360–361*

integrated marketing communications, *361–362*

Internet communications, *357–359*

public relations, *359–360*

sales promotions, *355–357*

media

alternatives. *See* media alternatives

changes in, *10*

primary medium, *149*

secondary media, *149*

media alternatives

assessment of, *147, 148–162, 148f*

magazines, *156–157*

newspapers, *154–155*

out-of-home advertising, *157–162*

radio, *153–154*

television, *149–152*

media brief

competitor media strategy, *134*

defined, *134*

market profile, *134*

media budget, *136*

media objectives, *136*

target market profile, *135*

media budget

allocation, by region, *142f–143f*

budget allocations, *147*

described, *136*

media buying, *148*

media buying principles

direct mail advertising, *389–391*

Internet advertising, *391–395*
magazine advertising, *373–377*
newspaper advertising, *367–373*
out-of-home advertising, *386–389*
radio advertising, *382–386*
television advertising, *377–382*
media calendar, *147*
media consumption trends, *9–10*
media coverage, *293*
media-delivered coupons, *232*
media execution
assessment of media alternatives, *147, 147f–148f*
blocking chart, *147*
defined, *146*
media buying, *148*
media calendar, *147*
media selection, *146–147*
media information resources
described, *395*
Internet data sources, *399–400*
magazines, *397–398*
newspaper resources, *398–399*
out-of-home media, *399*
radio resources, *397*
research data by individual media, *400*
television resources, *395–397*
media kit, *268*
media objectives, *136–138*
media plan
defined, *136*
described, *62*
media execution, *146–148*
media objectives, *136–138*
media strategy. *See* media strategy
structure and content, *136f–137f*
media planning
assessment of media alternatives, *147, 148–162, 147f–148f*
described, *134*
media brief, *134–136*
media plan. *See* media plan
model, *135f*
quantitative nature of, *136*
media schedule
alternatives, *143f*
blitz schedule, *145*
build-up schedule, *145*
even schedule, *145*
flight, *143*
gross rating points (GRPs), *145*
pulse schedule, *144*
seasonal schedule, *145*
skip schedule, *143*
media selection, *146–147*

media strategy
continuity, *146*
defined, *138*
frequency, *145*
geographic market priorities, *141–142*
nature of the message, *140–141*
profile-matching strategy, *140*
reach, *145*
rifle strategy, *140*
shotgun strategy, *140*
target market profile, *138–141*
timing of advertising, *143–145*
merchandising support, *226*
merge/purge process, *173, 390*
message
delivery complications, *101*
encoding, *101*
integrated approach, *200*
nature of, and media strategy, *140–141*
noise, *102*
transmission, *101*
micro-marketing, *19*
micro-segmentation, *19*
millennials, *28*
mission statement, *42*
mobile media
advergaming, *214–215*
cell phones, *12*
online gaming, *214–215*
text messaging, *212–214*
video messaging, *213–214*
modular agate line (MAL), *367*
modular agate units, *369*
monopolistically competitive, *37*
motive, *13–14*
multi-tasking, *9*
multiple purchases, *225*
mural advertisements, *159*

N
NADbank Inc., *399*
national advertising, *155*
national coverage, *142*
needs, *13–14*
negative appeals, *119, 119f*
network advertising, *150*
new clients, *293*
new product activity, *50*
new product development strategy, *45*
newsletter, *268*
newspapers
advantages and disadvantages, *155f–156f*
agate line, *367*

broadsheet, *154, 367*
casual rate, *369*
circulation, *154*
classified ads, *155*
clutter, *155*
colour charges, *372*
community newspapers, *155*
comparisons, for efficiency, *372–373, 373f*
cost calculations, *369–372f*
CPM (cost per thousand), *372–373*
formats, *155*
free dailies, *155*
information resources, *398–399*
line rate, *369*
media buying principles, *367–373*
modular agate line (MAL), *367*
modular agate units, *369*
NADbank Inc., *399*
national advertising, *155*
position charges, *372*
preprinted inserts, *155, 372*
rate card, *369, 369f*
rate schedules, *369*
reach, *154*
retail advertisers, *155*
space size, determination of, *368–369*
spot colour, *372*
standard-size page options, *367, 367f*
tabloid, *154, 367*
Nielsen Media Research, *396*
Nike, *294*
noise, *102*
non-probability sample, *341*
non-verbal communication, *320–321, 329*

O
objections, *328*
objectives
advertising objectives, *109*
corporate objectives, *43*
creative objectives, *114–115*
defined, *36*
event marketing, *297–298*
interactive communications, *197–202*
marketing communications objectives, *59*
marketing objectives, *52–54*
media objectives, *136–138*
public relations planning, *262–264*
research objectives, *341, 341f*
sales promotion objectives, *223, 225–226*

observation research, *343*

off-invoice allowances, *244*

oligopoly, *37*

on-pack self-coupon, *232*

on-site sampling, *235*

online communications

    see also interactive communications; interactive communications strategies

    advantages and disadvantages, *211f–212f*

    link to traditional communications and ecommerce, *194f–195f*

    rich media, *205*

    vs. traditional communications, *195*

online databases, *173–174*

online gaming, *214–215*

online selling, *314–314f*

online surveys, *346*

open-ended questions, *343*

open-response questions, *343*

operations, *305–306*

opinion-measure testing, *354–355*

opportunities, *48*

opt-in lists, *208*

order form, *176*

order taking, *313*

Oregon, state of, *356*

out-of-home advertising

    advantages and disadvantages of, *161f*

    arena and stadium advertising, *161*

    Canadian Outdoor Measurement Bureau (COMB), *399*

    cinema advertising, *162*

    described, *157–158*

    elevator advertising, *161*

    information resources, *399*

    media buying principles, *386–389*

    outdoor advertising, *158–160*

    transit advertising, *160*

    washroom advertising, *161*

outbound telemarketing, *181*

outcomes, *273*

outdoor advertising

    advantages, *160*

    backlit poster, *158–159, 158f–159f*

    banners, *159*

    billboards, *158*

    disadvantages, *160*

    electronic signs, *159*

    mail posters, *160*

    mural advertisements, *159*

    posters, *158*

    shotgun strategy, *160*

    spectacular, *159*

    superboard, *159*

    transit shelter advertising, *159*

outgrowths, *273*

outputs, *273*

overall goal, *107*

P

packaging

    convenience, *92*

    marketing the product, *90–92*

    product protection, *89*

    promotional offers, *91*

    revolution in, *88–89*

    role of, *88*

paid circulation, *156*

partnering, *29–31*

partnership selling, *318*

pay for performance model, *394–395*

pay-per-click advertising, *202–203*

PBA Worldwide, *398*

peer groups, *17*

penetration strategy, *43*

perception, *17, 112*

performance allowance, *244*

permission-based email, *208*

personal characteristics, *318–321, 320f*

personal interviews, *346*

personal selling

    see also personal selling strategies; selling

    business-to-business selling, *314*

    classifications of, *312, 313f*

    company knowledge, *323*

    competitor knowledge, *323*

    defined, *8, 312*

    described, *8*

    direct selling, *314*

    evolution of selling, *315–318*

    human communications element, *318–323*

    and integrated marketing communications, *312–314*

    knowledge, importance of, *322–323*

    online selling, *314–314f*

    order taking, *313*

    personal characteristics, *318–321, 320f*

    planning model, *316f*

    preparation, *322–323*

    product configuration, *323*

    product knowledge, *322*

    repeat transactions, *313*

    retail selling, *312–313*

    sales presentation, *321*

    salespeople. *See* salespeople

    single transaction, *313*

    success in, *330*

personal selling plan, *64*

personal selling strategies

    approach, *327*

    closing, *329–330, 329f*

    described, *325–326*

    follow-up, *330*

    handling objections, *328*

    pre-approach, *327*

    prospecting, *326–327*

    qualifying, *327*

    sales presentation, *327–328, 328f*

    steps in process, *326f*

personality, *15*

personalization, *177, 177f*

physiological testing, *355*

picture matching technology (PMT), *396*

planning the event. *See* event marketing planning

podcasting, *154*

point-of-purchase material, *245–246, 357f*

pop-under ads, *205*

pop-up ads, *205*

population, *341*

portable people meter (PPM), *396*

portal, *198*

position charges, *372, 376*

positioning

    channel positioning, *85*

    comparative positioning, *83*

    defined, *50, 78*

    establishment of, *76–78*

    head-on positioning, *83*

    image positioning, *85*

    importance of, *78f*

    innovation positioning, *83*

    leadership positioning, *82–83*

    lifestyle positioning, *85*

    marketing communications programs, *85–87*

    price positioning, *83–84*

    product differentiation, *81–82*

    value positioning, *83–84*

positioning strategy statement, *50–51, 79, 112–113*

positive appeals, *118–119*

post-buy analysis, *136*

post-testing, *352*

postage-paid return envelope, *176*

posters, *158, 386f*

pre-approach, *327*

pre-testing, *352*

preference, *111–112*

premium, *240–241, 245*

preprinted inserts, *155, 372*

presentation strategy, *318*
press conference, *268*
press release, *264f, 265f, 267, 267f*
price positioning, *83–84*
pricing strategy, *300–301*
primary data, *340*
primary medium, *149*
primary research, *340–349, 340f*
prime time, *378*
Print Measurement Bureau (PMB), *398*
probability sample, *341*
problem identification, *107*
problem solving, *325*
problem statement, *107*
Procter & Gamble, *344*
product advertising, *4–5*
product as hero, *126*
product (brand) analysis, *50*
product configuration, *323*
product demonstrations, *126*
product differentiation, *111, 322*
product differentiation strategy, *81–82*
product integration, *151*
product knowledge, *322*
product placement, *151, 258*
product promotional tours, *291*
product protection, *89*
product publicity, *257–258*
product samples, *234–236*
product seeding, *3, 258–259*
product strategy, *298–299*
production costs, *390*
productivity measures, *362*
profile-matching strategy, *140*
profit, *362*
promotional advertising, *6*
proposal, *298, 298f*
prospecting, *326–327*
psychographic information, *171*
psychographic profile, *52*
psychographic segmentation, *23–24, 24f–26f*
public affairs, *260–261*
public relations
    advantages, *274–275*
    branded content, *258*
    budget, *271–273*
    as communications medium, *274–276*
    community relations, *260–261, 260f*
    corporate communications, *254*
    as credible information source, *274*
    crisis situations, *257f*
    and customer relationships, *275*
    defined, *8, 253*
    described, *8*
    disadvantages, *275–276*
    evaluation of, *359–360*
    execution. *See* public relations execution
    external publics, *253*
    fundraising, *261*
    goal of, *253*
    internal publics, *253*
    lobbying, *261*
    measurement of effectiveness, *359–360*
    planning. *See* public relations planning
    product placement, *258*
    product seeding, *258–259*
    public affairs, *260–261*
    public relations plan, *64*
    publicity, *257–258*
    reputation management, *254–256*
    role of, *254–261, 264*
    sales, impact on, *274–275, 274f–275f*
    strategic role, *264*
    third-party endorsements, *274*
    tools. *See* public relations execution
public relations execution
    annual reports, *270*
    blog, *270–271*
    booklets, *269–270*
    brochure, *269*
    media kit, *268*
    newsletter, *268*
    press conference, *268*
    press release, *267, 267f*
    special interest reports, *270*
    unique and innovative techniques, *272f*
    websites, *268*
public relations plan, *64*
public relations planning
    borrowed-interest strategy, *265*
    described, *261–262*
    goals, *263–264*
    objectives, *262–264*
    process, *262–263*
    public relations execution, *266–271*
    public relations strategy, *264–265*
public relations strategy
    described, *264–266*
    evaluation, *273*
    measurement, *273*
    timeline, *271–273*
publicity, *257–258*
publisher's statement, *398*
pull, *221, 221f–222f*
pulse schedule, *144*
pupilometer test, *355*
push, *221*

Q
qualifying (customers), *327*
qualitative data, *345, 345f*
quantitative data, *345, 345f*

R
radio
    advantages, *153, 154f*
    BBM Bureau of Measurement, *397*
    buying radio time, *385–386*
    cost calculations, *385–386*
    dayparts, *383*
    described, *153*
    disadvantages, *154f*
    discounts, *383–384*
    format, *153*
    grid-rate schedules, *383*
    horizontal rotation, *383*
    information resources, *397*
    Internet radio, *154*
    media buying principles, *382–386*
    podcasting, *154*
    Radio Marketing Bureau, *397*
    reach plans, *383, 384*
    reach potential, *153*
    rotation plan, *19–383*
    satellite radio, *154*
    seasonal rate structures, *383*
    vertical rotation, *383*
Radio Marketing Bureau, *397*
rate card, *369, 369f, 378, 378f, 386f, 390f, 394f*
rate schedules, *369–374, 374f*
ratings, *396*
rating(s), *381*
reach, *145*
reach plans, *383, 384*
real self, *15*
rebates, *238–240*
recall tests, *353*
recency, *381*
recognition tests, *352–353*
recommendations, *349*
rectangular ad, *203*
redemption rate, *233, 233f*
reference groups, *17*
referral, *327*
regional coverage, *142*
regional markets, *49*
regular programming, *378*
regulatory influence, *40*
regulatory trends, *49*
rehearsal, *305*
related recall, *353*

relationship selling, *317–318*
reliability, *340*
repeat purchases, *232*
repeat transactions, *313*
reputation management, *254–256*
research. *See* marketing research
research objectives, *341, 341f*
response cards, *357*
response list, *173, 173f, 390*
retail advertisers, *155*
retail organizations, *73*
retail selling, *312–313*
rich media, *205*
rifle strategy, *140*
rotation plan, *19–383*
run of category, *393*
run of network, *394*
run of site, *394*
run sheet, *298, 300f*

S

safety, *307*
sales
    as benefit of event marketing, *293*
    brand sales, *361*
    profit, *362*
    public relations, impact of,
      274–275, 274f–275f
sales force, *314*
sales presentation, *321, 327–328, 328f*
sales promotion
    consumer promotions. *See* con-
      sumer promotions
    contests, *227f*
    defined, *6–7, 221*
    described, *6–7*
    display activity, *228f*
    evaluation, *355–357*
    measurement, *355–357*
    multiple purchases, encouragement
      of, *225*
    objectives, *223*
    planning, *222–224*
    pull, *221, 221f–222f*
    push, *221, 221f*
    strategy. *See* sales promotion strate-
      gy
    trade promotions. *See* trade promo-
      tions
    trial purchase, encouragement of,
      225f
sales promotion plan
    content of, *224f*
    defined, *224*
    described, *62*
    objectives, *225–226*
sales promotion planning

additional considerations, *247–248*
    brand equity, *248*
    brand image, *248*
    budget, *224*
    competitor activity profile, *223*
    described, *222*
    frequency of promotions, *248*
    market profile, *222*
    process, *223f*
    sales promotion objectives, *223*
    target market profile, *223*
sales promotion strategy
    consumer promotion execution,
      231–243
    described, *226–229*
    evaluation, *229–230, 230f*
    fulfillment, *229*
    logistics, *229*
    measurement, *229–230*
    trade promotions execution,
      243–247
sales volume trends, *50, 226*
salespeople
    follow-up service, *325*
    locating customers, *325*
    maintaining customers, *325*
    market intelligence, *325*
    problem solving, *325*
    responsibilities of, *325*
    roles of, *325*
    successful salespeople, *321*
sample, *341*
sample design, *341–343*
sample size, *341*
samples, *234–235*
sampling frame, *341*
satellite radio, *154*
schedules. *See* media schedule
Scott Paper, *344*
search advertising, *202–203*
seasonal analysis, *49*
seasonal rate structures, *383*
seasonal schedule, *145*
secondary media, *149*
secondary research, *395*
    see also media information resources
security, *307*
seeding. *See* product seeding
segmentation. *See* market segmentation
selection of media, *146–147*
selective direct mail, *177*
selective exposure, *17*
selective perception, *17*
selective retention, *17*
selective spots, *150*
selects, *173*

self-concept, *15*
self-image, *15, 319–320*
selling
    see also personal selling
    changes in selling strategies, *316*
    in changing business environment,
      330–333
    consultative selling, *316*
    evolution of, *315–318*
    partnership selling, *318*
    presentation strategy, *318*
    relationship selling, *317–318*
    relationships *vs.* products, *331*
    strategic selling, *317*
    as team effort, *330–331*
    and technology, *332–333*
session, *202*
setup, *306*
seventy poster, *160*
sexual appeals, *121–122, 122f*
shelf talker, *245, 245f*
Shoppers Drug Mart, *172*
shotgun strategy, *140, 160*
single-purchase refund, *239*
single transaction, *313*
site selection, *302–305*
skip schedule, *143*
skyscraper, *203*
slippage, *239*
slogans, *128, 129f*
social influences, *38*
social responsibility, *254, 254f, 362*
social trends, *49*
solo direct mail, *177*
sound, *305*
spam, *208*
special interest newsletters, *268*
special interest reports, *270*
special programming, *378*
spectacular, *159*
spiff, *245*
sponsored email, *208*
sponsorship, *8*
    see also event sponsorship
sports event marketing levels,
    281f–282f
sports marketing sponsorship, *281–286*
spot colour, *372*
stadium advertising, *161–162*
staffing, *305*
staging, *302–305*
stair risers, *160*
Starch readership test, *353*
statement stuffer, *177*
station domination, *160*
station posters, *160*

stickiness, *202*
strategic alliances, *45*
strategic planning
    competitor influence, *37–38*
    corporate objectives, *43*
    corporate plan, *41, 42–45*
    as cyclical process, *36*
    defined, *36*
    demographic influences, *38*
    economic influences, *36–37*
    external influences, *36f*
    factors influencing, *36–40*
    legal and regulatory influence, *40*
    links between various plans, *41f*
    marketing plan. *See* marketing plan
    marketing planning, *45–56*
    mission statement, *42*
    process, *41*
    social influences, *38*
    technology influence, *38–40*
strategic selling, *317*
strategies
    acquisition strategy, *45*
    borrowed-interest strategy, *265*
    branding strategy. *See* branding
        strategy
    competitor media strategy, *134*
    coverage strategies. *See* coverage
        strategies
    creative strategy, *115–119*
    defined, *36*
    development of, *45*
    direct mail, *177–178*
    event marketing, *298–301*
    interactive communications. *See*
        interactive communications
        strategies
    marketing communications strategy,
        59–64, 301
    marketing strategies, *54*
    media strategy, *138–146*
    personal selling. *See* personal selling
        strategies
    positioning strategy, *50–52*
        see also positioning
    presentation strategy, *318*
    pricing strategy, *300–301*
    product differentiation strategy,
        81–82
    product strategy, *298–299*
    profile-matching strategy, *140*
    public relations strategy, *264–265*
    rifle strategy, *140*
    sales promotion strategy. *See* sales
        promotion strategy
    shotgun strategy, *140, 160*

streaming media, *205*
strengths, *47*
style, *117–119*
super banner, *203*
superboard, *159*
superbrands, *88*
superbus advertising, *160*
superstitial, *205*
suppliers, *297*
supply and demand, *377–378*
support claims statement, *114–115*
survey methodology, *346–347, 347f*
survey research, *343*
sweepstakes, *236*
SWOT analysis
    competitor analysis, *50*
    described, *47–48*
    external influences, *49*
    market analysis, *49*
    product (brand) analysis, *50*
    target market analysis, *49*

T

tabloid, *154, 367*
tabulation, *348*
tactics, *36, 54*
taglines, *128*
target market analysis, *49*
target market profile, *52, 135,*
    138–141, 223
target markets, *19, 110–111*
    see also market segmentation
target reach, *293*
targeting requests, *394*
team effort, *330–331*
teardown, *306*
technology
    design, impact on, *94, 95f*
    influence of, *38–40*
    interactive outdoor advertising,
        159
    and selling, *332–333*
    trends, *49*
    virtual product placement, *258*
telemarketing
    call centre, *181*
    defined, *169, 314*
    described, *181*
    inbound telemarketing, *181*
    marketing roles of, *183f*
    negative image of, *183*
    outbound telemarketing, *181*
    primary advantage of, *182–183*
    roles, in personal selling, *314f*
telephone interviews, *346*
television

advantages and disadvantages, *151f*
BBM Bureau of Measurement,
    395–396
branded content, *151*
Canada's top TV shows, *379f*
changes, effects of, *152*
cluster profiling, *151*
commercial length, *378*
day time, *378*
digital channels, *149*
direct response television. *See* direct
    response television (DRTV)
discounts, *382*
entertainment sponsorships,
    286–288
fringe time, *378*
gross rating points (GRPs),
    381–382, 381f
information resources, *395–397*
local spots, *150*
media buying principles, *377–382*
media habits, changes in, *149*
network advertising, *150*
Nielsen Media Research, *396*
prime time, *378*
product integration, *151*
product placement, *151*
programs, types of, *378*
rate card, *378, 378f*
rating, *381*
recency, *381*
selective spots, *150*
shorter commercials, *152*
sponsorship, *150–151*
strategies for reaching viewers,
    151–152
supply and demand, *377–378*
technology, changes in, *149*
Television Bureau of Canada, *397*
time of day, *378*
volume discount, *382*
Television Bureau of Canada, *397*
TELUS, *294*
test marketing, *344*
testimonials, *126*
text messaging, *12, 212–214*
theory of motivation, *13*
third-party endorsements, *274*
third-party list, *208*
threats, *48*
Tim Hortons, *58*
timeline, *271–273*
timeline chart, *298*
timing of advertising. *See* media
    schedule
tip-in, *180*

TNS Media Intelligence, *400*
tone, *117–119*
torture test, *126*
tour events and sponsorships, *291*
trade allowances, *244*
trade promotions
    collateral material, *245*
    cooperative advertising allowance, *244*
    dealer display material, *245–246*
    dealer premiums, *245*
    defined, *221*
    execution, *243–247*
    performance allowance, *244*
    point-of-purchase material, *245–246*
    trade allowances, *244*
    trade shows, *246–247, 247f*
trade shows, *246–247, 247f*
trademark, *70*
traditional communications, *194f–195f*
transactions
    Internet, *201*
    repeat transactions, *313*
    single transaction, *313*
transit advertising

bus murals, *160*
interior cards, *160*
king poster, *160*
seventy poster, *160*
station posters, *160*
superbus advertising, *160*
transit shelter advertising, *159, 386f*
transmission, *101*
trial close, *329*
trial purchase, *109–110, 225f, 232*
trial-size packages, *234f–235f*

U
unique selling point (USP), *73*
universe, *341*
urban growth, *20*

V
validity, *340*
value-added sponsorships, *284*
value positioning, *83–84*
venue, *297*
venue marketing, *283–285f*
venue sponsorship, *283*
verbal skills, *320*
vertical rotation, *383*
video games, *214–215*

video messaging, *213–214*
viral marketing, *209*
virtual product placement, *258*
visit, *202, 358*
visitor, *202, 358–359*
voice-pitch analysis test, *355*
volume discount, *382, 384*

W
washroom advertising, *161*
weaknesses, *47*
web portal, *198*
webcasting, *211*
webisodes, *211*
websites, *209, 268*
West 49, *47*
women and marketing, *23*
World Wide Web, *194*
worldmark, *69*